Many misconceptions circulate in the West about Tantric religion, whether Buddhist or Hindu, mainly because scholars have relied exclusively on textual sources. Here, for the first time, is an account of how Tantric Buddhism works in practice. *Monk, Householder, and Tantric Priest* is a detailed ethnography of the Mahāyāna and Vajrayāna (Tantric) Buddhism of the Newars of the Kathmandu Valley, Nepal. It describes the way of life and social organization of the Hindu-Buddhist city of Lalitpur, the relationship of Buddhism to Hinduism, and the place of religion and ritual in the life of Newar Buddhists. The author shows how Newar Buddhism manages to combine within a single hierarchical system of thought and practice the apparently opposed ideals of celibacy and restraint on the one hand, and full participation in worldly activities on the other.

The study of the Newars has wide implications, for it allows us to grasp how Buddhism works and worked in its original context of caste and Hindu kingship. This is an important book which should appeal to Buddhologists and religious studies specialists, as well as to South Asianists, sociologists, and social anthropologists generally.

Cambridge Studies in Social and Cultural Anthropology

84

Monk, householder, and Tantric priest

A list of books in this series will be found at the end of the volume

MONK, HOUSEHOLDER, AND TANTRIC PRIEST

Newar Buddhism and its hierarchy of ritual

DAVID N. GELLNER

CAMBRIDGE
UNIVERSITY PRESS

Published by the Press Syndicate of the University of Cambridge
The Pitt Building, Trumpington Street, Cambridge CB2 1RP
40 West 20th Street, New York, NY 10011-4211, USA
10 Stamford Road, Oakleigh, Victoria 3166, Australia

First published 1992

Printed and bound in Great Britain by
Woolnough Bookbinding Ltd, Irthlingborough, Northamptonshire

A catalogue record for this book is available from the British Library

Library of Congress cataloguing in publication data

Gellner, David N.
Monk, householder, and Tantric priest: Newar Buddhism and its hierarchy of ritual / by David N. Gellner.
p. cm. – (Cambridge studies in social and cultural anthropology: 84)
Includes bibliographical references and index.
ISBN 0 521 38399 4
1. Buddhism–Nepal–Kathmandu Valley. 2. Kathmandu Valley (Nepal)–Religious life and customs. 3. Newar (Nepalese people)–Religion. I. Title. II. Series.
BQ396.K37G45 1992
294.3′095496–dc20 91–16259 CIP

ISBN 0 521 38399 4 hardback

SE

For Lola,
for my parents,
and for Jog Maya Shakya

Contents

Illustrations

Plates

Between pages 136 and 137, and 264 and 265

Figures

Tables

Preface

If, as Whitehead is supposed to have remarked, Western philosophy is a series of footnotes to Plato, the anthropology and sociology of religion form a series of footnotes to Durkheim and Weber. By 'Weber' I do not mean the mirror-image of vulgar Marxism which still lingers on in some quarters, nor yet the Weber who is invoked as an ancestor of interpretive anthropology. As I read him, Weber frequently writes like a (sophisticated) Marxist: he is at least as interested in coercion and the ideological use of 'constructed meanings' as he is in interpretation as such.

Both Weber and Durkheim had interesting things to say about Buddhism. Weber wrote at length about it in the long essay translated (and in many places mistranslated, beginning with the title) as *The Religion of India*: this indeed includes a page on Newar Buddhism. But, reliant on the secondary sources of his time, Weber underestimated the degree to which Buddhism always was a religion of the laity and he exaggerated the differences between ancient Buddhism and Mahāyāna Buddhism (I have discussed Weber on Hinduism and Buddhism elsewhere: Gellner 1982, 1988b). Durkheim, for his part, made some intelligent remarks about Buddhism in rejecting Tylor's definition of religion as belief in spiritual beings. However, determined to reduce all religious phenomena to a single essence, he did not see that salvation religions – not to mention those activities to be labelled instrumental religion below – might sometimes fail to fit his model.

I agree with that most anti-Durkheimian of authors, Evans-Pritchard, that however important it is to relate religious ideas and practices to social organization – and it is supremely important as I hope will be amply shown below – they cannot be reduced to a simple 'projection of the social order' (Evans-Pritchard 1956: 320). Thus in the middle sections of this book (chapters 6 through 10) description of Newar Buddhism 'in its own terms' predominates over analysis, whereas in the rest of the book the reverse is true. In fact, of course, the very organization of description implies, and is impossible without, analysis; but I have used what anthropologists call an emic structure (i.e. one of Newar Buddhists' own ideas) to organize the description, and this is as close as I found it possible to get to the approach of adherents themselves. I hope that this procedure, as well as the frequent cross-referencing by chapter sub-sections, will make a complex religion accessible, something Durkheim considered unattainable in the analysis of 'a confused mass of many cults' (Durkheim 1965: 17).

In giving detailed accounts of two specific rituals which outsiders are not permitted to observe in full (§9.3), I follow ritual handbooks. Elsewhere I have also made use of such evidence in conjunction with frequent observations of actual performances. I am fully aware of the problems of using such written sources in describing ritual; but I also believe that a full understanding of complex rituals can only be achieved if one takes into account the models and mnemonics used by those who have to carry them out. It is a mistake to think that such models are so idealized as to be of no help in comprehending 'what really happens'.

Over the years it has taken to write this book I have accumulated many debts, which it is a great pleasure to be able to acknowledge here. In the first place heartfelt thanks are due to the people of Kwā Bāhāḥ and Cikã Bahī, who accepted being studied with such good grace and often indeed with enthusiasm, and to the Centre for Nepalese and Asian Studies (CNAS), Tribhuvan University, which supported my research application and permitted me to be an affiliated scholar. I hope that this book will go some way towards repaying the trust extended to me. In particular I owe a special debt of gratitude to the late Kuber Muni Shakya, who passed away nine months after I began to live in his house, and to his wife, Jog Maya Shakya. Jog Maya exemplifies, both in my opinion and that of others who know her, the great virtues of an intelligent and tolerant Newar Buddhist piety. She taught me much about Newar Buddhism and I quote her often below. Kuber Muni, Jog Maya, their son Mangal Ratna (Jetha), and the rest of the family accepted me as one of themselves, while allowing me the freedom an anthropologist cannot do without. I cannot possibly mention all those Newars who befriended me and helped in whatever way they could, but five friends deserve especial thanks: Tirtha Lal Maharjan, Nirmal Man Tuladhar, Ratna Kaji Shakya (of Bākū Nani), Ratna Kaji Shakya (of Ānanda Bāhāḥ), and Bhai Ratna Vajracharya. In Kathmandu I was particularly helped by Subarna Man Tuladhar who was not only an excellent Newari teacher but also a continuing source of insights and explanations. Daya Ratna Shakya (alias Darasha Newami) undertook much survey work with great resourcefulness. *Paṇḍit* Asha Kaji Vajracharya allowed me to profit from his great knowledge of Newar ritual and culture.

I have not disguised the identity of the places where I did fieldwork. Local people would regard pseudonyms as undermining the whole purpose of doing research in the first place. Furthermore, I have in some cases named my informants, since educated Nepalese consider the foreign habit of not doing so to be at best discourteous and at worst dishonest. Asha Kaji specifically requested that information received from him be attributed. Since he is both a specialist in many of the topics treated only superficially here, and the author of many books, I consider his request entirely reasonable.

Two years of fieldwork in Nepal, May 1982 to May 1984, could not have been undertaken without the generous support of a Leverhulme Trust Fund Study Abroad Studentship. Unless otherwise specified, the ethnographic present of the text refers to that period. Before that, study had been supported by a DES Senior Studentship (as it was then), and afterwards by the Boden Fund (twenty-one months) and the Max Müller Fund (five months), both of Oxford. I am also grateful to my three Oxford colleges: Balliol, where this work was first conceived, Wolfson, where the bulk of the first draft was written, and St John's, where a Junior Research Fellowship provided the ideal conditions in which to complete and subsequently to revise it. The final revisions were made while holding a British Academy Postdoctoral Fellowship. Return trips to Nepal (December 1985, July–August 1986, July–September 1989) were wholly or partly funded by the Graduate Studies Committee, Oxford, the Spalding Trust, the British Academy, and the Max Müller Fund.

Richard Gombrich not only inspired and suggested this project, but supervised it and encouraged me in exemplary fashion throughout. Alexis Sanderson has, along with Asha Kaji, been an invaluable guide through the maze of Tantric Buddhism: his detailed comments on chapters 5, 9, and 10 have both enriched the analysis and saved me from many errors. Nick Allen and Michael Witzel examined the manuscript and made many helpful suggestions. Others who read all or part of it and made useful comments were: Frances Brown, Catherine Cantwell, Michael Carrithers, Patricia Crone, Chris Fuller, Ramesh Kunwar, Todd Lewis, Siegfried Lienhard, John Locke, Robert Mayer, Rajendra Pradhan, David Seyfort Ruegg, Gregory Sharkey, and Subarna Man Tuladhar. A particular debt of gratitude is owed to Declan Quigley and Jonathan Spencer who read through the manuscript at a late stage and suggested cuts. None of these friends, colleagues, and teachers can be held responsible for the errors which remain; for these, after the manner of Newar authors, I beg learned readers' forgiveness. I would also like to thank Carolyn Clarke for her drawings, one of which appears here as Figure 17, and Niels Gutschow for providing the maps, drawn either by himself or by his team in Nepal.

I have been aided immensely by the work of two scholars in particular: that of John Locke on Newar Buddhism, and that of Gérard Toffin on Newar society. John Locke provided unstinting guidance and advice while I was in the field. Gérard Toffin has been unfailingly supportive and encouraging since then. Both Declan Quigley and Rajendra Pradhan invited me to accompany them in their own fieldwork when I was a complete beginner, and each has been a longstanding source of help, encouragement, advice, and ideas. My parents have supported me in various crucial ways, and their visit to Nepal in the early stages of fieldwork was an auspicious beginning. My wife, Lola Martinez, not only read through the manuscript twice at a time when she was very busy, but has cheerfully put up with its intruding, in two different incarnations, on two equally important stages of our life together.

Note added in proof

Robert Levy's monumental *Mesocosm: Hinduism and the Organization of a Traditional Newar City in Nepal* (1990, Berkeley and Los Angeles: University of California Press) reached me too late for all but a brief mention here. It focuses on Hinduism in Bhaktapur, the most Hindu of the Newars' three cities. I would be flattered if the present work, focusing on Buddhism in Lalitpur, the most Buddhist of the three cities, were considered to complement Levy's *Mesocosm*. In general, it seems to me that what Levy writes about the social uses of Tantrism is consistent with the analysis advanced here.

A note on pronunciation and abbreviations

Pronunciation. The macron indicates a lengthened vowel. Thus *ā* is pronounced like the 'a' in 'father', *ī* as 'ee', *ū* as 'oo'. Short *a* is pronounced like the 'u' in 'sun'. The tilde (˜) and *candrabindu* (ँ) over a vowel, as well as *ṃ* or *ṁ* after it, all indicate a nasalization of the vowel. *ḥ* indicates a lengthening of the preceding vowel. Newari has two vowel sounds not found in Nepali or Sanskrit; they are written *-āy* and *-ay* respectively. The former is pronounced roughly like the English 'air', so that *kāy /kāe:/* (son) sounds somewhat like 'care', drawn out, and pronounced, as in southern British English, with no 'r' sound. The latter (*-ay*) sounds roughly like the 'ay' of 'pay'; *bhway* (feast) thus rhymes with 'whey'.

Newars generally fail to pronounce retroflex consonants (*ṭ, ṭh, ḍ, ḍh, ṇ*) any differently from the corresponding dental sounds (since retroflex consonants do not exist in Newari proper). Thus, in the present context, foreigners can safely do the same. *ś* and *ṣ* are both pronounced 'sh', or sometimes just as 's'. *Th* is an aspirated 't', and is *never* pronounced as in 'brother'. *V* is pronounced like 'w' in combination with other consonants (e.g. Svayambhū) but close to 'b' in other cases (e.g. Vajrācārya). *C* is pronounced like the first 'ch' of 'church' and never as 'k'; *ch* is pronounced like the English 'ch' with aspiration. *Ph* sounds like 'f' but is articulated bilabially. All other letters are pronounced more or less as an English-speaker would expect. The only exception to the generally phonetic spelling system is that *jña*, being awkward to pronounce, is said *gya*: thus *prajñā* (wisdom) is pronounced *pragyā*.

Diacritics have been omitted from personal names, and from the names of well-known kings, families, and places (e.g. 'Rana' not 'Rāṇā'). For maximum recognition the Sanskritic names of gods have been used. To translate is, if not to betray, to make choices with consequences for interpretation. The inconsistencies which may be noticed below are the result of trying to satisfy three conflicting imperatives: (i) to illustrate that Newars are as much part of South Asian culture as they feel themselves to be; (ii) to convey how Newars themselves pronounce Newari and view their own tradition; (iii) to communicate with non-specialists by, wherever possible, not overburdening the text with non-English words. A detailed justification of the orthography and transliteration adopted in this book is given in appendix 1 to chapter 1. For linguistically adequate accounts of Newari, the reader should consult Malla 1985a and Hale 1986.

Italicized words are, unless otherwise indicated, Newari; where two alternatives are cited, I have adopted the convention of giving the more Sanskritic and honorific term first, the more colloquial and/or etymologically Tibeto-Burman form second. The words 'Brahman', 'yoga', 'mandala', and 'mantra' I have considered sufficiently well known to treat as English (although the specific meaning of the latter two for Newars is discussed below); I have anglicized the rare mentions of Tibetan sects (e.g. Gelukpa). The convention used in works on Tibetan Buddhism of giving mantras in capital letters has been adopted, as has the South Asianist convention of writing caste names with capitals (thus 'Farmer' refers to the Maharjan caste, whereas a 'farmer' can come from any caste). I have also followed the South Asianist habit of using the English plural with local terms, except when the pronunciation resulting sounds to my ear especially barbarous (e.g. the *bahī*, not *bahī*s). I have used initial capital letters as a way of marking English translations of a technical expression in Newari, e.g. Observance for *vrata*, Monastic Initiation for *bare chuyegu*, and so on. The detailed index, giving both Newari terms and English equivalents, is meant to function also as a glossary. I have followed the usage of Nepalese writers in using 'Nepali' to refer only to the language and 'Nepalese' both as an adjective and as a noun referring to the people. 'Newari', be it noted, denotes only the language; the adjective is 'Newar'.

Abbreviations

BEFEO	*Bulletin de l'Ecole Française d'Extrême Orient*
BSOAS	*Bulletin of the School of Oriental and African Studies*, London
Bubi/Babi	These abbreviations form part of the identifying numbers of manuscripts belonging to the Asha Saphu Kuti, Raktakali, Kathmandu
BV	Buddhist Vaṃśāvalī, i.e. Cambridge University manuscript 1952A, translated loosely as Wright's *History of Nepal*
CIS	*Contributions to Indian Sociology*

CNS	*Contributions to Nepalese Studies*, published by the Centre for Nepalese and Asian Studies (CNAS), Tribhuvan University, Kathmandu
CNRS	Centre National de Recherche Scientifique, Paris
EJS	*European Journal of Sociology*
GOS	Gaekwad Oriental Series, Oriental Institute, Baroda
INAS	Institute for Nepalese and Asian Studies, now renamed the Centre for Nepalese and Asian Studies (CNAS)
JAS	*Journal of Asian Studies*
JIABS	*Journal of the International Association of Buddhist Studies*
JNRC	*Journal of the Nepal* [-German] *Research Centre*, Kathmandu
JRAI	*Journal of the Royal Anthropological Institute*
KSc	Kriyā Samuccaya (Chandra 1977)
NBP	Nepal Bauddha Prakashan, Kathmandu
NGMPP	The Nepal-German Manuscript Preservation Project; this prefixes the identifying numbers of manuscripts microfilmed under this project, copies of which are available from the National Archives, Kathmandu
Np.	Nepali
N.S.	Nepal Samvat, the era traditionally used by Newars, which began in 879 CE
Nw.	Newari
PV	*Pacific Viewpoint*
RRS	Regmi Research Series, Kathmandu
Skt.	Sanskrit
UMI	University Microfilms International
V.S.	Vikram Samvat, the official Nepalese era, which began in 57 BCE

1

Introduction

Let the closet student, then, give reasonable faith to the traveller, even upon this subject; . . . let him not suppose that the living followers of Buddha cannot be profitably interrogated touching the creed they live and die in; and, above all, let him not presume that a religion fixed, at its earliest period, by means of a noble written language, has no identity of character in the several countries where it is now professed . . .

Hodgson, 'European Speculations on Buddhism'
(Hodgson 1972 I: 100)

1.1 Aims and methods

This book is intended as a contribution to the anthropology of Mahāyāna Buddhism. It sets out to describe and analyse the Buddhism of the Newars of the Kathmandu Valley, Nepal, in the belief that this is of interest both in itself and because the Newars occupy a special place in Buddhist and South Asian history. Buddhism has all but died out in India, the land of its birth. Theravāda Buddhism, the 'doctrine of the elders', the oldest and most conservative form of Buddhism, survives in Burma, Thailand, Laos, Cambodia, and Sri Lanka. Mahāyāna Buddhism spread to Tibet, China, Korea, Vietnam, and Japan, as well as to Indonesia where it survives in a highly attenuated form in Bali. Only in the Kathmandu Valley can one still find Mahāyāna Buddhism within a South Asian cultural environment.[1] While there is an anthropological literature of very high quality on Theravāda Buddhism there is little on Mahāyāna Buddhism, and one aim of the present work is to begin to fill this gap.[2]

It was in search of this surviving remnant of South Asian Buddhism that Sylvain Lévi, the great French Sanskritist, visited Nepal in 1898 and wrote its history. Only in the Kathmandu Valley are there still Buddhists whose texts and ritual handbooks are in Sanskrit. These texts and rituals go back in an uninterrupted line to the great north Indian centres of Mahāyāna and Vajrayāna Buddhism of the late first millennium. The present study does not attempt to estimate exactly which aspects of Newar religion and culture go back to this period. That would be a separate historical investigation of its own, raising complex and controversial questions about long-term historical change and about structures which somehow manage to endure (or be reproduced) over a very long period. Nonetheless, the present study was undertaken in the belief that an understanding of Newar Buddhism would be of wide significance for the history of South Asia and for the history of Buddhism. This is what was expressed by Lévi (1905 I: 28) in his aphorism 'Nepal is India in the making.' Here, in the Kathmandu Valley, one could study 'as in a laboratory' the relationship of late Buddhism to Hinduism and to Hindu kingship, a dynamic process which culminated in India in the elimination of Buddhism.

It is a controversial question why Buddhism disappeared from India. P. Jaini (1980) has written a stimulating article reviewing, in the light of the survival of Jainism, the various theories that have been put forward to explain the disappearance of Buddhism and this is discussed further below (§7.5). Buddhism was already in decline when the Muslims arrived and destroyed the great monasteries of northern India, forcing those monks who survived to flee to Nepal and Tibet. In south India Buddhism was already moribund, absorbed and superseded by Hindu devotionalism. In north-east India (Bengal, Bihar, and Orissa) it is arguable that, but for the Muslim conquest, Buddhism might have survived much as it survived in Nepal.[3]

This perspective on Newar Buddhism has been taken up recently (Lienhard 1984; Snellgrove 1987: 375, 379–80), but rather more often foreign observers have interpreted Newar Buddhism as Hinduism in all but name (Snellgrove 1957: 106). Here then is the central problem:

(i) How does Newar Buddhism differ from the Hinduism with which it is surrounded?
(ii) How does Newar Buddhism differ from Theravāda Buddhism to which it is historically (though distantly) related, and with which in modern times it has once again come into contact?

The brief answer to the first question, to which Snellgrove in his earlier sketch of Newar Buddhism replied 'not at all', is that there are important differences of value and organization, as well as significant homologies. The brief answer to the second question is that there are surprising (because unexpected and unappreciated) continuities with Theravāda Buddhism, as well as obvious differences. Clearly, in order to answer these two questions fully, it is necessary to describe in detail how Newar Buddhism works. Those not interested in the conceptual issues raised by such an attempt may wish to turn directly to the next section (§1.2).

In comparing Newar Buddhism to Theravāda Buddhism, and in taking the latter as exemplifying non-Mahāyāna Buddhism, I am sure to be criticized by Indologists and Buddhologists. In my defence I should say that on this point I have deliberately adopted a sociological perspective. I am aware that ancient Buddhism before the rise of the Mahāyāna comprised many schools and ordination traditions, and that of these the Theravāda was only one (and not a very important one from the Mahāyāna point of view). I am also aware that, since the terms 'Theravāda' and 'Mahāyāna' refer to quite separate criteria of identity (ordination and allegiance to a class of scriptures respectively), it was possible in some places to be a Theravādin Mahāyānist (Snellgrove 1989: 8; Bechert 1989: 27). However, of the various pre-Mahāyāna traditions, only the Theravāda survives today as the practice that defines the religious identity of large groups of adherents, both monastic and lay. It is true that pre-Mahāyāna monastic codes, as well as other types of scripture, deriving from non-Theravāda traditions, survive within the Mahāyāna Buddhism of China, Tibet, and Japan. But none of these can be said to define an entire religious tradition,[4] and it is in the comparison of such complexes of practice and belief that I am interested.

In attempting to describe the religious life of a group of people, one is dealing with phenomena which are culturally specific. It is necessary, therefore, to include in one's description not just what people do, but what they think they are doing. Since Newars view their religion primarily as a set of practices, it is ritual and custom that hold the centre stage. Furthermore, since Newars defer to ritual experts, mostly priests, in these matters, and the priests make use of ritual handbooks based on scriptures, for a full understanding one has to take some account of written evidence. I have not tried to seek out the earliest or original version of ritual handbooks (or myths as the case may be), but have rather wanted to look at the texts in use today. My main aim has been to provide a synchronic account of Newar Buddhism. But it would have been both wrong and impossible to avoid references to the past. To have done so would have implied that Newar society and religion are unchanging and static; and it would have precluded an understanding of the dynamics of the present.

Description implies a translation of the Newars' categories. Inevitably it also implies analysis. For Newars, including for their religious specialists, although there have been traditional methods of analysis, the composition of a single serial account of their entire religion is a relatively new idea. Newar religion is lived in many different contexts. These contexts are usually kept apart, but also kept in place, by the rhythm of the annual and life cycles. Some local *paṇḍit*s, such as Ratna Bahadur Vajracharya (1972), Asha Kaji Vajracharya (1977), and Jog Muni Vajracharya (1979), have attempted serial accounts of Newar Buddhism in recent times. If doing anthropology were merely a question of translation I could have translated these works. But the resulting text would have been unsociological and esoteric, intelligible only to Newars, who do not need it.

In presenting Newar Buddhism in the form of a serial narrative for outsiders, it is necessary to impose order, to classify under different heads, to make connections and comparisons between different parts, and to separate what one considers central from what seems peripheral. (It is also necessary to cross-refer continually from one part to another, and this is why I have resorted to the apparatus of numbered section headings.) In each of these activities I am acutely aware of the possibility of misjudgement. I have therefore used a fundamental Newar Buddhist schema, that of the Three Ways, to organize the main body of the description (chapters 6 through 10). Each Way offers a path to salvation, as monk, householder, and Tantric practitioner respectively. Ultimately, all Three Ways are thought to be one: advanced Newar Buddhists are supposed to fulfil all three simultaneously.

What is meant by the Three Ways – and how it is possible to be both monk and Tantric! – is explained below (§4.2, 9.1, 9.2, 10.3, 10.4). For present purposes it is worth contrasting the Three Ways to the triads which have been used to organize two other studies of Asian religion. Spiro (1982) organized his exposition around the categories nibbanic, kammatic, and apotropaic Buddhism. These refer, respectively, to Buddhism orientated to gaining *nirvāṇa*, Buddhism orientated to improving one's *karma* and thus attaining heaven, and Buddhism used for magical and protective purposes.[5] For all Spiro's lucid exposition and superb ethnography, and in spite of the terms used, these are not in fact emic Burmese categories. Spiro set up three systems or subsystems according to the purposes for which Burmese Buddhism was practised; in fact each purpose can be accommodated within the one system, Buddhism, and the three types of purpose are not so exclusive as implied. Furthermore, Spiro wrongly identified only nibbanic Buddhism, i.e. Buddhism orientated to the attainment of *nirvāṇa*, as normative and scriptural (Gombrich 1972: 491). Unlike Spiro's categories, the categories used here are emic; in other words, they are used by Newar Buddhists themselves. Salvation is the goal in all Three Ways; but all three also have thisworldly uses. Together they form a hierarchy.

Another triad was used by Geertz in *The Religion of Java*. He distinguished three variants of Javanese religion: that of the peasants, that of the old urban ruling class, and that of the more strongly Muslim merchants and artisans. Were one to make a similar analysis of Newar religion one might attempt to distinguish a peasant variant, similar in villages and cities, and two high-caste urban variants, Hinduism and Buddhism. However, because the Newars' is a caste society, and castes like to differentiate themselves from one another, one could also identify as many variants as there are castes. In this book I have not tried to describe all the religious activity of the Newars in equal depth. Rather, I focus on what, in a more ambitious but less detailed analysis, might be considered one variant of the overall religious field.[6]

This brings us to the question of what is meant by 'Newar Buddhism'. 'Newar Buddhism' is short for 'the traditional Mahāyāna and Vajrayāna Buddhism practised by the Newars'. The Newars are an ethnic group, defined partly by language and culture and partly by their association with the Kathmandu Valley. The Valley was traditionally called, and still is called by many, 'Nepal': 'Newar' and 'Nepal' are etymologically identical (though this is evident to few today). As will be explained below (chapter 2), the definition of 'Buddhism' and 'Buddhist' as opposed to 'Hinduism' and 'Hindu' is far from simple in the Newar context. As a first approximation suffice it to say that some Newars are wholly Buddhist, others are wholly Hindu, but the majority of Newars participate in the rites and practices of both religions.

'Religion' in English translates three different Newari terms, all of which come from Sanskrit: *dharma*, *mārga*, and *mata*. The last two, literally path and doctrine respectively, are used, with rare exceptions, only in the expressions *buddhamārga* (or *-mata*) and *śivamārga* (or *-mata*), the paths of the Buddha and of Śiva respectively; and in the derivatives, *buddhamārgī* and *śivamārgī*, a follower of the path of the Buddha or follower of the path of Śiva respectively. The word *dharma* is much more widely used, to mean religion, ritual, duty, teaching, or religious merit (see below §4.3.1).

As such a broad term, *dharma* covers three analytically distinct (ideal) types of religion (see Figure 1).[7] These three types do indeed correspond, more or less, to distinctions made by Newars themselves (as is shown further below, §5.1.1, Figure 15). The first type of religion is soteriology or

Figure 1. Three types of religion. (Cf. Figure 15, on p. 137 below, which rearranges these terms in line with Newar conceptions.)

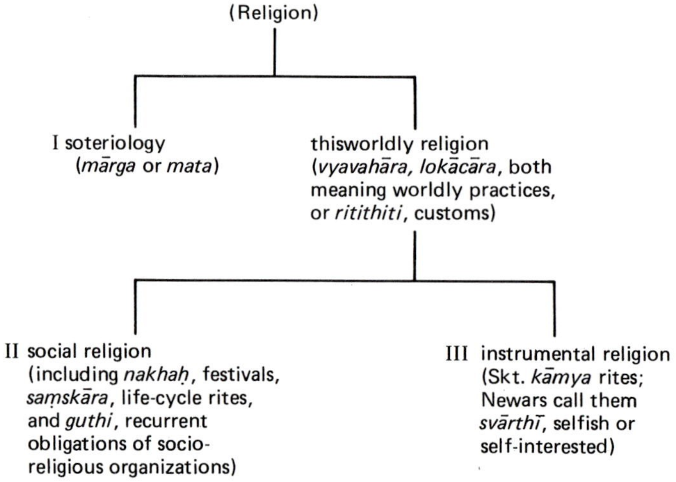

religion of salvation. This corresponds to *mārga* and, within Buddhism, to *yāna*, Way. The word 'salvation' is used in a Weberian manner, to refer to escape from all the ills of this world. Within worldly (i.e. non-soteriological) religion, I distinguish between social religion, on the one hand, and instrumental religion, on the other. Social religion is regular, occurring inevitably according to the cycle of the seasons and of the individual's life. Instrumental religion comprises action undertaken, usually on behalf of an individual, to make something happen, paradigmatically to prevent or overcome illness. Instrumental religion can be (and often is) seen as magic, but for analytical purposes a separate term is useful. Many Buddhists believe that instrumental religious rituals have an effect not because of the inherent power of the rite (as with magic), but because of certain attitudes of mind generated, or because compassionate divinities reward piety and good behaviour.

Both soteriology and instrumental religion are primarily the concern of the individual.[8] Social religion is primarily the religion of the group, be it city, caste, lineage, or family. In writing that a religion, e.g. Buddhism, is a soteriology, I depart from the technical language of theology in which a religion may *have* a soteriology but is not generally said to *be* a soteriology. My defence is again Weberian: these are ideal types. A religion which is a soteriology is not thereby debarred from being social and instrumental as well. Even Theravāda Buddhism, which Weber rightly saw to be as pure a soteriology as has ever been devised, still has room for some elements of social and instrumental religion.

All three types of religion may be called *dharma* in Newari. But a hierarchy is recognized whereby soteriology is the highest and truest *dharma*, and some Newars say that instrumental religion is 'not really *dharma*'. What they mean is that *dharma* ought not to be self-interested. Others also say that social religion is 'not really *dharma*'; they mean by this that people do it, not out of any soteriological intent, but merely because it is traditional in their caste and family (it is their *kuldharma*, 'family *dharma*'). In such a context non-soteriological religion is likely to be disparaged as mere 'worldly custom' (*vyavahāra*, *ritithiti*, or *lokācāra*).

As is probably the case in all world religions, rituals originally designed to promote salvation become universal within a given group and are therefore transformed into life-cycle rites. Such routinization may occur to varying degrees. Monastic Initiation is indeed a life-cycle rite for Śākyas and Vajrācāryas and primarily so, since the soteriological idiom with which it is associated (the Disciples' Way, explained below, §4.2) has been marginalized in Newar Buddhism. Tantric Initiation, on the other hand, although it seems to have been virtually universal among Vajrācāryas in the past, has never lost its strongly soteriological flavour. Some assert that dutiful performance of social religion, culminating in the divinizing rite of Old-Age Initiation (*burā jā̃kwa*), is itself salvific. This interplay between social religion and soteriology, the rites of the one being transformed into rites of the other, is part of the explanation for the polysemy of the word *dharma*.

In order to study Newar religion and society, with a focus on Buddhism, I lived with a Śākya family in Nāg Bāhāḥ, Lalitpur, for nineteen months in 1982–4, again for two weeks in December 1985, and for six weeks in the monsoon (the European summer) of 1986. Further fieldwork was carried out for two months in the monsoon of 1989; during this time I lived in Kathmandu. After a year in the field I was fluent enough in Newari to handle one-to-one conversations with relative ease. Newar culture is so complicated that, taken literally, participant observation sometimes seems like a contradiction in terms: either one observes or one participates, but to do both is impossible. This is true, in particular, of religious rites. The principle retains its validity however for studying the way of life as a whole.

In an urban environment it is impossible to follow Leach's (1982: 145) maxim: 'The first essential of intensive fieldwork is that the fieldworker should be able to recognize everyone in his vicinity . . .' Inevitably one's knowledge is broader – applicable to more people – but shallower than that of an anthropologist working in a village. Furthermore as Leach also points out, though with characteristic overstatement, the idea that all members of a society share the same culture 'is totally misleading. Almost all empirical societies . . . are socially stratified – by "social class", by "hereditary caste", by "hierarchy of rank" etc. – and each stratum in the system is marked by its own distinctive cultural attributes – linguistic usages, manners, styles of dress, food, housing, etc.' (Leach 1982: 43). Since viewpoints are multiple I have given, whenever possible, the caste, age, and sex of my informant. I was certainly limited to some extent by the fact that I was living with Buddhists. In the time available to me, working on my own in a heterogeneous city of nearly 80,000 people, research had to be focused in some way. A team of four, one each for the high-caste Hindus and Buddhists, one for the Maharjan peasant caste, and one for low castes, might have been able to complete a study of the city as a whole.[9] Even had I possessed superhuman energy, the very fact of living with high-caste Buddhists would have made an equally intensive study of other groups problematic, since I was, like a Newar though not to the same extent, identified by where and with whom I was living.

Partly because of the complexity of city life, but mainly because I set out to study religion, I have not written a standard-issue anthropological monograph. Many reservations have been expressed in recent years about the artificial completeness of its format; I do not necessarily share them. The only work close to such a monograph is Toffin's 700-page magnum opus, *Société et Religion chez les Néwar du Népal*. It is a magnificent achievement and an essential source; I refer to it frequently, and occasionally take issue with it, in what follows. Yet, massive and invaluable as Toffin's monograph is, it does not deal with the big cities of the Valley. Instead it focuses primarily on Pyangaon, a small, and in some ways atypical, village, and on Panauti, a small town which is in some ways more similar to medium-sized Newar villages than it is to the three cities of the Valley (cf. §1.2, 11.1 below). There is still room, then, for a monograph on Newar city life, though it is likely to be the result, like Toffin's *Société et Religion*, of repeated research trips over more than a decade.[10]

1.2 Historical background and contemporary context

The Kathmandu Valley is a roughly circular bowl at 1,350 metres (4,400 feet) in the Himalayan foothills. Its fertile soil enabled it to support an elaborate division of labour, a monarchical state (sometimes three states), and complex religious traditions imported from the Indian plains from at least the fifth century. All this, combined with its favourable climate half way between the snows of the high passes to the north and the malarial plains to the south, enabled it to control valuable trade routes between Tibet and India. It was an island of Indian urban 'high' culture in the otherwise relatively poor, sparsely populated, and rustic Himalayan foothills.

Today the Kathmandu Valley houses the capital of the modern state of Nepal, which goes back (give or take several boundary adjustments) to 1769. The contrast between the wealth, cultural elaboration, and amenities of the Valley, on the one hand, and the poverty and backwardness of the rest of the middle hills, on the other, remains as strong as ever. How the cities of the Kathmandu Valley appear to many foreigners, as well as the way they are viewed by those from the hills, is captured in a recent potboiler:

> Kathmandu is a funny city. When you first arrive there from the West, it seems like the most ramshackle and unsanitary place imaginable: the buildings are poorly constructed of old brick, and there are weed patches growing out of the roofs; the hotel rooms are bare pits; all the food you can find tastes like cardboard, and often makes you sick; and there are sewage heaps here and there in the mud streets, where dogs and cows are scavenging. It really seems primitive.
>
> Then you go out for a month or two in the mountains, on a trek or a climb. And when you return to Kathmandu, the place is utterly transformed. The only likely explanation is that while you were gone they took the city away and replaced it with one that looks the same on the outside, but is completely different in substance. The accommodations are luxurious beyond belief; the food is superb; the people look prosperous, and their city is a marvel of architectural sophistication. Kathmandu! What a metropolis! (Robinson 1989: 141)

The history of the Kathmandu Valley can be divided into five periods according to dynasty (see Table 1.1). The first period is that of three 'prehistorical' dynasties: the Gopālas, the Ahīrs (or Mahiṣapālas), and the Kirātas, known primarily from traditional chronicles. Oral accounts, in my experience, mention only the last, the Kirātas.[11] Historians argue that at least the Kirātas must be genuinely historical since the kings' names listed by the chroniclers are all unSanskritic.[12] For the Licchavi period, from the fifth to ninth centuries, there is a corpus of around 200 inscriptions from which one can learn much, although they leave tantalizing gaps. There are far fewer sources for the Ṭhakurī period, from the ninth century to 1200: it seems to have been a time of political decentralization, perhaps even disintegration. For the Malla period, 1200–1768, there is a mass of documentary evidence, only part of which has been published. The same is true of the period since 1769 when Prithvi Narayan Shah, ancestor of the present King, finally conquered, after years of struggle, the divided Malla

Table 1.1 *Main historical periods and some important recent dates.*

Dynasty	*Dates*
Gopāla ('cowherd')	Pre-fifth century,
Ahīr (Mahiṣapāla, 'buffalo-herd')	mythical or semi-mythical
Kirāta	dynasties.
Licchavi	5th–9th centuries
Ṭhakurī	9th century–1200
Malla	1200–1768
Shah	1769–present (Rana period: 1846–1951)

Recent Dates	
1769	Prithvi Narayan Shah's conquest of the Kathmandu Valley establishes the modern state of Nepal.
1846	Jang Bahadur Rana seizes power and establishes hereditary Rana Prime Ministership.
1854	Jang Bahadur promulgates Law Code (Muluki Ain).
1933	Earthquake devastates the Valley.
1951	Overthrow of the Ranas, and the coming of 'democracy'.
1955	King Tribhuvan dies; King Mahendra succeeds him. India completes construction of the Tribhuvan Rajpath metalled (Np. 'pitch') road linking Kathmandu to India.
1960	After one year of the elected Congress government, King Mahendra imprisons Prime Minister Koirala, and establishes Partyless Panchayat Democracy.
1964	Land Reform guarantees the security of tenants and limits their obligations to the annual provision of twenty-three *pāthīs* of paddy per *ropanī* (on the best-quality land).
1972	Death of King Mahendra; King Birendra assumes the throne.
1980	After political disturbances, a referendum is held on whether to continue the partyless system. The partyless system wins by 55% to 45%. The King has conceded direct elections to the National Assembly in any case.

kingdoms of the Kathmandu Valley. In the years immediately following 1769 the present state of Nepal was established. From 1846 to 1951 the Rana family were hereditary prime ministers and effective rulers of Nepal: the Shah kings were kept under tight control. In 1951 the present King's grandfather, Tribhuvan, fled to the Indian Embassy and, with Indian support, brought down the Rana regime.[13]

The modern state of Nepal is shaped like an elongated rectangle lying north-west to south-east along the Himalayas. To the north is Tibet, part of the People's Republic of China; to the south, west, and east lies India. Both the shape of Nepal and the fact that all natural trade routes run north–south along river valleys, not east–west, are strategically important. Not only is Nepal culturally dominated by Indian influences, it is inevitably tied in to the Indian economy, with little room for independent manœuvre. Thus Nepal's foreign policy is based on non-alignment and attempts to counterbalance overwhelming Indian influence.

Geographically Nepal comprises four distinct zones. From north to

Figure 2. Map of Nepal.

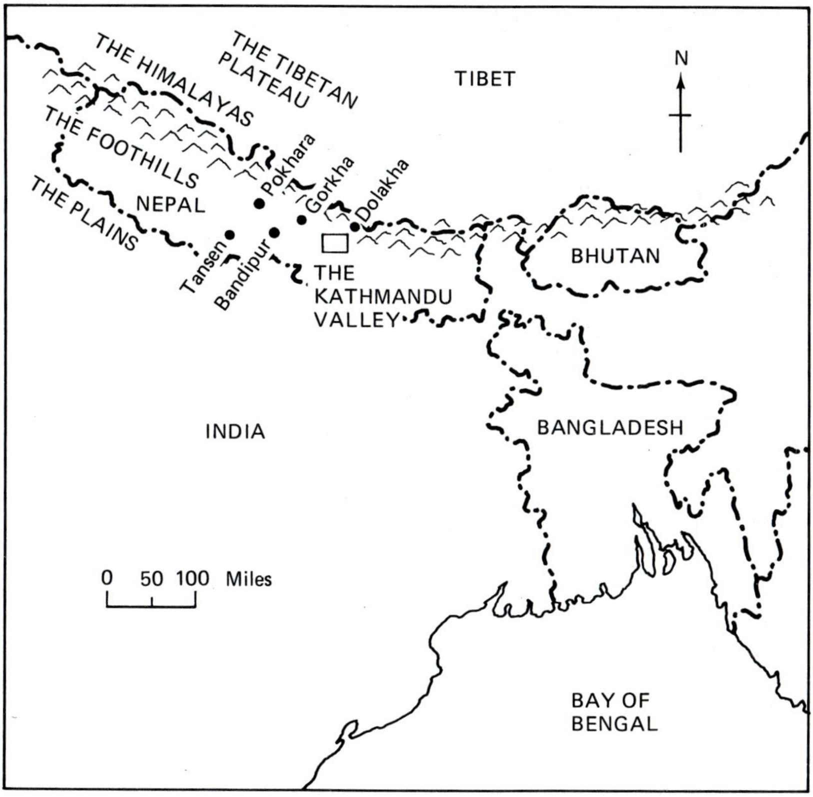

south they are: some valleys on the northern side of the Himalayas, the Himalayas themselves, the middle hills (the Himalayan foothills), and the Tarai (the flat Gangetic plain). The climate of the high valleys is subalpine, of the middle hills temperate, and of the Tarai subtropical. Contrary to what one might expect, the high Himalayas do not form a watershed: a few rivers rising on the Tibetan plateau cut through the high mountains. Even so, the trade routes leading up to Tibet were arduous and dangerous in the past since the valleys are often narrow and the routes lead over high passes. The northernmost valleys, though politically within Nepal, are ethnically and culturally Tibetan. Similarly, at the other end of the country it is equally true that political and cultural boundaries fail to coincide.

The Tarai was ceded to Nepal by the British East India Company in 1816, since they realized that the aristocracy of Nepal would need large estates to make the new state of Nepal viable. The extensive forests of the Tarai formed a malarial barrier which the Shah and Rana rulers were happy to maintain in order to discourage any ideas of invasion the British might harbour. With the eradication of malaria there has been considerable migration from the hills of Nepal into the Tarai, but the bulk of the population is still linguistically and culturally continuous with groups just over the border in India. Consequently they are often regarded as Indians, and are in effect treated as second-class citizens in much of the citizenship legislation of Nepal (Gaige 1975: chapter 5), notwithstanding the fact that the Tarai produces 59% of Nepal's GDP and 79% of government revenue (ibid.: xv).

The majority of Nepal's population lives in the middle hills. The culturally and politically dominant ethnic group is known as Parbatiyā, meaning 'hill people'. They tend to be called Indo-Nepalese in French-language publications, and one or two Anglophone writers have followed this usage. Others refer to them as 'Indo-Aryan'. I prefer to avoid both these usages, since at worst they imply that language and race (or genetic inheritance) must always go together, and at best they suggest that the Parbatiyās' culture is closer to that of India than that of other groups in Nepal. This latter assumption is simplistic and debatable, especially so when Parbatiyās are compared to Newars.

The Parbatiyā caste system is relatively simple. The main castes are Brahman (pronounced 'Bāhun') and Chetri (the local pronunciation of Kṣatriya). Associated with them are several Untouchable artisan castes (principally Damāī̐, Kāmī, and Sārkī, who are Tailors, Blacksmiths, and Leatherworkers respectively). There is a small royal caste, Ṭhakurī, a Kṣatriya sub-caste higher than the Chetris, from which the King of Nepal must come by law. Jang Bahadur Rana attempted (and largely succeeded) to have his branch of the Kunwar clan raised to the status of Ṭhakurī, from that of Chetri, by having the King grant them the title 'Rana', and by arranging numerous marriages between his relatives and the royal family. The Nepali language was known traditionally as *khas kurā*, meaning 'the language of the Khas'.[14] The Newari equivalent, *khẽy bhāy*, is still frequently used in Newari, as is the alternative *parti bhāy* ('language of the Parbatiyās'). 'Khas' is the old name for the Chetris, but they now consider it insulting (Newars apply the term *khẽy* to all Parbatiyās). The name 'Gorkhālī' is used both as a name for Parbatiyās and for the Nepali language; the reason is that the Shah dynasty came from the town of Gorkha about forty miles to the west of Kathmandu. The English 'Gurkha' is a mispronunciation of this. It is something of a paradox, then, that British policy was (and is) not to recruit Parbatiyās into the Gurkhas, but rather certain of the so-called hill tribes.

Unlike the Parbatiyās who are found in large numbers in most of the middle hills, these hill tribes tend to be concentrated in particular regions. Some 'tribes' still speak their own Tibeto-Burman languages; others, or many members of others, now speak only Nepali. The most well-known hill tribes are the Magars and Gurungs to the west of the Valley, the Tamangs all around it, and the Rais and Limbus to the east. Historically there has long been a process of migration eastwards along the Himalayas. Even in the areas of their greatest concentrations, the 'tribes' now live intermingled with Parbatiyās and other immigrants, especially Parbatiyā low-caste specialists settled on the edge of their villages. The further east one goes the greater the melting-pot effect. Outside of Nepal, in Darjeeling, Sikkim, Bhutan, and Assam, all Nepalese tend to blend together, all speaking only Nepali. Many Newars have joined this migration eastwards. They have also spread in all directions throughout Nepal, where they are renowned as a trading and shopkeeping group. They tend to dominate the bazaar towns of the middle hills (except areas around the Thak Khola Valley, where the local Thakali traders were evidently able to keep them out).

All these various ethnic groups were absorbed into the Parbatiyā hierarchy above the Untouchables but below the Chetris. This process was ratified and extended by Jang Bahadur Rana's Law Code of 1854 (Höfer 1979). Associated with this there has been a cultural process of Sanskritization, still continuing today and encouraged by education and the radio, whereby the hill tribes have gradually adopted the culture and the language of the dominant Parbatiyās.

The Newars proved a classificatory problem for the compilers of the Law Code and have remained one for anthropologists and others ever since. They are divided into many castes, far more than the Parbatiyās. Their social structure, urban life-style, literacy, and artistic achievements make the Newars quite unlike the hill tribes, with whom they are often classed simply on the grounds of their Tibeto-Burman language, Newari.[15] Today the Newars may well be in a slight minority in the place they consider theirs, the Kathmandu Valley. Exactly what the proportions are is impossible to know since, even if one accepts the figures as reliable (a generous assumption), Nepalese censuses ask only for mother tongue and not for ethnicity. Consequently many Newars are registered, often correctly, as Nepali-speaking. Probably about half of all Newars live outside the Valley, and very many of these have assimilated completely to Parbatiyā culture.

Within the Kathmandu Valley there is now a vociferous movement of Newar cultural nationalism, seeking to preserve Newar culture and the Newari language. Much of its effort goes into literary production: Newari plays, poems, novels, short stories, magazines, and a few comics. There are at least two Newari weekly newspapers and since 1988 there is a small daily newspaper as well. K.P. Malla's bibliographies (1979a: 31; 1984a: 2–3) list 1,306 books published in Newari between 1909 and 1983. Compared to the number of books and newspapers in Nepali these figures are not very impressive. Nonetheless it is far more than appears in any other minority language of Nepal (with the possible exception of Maithili, spoken in the Tarai).[16] Newar cultural nationalists are quick to point out that there are no government grants or subsidies for publications in Newari and that they have to raise all the finance themselves – an altruistic and often politically risky labour of love. It is also true that of those Newars who are literate, many, if not most, are more comfortable reading in Nepali than in Newari, because they have been educated exclusively in the former. In fact many cannot read in their mother tongue at all. Recently Newar cultural nationalists have joined with intellectuals from other minority groups to call for primary education in the mother tongue (as it often was, among the Newars at least, until the late 1960s).

The most visible public movement in which Newar cultural nationalists are involved is that to have the Nepal Samvat (era) recognized as the national era instead of the current official and 'foreign' era, the Vikram Samvat. This, they claim, is not a specifically Newar issue, though it is certainly perceived as such within the Valley where the annual demonstration around the three cities, Kathmandu, Bhaktapur, and Lalitpur, is participated in largely by Newars. Non-Newars call this procession *bhintunā*, since this ('Good wishes!' in Newari) is part of one of the slogans most frequently chanted by the men and boys as they circulate in trucks and cars, on motorcycles, bicycles, and tractors.[17]

There is another tendency, too diverse to compose a single movement, which is related to, and yet distinct from, Newar cultural nationalism. It focuses on Buddhism. Many Buddhist intellectuals are more interested either in reviving traditional Newar Buddhism or in propagating the relatively newly introduced Theravāda Buddhism (cf. §11.3 below). Such Buddhist activists frequently make use of Newari. Indeed it is Buddhist Newars, rather than Hindu Newars, who tend to publish religious works in Newari. Thus of the 1,306 printed Newari works mentioned above, 555 were on religion and all but twenty-two of these were Buddhist. Newar Hindus, by contrast, tend to publish in Nepali since they share their

Hinduism with Parbatiyās; often indeed they make use of the numerous Hindu devotional works published in India in Hindi.

However, although Buddhist activists are perhaps the biggest single group making use of Newari, they do not place great value on the language itself, and are just as happy to use Nepali where that enables them to communicate their Buddhist message more easily. Their magazines normally carry articles in Nepali and Newari side by side. There are some Buddhist Newars who are both Buddhist activists *and* Newar cultural nationalists, but on the whole their prime loyalty lies either with the religion or with the language. Even among the prominent Newari poets, many write also in Nepali. It is probably significant however, that it is those from Hindu backgrounds who do this, whereas those of a Buddhist background are more likely to write only in Newari.

Most Newars are not very involved either in Newar cultural nationalism or in Buddhist activism. The limit of their participation is to take part in the New Year's demonstration, to attend a programme of speeches or a quiz laid on by Buddhist activists, or to peruse occasionally a newspaper or other publication in Newari. What has affected all Newars in different ways is the gradual intensification of Newar cultural self-consciousness, a process going back at least to 1769 and the conquest of the Valley by Parbatiyās. In Nepal as a whole, Newars, at least high-caste (and especially Hindu) Newars, are very successful. They, along with Parbatiyā Brahmans and Chetris, hold most of the top jobs in the country, so that a recent author has referred, with some justice, to 'the Chetri-Brahmin-Newar "establishment"'.[18] Newars have certainly benefited from their traditions of literacy and from their proximity to the rulers of the country. Although probably only something of the order of 6% of the population of the country as a whole, they account for roughly 30% of all university teachers and civil servants. Their representation within commerce and industry may be even higher than this. Nonetheless, Newars often feel that they are a disadvantaged minority, because the effective selection pool for many of these posts is the Kathmandu Valley, where, as we have seen, they make up about half the population.

Newar identity today is starkly and obviously relational. Newars now define themselves as 'not Parbatiyā'. The prime marker of ethnic identification is, in the Nepalese context, language. Since the Parbatiyās' language is now called Nepali, it is not uncommon to hear young Newars say, 'I'm not Nepalese, I'm a Newar' (and they may say this even if they themselves do not speak Newari, or only speak it badly). Some castes, especially Newar Brahmans, but also to a degree the high Hindu caste of

Śreṣṭhas, are generally more assimilationist than other Newars. They are readier than others to adopt Parbatiyā customs and to speak Nepali, rather than Newari, to their children. Nonetheless, Śreṣṭhas still consider themselves Newars, and indeed are often taken to be, and consider themselves, the typical and paradigmatic Newars. There is considerable historical evidence that from the mid-seventeenth century (its earliest occurrence) to the nineteenth century the term 'Newar' was used only of those groups now called Śreṣṭha (Gellner 1986: 140–1). I suspect that many ethnic terms in modern South Asia originated in this way as names of the Kṣatriya or noble caste in the region in question.

By a familiar kind of oppositional logic, Newar cultural nationalists wish to emphasize and accentuate the Newar sense of being 'not Parbatiyā'. Consequently there is great concern with the purity of the Newari language. In a reversal of at least 1,500 years of Sanskritization, Tibeto-Burman neologisms are created for modern and abstract concepts. But Indo-European influence has gone so deep in Newari that if one were really to purge the language of everything which was not strictly Tibeto-Burman in origin, one would be unable to speak at all except about very basic bodily functions and movements. Many kin terms, virtually all religious vocabulary, and all abstract concepts would go. Thus the more 'pure' Newari an intellectual speaks, the further what he says is from the language of ordinary Newars.

The Nepali language suffers from a parallel paradox, also arising from nationalistic concerns. Being an Indo-European language it seems more natural to borrow its new concepts from Sanskrit. But this, as K.P. Malla points out (1979b: 144), leads 'to the paradox of Nepali linguistic nationalism [which] is that the broader the scope of Nepali, the less it sounds like a language of Nepal'. In fact it ends up sounding like the very language from which Nepalese nationalists wish to differentiate it, namely Hindi. At one time this fact provoked a kind of linguistic populist stance on the part of some Nepalese intellectuals, and they proposed, where a Sanskrit loanword was unavoidable, to borrow one which was different from that used in Hindi (Hutt 1988: 59). The advocates of Nepali and Newari share with each other, and no doubt with intellectuals throughout the subcontinent, a rhetoric of devotional love for their mother tongue and culture.

The name 'Nepal' applied traditionally only to the Kathmandu Valley and many hill Nepalese still say 'I'm off to Nepal' when they are going to Kathmandu. It was the British who first extended to the whole of the territory ruled by the Shah dynasty the name of the place which housed their capital. This usage was taken up by the Nepalese state itself only a century later in the 1920s.[19] The term 'Nepal' (Skt. *nepālāḥ*) seems to have begun as an ethnic term, Tibeto-Burman in origin, used of the buffalo- and/or cattle-herders of the Tistung valley, just outside the Kathmandu Valley on the old path down to India (Malla 1984b: 68). 'Nepal' came quickly to denote the Kathmandu Valley and it was always given a Sanskritic etymology in the charter myths and legends of the Valley's origin. The etymology most frequently given in nineteenth-century chronicles (and now in history textbooks) derives 'Nepal' from the name of a sage, Ne, who protected (*pāl*) the Valley; he is also credited with initiating the rule of the Gopāla dynasty (Hasrat 1970: 33). Oral tradition cites more frequently another etymology: '*niyam pāl*', 'keeping the rules' (see §7.1 below).

In the Malla period the language of the Valley was known formally as *deśa-bhāṣā* ('the language of the country') or as *nepāla-bhāṣā* ('the language of Nepal'). Colloquially it became known as, and is still called, *newā-bhāy*. By a kind of back-formation, 'Newā' or 'Newar' came to denote those who spoke *newā-bhāy*. A distinction thus grew up between the people (Newars) and the place (Nepal). The first Newar cultural nationalist, Dharmaditya Dharmacharyya, attempted to tie the two together by disputing the decision of the government to designate the Parbatiyās' language, till then called Gorkhālī, as Nepali, and by reviving the old name of Newari, Nepal Bhāṣā (Gellner 1986).

The historical and ethnic awareness of the Newars who are the subject of this book does not encompass all the periods and details discussed so far. They believe that the Valley was once a lake full of holy serpents (*nāga*) and that it was emptied by the *bodhisattva* Mañjuśrī cutting through the gorge at Kotwal. Both before and after this various Buddhas visited the Valley, thus sacralizing its important landmarks. These associations are outlined below (§7.1). Moving to more historic times, local people consider that the Kirātas were uncivilized anti-Buddhist kings. There are various reminders of the Kirāta period, in particular a mound in Patuko near the centre of Lalitpur, where the Kirātas' palace is said to have been; one caste, the Vyañjankārs, are said to be descended from Kirātas. Later on there was a period of many small-scale Vaiśya kings, some of whose descendants, the Thaku Jujus, still have important ceremonial functions (e.g. as the sponsor of the five-yearly Samyak festival in Lalitpur). Many local myths feature the destruction by fire of a city called Viśālnagar and the flight of particular groups to Lalitpur at about this period. Later still was the period of Malla or 'Newar' kings ruling in each of the three cities of Kathmandu, Lalitpur, and Bhaktapur. Several of them are still part of popular folk memory, such as Siddhi

Narasiṃha and his son Śrī Nivāsa. Eventually the Newar kings were defeated and replaced by Parbatiyā ones. During the time of the latter there was the Rana period, which is still remembered by those aged forty-five or more. For many it was a time of poverty, and for peasant farmers especially so. It was also a time when people feared authority greatly and therefore – so it is claimed – officials took fewer bribes. For today's older generation, the end of the Rana regime in 1951 marked a turning point in their lives. Another temporal landmark was the great earthquake of 1933.

Before 1951 caste and caste traditions, which included much of what counts as Newar Buddhism, were supported by the force of law. It was illegal to live by a trade or profession which was traditionally the exclusive preserve of another caste. The Rana period seems to have frozen the Newars' culture and caste hierarchy. Not only were caste traditions regulated by law, the Newars found themselves encapsulated within a political system which excluded all but a few of them from positions of influence. It is very hard to be sure, but one suspects that in the Malla period, before 1769, Newar culture and society were somewhat more fluid, although even then new practices were no doubt justified primarily in terms of primordial tradition.

There are three cities in the Kathmandu Valley each of which, as noted above, was the seat of a royal kingdom in the later Malla period: Kathmandu itself, Lalitpur, and Bhaktapur. These are the modern official names. Lalitpur, where I did most of my research, is known as 'Yala' or 'Yela' in Newari, 'Pāṭan' in Nepali, and 'Lalitapaṭṭana' (or some variant) in inscriptions and other historical sources. There are numerous Newar villages surrounding these three cities. The villages display the same urban life-style as the towns: that is, they are nucleated, and have the same kind of social organization and culture.[20] A Newar peasant prefers to live next door to his kin and an hour's walk from his fields rather than the other way around. Normally these villages are tied to one or other of the cities by regular religious and ritual occasions: masked dances of the Mother Goddesses, pilgrimage routes, and priestly services. There are other Newar settlements larger than villages but not so large as the three big cities. They approach the cities in the number of castes present, and they mark their aspiration to the status of city in various ritual ways, primarily by the presence, if only in ritual, of a place designated as a 'royal palace'. Examples of such towns are Kirtipur, Thimi, Banepa, and Panauti.[21]

In addition to these three types of settlement within the Kathmandu Valley – one-time royal cities, aspiring towns, and villages – there are several other types of Newar settlement found outside the Valley. It has

Figure 3. Map of the Kathmandu Valley.

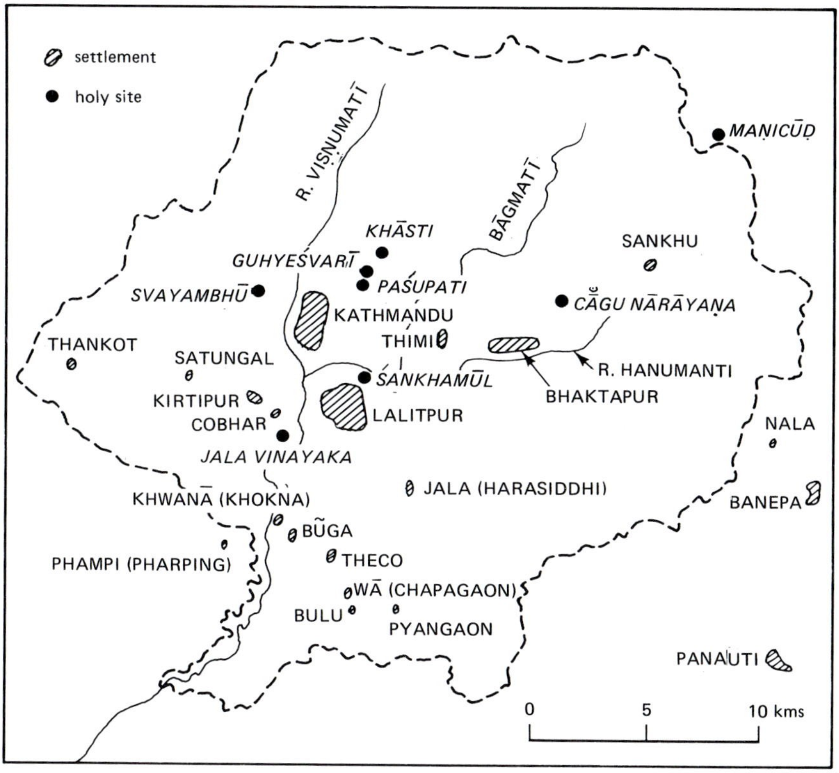

already been remarked that throughout the Nepalese hills the Newars are the principal group involved in the retail trade. This Newar diaspora is the product of emigration from the Valley occurring continuously since 1769. In a few cases – the Newar bazaar in Gorkha is a case in point – such settlements even predate 1769. One can distinguish: (i) bazaar towns near the Valley where Newar culture and the Newari language are largely retained; (ii) bazaar towns far from the Valley – such as Dailekh studied by Lionel Caplan (1975) – where Newar culture and Newari are entirely lost; (iii) peasant villages throughout Nepal, but principally near old trade routes, which are Nepali-speaking (like category ii) and are to all intents and purposes assimilated to Parbatiyā culture.[22]

Nowadays the ancient cities of Kathmandu and Lalitpur have become in effect a single conurbation enclosed by the ring road donated by the People's Republic of China. However, the Newar inhabitants of each city still maintain a strong sense of difference and each city has a separate local council. The Valley is dotted with the settlements of Parbatiyās, who, unlike Newars, do not traditionally live in nucleated settlements. Their farm-houses are spread out all over the Valley; a Parbatiyā village lacks the architectural density and urban 'feel' of a Newar village.

The population of the Kathmandu Valley is today much greater than can be supported by its own agricultural output. The Valley houses most of the civil service of the modern Nepalese state, as well as numerous foreign aid organizations and diplomatic missions. Tourism is a very important earner of foreign currency. During the early 1980s on average about 55,000 Indian and 125,000 other tourists came to Nepal each year, and the vast majority came by air, i.e. via Kathmandu. The trend in tourist numbers, in spite of occasional dips, was generally upwards (HMG 1988: 132ff.). Tourism has been particularly important for the Vajrācāryas and Śākyas. Many of them are artisans whose livelihood now largely depends on foreign and tourist demand for the curios, statues, and jewellery they produce.

Foreign aid finances almost the whole of the Nepalese government's development budget. Development, such as it is, has had a much more dramatic effect in the Valley than elsewhere. The whole of the Valley has electricity and metalled roads lead to many of its villages. Unlike more remote areas of the rest of Nepal, Land Reform (1964) has had a real effect.[23] There are in the Valley jobs and commercial opportunities, educational facilities and hospitals, the like of which are unknown in the hills. There has been rapid population growth in recent years; the population of Kathmandu went up from roughly 150,000 in 1971 to over 235,000 in 1981 (cf. Table 1.2 below). The population of Lalitpur increased from 59,000 to nearly 80,000 in the same period. Between 1980 and 1984 Nepal had the second-highest annual population growth rate in South Asia (2.6% compared to Pakistan's 3%) and the highest urban growth rate at 8.2% (UNICEF 1987: 10).

All of this means that the Valley is changing rapidly. Change is most obvious in the replacement of traditional three- or four-storey houses of brick, ornately carved wooden windows, and tile, by anything from five- to nine-storey ones of cement and concrete. Around the ancient centres of Kathmandu and Lalitpur every spare plot of rich riceland is disappearing under the remorseless advance of housing. Already in an article first published in 1967 K.P. Malla commented on the new suburbia where 'pseudo-smart bungalows are cropping up – many of them in the form of brick edifices plastered with cement and painted with garish colours of all shades.'[24] Kathmandu, which within recent memory was a sleepy town with its few modern boulevards often empty, is now a noisy, overcrowded, and gigantic bazaar, with (by the late 1980s) seemingly permanent traffic jams. Where once it was an entrepôt between Tibet and India, it is now the nearest point where Indians can buy Japanese goods brought in from Hong Kong and Bangkok.

Social change, though less obvious than the transformation of the old architectural forms, is also occurring. To give one of many possible examples, the vast majority of women older than fifty-five are illiterate; when they were young, girls were not taught to read. Nowadays a high-caste girl who has not passed her (secondary) school leaving certificate (SLC) will find it counting against her in the marriage stakes.

Social change has of course affected religious practices, and this is mentioned where appropriate. The present study is primarily concerned with what Buddhist Newars consider to be their traditional religious practices, rather than with their transformation under modern conditions. It is necessary, therefore, to backtrack and consider again, in the light of the context just outlined, that period when, so far as it is possible to tell today, the practices that Newars themselves consider to be 'traditional Newar culture' were created.

Local chronicles (*vaṃśāvalī*) ascribe great importance to Sthiti Malla (also known as Jaya Sthiti Malla), who ruled the Kathmandu Valley from 1382 to 1395. Scholars debate whether his reign was as significant as folk tradition presents it. Newar tradition has probably settled on Sthiti Malla as the origination of traditional custom because of his name (*sthiti* or *thiti* means 'custom' or 'regulations').[25] Nonetheless, it seems that it was indeed around this period that much of what is now considered central to Newar culture was created or put together from old materials. For instance, the Svayambhū Purāṇa, which is a fundamental charter for present-day Newar Buddhist practice, probably dates from this period. The Svasthānī *vrata* (the Observance of the goddess Svasthānī) also emerged at this time: it was invented by Newars, possibly by Vajrācāryas, but is now fundamental to female Hindu piety throughout modern Nepal (Bennett 1983; Iltis 1985). One can speculate that the Muslim conquest of north India led to a greater awareness of the need to provide a local rationale for Buddhism and Hinduism, now that the sources of the one were destroyed and of the other weakened. Similarly after 1769, when the Parbatiyās conquered the Newars, there was, as already mentioned, a heightened awareness of local – and eventually consciously Newar – identity.[26]

It was probably also around the time of Sthiti Malla, or shortly after, that the last celibate monks within Newar Buddhism died out. Thereafter Newars who wished to be monks or nuns in the conventional sense had to enter the Tibetan Buddhist orders. Local tradition ascribes the extinction of permanently celibate monks to Śaṅkara Ācārya or to Sthiti Malla (see §3.3 below). It is represented as a violent iconoclastic change. In fact monks probably coexisted with married Vajrācārya priests for a long period, until the monks finally disappeared in the fourteenth or fifteenth century. It is not clear when married monks and Vajrācāryas first appeared in Nepal: perhaps in the tenth or eleventh century. The wife of King Meghavāhana of Kashmir built a monastery half of which was destined for married monks as early as the fifth or sixth century.[27] Kölver and Śākya (1985: 190–2) cite a document of 1069 (N.S. 189) which records the mortgage of land, including the property of her husband, by a Buddhist nun: they are inclined to believe (ibid.: 62) that her husband was still alive, which, if so, would prove the existence of married monks in eleventh-century Nepal. This, however, is far from certain; Śākya women today are never thought of as married nuns, whereas Śākya men *are* meant to be seen, in ways described below, as married monks. In any case, by the fifteenth century what is recognizably the present Newar Buddhist system was well established. A manuscript of 1440–1 from Oṁ Bāhāḥ, Lalitpur, specifies that sons of lower-caste mothers are not to be initiated. As Locke points out, 'this is a clear statement of three facts: the members of the *saṅgha* are married and have sons, membership in the *saṅgha* is limited to sons of members, and pure caste status is a prerequisite for initiation'.[28]

1.3 The setting of the study

In order to study Newar Buddhism I went to Lalitpur, the city which is commonly known to be the most Buddhist of the three in the Valley. According to the census of 1981, 17.2% of Lalitpur's population is Buddhist compared to 13.6% in Kathmandu and 3.6% in Bhaktapur. The corresponding figures for 1971 are respectively 32.5%, 24.5%, and 7.5%. In fact Lalitpur is very much more than one sixth Buddhist (if one believes the 1981 census) or one third Buddhist (if one believes the 1971 census); the significance of the census figures is discussed below (§2.7). Within Lalitpur I decided to focus my research on the members of Kwā Bāhāḥ, the largest and arguably the most important of Lalitpur's large monasteries (*bāhāḥ*). Later I also investigated Cikã Bahī which, as it turned out, has more members than any other of the *bahī* class of monasteries, and has preserved best the distinctive traditions of the *bahī*.[29] Membership in these monasteries is determined by patrilineal descent. Small Monastic Communities (*saṃgha, sã*) sometimes operate as exogamous patrilineal descent

Table 1.2 *1981 figures on population, mother tongue, and religion for the three cities (town panchayats) of Lalitpur, Kathmandu, and Bhaktapur.*

	Lalitpur		*Kathmandu*		*Bhaktapur*	
Total households	12,301		35,985		7,270	
Total population	79,875		235,160		48,472	
Newari mother tongue	40,817	(51.1%)	84,287	(35.8%)	40,459	(83.5%)
Nepali mother tongue	31,110	(38.9%)	119,050	(50.6%)	6,796	(14%)
Hindu	64,422	(80.7%)	195,299	(83%)	45,987	(94.9%)
Buddhist	13,370	(16.7%)	30,735	(13.1%)	1,727	(3.6%)

Source: HMG 1984: Tables 1, 9, and 10.

groups. Large monasteries like Kwā Bāhāḥ, on the other hand, do not, and marriage is permitted between members.

The city of Lalitpur, like other Newar settlements, is divided into numerous named localities. Streets are narrow, often being just wide enough for one car to pass down at a time. There are many lanes (*galli*) which are impassable by car. The streets of Lalitpur are laid out roughly in a grid pattern and it is likely that, as in other Newar settlements, the city developed in accordance with Hindu scriptural models.[30] Today there is a paradoxical contrast between the old cities of Kathmandu and Lalitpur, both laid out in a relatively regular grid pattern hundreds of years ago, and the new modern suburbs built all around them, which have grown up higgledy-piggledy along winding roads according to no plan and by a 'natural' process of accretion. Only on two sides, the north and east, does Lalitpur retain a considerable number of rice fields still, and it is only a matter of time before urban infill spreads there too.

Within the city of Lalitpur localities are centred either on a crossroads with temples and a dance platform (*dabu*) or on a Buddhist monastery. Whereas Hindu temples tend to be sited at crossroads and to stand on several layered plinths in order to make them as prominent as possible, Buddhist monasteries are characteristically formed by an enclosed courtyard which has to be entered, thereby leaving the street behind. Streets and lanes do not normally have names (an exception is a lane opposite the palace called No Head Lane, *mwaḥmaru galli*, because it has a shrine to the decapitated goddess, Chinnamastā). Recently (1989) a tourist map of

Kathmandu was published by foreigners which produced a comic effect by squeezing all the locality names onto streets.

Attachment to one's own place, what the Italians call *campanilismo*, is strong. Once the anthropologist comes to live in one place, as will be discussed further below (§11.1), the inhabitants of that place count him or her as one of theirs, and are not happy to be deserted.[31] In Lalitpur I lived in Nāg Bāhāḥ, a large well-known courtyard (not a monastery in spite of the name). It is one of a series of courtyards adjacent to Kwā Bāhāḥ and it is inhabited almost exclusively by Śākya and a few Vajrācārya members of Kwā Bāhāḥ. The other inhabitants are several families of Nāpits (Barbers) and one Maharjan (Farmer) household.

In Nāg Bāhāḥ most of the inhabitants are artisans, but a large number keep shops of different sorts, and a few have salaried government jobs. There is also a larger number of rich traders, including members of the well-known Dhakhwa clan, than is normal for a single residential quarter (*twāḥ*) of the city and this gives rise to the popular image of Nāg Bāhāḥ as a rich man's (*sāhu*) area. It is true that it is better kept than most other parts of the city. Nāg Bāhāḥ has what the locals call a 'park' with rose bushes, trees, and an enclosure in the centre, alongside the numerous votive *caitya*s (Buddhist cult objects); it is paved with bricks and acquired covered drains earlier than most other parts of the city. The inhabitants take pride in its appearance, though what counts as clean in Nepal (depositing rubbish outside where Sweepers can collect it eventually) might not be reckoned so by a Westerner, just as some of what Westerners consider clean (e.g. washing dishes in still water) is thought dirty and impure by Newars.

The Newar norm, both in the moral and in the statistical sense, is the patrilineal joint family (Quigley 1985a). Quigley shows clearly that three quarters of high-caste Newars in Dhulikhel, and nearly half of the (low) Khaḍgī caste, live in some kind of joint family. As he rightly stresses, those who live in a nuclear family do so because they are at a particular point in the domestic cycle. When the sons marry and have children, the household is expected to stay together. Indeed it is not uncommon for four generations to live together.

Beyond the household there is the patrilineage, all members of which share a common lineage nickname. I shall use the term 'clan' when the lineage is large enough to have sections (*kawaḥ*) the size of ordinary lineages (cf. §2.6 below). There are sometimes other clans or lineages, with different nicknames, which are also remembered to be related patrilineally, though exact links can no longer be demonstrated. Within the clan or lineage three categories are recognized: distant kin (*tāpā phuki*), kin (*phuki*), and close or 'bone marrow' kin (*syā phuki*). For distant kin only the remotest of death obligations are observed; for kin, seven days' mourning is observed; for close kin, forty-five days' (see Table 7.5). Other ritual observances are more a matter of choice, and may or may not be performed with kin in general. This depends on the state of the cooperative institution (*guthi*) for the worship of the Lineage Deity (§8.2.4).

Kinship terms distinguish all generations up to grandparents and down to great-grandchildren and beyond; they also distinguish consanguines from affines.[32] Generally too, wife-takers are clearly distinguished from wife-givers. The only exception to this is that the word for mother's brother (*pāju*) is the same as that for the father's sister's husband. The two are not confused in Newars' minds. (If the latter needs to be specified with more precision he is called *jicā pāju*.) Nonetheless, the equivalence remains as a hint that in the long-distant past the Newars may well have practised cross-cousin marriage. Today it is considered shocking and taboo, although it is known that neighbouring groups, such as the Tamangs, practise it; and certain groups within Newar society are accused of practising it (Lalitpur Vyañjankārs, Dhulikhel Śreṣṭhas, Pyangaon Maharjans).

Like the traditional Japanese joint family (Bachnik 1983), the Newar joint family is a kind of corporation. The head of the household may not sell family property without the agreement of his sons who are coparceners. However, unlike the Japanese case, the Newar joint family does not survive the death of all its members. In Japan the ideal is that only one son inherits; the others have to leave and set up branch houses. The Japanese household continues, as the same household, over many generations. Among the Newars, as generally in South Asia, all sons inherit equally, so that when the property of a joint household in which there are three brothers is divided, three new households result, and the old household is no more. This is made public to all and sundry when the old house is divided into three with internal partitions and separate entrances.

It is very common for the splitting up of a Newar joint family and the consequent division of property to occasion bitter disputes between brothers.[33] Since houses are frequently divided down the middle, households often live immediately next door to their nearest patrilineal kin. When conducting my house-to-house survey I discovered that in a surprising number of cases such close kin are not on speaking terms ('imita nã ma wā', 'we don't speak to them'). Newars are aware that in their culture there is no unproblematic way for divisions to be made, and they often compare their own society unfavourably with that of the Parbatiyās. Among Parbatiyās, Newars say, division more often occurs amicably and before the death of the parents. If a Parbatiyā man is successful, he will pull his brothers up with him. A Newar man in the same position is often on such bad terms with his brothers that he refuses to help them. In fact Parbatiyās also quarrel to the point of not speaking (Bennett 1983: 179, 205). Whether there is anything to the Newar perception of Parbatiyās, other than a Newar sense of difference and of their own disunity, is impossible to say. It would be wrong to imagine that brothers are always on bad terms, but, equally, it is a rare division of property which leaves no resentments at all in its wake.

Authority in the household is vested in the senior male, and in his wife who keeps the keys to the storeroom. Keys have great symbolic importance in Newar society, as will be seen again below (pp. 156, 233). Since houses are rarely left empty and since valuables are always locked away, it is often young and powerless members of the family who are suspected of petty theft. When a man is old and if his wife has died, he will hand over the headship of the household to his son. Authority within the household is represented in many ways. One, already noted, is the practice of sitting in order of seniority, first men, then women, during feasts. Another is the formal deference of 'bowing down' to elders. This may be done in two ways: 'bowing down to the feet' (i.e. so that the forehead actually touches the foot) ('tuti bhāgi yāye'; in Kathmandu also called 'tuti ani yāye'); or 'bending the head' ('chyā̃ kwachuye') while saying 'bhāgi yāy' ('I bow down [to you]').

The rules for bowing down to elders are complicated and vary from caste to caste. In general it is said that men should bow down to the feet of all those, both male and female, of generations senior to them in the household. Technically they should do so to elder brothers as well. In practice they bow down only on formal occasions when receiving a blessing from the elder in the shape of powder (*sinhaḥ*) placed on the forehead and a flower given into the right hand. On such occasions – including rituals carried out in cooperation with patrilineally related households where the blessing is distributed by the most senior male present – they bend down towards the feet but are likely to be prevented by the senior from actually touching the feet if they make a serious attempt to do so.[34] On other occasions, for instance when meeting senior agnatic or affinal relatives in public, a man should show deference by inclining his head (though with the mother's brother more informality is allowed). A similar deference should be shown to one's family priest and to his wife. After the death of their mother or father, while the corpse is lying on the funeral pyre, men must make clear and unambiguous obeisance to their parents' feet (accompanied by cries or sobs).

Unmarried women have to bow down only to the feet of their mother and father, and to no one else. Married women, however, have to show ritualized deference to more people and more often than anyone. Among most Newars, every day before eating, they have to bow down to the feet of their husband, all the husband's elder brothers (providing they are in the same household), their husband's mother and father, and all others of senior generations within the household. In some families they have to bow down to their husband's elder brothers' wives as well; in others they do this only on feast days. By contrast, among urban Śreṣṭhas (high-caste Hindu Newars) as among Parbatiyās, the young married woman has to bow down to the feet only of her husband and her mother-in-law. It will be seen from this that the body is hierarchized, like space in general. The right side ranks above the left: a wife should keep her husband to her right, to show respect, just as one circumambulates a deity clockwise, for the same reason. Inside the house, one should never step over the body of a senior and in order to avoid doing so while descending the stairs one should shout 'Binābi!' as a warning.

It is worth noting that the terminology of kinship and seniority carries over into other spheres. The elders of a Buddhist monastery, and sometimes those of a *guthi*, are called 'grandfathers' (*āju*). Newar Brahmans are addressed as 'grandfather' using the Nepali word (*bājyā*). Some goddesses are called 'grandmother' (*aji*), particularly Hārītī and Tantric goddesses. Some gods are called 'grandfather', particularly Bhairava, Indra, Dīpaṅkara, and Tantric gods. A conflation of gods and ancestors occurs in some Tantric shrines where effigies of the founders are kept and worshipped during rituals there.

Marriage is almost invariably viri- and patrilocal.[35] The number of people a married woman has to bow down to, and the fact that she must do it every day before eating, is a graphic expression of her low status in her new home, at least in the first years of marriage. It would be a mistake, however, to deduce from the fact that daughters-in-law (*bhaumacā, bhamcā*) bow down to fewer people in Śreṣṭha or Parbatiyā households that they have higher status or more security there: if anything the reverse is true.

A general rule is often cited by Newars to the effect that they may not marry anyone within seven generations, i.e. anyone descended through males or females from a common ancestor, counting up inclusively from ego for seven generations. In practice, since the society is organized patrilineally, no female of a family of the same clan or lineage, or of a clan which is remembered to be agnatically related, may be married, however distant the relationship. By contrast, when relationships are traced through females, people usually remember only five or so generations. One may even marry into one's mother's brother's clan providing the clan does not observe rituals together and providing, so far as is known, the relationship is more distant than seven generations (i.e. fifth cousinhood). At the margin the rules have relaxed in recent years, but marriage with close cousins is still considered incestuous and highly shameful. Cousins who wish to marry have no choice but to run away and never return.

A newly married bride has to behave in a submissive and compliant manner. She has to do most of the hard work cleaning, washing, and cooking in the family. Among the farming castes she has to work in the fields. Her status only rises when she has had a son. It is not only because sons are given greater value generally that women prefer them. They have a material incentive in that only if they have a son will they themselves be able to acquire a daughter-in-law. On the other hand, daughters are also treated with love, and a first-born daughter is especially welcomed on the grounds that she will be able to perform Younger Brother Worship (Kijā Pūjā) to her hoped-for future younger brothers.

A mother-in-law expects her daughter-in-law to be deferential, but she is at the same time likely to suspect her of wishing to monopolize her son's affections and engineer a split. Once married, a woman can no longer pursue education and rarely can she continue to work outside the house. Her place is to ensure the cleanliness and ritual purity of the home, to bear children, and to care for them. Men do the shopping and take care of the shop if the family has one. High-caste women therefore have no excuse to be outside the house, except to fetch water (increasingly unnecessary as houses have taps installed) or for religious purposes. This relative seclusion, though much less severe than in much of north India, is part of the explanation for upper-caste women's keen participation in religious activities which give them a valid and meritorious reason to meet other women and see at least some of the world outside.

As Quigley (1985a: 41) has noted, the strength and importance of the household in Newar society is reflected and expressed in the careful organization of space in the house, a topic which has been discussed by many observers.[36] Newar city houses are by tradition of four storeys (see Fig. 4). The ground floor (*cheli*) is used for storage, for such activities as weaving, and as a shop if the house fronts onto a street. In the past it was where grain was husked, before electric mills came in. Now that the idea of having such an impure place inside the house has been accepted, the WC is normally on the ground floor. On the next floor up (the *mātã*) are bedrooms and a reception room. On the second floor (*cwatã*, third floor in US English), there is a large room used for eating feasts when there are invited

Figure 4. Symbolic associations of space within the Newar house (adapted from Barré *et al.* 1981: 163). This arrangement represents one possible layout. In some cases the hearth is at the front of the *baigaḥ*, and there is a god-room behind it (see Gutschow *et al.* 1987: 135).

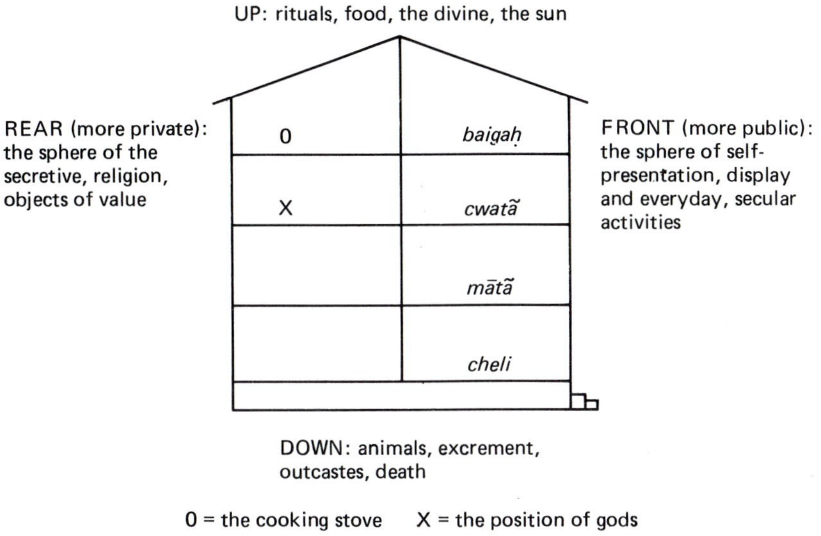

guests. The kitchen is usually under the roof on the top floor (*baigaḥ*), but in some cases it is in a separate room on the second floor at the back. A god-room or shrine room is also near the top and back of the house. A tiled verandah on the top floor, where clothes may be dried and women may sit in the sun in privacy, is a common feature.

Very low castes are not permitted to enter the houses of higher castes. Touchable but impure castes may enter but not ascend the stairs. Low but clean castes may come up to the first-floor landing or reception room. Castes of equal or higher status may come up to the second floor to be feasted and entertained. Lower castes will have food brought down to the first floor. Entry into the kitchen is reserved for one's own relatives, and on occasion to caste fellows. According to Shepard (1985: 25, 211), castes in the middle of the hierarchy, such as the Śilpakārs with whom she worked, do not agree on whether higher castes may enter their attic/kitchen: some say that they may, others that they may not. It is in any case a hypothetical question, unlikely to arise in the normal run of things.

When a house is built, elaborate rituals have to be carried out and auspicious times and auspicious directions determined. Nails with protective *yantras* (five-coloured thread inside an envelope of paper) and a peacock feather are hammered in over the lintel by the family priest to keep out evil spirits. Slusser (1982: 420–1) has published an extract from the ritual of consecration of the house in which a series of correspondences are made between different gods and all the parts of the house, as well as with objects within it. Some of these are known by lay people. The three main floors are identified as the underworld, world of mortals, and heaven respectively, a correspondence which makes very clear the hierarchy of space within the house. These broad associations, shared by all Newars alike, have survived the considerable modifications in the details of the organization of space consequent on the emergence of modern house styles and the use of modern building techniques.

As with the organization of space, so also where food is concerned there is a complex set of symbolic associations. Four principal types of food can be distinguished. Traditionally the two main meals of the day, consisting of boiled rice (*jā*), lentil soup (*kẽ*), vegetables (*tarkāri*), and chutney (*acār*), are eaten around 10 a.m. and 6 or 7 p.m. (These times may vary considerably for farmers.) The different members of the family do not eat together, but come in as convenient. Women tend to eat after men, and a woman ought never to eat before her husband. The youngest daughter-in-law in the house usually does the cooking and eats last, and she may go hungry if there is not sufficient left over. Cooked rice is the food most susceptible to impurity. It is eaten quickly without talking and with considerable concern for privacy. This attitude, and the associated purity beliefs, are shared with Parbatiyās (Bennett 1983: 40–1), and are indeed general in South Asia. The need to shield oneself from the eyes of outsiders when eating boiled rice may also, in many cases, reflect a fear of witchcraft.

The food eaten at feasts (*bhway*, Skt. *bhojana*) contrasts sharply with this. The staple is beaten rice (*baji*, Np. *ciurā*), which may be shared with others of different (but clean) caste. It is much less susceptible to impurity, presumably because it has been dried in the sun and no longer requires contact with water. For feasts within the family the whole household must eat together, as already noted. As well as being occasions of enjoyment, feasts also require more formality; care is taken to sit people, at least the older people, in order of seniority (see Plate 8). Feast food is often eaten outside the house in mixed company; such feasts are held out of doors in full view of non-participants. The atmosphere is very different from that of an everyday rice meal. One eats slowly, not hurriedly. At many types of feast one chats and jokes with other feasters. There are as many as fifteen dishes (or even more) including numerous buffalo meat, vegetable, and bean preparations. Alcohol is served, both milky rice-beer (*thwã̊*) and powerful spirits (*aylāḥ*). On rare occasions, e.g. when all participants in a *guthi* are sure of each other's status, the two opposed types of food may be combined in a 'rice feast' (*jābhway*).

Newar feasts are held extremely often, even nowadays when people are very conscious of the cost, and there is a widespread tendency to substitute less elaborate versions of feast food for a full-blown feast. There is a Nepali proverb 'The Chetri [or Parbatiyā, or nawab] ruins himself through luxury, the Newar by feasting.' Newars themselves frequently quoted it to me, in an ironic and almost apologetic tone, when I attended their feasts.

In many ways the snacks that people eat in the middle of the day, consisting of beaten rice with pastries or vegetables, and tea, are a mediating category between boiled rice and feast food. More everyday and much less elaborate than feasts, they are nonetheless not consumed in the constrained and concentrated manner of main rice meals. Snacks taken outside the house in eating houses and restaurants fall into the same category. Real, sustaining food is, however, boiled rice. To eat properly is to eat boiled rice. The principal greeting in the street is 'Have you eaten rice?' Unlike most inhabitants of the hills of Nepal, only a few Newars cannot afford rice and instead eat maize flour boiled into a kind of porridge called *ḍhiṁḍo*.

One final type of food needs to be mentioned. It might be called 'fast food', if that did not have other connotations in English. This is the food eaten while performing an Observance (*vrata*); for the duration of the Observance one may eat only one meal per day of this pure food (*pālã*; Skt. *pālana*, 'keeping [as of a vow]'). It consists of rice cooked in milk and ghee, fruits, and pastries. Such rice is much more inherently pure than rice cooked in water, and it can safely be eaten in public and in the presence of outsiders. Salt, onions, tomatoes, garlic, beans, spices, meat, and alcohol are all forbidden. Such foods are known formally as 'meaty' (*āmiṣ*); colloquially the prohibition is expressed by saying 'it is forbidden to eat salt' ('cibhyāḥ' or 'cisawāḥ naye ma jyū'). The distinction between these two types of sacred food – the feast type and the pure type – will be seen below to be highly significant for the structure of Newar Buddhism (§§4.2, 5.2.1, 7.5, 10.5).

Most of the men of Nāg Bāhāḥ are, as already noted, artisans. In most cases this means that they work at home, for themselves. In a small number of cases they work for a big exporter in a small workshop or factory. The normal pattern, however, is to work on commission from exporters or shopkeepers. In the case of gold- and silversmiths, work is commissioned also by individual Nepalese. Sometimes artisans have shops of their own and work there; goldsmiths do this regularly. Some shopkeepers have shops in Kathmandu, but most rent them in Lalitpur, a few minutes walk from where they live. Daily life goes on, therefore, in or very near the home.

It is noteworthy, as Quigley (1985a: 33) has stressed for Dhulikhel traders, that, with the exception of farmers' informal cooperative labour groups,[37] the very high degree of cooperation which Newars display in religion, ritual, and social affairs, is virtually never translated into economic cooperation. Buddhist Newars are admired by others for the degree of 'unity' they show in cultural matters; and they are numerically overwhelmingly predominant in the manufacture and retail of curios, silverwork, and other types of artisan work. And yet economic cooperation is simply not on the agenda (cf. §8.2.1). Cultural cohesiveness (both of kin and of wider groups) seems to be predicated on economic competition. Friends and relatives do sometimes go into business together as partners, but bitter disputes often result from such cooperation.

Although there is a great deal of cooperation in social and cultural matters, there is also competition for prestige at many different levels. Anthropologists of South Asia have not written extensively about honour and shame, as those of the Mediterranean have, perhaps because there is so much else to write about. Nonetheless, the pursuit of social honour is an important fact of everyday Newar life. There have been attempts, both by the government and by organizations representing Śākyas and Vajrācāryas throughout Lalitpur, to limit the amount of display and the number of guests invited at life-cycle rituals, especially at weddings. Where weddings are concerned, they have certainly failed, and the relentless inflation of what the neighbours expect has led to some considerable changes in the way they are celebrated. No one invites the (Newar) Kāpālī musicians who are employed for more traditional religious occasions; instead a Parbatiyā low-caste band plays Hindi film tunes on Western instruments. Instead of the traditional sit-down feast of beaten rice and buffalo meat cooked by friends and relatives, there is, increasingly, a stand-up buffet of pilao rice and other dishes cooked by a specialist from a tourist hotel (a procedure which discards the old concerns with purity). The whole affair is now (1989) known in Newari as a 'party' and finished off with disco dancing.

Honour (*ijat*) is shared by households, so that the whole house loses face if, say, a daughter runs off with a low-caste man. This is referred to as one's honour or one's nose 'going' (a common north Indian metaphor). If a member of the household does well it reflects on the whole household. In the pursuit of worldly success it is considered necessary to be *calāk*, clever or even 'cunning'. Indeed S.M. Joshi (1987: s.v.) defines the term thus: 'someone no one is able to trick or deceive'. It is recognized that earning a living (for men) or bringing up children (for women) precludes full involvement in religion. A woman's role may be seen as basically altruistic (though motivated by a desire to have someone to care for her in old age). A man's involves doing for the sake of his family (like Cavour for his country) things he ought not to do if his own spiritual welfare were the foremost concern. The truly religiously motivated are not supposed to care about making money or having a good reputation. A rich man who makes a spectacular religious donation without being otherwise obviously pious is particularly likely to be susceptible to the charge that it was done only for show.

Nevertheless Śākyas and Vajrācāryas have found ways of combining everyday life and religion. For practising Vajrācārya priests this is easy, though the number who live from that alone is now very small (§9.2, 11.5). In the past artisans used to chant Buddhist hymns while they worked. The life of an artisan or shopkeeper is indeed such as to permit a considerable amount of religious activity. A young Maharjan man said to me: 'Most people are Hindu in orientation: they worship for what they can get. Buddhists [he meant Śākyas and Vajrācāryas], though, are concerned to propagate ("pracār yāye") the Buddha and their own caste. They are mostly Śākyas and the Buddha is one of theirs.' This is interesting, not only for the acceptance of the Śākyas' claim to be descended from the Buddha's clan (§2.4), but because it suggests a difference in religious orientation between the Śākya-and-Vajrācārya combine and other Newars. It would be quite wrong to suppose that Śākyas and Vajrācāryas never worship for a specific worldly benefit, or that other Newars never practise in an otherworldly, expressive mode. But the balance or mixture between the two is probably such that Śākyas and Vajrācāryas do perform more ritual as an expression of their Buddhist identity, i.e. for what they would see as soteriological purposes, than other castes (cf. §2.5, 11.2 below). I was frequently impressed at the amount of time, energy, and money expended by Buddhists on religion and ritual – even now, when, by all accounts, these things have been considerably reduced in scale compared to forty or fifty years ago.

The place of religion in the life-cycle of individuals was brought home to me on a return trip to Nepal in 1989. I and my wife met an old friend, Ratna, on the bus from Lalitpur to Kathmandu. He and his father are successful silversmiths, and his father is an extremely pious Tibetan Buddhist practitioner. Both Ratna's parents spend every moment when they are not at work doing Tibetan Buddhist rituals and reading Tibetan Buddhist texts. Ratna, by contrast, had long had an interest in Goenke's *vipassanā* meditation, camps for which are run once a year in Kathmandu. (The difference in preferred religious idiom between father and son might be read as a low-key assertion of the younger generation's independence.) I had attended Ratna's wedding in 1984 and by 1989, aged thirty-two, he had two small children. I asked him if he still meditated and he said:

> No, I don't have time. I used to do it when I got up, at 5 a.m. Now I only rise at 7 a.m. But I'll start again soon. From about the age of thirty-five one should learn how to be detached ('tyāg yāye'), one should stop doing business so much. You have to get rid of the taste (*ras*) for life. You have to make your *man* (mind, sentiments) unattached. You have to do some *dharma* as you get older. Which do you go to, church or *gumbā* [Tibetan Buddhist monastery]?

I tried, feebly, to say that my work, studying, was my *dharma*, and he put me firmly in my place:

> Studying isn't *dharma*. You can have PhDs in seven different subjects and it won't do you any good!

With this warning, we can proceed to look at the caste context of Newar Buddhism.

Appendix 1 to chapter 1: A method of transliterating Newari

Grammatically and historically Newari is a Tibeto-Burman tongue. However, since Newars have been within the ambit of South Asian civilization for at least 1600 years, and since north India is dominated linguistically by Indo-European languages, Newari has been strongly influenced by them. Newari takes its abstract concepts from Sanskrit or (especially in the case of legal terms) from Persian. These often enter the language indirectly, through Hindi and Nepali. Most religious concepts derive from Sanskrit, since Sanskrit is the language of scripture and liturgy both for Buddhists and for Hindus. The more honorifically or abstractly a Newar attempts to speak, the more loanwords will be used. Only with the recent appearance of Newar cultural nationalism is this convention broken, by the invention of Newari neologisms to replace the loanwords, a practice which rarely succeeds in entering colloquial speech (Gellner 1986).

Those familiar with other South Asian languages will recognize many of the italicized terms. Where two or more equivalent terms are given, I list first the Sanskrit *tatsama*s (words in the same form as in Sanskrit); then the *tadbhava*s (words deriving from Sanskrit, but taking a different form); and, finally, the pure Newari words. As a general rule, the closer a word is to Sanskrit, the more honorific its usage.

Newari is written today in the Devanagari script, like Nepali and Hindi. There is no standard roman transliteration for Newari (or for Nepali, for that matter). Since Newari has such profound links to Sanskrit, while yet remaining an independent language, every system has some drawbacks. To be entirely systematic in using the Sanskrit system would mean that *kāy* (son) would be spelt *kāya* (a doctrinal Buddhist word for 'body'), when the two are pronounced very differently. On the other hand, to use a system which ignored Newari's links with Sanskrit would obscure connections and parallels with other parts of South Asia.

Thus I transliterate Newari using the method standard for Sanskrit, with the following three modifications.

(i) व is transliterated as 'wa' where it appears in *tadbhavas* or pure Newari words. In such words व always represents a 'w' sound; 'b' is always written ब. (In the past the Hindi व़ was sometimes used to mark the pronunciation 'wa', but this convention is only rarely used today.) In Sanskrit *tatsamas* the pronunciation varies: initial व is pronounced 'b'; when it comes second in a conjunct consonant it is pronounced 'w'. I have transliterated Sanskrit *tatsamas* in the standard way for maximum recognition.

(ii) There is no easy answer to the question of whether or not to include the inherent 'a' at the end of words. It is rarely pronounced by Newars. If one is transliterating a manuscript one must of course include it unless it is cancelled by a *virāma*. In the present case one is attempting both to represent a written form and to give some guide to pronunciation. To include the inherent 'a' in every case would mean that *jāt* (caste) was confused with *jāta* (horoscope), *tol* (locality) with *tola* (a unit of weight), and, as noted above, *kāy* (son) with *kāya* (a Buddhist 'theological' concept). Consequently I have included the final 'a' in pure Newari words and in *tadbhavas* only if it is pronounced. In Sanskrit *tatsamas* I have found it impossible to be absolutely consistent. It is included in some cases, either because the word is well known to Westerners in that form, or because the word is not so frequently used in Newari (*nirvāṇa*, *saṃsāra*, *mārga*, *bhuvana*, *pīṭha*, Avalokiteśvara, Nārāyaṇa, Bhairava). Foreigners who pronounce it unstressed, where Newars would omit it, will still be understood. In other cases, I have judged that giving a guide to pronunciation is more important than Sanskritic consistency, and so I have written: *purohit*, *paṇḍit*, *pāp*, *prasād*, *jal*, *samay*, *doṣ*, *bhūt*, *pret*, Kumār, Gaṇeś, Bhīmsen, Matsyendranāth, and so on. In some cases it has not been possible to avoid the term appearing in two forms. Thus generally I write *dān* since that is how Newars pronounce it, but on occasion, in a scriptural context, it is written *dāna*. I comfort myself with the thought that the very inconsistency in transliteration conveys an important fact about Newar culture. The final 'a' has always been included where it is pronounced (e.g. *dharma*, *moha*, *karma*, Karuṇāmaya, *mokṣa*). It is omitted in the names of castes where it is not pronounced.

(iii) There are two other common conventions for the transliteration of Newari: the use of a colon to represent the *visarga* (which in Newari indicates the lengthening of the preceding vowel); and the use of a tilde to represent both *candrabindu* (ँ) and *anusvara* (the dot indicating nasalization). The colon simply leads to confusion: people think it is a colon, so it is eschewed in favour of the Sanskrit convention (*ḥ*). The tilde has been reserved for the more common *anusvara*; the *candrabindu* is represented by itself.

So much for principles of transliteration. Which Newari spelling should one follow? This is indeed a problem because Newari orthography is not yet standardized (though the situation is not as chaotic as it is sometimes represented to be). Fortunately Thakur Lal Manandhar has recently published a Newari–English dictionary (Manandhar 1986). It is the first serious attempt of its kind. I have tried to follow its orthography since at least for the immediate future it is likely to be treated as standard. Where it provides no guidance I have turned to Satya Mohan Joshi's Newari-Newari dictionary (S.M. Joshi 1987). For Nepali I have followed the Royal Nepal Academy's *Nepālī Bṛhat Śabdakoś* (Pokharel *et al.* 1983).

Newar intellectuals who work on Newari are naturally ahead of other Newars in their usages. For instance, Newari has no retroflex consonants: it uses the dental letters to represent its palatal sounds. Nonetheless, influenced by their education in Nepali, most Newars automatically write *guṭhi* rather than *guthi*, *pāṭh* rather than *pāth* and so on. I have followed Manandhar in using the dental letters, since his convention is being accepted as standard.

In three ways I have not followed Manandhar's spellings.

(i) As noted above, Sanskrit *tatsama*s are spelt as in Sanskrit, i.e. with retroflex consonants if they have them.

(ii) Just as there are no retroflex consonants in Newari, so there is no open 'o' sound. The Devanagari 'o' was used traditionally for two different sounds: a lengthened 'a', now represented by 'aḥ', and a 'wa' sound now represented by 'wa'. Thus *laḥ* (water) could be written *lo*, and *cwane* (to live, to stay) was usually written *cone*. I have followed Manandhar's modern orthography, which rejects these old spellings, except in some caste names and in locality names. Thus I have written 'Jogi' not 'Jwagi' and 'Puco' not 'Pucwa'. (I have, however, written 'Dyaḥlā' rather than 'Dyolā'.) In these cases I have given priority to the way that the members of the caste, or the inhabitants of the area, would spell the name themselves.

(iii) Manandhar often gives preference to *tadbhava* forms of Sanskrit loanwords, rather than to *tatsama*s. No doubt this is motivated by the thought that they are close to what Newars actually say, and so should be recognized as the correct Newari, as opposed to the Sanskrit, form. Turner (1980: xviii) had the same instincts in compiling a dictionary of Nepali. Turner's preference has not prevailed. It is the *tatsama* forms which are recognized as correct Nepali. In the same way, desirable though that end may be, I do not believe that what is Sanskritically incorrect will ever be accepted as correct Newari, except in certain well-established cases. So I have written *vrata* not *barta* as Manandhar does, and so on with other Sanskrit *tatsama*s.

Appendix 2 to chapter 1: The calendar

The official calendar in use in Nepal today is the Vikram Samvat (V.S.), which began in 57 BCE. Newars frequently use the Nepal Samvat (N.S.), which began in 879 CE. Thus 1983 CE corresponded to Vikram Samvat 2039–40 and Nepal Samvat 1103–4. Where no letters adjoin the date it may be presumed to be of the common era (i.e. that which, from a Christian viewpoint, is designated 'AD').

As in the Gregorian calendar, there are twelve months in the year. Beginning with the new year according to the V.S., they are, in the abbreviated Sanskritic form of the pocket calendars used by many Newars: Vaiśākh (which usually begins in April), Jyeṣṭh, Āṣāḍh, Śrāvaṇ, Bhādra, Āśvin, Kārttik, Mārga (Mangsīr), Pauṣ, Māgh, Phāgun, Caitra. Months are calculated both according to the solar and according to the lunar cycle, and between the two there is only partial overlap. In other words, it may still be Vaiśākh according to the solar calendar after Jyeṣṭh has already begun according to the lunar cycle. The solar calendar is used for all official purposes (government business etc.); the lunar calendar is used to determine religious events. The first day of the solar month (*saṃkrānti*, *sãnhū*) is also of religious significance.

The lunar month is divided into two halves, a dark (*kṛṣṇa*) half in which the moon is waning, leading up to the new-moon day (*amāvāsyā*, *amāy*), and a bright (*śukla*) half, of the waxing moon, leading up to the full-moon day (*pūrṇimā*, *punhī*). The first day of the fortnight is called *pāru* (Skt. *pratipadā*). Each subsequent day (*tithi*) is named in Newari by a Sanskrit ordinal number from two to fourteen. The date for a given festival or religious observance is specified with the month, the half, and then the day (for numerous examples, see below, Table 7.9). Clearly, since the lunar month is twenty-eight days long, there cannot always be fifteen days (including the new-moon and full-moon days respectively) in each half. Thus the two halves may vary from thirteen to sixteen days in length. Sometimes one of the lunar days is elided, and at others it is repeated. If there is any doubt on which day a given festival should be observed, an astrologer is consulted.

There are Newari names of each of these months, namely, Bachalā, Tachalā, Dillā, Gũlā, Yãlā, Kaulā, Kachalā, Thı̃lā, Pohẽlā, Silā, Cillā, and Caulā. However, although many of the older generation still know these names, and although they are used self-consciously by Newar cultural enthusiasts, most literate Newars, as well as many others, do not generally use them. Part of the reason is that they are used exclusively with an older system (associated with the Nepal Samvat) according to which the month begins with the bright half and ends with the dark half, rather than the other way around. This older system, ending with the dark half, is common in Bengal, Maharashtra, and south India; the new system, ending with the bright half, is used in north India and Andhra (Kane 1941 V: 641). The consequence of this simultaneous use of two systems is that, although Bachalā is the Newari name for Vaiśākh, in the combined system now in use Bachalā only covers the second (bright) half of Vaiśākh. The second (dark) half of Bachalā corresponds to the first (dark) half of Jyeṣṭh. Most Newars respond to this confusing situation by using the Sanskritic, and forgetting the Newari, names.

A further complication is that the Nepal Samvat system begins with Kachalā (i.e. half way through Kārttik), and not in Vaiśākh. In other words, the N.S. new year falls in November, whereas the V.S. new year falls in April. Most Newars do generally remember which N.S. year it is, partly because of the demonstrations every year to have the Nepal Samvat given official recognition. For further details on the calendar, see Slusser 1982: 381–91.

2

Caste and religious affiliation

[In complex religions] neither the thought nor the activity of the religion is evenly distributed among the believers; according to the men, the environment and the circumstances, the beliefs as well as the rites are thought of in different ways.

Emile Durkheim, *The Elementary Forms of the Religious Life*, p. 17.

As inheritors of Greek logic and Jewish monotheism we instinctively apply the principle of contradiction to religious beliefs; for us gods and worshippers are classified in closed sets, which we consider exclusive to the point of antagonism. Statisticians, proceeding in a laughably literal-minded manner, calculate the total number of Buddhists, Confucians, or Shintoists. An Indian (*Hindou*), a Chinaman, or a Japanese would be incapable of understanding them.

Sylvain Lévi, *Le Népal*, vol. I, p. 317.

2.1 Newar castes

The story is often told of the foreigner visiting the Kathmandu Valley who asks a Newar whether he is a Hindu or a Buddhist, and gets the simple but confusing reply 'Yes'. Many foreigners have wrongly concluded that it is the Newars who are confused, and some have gone on to write diatribes against Newar Buddhism, suggesting that it is wholly and disgustingly corrupt (Oldfield 1981 II: 80) or that it is Hinduism in all but name (Snellgrove 1957: 106). It is not my concern to combat the negative value judgements implied in these views but rather to demonstrate the descriptive inadequacy which has been the consequence of such disdain. This inadequacy is of two sorts, empirical and theoretical. Empirically, Newar Buddhism has been described without any reference to Newar Buddhists' own values and

Figure 5. Map of Lalitpur: the old city. Most of the land to the north, west, and south of the old city is today built up. Map: N. Gutschow. 1 Puco (Pulcok), 2 Pāṭan Ḍhokā, 3 Nyākhācuk, 4 Nāg Bāhāḥ, 5 Kumbheśvar, 6 Śaṅkhamūl, 7 Cāmuṇḍā (Sikabahidyaḥ), 8 Ilā Nani, 9 Kwā Bāhāḥ, 10 Konti, 11 Cikā̃ Bahī, 12 Cyāsaḥ, 13 Bu Bāhāḥ, 14 Haugaḥ, 15 Palace, 16 Hakha, 17 Ta Bāhāḥ (Matsyendranāth-Karuṇāmaya), 18 Tanga, 19 Tanga Bāhāḥ (Cākwāḥdyaḥ), 20 Guita, 21 Bāl Kumārī, 22 Bhī̃chẽ Bāhāḥ, 23 Lagankhel, 24 Uku Bāhaḥ, 25 Southern 'Aśokan' *stūpa* (Lagā̃ Thūr), 26 Mahālakṣmī.

beliefs; theoretically, such descriptions presuppose a Judaeo-Christian definition of religion and religious allegiance which hinders comprehension of Asian realities. (On this latter point, see further below, §3.7.)

The modernist claim that Buddhism is not a religion presupposes the same Judaeo-Christian definition of religion. It would be wrong, however, to presume that Newar Buddhists do not themselves make judgements about the merits of different types of Buddhism; they even allow, explicitly or implicitly, that their tradition falls short in certain respects (§2.4, 3.3). But Newars themselves almost never share the radical Protestant-derived rejection of ritual and spiritual hierarchy which seems to inform so many foreigners' judgements. Their criticism is not of the tradition as such, but of the learning and application of its present-day practitioners (§11.5).

The foreigner's either/or question does not only smuggle in an ethnocentric concept of religion, and, in its exclusive use of the conjunction 'or', a disregard for context. We also make a mistake if we assume that we can talk of Newars as such, without specifying caste. Caste is, even today, the single most important determinant of a person's attitudes, particularly of his or her religious identifications. This chapter attempts to show how this is so. The following chapter then attempts to explain how Buddhism and Hinduism are to be understood in relation to each other and suggests thereby a more appropriate way of approaching the two religions.

In order to get the definitional question, who is a Hindu and who a Buddhist, into focus, we have to map the distinction between three kinds of religion outlined in Figure 1 onto a model of the Newar caste hierarchy. Figures 6 and 7 present such a model for the city of Lalitpur. There are two big horizontal cleavages at the bottom of the hierarchy. At the very bottom are the Untouchables, literally 'those who may not be touched' ('thiye ma jyūpī'); their touch requires purification. Above these, but still impure, are those castes who are not Untouchables but are 'water-unacceptable' ('laḥ calay ma jupī').[1] Clean castes, i.e. all the rest, accept water from each other, but cooked rice, feast food, and shared cigarettes or hookahs are subject to complex purity rules.[2]

From the Indian perspective the single most striking fact about this hierarchy is that it is twin-headed. There are two competing priestly or religious castes, the Rājopādhyāya Brahmans on the one side and, on the other, the Vajrācārya-Śākya caste. Just as the Brahmans are the guardians, propagators, and indeed embodiment of Hinduism, so too are the Vajrācāryas and Śākyas of traditional Buddhism in the Kathmandu Valley. Only Brahmans, Śākyas, Vajrācāryas, kings, monks, and revered ascetics are addressed with the honorific auxiliary *bijyāye*. The superiority of Śākyas and Vajrācāryas to non-priestly castes, including Śreṣṭhas, was evidently built in to traditional Newar culture, even though it is denied by Śreṣṭhas today.[3]

Another way of describing the fact that the Newar caste system is double-

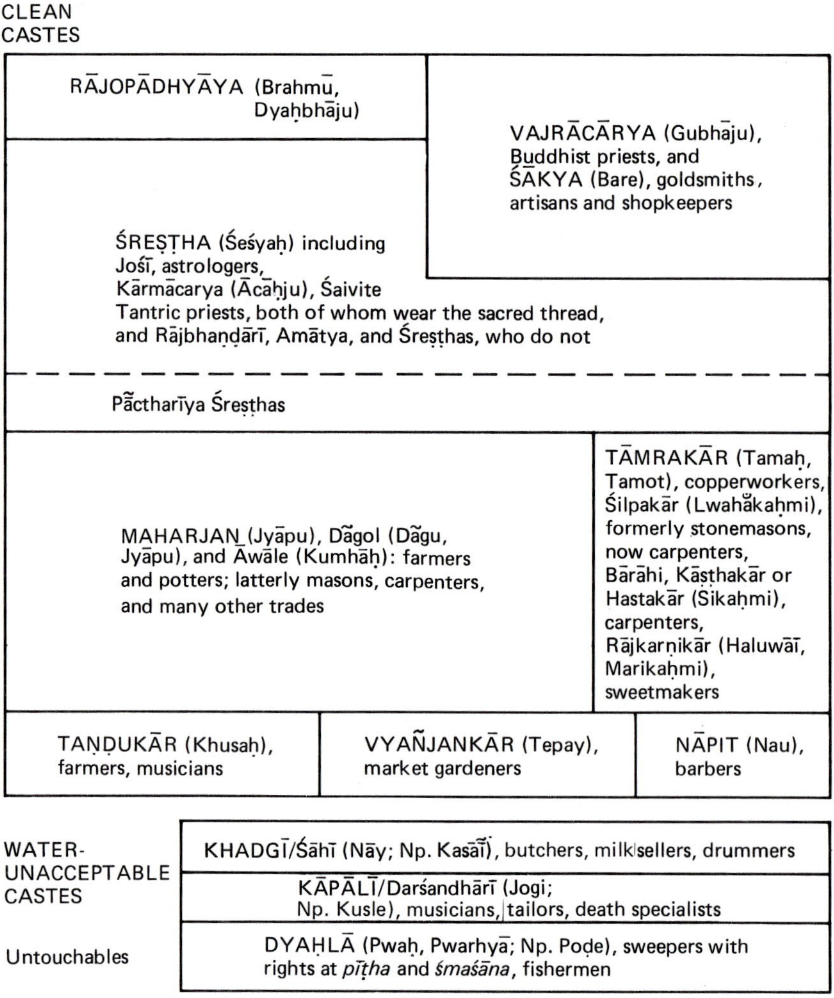

Figure 6. Principal Newar castes in Lalitpur (Nw. Yala, Np. Pāṭan).
Notes:
(a) Area is a very approximate representation of numerical strength based on previous surveys (carried out in Kathmandu and Bhaktapur) and on informed guesswork.
(b) The broken line indicates the existence of formalized hierarchy within the caste.
(c) Sanskrit-derived caste names are given first; colloquial non-honorific equivalents follow in parentheses. Caste names which are used in the text for the caste as a whole are given in capitals. Some very small castes have been omitted.
(d) The relative status of castes depicted side by side is debated.
(e) Rājopādhyāyas serve as family priests to Rājopādhyāyas, Jośīs,

headed is to say that it has two competing centres. This way of speaking is perhaps closer to local concepts. What Cantlie writes about Assam is in part also true of Nepal:

> The Assamese do not have a word for [hierarchy]. Anthropologists usually represent the order of castes in their village in a vertically-ranked series with the highest at the top and the lowest at the bottom. The associated visual image is a ladder-like construction and castes are spoken of as moving 'up' and 'down' the hierarchy. In Assam, however, castes are said to be 'big' or 'little', not 'high' or 'low', and the associated visual image is a circle with the 'biggest' castes in the centre, the 'smaller' castes in the surrounding rings, and the untouchables outside altogether (the ideal plan of cities and temples is of a similar kind). The implications of this model are not those of a ranked series of status groups, but of a moral universe with a sacred and protected centre inhabited by the Brahman as the possessor of knowledge. (Cantlie 1984: 305–6)

In Nepal also high and low castes are often referred to as 'big' and 'little' castes respectively; but interestingly this usage is confined to Nepali. In Newari, although such terminology is understood, the idiomatic way to refer to high and low castes is *thajāt* and *kujāt*; and these mean precisely 'high caste' and 'low caste' respectively (though the latter term has considerable pejorative force, and should not be used by foreigners).[4] In Nepal there is a tradition of listing castes in order. Ladder-like symbolism is a native, and not just an anthropological, construction.[5] The Newars do have a term for the caste system (*jāti vyavasthā*); the regulation of this system is represented in myth and folk history as the duty of the king (Greenwold 1975).

These local differences apart, Cantlie has pointed out something important, which applies equally to the caste system of the Newars: it is expressed through the model of the maṇḍala or sacred diagram (a more precise definition is given below, §7.1). Newars themselves use the term *maṇḍala* or *mandaḥ*; for them it refers primarily to the powder diagrams drawn by priests during complex rituals. They are aware also that it is a

---

Karmācāryas, Amātyas, Rājbhaṇḍārīs, some Śreṣṭhas, Tāmrakārs, and some Bārāhi. Vajrācāryas serve as family priests to Vajrācāryas, Śākyas, some Śreṣṭhas, Maharjans, Rājkarṇikārs, Śilpakārs, some Bārāhi, all Āwāles, Taṇḍukārs, Vyañjankārs, and Nāpits. Taṇḍukār (Nāy Gubhāju of Konti) serve as family priests to Khaḍgī. Khaḍgī women are toenail cutters for Vyañjankārs and Taṇḍukārs.

(f) Previous tables of Newar castes may be found in Rosser 1966: 85–6, 89; M.R. Allen 1973: 5; Greenwold 1974a: 103–4; Gutschow and Kölver 1975: 56–8; K.P. Chattopadhyay 1980: 53ff.; Barré *et al.* 1981: 26, 28; Gutschow 1982: 45; and Toffin (the latest and best) 1984: 231, 261, 279.

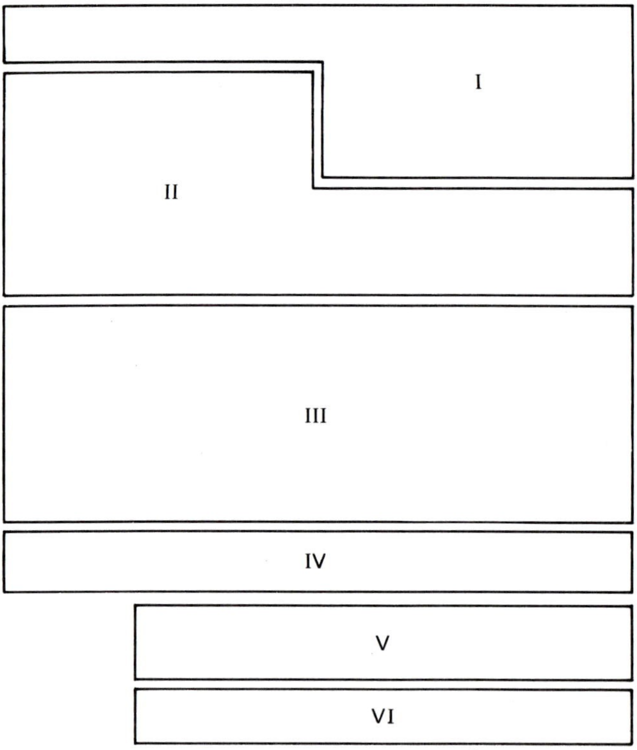

Figure 7. Six major subdivisions in the caste hierarchy and the criteria used to make them.

Notes:

I: Subdivision I comprises priests entitled to the honorific auxiliary *bijyāye* (from Skt. *vijaya*, 'victory', plus *yāye*, 'to do'); they are never addressed with the ordinary honorific auxiliary, *diye*. Karmācārya priests (who belong in block II) are addressed with *bijyāye*, but only in a priestly context and only by those families whose priest they are.

II: I and II together are those castes entitled either to full Tantric Initiation (Buddhist or Hindu) and/or to wear the Hindu sacred thread. These castes (I and II) are today referred to by lower castes as *bhājupī̃*, 'gentlemen', although historical records do not, it seems, show Śākyas and Vajrācāryas using this title (John Locke, personal communication).

III: Groups I, II, and III have their toenails cut by a Nāpit woman. (Traditionally, and still in many cases, she would visit regularly; for everyone the service is essential at major life-cycle rituals.)

IV: The castes in this category (all those above Khaḍgī and below Maharjans) have their toenails cut by a Khaḍgī woman, except for Nāpits, who have their own intracaste specialists.

V: This group comprises those from whom castes I–IV will not accept water, but whose touch does not require purification.

VI: 'Clean' castes (I–IV) will not accept water from these castes and, if touched by them, are supposed to purify themselves.

pervasive symbol, found in many contexts.[6] This mandala model is essentially spatial and indeed underlies the organization of the city and the temple.[7] Its application to the Kathmandu Valley as a whole is discussed below (§7.1). It has been persuasively argued that it also underlies the layout of space within the household (Barré *et al.* 1981: 162–3). Shepard (1985) has pointed out that even the Newars' sunken water fountains (*gā hitī*) reflect this pattern; thus, they may be seen as mirror images of the characteristic temple form. She dubs this extensive use of the mandala symbol 'mandalization' and elegantly analyses the mandala form into three basic and interconnected elements: boundedness, hierarchy, and the importance of the centre (Shepard 1985: 121).

This theme – the ritual organization of space according to the mandala model – has been explored by Zanen in relation to the layout of the town of Sankhu, in the north-east of the Valley. Zanen (1986: 150) analyses it into six underlying elements:

(i) the palace at the centre;
(ii) the division of the town into two halves;
(iii) an eightfold division of the town, each unit with a Mother Goddess;
(iv) a fourfold division of the town each attached to one of four gates;
(v) an outer circle of Eight Mother Goddesses and eight cremation grounds, surrounding the town;
(vi) a festival route (*pradakṣiṇā patha*) within the town.

Lalitpur does not share precisely these elements, except for (i) and (vi). It would have easily lent itself to a binary division of upper against lower town, as is graphically demonstrated for Bhaktapur during the annual tug-of-war there on Khai Sãnhū. In fact, the ritual division is either into three (separate sections for observing the Matsyendra festival) or four (four sections, each observing Yẽnyāḥ on successive days). Neither inside nor outside the city do the Eight Mother Goddesses produce an eightfold division. There is a set of them around the city, but three are notional stones and only three have cremation grounds attached (producing another threefold division). Gutschow's research suggests that underlying the organization of Lalitpur there is also a system of twenty-four localities.[8] That even children perceive their environment in terms of the geometric arrangements of shrines in the city is suggested by the drawing published in the attractive book by Barré *et al.*, *Panauti, une ville au Népal.*[9]

Caste also relates to the layout of space. The higher the caste, the greater the access to the centre. One representation of the ideal layout of a Newar city, taken from the thesis of an anthropologist who is himself a Newar, is

Figure 8. One conception of the ideal plan of a Newar city (adapted from R.P. Pradhan 1986: 381).

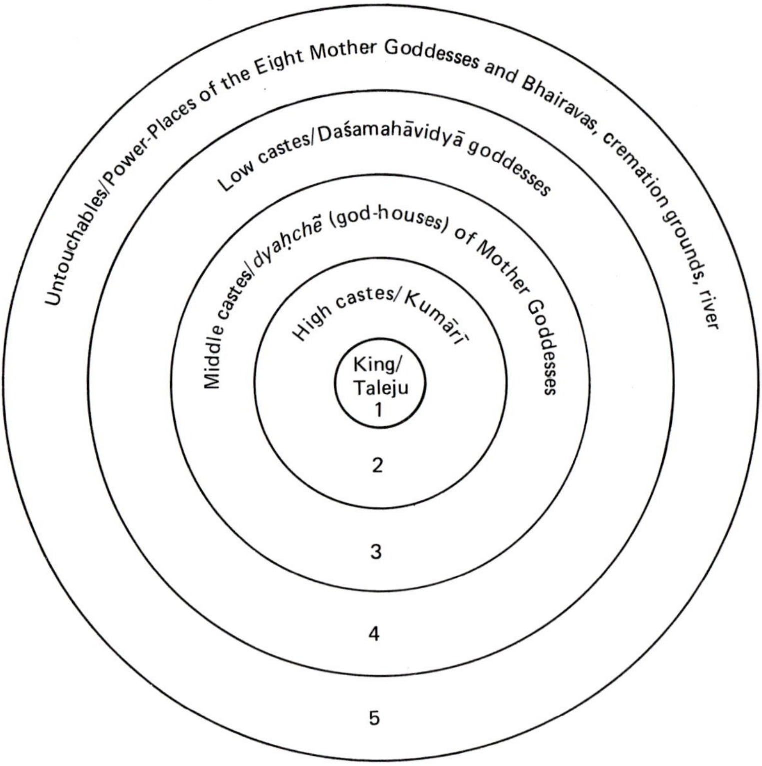

given in Figure 8. This shows the King in the centre. In Lalitpur the royal palace is indeed right in the centre of the city; but in Kathmandu it is slightly off centre and in Bhaktapur markedly so. Nonetheless, the Malla kings found ways of demonstrating ritually that the palace, wherever it was, was the centre. Likewise, for high castes with secret Tantric shrines, the whole city was conceived as a mandala with their shrine as the centre.

Both 'highness' and 'centrality' are concepts which different high castes can manipulate, within limits, according to context. As in south India (Dirks 1987: 291), the presence of the King – were he included – would make the rank order shown in Figure 6 problematic: as a Kṣatriya he would rank below Brahmans, but as King he ranks first in the kingdom.[10] Since Lalitpur has not been a separate kingdom since 1768, this complex question of the King's position can be set aside for present purposes.

Each of the main castes of Lalitpur now needs to be introduced. Some

Westerners have called Vajrācāryas and Śākyas 'Buddhist Brahmans' (Lévi 1905 I: 226; Greenwold 1974a). In fact this is apt only for the Vajrācāryas, as they alone may act as priests for others (*purohit*) and have hereditary parishioners (*jajmān*, *jaymā*). Although Śākyas may not be family priests, they are in other respects the equals of the Vajrācāryas. There are status differences based on education, wealth, and so on, but the Vajrācāryas and Śākyas otherwise lack the numerous internal grades of status characteristic of the large and influential Hindu high caste, the Śreṣṭhas. Most Śākyas are artisans, as are most Vajrācāryas in Lalitpur (only a minority are full-time priests). Goldsmithing used to be one of the most widely practised trades, although this has fallen off as the price of gold has increased. Others are, and have always been, god-makers, carpenters, coppersmiths, or silversmiths. A substantial minority are shopkeepers and traders. Nowadays they dominate the tourist-directed 'curio' trade, both as artisans and as retailers. In principle there is no bar on intermarriage between Vajrācāryas and Śākyas, though there are a few constraints in practice. That is, all agree that intermarriage is permitted, and it does indeed take place, but it is less frequent than would be the case if it were completely free between the two sub-groups (§9.2).

There are several important asymmetries between these two top castes, the Brahmans and the Vajrācārya-Śākya combine, the most important being size: there are very few Rājopādhyāya Brahmans, so few indeed that it is difficult for them to find marriage partners who are not within the proscribed kinship range.[11] Thus when the Buddhists, the Śākyas and Vajrācāryas, think of Hindus, they think primarily not of the Brahmans, but of the Śreṣṭhas. Nonetheless, the Rājopādhyāyas have an extremely important place in Newar culture, and when I speak of Brahmans, without qualification, I refer to these Newari-speaking Rājopādhyāyas, and not to the (very numerous) Nepali-speaking Parbatiyā Brahmans.

The Śreṣṭhas are not a priestly caste, in spite of the fact that among their number are both Jośī, astrologers, and Karmācārya, Tantric Śaivite priests. Their self-image is thoroughly Kṣatriya, since they are descended from the groups which governed the Malla kingdoms of Nepal (*c.* 1200–1769).[12] In Rana times (1846–1951) many Śreṣṭhas attained positions of influence, and in modern Nepal they are the group of Newars with the largest numbers in the civil service, business, and the professions. Not surprisingly, they are the best educated and the most westernized. This means that they are also the group which has been most influenced in language and culture by the non-Newar ruling class of Nepal. The dominant Parbatiyās do not however accept them as Kṣatriyas, a judgement which was law in the Rana period

(Höfer 1979: 138). For ordinary Newars, however, they represent the social apex to which upwardly mobile middle-ranking castes aspire. Although ordinary Newars respect Vajrācāryas and Śākyas, they are, like Brahmans, a sacerdotal caste, and their way of life is not normally a model to be emulated.

Śreṣṭhas are a particularly heterogeneous caste, a common feature of prestigious Kṣatriya castes in north India also (Parry 1979). Urban Śreṣṭhas are traditionally divided into two ranked sub-castes, the higher known as Chatharīya or 'six *thar*' and the lower as Pā̃ctharīya or 'five *thar*'.[13] The latter are believed to be the offspring of Chatharīya fathers by lower-caste mothers. In theory the two sub-castes are not supposed to intermarry.

In reality the internal structure (if one can use such a term of a fluid situation) of the Śreṣṭha caste is very complex. In the past a large number of status distinctions were recognized within both Chatharīya and Pā̃ctharīya sub-castes, so that at the margin it was possible to talk of four-*thar* or three-and-a-half-*thar* Śreṣṭhas (Rosser 1966: 101). Only recently Toffin (1984: 378) was able to distinguish four grades of status within the Pā̃ctharīya group in Panauti. It would be a mistake to imagine, however, that these four grades have an 'objective reality' in the sense of being accepted as real by everyone. On the contrary, they are the subject of eternal debate and each interested party has a different view of the whole. Because of the large number of Pā̃ctharīya Śreṣṭhas, Chatharīya Śreṣṭhas in Panauti (Toffin 1984: 261, 38 n. 9) – and probably Bhaktapur Chatharīya Śreṣṭhas also – deny that they themselves are Śreṣṭhas, restricting this term to the parvenu Pā̃ctharīyas. In Lalitpur, however, Chatharīya Śreṣṭhas do not reject the 'Śreṣṭha' label. Those who do not have some other Sanskritic surname, such as Amātya, Rājbhaṇḍārī, Jośī, or Karmācārya, use 'Śreṣṭha' as a surname in preference to their non-honorific nickname. These latter are often not very flattering: examples are Nyāchyā̃ ('fish head'), Cipālu ('salt and ginger'), and Lākhe ('demon'). Food nicknames are said to derive from the dishes which that particular family had to provide at feasts for the Malla King Siddhi Narasiṃha (who ruled Lalitpur from 1620 to 1661).

Inside or near the Valley, but outside the cities, there are large numbers of 'village' Śreṣṭhas who are peasants or small traders, though a few are also very rich. They are often ignorant of the Chatharīya/Pā̃ctharīya distinction (Quigley 1984: 39) unless they have moved to Kathmandu. There are also many 'hill' Śreṣṭhas, who are likewise traders and peasants, throughout the hills of Nepal.[14] Many of these are social climbers who have adopted the name Śreṣṭha to hide a low-caste origin. Others have succeeded in maintaining a high status they always enjoyed and refuse to intermarry with the former, while themselves often finding it impossible to make alliances inside the Kathmandu Valley. These village and hill Śreṣṭhas aspire to the social position of the urban Chatharīya Śreṣṭhas, and favour the same kinds of religion, but rarely intermarry with them.

Below the Śreṣṭhas is the large farmer caste, which in Lalitpur takes the surnames Maharjan and Dãgol (I shall refer to them all as 'Maharjan'). They are still largely farmers, though some have taken up other trades, and a few have jobs in the bureaucracy. They perform numerous socio-religious services for the higher castes, Śreṣṭha, Brahman, Vajrācārya and Śākya, whom they sometimes call collectively *bhājupī̃*, gentlemen. These services include cremation at death, carrying loads in all religious contexts, and acting as midwife at birth. The fact that only they may provide these services for the high castes, as well as the fact that only they may provide similar services for important deities (such as building and climbing up the chariot of Karuṇāmaya-Matsyendranāth), are cited as proof to substantiate their high status within the middle part of the hierarchy, and to deflate the claims of the Tāmrakār *et al.* to take precedence over them. According to a group of Maharjans and Dãgols I asked about this, 'There is no difference between Maharjans and Dãgols, except that "Dãgol" means "a good/reliable person specially chosen" (*bhī̃mha lyeyāḥ taḥgu*).' In spite of this general feeling that Dãgols rank slightly higher than Maharjans it is in general impossible to establish any caste-like division between them. The Āwāles, on the other hand, are considered slightly inferior in rank, and some Maharjans say that their ritual duties require them not to marry with Āwāles.[15]

The Tāmrakār *et al.* claim to be superior in status to the Maharjans. In their favour it must be said that they receive Tantric Initiation, which in the normal run of things Maharjans may not. The Tāmrakārs are strong Hindus,[16] but the other caste sub-groups, with whom they intermarry – Śilpakār, Rājkarṇikār, Kāṣṭhakār, and Bārāhi – are Buddhist. Their Buddhist tendencies have been accentuated in recent times by the claim of the whole Tāmrakār *et al.* caste to be one caste with the Tulādhar *et al.* (Urāy) in Kathmandu. Nowadays this claim is for the most part accepted by the latter, who do not like to insist on fine distinctions of status in what is agreed to be a democratic age. Tell-tale signs remain, however, to show that in the past Tāmrakār *et al.* did not have the same high status as the Tulādhar *et al.* One such sign is the fact of disputed status *vis-à-vis* the Maharjans; another is the fact that Tāmrakār *et al.* are not known in Lalitpur as 'Urāy' as the Tulādhar *et al.* are, and they do not share all the same minor customs (as endogamous groups frequently do). A third sign is that, unlike Tulādhar *et al.*, Tāmrakār *et al.* may only take an abbreviated form of Tantric Initiation and may not take the same form as Śākyas and Vajrācāryas. Finally, older informants remembered a dispute over precedence which took place in Rana times between two women, one Maharjan, one Tāmrakār *et al.*, who were performing a month-long fast ('māy apasã cwane') in Kwā Bāhāḥ; it was decided that the Maharjan was superior.[17]

At the bottom of the clean caste group come a number of small castes. Some very small castes – Karamjit (Bhāḥ), Citrakār (Pũ), Nakarmī (Kau), Mālī (Gathu), Rañjitkār (Cipā), Rajaka (Dhobi, Dhubyā), Carmakār (Kulu), and Cyāmkhalaḥ (Cyāme) – have been omitted from the table. I do not have data on their relative ranking, though the last three come in the 'water-unacceptable' group. Taṇḍukār, Vyañjankār, and Nāpit are all of roughly equal rank, as are the Citrakār and Nakarmī, not included here. All these are small castes which do not intermarry. Any rank order between them is inevitably artificial. The Taṇḍukār and Vyañjankār could well be regarded as Maharjan (Jyāpu) sub-castes, formed by fission on the basis of intermarriage, locality, and/or ritual specialization.[18]

Among those from whom the clean castes may not accept water, the Khaḍgī, traditionally milksellers, drummers, and butchers, are clearly the aristocrats. Unlike the rest they are not untouchable, and they may live inside the old city walls.[19] They are relatively numerous and some of them are very well off these days. At the bottom there is a difference between the Dyaḥlā and the Cyāmkhalaḥ who refuse to intermarry. In Lalitpur, unlike Kathmandu, the Cyāmkhalaḥ are not very numerous. Higher castes invariably state that the Cyāmkhalaḥ are the lowest of all, but, surprisingly, the Dyaḥlā themselves do not claim to be higher than them. The Dyaḥlā point out that the Ranas employed Cyāmkhalaḥs as sweepers in their palaces, and refused to let Dyaḥlās in, because the latter had to provide the public executioner from among their number. Both Kāpālī and Dyaḥlā are the temple priests of certain important shrines (Bhīmsen and some Mother Goddess temples within the city walls in the case of Kāpālī, Mother Goddess shrines outside the city in the case of Dyaḥlā). As in south India (Dirks 1987: 278), it is not polluting to accept the deity's blessed substances (*prasād*) from their hands.

2.2 *Śivamārgī* and *buddhamārgī*, Hindu and Buddhist

The main Newari words which are usually translated as 'Hindu' and 'Buddhist' are respectively, as already mentioned in chapter 1, *śivamārgī* and *buddhamārgī*, that is those who 'follow the path of Śiva' and those who 'follow the path of the Buddha'. Alternative terms often used are *śivamat*, 'following the doctrine of Śiva', and *buddhamat*, 'following the doctrine of the Buddha'. As with most religious vocabulary (specifically that relating to the Great Traditions) both of these sets of terms are Sanskrit. It is noteworthy that although the two religions fulfil a large range of social functions, the local defining terms are soteriological. Which of these two categories a Newar falls into is determined by the identity of his or her hereditary family priest (*purohit*). Those with a Vajrācārya priest are *buddhamārgī* and those with a Rājopādhyāya Brahman priest are *śiva-mārgī*. This in turn determines the symbols painted over the main doorway of one's house at marriage, or at the Old-Age Initiation called *burā jãkwa*. Those who are *buddhamārgī* have the Five Buddhas (*pañcabuddha*); *śivamārgī* Newars have the Hindu trinity (*trimūrti*: Brahmā, Viṣṇu, Maheśvara) with Maheśvara (Śiva) in the centre, and flanked on the outside by Gaṇeś and Kumār, Śiva's sons.

It is not possible to have more than one family priest. He has a right to be called for all regular life-cycle rituals and to receive the requisite fee (*dakṣ-iṇā*). For optional ceremonies, however, one may invite whomsoever one pleases. In theory it is not possible to change one's family priest. Traditionally priests have inherited and sold rights over parishioners like other property; today the relative value of such rights has fallen considerably. In fact it does sometimes happen that a Newar manages to persuade another priest to come even when he ought to be inviting his *purohit*. Rosser (1966) has described at length two different cases where this has occurred. (a) During a famous caste dispute in the 1920s and 30s within the Buddhist community of Kathmandu, many of the Tulādhar *et al.* and some Śākyas switched from one Vajrācārya to another (cf. §8.2.3). (b) There is a continual, slow drift from (Buddhist) Vajrācārya priests to (Hindu) Rājopādhyāya or Parbatiyā Brahman priests on the part of previously *buddhamārgī* Maharjans or Śreṣṭhas who express their upwardly mobile aspirations by this substitution. The lesson of these cases is that it is very difficult for priests to prevent this happening either when the parishioner has enough money to entice another priest, or when a group of parishioners is sufficiently determined. However, just because it is not supposed to happen, it is very difficult to get a precise idea of how prevalent it is.

An important factor in the defeat of the Kathmandu Vajrācāryas in this dispute with the Tulādhar *et al.* was the fact that even thoroughly Buddhist patrons, who would not consider employing Brahmans, had an alternative, namely Tibetan monks, for their optional piety. Resentment against the Vajrācāryas certainly played a part in the support given to Theravāda monks and nuns in the years that followed. Now that Theravāda monks and nuns are well established in the Valley, Vajrācāryas no longer offer the only Buddhist alternative, at least for those (still few) willing to use Theravādins for life-cycle rituals.

In addition to this traditional terminology of *buddhamārgī* and *śiva-mārgī*, there is now a more modern one, an opposition between *buddhadharma* and *hindudharma*, a distinction which does not correspond exactly to that between *buddhamārgī* and *śivamārgī*. This has been introduced primarily by the government, through its decennial censuses, in which religion (*dharma*) is asked for, and in its various politico-religious campaigns. These campaigns present Nepal as the only Hindu kingdom in the world (*ekmātra hindu rājya*) and tacitly encourage the traditional belief that the King is a partial incarnation of Viṣṇu.[20] It has long been clear that there are advantages to being Hindu. The only castes whose members would find it almost unthinkable to claim to be Hindu are the Vajrācāryas and Śākyas themselves, and in addition, in Kathmandu, the Tulādhar *et al.* (Urāy). All other castes can and normally do register themselves as Hindu. I have even heard of a Vajrācārya applying for an important job writing his religion as Hindu. In this context one may hear a Nepali proverb cited: *jasko śakti usko bhakti*. This is the exact equivalent of the Latin *cuius regio eius religio*, but because it is a folk observation, not a legal principle used to decide religious allegiances after the Thirty Years War, it is best translated as '[People tend to adopt] the devotional style of whoever holds power.'

The modern insistence on single, context-free religious identities has produced a seeming paradox: large numbers of people with Buddhist priests, whose rituals are normally in a Buddhist idiom, claim to be Hindus. What one might be inclined to see as an inconsistency actually bothers most Newars very little, because the traditional context in which they carry on religious and social activity has little or nothing to do with the official context in which they say they are Hindus. Most of them if challenged would take the government view that Buddhism is a form of Hinduism. This view, as we shall see (§3.3), has ancient precedents. It is institutionalized at certain important shrines, such as Vajrayoginī in Sankhu, Cā̃gu Nārāyaṇa, Paśupati, and Guhyeśvarī: Muslims, Untouchables, and all Westerners are excluded, but Buddhists, including Tibetan Buddhists, are admitted.[21] The notices say 'Hindus only' and never refer to Buddhists.

Of course it is not only people who may be divided into Hindu and Buddhist. Each religion has its own deities, rites, festivals, texts, and priests. (Whether or in what way these differences imply a difference of fundamental values is controversial: I argue that they do, §2.5, 11.2.) A glance at Table

3.2 below will show that while it is possible to designate certain deities as clearly Hindu (class A), and others as Buddhist (class B), the rest are really both. The deities of class C, and even of class D, cannot be said to be primarily of one or of the other, though, like many things in Newar religion and society, this is disputed by some. Each religion has a distinct view of the other (see below, §3.3–3.6); thus Hindu gods are accepted in the Buddhist scheme of things and vice versa, but the ways in which this is effected are not identical. What I have said of deities applies also to festivals, myths, and rites: some are clearly Hindu, others clearly Buddhist, and some not clearly either. Depending on context we may want to say that a custom or myth is neither Hindu nor Buddhist, or that it is the common property of both religions.

2.3 The Śreṣṭhas between Buddhism and Hinduism

Tension between Buddhist and Hindu identity is acutely felt only by Śreṣṭhas (and it would be wrong to imagine even them having sleepless nights over it). Large numbers of them, both in Kathmandu and in Lalitpur, have Vajrācārya priests. This was tacitly recognized in the updated version of the 1854 Law Code, issued in 1953, which forbade Hindus to marry Buddhists or to take Buddhist Tantric Initiation unless this was traditional in their caste.[22] And yet, as I intimated earlier, for Newars they are paradigmatic Hindus. Here is a real paradox, which is not merely the result of a juxtaposition of traditional and modern, or of the fact that the Śreṣṭhas are the most westernized Newars. The explanation of it has to do with the Śreṣṭhas' identity as Kṣatriyas, that is to say as rulers. As a middle-aged Śākya man remarked to me, Hinduism (*śivadharma*) is the religion of rulership (*rājnaitik dharma*). This is certainly so: in the Malla kingdoms which preceded the present dynasty (i.e. before 1769) the kings and their immediate entourage were all *śivamārgī*, but it seems that the great majority of their subjects were *buddhamārgī*.[23] This is clear from the fact that most Newars in Kathmandu and Lalitpur still are *buddhamārgī*, and from the extremely small number of Rājopādhyāya Brahmans.

It is not true that those defined locally as Kṣatriyas must, in all South Asian contexts, be Hindus. There are many historical examples of kings who preferred Buddhism or Jainism. Nonetheless it was probably inevitable that the rulers of the Kathmandu Valley during the Malla period should be Hindu: they wished to tie themselves in to the north Indian status hierarchy, and it would have been anomalous to declare themselves Buddhist. Indeed, as today, to do so would have risked being aligned with the low-status (because yak-eating and indifferent to ritual pollution)

Tibetans. At the same time the rulers did not necessarily have an interest in their subjects all abandoning their Vajrācārya priests and starting to use Brahmans. Providing they respected caste and status, which they did, the difference of priests may well have been considered a useful one, functioning to distinguish the rulers from the ruled.

During this period power was extremely decentralized, and for long periods – from 1482 to 1620 and from 1705 to 1768 – Lalitpur, even though it had a nominal ruler, proved completely ungovernable.[24] In this period also Vajrācāryas and Śākyas were evidently numerous; as today, they far outnumbered Brahmans, and must have been in control, through their monasteries, of much land, thus holding the allegiance of many tenant farmers. It is certainly a plausible hypothesis that Lalitpur's relative ungovernability had something to do with the strength of Buddhism there. Inscriptions show that, before the present dynasty established its rule in the Kathmandu Valley in 1769, Śreṣṭhas made numerous donations to Buddhist monasteries, established *caitya*s (Buddhist cult objects), and fed monks (i.e. Vajrācāryas and Śākyas), as well as establishing Hindu temples and cults. Perhaps those Śreṣṭhas who have Buddhist priests today, i.e. are *buddhamārgī*, are descended from those nobles who 'played the Buddhist card' in the political struggles of Malla Nepal. Perhaps also they are descended from nobles who were once out of favour, and the local powerholders forbade Brahmans to serve them as priests, in order to inflict lower status on them. That, at any rate, such an idea may have been present is indicated by a chronicle cited by D.R. Regmi (1965 I: 644): among the many caste rules it ascribes to Sthiti Malla, it records that Brahmans were forbidden to act as priests to 'castes other than the Kṣatriyas and Śreṣṭhas'.

Whatever may turn out when historical evidence is available, it seems clear that the Buddhist allegiance, now deeply eroded, of many Śreṣṭhas in Kathmandu and Lalitpur, has to do with the extreme political decentralization of the Malla period. The ancestors of *buddhamārgī* Śreṣṭhas were big men, but on such a local scale that the appropriate idiom of their largesse was Buddhist. When the small Malla kingdoms disappeared it was inevitable that the Śreṣṭhas' Kṣatriya identity would lead them away from Buddhism; it is perhaps a tribute to the power of tradition that so much of their Buddhist past survives. Given the Śreṣṭhas' present-day preferences, a purely synchronic account of Newar religion would be quite unable to explain why some Śreṣṭhas have Buddhist priests, take Buddhist Tantric Initiation, and support Buddhist *guthi*s (socio-religious associations described below, chapter 8).

Thus one reason for the association of Śreṣṭhas and Hinduism has to do with their high status. High social status and Hinduism went hand in hand even in the Malla period. The connection became still stronger thereafter. A good example of this was a table drawn up by a Jośī interested in such matters, in which he had amalgamated the 'thirty-six castes' into a single hierarchy. This is a conventional number and in order to make it come out right he had had to mix up in an unsystematic way the data of his own experience with certain historical sources (primarily, it seemed, the chronicle, the Bhāṣā Vaṃśāvalī, published by Paudel and Lamshal, or a tradition cognate with it). The top ten castes beginning with Rājopādhyāya Brahman he listed as *śivamārgī*, and the remaining twenty-six, beginning with Vajrācārya and ending with Caṇḍāla at the bottom, he listed as *buddhamārgī*. When I protested that the Tāmrakār, whom he placed thirteenth, i.e. third among the castes he classed as *buddhamārgī*, were in fact surely *śivamārgī* (as indeed they are in Lalitpur) he replied: they may have Brahman priests but they honour the Buddha. But by this criterion, the Śreṣṭha, listed ninth, ought *a fortiori* to have been classed as *buddhamārgī*. Evidently for this Jośī, religion was a simple function of caste status. Incidentally, his table, which put the Jośīs second, inferior only to Rājopādhyāya Brahmans, and placed first among Kṣatriyas, also illustrated how the details of the caste hierarchy depend very much on the perspective of the informant.

A second reason why Chatharīya Śreṣṭhas are considered to be paradigmatic Hindus is that certain of them, particularly Jośī and Karmācārya, are indeed strong and unequivocal Hindus. Those who intermarry with them are usually connected by association in the minds of other Newars.[25]

2.4 Buddhist religious identity

'The monks are the Buddhist elite. They are the only Buddhists in the proper sense of the word.' M. Allen begins his article on Buddhism in Nepal with this quotation from Conze (1960: 53), but he concludes by saying that the Vajrācāryas and Śākyas 'are, and perhaps have been ever since they forsook monasticism, Buddhists of such a highly eclectic kind that formal identification is no longer a simple matter' (Allen 1973: 14). It should be clear from the discussion above that this judgement is correct of *buddhamārgī* castes *other than* Vajrācārya and Śākya: for other castes identification is indeed complex. From the Buddhist (i.e. Śākya and Vajrācārya) point of view, other castes are (lay) householders: their devotion to Buddhist deities is entirely praiseworthy and to be encouraged, but if they should also show attachment to Hindu deities, if they should imitate royal customs, or sacrifice animals, this is not in the least surprising.

It is precisely with the Vajrācāryas and Śākyas that identification is straightforward: they are Buddhists. Now that the Western term 'Buddhist' has entered the language, they often use it themselves as a shorthand way of referring to Vajrācāryas and Śākyas. Thus they sometimes explain the Monastic Initiation ritual, through which all males of the caste pass as a boy, as 'becoming a Buddhist'. It is important to see that the reason for the Vajrācāryas' and Śākyas' unequivocal Buddhist identity is that they are monks, albeit married, part-time ones. Substitute 'Vajrācāryas and Śākyas' for 'monks' in Conze's statement (above), and it captures an important truth about traditional Nepal.

Monastic status begins with Monastic Initiation, in which Śākya and Vajrācārya boys spend four days as monks. It is re-affirmed annually at the festival of Pañcadān in which they go from house to house, locality to locality, begging alms (§6.3). It is also re-affirmed whenever a Vajrācārya or Śākya performs an Observance or life-cycle ritual and has his head shaved. They, and only they, have the whole head shaved, leaving no topknot (*ānsā*). This difference is the one most frequently referred to in intercaste groups, and it is always possible to get a laugh by calling Vajrācāryas and Śākyas 'those without topknots'. It is symbolic of course of their monastic status, which sets them off sharply against all others. In the past Vajrācāryas and Śākyas kept their heads permanently shaved (Oldfield 1981 II: 77, 139); even thirty or forty years ago they would have it shaved for every major life-cycle ritual.

Vajrācāryas and Śākyas are also set off from all other Newars by their conception of caste. Other castes have a myth which posits a single social origin. The Rājkarṇikārs (Sweetmakers) believe they are the descendants of Brahman immigrants from India. High-caste Śreṣṭhas believe that they arrived in Nepal as courtiers of Hari Siṃha Deva of Mithila in the fourteenth century. The Khaḍgī believe that they are descended from one of these same courtiers, or even a son of the King himself, who was chosen to sacrifice a buffalo to Taleju because he happened to be found defecating with his face to the sun; their non-honorific name, Nāy, derives, they claim, from 'Nayar' (the famous south Indian Kṣatriya group).

For Śākyas and Vajrācāryas other castes are all householders of the four *varṇa*s (Brahman, Kṣatriya, Vaiśya, and Śūdra), but they themselves stand outside this fourfold system of priests, kings, traders, and menial castes. They have their origin in all four categories. Thus some of the Vajrācāryas of Bu Bāhāḥ are supposed to be Brahmans, the Śākyas of Uku Bāhāḥ claim to be descendants of the king who founded it and then took vows and lived there, the Vajrācāryas of Dhum Bāhāḥ are commonly thought to be descended from Barbers (Nāpit) and the Śākyas of Michu Bāhāḥ are said to be descended from Farmers (Maharjan).[26] These varied mythical caste origins of the Śākyas and Vajrācāryas exist on the level of hearsay and myth: they do not affect the status of individuals or families. No one tries to reconcile these accounts with the idea that the Śākyas are descended from the Buddha's kinsmen. Nor does anyone see a contradiction between the tradition that Śākyas and Vajrācāryas come from all four *varṇa*s and the alternative tradition, cited when their status is in question, that they are descended from Brahmans and Kṣatriyas ordained by the Buddha Krakucchanda.

Attempts to place the Vajrācāryas and Śākyas as they are today within the *varṇa* system are forced. A Newar Brahman told me that the Vajrācāryas are the Buddhists' Brahmans and the Śākyas their Kṣatriyas. In fact this is just an analogy and does not really work: even at the time of Sthiti Malla they were not included in the list of sixty-four castes.[27] This is because of their monastic identity; and it also explains why Locke (1980: 12) was told that Vajrācāryas and Śākyas belong outside the caste hierarchy, although in fact, in their life as householders, they are inevitably and frequently concerned with their caste status.

Vajrācāryas and Śākyas are, then, householder Buddhist monks and this fact ought to prevent us from making a common mistake. There is a tendency, to which Newars are prone, though not as badly as Western observers, to see the difference between Buddhism and Hinduism purely in terms of the monk-householder distinction. Anything which householders do is not really Buddhism, on this view, but a second best, a capitulation to Hinduism (or whatever is locally defined as the other religion). Buddhist modernists make use of this tendency, and condemn everything not conforming to their canons of orthodoxy as Hinduism.[28]

At the same time it is important to realize how strongly the monastic ideal exists also as a part of Mahāyāna and Vajrayāna Buddhism, which stress the equal validity or superiority of being a Buddhist householder. Jog Maya told me that being a householder was, from the religious point of view, no less ('kam ma ju') than being a monk or nun, and she meant, I think, that in many ways it was a harder path: not only difficult ritual obligations but also lifelong family responsibilities to be fulfilled. It is therefore wrong to make the equation monasticism = Buddhism. It is wrong even for the Buddhism depicted in the Pali canon[29] and *a fortiori* it is wrong for Mahāyāna and Vajrayāna Buddhism. Whereas in Theravāda Buddhism celibate monasticism is the highest religious role and debate centres on how ascetic monks should be, within Mahāyāna Buddhism there are many opposing views. In Tibet, with the rise of the Gelukpa, celibate monasticism has the highest prestige for many, but there are simultaneously many countervailing views, with which the Newars are more in agreement. In Newar Buddhism celibate monasticism, while authentically Buddhist, is a first step towards higher statuses (§4.2, chapter 6).

2.5 Some differences between Hinduism and Buddhism

I have pointed out that the number of Brahmans is very small compared to the number of Vajrācāryas and Śākyas; and this is part of the explanation for the ambivalent position of some Śreṣṭhas between Hinduism and Buddhism. There are many other differences between the two religions, some of which are no more than cultural markers, while others reflect, or derive from, the distinct value-orientations of the two religions.

In the organization of priestly functions in the two religions there is a striking asymmetry. Whereas the Vajrācārya combines within himself the roles of teacher (*guru*) and priest of all kinds, the Śaivites have an extreme specialization of priestly functions.[30] (i) The highest-status priest is the Rājopādhyāya *guru*, who gives the Gāyatrī mantra at the caste-initiation rite (*vratabandha*), and must be invited on many other ritual occasions. (ii) Another Rājopādhyāya Brahman, the family priest (*purohit*), actually performs life-cycle rituals. (iii) High-caste Karmācāryas perform the Tantric worship of certain important goddesses and in the past, when there was a demand for them, carried out secret Tantric rituals for Hindu patrons in their homes. (iv) A lower-caste Karmācārya group (Ghaḥsū Ācāḥju) provides priests who help the Rājopādhyāya perform worship involving blood sacrifice, and who carry out the purifying Fire Sacrifice on the thirteenth day after death. (v) Each high-caste *śivamārgī* patron (*jajmān*) also has his own astrologer, Jośī, who must be called to rituals and receive a sacrificial fee (*dakṣiṇā*), just like the Brahman and Karmācārya. (vi) Priestly services from low-caste death-specialists are also duplicated: Hindus are served both by Kāpālī (Jogi) and by Karamjit (Bhāḥ) (= Mahābrāhmaṇ).

This may be contrasted with Śākyas and Vajrācāryas themselves in their role as patron. They require only a family priest, a Barber, and a Kāpālī (Jogi). With these three, they say, they have all they need. If they own rice land they also have a Maharjan tenant (*mhay*) who carries messages and helps at major rituals. Even in the past it seems that they had no other *jajmānī* relations.[31] Buddhists do not have a separate hereditary relationship with a *guru* as opposed to their family priest.

Two explanations for the multiplication of Śaivite priests spring to mind.

On the sociological level, it is to be connected to the 'conspicuous religious consumption' expected from South Asian kings and their courtiers. (Ordinary Newars call at most one priest, except on the most extravagant occasions, and often indeed the elder of the lineage, *thakāli*, acts as priest.) High-caste Hindus are fulfilling the role of Kṣatriyas, and to do that they have to have *jajmānī* links to as many specialists as possible. Secondly, from the historical point of view, Hinduism has always tended to multiply priests. The Rājopādhyāya-Karmācārya bifurcation reflects Brahman reservations about Tantrism, which they embraced less wholeheartedly than the Vajrācāryas.[32] This relative (though only relative) hostility towards Tantrism on the part of Brahmans (but not on the part of kings) may be observed in Table 3.2. In the Buddhist case the highest level of the caste hierarchy monopolizes the Tantric shrines while the non-Tantric deities may equally be served by Śākyas. With the Hindus, it is the non-Tantric deities (Mahādeva, Nārāyaṇa, and Kṛṣṇa) who are the preserve of the highest level alone.

As far as religious observances go, there are a few which are the sole property of one religion or the other. Thus only high-caste Hindus perform Govardhana Pūjā to Kṛṣṇa, and only high-caste Buddhists observe Disī Pūjā (the winter equinox when the esoteric deity Cakrasaṃvara is worshipped). But in these cases the festival is no concern of ordinary Newars. Where ordinary Newars take part in a given festival, or follow a particular practice, then the two religions provide either alternative explanations of the same practice, or alternative but functionally equivalent practices. The former (different names for, and explanations of, the same phenomenon) is discussed below (§3.2). Here are some examples of the latter.

To make merit for recently deceased relatives, Hindus take part in Sā Pāru (Np. Gāī Jātrā); Lalitpur Buddhists participate in Matayā, the following day, and Kathmandu Buddhists observe the custom of *upākhu wanegu* almost a month later. Hindus greet each other by saying 'Nārāyaṇa' (the most common name of Viṣṇu), while Buddhists say 'Tāremām'[33] or 'Bhagvān śarṇa' ('The Lord [Buddha] is my refuge'). Hindus perform an Observance (*vrata*) to Nārāyaṇa on the eleventh day of the month (*ekādaśī*), whereas the most common Buddhist Observance is to Amoghapāśa Lokeśvara on the eighth (*aṣṭamī*).

At the level of custom also there are many minor but noticeable differences between high-caste Hindus and Buddhists. Certain types of jewellery (e.g. the bride wearing a golden *lũswã* in her hair at her wedding) are typically Buddhist. At Kijā Pūjā (younger brother worship) Buddhist men go to visit their married elder sisters, to receive worship and give the required gifts, but Hindu elder sisters must come to visit their brothers. At feasts Buddhists employ at most one or two cooks, and rely on the help of close friends and relatives to cook and serve the food. When the guests arrive they eat outside in a courtyard or monastery and all receive equal treatment, except that proximity to the deity (who is presented with several portions of the feast) at the head of the first line indicates seniority. Hindus by contrast employ a whole group of servers who are high-caste and specialize in this profession; the guests come at different times, often over several days, and are served indoors in small separate sittings according to their status.

There are in addition some differences of linguistic usage. For example, for plate, Buddhists say *demā*, Hindus, *bhū*; for spatula, most Buddhists say *catā̃*, Hindus, *panyū*. In themselves these differences are trivial, but, like differences of accent and vocabulary in Newari generally, they are a frequent topic of conversation. Hindus make greater use of Nepali kinship terms, and indeed are far more likely to speak Nepali to their children, whereas Buddhists remain more attached to Newari.

In many cases the practices of other Newars are in accord with high-caste Buddhists rather than those of high-caste Hindus: in their feasts, in their attachment to Newari, and, in Lalitpur at least, in much of their social religion too.[34] What is the significance of this? Partly it is a reflection of the fact that, until the arrival of Theravāda Buddhism in the 1930s, local Buddhism had been isolated from substantial external Buddhist influence for hundreds of years.[35] Hinduism by contrast is partly defined by the fact that it derives its legitimacy from the Great Tradition to the south. Hindu linguistic usage, the greater emphasis which Hindus put on hierarchy, and the gods and practices which they prefer – all these factors weaken the ties of Hindus to Newar culture and, for them, devalue the purely local. Paradoxically Buddhism, supposedly the more universalist religion, turned in on itself. This precluded the rise of new cults under external influence.[36] It also meant that Śākya and Vajrācārya traditions reflected and reinforced what were, presumably, pre-existing Newar attachments to equality within *guthi* and status groups, and to isogamy as opposed to hypergamy.[37] High-caste Hindus, by contrast, have been open to new styles of religion and social practice, both coming from India and from the influence of the dominant Parbatiyās after 1769. Their Hindu identity made them more likely to apply criteria of hierarchy within the caste, just as their Kṣatriya conduct produced numerous imitators and half-caste assimilators.

The internal equality of Vajrācāryas and Śākyas when compared to

Śreṣṭhas, and the reason for it, were recognized in the Buddhist chronicle translated as Wright's *History of Nepal* in the passage dealing with Sthiti Malla's caste 'reforms':

Although they (*vãdya*) are Brahman and Kṣatriya [in origin], they are [all] one, there is no difference [between them]; their religion (*dharma*), rituals (*karma*), death rites (*kriyā*), marriage ceremonies (*vihā*), rules of eating (*dālbhāt*) are all the same. Renouncers (*sãnyāsī*) are also like that. Taking all this into consideration, they decided that there was no decision on caste to be made (*jāt tirṇay* [for *nirṇay*] *garnu chaina*) in the case of Vãdyas [Vajrācāryas and Śākyas] or in the case of renouncers.[38]

2.6 Caste identities and the problem of names

Newar castes have at least two different names: a purely Newari one, which is non-honorific, and therefore familiar, and a Sanskrit-derived one. The latter tends to describe the caste's religious function or its traditional profession, and on that account is a matter of collective pride. It is therefore polite to refer to a Newar's caste in his or her presence by using the honorific term; the non-honorific name is used in the third person. The honorific caste name is therefore used as a surname by most Newars. The traditional process by which Sanskrit loanwords were used as honorifics in Newari has been compounded in the last two centuries by the adoption of Nepali loans for the same purpose. This explains why the misapprehension can arise that a caste's honorific name is Nepali, and its non-honorific equivalent is Newari (see Fürer-Haimendorf 1956: 26).

The exceptions in a sense prove the rule that Sanskrit-derived surnames are more honorific. Some high-caste Hindus from Bhaktapur and a few others from Kathmandu and Lalitpur (e.g. among Śākyas, the Dhakhwa clan) prefer to use the name of their own particular lineage or clan (*kulnā̃*) as a surname. This is always a Newari term, which usually started life as a nickname (Dhakhwa, *dhāḥ-khwā*, means drum-face). The families which use these names are so well known, and of such high standing, that they have nothing to lose and something to gain from marking themselves off from their caste fellows in this way. (One may compare the way in which the top Kṣatriya families among the Parbatiyās, the Ranas and Ṭhakurīs, refuse the Chetri/Kṣatriya label: Bista 1972: 26–7.) Since, however, the lineage name is often unflattering, less distinguished Newars in the western part of the Valley usually avoid using it of themselves. In Bhaktapur and Dhulikhel, and other parts in the eastern half of the Valley, these lineage names are generally used and acknowledged more openly.

In the very recent past, some members of the Newari language movement have started to sign their name using the non-honorific caste term, much in the same spirit as the Black Pride movement started using the term 'black'. They call themselves Gubhāju instead of Vajrācārya, Tamaḥ instead of Tāmrakār, Jyāpu instead of Maharjan. 'Bare' is evidently too pejorative in its overtones: Śākyas use the archaic 'Vandya' or 'Bandya' instead. This unprecedented move is part of a general attempt both in writing and in high-register speech to use only Newari roots and to exclude words which come from Sanskrit, Persian, and especially Nepali.

There has been a tendency in modern times to the homogenization of caste names: what used to be Brahmacarya Bhikṣu, Śākyabhikṣu, and Śākyavaṃśa (§6.1) are all Śākya today. Similarly, many Hindus take 'Śreṣṭha' and not a few Buddhists 'Tulādhar' as their surnames today who would not have done so in the past. Most of those who do this are upwardly mobile, as described by Rosser (1966); others are the offspring of high-caste fathers and lower-caste mothers; but some are high-caste families who have started to move in a modern technocratic world in which their traditional locally recognized lineage name makes no sense.

Newars use two different terms to refer to caste: *jāt* and *thar*. The former is the more basic and general, the latter is honorific. Thus, in asking a Newar their caste, it is polite to ask for their *thar*, blunt and rude to ask for *jāt*. It is probably for this reason that, if one asks for someone's *thar*, there is a presumption that the honorific, Sanskrit-derived name will be given. If one asks for *jāt*, there is a presumption that the non-honorific term, usually used only in reference by non-members of the caste, will be given. These are only presumptions, and the speaker can always assume ignorance on the part of the questioner and reply with any epithet they like. They may even say 'I am Nepalese', meaning by this that caste differences are unimportant in modern Nepal, and one should not be asking.

Within castes three types of groups larger than the household can be distinguished; in order of decreasing size they are: sub-castes, caste sub-groups (to be explained presently), and clans or lineages. The terms *jāt* and *thar* may be used for any one of these; but it is my impression that *jāt* is rather rarely applied to the smallest unit, the clan or lineage, whereas *thar* occasionally is so applied. The reason for this seems to be that some castes as a whole lack an honorific name: only caste sub-groups have them. Consequently there is a slight presumption that *thar* (the honorific term) refers to a smaller unit than *jāt*. This flexibility of the terms we translate as 'caste', 'sub-caste', and so on, is found throughout South Asia (Dumont 1980: 62–3).

The first type of unit within the caste is the endogamous sub-caste. The main example here is the division of Śreṣṭhas into Chatharīya and Pãctharīya. (One must remember, however, that although these two groups are represented as two distinct and endogamous sub-castes there is inevitably a fuzzy margin between them.) Other Newar castes, with the arguable exception of the Maharjans, lack sub-caste divisions. Secondly, there are what I call caste sub-groups, which are neither endogamous (like sub-castes) nor exogamous (like clans or lineages). They are groups sharing the same surname and the same socio-religious identity. The different caste sub-groups within a caste are often ranked, the claims to superior status being expressed religiously. The gradations may well be contested, but in any case they are very slight and do not impede normal intermarriage. (Thus, unlike Greenwold 1974a: 108, or Toffin 1984: 388, I prefer *not* to call these groups sub-castes.) It is these caste sub-group surnames which are most often given as a person's *thar*.

Among the Chatharīya Śreṣṭhas there are several such caste sub-groups: Jośī, Rājbhaṇḍārī, Amātya, and so on. These three are defined by their role, now or in the past, as astrologers, royal storekeepers, and ministers respectively. Caste sub-groups are not exogamous. They may indeed (but need not) have a slight preference for endogamy because they often consider themselves a caste, with a common socio-religious identity.[39] Traditional lists of castes, as found in the Nepali chronicles of the nineteenth century, cite them as separate castes. It is only for the sake of analytical precision that they have not been called castes here.

Śākyas and Vajrācāryas are caste sub-groups of this sort. In the past there were others (§6.1), but they are all considered to be Śākyas today. The five groups making up the Tāmrakār *et al.* are certainly caste sub-groups. Among Maharjans, the Dãgol do not so clearly constitute such a group, since they have no city-wide organization, common shrine, or clear public ritual defining them as separate from those using 'Maharjan' as a surname. The Āwāles, on the other hand, are moving from being considered a Maharjan sub-caste to acceptance as a caste sub-group within the Maharjans.

A third type of grouping within castes, much smaller than the caste sub-group, is the clan or lineage. This is strictly exogamous. It is often defined by the addition of a place-name to a caste sub-group name. For example, the Jośīs of Lalitpur are divided into six exogamous clans or lineages each based in a given locality. The degree to which clans function as a unit varies enormously. Some, like the Dhakhwas, can still trace how they are all related; they hold considerable assets in common, come together every year to perform Lineage Deity Worship and other rituals (§8.2.5), and observe death pollution for each other. Other clans are little more than common nicknames: only the most minimal restrictions are observed, if at all, on the death of another member; no rituals are performed together and no land is held in common; apart from avoiding intermarriage, no further obligations towards each other are recognized. Some clans, with different names, are remembered to be related agnatically. Until very recently marriage was avoided between such clans and it was punished as incest by expulsion from the family if it occurred. Today, however, such marriages, if strongly desired by the couple, are sometimes permitted.

There is no sharp distinction between clan and lineage made in Newari: both are equally *kul* or *khalaḥ*. We may wish to call clans those groups which are large enough to have sub-lineages or segments (*kawaḥ*) within them. Lineages, then, are those agnatic groups with a single nickname which are not large enough to have subdivisions of this sort. In the case of lineages precise genealogical links often are remembered, because the unit is smaller. Where clans are concerned such links are often not remembered if the clan is large and the *kawaḥ* units do the work of organization. Even where exact links are not known families remember whether other clan members are *phuki* (kin) or *tāpā phuki* (distant kin), since it is necessary to know this at the time of death (see below, Table 7.5). In the past there was no doubt a cycle whereby clans broke up into separate named lineages after reaching a certain size, and lineages gradually grew into clans. Today the aspiration for clan solidarity is more questioned and less put into practice.

The names of clans and lineages are usually regarded as informal and most of them clearly began as nicknames. Only rarely nowadays are they used as surnames, as by the Dhakhwas. Except for the Dhakhwas, it is very rare for Śākyas or Vajrācāryas to refer to their clan or lineage as their *thar*. A Śākya or Vajrācārya asked for their *thar* will nearly always reply 'Śākya' or 'Vajrācārya'. By contrast it is my impression that it is more common for Śreṣṭhas to give their lineage or clan name (such as Nyāchyã, 'fish head', or Kisī, 'elephant') as their *thar*, rather than their caste or caste sub-group.[40]

The crucial fact underlying the distinction between caste and caste sub-group is that outsiders lump together what insiders distinguish, even though they are often aware that the insiders themselves make finer distinctions. (This is true of other contexts too and is indeed a general principle of caste societies: Mayer 1966: 5, 159–60; Parry 1979: 231–4.) Thus the Vajrācārya and Śākya caste is called 'Bare' by high-caste Hindus, 'Bā̃ḍā' (a Nepalization of 'Bare') by Nepali-speakers, and 'Gubhāju' by farmers and lower castes.[41] They themselves tend to use 'Gubhāju' to mean Vajrācārya, and they insist that 'Bare' refers exclusively to Śākyas; but since 'Bare' is considered, more even than most non-honorific names, to be

Figure 9. Segmentary names: terms used to refer to the Vajrācārya-Śākya caste by outsiders and by themselves. The box represents the top Buddhist caste with its two caste sub-groups; the terms they use to refer to themselves and which they consider equivalent are shown inside the box. Non-members use a single term to refer to the whole caste, and these are given outside the box.

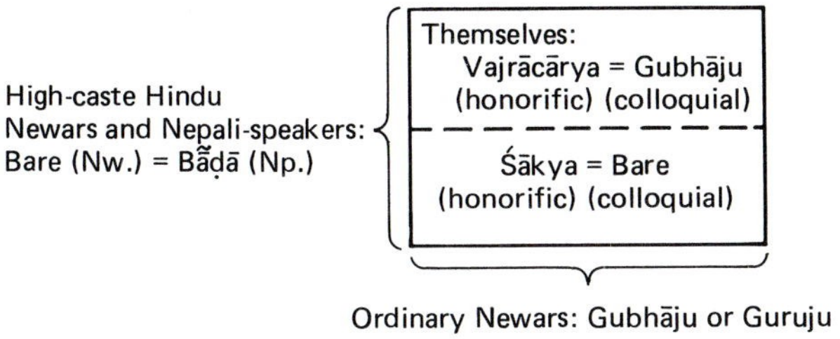

disrespectful, even occasionally insulting, they usually only use it in certain stock phrases. High-caste Hindus deny them respect in using the term 'Bare', which Vajrācāryas and Śākyas resent. Similarly, out of respect, middle and lower castes extend the priestly name 'Gubhāju' to all of them, whether they are Vajrācārya or Śākya. Consequently (as a further complication) Śākyas living in farmer-dominated areas often imitate their usage and refer to themselves as 'Gubhāju' too. In Kathmandu, however, 'Gubhāju' tends to be used only of Vajrācāryas, even by lower castes, and it is 'Guruju', in Lalitpur primarily a term of address, which is used for Śākyas and Vajrācāryas alike as an honorific term both of reference and address. These various usages are summarized in Figure 9.

There is therefore no unambiguous usage, except always to say 'Vajrācārya and Śākya'. Locke (1980, 1985) follows Allen (1973) and Greenwold (1974a, 1974b) in using 'Bare' to refer to the caste as a whole. I prefer to be more precise and to avoid taking sides where a concept is 'essentially contested', even at the cost of being more long winded.[42]

As another illustration of the same indeterminacy, we can take the Chatharīya Śreṣṭhas. If you ask some of them whether they are Śreṣṭha, they will say, 'No, I'm Karmācārya' or 'No, I'm Rājbhaṇḍārī' because these particular caste sub-groups do not take 'Śreṣṭha' as a surname, unlike others of their caste. Nevertheless they do all form one intermarrying unit, and non-Śreṣṭhas lump them all together as 'Śeśyaḥ'. There is ambiguity because the term 'Śreṣṭha', like 'Gubhāju' and 'Bare' suffers from markedness (having a broader and a narrower application): outsiders refer to them all by a term which for insiders designates only one caste sub-group. As with Vajrācāryas and Śākyas, lower castes are respectful and tend to say 'Śreṣṭha', while Vajrācāryas and Śākyas tend to say 'Śeśyaḥ'.

Thus, the terminology of caste and caste sub-group distinguishes two levels which Newari usage does not itself clearly differentiate. The examples just given show that Newars themselves identify with the caste sub-group; they identify it as their caste. What is here called caste, viz. the marriage circle formed by a collection of caste sub-groups (where such exist), sometimes has no single name for itself, as the titles 'Tulādhar *et al.*' and 'Tāmrakār *et al.*', and the conjunction 'Śākyas and Vajrācāryas' all illustrate. In attempting to be precise, and to avoid having to rely on context to clarify the radically ambiguous reference of the terms used, such periphrases are unfortunately necessary. Within the culture the three analytical categories, caste, sub-caste, and caste sub-group, are all equally *jāt*.

2.7 The determinants of religious identity

We are now at last in a position to label Newars as Hindu or Buddhist in a tolerably systematic fashion. Taking the three types of religion distinguished in chapter 1, and subdividing social religion into two, we have four distinct contexts:

Instrumental context

At the instrumental end of the spectrum the terms 'Hindu' and 'Buddhist' are almost irrelevant. When Newars seek an urgent cure for some worldly ill, they usually do not stop to consider whether it is Hindu or Buddhist. If there is more time to reflect, but there is still a particular end in view, the religious identity of the rite or practitioner sponsored is more significant. It is also true that the castes with a social identity strongly in one or other camp are more likely to seek help from someone identified with their own religion. It is improbable that a Brahman would come to see a Śākya woman possessed by Vajrayoginī and Hārītī; but it is not impossible if everything else had been tried and failed. I have evidence of the converse at least: a young Śākya man in search of a cure for extreme short-sightedness had visited, he claimed profitably, a probably low-caste woman (she refused to discuss her past history) who proclaimed herself to be Śivaśakti, the supreme (Hindu) godhead. Another Śākya man was one of her principal disciples.

Traditional social context

In the sphere of social religion it is always possible to specify precisely a person's religion, but caste and context must be cited too. Social religion includes recurrent festivals and life-cycle rituals, in which one acts as a member of one's caste. As we have seen, there are differences even between the caste sub-groups which go to make up a caste: Jośīs are unequivocal Hindus, whereas many Śreṣṭhas have Vajrācārya priests (and therefore are *buddhamārgī*), support Buddhist festivals, and take Buddhist Tantric Initiation (but still call themselves Hindu). Similarly, the Tāmrakārs are self-consciously Hindu and have Rājopādhyāya priests, while Rājkarṇikārs and Śilpakārs, with whom they intermarry, are Buddhists, though less unequivocally so.

As one goes down the caste hierarchy it is less and less realistic to force an answer to the either/or question. The Maharjans all have Vajrācārya priests in Lalitpur. But they too return 'Hindu' on the census form. They can distinguish between Hindu and Buddhist deities and know that high castes identify themselves as Hindu or Buddhist. But they insist on being both. Most of them are simple farmers who are extremely uncomfortable with theoretical questions.[43] For them at least it is certainly true that religion is a matter of action, not belief; and those actions – rituals, festivals, and music-making – which were good enough for their forebears are good enough for most of them: speech-making, confessions of faith, and soteriology are left to the high castes.

The equal honour that Maharjans render to both religions is nicely illustrated by the programme of the Ī Bahī area Maharjan music group. It plays every day for the Buddhist holy month of Gū̃lā beside the northern *stūpa* of Lalitpur. Then two weeks later it begins to play again for a month, this time to celebrate Mohanī (Np. Dasaĩ), the most important Hindu festival (known in India as Durgā Pūjā or Navarātrī), at the shrine (*pīṭha*) of the Mother Goddess Cāmuṇḍā (Sikābahīdyaḥ) outside the town, two minutes walk from the aforesaid *stūpa*. As the son of the group's leader put it to me: 'We honour both religions; we join the procession for Buddha Jayantī, but we come along drunk, which the [Theravāda] monks don't like.'

What is important to see here is that Newar religion is an extremely social matter – almost every social occasion is also to some extent religious – and that this kind of religion is determined by one's caste. Only the higher castes insist on using Hindu or Buddhist forms to express this, and even they are capable of considerable subtle ambiguity. The middle and lower castes are on the whole happy that their social occasions are sanctified, and prefer not to raise the question of which religion is doing the sanctifying.

Modern social context

This covers the ascriptions made during the census, or in the newspapers, or in the discussion of the young and educated. For the uneducated this kind of identity is relatively unimportant. But for those with education and aspirations to government jobs it is a matter of immediate significance. Buddhism is often associated in the minds of high-caste Hindu Newars with educational backwardness, obscurantism, and low social prestige. This goes a long way towards explaining the emotional appeal of an assertive Buddhist modernism for those who are stuck with a Buddhist identity.[44]

Soteriology

With soteriology we come to an element of personal choice. Some pious individuals prefer Buddhism, others Hinduism. Except in one or two cases, influenced by neo-Hindu ecumenism, the pious are normally partisan. Newars themselves would consider it anomalous for a Vajrācārya or a Śākya to become a pious Hindu, and today at least it is very rare for a Brahman to become a pious Buddhist: in both cases it would require the convert to be impervious to social pressure.[45] But with all other castes this is not so: there are Śreṣṭhas who take a strong and intellectual interest in Buddhism, and others who do the same for Hinduism. I know of a Jośī who is a Tibetan Mahāyāna monk and another who is a prominent Buddhist intellectual, although the caste identity of Jośīs is strongly Hindu. Some Maharjans are keen devotees of Buddhist events organized by Śākyas and Vajrācāryas, or of Theravāda Buddhism; others become pious Hindus; but the vast majority of their caste fellows do not have soteriological interests, and if challenged say that the strict fulfilment of their social religion is all the soteriology they need.

It is true that much optional religious activity has social ends in view, so that there is a grey area between social and soteriological religion. And in a society in which social identities are defined religiously almost every expression of soteriological piety has social implications, simply by virtue of the idiom in which it is expressed. Often indeed, certain soteriological devotions, different from those of other caste members, are passed down in the family.

In spite of these qualifications, individuals can have religious attachments independent of their social identity, though most do not choose to make them. Even for Śākyas and Vajrācāryas, who must be Buddhists, there is a choice to be made between the traditional Vajrayāna of the Vajrācāryas, the powerful and impressive Tibetan tradition, and the newly imported Theravāda movement. As Jog Maya remarked to me, there are religions enough for everyone to choose, just like vegetables in the morning bazaar.

In what follows, therefore, when I say 'Buddhists' I mean Vajrācāryas and Śākyas, plus those individuals of other castes who have a strong

Figure 10. Three ways of describing Newar religious affiliation.

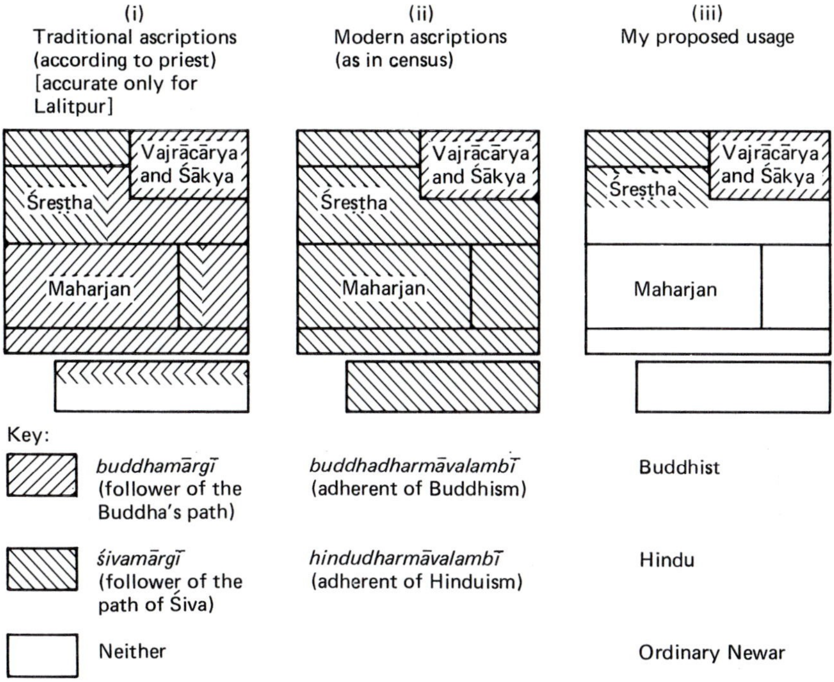

personal identification with Buddhism. By 'Hindu' I refer to Brahmans and Śreṣṭhas, plus those others with strong Hindu leanings. All other Newars I shall refer to as 'ordinary Newars'. They are perhaps typified by the Farmer who observes the customs and festivals traditional to his caste and leaves all Sanskritic niceties to the higher castes. 'The traditions of his caste' include activities which might be classified as Buddhist, Hindu, both at once, or neither: he is not concerned with such distinctions; for him they are all equally the religion of his family (*kuldharma*) which he has inherited and which it is his duty to maintain.

There are three different ways of dividing Newars into the Hindu and Buddhist camps, and these are summarized in Figure 10. The figure shows a simplified version of the caste hierarchy given in Figures 6 and 7; I shall use the terms *śivamārgī* and *buddhamārgī* as shorthand for 'those with Brahman priests' and 'those with Vajrācārya priests' respectively as shown in Figure 10(i). The terms used in Figure 10(ii), *buddhadharmāvalambī* and *hindudharmāvalambī*, are new, but the idea of looking at it this way is not. The sentiment that only Vajrācāryas and Śākyas are really Buddhists has been discussed above (§2.4). In defence of my proposed terminology, illustrated in Figure 10(iii), I should say that I seek to use the terms in a way that reflects real differences of value-orientation and this requires the category, the largest of the three, of 'ordinary Newars' who are neither exclusively Buddhist nor exclusively Hindu. If I sometimes use the terms 'folk religion' or 'popular religion' for the practices of ordinary Newars, I do so merely in order to give them a label. I do not thereby imply, as others sometimes have (Lienhard 1978: 249; Van Kooij 1978: 5; Toffin 1984: 432–3; Locke 1989: 95), that such practices are to be understood as a residue, and that by studying them we can understand what pre-Buddhist and pre-Hindu religion was like in Nepal.

It should be clear, then, that there is a distinction made between Hinduism and Buddhism in the culture. Matters are complicated not only by conflicting definitional criteria but by the fact that the middle and lower castes usually prefer not to apply the concepts in an exclusive way to themselves and their own traditions; nevertheless they understand the concepts. Not surprisingly, they tend to think of Buddhism and Hinduism mainly in terms of what Śākyas and Vajrācāryas, on the one hand, and Brahmans and Śreṣṭhas, on the other, do. Those of them who take an especial interest in religion become, as I have pointed out, either pious Buddhists, or pious Hindus, but not both at once.[46] This shows that it is only in their social religion that they prefer to remain equidistant, and even here everyone knows that one may have only one family priest, either a Brahman or a Vajrācārya, and not both. Soteriologically, Newars know that it is one or the other. It is clearly apt that the local terms define the two religions soteriologically – as alternative paths (*mārga*) or doctrines (*mata*).

3

The relation of Hinduism and Buddhism: competition and coexistence

> Upon the whole, therefore, I deem it certain, as well that the types of Sivaism and Buddhism are frequently the same, *as that the things typified are, always more or less, and generally radically different.*
>
> Hodgson, 'On the Extreme Resemblance that Prevails between Many of the Symbols of Buddhism and Saivism' [italics and spelling as in the original] (Hodgson 1972 I: 137).

> The Brahmans carried out a flanking movement against the Buddha; unable to topple their adversary, they resigned themselves to accepting him in order to absorb him.
>
> Lévi, *Le Népal*, vol. I, pp. 371–2.

3.1 The structure of the Newar pantheon

Anthropologists studying Hinduism have generally identified six distinct levels in the pantheon.[1] These may be listed as follows:

(i) an undifferentiated godhead, named simply *īśvara* or *bhagavān*;
(ii) the great gods, Śiva and Viṣṇu, and the goddess (Devī) in her form as Pārvatī, Śiva's wife;
(iii) the sons of Śiva and Pārvatī: Gaṇeś and Kumār;
(iv) fierce forms of Śiva (i.e. Bhairava) and Devī (the Eight Mother Goddesses, including Kālī; Durgā);
(v) fierce or capricious non-Sanskritic guardian deities, such as village goddesses and lineage deities; holy serpents (*nāga*), sages (*ṛṣi*), the earth god (*bhūmi*), ancestors (*pitṛ*);
(vi) ghosts (*bhūt*, *pret*) and demons (*rākṣasa*) and others.

The levels are differentiated not only by the nature of the gods or demons themselves, but also according to the means and the media through which

Figure 11. One way of representing the main part of the pantheon as structured by a series of oppositions. Letters refer to subdivisions shown in Figure 12.

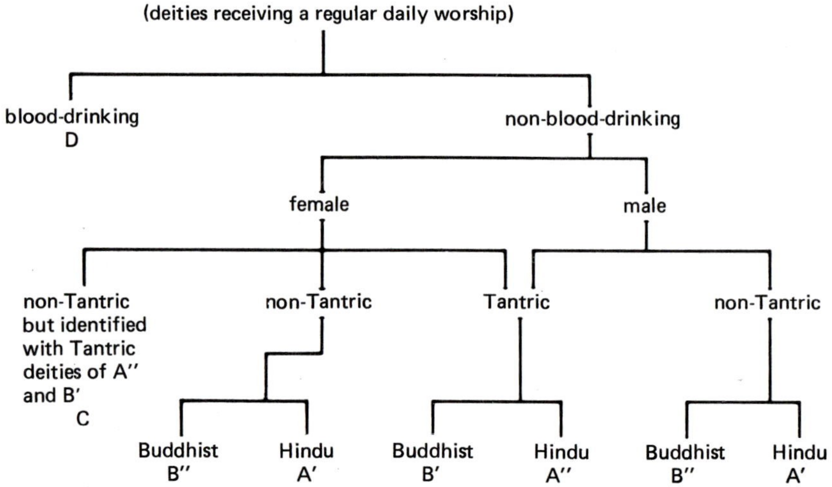

people interact with them. The abstract level (i) receives no cult. Levels (ii) and (iii) accept only pure, vegetarian offerings. The gods of level (iv) require animal sacrifice and alcohol. The heterogeneous members of category (v) are worshipped with various substances, and only in some cases (village goddesses, lineage deities) with animal sacrifice. The ghosts and demons of level (vi) receive extremely impure offerings: leftovers, entrails, congealed blood, broken rice.

These six levels are broadly valid for the Newars also. For completeness one needs to add to level (ii) the various Buddhas and *bodhisattva*s. When the suffix *-dyaḥ* (deity) is added to *bhagavān* it refers, for Newars, specifically to Lord Buddha. 'Bhagavatī', the feminine form of the same title, on the other hand, refers primarily to the Hindu goddess, Durgā. Levels (ii), (iii), and (iv), which include all those divinities receiving a regular daily cult, are structured slightly differently, and in a more complex manner, among the Newars, and this is shown in Figures 11 and 12.

Among the Newars Gaṇeś receives blood sacrifice; his brother, Kumār, is placed in the same category, by Buddhists at least, but is not sufficiently important to have a separate cult. Newars call 'fierce' gods *hiphaḥ dyaḥ*, 'blood-receiving deities': when an animal is sacrificed to them, its throat has to be cut on the under side so that the blood spurts over the icon of the deity in a continuous stream. Level (v) also includes various nameless deities worshipped for a specific purpose: for instance, the famous 'toothache

Figure 12. The structure of the Hindu-Buddhist pantheon of Lalitpur according to which castes perform daily worship and/or keep the daily offerings (i.e. have the right to be god-guardian, *pūjārī* or *dyaḥpāḥlāḥ*).
Notes:
(a) All the gods mentioned have at least one temple in Lalitpur, except three, Guhyeśvarī, Bijeśvarī, and Hārītī, whose temples are in Kathmandu.
(b) Sometimes a Śākya elder may perform the daily worship of a Buddhist Tantric deity, rather than have a Vajrācārya perform it, if there are no Vajrācāryas in the monastery or *guthi* in question.
(c) All Buddhists, except hardline Theravāda modernists, would accept both categories B and C as Buddhist deities. Many Buddhists would deny that the gods of category D are Buddhist; others say that the point of Mahāyāna Buddhism is to worship all gods. Practising Vajrācārya priests, whose parishioners worship category D gods, are particularly likely to insist on this.

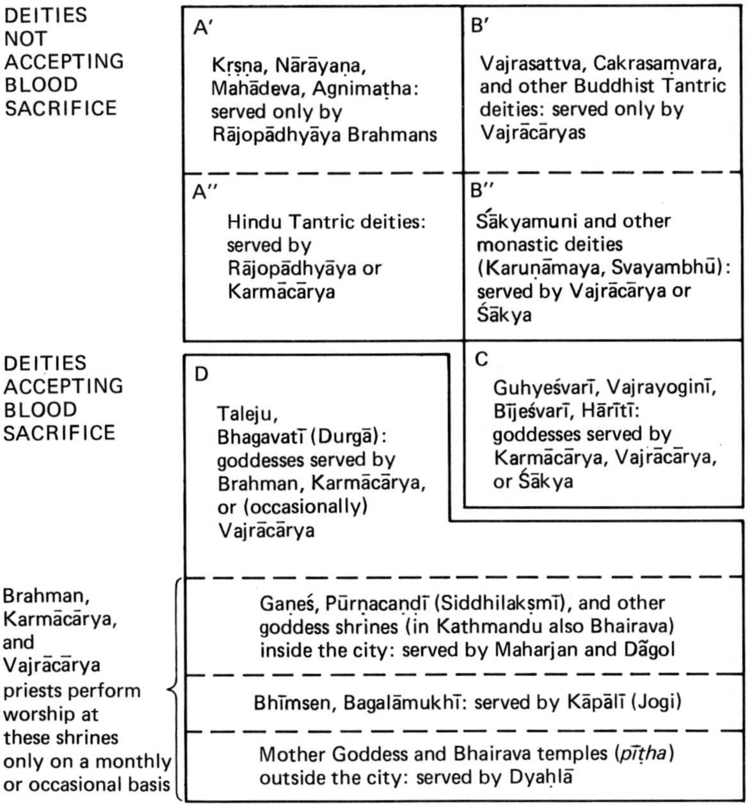

deity' in Thāymadu (Bangemudha), Kathmandu, where a nail is hammered in for relief from toothache. In category (vi) there are also various spooks or spirits: the hairy black *khyāḥ* who blocks your way in the dark; the *kawã*, a skeleton with a penis met outdoors at night;[2] the *kickinni*, a seductive female with reversed feet who causes the weakening and death of men who fall for her. *Pret* are often simply called *sika* (from *siye*, to die), spirits of the dead who fail to be reborn and return to haunt their families.

The structure of the main part of the pantheon, levels (ii), (iii), and (iv), can be derived from four oppositions: Hindu/Buddhist, male/female, blood-drinking/non-blood-drinking, Tantric/non-Tantric.[3] These are represented in Figure 11. The deities who do not accept sacrifice are considered superior to the blood-drinking ones. But there are differing views on the relation of Tantric to non-Tantric deities, and there are times and contexts when female deities are considered superior to male. Thus if there is a tendency for all oppositions to be hierarchically biased towards one pole or the other,[4] there is scope too for different points of view based on favouring the opposite pole. The Hindu/Buddhist distinction is hardly the most important one, or, rather, becomes important only at a certain level. As Lévi (1905 I: 319) wrote: 'A rigid classification which simplistically divided divinities up under the headings, Buddhism, Śaivism, and Vaiṣṇavism, would be a pure nonsense; under different names, and at different levels, the same gods are for the most part common to different confessions (*églises*).'

In Figure 12 deities are listed in various groups, firstly according to whether or not they accept blood sacrifice, and secondly according to which caste provides the 'guardians' or 'turn-holders' (*dyaḥpāḥlāḥ*)[5] who perform daily worship (*nitya pūjā*) and keep the offerings that other worshippers may bring. Figure 12 includes all deities of any importance except Kumārī, whose special position requires separate discussion (§3.2, 3.4).

Several other points need to be made about Figures 11 and 12. It is the high male deities who tend to represent the absolute and transcendent aspects of religion, and the holiest shrines of this sort, such as Svayambhū and Paśupati, are usually found outside the cities, on hilltops or by holy rivers. In general the gods of categories C and D are much more likely to respond to requests for immediate and self-interested results, although the *bodhisattvas* of B'' may respond with help for ends which do not involve harm to other people. With all gods there are some forms which are the focus of group identity and other large important shrines which attract all comers regardless of group membership. One might be tempted to say that the fierce gods and goddesses of categories C and D are more liable to be used as such Durkheimian foci of group identity and loyalty, but there are many counter-instances. The use of Tantric deities (A'', B') for such purposes is discussed below (§11.1). The Buddhist deities (B'') of large monasteries *both* define the group formed by the Śākya and/or Vajrācārya membership *and* attract worship from outsiders, regardless of group membership.

The deities of category D are both male and female, but predominantly female. They may be approached and worshipped by anyone. At the same time they play an important role in Tantric rituals, that is, rituals with essentially esoteric content. The goddesses of category C are in an intermediate, perhaps even mediating, position, probably for historical reasons. It seems that they were once Buddhist Tantric deities, sited in monasteries, who have become popular deities too.[6] This accounts for the fact that they do not accept blood sacrifice directly, unlike the goddesses of category D. (At Vajrayoginī and Guhyeśvarī it is however made to a Bhairava in their vicinity.) Were it not for the presence of Buddhism as a separately organized Great Tradition it seems likely that they would have been absorbed into category D.

Hārītī has also been placed in category C because of her position as a female deity not accepting blood sacrifice (though she does accept ducks' eggs). She is not however exactly the same as Bījeśvarī or Vajrayoginī: it is remembered that she is a demonness (*yakṣiṇī*) converted to Buddhism. (This is the only well-known case of such promotion among the Newars, a phenomenon which in Sri Lanka appears to be both relatively frequent and historically traceable: Obeyesekere 1984: 68.) Consequently Hārītī lacks the identification with the female Tantric deities of categories A'' and B' which is frequently made for the other goddesses of category C.

The goddesses who belong in category A' and B'', who are non-Tantric and non-blood-drinking, such as Pārvatī, Sarasvatī, and Tārā, are, in large part, reflections of the pure male divinities of the same category. They do not have large, important temples of their own. The Buddhist deity Mahākāla (also called Mahā̃kāḥdyaḥ by Newars) is popularly conflated with Bhairava (of category D). As publicly enshrined, e.g. at the Tundhikhel in Kathmandu, Mahākāla belongs in category C.

The Tantric/non-Tantric distinction is merely one way in which a more general distinction between the inner and outer is made in Newar society. Thus M. Allen writes:

> A number of informants, both Hindu and Buddhist, stressed the importance of the distinction between *guhya* and *bahira*. *Guhya* refers to all that is inner or secret while *bahira* connotes things that are outer or open. The dichotomy is fundamental not

only to all forms of Tantricism but to the very fabric of Newar social life. Group membership is commonly defined by ritual initiation and social boundaries are maintained by secrecy and closure . . . For a Newar Buddhist the most basic inner/outer dichotomy is that between tantric and non-tantric . . . The inner/outer distinction is relative, not absolute . . . (Allen 1975: 56–7)

Perhaps Allen should have written that the Tantric/non-Tantric distinction is the most *important* of the inner/outer dichotomies, since the most basic, in the sense of most literal, is between the deities inside the city and those outside it.[7] At another level, all the blood-drinking deities, even those inside the city, are impure, outer deities. But at the highest level, that is within the category of male, non-blood-drinking deities, the inner/outer dichotomy is precisely the Tantric/non-Tantric one.

In a recent analysis, Fuller (1988: 26) has shown how local goddesses in south India are 'segmented' into three forms during different stages of their cult and annual festival: a high vegetarian form, an intermediate meat-eating form, and a low form which receives animal sacrifice. Among the Newars one does not find a divinity with a single name sometimes receiving blood sacrifice, sometimes not. But under different names the same process is common. We have already noted how a Bhairava in the vicinity of an important god frequently receives blood sacrifice: this occurs at Paśupati and Vajrayoginī, and a string is tied from the Bhairava stone to the main image; Bū̃gadyaḥ (Karuṇāmaya) has animal sacrifice performed to the wheels of his chariot, which are identified with four Bhairavas. In the case of Śiva (Paśupati) it is clearly recognized by Newars that Bhairava is his low form. Likewise Vasundharā, the Buddhist goddess of wealth, who receives only pure offerings, is sometimes identified with Mahālakṣmī, one of the Eight Mothers, who receives animal sacrifice (cf. §3.2 on Kumārī). In the same way, Tantric forms of these divinities (i.e. the esoteric icons enshrined in *āgå̃*, Tantric shrines of limited access) correspond to Fuller's 'intermediate' form: they require meat and alcohol but do not accept animal sacrifice. However, as secret inner divinities, far from being intermediate, they are seen as the highest, or at any rate the most profound, version of the deity.

It should be clear from a comparison of Figure 12 with Figure 6 (§2.1), that there is a certain similarity of structure between the divine hierarchy and the caste hierarchy.[8] However, as Toffin (1984: 598) points out, 'It would be wrong to represent the homology as a correspondence, element by element.' The city is too large, and the number of castes too great, for the homology to be precise, for it to be possible to 'read off' social structure from the divine hierarchy or vice versa. Another reason for this is that the two scriptural religions in their universalist aspect invite worship from all comers, so that the homology, encouraged by the social functions of Newar religion, continually breaks down.

The tendency for particular castes to be identified with particular gods can be illustrated by the case of the elephant-headed god, Gaṇeś. What goes for him goes *a fortiori* for high Buddhist or Hindu deities. The worship of Gaṇeś is universal in Newar society but, as might be guessed from Figure 12, it is particularly popular with the Farmer caste. Just as the guardian (*dyaḥpāḥlāḥ*) of a category B god must always be a Śākya or Vajrācārya, and of Mahādeva or Nārāyaṇa a Brahman, so the guardian of Gaṇeś shrines is usually a Maharjan. One of the ways of expressing piety and earning merit in Newar society is the practice of regular morning visits to a particular deity's temple over a fixed period of time. Buddhists usually perform this during the month of Gũlā, to Svayambhū, and during the month of Kārttik, either to Svayambhū or to Ādināth Lokeśvara on Cobhār hill. Both Hindus and Buddhists visit the temple of Mahālakṣmī to the south of the city every morning during the month leading up to Mohanī. Some of the Farmer caste take part in all of these, but it is they who dominate a four-month period of visits to the Gaṇeś at Kwenā (Kwenā-dyaḥ or Jala Vinayaka) every Tuesday (the day holy to Gaṇeś) during the *caturmāsa*.[9] The Maharjan who was guardian of the subsidiary Jala Vinayaka shrine in Lalitpur told me that he, Gaṇeś, is the real Lord of the universe (*jagadīśvara*) because he was here (as Jala Vinayaka) from the beginning, even at the time when Nepal was a lake, unlike all your Buddhas and Bhagavāns which were established only later by rich men.

Most Newars worship gods of all four categories shown in Figure 12 at some time or other, with the exception that access to secret Tantric deities is restricted to high castes. Even if they themselves may not do so directly, all clean castes have rituals to Tantric deities performed on their behalf by their family priest. For Newar Buddhists the Buddhas and important *bodhisattvas* (Karuṇāmaya, Mañjuśrī, and Tārā) occupy the highest level of the pantheon, below the undifferentiated absolute. Below them are the lesser *bodhisattvas*, including Śiva and Viṣṇu. The rest of the pantheon is in common with Hindus. The idea that different *bodhisattvas* are the 'sons' of the five Buddhas or Tathāgatas is known to pious Buddhists, but it is hardly the first and most important aspect of their belief system, as some presentations of Newar Buddhism suggest.

One might suppose that Brahmans would never worship Buddhist deities, but even here caution is in order: the Hindu pilgrimage text, the Nepāla Māhātmya, recommends that pilgrims visit Vajrayoginī, who is described as a form of Pārvatī, and Svayambhū. Svayambhū is described simply as a Buddhist site, with no attempt to pretend it is 'really' Hindu (Lévi 1905 I: 390; Brinkhaus 1980: 281); elsewhere, however, the text says that to worship the Buddha is to worship Śiva and that the Buddha is a form of Viṣṇu (Lévi 1905 I: 318). Pratāp Malla, King of Kathmandu between 1641 and 1674, recorded publicly that he worshipped Svayambhū as a form of Śiva (D.R. Regmi 1965 II: 569). A Brahman told me that underneath Svayambhū's *stūpa* there is actually a *liṅga* (the rounded cylindrical cult object which is the most common representation of Śiva). This clearly shows, as should become clear in what follows, that different actors evaluate the pantheon in different ways. The hierarchy illustrated in Figure 12 is not rigid: there is plenty of room for debate about who is the highest god and how other gods are related to him or her.

3.2 The multivalency of symbols

The multiple identity of the deities of Nepal can be approached, as with castes, by considering the question of names. The most Sanskritic deities do not usually have a colloquial Newari name, but they may well have alternative Sanskrit epithets: thus Guhyeśvarī is known to all under this name, but high-caste Hindus probably worship her as Kubjikā or Guhyakālī;[10] Buddhists identify her as Nairātmyā, consort of Hevajra. Mahādeva (Mahādyaḥ) is always called that, but Buddhists worship him as the *bodhisattva* Vajrapāṇi (particularly in the cycle of Observances to the Eight Passionless Ones, *aṣṭavaitarāga*). Important male gods are often known by their Sanskritic name with suffix *-dyaḥ*. Thus Bhīmsen is known as Bhīdyaḥ, Gaṇeś as Ganedyaḥ, Nārāyaṇa as Nārāindyaḥ and so on.

Many other gods have alternative Newari names. Bhairava is known both as Bhairaḥdyaḥ and as Harkhā̃dyaḥ. The main deity of a monastery, who is most commonly Śākyamuni Buddha with the earth-touching gesture, is usually called *kwābāju* in Lalitpur and *kwāḥpāḥdyaḥ* in Kathmandu.[11] The Dīpaṅkara images made to celebrate the festival of Samyak are known as *samedyaḥ*, *kwiyampāju*, or simply *ājudyaḥ* ('grandfather god').

For certain deities – those of level (v) – the Newari term is the main one, the Sanskrit name being secondary, little known, possibly in dispute, and often just attributed on the spot to satisfy the researcher. This is so in particular of *digu dyaḥ*, Lineage Deities. This is a generic term, rendered by *kuladevatā* in both Sanskrit and Nepali. In normal speech the deities are just called *digu dyaḥ*. Quigley (1985b: 27–8) describes well the confusion which can result from insistent questions about the identity of a Newar's *digu dyaḥ*. Not surprisingly, the high castes are usually much clearer in their minds than other Newars that their Lineage Deity has a definite Sanskritic identity. In the case of the members of Kwā Bāhāḥ it is Jyotirūpa Svayambhū (also called Ādibuddha) enshrined in the centre of the monastery, but they always refer to it in ordinary speech as *digu dyaḥ*. Other such deities are the *kalaḥ wāye dyaḥ* (Remains Deity) and the *chwāsā* or *chwāsā dyaḥ*. The former simply means 'the god where the ritual basket is thrown', and is the spot where the leftovers of a feast are thrown. It is identified in Buddhist liturgy as Dhūmāṅgārī or Ugracaṇḍī, but only priests are aware of this. The *chwāsā* is the spot where inauspicious objects such as a child's umbilical cord or the clothes of a dead person are placed.[12] Because of this connection to early childhood the *chwāsā* is often identified with Hārītī.

The trivalency of Newar religious symbols is best illustrated by the example of Karuṇāmaya-Matsyendranāth (see Plate 3). Buddhists nearly always refer to him as Karuṇāmaya. Others call him 'Būgadyaḥ' (i.e. 'the god of Būga', the village where he spends half the year) in normal speech, and Matsyendranāth (or Macchendranāth) or Karuṇāmaya at other times, depending on context.[13] He is so important that he has a special name, *bābādyaḥ*, in the Newars' children's language (an extensive alternative vocabulary with which young children are taught to speak). Hindus usually think of him as a form of Śiva, though the Brahmans of Lalitpur like to relate a story which illustrates his identity with Kṛṣṇa. Here, therefore, because the deity is equally important to (i) Hindus, (ii) Buddhists, and (iii) ordinary Newars, he has three separate, equally common names: (i) Matsyendranāth, (ii) Karuṇāmaya, (iii) Būgadyaḥ.[14]

The goddess Kumārī illustrates another possibility: she too is essential to all Newars, but in this case the deity has just one name in common use. No doubt this is possible because the name Kumārī (meaning 'virgin') is on the one hand Sanskritic, but on the other, of itself aligns her neither with Buddhism nor with Hinduism. Theologically inclined Buddhists say that she is Vajradevī, while Hindus consider her to be Taleju, Lakṣmī, or Durgā (and no doubt also some other Śaivite Tantric goddess – perhaps Guhyakālī?) depending on context.

Trivalency is also evident in the different attitudes towards the deities of category D in Figure 12. They are defined by the fact that they accept blood sacrifice. For most ordinary Newars they are simply powerful gods whom it is wise to propitiate. The two scriptural religions, however, regard them differently. The Hindu view can be illustrated with the example of a Śreṣṭha who expressed his distaste for Power-Place Worship (*pīṭha pūjā*), which is precisely the annual propitiation of all category D gods within Lalitpur: this is all self-interested, *tāmasik* religion, he said. By using the three-fold hierarchical system of the *guṇa*s, classical Hindu concepts of which the *tāmasik* is the lowest, he tacitly accepted Power-Place Worship as Hindu, but of the lowest type. Contrast this with the Buddhist attitude (frequently expressed) which says simply that Power-Place Worship is not Buddhist, nor are the Eight Mother Goddesses. This of course is the exoteric view. From a Tantric (esoteric) point of view, all deities, indeed all things, are manifestations of the absolute. This explains how one of the elders (*āju*, literally grandfathers) of Cikã Bahī could explain, as if letting me into a secret, that the Mother Goddess Bāl Kumārī was the same as the Tantric deity in his family *āgã̊*, which was why his grandfather had set up a *guthi* to worship Bāl Kumārī. This same identity is implied by the practice of taking offerings to Kumārī to the shrine of Bāl Kumārī which occurs during the annual performance of the Observance of Vasundharā in Cikã Bahī.

The 'one god – multiple names' theme was evident in a conversation, at which I was present, between an assertive Jośī and a rather less articulate Vajrācārya. The discussion took place after the feast to celebrate the end of the annual Power-Place Worship referred to above. The Jośī had made a map showing all the *pīgã dyaḥ* of Lalitpur, and participates every year as a guide. The Vajrācārya had taken part as the family priest of Krishna Lal Maharjan who had acted as the main sponsor (*kaji*) of the event (see Plate 2). Krishna Lal took this role by virtue of being the leader of the Maharjan music group of Gaḥchẽ, the locality which had elected to organize the city-wide ritual this year. After the feast, held in the Karuṇā cuka courtyard of Ī Bahī, the Jośī, Vajrācārya, several young Maharjans, and I retired to Krishna Lal's house, while the music group continued to play outside. The following is a small part of the discussion which ensued (which I wrote down from memory immediately afterwards).

JOŚĪ: The *pīṭha devatā* [*pīgã dyaḥ*], who are the Eight Mothers (*aṣṭamātṛkā*) are the greatest gods of Nepal. If you look at Paśupati, the south face is Bhairab, the others are Brahmā, Viṣṇu, Maheśvar, and on top – it's Bhagavatī!
VAJRĀCĀRYA: From our point of view these are the Pañcabuddha. And we worship Nārāyaṇ as Ārya Avalokiteśvar, Mahādyaḥ as Vajrapāṇi Bodhisattva.
JOŚĪ: We also accept the Buddha. I didn't stop my daughters going on [the Buddhist procession of] Matayā, because the Buddha is a form of Mahālakṣmī. [Switching to Nepali:] Mahālakṣmī took his form. I can prove it with scripture (*ślok*). And who is Mahālakṣmī? Bhagavatī. The Buddha doesn't have a moustache [and so is a female incarnation]. But if she takes a male form such as Narasiṃha, she has a moustache . . . [switching back to Newari after protests from the young Maharjans:] Bhagavatī-Mahālakṣmī is the greatest god.

VAJRĀCĀRYA: No she isn't, of the Eight Mothers she is the last one [he tries to list the eight in canonical order but gets in a hopeless muddle].
OTHERS: Well, here at least is a definite contradiction [between Hinduism and Buddhism].
JOŚĪ: In any case, ultimately there's only one Lord (*īśvar*). Buddhism is no different, whatever the surface differences.
VAJRĀCĀRYA: Yes, there's no difference.
JOŚĪ: The biggest festival in every country, whether Nepal, India, or the West – we don't know what happens in China – is Mohanī, Dasaĩ. And the principal deities in that (festival) are the Eight Mother Goddesses, the Gã Pyākhã who dance in Lalitpur; they are (none other than) the Daśamahāvidyā. Now Buddhists say: do not commit violence (*hiṃsā*) but where their Tantric gods (*āgǎ dyaḥ*) are concerned, violence is absolutely essential.[15] Please don't be angry at what I say, Guruju. [All nod their heads, including the Vajrācārya.]
VAJRĀCĀRYA: Yes, but we don't call our god Bhagavatī . . .
JOŚĪ: Whatever you call it, the deity is the same.

3.3 Hinduism dominating Buddhism

It has been shown how there are competing explanations and epithets for particular deities, festivals, and other practices and how these reflect the different points of view, not just of the two scriptural religions, but of 'ordinary Newars' too. Sanskritic, Great Traditional explanations or identifications are always considered more proper, formal, and correct than those phrased in colloquial Newari. The latter are used as a shorthand or as a way of avoiding formal commitment to one or other specific Sanskritic identity. All are aware that Buddhist and Hindu explanations compete. In some cases, Hindu explanations predominate over Buddhist ones, and in others Buddhist ones are the most widely accepted.

The elephant-headed god, Gaṇeś, is nearly always represented on the Newars' ritual oil lamp, *sukundā*,[16] and both Buddhists and Hindus normally begin any ritual or complex act of worship by lighting the oil lamp and making offerings to the image of Gaṇeś. Nearly all Newars will explain this by saying that Gaṇeś has to be offered worship before anyone else, and will go on, if pressed, to cite local versions of the well-known Hindu stories of how Gaṇeś won this right. They may also point out that the worship of Gaṇeś removes the obstacles to any undertaking. When a Brahman does a *pūjā* this offering is indeed made to Gaṇeś, and the priest utters the words *maṅgalamūrtaye namaḥ* (Obeisance to him who is the incarnation of auspiciousness) (Kayastha 1980: *ga*). Only practising Vajrācārya priests and a few other well-informed Buddhists are aware of the fact that in Buddhist rituals, when the sponsor (*jaymā*) makes offerings to the figure of Gaṇeś, he is actually worshipping the fire-god, Agni, who is the representative of the sun (Surdyaḥ, Skt. Sūrya). This is what is 'actually happening' in the sense that this is what the liturgical utterance of the priest indicates. Gaṇeś is indeed worshipped during Buddhist rituals, but he is only represented by a small cone of rice (*gwaḥjā*, what is known in Tibetan as *torma*) and is classed along with the Eight Mothers and Bhairava, as indeed he should be from the Buddhist point of view, since he accepts blood sacrifice. The popular understanding, that it is Gaṇeś, rather than the lamp itself, which is being worshipped, is supported by a local myth that the figure of Gaṇeś on the lamp represents the local incarnation of Gaṇeś already referred to, Jala Vinayaka (Kwenādyaḥ), who caused problems for the spiritual exercises of Oḍḍiyānācārya [=Padmasambhava] because the latter had not invited him along with all the other gods. To appease his anger Oḍḍiyānācārya laid down that Jala Vinayaka should be worshipped before any undertaking.

Here then we have a case where the Hindu view of things is overwhelmingly dominant, to such an extent that the *sukundā* is nearly always made (usually by Buddhist artisans) with Gaṇeś represented on it. In fact, Buddhism is not always concerned to combat this dominance; but in any case, here it is clear and unambiguous.

Another example, of a different kind, is the name of a courtyard next to Kwā Bāhāḥ in Lalitpur. It is known to all as Sasu Nani, *nani* being the Newari for a small courtyard, and 'Sasu' deriving from 'Sasudyaḥ', the Newari name of the Hindu goddess of learning, Sarasvatī. In writing or official contexts the courtyard is known nowadays as Sarasvatī Nani. (When I was surveying the inhabitants they ticked me off for writing down the colloquial form 'Sasu Nani'.) In old inscriptions, however, it is known as Vāgīśvara Vihāra, the monastery of Vāgīśvara, the latter being an epithet of Mañjuśrī, the Buddhist *bodisattva* of wisdom. Now there is indeed a temple to Mañjuśrī in the middle of the courtyard, which gives it its name, and everyone knows very well that it is he. But Newars all habitually conflate Mañjuśrī and Sarasvatī, and all of them, Hindu, Buddhist, and ordinary Newar alike, worship him/her on the festival of Śrī Pañcamī, for success at school or in their professional vocation. Both deities are known in Newari as Sasudyaḥ. Here again the Hindu version is clearly dominant, though not so completely as in the previous example. Unlike the case of the oil lamp, Buddhists, though they may say 'Sasudyaḥ', know very well who Mañjuśrī is and what he stands for. Furthermore, the most important site for the worship of Sasudyaḥ on Śrī Pañcamī, Mañjuśrīthān behind Svayambhū, is unambiguously Buddhist.

The religious identity of some rites is hotly debated and the question of Hindu dominance where they are concerned is therefore essentially contested. Most Hindus and many Buddhists would claim that the death rite of Ancestor Worship (*śrāddha*) is a Hindu practice, and that it is merely through Hindu influence that Buddhists practise it. Consequently many (though by no means all) Buddhists have given up performing Ancestor Worship annually beyond the two-year anniversary (*nidā tithi*); and they have given up performing an annual *sohra śrāddha* for all their ancestors collectively. I have heard both a Brahman and a Vajrācārya (on separate occasions) blame this on the Theravāda monks preaching against Ancestor Worship. Each of them castigated the monks as selfish, living off others' gifts and providing nothing in return.

Many Vajrācāryas and many traditionally inclined Śākyas, however, would deny that Buddhist Ancestor Worship is a Hindu practice, since the deities invoked are thoroughly Buddhist, as are the mantras used. It is true that Buddhism has nowhere condemned outright the desire to benefit one's ancestors through ritual action. Indeed Buddhist householders are seen performing Ancestor Worship in the Pali canon. To this extent Newar Buddhist traditionalists are right. However, in the Pali canon it is evidently a question of endorsing an existing pre-Buddhist practice as worldly custom, while recommending other, Buddhist practices for salvation. As with the Buddhist Fire Sacrifice (§5.3), Buddhist Ancestor Worship, as found in Nepal, would seem to be an adoption and reworking of a Hindu ritual (§7.3). Where the Theravādin tradition had to perform some interesting theological gymnastics to square gift-giving on behalf of one's ancestors with Theravādin beliefs about the inevitability of reaping one's own karmic fruit (Gombrich 1971: 226f.), Nepalese Buddhism (and perhaps Indian Buddhism before it?) has straightforwardly endorsed the householder's desire to benefit his ancestors, and gone on to cast the ritual by which they are 'fed' in a Buddhist idiom.

The degree to which Hindu ways of thinking predominate over Buddhist varies from individual to individual, as well as according to context. A Śākya man once explained a Monastic Initiation ceremony we were both watching, by saying that the boy's maternal uncle (*pāju*) had to stop him from running away and becoming a monk. He was interpreting the ritual in terms of Loincloth Worship (modelled on *upanayana*) which all Newars except Śākyas and Vajrācāryas pass through in order to be incorporated into their caste. Unlike in Loincloth Worship, a pretence of running away and being caught by the maternal uncle does not occur in Monastic Initiation, and it was unusual for this Śākya not to know that. In fact I think he must have known it, but because he was addressing an outsider he quite naturally and unselfconsciously made use of Hindu categories.

Thus apparent Hinduization may in fact be a question of context. A good example of this is the god Karuṇāmaya-Matsyendranāth. Buddhists tend to use the name 'Matsyendranāth' when they are speaking to non-Newars, Indians or Westerners, even though they invariably call him 'Karuṇāmaya' between themselves.[17] (In the same way they will automatically speak in Nepali, not Newari, to outsiders, and I frequently had the experience with Newars I did not know of addressing them in Newari and receiving answers in Nepali.) This reflects the fact that Buddhists are used to being a small minority in a Hindu context, and are used to explaining their own religion and customs in terms which they expect others to understand.

Nonetheless Buddhists certainly do not deny, and indeed often assert, that they have been dominated by Hindus and influenced by Hinduism. This is expressed mythologically in the figure of Śaṅkara Ācārya. Wright's chronicle, written in Lalitpur, records the visit of Śaṅkara Ācārya to Nepal, and his 'defeat' of the *buddhamārgī*s (Wright 1972: 120). This story is extremely well known to Buddhists in Nepal. Also still current is the story Hodgson was told that Śaṅkara proceeded to Tibet, where he was defeated by the Dalai Lama (Hodgson 1972: 48; in Wright 1972: 152–3, this story is told of a later incarnation of Śaṅkara). He is also blamed for the involvement of Buddhists in animal sacrifice (Hasrat 1970: 39). It is particularly interesting that very similar myths occur among Newar Hindus. Newar Brahmans say that just prior to the arrival of Śaṅkara Ācārya they were persecuted by the 'Bānre', i.e. the Śākyas and Vajrācāryas, who tore off their sacred threads and nearly exterminated them (Toffin n.d.). Likewise a Rājbhaṇḍārī from Kathmandu blamed Śaṅkara Ācārya's influence and doctrine (*mat*) for attracting other Chatharīya Śreṣṭhas away from their traditional Tantric (Śākta) religion and into an alcohol- and sacrifice-free Vedicism.

These myths belong to the Malla period, and not to the time of the famous Advaitin Śaṅkara (probably eighth century) when of course Tibet had barely been converted to Buddhism, and certainly did not yet represent, as it eventually came to do, a stronghold of Buddhist learning and spiritual attainment. It is likely that these stories represent mythological versions of an event which really occurred. In the early twelfth century CE the head of the Kāśī monastery of Rudraśaivas came twice to the Kathmandu Valley. He evidently had considerable influence; the King's sons received Tantric Initiation from him and he introduced Tantric forms of worship at Paśupati (D.V. Vajracharya 1980: 217).

The other bogey figure in Buddhist mythology is Sthiti Malla (reigned 1382–95). Sometimes it is he, instead of Śaṅkara Ācārya, who is said to have caused the Vajrācāryas and Śākyas to forsake monasticism by taking wives. He is often said to have forced them to take up demeaning jobs, such as goldsmithing, which are normally only performed by Untouchables.[18] For Hindus Sthiti Malla is a social reformer who introduced or regulated the system of castes, and this no doubt accounts for his negative image with the Buddhists. According to one version it was Sthiti Malla who introduced the Newars to the use of buffalo meat, by sacrificing a buffalo to Taleju and falsely persuading Buddhists that no ritual is complete without buffalo meat as the goddess' blessed food (*prasād*) (A.K. Vajracharya 1980: 66–7, 79).

3.4 Examples of Buddhist predominance

While in some cases Hindu dominance is unambiguous or straightforward, there are other features of Newar religion which might well be taken to indicate Buddhist predominance. Two cults of central importance in Newar religion, those of Kumārī and of Karuṇāmaya-Matsyendranāth, are very largely in the hands of Buddhists.

Kumārī as a deity is not limited to the well-known living goddesses to whom Michael Allen (1975) devoted his excellent book; these girls are simply human manifestations of a much wider cult which affects almost every Newar and is much older (Lienhard 1978: 260). For *buddhamārgī* and *śivamārgī* alike, several auspicious life-cycle rituals, and most Observances (§6.5), end with the worship of Kumārī. She is represented by a plate piled high with all the dishes to be served in the feast which will follow. In Lalitpur the plate is then taken by the senior women of the household to the traditional Kumārī shrine of the family. This shrine is nearly always either in the house of a Vajrācārya or inside a Buddhist monastery.[19] When the plate is taken to the shrine, the guardian or owner of the shrine performs further worship on behalf of the women, who are not allowed inside the room where the god is kept. The owner of the shrine receives their offerings and keeps the food, consuming it with his family as the goddess' blessing (*prasād*).

The Tantric nature of the Kumārī's identity is indicated further by the fact that in the initial act of worship (*kumārī pūjā*), by the family priest, two other feast shares are laid out on either side of the Kumārī's share, and these are said to be to Siṃhinī and Byaṅghinī (Skt. Vyāghriṇī). These are door-guardians of Buddhist Tantric shrines. The important point here is that we have a cult of central importance which is almost entirely in the hands of Buddhists. This probably explains the fact, which Slusser (1982: 315) finds so puzzling, that the Royal Kumārīs, the famous 'living goddesses' worshipped by Hindus as Taleju/Durgā, must be chosen from among Vajrācāryas or Śākyas.

The priests of Karuṇāmaya-Matsyendranāth are Śākyas and Vajrācāryas from the village of Bũga. Non-Newar Nepalese and foreigners may be (and usually are) ignorant of the fact that the deity's priests are Buddhist, but there can be very few Newars who are unaware of it. The Brahman myth which posits his identity with Kṛṣṇa is transparently a charter for Brahmans to worship a Buddhist deity. Within Newar society it is the Buddhist version which is dominant, and the Hindus who have accommodated to it.

This does not contradict what was stated in the previous section: it is within the wider Nepalese society that the Hindu view of the god as Matsyendranāth is the dominant one, and the reasons for this are clear. There are no Buddhists among the dominant castes of Nepal, and in any case they know of the god only through the King's presence at the 'showing of the vest' at its end. The identification of Karuṇāmaya as Matsyendranāth goes back at least to 1677, but it received further reinforcement after 1769 with the arrival of the Shah dynasty from Gorkha: since Matsyendranāth is held to have been the *guru* of Gorakhnāth, the patron saint of the Gorkhālī dynasty, the prevalence of the Hindu version in Nepal as a whole both expresses and is reinforced by Parbatiyā dominance.[20]

An even more striking example of Buddhist dominance, within the limited area of Lalitpur city, is given by the annual festival called Matayā ('festival of lights').[21] The Jośī who permitted his daughters to take part in Matayā because he believes that the Buddha is a form of Mahālakṣmī/Bhagavatī has already been quoted. What no one contests is the thoroughly Buddhist nature of the festival, which consists in visiting all the *caitya*s of Lalitpur, a proceeding that takes about fifteen hours. *Caitya*s (more colloquially, *cibhā dyaḥ*) are the most basic Buddhist cult object; there are different styles, but most commonly they show four of the five Buddhas, one on each side (the fifth is considered either to be inside the *caitya*, or to be represented by the thing as a whole). Matayā is participated in primarily by those who have had a death in the family, and the most esteemed offering is light (hence the name of the festival) in the dead person's name, a thoroughly Buddhist practice. Matayā and the chariot festival of Karuṇāmaya-Matsyendranāth are the two most important religious celebrations of the year in Lalitpur, in that they attract the largest numbers of participants and the greatest enthusiasm.

3.5 Buddhism and Hinduism 'in harmony'

It is one of the touristic, journalistic, and school-book clichés of modern Nepal that Buddhism and Hinduism exist there in peaceful harmony. What this corresponds to traditionally is a strong measure of moral and religious relativism. I was often told by elderly people that every country has its own *dharma*, that the same sun shines on all men alike, or that the names might be different but there is only one god. Of course, one is told these things when one's interlocutor is well disposed and inclined to minimize differences. I well remember taking a photograph when I should have refrained, and being told by an irate Śākya, 'We don't need your religion and you don't need ours.' What is common to this sentiment (widely felt, I believe, if more rarely expressed) and those referred to above, is the idea that each people has its own *dharma* which satisfies universal needs in a way particular to it.

This spirit of relativism is very pervasive, for it is not only that different castes do things in different ways. Even within a caste each locality, each *guthi*, and ultimately each family may have its own way of doing things, its own peculiar traditions, known only to it, and kept up out of a pride in difference and the need to distinguish oneself from outsiders. A Rājopādhyāya Brahman explained:

> We Nepalese have to follow the god's law (*kānun*) like a legal system, but everyone has their own system. Everyone is likely to have a prohibition peculiar to them which their own personal god (*iṣṭadevatā*) has imposed. In our family we are not allowed to make *yaḥmari* [a kind of rice cake] to worship Dhanalakṣmī on Yaḥmari Punhī as everyone else does, though others may bring them to us from their house.

This relativism can be, and occasionally is, extended to any religion. But normally Hinduism and Buddhism are considered to share a charmed inner circle, of truer or higher religion.[22] Other religions may be all very well for their adherents, but in fact they are a lower version of Hinduism or Buddhism, as the case may be. One of the reasons why this relativism is tacitly restricted to the Hinduism and Buddhism of the Valley is that the two religions share many concepts. Another is that they share the belief that the religious life, at least as far as householders are concerned, is one of regular rituals and frequent fasts and is in general hedged round by a large number of obligations (*niyam*).

Newar Hindus and Buddhists do indeed share many religious concepts: what it is to worship a deity, the duties of a priest, the value of religious devotion, and a single religious calendar, to name a few. It would be wrong however to conclude from this that the two religions are really one. When I pointed out to the women of the household where I was staying that Brahmans use all the same ritual implements as Vajrācāryas (see below, §5.3, Table 5.4), they denied my implication that Buddhist and Hindu ritual were, on this account, just the same. For them the use of these implements constitutes worship as such: the fact that both religions make use of the same implements no more means that the rituals or religions are identical, than the fact that the English and French both use knives and forks implies that their attitudes to food and eating are the same.

What Buddhism and Hinduism have in common tends simply to define Newars' baseline concepts. By this I mean that their whole experience of religion is either of Hinduism or of Buddhism. If you ask them what religion is, or what ritual is for, it is hardly surprising that their answer will be based on what Hindus and Buddhists do. Neither religion inculcates a catechism which would provide ready-made answers to such questions; for all Newars religious education, directed primarily at girls, is practical, not doctrinal, consisting mainly of teaching them how to carry out daily worship. Those who have travelled, particularly upper-caste men, and the younger generation educated in the Western style, know very well that rituals and religions differ in different countries. Indeed it is among these groups that one finds religious modernists, intent on reshaping their own traditions in line with Western (often Protestant in flavour) religious conceptions.

Since Hinduism and Buddhism between them dominate Newar religion, this means that other religions are correspondingly marginal. The Newar attitude towards Muslims, a number of whom have been living among them since at least the first half of the eighteenth century,[23] illustrates well their feeling that other religions, although perhaps valid for their adherents, are in some way unnatural. Muslims, one is frequently told, are upside-down (*ultā*): at funerals they laugh instead of crying; when they wash their faces or arms they do it from the bottom upwards; and after the death of her husband a Muslim widow will wear lipstick and leather shoes. I was not able to check whether these charges are just or not. The point is that, for Newars, Muslims reverse the natural order of things to which both Buddhists and Hindus conform.[24] This view of Muslim customs as 'diametrically opposed' to Hinduism is pervasive in South Asia and goes back at least to the twelfth century when it was articulated by al-Biruni (Gaborieau 1972: 91, 93; 1985: 8–9).

Now that Westerners (*ãgrejī* or, increasingly, *amrikān*) have become an identifiable category, certain ideas about them have become widespread. In a way they are assimilated to low castes and villagers. They are seen as a lower form of humanity because they lack rules, have little or no religion (*dharma*), eat snake meat, and spend the whole of their time, like beasts, merely satisfying wants. I lost count of the number of times that Newars said to me, while I was observing some religious activity or other: 'You [meaning: you Westerners] have an easy time of it. You don't have to do any of this, do you?' However, Westerners are also somewhat anomalous because, unlike hill people or villagers, they are rich and powerful, and it is the perception of this, along with deeper structural changes, which has brought about a gradual and persistent erosion of the vast number of Observances, festivals, taboos, and other religious practices of high-caste Newars.

High status and a large number of religious obligations are inseparably linked in Newar minds.[25] The higher the caste, the greater the amount of time and effort devoted to religion. The low unclean castes, like villagers in the hills, are said to have no religious obligations; they do not perform any purifying life-cycle rites (*saṃskāra*) and this explains their low status. No wonder the Untouchable Dyaḥlā are getting rich these days, people say, when they have no obligations and can save all their excess income.

A story illustrates the same theme, that high status requires much ritual activity, though the point my informant wished to make was that people usually perform religious practices without knowing what they mean. In the small bazaar towns of the Nepalese hills there are many Śākyas and Vajrācāryas carrying on their traditional trade as goldsmiths. The only competition they get is from the occasional Sunār, a subdivision of the Parbatiyā Untouchable group, the Kāmī (Gaborieau 1978: 219). According to my informant, a Śākya goldsmith in Triśūlī (Nw. Sā̃gu), the Sunār claim to be the offspring of Śākyas and Vajrācāryas:[26]

One day a Sunār came to a Śākya goldsmith and claimed to be his caste fellow. He was told: 'Śākyas have to do a lot of ritual (*pūjā*). You do not do any: that is why we are high caste and you are low.' So the Sunār came to watch the Śākya performing his morning worship, in order to copy him. The Śākya performed the placing of mantras on the body (*mantranyāsa*) which the Sunār carefully committed to memory. But in the middle the Śākya also scratched his leg and the Sunār, not understanding what he was seeing, went away and always used to scratch his leg at that point in his *pūjā*!

In order to minimize the differences between Hinduism and Buddhism when it suits them, Newars emphasize the fact of piety and ritual, and ignore differences of content. What is important is to be persistent in one's religious attachments (*ekcitta*), and to keep a large number of rules. The outward form, the particular mantra, the deity in whose name it is recited, or the tradition from which one receives initiation are not so significant. This is relativism, but a relativism which only extends to those religions which give mantras and Tantric Initiation. Other religions remain, even if only implicitly, beyond the pale.

One of the contexts in which Hindus and Buddhists sometimes come together is the *sā̃nhū guthi*. *Guthi*s are socio-religious organizations with a fixed (male) membership (see below, chapter 8). The most common and pervasive *guthi*s – death *guthi*s, Lineage Deity *guthi*s – are strictly monocaste, but there are some, more optional *guthi*s which bring together members of different castes for a common religious purpose. Thus *sā̃nhū guthi*s are set up for the worship of Karuṇāmaya-Matsyendranāth on the first of every solar month (*sā̃nhū* or *sā̃lhū*; Np. and Skt. *saṃkrānti*). Another type of *guthi* which commonly has intercaste interdenominational membership is that for worship at the festival of Yẽnyāḥ (Indra Jātrā). The most striking example, however, because it concerns the priests of the two religions, is a *guthi* shared by the Vajrācāryas of Bu Bāhāḥ and the Rājopādhyāya Brahmans connected to the Agnimaṭha (a shrine in Lalitpur where a Fire Sacrifice is permanently kept alight). At the annual ritual, it is said that the Brahman and Vajrācārya elders take turns to sit in the seniormost position. Mythologically the *guthi* is explained by the tradition that there were two Brahman brothers: one became a Buddhist and founded Bu Bāhāḥ, the other remained attached to Hinduism (*sanātana dharma*) and founded the Agnimaṭha.[27]

The myth of Bu Bāhāḥ's origin also illustrates, as do many other stories, the equivalence of Vajrācāryas and Brahmans.[28] A Śākya from Lalitpur who now lives in Gangtok, Sikkim, where there are no Vajrācāryas, gave me this example from his own conduct: for life-cycle rituals he calls Tibetan lamas to the house, but on the anniversaries of his parents' deaths, he calls on an Indian Brahman to make the minimum required prestation (*nislāḥ*) in their name. These examples of the equivalence of Vajrācāryas and Brahmans are typical of the relativistic view expressed in interdenominational contexts. When Hindus or Buddhists are on their own however, if they compare Brahmans and Vajrācāryas at all, they are much more likely to denigrate one and praise the other.

A new modern spirit rejects this happy relativism. When I asked Jog Maya how Mahālakṣmī, a blood-drinking Mother Goddess, could be identified with Vasundharā (as she is), she replied that gods are perhaps like us: sometimes we eat feasts which include meat and alcohol, and at other times we fast and give up these things. Buddhist – and indeed Hindu – modernism strongly opposes this kind of position: to be a vegetarian at one time, carnivorous and alcohol-consuming at another, to be Buddhist in one context, a Hindu in another, is sheer hypocrisy in its view.

It is the official government view, expressed in textbooks, on the radio and at government-sponsored Hindu conferences, that Buddhism, Sikhism, and Jainism are branches of Hinduism. The Buddha himself is claimed as one of the greatest sons of Nepal, and as a messenger of peace (*śāntidūta*). That the Buddha was born in Nepal is often mentioned in the context of King Birendra's diplomatic initiative to have Nepal recognized internationally as an unmilitarized Zone of Peace.[29] Traditional Newar Buddhists can see nothing wrong in this; but some of the younger generation, those one can call Buddhist modernists, campaign against the claim that Buddhism is a branch of Hinduism. In their view Buddhism and Hinduism should only meet on a basis of equality and a presupposition of difference. Thus, in 1984, the appearance of a (Hindu) Kṛṣṇa Bhajan (Hymn-singing) group in a Buddha Jayantī procession (celebrating the Buddha's enlightenment) drew strong protests from those who saw it as a plot to spread the government view of Buddhism.

These protests received the following impassioned reply from Madan Mohan Mishra, a Newar Brahman of Lalitpur and Newari poet. It is worth quoting at some length, because the traditional, relativist view is rarely articulated in print, whereas the modern anti-relativist one can be seen any day of the week:

> Among Nepalese who call themselves Buddhist some worship Kumārī, others honour Śiva himself as their chosen deity (*iṣṭadevatā*). During Gũlā the [Buddhist] Jñānmālā Bhajan group comes and plays at the [Hindu] Nārāyaṇa Bhajan group's. Are the Jñānmālā group now going to seize the Harinām people [i.e. Hindus] as soon as they say 'Tāremām' [i.e. 'hello' in Buddhist idiom] and drag them off to the police station? . . . In the articles which have appeared in [the journals] *Ināp* and *Śānti Vijaya* I see a plot to set Newars against each other . . . Those who go round making distinctions between Śreṣṭha-gods (*syasyo dyaḥ*) and Vajrācārya-and-Śākya-gods (*bare dyaḥ*) flatly contradict the teaching both of Bhagavān Buddha and of the Vedas . . . If we fight among ourselves it is the Christians who will take advantage: Buddhists must keep up the Buddha's teachings, the Hindus what is Hindu . . . Among the many monasteries made for him is Bu Bāhāḥ, Lakṣmīvarṇa-saṃskārita Yaśodharā Mahāvihāra, and even today there is still a *guthi* in which Vajrācāryas and Brahmans sit side by side and eat together. If this is not Hindu-Buddhist unity, what is? For so many years there has been no controversy. How is it that only now these new-style Buddhists have dug it up? If the Jñānmālā Bhajan is joined by other *bhajan* groups on Buddha Jayantī, and if they sing 'Hare Rām', there is no need to be surprised. If Bhagavān Buddha, who brought joy to the hearts of the good (*sādhu*) and put in motion a river of wisdom, is praised with the epithet 'Rām', so what? 'Rām' was not only the name of the son of King Daśaratha, but is also used of Bhagavān Tathāgata himself, Yours etc.[30]

This section has described a general spirit of relativism, and also how that relativism coexists with the presumption that Buddhism and Hinduism, as practised by the higher castes, are better than other religions. It is necessary to point out, however, that this relativism has definite limits: while everybody assumes that each *guthi*, each temple, and even each family may have its own traditions, and keeping these up is indeed part of one's religious duty, these traditions are by no means the whole of one's duty. In other words, the lopsidedness of this relativism reflects some shared notions about religion and morality.

Basic religious concepts, such as *dharma*, *pāp*, *karma*, *dān*, rebirth, and the possibility of release (*nirvāṇa*, *mokṣa*, *mukti*, *taray juye*), as well as ideas about religious methods (*pūjā*, *bhakti*, *niyam*), are shared by all Newars. Some of these concepts are described, from the Buddhist point of view, below (§4.1, 4.3). Many Hindus would assent to the formulations given there, at least in outline.

3.6 Buddhist myth and iconography which attempt to subordinate Hinduism

With Buddhism and Hinduism sharing many basic principles it is hardly surprising that they are also in strong competition. The priestly class of each religion covets the souls and patronage of the others' parishioners. Even though it is very difficult to change one's family priest, there is sufficient flexibility in optional religious observances for Vajrācāryas to have experienced a significant decline in the demand for their services. They have lost out to Brahmans, to Theravāda monks, and to Tibetan Mahāyāna monks and because of an overall decline in religious practices in the last fifty years. Competitive pressure is not all one way however: I have already suggested, taking examples which are common to all Newars, that in one or two significant cases Buddhism can be said to dominate Hinduism rather than the other way around. Buddhists and Hindus themselves are often on good terms, and minimize the differences between their respective religions, but their myths and icons often seem calculated to keep them apart. Evidently each religion uses similar means to try and subordinate or overcode the practices, icons, and myths of the other.

Iconography is a fertile field for the borrowing of symbols and motifs belonging to the other religion and reworking them within a new framework. One Nepalese iconographic form which is, it seems to me, a clear copy, is that of the *bodhisattva* Sṛṣṭikartṛlokeśvara. The icon shows Avalokiteśvara emitting from his body all the Hindu gods. A famous example of this form appears on the gold window of the Lalitpur royal palace. At first glance his form is very similar to the Hindu icon of Nārāyaṇa or Ardhanarīśvara surrounded by the ten *avatāras*. It is no accident then that a young Maharjan friend spontaneously identified a statue at Śaṅkhamūl, which was in fact Sṛṣṭikartṛlokeśvara, as 'Nārāyan-dyaḥ'. This iconographic form, deliberately ambivalent though it is, expresses for Buddhists in a theistic way the subordination of Hinduism to Buddhism.

Newars believe that Avalokiteśvara, the embodiment of compassion, takes whatever form is necessary to save suffering beings. The identification of Karuṇāmaya-Matsyendranāth with Kṛṣṇa made by local Hindus has already been mentioned (§3.2). Thus, just as Hindus can worship Buddhist divinities as Hindu gods, Buddhists can equally worship Hindu gods and justify it by saying that they are 'really' worshipping Avalokiteśvara. At the same time, Avalokiteśvara, although identified with them, remains superior. The local Buddhist myth admits that Nārāyaṇa brings the rice crop but insists that only Karuṇāmaya (i.e. Avalokiteśvara) can bring rain and ensure that there is rice inside the husks (A.K. Vajracharya 1980: 7–8; Locke 1973: 42).

The connection between Avalokiteśvara and Śiva, reinforced by the identification made between the local Avalokiteśvara and Matsyendranāth (a deified Śaivite ascetic), is ancient. Avalokiteśvara's iconographic form was strongly influenced by that of Śiva.[31] Avalokiteśvara shares with Śiva the epithets *īśvara*, *maheśvara*, and *lokeśvara* ('lord', 'great lord', and 'lord of the world' respectively). The scripture, the Kāraṇḍavyūha, which is the source for the icon of Sṛṣṭikartṛlokeśvara, is also one of the main sources of the doctrine that Avalokiteśvara saves all suffering beings in whatever form is necessary. Even originally this seems to have been a justification of worshipping Śiva as a *bodhisattva* and as a form of Avalokiteśvara (Thomas 1933: 193). One consequence of this Buddhist strategy was that, once Buddhism was destroyed in India, its cults were easily absorbed by Hinduism.[32] In Nepal, on the other hand, it has enabled Buddhism to persist in a strongly Hindu context.

Another case of deliberate ambiguity, which lacks canonical legitimization and perhaps therefore constitutes genuine syncretism, combines a Buddhist *caitya* and a Hindu *śivaliṅga*. The *śivaliṅga* is a common and basic Hindu cult object, as the *caitya* is to Buddhism. This type of *caitya* rises out of a lotus on top of a water-course (*jaladhārā*) of exactly the same shape and orientation (to the north) as that of a *śivaliṅga*. There are numerous examples of such *caitya*s in Kathmandu, but I know of only one in Lalitpur (in Bhelāchẽ *twāḥ*, by the Bhairava temple). It is clear that an identity is being implied by this form, though Buddhists usually deny it. On stylistic grounds it seems probable that all of these *caitya*s can be assigned to the Rana period (i.e. after 1846), a period of intensified Hinduization.

What is striking is that even in those elements that do seem to be borrowed, such as the icon of Sṛṣṭikartṛlokeśvara, the point is to express

Buddhist superiority. Numerous myths represent this, such as that of Virūpākṣa, in which Paśupati is saved from the destructive consequences of Virūpākṣa's wrath by the compassionate intervention of Karuṇāmaya (Wright 1972: 91–2; Slusser 1982: 228; Vaidya 1986: chapter 32). The iconographic form of Harihariharivāhana-lokeśvara is a graphic expression of this superiority, with Lokeśvara riding on Nārāyaṇa's shoulders, a form which, Newar Buddhists admit, is guaranteed to annoy Hindus.[33]

The idea that Nārāyaṇa and Mahādeva are *bodhisattvas*, advanced beings, but inferior by far to the Buddha himself, is well understood by Buddhists. Jog Maya told me: 'One should honour all the gods, but if you worship the Lord Buddha, that takes care of Mahādyaḥ and Nārāyaṇa, because they are subservient to him (*bhagavānyāta cākari yāyepī*).' A Vajrācārya priest said:

We [Buddhists] worship the Eight Mother Goddesses, but (only) as guardians of the directions. Vārāhī [one of the eight] is not the same as [the Buddhist Tantric goddess] Vajravārāhī. The latter only has the face of a boar on one side [not as her principal head as Vārāhī does]. It is the same with the Ten Wrathful Ones (*daśakrodha*), who are men, as the Eight Mothers are women. They are also worshipped by *śivamārgīs*. For us they are just guardians of the directions. Just as the king has doorkeepers who are fed, but less (than the king), so we worship them [the Wrathful Ones], but less (than the Buddha). In the same way we worship the Hindu Trinity (*trimūrti*) as the throne (*āsan*) of Cakrasaṃvara!

Hodgson's *paṇḍit*, Amṛtānanda, expressed it thus:

Adi-Buddha may be considered a king, who gives orders; and the five Buddhas and other divinities of heaven, his ministers, who execute his orders; and we, poor mortals, his subjects, servants and slaves. In this way the business of the world is distributed among the deities, each having his proper functions; and Adi-Buddha has no concern with it. (Hodgson 1972 I: 46)

A Śākya man went further and said that whereas Hindu gods are all of this world (*laukika*) and must go through rebirth, the Buddha is transcendental (*lokottara*); an absolute god (*īśvara*) and gods, he went on, have nothing to do with Buddhism.[34] The same kind of argument was put by the Newar Buddhist *paṇḍit* Jog Muni Vajracharya (1979: 3):

Worldly religious action (*saṃvṛtti mārga*) can lead one to be an emperor or an Indra [the highest worldly level] but once one's merit (*puṇya*) is exhausted, one will inevitably be reborn. Hence the wise (*jñānī paṇḍit*) follow the path of the ultimate, the *nirvāṇa* of the completely enlightened Buddha.

The subordination of Hindu divinities to the Buddha is expressed iconographically in many places (e.g. on the struts displaying Nārāyaṇa and Mahādeva at the entrance to Kwā Bāhāḥ), but particularly in the representation of the Buddha's enlightenment, known locally as Lumbinī Jātrā, which is painted on many walls in Lalitpur and occurs in many other contexts also.[35] In this, in an idea going back to the Pali canon in its essentials, the Hindu gods salute the Buddha and celebrate his achievement in attaining enlightenment. Traditionally the Matayā festival, mentioned above, celebrates the Buddha's defeat of the Māras and attainment of enlightenment.[36] As part of the procession, groups of young men dress up outlandishly, put on face masks and behave, by local standards, in ways which break the rules of decorum. They are said to represent the Māras ('destroyers', i.e. demon tempters). A Farmer man also goes along every year dressed as Mahādeva, and he too is supposed to be rendering homage to Lord Buddha.

Competition between the two religions is expressed in the following story, well known in the locality, from Kwā Bāhāḥ, Lalitpur:

> The Casalāju [the most senior Vajrācārya of Kwā Bāhāḥ] was competing tantrically with a Brahman at the temple of Cāmuṇḍā [the *pīṭha* of the Vajrācāryas of Kwā Bāhāḥ] outside the northern gate of the city, near the burning ground. The Brahman was on the point of winning so the Casalāju ran away, and the Brahman pursued him. When they reached the road outside the main entrance to Kwā Bāhāḥ, the Casalāju's wife rushed out and threw her sari over the Brahman. Her husband was then able to bind him magically to the spot ('tāran taye') and they sacrificed him to the Bhairava on the door.

Some say that the Brahman's head is under the long oblong paving stone in the middle of the foyer of Kwā Bāhāḥ; others say that his head is upstairs in the shrine of Yogāmbara, and it is his bones which are under the paving stone. According to local Buddhists, this explains why Brahmans will never come into the main door, and if they do have to enter Kwā Bāhāḥ, e.g. at Kṛṣṇa Pūjā, why they come in the back door. A Brahman confirmed that they come in the back door; but he said the reason was that when you go in the main door you have to go underneath a *caitya*, and *caitya*s contain impure (*aśuddha*) things such as bones.

This Buddhist story and the local practices justified by it are examples of mutual hostility between Brahmans and Buddhists. The story also illustrates the important place of the Vajrācārya's wife: it is only thanks to her that he defeats the Brahman. The Brahman's reaction shows how attitudes differ: what is a holy relic (bones in a *caitya*) to the Buddhist is impure to the Brahman.

At the everyday level of social interaction, it is Śreṣṭhas, not Brahmans, who are thought of as the most representative Hindus, as pointed out above (§2.1). In Lalitpur Buddhist hostility to Śreṣṭhas is no doubt also given emotional force by the simple distrust and dislike of two large and dominant castes competing with each other for resources, influence, and, as shopkeepers, for custom. Thus a middle-aged Śākya woman described another family (Śākyas as it happened) as 'a bad lot (*duṣmān*), just like Śreṣṭhas'. Conversely, Riley-Smith (1982: 125) was told by a Śreṣṭha, 'to see a tiger look in the face of a cat, to see a thief look at the face of a Śākya'.[37] It also reflects a basic conflict over status: as a priestly caste entitled to the honorific *bijyāye*, Vajrācāryas and Śākyas consider themselves superior to Śreṣṭhas. They therefore resent the fact that Śreṣṭhas refuse to eat rice cooked by them and in other ways treat them as social inferiors.

3.7 Conceptualizing the relation between Buddhism and Hinduism

The problem of how best to think about the relationship of Buddhism and Hinduism among the Newars raises many issues which have concerned students of religion and society in South Asia. Can Hinduism be considered a single religion? What relationship is there between two Great Traditions such as Buddhism and Hinduism? Is syncretism a valid concept in South Asia, and if so, in which contexts, practices, and traditions can it be discerned? Can some groups (e.g. priests) be said to be more orthodox than others, and can a tradition as a whole be labelled heterodox? Needless to say, there are unlikely to be definitive answers to these questions, but some suggestions can at least be made as far as the Newars are concerned.

The very term 'Hindu' is sometimes attacked. In origin a Persian word meaning 'Indian', it was taken up rather late by Hindus themselves. In the Newar case, however, since there are not institutionalized divisions between Śaivas and Vaiṣṇavas as there are in some other parts of South Asia, there would seem to be no harm in using 'Hindu' in the way proposed above (§2.7), or in using 'Hinduism', as Nepalese themselves now do either with the English word or with its local equivalent, *hindudharma*, as a translation of *śivadharma* or *śivamārga*. One must remember, however, that Hinduism is far from being a monolith. It provides in abundance all three types of religion distinguished in chapter 1. Thus potentially it provides different soteriological and doctrinal systems. In Nepal the systems or 'sects' known as Śaiva (focusing on Śiva) and Śākta (focusing on Śiva's consort) are dominant (and it would be argued by many that they are two aspects of the same orientation). Nonetheless, the underlying ground of Hindu pluralism – the existence of several great gods in numerous forms, which are differently valorized by different devotees – is also very much present. The same processes of competition, incorporation, and attempted subordination, which have been described above for the relation between Buddhism and Hinduism, are found equally *within* Hinduism, in the relationship between Śaivism and Vaiṣṇavism.[38]

Many observers have approached Newar Buddhism, as they have Buddhism in other cultures, with the expectation that it should be a simple, austere, egalitarian, all-encompassing faith, defined by its own specific doctrines. As in other Asian countries, they have not been reticent in registering their disappointment and disapproval that Newar Buddhism does not fit this Protestant stereotype of what a religion should be.[39] They have, therefore, described Newar Buddhism in terms of its 'decline and fall' from an earlier pristine state. In many formulations it seems very doubtful that the pristine state ever existed. As Locke has pointed out (1985: 484a), Snellgrove's (1957: 102) postulate that Lalitpur before 1200 was a Buddhist monastic 'university-city' has been extremely influential, even though there is no evidence for it (and tempting though architectural comparisons of Newar Buddhist courtyards with Oxbridge quadrangles may be).

The basic problem with these descriptions in terms of 'decline and fall' is not the use of the word 'decline' as such (nor is it the use of more emotive substitutes such as 'degeneration' or 'corruption'). It is clear that there *have* been times when Newar Buddhism, compared to Hinduism, has been on the decline: the Rana period is an obvious example. Contemporary changes, which perhaps call for a rather stronger term, are discussed below (§11.5). Great Traditions with transcendent ideals and institutions for preserving them frequently do experience cycles of decline and reform (though I prefer Weber's term, routinization, for the former).[40] In the fifteenth century Tibetan Buddhism experienced a kind of renewal with the founding of the Gelukpa Order and its emphasis on strict monasticism. The Gelukpas did not however reject the Tantras, but merely restricted their use. It therefore represented an orthopractic fundamentalism, not a scripturalist or egalitarian Reformation, and was if anything more elitist than what went before (Kvaerne 1984: 264), as Buddhist reform movements tend to be. It is unlikely that Newar Buddhists could ever have launched such a movement of monastic renewal without considerable outside influence, since their material resource base has always been relatively small.

The main criticism of most of those who have written in the 'decline and fall' vein is that they have imported too many ethnocentric expectations and have, therefore, failed to take account of Newars' own understanding of these issues. The latter point (Newars' own views) can be dealt with fairly quickly.

We have seen (§3.3) that in certain myths Newar Buddhism itself presents a view of its own decline and domination by Hinduism. The myths see the decline in terms of the loss of celibacy, loss of learning, and loss of control over certain temples (e.g. Paśupati). It would be wrong to conclude that Newar Buddhists agree with foreigners in condemning their own tradition.

Far more important in most contexts than myths of decline are the Three Ways (see below, §4.2), admiration of Vajrācāryas and Tantrism, and the rejection of celibacy (§9.2). Furthermore, local perceptions of decline refer only to the Buddhist clergy, that is, to Śākyas and Vajrācāryas, and not to other *buddhamārgī* castes (lower castes with Vajrācārya priests).[41]

The theoretical (as opposed to the ethnographic) shortcomings of the 'decline and fall' type of analysis cannot be dismissed quite so succinctly. Students of Buddhism, wherever they work, are familiar with the claim that Buddhism as practised is corrupt and degenerate. This charge is as common in writings about Theravāda Buddhism as it is in those about Mahāyāna Buddhism but it must be Vajrayāna Buddhism which has excited the most colourful and censorious language (e.g. Waddell 1978: ix, 15; Oldfield 1981 II: 80). The same kind of descriptions are often found in studies of popular Islam, but more rarely in scholarly descriptions of Hinduism.

Charges of corruption and degeneracy originate in the assumption that the religion in question is supposed to be egalitarian, ascetic, and hostile to magic, but in practice displays the opposite tendency in every case. In the study of Buddhism it is important to be clear about the ways in which it differs from Protestantism or Islam. Buddhism maintains a conceptual separation of soteriology from thisworldly religion, permitting magic and instrumental worship in the latter. It is universalist, but in a logically distinct sense from Protestantism or Islam. Buddhism teaches that *any* human being can attain enlightenment but does not envisage – in spite of the change of emphasis in the Mahāyāna – that *all* could do so at any one time. Virtuosi, meditating for enlightenment, are a very small proportion indeed of recognized Buddhists. For example, Snellgrove (1987: 90) quotes a Mahāyānist text which prescribes generosity (i.e. alms-giving) for the 'lowly', the practice of morality for the middling, and tranquillity (i.e. meditation) for the advanced. Thus, spiritual hierarchy is built into Buddhism, and was so, even in the time of the Buddha himself (Gombrich 1988: 73–4). The egalitarian, meditation-centred version of Buddhism is a modernist innovation.

Another term frequently used of Newar Buddhism is 'syncretism'. Gombrich (1971: chapter 1) has discussed at length the question of whether Theravāda Buddhism is syncretic. His answer is that it is not, if we use a neutral definition of syncretism as the adoption by a religion of elements which contradict its basic framework. The common perception of Theravāda Buddhism as syncretic presumes that it is similar to Christianity, combining soteriology, social, and instrumental religion within a single exclusive and monotheistic framework, and that it must therefore be hostile to the use of any other system, even for instrumental ends. If this were so, the worship of Hindu deities by Buddhists would indeed be syncretic. In fact Buddhism is primarily a soteriology and Theravāda Buddhism in particular provides for very few worldly ends. Consequently 'Buddhism in real life is *accretive*' (Gombrich 1971: 49; emphasis in the original). That is, it always coexists with some non-Buddhist system which provides for Buddhists' worldly needs. As long as Buddhists do not worship Hindu gods *for salvation* they do not break the Buddhist framework.

A similar, though more complex, argument can be made about the Mahāyāna Buddhism of the Newars. If one insists on a Western definition of religion, it is syncretic. If one is a Theravāda Buddhist, its incorporation of Hindu elements, its invention of parallel rites, and above all the soteriologically central position of Tantric deities and rituals, will appear syncretistic. If one accepts Mahāyāna Buddhists' own view of what religion is – a soteriology that makes use of every means to lead suffering beings onto the Buddhist path – it is not syncretic. The Mahāyāna doctrine of 'skill in means' explains how a *bodhisattva* will appear in any form necessary, even that of a Hindu god or seducer, in order to bring beings to salvation.

This doctrine has given Mahāyāna Buddhism the flexibility to spread throughout Asia. In doing so it has related to local religions in the same way everywhere.[42] This underlying logic has probably been contravened in Bali so that one can speak, without reservation, of syncretism there (Ensink 1978). In Nepal, by contrast, high-caste Newars do not regard the gods and rites of one religion as simply substitutable by those of the other. Ordinary Newars on the other hand do tend to have a syncretic attitude to their religion.

What this shows is that the term 'syncretic', if it is to be used, has to be handled critically and with an awareness of context. Thus, Lienhard's (1978) analysis of the relationship of Buddhism and Hinduism among the Newars into three separate processes is particularly welcome. The three are: borrowing from one religion to another (p. 244: 'in most cases Śaivism was the donor, Buddhism the recipient'); parallelism, by which functional equivalents are developed in one religion of the cults or rites of the other; and thirdly, identification, whereby a single cult is frequented by all under different names. Parallelism has been discussed above (§2.2, 2.5; see also §7.2). Identification, which I have called the multivalency of symbols (§3.2–4), surely has to be seen as *competitive*: it is a question of domination, with sometimes one, sometimes the other religion having the conceptual upper hand. As Lienhard (1978: 256) points out, the case of Mañjuśrī-Sarasvatī (Sasudyaḥ) illustrates both parallelism and multivalency (identification), since the deity is both separate and conflated at once. Borrowing, on the other hand, is a principle of a different order, raising questions of origin and history which have to be assessed separately in each case. None of Lienhard's three processes comprises syncretism on the argument given above, but it is not necessary to labour that point. What is important is that Lienhard's analysis represents an advance in precision in the task of conceptualizing relations between the two religions.

Another attack on the term 'syncretic' has been made by Brinkhaus (1980) who criticizes Sylvain Lévi's statement (1905 I: 204) that the Nepāla Māhātmya (the Hindu pilgrimage text) 'faithfully reflects the eclectic syncretism which has nearly always prevailed in Nepal'. On the contrary, Brinkhaus argues, the three passages in question reflect 'rather a special form of conflict and an inclusivistic attempt to resolve this conflict'. Brinkhaus sees this as a form of Paul Hacker's 'inclusivism': 'This manner of confrontation does not raise doubts about the validity of an alien religion, which has an independent existence and its own set of traditions, but rather attempts to incorporate and, at the same time, to subordinate this religion to one's own' (Brinkhaus 1980: 279). Dumont's concept of hierarchical encompassment, by which the superior pole of an opposition absorbs within itself at a higher level what is opposed to it at the lower one, is, I would argue, a formalization of this mode of thought. Whether or not Dumont is right that this is the best way to think about intercaste relations (still a controversial question in the anthropology of South Asia), it is, I submit, how interreligious relations are conceptualized within South Asian religious thought. It is also, as noted above, how relations between Śaivism and Vaiṣṇavism are viewed within Hinduism, and also, as will be seen below (§4.2), how relations between different Ways within Buddhism can be understood.

However one wants to label this process – deliberate syncretism, overcoding, encompassment, inclusivism, competitive acceptance – Sylvain Lévi made some highly suggestive comments in the introduction to *Le Népal* on the institutional and ideological factors which enabled Hindu inclusivism to prevail over Buddhism in India. The development of monastic theocracy in Tibet, as well as monastic landlordism in Theravāda Buddhist countries, is perhaps the unspoken background to Lévi's remarks. In comparison to Buddhism, Lévi wrote, the Brahman appeared

> as a counterpoise and a safeguard. The Buddhist monasteries were incessantly enriched by pious donations, and, thanks to their longevity, stability, and organization were powerful institutions, the lords of souls and of vast estates. They checkmated temporal authority and even threatened to destroy it. The Brahman

gave it less to fear: he had taken no vow and was bound by no contract; he was free, independent, and alone; he could move with the times and he founded no order; he did not live in a community . . . He did not dream of human brotherhood or universal salvation; he aimed only at his own supremacy, and, as the basis for it, the caste system; he carried his institutions, beliefs, and laws within himself . . . (Lévi 1905 I: 30).

The prisoner of its own pretensions, and ambitious to legitimize them with prestigious marriage alliances, the royal family multiplied the symbols of its own orthodoxy and isolated itself behind self-made barriers. Starting from the top down, this tendency gradually took over; the Brahman, realist that he was, played (and he was bound to win) on the meanest human sentiments: vanity, contempt, and the desire to distinguish oneself from others. Society divided itself up into castes group by group, at first basing them on different professions; it was happy to accept a hierarchy in which nearly everyone had someone below himself to despise. With this, the battle [against Buddhism] was won. (ibid.: 32)

Thus Hinduism attempted to shape and absorb Buddhism, to relativize its claims, to assign it a place in a hierarchy which at the same time subordinated it to Hindu values. This explains the rules which Hindu kings in Nepal imposed on Buddhists, the acceptance of Karuṇāmaya as Matsyendranāth or Kṛṣṇa, and even the kings' occasional use of Vajrācārya priests. Since Hinduism is based on the relativistic spirit described above (§3.5), it can easily absorb a particular group, even if that group does not use Brahmans, by assigning it an inferior rank. The modern view of Buddhism as a 'branch' of Hinduism is no more than a formalization of this.

Thus we can understand Nepalese religious history, indeed the history of South Asia as a whole, as the gradual process by which Hinduism succeeded in 'encompassing' Buddhism and other 'heterodoxies'. If, following Lévi, we see this as a historical process, half-complete and still working itself out in Nepal, then even those aspects which seem to demonstrate Buddhist predominance – the cult of Karuṇāmaya-Matsyendranāth, Kumārī worship, and so on – can be fitted neatly into the framework: they are Buddhist cults which Hinduism has accepted as its own, as a prelude to taking them over entirely. The fact that Karuṇāmaya is known to the outside world almost exclusively as 'Matsyendranāth' is a sign of its success.

At the same time Newar Buddhism attempts to subordinate Hinduism by similar means (§3.6).[43] Yet there are important differences. Buddhism has a tendency to reject folk practices which Hinduism easily accepts as low forms of Hinduism (§3.2). In its attempt to prevent its laity abandoning it, and in order to avoid persecution, Newar Buddhism has put forward a

Hindu-seeming front, and encouraged parallelism and multivalent symbols. It has evolved a subtle and effective hierarchy of Three Ways (§4.2). It has incorporated Tantrism further than Hinduism (§11.2, 11.3); but at the same time it has preserved an independent Buddhist identity. It makes use of hierarchical logic internally (in the structure of the Three Ways), but is ambivalent about including Hinduism also, at the lowest level (whereas Hinduism is not ambivalent about including Buddhism at *its* lower levels). While competition is evident in all these ways, it is never so extreme as to preclude peaceful coexistence. Competition is pursued within a shared framework of common shrines (multivalent symbols), parallel rites and cults, and very similar presuppositions about the nature and ends of religion. These ideological features, so clearly displayed in Nepal, may well be as old as Mahāyāna Buddhism itself.

4

Basic notions of Newar Buddhism

It would be easy to multiply examples of this tendency to unrestrained adoration, unencumbered by system or theory.

Sylvain Lévi, *Le Népal*, vol. I, p. 319.

The primary motive for doing well, and worshipping Buddha, according to the scriptures, is the hope of attaining *Mukti* and *Moksha*, becoming Nirvána, and being freed from transmigrations: these exalted blessings cannot be had without the love of God; therefore they, who make themselves accepted of God, are true saints, and are rarely found; and between them and Buddha there is no difference, because they will eventually become Buddhas . . .

Amṛtānanda in Hodgson's *Sketch of Buddhism* (1972 I: 50).

4.1 A religion of worship

It is arguable that whereas gift-giving (*dān*) is stressed differently in Buddhism and Hinduism (§4.3.2), both religions are equally built on worship. Worship is perhaps the religious act *par excellence*, and pervades Newar society, both within and outside the organized frame of the two scriptural religions. Hinduism and Buddhism can be seen as two competing systems trying to channel, capture, conceptualize, and profit from a vast, amorphous, and autonomous mass of worship.[1] Where Hinduism alone provides the Great Tradition, simple worship appears as a basic Hindu religious act (Babb 1975: 33). Among the Newars it is only possible to see *pūjā* as basically Hindu, and not Buddhist, from an inclusivist Hindu or from an extreme Theravāda Buddhist modernist point of view. Worship is in fact fundamental to each of the Three Ways of traditional Newar Buddhism. Before proceeding in the next section to a preliminary discussion of the Three Ways, worship as such must be described.

Worship means 'worship of the gods', and many Newars say that religion (*dharma*) means worshipping the gods. By extension, however, worship is also offered to *gurus*, elders, younger brothers (by elder sisters), and other superiors. As Östör (1980: 50, 52) notes for Bengal, in offering *pūjā* to a god there is an explicit analogy with receiving a guest, and *pūjā* is 'built around service, respect, and honor'.

The simplest worship consists of bowing one's head with one's hands together; also indicative of respect, though not constituting worship as such, is the practice of keeping the deity or other superior to one's right. If offerings are made the simplest is a few grains of rice or, nowadays, a coin. A more elaborate worship is accomplished by offering a set of five things together called the Five Offerings (*pañcopacāra pūjā*): flowers, incense, light, red vermilion or yellow saffron powder, and food (e.g. rice, sweets, or fruit).[2] To these may be added an offering of water representing the bathing of the feet (*pādyārgha* or *argha*), and thread tied in a circle (*jajãkā*) which represents cloth. In his book on materials required for Buddhist *pūjā*s in Kathmandu, Ratna Kaji Vajracharya (1980: 1) distinguishes the Five Offerings from the Five Gifts (*pañcopahāra*): the latter are five substances meant to satisfy the five senses, viz. the Mirror (see below, Table 5.5) for form, the bell for sound, vermilion or saffron paste for smell, food for taste, and thread (*jajãkā*) for touch.

All the offerings so far considered may be made by an individual on his or her own; but in rituals which require the specialist services of a priest the number of offerings increases rapidly. Some offerings are kept at home by each family, others may be bought at shops which specialize in the sale of ritual requisites, and some are so unusual – such as the rhinoceros meat required when performing Ancestor Worship – that the priest will bring along a minute quantity himself. As noted above, certain deities accept animal sacrifice: the various Hindu goddesses (e.g. the Eight Mother Goddesses and the Nine Durgās), Bhairava, Gaṇeś, and Bhīmsen. To sacrifice an animal to high and pure deities – Mahādeva (Śiva), Nārāyaṇa (Viṣṇu), the Buddha or *bodhisattvas* – would be a heinous sin. Tantric deities do not normally receive actual blood sacrifice, but must be offered cooked meat and alcohol.

The offerings made in worship must be new and fresh ('pū ma juye', 'not used'). Offering a half-eaten banana would be a terrible insult, contradicting the basic emotional attitude of worship: respectful acknowledgement of one's inferiority and, often only implicitly, a request for protection. Likewise the offering must be kept pure (*śuddha*, *nī*), that is, it must be kept away from contact with impurity, a category which, as in the rest of South

Asia, includes saliva, excrement, menstruating women, dogs, leather, Untouchables, the soles of the feet, and so on. When worship has been performed it is usual to receive back some of the offerings as a blessing (*prasād*): red or yellow powder (*sinhaḥ*) as a spot on the forehead, flowers to put behind the ear (right for men, left for women), water or food – including in certain circumstances the meat of a sacrificed animal – to consume.

Most Newars just laugh when asked if the *prasād* could be considered the god's polluted food (*cipa*). They have never thought of it that way. Subarna Man Tuladhar's response to this suggestion was to say: 'Certainly not: it is supposed to be a symbol (*pratīk*) of the god.' In support of this interpretation one can cite the fact that food which is to be offered to a particular deity is often first worshipped *as* that deity (as, for instance, in the Kumārī Pūjā discussed above, §3.4). In asking this question I had in mind Babb's (1975: 56) theory that *prasād* is considered to be the divinity's polluted food. Fuller (1979: 470–1) has criticized this interpretation convincingly, pointing out that the relationship between temple priest and deity is more like that of wife to husband than of low caste to high. Furthermore, food exchange is not central to worship in temples: devotees receive powder, flowers, and holy water, but only occasionally are they given items of food. This is so in Nepal also. It is only in complex rituals, such as Observances, or in rituals participated in as a group, that the consumption of food is essential. It will be seen below (§10.5) how, after a Tantric ritual, the *human participants*' polluted food must itself be worshipped and deposited at a Remains Deity.

Worship is divided in the Mahāyānist scheme of things into seven limbs (*aṅga*). The Newar Buddhist is not explicitly taught this, but it is expounded in a set of Sanskrit verses (*gāthā*), called the Bhadracarī, which are extremely well known, being recited regularly on behalf of a dead person and sometimes by pious Buddhists as part of their daily devotions.[3] Before the introduction of printing, this text, sometimes reduced to its opening and concluding verses, was frequently copied by hand.

Vandana-pūjana-deśanatāyā anumodhanādhyeṣaṇa-yācanatāyā
Yac ca śubham mayi saṃcitu kiṃ cit bodhayanāmayami ahu sarvam.

By means of (i) Bowing down, (ii) Making offerings, (iii) Confession of Sins, (iv) Rejoicing in merit, (v) Requesting teaching, and (vi) Entreating, whatever merit I accumulate, all that I dedicate towards enlightenment.[4]

The seventh limb of worship is the Dedication of Merit to others (*pariṇāmaṇā*), which occurs at the end of the verses, when the merit gained by reciting is transferred to the dead person. Of the seven limbs, the first two are connected to the act of Worship itself (Bowing down and Making offerings); the rest are clearly designed to tie this act of worship in to an altruistic moral system. This schema continues in Tibet (Dhargyey 1974: 214–22): the sixth limb, Entreating, is explained as 'requesting the Guru to live long' (ibid.: 220). Among the Newars there is a popular ritual (the *satwaḥ pūjā*) to Avalokiteśvara and Tārā, often performed before the chariot of Karuṇāmaya-Matsyendranāth; it is named (according to the learned) after these seven branches of worship.[5]

Verses five and six of the Bhadracarī describe vividly the act of worship as indeed it is practised today:

Puṣpavarebhiḥ ca mālyavarebhiḥ vādya-vilepana-chatra-varebhiḥ
Dīpavarebhiḥ ca dhūpavarebhiḥ pūjataneṣu jināna karomi
Vastravarebhiḥ ca gandhavarebhiś cūrṇapuṭebhiś ca merusamebhiḥ
Sarvaviśiṣṭa-viyūha-varebhiḥ pūjataneṣu jināna karomi.

With the best of flowers and the best of garlands, with the best of music, unguents, and parasols,
With the best of lamps and incense I worship the Victorious Ones [i.e. the Buddhas],
With the best of garments and the best of perfumes, and ground powder[6] piled high as Mount Meru,
With all the best and outstanding splendours I worship the Victorious Ones.

What I have called ritual is often just a complex form of worship, so complex that it requires a class of specialists to perform it. In the case of Newar Buddhism and Hinduism this is true in the very specific sense that rituals are built up out of numerous small individual acts of worship arranged in sets (§5.2.4). In these complex rituals the priest tells his patron what offering to make and utters the relevant salutation in Sanskrit on his behalf.

4.2 The Three Ways of Buddhism and what they mean for Newars

The analysis of Newar Buddhism which follows in subsequent chapters is arranged according to three levels within it. These levels, called *yāna*, Skt. 'way', form a ritual and ideological hierarchy. From lowest to highest they are: the Way of the Disciples (*śrāvakayāna*), the Great Way (*mahāyāna*), and the Diamond Way (*vajrayāna*). These three levels also represent a historical development, the Disciples' Way being the earliest and the Diamond Way the latest form of Buddhism. Thus the doctrine of different Ways does not merely integrate different practices within a single overall structure; it also provides a religious interpretation of Buddhism's own history. Here I give a brief and schematic summary of this history, so that the analysis which follows will make sense.

Mahāyāna Buddhism, or the Buddhism of the Great Way, arose around the turn of the common era.[7] It saw itself as just that, a greater and more catholic way than the Buddhism taught up till then. The word *yāna* is often translated as 'vehicle', so that books on Buddhism refer to the Great Vehicle and the Lesser Vehicle. I prefer to translate the word as 'way', which highlights the fact that *yāna* has the same soteriological implications as *mārga*, path; the former, however, is used only to describe subdivisions within Buddhism and never, like the latter, for non-Buddhist teachings.

Of all the pre-Mahāyāna Buddhist schools in India (which traditionally numbered eighteen but in fact were more numerous) only one has survived, the Theravāda. Its name means 'doctrine of the elders' (from Pali *thera* = Skt. *sthavira*), which expresses the fact that it was proud to be the most conservative of all the ancient Buddhist schools. Modern scholarship has popularized the term Hīnayāna, Lesser Way, for the pre-Mahāyānist schools, since this represents the balancing term for 'Great Way'. However, since the word 'Hīnayāna' has pejorative overtones, and was indeed a polemical invention of the Mahāyāna, it is only used in a Mahāyānist context. Buddhists from Sri Lanka, Burma, and Thailand always refer to their own religion as Theravāda Buddhism, never as Hīnayāna.

The Mahāyāna went beyond early Buddhism in two fundamental ways, one philosophical and one theological (perhaps one should say Buddhological). Philosophically it put the doctrine of the emptiness (*śūnyatā*) of all phenomena in the central position previously occupied by the earlier doctrine of non-self (*anātmā*), which had been, and is still by Theravāda Buddhists, applied principally to the human individual.[8] Mahāyāna Buddhists criticized the non-Mahāyāna schools for raising their analysis of the constituent elements of the universe into a philosophic realism. Through the application of a radical negative dialectic attacking all views, it claimed to represent the Buddha's true teaching of the Middle Way. By emphasizing the conditional nature of all things, even ultimately of the Buddhist scriptures themselves, the early Mahāyāna paved the way for the subsequent development of Buddhist idealism; and it also provided a large part of the philosophical justification for the mystic antinomianism of the Tantras.

Even more important than this philosophical paradigm shift was a change in attitude to the *bodhisattva*. In all forms of Buddhism three types of enlightened being are recognized: the *samyaksambuddha*, a fully enlightened Buddha who discovers the way to *nirvāṇa* and teaches it to others; the *pratyekabuddha*, Solitary Buddha, who attains enlightenment but does not teach others; and the *arhat*, someone who reaches *nirvāṇa* by following the teaching he (and it is usually he) has learnt from a fully enlightened Buddha. Both in Theravāda Buddhism and in the Mahāyāna, one who aims at becoming a fully enlightened Buddha has to work his way over many rebirths, gradually acquiring the merit to fulfil his intention; and during these many rebirths in which he aims at becoming a *samyaksambuddha* he is known as a *bodhisattva*.

The crucial innovation of the Mahāyāna was to expand the application of the *bodhisattva* concept. In Theravāda Buddhism it applies, in the fourth and lowest stage (*kali yuga*) of our world-age, only to Śākyamuni Buddha and to the future Buddha, Maitreya. Theravāda Buddhists encounter the *bodhisattva* only in Rebirth (Jātaka) stories of the Buddha's previous lives. Perhaps the most popular and at the same time most poignant is the story of the future Buddha as Prince Viśvantara, who went so far in gift-giving that he not only gave away all his material possessions but his wife and children too. The story is well known to both Theravāda and Mahāyāna Buddhists (Cone and Gombrich 1977; Lienhard 1980). But in Theravāda Buddhism the *bodhisattva*-concept is essentially retrospective and, though the virtues of a *bodhisattva* are exemplary (albeit exaggerated) for all Theravāda Buddhists, his status is not.

Mahāyāna Buddhism made *bodhisattva*-hood the aim of all good Buddhists: Mahāyāna Buddhists take a vow to become a Buddha for the sake of all beings and to strive for the welfare of others.[9] Some of the early texts of the Mahāyāna refer to it as the *bodhisattvayāna*, the Way of the Bodhisattvas, and thus oppose it to the *pratyekabuddhayāna*, the Way of the Solitary Buddhas, and to the *śrāvakayāna*, the Way of the Disciples (literally 'hearers', because they merely hear the law as preached by a fully enlightened Buddha: Dayal 1970: 10–11). At the same time Mahāyāna texts point out that there is only one path and one Buddha, and that the Mahāyāna represents only an elaboration, and not a rejection, of the Śrāvakayāna. These texts are known and quoted by Newar Buddhist *paṇḍits*.[10]

The integration of these different Ways within one framework means that the goal of attaining enlightenment for oneself, as in the Śrāvakayāna, is considered both selfish and undesirable. For the Mahāyāna the *nirvāṇa* of the 'disciples' is merely a 'resting place' and not the final goal.[11] The Mahāyāna ideal of Buddha-hood for all is also understood by other Newars. Riley-Smith, who worked with the image-casting Śākyas of Uku Bāhāḥ, asked one of his informants whether the recently deceased senior of

Uku Bāhāḥ would become a *bodhisattva*: 'He may become a Buddha. All men may become Buddhas through *dharma*, which takes away *pāp* [sin] (laughter). *Pāp* is like mud around a *dyo* [*dyaḥ*, god], a *mūrti* (statue), isn't it? When the mud is broken the Buddha is seen.'[12] I asked Jog Maya, 'Which is the easiest Way (*yāna*)?' She replied:

There are three Ways: the Disciples' Way, the Great Way, and the Diamond Way. There's also the Way of the Solitary (Buddhas). *Paṇḍit*s say that one shouldn't mock others. All are the Buddha's teaching, whichever you practise. The Great Way is higher, though. The Disciples' Way is easiest because they only have to worship the Buddha, whereas in the Great Way there are Tārā and all the rest, and one has to read so many books. The [Theravāda] monks say that getting to the stage of being an *arhat* (*arhatpad*) is enough, but in the Great Way one has to attain the stage of complete enlightenment (*samyaksambuddhapad*). To reach that one has to be a *bodhisattva* and fulfil the Ten Perfections. The monks say that all one has to do is meditate (do *bhāvanā*). That's all very well, but one has to attain the Four Trances (*caturdhyān*) and the Perfections too.

The concept of the *bodhisattva* was extremely fertile, for it managed to unite two phenomena which are sociologically quite distinct. On the one hand it provided an altruistic rationale for increasing involvement in lay and worldly religious action on the part of Buddhist clergy (whether celibate or not) and indeed accelerated the development of a married clergy (since the *bodhisattva* of the Rebirth stories is many things – including women[13] and animals – but only rarely a monk). On the other hand, the *bodhisattva* doctrine permitted the development of a pantheon of Buddhist saints whose essential nature and whose iconographic form was often derived from attributes of the Buddha.

These *bodhisattva*s are so compassionate that they will answer the call of any being who invokes their aid and so advanced spiritually that they have the power to do so at will. The most important of these is Avalokiteśvara, as he is usually known in the West. He became the patron saint of Tibet and has virtually the same status in the Kathmandu Valley. Newar Buddhists call him Karuṇāmaya, 'embodiment of compassion'. The second most important *bodhisattva* is Mañjuśrī, *bodhisattva* of wisdom, with whom Avalokiteśvara is often paired. As a secondary elaboration, in Tibet high lamas are considered to be *bodhisattva*s and elsewhere (Nepal, Sri Lanka, Thailand, China) kings are too.[14] *Bodhisattva*s such as Avalokiteśvara and Mañjuśrī, unlike Śākyamuni himself, are not thought of as human beings with a history of rebirths and gradual spiritual attainment. They appeared suddenly in South Asian history, as they do to the unsophisticated Buddhist layman today, as fully formed divinities to be petitioned.

Harrison (1987) suggests that the development of these celestial

Figure 13. The interrelationship of the different Ways of Newar Buddhism. Terms given in parenthesis are alternatives. Terms underlined are the ones generally used by Newar Buddhists. The broken line indicates that the Sahajayāna is sometimes considered to be a higher Way, above even the Vajrayāna. The word 'Mahāyāna' is polysemic. In its broader sense it includes what is otherwise opposed to it, the Śrāvakayāna (in line with the hierarchical logic mentioned above, §3.7). 'Hīnayāna' is not much used but is included here as it is well known from the Western literature on Buddhism.

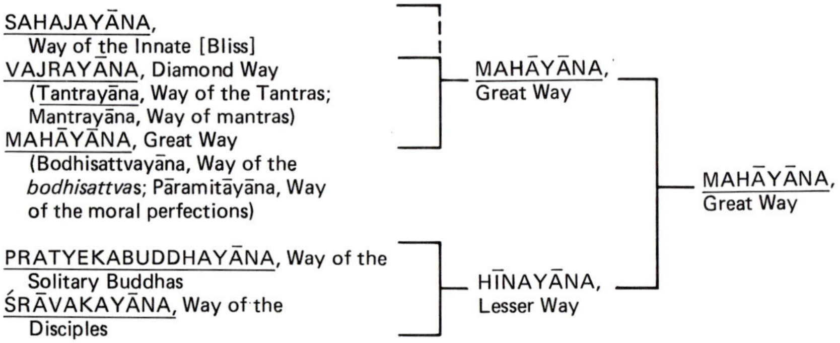

*bodhisattva*s, as they are often called, occurred only after the emergence of the *bodhisattva* as a soteriological ideal. Whatever the order of their emergence, the cult of the celestial *bodhisattva*s was intended to satisfy lay religious needs, whereas 'teachings about the actual practice of the Bodhisattva career are directed primarily towards monks' (Snellgrove 1987: 63). With the rise of the Vajrayāna, however, even the householder was enabled to follow this path.

Figure 13 summarizes the most important Ways as conceived by Newar Buddhists. The term Pratyekabuddhayāna (Way of the Solitary Buddhas) is a scholarly elaboration. Solitary Buddhas do not, by definition, establish the teaching, they merely practise it. From a sociological point of view the Way of the Solitary Buddhas simply expresses the belief of Buddhists that somewhere there always are, even in periods when Buddhism is not established as a religion, holy men attaining enlightenment. Consequently Hīnayāna and Śrāvakayāna are virtually synonymous. I retain the latter term since it is the one preferred by Newar Buddhists. They usually list the Ways thus: Śrāvakayāna, Pratyekabuddhayāna, Mahāyāna, and Vajrayāna. The final Way shown in the table, Sahajayāna, the Way of the Innate (Bliss), is a category normally cited only by learned Vajrācāryas.[15]

The older generation of Newar Buddhists use 'Śrāvakayāna' (and not 'Hīnayāna') to refer to Theravāda monks established in Nepal since the

1950s. For the sake of clarity I shall not copy their usage, but retain 'Śrāvakayāna' for the monastic part of traditional Newar Buddhist practice. One must remember, however, that the equivalence of Theravāda and Śrāvakayāna is an important part of Mahāyānist ideology. The term 'Mahāyāna' is sometimes, though less systematically, used by Newars to refer to Tibetan Buddhism, as opposed to the Vajrayāna Buddhism of Nepal. The reason for this must be that Newar Buddhists, as laymen patronizing Tibetan monks, tend to come in contact only with the Mahāyānist side of Tibetan Buddhism. (In fact, Tibetan Buddhism is no less Vajrayānist than that of the Newars.)

'Vajrayāna' and 'Tantrayāna' refer to Buddhism based on the Tantras. These texts were composed or redacted later than the basic Sūtras of Mahāyāna Buddhism. Snellgrove (1957: 56) writes that Tibetan Buddhist practitioners (i.e. monks or lamas) sometimes ask whether one follows the Sūtras or the Tantras, in other words, whether one practises according to the Mahāyāna or the Vajrayāna. In Nepal, since so much of religion is ascribed not achieved, this is not a usual question. There is rather a feeling, articulated to me by several Newar Buddhists, that Śākyas follow the Mahāyāna and Vajrācāryas follow the Vajrayāna. This is rather inexact, though the reason for the association should become clear in what follows.

The Diamond Way is in fact a specialized, privileged, and esoteric path within the Great Way. It will be shown below (§5.3, Table 5.2, and chapters 9 and 10) what this means in terms of ritual. Ideologically it means that the practitioner of the Diamond Way attempts to fulfil the ends of the Great Way by other means. These means may be frightening and dangerous, and are at least burdensome and difficult. But if successful they enable the practitioner to attain enlightenment in this life, rather than over the many thousands of lives required to attain Buddha-hood in the Great Way. A summary of what these distinctions mean to the Newars is given in Table 4.1.

The different deities of Newar Buddhism can be assigned to different Ways: the Buddha, Śākyamuni, belongs to the Way of the Disciples, the *bodhisattvas* to the Great Way, and 'Great Buddha' Vajrasattva and the esoteric deities to the Diamond Way. Similarly the architecture of the Buddhist monastery, with its three shrines, to Śākyamuni, to the *bodhisattva* Amoghapāśa Lokeśvara, and the Tantric shrine, was several times explained to me as reflecting the same hierarchy. It has been mentioned above that the Three Ways also provide a model of Buddhist history. As a matter of historical fact the types of Buddhism represented by the Three Ways did arise in that order. Even though the later texts present

Table 4.1 *Summary of the different practices falling under the head of the Three Ways (*yāna*) in Newar Buddhism.*

The Way of the Disciples (Śrāvakayāna):	Monasticism, ascetic rule-observance, worship of the Buddha.
The Great Way (Mahāyāna):	worship of all the gods, fulfilment of hereditary householder duties, including festivals and life-cycle rites, acquiring merit through donations (*dān*), cultivation of the moral perfections in accord with the ideal of the *bodhisattva.*
The Diamond Way (Vajrayāna):	worship of Tantric deities, taking Tantric Initiation (*dīkṣā*), acquiring magical powers and advanced spiritual states by strict rule-bound devotion to powerful deities or their exoteric manifestations.

themselves as taught by the Buddha himself, some Newars do see the Great Way and Diamond Way as a later adaptation of the Way of the Disciples; that is, they understand the conceptual levels as simultaneously expressing a chronological development. This may be due to the influence of the Theravāda monks and nuns now active in Nepal, but it may equally be due to more traditional teachings. Newar *paṇḍit*s explain that the Buddha himself taught the Three Ways, but in sequential order and in different places (see below, §9.1). Furthermore, this structure of the Three Ways is built into Newar rituals and in particular to the sequence whereby a young Vajrācārya passes first through Monastic Initiation, then becomes a householder, and finally undergoes the Consecration of a Vajra-master (§9.3; Locke 1975: 18). On the traditional Newar Buddhist view, then, all Three Ways were taught by the Buddha; the differences between them are explained by the fact that the Buddha adapted his message to the capabilities and needs of his listeners.

4.3 A survey of religious concepts

We have seen above (§2.7) that Buddhism and Hinduism are defined in Newar culture as alternative paths (*mārga*), but also as doctrines or creeds (*mata*). They are primarily sets of practices, but the idea persists that they are founded each on their own set of doctrines laid down by, or revealed to, their founder. There are, however, no institutional means for overseeing doctrine, and the unity and uniformity of Newar Buddhism are ensured by loyalty to the Vajrācāryas' rituals rather than to doctrine.

Before describing the role of doctrine in Newar Buddhist practice, it is worth considering briefly the question of ritual uniformity. The only organization even remotely resembling a church in Newar Buddhism is the Ācārya Guthi (Association of all Vajrācāryas) of Kathmandu.[16] In Lalitpur there is no association of all Vajrācāryas of the city, but each monastery with large numbers of Vajrācārya members has its own Association of Vajrācāryas. Traditionally these associations were supposed to regulate ritual and oversee relations between priests and their parishioners. Today the associations never seem to exert authority on these matters and continue only their ritual and status functions. The probable reasons for this are the decline of deference towards priests and the decreasing importance of ritual. Even in the heyday of traditional Newar Buddhism, however, there certainly existed different ritual traditions. The Vajrācāryas of Bu Bāhāḥ, and Vajrācāryas of other monasteries taught by them, perform rites in one way; the Vajrācāryas of Kwā Bāhāḥ perform the same rites with certain variants and in a slightly different order. There is no body in Lalitpur with the authority to arbitrate between these different traditions. The existence of the Association of all Vajrācāryas in Kathmandu may mean that there are fewer variants there in the way that Buddhist rituals are performed.

As far as the laity is concerned, these differences are unimportant. They are usually ignorant of them. Priests, on the other hand, know that rituals are performed differently by the priests of other monasteries and occasionally discuss the differences. They also know that every ritual has shorter, more basic forms and longer, more elaborate versions. They do not dilate on the different ways rituals are performed to the laity. The idea that ritual ought to be uniform certainly exists.[17] In spite of surface differences there is a unity of fundamental principle underlying all Newar Buddhist ritual.

Ritual is taught to young Vajrācāryas by their fathers or uncles, or by a learned teacher chosen for the purpose. They are made to memorize the Sanskrit utterances accompanying each ritual gesture or act. Doctrine is only taught in an *ad hoc* way, so that the practising priest can answer casual questions about the ritual asked by the laity. The laity receives no explicit teaching on doctrine. Laymen and women, particularly women, are taught by their mothers to make basic offerings. All other learning is a matter of personal choice.

In the past, before the establishment of schools, boys of the high, literate castes would practise their writing skills by copying religious texts. These would often be Sanskrit hymns (*stotra*, *tutaḥ*) recited in worship, but the

Cāṇakya Sāra Saṃgraha (proverbs and other worldly wisdom ascribed to Cāṇakya) was a very popular beginners' text both for Buddhists and for Hindus. Among Buddhists, the Bhadracarī, the Nāmasaṃgīti, and explanations of the Ten Unproductive Sins with Newari glosses were all copied frequently.

On certain occasions learned Vajrācāryas are invited to read and explain popular texts, usually Rebirth stories (*jātaka* and *avadāna*). Through this medium doctrinal notions are diffused. These readings are rare, however, compared to the preaching of the modern Theravāda movement. There are also a few discussion groups who meet to read and discuss canonical texts under the guidance of a *guru*. Nowadays they use printed versions, e.g. of commentaries on the Bodhicaryāvatāra. Such study, for those who were interested, no doubt took place in the past also. In short, learning doctrine was an informal and *ad hoc* process, a matter of personal choice. By contrast, at different levels according to background and gender, a basic minimum knowledge of ritual was explicitly taught in the family.

Consequently, opinions on doctrinal matters vary widely. All admit that there are others who know more than they do, and discussion of doctrine is open-ended and tolerant.[18] Nonetheless certain key notions are held in common. An attempt must therefore be made to sketch these notions.

4.3.1 Dharma, pāp, *and* karma

Dharma is used in Newari equally for any religious observance and, more generally, for morally and religiously good behaviour, the opposite of *pāp*, sin.[19] The first sense of *dharma* may be illustrated by the Vajrācārya priest who said: 'Whatever *dharma* you do, you must always begin by performing the *guru maṇḍala*.' The colloquial term for an Observance, *dhalā̃*, otherwise known as *vrata*, derives from *dharma*. So, to perform the Observance of a god or goddess is literally to activate (*dane*) their *dharma*. The second meaning of *dharma* is obvious in the negative condemnation of someone as 'without *dharma*', by which is meant morally unscrupulous. That someone who treats people badly is nonetheless punctilious in their religious practices is a paradox in Newari usage (e.g. 'he does all that *dharma* but is *pāpī*', said with strong disapproval). Newars may say of someone 'his *dharma* is strong', which implies both that he spends a lot of time and effort on religion, and that he is a trustworthy and dependable person.

When someone does a meritorious act, one says: 'dharma lāī', it will bring *dharma*. Here *dharma* is being used as an exact equivalent of what in Theravāda Buddhist societies and in Newar Buddhist scriptures is normally called *puṇya*, merit. Newari usage conflates the act which brings merit and the merit itself, a usage with ancient Indian precedents.[20] The term *puṇya*, religious merit, is known but is not used in ordinary speech, i.e. where the speaker is not being self-consciously scriptural. In ordinary speech *dharma* and *pāp* are opposites, both in describing behaviour and in denoting the results of that behaviour.[21]

Some of the things Buddhists say about *dharma* may be illustrated by the following quotations:

Karuṇāmaya [Matsyendranāth] receives the ten sacraments (*daśakarma*) because we have ten orifices in our body. If it weren't for (doing) *dharma* they'd grow too small to emit their respective fluids and we'd die. (Vajrācārya priest of Cobhār Lokeśvara)

There was a king who had Yama, king of the dead, as his fictive kin brother (*twāy*) and he thought to himself: 'My friend will tell me when I have to come, and I'll do *dharma* then.' So he didn't think of *dharma* or of death, and piled up riches and kingdoms. Then one day he became ill and called his friend: 'Why didn't you tell me?' Yama replied: 'I did, I sent you a letter every day. Didn't you notice the white hair, the failing teeth, and so on?' These were the signs he should have heeded but did not. (Newar monk in the Tibetan tradition, preaching after a death in the family)

The Buddha's teaching is not to indulge in merry-making (*mwaḥj*), not to chase girls, wealth, or tasty food, but to do *dharma* and follow the path to heaven. (55-year-old Vajrācārya priest)

People say that those who know what is right and wrong (*tyaḥ* and *ma tyaḥ*), and do what is good (*bhĩgu*), have the Perfection of Wisdom or have seen the Perfection of Wisdom. Those people who are always fighting haven't, and don't know any *dharma*. But you can't actually see her, or if you do see her, there's nothing there (*chũ ma ru*). She's emptiness (*śūnyatā*) and *dharma*. (Jog Maya Shakya)

Dharma is getting rid of desire, anger, greed, delusion, and affection (*kāma, krodha, lobha, moha, māyā*).[22] If you get rid of these you will obtain power. You must not hurt others' feelings. That is *dharma*, not any of this new-fangled stuff [Theravāda monasticism etc.]. (middle-aged Vajrācārya priest)

Some people have started to take the horoscopes (of prospective bride and groom) to the astrologer and say to him, 'Make them fit for us', and he does it for them. This is against our *dharma*. It may be all right to do that in Britain, but this is a place with many gods ('dyaḥ yekwa dūgu thāy'). (Tirtha Lal Maharjan)

For Buddhists *dharma* also refers to *the* Dharma, that is, the teaching of Lord Buddha, and, as suggested by Jog Maya, this is personified in the figure of the goddess, the Perfection of Wisdom. She is considered to be a form of Tārā. In very many of the tympana over the doors of Buddhist shrines in the Valley, she represents the Dharma, as Avalokiteśvara represents the Saṃgha (Monastic Community). The two of them flank the Buddha, thus constituting the Three Jewels (*triratna*) of Buddhism: Buddha, Dharma, Saṃgha.

At death one's rebirth is determined by the balance of *dharma* as opposed to *pāp* (for the various possible rebirths, see below, §4.3.11). This Newar Buddhist conception – which would be accepted equally by Hindus – is graphically illustrated at Itum Bāhāḥ, in Kathmandu, every year during the month of Gũlā. On Sā Pāru (Np. Gāī Jātrā), the day when the doors of Yama's kingdom are believed by Hindus and Buddhists alike to be open for the dead, a senior of the monastery uses toy models on show to explain to children and other onlookers what happens at death. The soul (*ātmā*) of the dying person drinks from the waterspout known as Dãlāy Hitī,[23] and Citragupta, the clerk in the land of the dead, consults his book to see if the dying person has any life (*āyu*) left to run. If he has, he is sent back, and the traditional doctor (*vaidya*) feeling his pulse announces: 'No, his time hasn't come yet.' Beside Citragupta is a pair of scales marked on either side *dharma* and *pāp*; the balance, says the elder, will determine the dead person's rebirth, whether in hell (*naraka*), as a horsefly, or wherever.[24]

These conceptions are not confined to the learned. An eighty-year-old peasant, Shiva Lal Maharjan, gave me the following account of an experience he had when young:

> I was very ill. I was taken up. There were two high walls and on the right a long line of men playing musical instruments and on the left a line of women dancing. Then they all sat down behind curtains and ate *samay baji*.[25] But I wasn't given anything: no meat, no beaten rice, no ginger, no soyabeans, no black-eye beans. They just threw down some popped rice (*syābaji*). Then I went to the water spout to drink but the people guarding it sent me away, saying 'We won't let you drink!' If I had eaten *samay baji*, or drunk the water, that would have been it. But I had life (*āyu*) left still.

A materialist view of sin, such as that implied by the pair of scales, is common. Earthquakes are said to occur because the earth is heavy with sins. Just as *dharma* can mean ritual action, so the paradigmatic *pāp* as illustrated in religious stories is usually hostility to gods and ritual. Equally common in ordinary parlance is the sentiment that *pāp* consists in harming (*syãke*) or causing suffering ('dukha biye') to other people. This is no doubt reinforced by a Buddhist canonical teaching, widely reproduced by literate Newar Buddhists, that there are Ten Unproductive Sins (*daśākuśala pāpa*). In order, these are: harming living beings, taking what is not given (i.e. theft), sexual misconduct, telling lies, slander, speaking harshly and aggressively, gossiping and other frivolous talk, covetousness, malevolence, and adherence to false doctrines.[26] The first three are said to be sins of the body, the next four sins of speech, and the final three sins of the mind. It will be seen that the first four are the sins which lay people in other Buddhist cultures undertake to avoid when they utter the Five Precepts.[27] Newar Buddhists do not in fact take these Precepts regularly, unless they are devotees of the Theravāda movement or participate in Observances organized by monks of the Tibetan tradition. Nonetheless, in a ritualized fashion, the content, and sometimes the actual wording, of the Precepts, Five, Eight, and Ten, are incorporated into the practice of Observances and Monastic Initiation. During the 'stories' or 'explanations' read out at such Observances the participants are exhorted to avoid the Ten Unproductive Sins.

Thus sin (*pāp*) is viewed anywhere on a spectrum from being a material substance to being an ethical quality of one's actions towards other living beings (and often both simultaneously). When it comes to the *results* of sin, however, all agree that these must be material in nature. It is taken as axiomatic that the general conditions of one's life – high caste or low, rich or poor, lucky or unlucky – are determined by one's *karma*. In situations where there is nothing to be done Newars often say, 'It's all written in one's *karma*' or 'Everyone has to experience their own *karma*',[28] and they tap their forehead where one's *karma* is supposed to be written at birth by Citragupta, Yama's messenger. This is not a fatalistic belief, for the *karma* doctrine is not used to advocate resignation to others. One would not normally say to another, 'There is nothing you can do about it, it is all in your own *karma*.' If the *karma* doctrine is urged on others, it is with precisely the opposite force: all fortunes and misfortunes are the result of one's own *karma*, therefore pull yourself together, devote yourself to the gods and doing *dharma*, and it will be all right. It is only when a person wishes to reconcile him or herself to something that has already happened and cannot be avoided that the fatalistic overtone is used. Newars often enjoy teasing one another, but I do not think they would be so rude as to taunt one another with their bad *karma*.[29]

Not only are *karma*'s effects material in nature; it is believed, as in other Buddhist societies (e.g. Ortner 1978: 111), that rewards and punishments are inevitably fitting. One of the justifications given by Newar peasants for not ploughing is that in a future life they will have to suffer the same treatment as they mete out to their animals.[30] Priestly texts encourage the laity in the belief that those who steal will themselves suffer poverty, those who commit adultery will lack offspring, and so on.

4.3.2 Dān

In Mahāyāna Buddhism there is a canonical list of virtues known as the Six or Ten Perfections (*pāramitā*): it begins with *dāna* (charity, giving) and proceeds through morality (*śīla*), forbearance (*kṣānti*), energy (*vīrya*), and meditation (*dhyāna*), culminating in wisdom (*prajñā*). The four which bring the list up to ten – skill in means (*upāya*), resolution, strength, and knowledge – are supplementary to the first six, and historically later additions; wisdom remains the ultimate attainment. When one has perfected all these, one has fulfilled the *bodhisattva* path.[31] This list is one of the most well-known sets of Buddhological concepts among Newar Buddhists. The final perfection, wisdom, is personified as a goddess and identified with the Dharma or Buddhist teaching, as mentioned above. The ten elders of Kwā Bāhāḥ monastery are frequently referred to as the Ten Perfections (while elders in smaller monasteries with only five elders are identified with the Five Buddhas). The best-known and simplest chanted hymn (*tutaḥ*) is a praise of the Ten Perfections (the 'Dānabalena') and it is recited daily as part of the liturgy performed before enshrined Buddha images.

The scriptures of Mahāyāna Buddhism go into great detail over the lengths *bodhisattva*s go to in practising these perfections. The Buddha's previous birth as Viśvantara, in which he gave away his kingdom, wife, and children, has already been mentioned. Newar Buddhists frequently go on pilgrimage to Namobuddha, near Panauti, where they believe the Buddha as Mahāsattva fed his body to starving tiger cubs, and to Maṇicūḍ, where he is said to have given his head to be split open, as there was a jewel inside which would save the kingdom.[32]

Alongside these exemplars of extraordinary giving (and forebearance), Buddhist scriptures also lavish praise on all the possible types of gift-giving which the Buddhist laity may perform towards the Monastic Community. The verses with which Śākyas and Vajrācāryas, in their role as monks, are supposed to accept gifts from the laity promise a material return, either in this life or a future one (see below, chapter 6, appendix). What Mauss observed of Hinduism applies equally to Mahāyāna Buddhism:

> Food given away means that food will return to the donor in this world; it also means food for him in the other world and in his series of reincarnations. Water, wells and springs given away are insurance against thirst . . . Such economic theology is developed at great length in the rolling periods of the innumerable cantos, and neither the codes nor the epics ever tire of the subject. (Mauss 1954: 55)

The principal institutional setting for the giving of gifts to the Monastic Community is the festival of Pañcadān, described below (§6.3). In most cases, it is the good intentions of the donors, and the merit received by them, which receive stress. However, a Śākya who had himself sponsored Optional Pañcadān, gift-giving to Śākyas and Vajrācāryas on a massive scale, discussed a similar occasion in Kathmandu a few years previously. The Śākya man chosen to receive the most munificent gift of land, a house, and money did not even know how to recite the appropriate alms-receiving verse (*dānavākya*), could not digest the gift, and consequently went mad.

One might wonder whether this belief, that gifts are difficult to digest, implies the Hindu belief, so well described by Parry (1980, 1986), for funeral priests and other religious specialists in Benares, and Raheja (1988a), for almost every prestation and ritual action between and within castes in a village in western Uttar Pradesh: namely, that the recipient accepts the sin of the donor along with the gift. Two points, made by Parry and Raheja for north India, definitely apply to the Newars: (a) accepting *dān*, especially an unusually large *dān*, can be problematic; (b) castes of ritual specialists often regard the obligation to accept *dān* from their patrons or parishioners as an unpleasant duty, which is, if possible, to be avoided.[33]

However, at least four points can be made against applying what can for convenience be called the Parry-Raheja model to the Newars wholesale (and it may be that some of these qualifications will turn out to be applicable elsewhere in South Asia).

Different Opinions

There is a considerable diversity of opinion on the question of what, if anything, is transferred along with the *dān*. Many Newars, Hindu and Buddhist, high caste and low, flatly deny that either sin (*pāp*) or inauspiciousness (*aśubh*, *aśānti*, *mabhīgu*) is accepted by the recipient. Some laugh and say 'How easy if one could give away sin like that!' and they argue that if such bad things were inevitably passed on in *dān*, no one would ever accept it and no one would ever agree to be a priest. Others allow that such a transfer may occur, but say that it will not, provided the *dān* is 'digested'.

Transfer of evil can be prevented

There are methods of preventing any unwanted transfer. In the first place, the recipient of *dān* should recite a blessing (or at least silently think one) and hope that the donor receives whatever they wish for. In this way a return is made for the gift. There is a requisite verse for each item given. *Paṇḍit* Asha Kaji Vajracharya related how a family priest had come to ask him what to recite as a rich parishioner was about to give him a radio as part of the *dān* after a death in the family (he answered: *dūryantra*, 'distance machine'; i.e. insert the word *dūryantra* in a pre-existing verse). Secondly, the recipient should never specify what must be given, but accept willingly whatever is offered. Thirdly, those who receive *dān* must themselves give *dān* to their own *gurus* and others. Not to do so is to behave like a ghost (*pret*), not a man. Fourthly, if the *dān* is being given to get rid of inauspiciousness, a part of all food items is thrown at the *chwāsā* stone. Likewise, all items given in the name of a dead person are left out overnight before use (food is left on the balcony where crows can eat it). In these ways no evil is transferred. Some people do say that priests today no longer know how to recite properly, and that is why so many of them are physically unattractive. But most Newars do not believe that this is generally so.

Types of dān

Dān can be either auspicious or inauspicious. It also varies according to whether it is regular (given in the normal run of things) and irregular (occasioned by a crisis or by a desire to perform some supererogatory act of merit). Some *dān* is given precisely to avoid a great calamity. Here the possibility that a transfer may occur means that only a Dyaḥlā will accept it. In this category, also, are the rice and old clothes given during an eclipse (*grahadān*). *Dān* given immediately after death is also inauspicious, and in many cases Kāpālīs no longer take the clothes thrown at the *chwāsā*, but a Dyaḥlā does so instead (§7.3). Other *dān*, however, whether given annually at, say, Pañcadān, or optionally, at the time of one's own choosing, is given with the positive aim of gaining merit, and not in the hope of avoiding any specific evil. Consequently the stigma attached to accepting it is much less.[34]

In the case of such auspicious *dān*, even if the recipient does accrue sin by not reading the requisite blessing, it is not necessarily a question of accepting the *donor's* sin. It is true that today many Śākyas and Vajrācāryas feel shame about accepting such auspicious *dān* as given in the Pañcadān festival. The same is so *a fortiori* for many ritual specialists, especially those associated with death (e.g. the Karamjit and Kāpālī). In the past, on the other hand, even these professions could be a source of pride. Today there are still many priests and ritual specialists who have no economic need to carry on their religious role, but yet continue to do so, because they think it would be wrong to abandon their patrons and relinquish their caste duties.

Dān *as an exchange*

The positive aspects of *dān* are frequently stressed. They include future material benefits, and the cultivation of mental states – non-attachment to material goods, altruism, and good will – which themselves bring benefits. Thus, *dān* is viewed more as an asymmetrical exchange – of blessing for gift – or as an investment with delayed returns, than as a pure gift with both positive and negative aspects. At a higher level, there is an attempt to get away from any idea of exchange. In Catholicism this means modelling relations with God on the close and uncalculating kin relations – generalized reciprocity, to use Sahlins' term (1974: 193) – obtaining within the family (Christian 1989: 171). By contrast, in Mahāyāna, as in Theravāda, Buddhism, one carries out what looks externally like a transaction (making offerings to a statue), but actually there is no recipient. Exchange is left behind altogether. In Theravāda this is accomplished by the teaching that the Buddha is in *nirvāṇa* and therefore cannot influence the world or accept anything; in Mahāyāna Buddhism the same conclusion is drawn from the doctrine of universal void or emptiness. Interestingly, Jainism evolved the same theory of offerings, in which 'nothing is "received," no one is "propitiated"' (Jaini 1979: 296).

Unlike the situation described by Raheja, among the Newars *dān* is never given to relatives. Prestations to the paternal aunt, for instance, are considered to be a payment in return for ritual services, just like *dakṣiṇā* (stipend) to one's family priest, and like all prestations to other ritual specialists which are not specifically *dān*. Relatives would not like to receive *dān*, Newars say; they are 'one's own people' (*thaḥpī̃*). The only exception occurs during life-cycle rites: Loincloth Worship or Monastic Initiation for boys, Mock Marriage for girls, Old-Age Initiation for old people. In these cases, as if to emphasize their liminality, those passing through the rite *must* receive *dān* from mothers, aunts, or daughters (depending on the rite).

It is possible that these differences with north India (if differences they genuinely are) may be due in part to the presence of Buddhism among the Newars. In Theravāda Buddhism there is always great stress on the fact that what the laity receives in return for *dān* is the far greater gift of religious teaching. Mahāyāna Buddhism continues the stress on the positive aspects and material benefits of gift-giving, as well as on the importance of good intentions and non-attachment. Ultimately these good intentions are what *dān* is all about, and not the desire for benefits (Gombrich 1971: 246–52). It is very evident that Raheja's Hindu villagers view life as a zero-sum game: in almost every case, avoiding inauspiciousness means passing it on to someone else. Buddhism, by contrast, is built on the rejection of such negative reciprocity: the practice of 'rejoicing in merit' (*anumodana*), mentioned above (§4.1) as one of the 'limbs' of worship, allows for good results to accrue *ad infinitum* as the pious rejoice in each other's acquisition of merit. As Gombrich (1988: 126) remarks, 'In Buddhist spiritual economics you gain by giving away.' While this practice is not formalized strongly in their tradition, as it is in Theravāda countries, the Newars share an emphasis on the religious value of good intentions. Although in some contexts they do tend to view life as zero-sum, this is by no means the pervasive theme it appears to be in Raheja's work. Traditionally, Buddhist monks are supposed to be above considerations of auspiciousness and inauspiciousness, and, while this is rarely true in practice, it has had an effect on the attitude of Buddhism to gift-giving.

In spite of all these continuities with Theravāda Buddhism, there is in Newar Buddhism no attempt to avoid the appearance of exchange – ritual services for goods – which sometimes occurs in Theravāda contexts (Tambiah 1970: 347–8; Strenski 1983: 472). At the lowest level Mahāyāna Buddhism positively encourages, as Theravāda does not, a spiritual accounting which sees merit as automatic. It is characteristic of Mahāyāna Buddhism to express something in a materialistic, Hindu-sounding way at the simplest level, but to see this as mere metaphor ('skilful means') on a more sophisticated, more strictly Buddhist level. From this point of view, where Buddhism and functionalism converge, the point of the belief in the necessity of 'digesting' *dān* is to encourage young Śākyas and Vajrācāryas to memorize the alms-receiving verses. The more strictly Buddhist view focuses on the intentions of the donor and recipient. Jog Maya emphasized the importance of intentions by saying:

> As long as you make offerings or pray with expectations for yourself (*āśikā*) you must continue to go round in *saṃsāra*. You are sowing the seed of another birth, of sin. Only if you do it as *dharma*, without expectations for yourself, but rather for the good of all beings, will you be saved.

4.3.3 Non-violence, intentions, and animal sacrifice

The importance of intention is also clear if we consider what many Newars believe to be the paramount Buddhist virtue, *ahiṃsā*. This is often translated as 'non-violence', but more precisely it means 'absence of desire to kill or harm'. Both meanings are intended in Newar Buddhists' usage. Elderly and many middle-aged Newar Buddhists are careful not to kill small insects, and to prevent small children in their care from doing so.

Paṇḍit Asha Kaji Vajracharya (1972: *ga*) defines *hiṃsā* (the opposite of *ahiṃsā*) as

> cutting the body of a living being and splitting it in two. This sort of sin is the seed which requires one to experience hell for aeons and aeons. One should avoid the evil work (*kukarma*) of *hiṃsā*; that is to say, one should avoid those who live by hunting and those who gain their living by and commit such unwholesome violent work as killing other living beings and selling their meat. That conduct which consists in avoiding such people and being able to give up the consumption of alcohol and meat is what is called genuine (*sakaligu*) Mahāyāna Buddhadharma.

In other contexts the same author likes to quote the verse:

Ahiṃsā paramo dharma ahiṃsā paramo gatiḥ
Ahiṃsā paramaṃ jñānam ahiṃsā paramaṃ padam.
Ahiṃsā is the highest *dharma*, *ahiṃsā* is the highest destination.
Ahiṃsā is the highest knowledge, *ahiṃsā* is the highest place.[35]

The prominence which this value is given and the vehemence with which it is expressed are due in part to the modern Theravāda movement which campaigns against animal sacrifice and announces in the pages of its journals, as a victory in this campaign, every indication that Buddhists (or others) have abandoned the practice. Traditionally many Śākya and Vajrācārya artisans sacrificed a duck to a statue of Bhīmsen in their house or workshop once a year. This custom has almost totally stopped; many ascribe its suppression to the influence of Kyanche Lama, a Tibetan who came to the Valley in 1923 (Rosser 1966: 105ff.), rather than to the Theravāda movement. Vajrācārya priests still have to oversee the sacrifice of animals, often goats, on behalf of their parishioners, although they are now made to feel uncomfortable about this.

What has happened is a shift in the boundary between what is defined as Buddhist and non-Buddhist. Traditionally animal sacrifice was acceptable to Śākyas and Vajrācāryas, but only in what was defined as a non-Buddhist context, in this case the worship of Bhīmsen for success in one's business. It has always been taboo to offer blood sacrifice to specifically Buddhist deities, whether exoteric or esoteric. Even so Hindu a source as the nineteenth-century chronicle, the Bhāṣā Vaṃśāvalī (Paudel and Lamshal 1963 I: 33), links the teaching of *ahiṃsā* to the Buddha, whom it represents as an *avatār* of Viṣṇu. Today it is difficult for Buddhists, at least for Śākyas, Vajrācāryas, and those attached to the Theravāda movement, to sacrifice animals at any time or in any context. Vegetarianism on the other hand is, as it has always been, an optional practice with only minor religious merit being attached to it.

What has remained constant is the Buddhist focus on intention. Traditionally, the sponsor of an animal sacrifice attempts to avoid the sin involved by not cutting the animal's neck himself. The butcher attempts to avoid the sin by waiting until the sponsor gives the word. It is widely known that the Buddha permitted his monks to eat meat providing they had not seen it being killed, nor had ordered it to be killed, nor had any suspicion that it had been killed for them.[36] Consequently, most Newar Buddhists eat meat, and they believe that the sin is wholly the butcher's, at whose shop they buy it. Whether or not they eat it, they have to cook it, since it is essential in many Buddhist rituals.

4.3.4 **Tyaḥ** ***and*** **ma tyaḥ**

In Newari, religious prohibitions are expressed by the verb *tyaye* in the negative: *ma tyaḥ*. Unlike the auxiliary *ma jyū* which means simply that one ought not to do something, without of itself implying a particular reason, use of *ma tyaḥ* implies a specifically religious reason. Since the religion of the Newars includes Buddhism, Hinduism, and much 'local' or 'folk' tradition, many things, and not just Buddhist ethical demands, are expressed by using *ma tyaḥ*. Among these are beliefs that the observer is inclined to class as superstitions (e.g. that it is *ma tyaḥ* to travel on a Saturday, or to return home on Tuesday, or bathe on a Sunday) as well as other beliefs which relate to ideas of purity and pollution (e.g. that it is *ma tyaḥ* to blow out a candle or similar flame because one's spittle is likely to come into contact with fire, which is holy). So many of these beliefs are now no longer taken seriously that many people complain, 'Nowadays *ma tyaḥ* means that one must do it.' Nonetheless the expression still has considerable moral force. The following example is typical:

> Of all living beings only mankind has intelligence (*jñān*). Nevertheless not all of them have the same nature (*svabhāv*). Some men behave well (*sādhu sant*) while others have a primitive, violent, and animal-like (*jaṅgalī hiṃsak paśu*) nature. The latter ignore what is right and wrong (*thwa yāye tyaḥ thwa yāye ma tyaḥ*), and cause suffering through their unnecessary and thoughtless evil acts.[37]

Certain ethical rules which Newar Buddhists would recognize as specific to their society are also said to be *ma tyaḥ*. For instance, taking money or earnings belonging to daughters of the family (*mhyāymasta*): since they will marry out, daughters have no right to inherit the family property; thus it is considered wrong to take anything from them. Rather, a brother has a lifelong obligation to feed his sisters, and their children, at any festival held in his house.

Some traditionally minded Buddhists regard all these different prohibitions as equally part of Nepal's ancient *dharma*. Others dismiss them as worldly custom (*vyavahār*, *lokācār*), preferring to call *dharma*, or *Buddhadharma*, only what is strictly to.do with salvation. All tend to agree on the importance of being consistent and devoted (*ekcitta*) in one's preferred form of religiosity, whatever that may be.

4.3.5 Auspiciousness, inauspiciousness, and protection from misfortune

Newars, whether Buddhist, Hindu, or both, believe that there are auspicious and inauspicious events, times, and places, and that if no care is taken to counteract any inauspiciousness one may have incurred, bad consequences will ensue. The terms *aśubh* and *mabhīgu* refer to inauspiciousness in general; *aśānti*, 'lack of peace', denotes the state, usually of a home, of inauspiciousness; an inauspicious event which simply occurs, i.e. a bad omen, is called a *bichuk*; an event caused by a person is *alachin*, and a person may also be *alachinā*, i.e. not *lachin* or possessing good qualities (Skt. *lakṣaṇa*). In general everything associated with death is inauspicious. A widow is always inauspicious and may never give *sagã*, the good-luck offerings which end important rituals and mark a departure abroad. It is she who has to cook the inauspicious rice which is used to make the riceballs (*piṇḍa*) offered in Ancestor Worship.

Astrologers are consulted about the auspicious place to build a house, and about the auspicious time (*sāit*) for any important life-cycle ritual (basically rituals of adulthood, marriage, and Old-Age Initiation). Most Newars, and all high-caste ones, show the horoscopes of prospective bride and groom to an astrologer before a wedding is fixed. Astrologers are frequently consulted if things are not going well at home, i.e. for what Westerners would consider psychological and social problems. The most famous and prestigious astrologers tend to come from the Jośī (Astrologer) caste, but many Vajrācāryas also practise as astrologers, often combining it with healing (§11.4).

Newar Buddhists seek protection from danger either from Karuṇāmaya, whose compassion will lead him to help, or from Tārā, whose name means saviouress. In Kwā Bāhāḥ she is worshipped in the form of the text-cum-goddess, the Perfection of Wisdom: the reading of the text is supposed to be particularly effective in the case of illness (Gellner in press). There is a list of eight dangers (*aṣṭa mahābhaya*) from which Tārā saves (kings, thieves, enemies, lightning, fire, wind, water, and earthquakes).[38] With her is associated a Newar Buddhist text, the Tārā Pārājikā, which gives details of what to do in various cases of inauspiciousness, e.g. a serpent crossing one's path, seeing a dog defecate, or a spire fall from a temple. The methods of attaining peace (*śānti*) are represented as having been taught to Tārā by the Lord Buddha himself. It is interesting to note that a similar text dealing with questions of caste and purity, the Mañjuśrī Pārājikā, is represented as having been taught by Lord Buddha to Mañjuśrī.

In times of particular misfortune Newar Buddhists have their family priest perform a worship of the nine planets (*navagraha pūjā*). This is still done today, but rather less than in the past. Two other protective practices, which literate laymen could carry out by themselves, were the worship of the Buddhist forms of the seven days of the week and of the Five Protective Goddesses (Pañcarakṣā). These were worshipped by reciting the texts named after them; but both practices are very markedly in decline.[39]

These texts are built around *dhāraṇīs*, mantric prayers often misleadingly called spells. As a translation of *dhāraṇī*, 'spell' is too instrumental and 'hymn' is not instrumental enough; 'prayer' is too personal, and does not capture the connotation that these particular syllables are appropriate for this situation, and no others. Snellgrove (1987: 122) translates it as 'mnemonic', the point being that they 'hold . . . the meaning succinctly of an intention which in normal speech would need to be much more prolix'. A few such *dhāraṇī* are still very much in use by Newar Buddhists, though it is no longer true that every Śākya and Vajrācārya household has hand-copied texts containing them. The best known is the Durgatipariśodhana ('the purification [i.e. prevention] of all evil rebirths'). Many Newars know it by heart as it is recited again and again at the time of a death and immediately after:

Oṁ namo bhagavate sarvadurgatipariśodhanarājāya tathāgatāya arhatyai samyaksambuddhāya tadyathā śodhane śodhane viśodhane viśodhane sarvapāpa viśodhane sarvabhaya viśodhane śuddhe viśuddhe sarvapāpa viśuddhe sarvakarmāvaraṇa śodhane svāhā.

As with other mantras, the grammar is irregular, but the vocabulary is well known. The translation, which is therefore imprecise and intuitive, is roughly as follows:

OṀ Obeisance to the Lord, the Attained One, noble one, completely enlightened Buddha, King He-who-purifies-all-evil-destinies. In the same way, purify, purify, thoroughly purify, thoroughly purify, thoroughly purify all sins, thoroughly purify all dangers, purified, thoroughly purified, all sins purified, purify all obstructions to *karma* SVĀHĀ.

The recitation of this *dhāraṇī* is said to remove the sin of the dead person and to help them attain Sukhāvatī, the heaven of Amitābha Buddha. Other *dhāraṇīs* have the same or similar structure. Tārā's is read against ghosts, Bhaiṣajyaguru's against illness, Vairocana's is sometimes read as part of the daily worship of a Buddha image, Aparamitā's is read on one's birthday and for long life, and Amitābha's is read, some time after a death, to help the dead person to attain Sukhāvatī.

4.3.6 Bodhisattva

The term *bodhisattva* has been introduced above (§4.2). One way in which the path to salvation is undertaken is the *bodhisattva* vow, that is, the vow to become a Buddha in order to save and uplift all beings. This meaning of *bodhisattva* is known only to the pious and to the high castes. The *bodhisattva* vow is built into the structure of the *guru maṇḍala* rite, but most lay people do not know this. The more knowledgeable laity know that

Karuṇāmaya, and other divine personages such as Śākyamuni before his enlightenment, Maitrī (Maitreya, the future Buddha of this world age), and Mañjuśrī, are *bodhisattvas*. Interestingly, *bodhisattvas* of the first rank, i.e. Karuṇāmaya and Mañjuśrī, do not have 'Bodhisattva' appended to their name, whereas more obscure *bodhisattvas*, such as Maitrī, Vajrapāṇi, Ratnapāṇi, and Śvetaketu, do.

4.3.7 Siddha, siddhi

Much better known is the word *siddha*, 'perfected' or 'accomplished person'. This is used of various saints, who combine being *bodhisattvas* with Tantric accomplishments/powers (*siddhi*), a double legitimization which is particularly important for Vajrācāryas (§9.2). Such saints I shall refer to as Realized Ones. Furthermore, almost any individual or even an inanimate object may 'become *siddha*' and be worshipped as a god: this expression is often used to explain why a particular stone is worshipped. The word *siddhi* is used, not just for magical powers acquired by holy personages, but for spiritual, or spiritually related, attainment in general. A teacher of Āyurveda may tell his pupil that he will acquire no *siddhi* if he treats his books so disrespectfully; I heard an old Tulādhar man tell the participants in an Observance of making clay *caityas* that if they wore shoes to carry them to the river there would be no *siddhi* from the rite.

4.3.8 Gods

Bodhisattvas and *siddhas* are considered to be gods, as is the Buddha, Śākyamuni. In the Buddha's case it is known that as Sarvārthasiddhi, before his enlightenment, and in many previous births, he was a man (or woman or animal). In Kathmandu, at least, the main Śākyamuni image of a Buddhist monastery is regularly referred to as *kwāḥpāḥdyaḥ* (in Lalitpur, *kwābāju* seemed more common). The Five Buddhas (*pañcabuddha* or *pañcatathāgata*) represented on *caityas* are actually called *bhagavāndyaḥ* ('Lord [Buddha] god'). The great *bodhisattvas* are certainly conceived of as gods, although, interestingly, the Newari suffix *dyaḥ*, meaning god, is not appended to their Sanskritic names, as it is to the names of the great Hindu gods.

In many accounts of Newar Buddhism by Westerners it is said to be essentially monotheistic, being based on a belief in the divine supremacy of Ādibuddha 'as the sole and self-existing spirit pervading the Universe' (Oldfield 1981 II: 86). The text, the Guṇakāraṇḍavyūha, does have an account of the creation of the world by Ādibuddha, a local derivative of which is quoted below (§10.3). This clearly parallels the role of Viṣṇu in Hinduism. But this is only one text, which is rarely invoked, and it is a gross misrepresentation to see Newar Buddhism as a theism whose cardinal tenet is belief in Ādibuddha.[40]

Occasionally the theistic term *īśvara*, 'lord', is used, though Buddhists tend only to use it in exclamations when under pressure (*he īśvar*!). Learned and modern-educated Buddhists know that Buddhism is supposed to be *anīśvaravāda*, a non-theistic doctrine. For ordinary Buddhists the term *īśvara* is ambiguous between the various great gods, i.e. gods considered to be soteriological, and can be used to imply a kind of monism. Such monism can also be asserted without using the word *īśvara*. Thus Jog Maya said: 'If you look in the Svayambhū Purāṇa you will see that Karuṇāmaya, Nāmasaṃgīti, and Cakrasaṃvara are all one.'

Between these and lower gods there is a great gap. Thus few Newars would agree with Gombrich's (1971: 46) Theravādin monk that 'gods are nothing to do with religion'; such a sentiment certainly can be heard, however, with regard to lower gods. Others say that gods are simply men who have 'crossed over' (*taray juye*). There is therefore considerable variation in the way the gods are perceived, and the line between gods and men is far from absolute. It will be shown below (§8.2.4, 9.3.5, 10.2) how, in the context of Tantric ritual, men and women come to be identified with and possessed by the gods.

Devotion (*bhakti*) to the gods is considered a great virtue. The expression of devotion is service (*sevā*). Public ecstatic forms of *bhakti*, common in south India, are rare among the Newars. There is, however, an annual tongue-boring of one man in honour of the goddess Mahālakṣmī, in the village of Bode (Anderson 1977: 48). Towards more specifically Buddhist deities, more restrained forms of devotion are expected, but here too the idea is that selfless devotion and a willingness to put up with hardship brings one close to god. (I well remember a Maharjan woman remarking sharply to someone who had pointed out that fasting is hard, 'Do you think that *dharma* is just doing whatever you like, then?') There is an obvious parallel between the way a god's favour is believed to be won by constant, unremitting devotion, and the way in which a political patron may be won over, and persuaded to grant favours or a job. In this profane context, behaving obsequiously and solicitously is called 'cākari yāye'.[41] The political analogy can be introduced irreverently into a religious context, as when worshipping a god for a specific result is referred to jocularly as 'ghūs nakegu' (literally 'feeding a bribe').

4.3.9 Śakti

The female consort of a male god is referred to as *śakti*. This usage derives ultimately from the Hindu Tantras, which is why a Tantric devotee of the

Hindu goddess is called a Śākta. The term is never found in Buddhist Tantric scriptures, but it is freely used by Newar Buddhists in this sense. By extension, Newars also use the word, on occasion and often half-jocularly, to mean 'wife'. This meaning is so well established that *śakti* is rarely used to mean 'power', although it has been adopted, as in India, to translate 'electricity', as in 'Electricity Corporation'. Nowadays in non-religious contexts the English word 'power' is used. In a perhaps related sense the words *sat* (pronounced *śat*), Skt. 'truth', and *satya*, same meaning, are used. If it rains, as it is traditionally supposed to do, on the day that Karuṇāmaya is placed on his chariot for the Matsyendra Jātrā, this is attributed to his *sat* (*Bũgadyaḥyā sat* or simply *dyaḥyā sat*).

4.3.10 Taray juye, nirvāṇa

The aim of the religious life is referred to most vaguely using the verb *taray juye*, to cross over. This leaves open the nature of the destination, something about which Newar Buddhists readily admit their incompetence to judge. Old people say that the merit of the group (*khalaḥ*) which meets every morning to recite the Nāmasaṃgīti in Kwā Bāhāḥ is such that even the cows who eat the discarded leaf plates from the group's annual feast are saved. At times of death a more precise destination is aimed at, namely the world (*bhuvana*) presided over by Amitābha. This is Sukhāvatī, the realm of happiness where the *bodhisattva* who is Amitābha's 'son', Karuṇāmaya, is also to be found. The Vajrācārya priest of Cobhār Lokeśvara, while explaining to me how Karuṇāmaya saves people from the sixteen hells and takes them to Sukhāvatī, continued:

> If we abandon passion, hatred, delusion, affection, anger, and greed (*rāga, dveṣa, moha, māyā, krodha, lobha*) we obtain Sukhāvatī now. We shoot directly up to Sukhāvatī instantly.

Some assert that this is the same as *nirvāṇa*, but others are not so sure. Some confusion exists about *nirvāṇa*, a term which one occasionally hears pronounced *nirmāṇ* (sic).[42] On the one hand, *nirvāṇ juye* is used as a euphemism for the dead so that some believe it simply means 'to die'; on the other hand, most know, and say immediately, that *nirvāṇa* means not coming back, i.e. not being reborn. Jog Maya argued as follows:

> *Nirvāṇa* means not having to come back. Sukhāvatī *bhuvan* is the place of Amitābha-Karuṇāmaya [sic], who is the god most worthy of respect and saves even the ghosts (*pret*) and is a *bodhisattva*. In order to become a Buddha you have to be a *bodhisattva* and fulfil the moral perfections, and for that you need to take birth outside Sukhāvatī [so *nirvāṇa* and Sukhāvatī are not the same].

On the other hand, a Vajrācārya man who works in a bank quoted the

Dhammapada's '*nirvāṇa* is the highest happiness (*sukha*)' and argued that this must be the same as Sukhāvatī: since there is no mental or bodily suffering in Sukhāvatī what difference is there between this and *nirvāṇa*?

Other Sanskrit terms used in learned and pious talk for the state of liberation are: *nirvāṇapada, Buddhapada, mokṣa, mukti.*

4.3.11 The six 'destinations' or rebirths

Ideas of hell (*naraka*) are equally imprecise. One Vajrācārya priest said that Yama rules over hell and there are four doors, of which the northern one is the best to enter. According to doctrine, known and explained by the learned, there are six possible 'destinations' or rebirths (*gati*) after death: gods (*deva*), demons (*daitya*),[43] men (*manuṣya*), animals (*tiryak*), ghosts (*preta*), and hell (*naraka*).[44] In the context of devotion to Karuṇāmaya it is often said that reciting his six-syllabled mantra (OṂ MAṆI PADME HŪṂ) frees one from each of the six rebirths.

The term *agati*, literally 'lacking rebirth', tends to be used of a person who ends up as a ghost through an untimely death. Girls who die during the course of the twelve-day Confinement ceremony, and have to be buried in the basement of the house where this occurs, since they may not be taken out where men will see them, are thought to become particularly troublesome and long-lasting ghosts of this sort.

4.4 The hierarchy of interpretations

It may be wondered by those who know other Buddhist societies, whether Newar Buddhists believe it is possible to transfer merit. The answer to this question is similar to the answer to the question whether Newar Buddhists regard the Buddha as man or god. It can best be approached by first considering Gombrich's (1971: 4–5) distinction between cognitive and affective beliefs. In Theravāda Buddhism the cognitive position, that is, the scriptural teaching which Theravāda Buddhists believe on a conscious and cognitive level, is that merit cannot be transferred and that the Buddha was a man who is now dead and enlightened and is therefore beyond the reach of prayer or entreaty. All that can be done is to give the dead the opportunity to rejoice in merit, should they happen to be ghosts hanging around the vicinity. They will thereby gain merit themselves to allow them to improve their position. It is fair to conclude however that, affectively or unconsciously, Theravāda Buddhists 'believe' that merit can be transferred and that the Buddha is more than merely a supremely meritorious dead man, since they keep up certain ritual activities which imply the beliefs that cognitively they reject (Gombrich 1971: 226–43; cf. Obeyesekere 1966: 5, 8).

Southwold (1983: 167–8), while allowing that this interpretation is 'rather persuasive', has criticized Gombrich's distinction for confusing emotions with beliefs, and for implying that Theravāda Buddhists do not really believe what they say they believe. It may well be that referring to 'affective beliefs' is terminologically unfortunate; but that is no reason to deny that one may 'feel that' as well as 'think that' something is the case. Nor does the distinction require one to say that Theravādins 'really believe' what they feel to be so, whereas what they say they believe is an illusion. The heart may have its reasons, and these may simply conflict with the head, without necessarily being primary in a causal or any other sense. Spiro (1982: 153–4), confronted by Theravāda Buddhism in Burma, comes up with a similar distinction between belief, on the one hand, and conviction or motivation, on the other: in his case, however, he is concerned to explain the latter in terms of childhood experience. From a very different perspective, Collins (1982: 152) argues that the distinction between cognitive and affective beliefs is required by the very structure of Theravāda Buddhism as an intellectual and religious system. Theravāda Buddhism teaches that one has no self; yet it tacitly permits the affective notion that there is a perduring self, transmigrating over many births, in order to impart the many moral teachings Buddhists need to learn and accept before they are ready to go ahead and truly internalize the truth of non-self through meditation.

It seems that one of the crucial innovations of Mahāyāna Buddhism was to abandon the stress on maintaining the cognitive position. Although in Mahāyāna Buddhism the cognitive position of Theravāda Buddhism continued, it was no longer taboo to refer to the Buddha as if he were a god, or to assert explicitly, in order to encourage lay devotion, that merit can be transferred. Instead of two beliefs, one cognitive, avowed, and universally accepted, the other affective, implicit, and inferable only in certain cases, we have instead a *hierarchy* of avowed cognitive beliefs, sometimes indeed held simultaneously. By scripture and in ritual the laity are encouraged to devotion based on the lowest and most literal-minded level of belief.

This shift of emphasis means that the doctrinal position of Mahāyāna Buddhism is much less clear than that of Theravāda Buddhism. One consequence has been the emergence of elaborate ritual, which directly satisfies lay needs to see the Buddha as a god and to transfer merit. Newar Buddhists certainly believe that they can assist their ancestors through performing Ancestor Worship and other rites described below (§7.3). A Vajrācārya priest argued to me and to others present at a regular performance that the ancestors would benefit wherever they were, that is, even if they had been reborn. All Vajrācāryas routinely argue this way. The argument is probably as old as any justification of ritual in India: it is found in the Viṣṇudharmasūtra (Kane 1941 IV: 340). However I also heard a Śākya woman arguing to her Vajrācārya priest that surely her deceased mother was reborn now, so that it was no longer necessary to give him the annual *nislāḥ* prestation; the priest wisely kept silent.

This argument depends on the view that gifts can only benefit the dead if they are ghosts (*pret*) and not otherwise (in that case only the givers benefit, because of their good intentions). Lewis (1984: 324) reports that Asan Tulādhars believe that '*śrāddha* offerings have no effectiveness unless the deceased is a *preta* . . . [I]f the dead are not *preta*s, then the offerings go to actual non-kin *preta*s, which is still meritorious for the dead and the living.' The argument that only ghosts can benefit from such offerings is, as noted above, a Theravāda doctrine. Undoubtedly the preaching of the Theravāda monks and nuns has had an effect on what Newar Buddhists believe today. This means that we cannot be sure what they believed fifty years ago: did some believe then, as they do now, that Ancestor Worship could not help ancestors at all unless they were a ghost? Or did they all accept the priestly assurance that the rite had an automatic effect experienced by the ancestors wherever they might be?

A similar ambivalence exists over the question of the Buddha's divinity. As pointed out above, unlike *bodhisattva*s, but like the great gods of Hinduism, the Buddha is in some contexts referred to with the suffix *dyaḥ* meaning god. At the same time it is common to hear the sentiment that the Buddha was a man. This indeed is the teaching of the Rebirth stories that Vajrācāryas recount to audiences of the pious. And it is *a fortiori* the message of the Theravāda monks. Newar Buddhists find themselves in a complex religious system which lays down numerous rituals of different sorts directed at numerous deities. Unlike Theravāda Buddhism, there is no single, repeatedly inculcated, doctrinal position on these practices. Rather there is a whole hierarchy of views from which one is free to articulate one's own preferred understanding of the purpose of it all. What in Theravāda societies the observer has to infer as an affective 'belief' or feeling is here explicitly stated; the degree to which it is considered to be a hortatory metaphor or taken as literally true varies according to context and actor.

5

Basic rituals of Newar Buddhism

Buddhism is basically a performing art.

Beyer, *The Cult of Tārā*, p. xii. (Copyright © 1973, The Regents of the University of California.)

In Chattisgarh religion is a thing done, not a thing believed . . .

Babb, *The Divine Hierarchy*, p. 31.

5.1 Sociological definitions

5.1.1 A sociological typology of ritual and ritual action

If worship is the most basic religious act, ritual may be defined as the combination of acts of worship of different sorts to form a whole. This omits any reference to the purpose, or rather purposes, of ritual; these will be dealt with below. As a preliminary approach, the different types of ritual encountered in Newar Buddhism are summarized in Figure 14.

The first and most important distinction for Newar Buddhists is that between obligatory and optional practices. The two types interact in that one may, as an act of free choice, undertake rituals which will henceforth be one's obligatory duty. Tantric Initiation, which in itself is optional, commits one to a burdensome regular daily worship for the rest of one's life; and for certain specified roles (practising Vajrācārya priests, monastery elders) taking initiation is itself compulsory. An ancestor's optional piety in founding a *guthi*, saddles his descendants with recurrent *guthi* obligations.

To do something optionally is usually expressed in Newari as doing a *pharmās* (or *pharmāy*), a word which derives from Persian via the Hindi *farmaiś*.[1] Doing what is obligatory is expressed simply by use of the Newari auxiliary verb *māle*. This is used with quite surprising frequency. I was taken aback during the festival of Mohanī when kites are flown from what

Figure 14. The main types of complex ritual among the Newars. Those rites normally or often requiring the presence of a priest have been marked with an asterisk.

Regular worship (*nitya pūjā*) – of an enshrined deity (*khe cā̃ykegu*) – of one's personal deity (*nhịkā̃ yā̃yegu*) Calendar festivals (*varṣakriyā, nakhaḥ cakhaḥ*) *Guthi* obligations (*guthipā*)* Life-cycle rituals (*saṃskāra, daśakarma*)*	OBLIGATORY
Chariot and palanquin festivals (*rath-* and *khatjātrā*)* Dance performances (*nāṭaka, pyākhā̃*)*	OBLIGATORY FOR PARTICIPANTS, OPTIONAL FOR SPECTATORS
Observances (*vrata, dhalā̃ danegu*)* Devotion to a deity (*sevā*), including recitation of chanted praises (*stotra, tutaḥ*) and participation in hymn singing (*bhajan*) Donation (to a temple, to monks, to a priest) (*dān*)* Tantric Initiation (*dīkṣā, dekhā*)* Text-reading (*pāth yākegu* or *pāthyākegu*)* Apotropaic rites such as Worship of the Nine Planets (*navagraha pūjā*)*	OPTIONAL

seems like every rooftop in Lalitpur, to be asked whether we in Britain also have to fly kites.[2] 'Have to?' I wanted to reply, 'What's "have to" got to do with it?' I found it hard to reconcile with the use of the verb denoting obligation the obvious pleasure the young men and boys of Lalitpur were deriving from flying kites (and from their attempts to cut the string of others' kites by rubbing their own string with paste and ground-up glass). I was still more surprised a few days later that, with Mohanī over, there was not a single kite to be seen, although conditions were still perfect for flying them. For Newars it is natural to describe all activity which occurs regularly as being 'done because it has to be done', i.e. it is part of tradition; no one would think of concluding from this that they should not enjoy it. Even kite-flying falls within this religious framework and even young men and boys, who normally show no special interest in religion, accept this; people say that kites have to be flown at Mohanī to let Indra (the god of rain) know that it has rained enough, that the monsoon may finish. Furthermore, it is entirely natural for Newars to think that what one group – caste, ethnic group, lineage, or family – has to do, others do not (as described above, §3.5).

Chariot festivals and dance performances fall between compulsory and

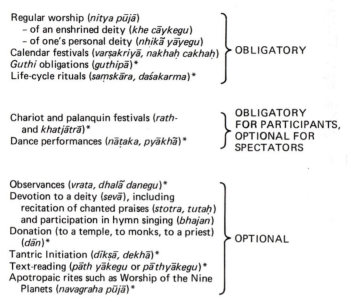

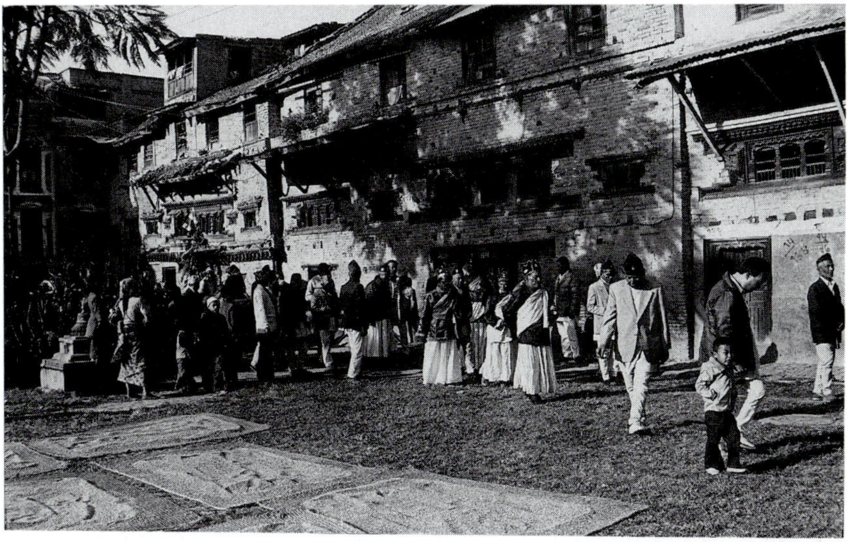

Plate 1. The annual procession of the deity of Kwā Bāhāḥ as it passes through Nyākhācuk. This takes place before the feast of all the members of Kwā Bāhāh on Kārttik śukla 10. A small silver image is carried in a palanquin as a representative of the main deity and the procession is led by the elders of the monastery. Offerings are thrown to the deity from windows; the more devout descend and make offerings directly onto the palanquin.

Plate 2. Power-Place Worship. At the end of the procession of devotees comes the sponsor (*kaji*), here Krishna Lal Maharjan, the head of the Maharjan music group of Ī Bahī Thūr in the north of Lalitpur. Assisted by his Vajrācārya priest he offers holy water, puffed rice, and white jasmine ('argha yāye') to each shrine. This is the shrine known as 'the gate of Yama [Lord of the underworld]'. In the background is the temple of Cākwāḥdyaḥ, Tanga Bāhāh.

Plate 3. The chariot festival of Karuṇāmaya-Matsyendranāth as it passes through Thaina. The chariot of Karuṇāmaya comes first, that of Cākwāḥdyaḥ behind. (Photo by Stephen D. Ryan.)

Plate 4. Two young girls make clay *caitya*s as part of the Observance of (making) a Hundred Thousand Caityas. This is performed every year during the month of Gū̃lā in Cikā̃ Bahī, Lalitpur. Every morning women come to make *caitya*s. At the end of the month there is a two-day fast and worship and on the final day of Gū̃lā the *caitya*s are taken in procession and consigned to the holy river Bāgmatī.

Plate 5. A lineage of Maharjans performing their Lineage Deity Worship on Guita hill, Lalitpur, on the festival of Pāsā Cahre (Piśāca Caturdaśī). Other Farmer lineages can be seen doing the same in the background.

Plate 6. The shrine of Caṇḍamahāroṣaṇa, labelled as Śaṃkaṭā, in Ilā Nani. Caṇḍamahāroṣaṇa acts as a public face of Cakrasaṃvara and his consort, Vajravārāhī, who are enshrined immediately above him in the Kwā Bāhāḥ subsidiary Tantric shrine.

Plate 7. The Tantric god-house (*āgȧ̆ chẽ*) of a lineage of Śākyas who are members of Kwā Bāhāḥ. Most of them live in Nāg Bāhāḥ or Ilā Nani. This lineage no longer performs Tantric worships together. In the past they would have met here several times a year. The election posters date from the local elections held earlier that year (1986).

Plate 8. The senior (unwidowed) woman of a Śākya lineage comprising three households offers *pācāku* after a ritual (in this case a Sixteen Ancestor Worship endowed by *guthi*). The family priest sits at the head of the line, then his assistant, then the senior male who acted as sponsor (*jaymā*), then other males present, in order of seniority.

Plate 9. A well-known Vajrācārya Tantric healer, here treating a Tamang woman who complained that her breast-milk did not flow.

Figure 15. Types of religion from the point of view of the individual Newar Buddhist (cf. Figure 1).

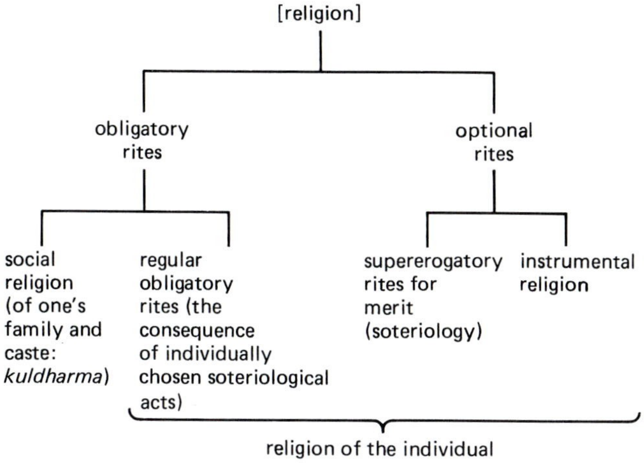

optional practices. They are usually obligatory for the main participants or dancers, and there may be aspects of them (e.g. holding a family feast) which are obligatory for others too; but watching them and coming for worship are for the most part optional.

The distinction between obligatory and optional rites is part of the everyday language of all Newars. It reflects in part the religious typology outlined in the introduction. One has to perform the rites of social religion because one is a member of a given group: these comprise the obligatory rites. Optional rites are typically performed by individuals, seeking either merit or salvation (soteriological religion), or some worldly end, most commonly the cure of an illness (instrumental religion). Thus one could turn Figure 1 of chapter 1 upside down as shown in Figure 15 in order to represent the distinctions made by Newars.[3]

There is a Hindu scriptural typology, accepted both by Vedic and by Tantric theorists, which divides ritual into the regular (*nitya*), the occasional (*naimittika*), and the desire-fulfilling (*kāmya*) (Gupta 1979: 124–6). Occasional ritual refers to the elaborate rites performed to one's chosen deity on holy days. Regular ritual is the abbreviated form of the occasional rite and is performed on ordinary days. Alternatively, 'regular' ritual covers both what occurs daily and that performed on holy days, whereas 'occasional ritual' refers to any rite which has to be held because of a non-regular 'occasion' (Skt. *nimitta*), e.g. initiations, consecrations, expiations, or popular festivals.[4] In all interpretations, desire-fulfilling rituals are those performed in order to obtain a particular worldly benefit. These scriptural typologies are narrower than that used by Newars because they focus strictly on the individual: desire-fulfilling rites correspond to what I call instrumental religion, but regular and occasional rites are only one type of obligatory rite (that incumbent upon the individual) and leave out of account the inherited religion of the group.

This tends to confirm Dumont's (1980: 275) suggestion that within Indian religion the renouncer, or individual-outside-the-world, was the creator and innovator whereas the Brahman-within-the-world merely preserved what the renouncer created. At any rate, the creators of learned concepts, whether technically renouncers or not, seem always to have adopted an individualistic, and not a group-orientated, viewpoint in the analysis of ritual.[5] This is equally true of Tantric scriptures, even though, as discussed below (chapter 11), Tantric ritual is used as the religion of groups and to sanctify group boundaries. Not only do traditional Hindu typologies take the viewpoint of the individual, they presume an advanced and serious practitioner. Thus they ignore the possibility of non-repeated, supererogatory religious action (as typically by a lay person): for example, performing or sponsoring a meritorious rite once, without undertaking subsequent obligations. In other words, the scriptural classifications have no term for 'optional' other than *kāmya*, 'desire-fulfilling', i.e. those rites which I have labelled instrumental.

The sceptic may well ask here: How distinct are these types of ritual? Are no soteriological or instrumental rites compulsory? Are there no group rituals which are soteriological or instrumental in intention? The answer is 'Yes' to both the latter questions. In the past it seems that nearly all Vajrācāryas took Tantric Initiation and it must therefore have been treated like an obligatory life-cycle rite. Monastic Initiation was in origin an optional rite – and this is remembered – but it has become a compulsory, life-cycle ritual. It is harder to think of instrumental rites which are compulsory or of compulsory rites which began life as instrumental rites, but it is certainly true that specific parts of compulsory rites are instrumental (e.g. those actions intended to prevent supernatural obstacles). There are also examples of soteriological and instrumental rites carried out by groups. For instance, the organization of many Observances is a complex and expensive affair and is therefore often carried out collectively. It is also common for *guthi*s to be established to ensure the annual performance of the rite (e.g. the annual Observance to Vasundharā). But in each case, except for members of the *guthi*, participation is optional; and even membership of the *guthi* is optional. Overtly,

Observances are about acquiring merit and can be classed as soteriological. It is well known, however, that many women who participate are motivated instrumentally, that is, they participate for self-regarding worldly ends, such as the birth of a son; and in this they are encouraged by the scriptures, the myths, and the priests of Newar Buddhism. In the past it sometimes happened that a group rite would be performed for explicit instrumental ends: during an epidemic a locality would get together and worship the local protective deity (*kṣetrapāl*).

These examples of group activity do not undermine the basic typology. They do not invalidate the general rule that instrumental and soteriological religious action is optional, whereas social religion is obligatory and imposed on the individual by virtue of group membership. In the putative counterexamples considered, the groups were not permanent but simply collections of individuals pooling their effort. Furthermore, the processes of social life are complex: the fact that a rite originally intended as soteriological has become social, or that social rites are occasionally justified in soteriological or even instrumental terms, does not of itself show the terminology to be inappropriate. It shows rather that the typology is made up of ideal types; actual social processes are usually justified in terms of more than one type, and the determination of which is predominant is a question of emphasis and interpretation.

5.1.2 An analysis of religious roles

Religious roles come in different forms and, as an added complication, the same set of relations can be described in alternative and incommensurable ways. The most commonly used vocabulary is that of family priest (*purohit*) and hereditary patron (*jajmān, jaymā*). These are Hindu terms, Vedic in origin, familiar throughout South Asia. The etymology of the term for patron (Skt. *yajamāna*) is 'one who sacrifices for his own benefit (by means of others)' as opposed to ritual specialists who sacrifice on behalf of their patron. Priests, Barbers, and Kāpālī all refer to those families which are obliged to call them on specified ritual occasions as 'their *jajmān*'. In complex rituals when a Vajrācārya priest performs a ritual for his patron, *jajmān* designates a ritual role: the *jajmān* sits next to the priest, keeping him on his or her right-hand side, and performs the ritual according to the priest's instructions. In this sense the short form *jaymā* is more often used ('jaymā cwane', to take the role of *jaymā*). Normally the (male) head of household (or lineage) should fill this role, but if he is too busy a younger man or senior female may do so (see Plate 12). Both priest and *jaymā* have to fast until the ritual is over.

Table 5.1 *Five ways of describing roles in the religion of Newar Buddhists.*

Context	Monastic (Way of Disciples)	Temple	Other Buddhist rituals (Great Way and Diamond Way)	Social relations (Hindu)	Medical
Superior role	*bhikṣu* (monk)	*dyaḥpāḥlāḥ* or *pūjārī* (temple priest)	*guru* (teacher)	*purohit* (family priest)	*vaidya* (healer)
Inferior role	*upāsak* (layman), *gṛhasthī* (house-holder)	*bhakta* or *bhaktajan* (devotee[s])	*śiṣya* (pupil)	*jajmān* or *jaymā* (patron, sponsor or parish-ioner)	*kyā̃ waipī̃* (lit. those who come to show, patients)
Prestation from inferior to superior	*dān* (alms)	*chāyegu* or *pūjā sārdām* (offerings)	*dakṣiṇā* (fee) and *dān*	mainly *dakṣiṇā*, on occasion *dān*	*dā̃* money (or goods)
In return	blessing	*prasād* of deity	ritual, teaching, blessing	ritual, teaching, blessing	cure, counter-magic
Examples of context	Pañcadān, Samyak (§6.3)	Temple worship (§6.2)	Observances (§7.5), Tantric Initiation (§9.3)	Any life-cycle rite (§7.2–3)	When ill or other crisis (§11.4)

This framework of priest and patron is the most obvious one, but to remain within it, and to treat it as a sufficient description of Newar Buddhism, would be a mistake; the same mistake as to accept as definitive the Hindu names, such as Matsyendranāth, which Buddhists use for the consumption of outsiders. Built into Newar Buddhists' rites are two other types of vocabulary, and there are at least two further religious or quasi-religious frameworks which also need to be mentioned. All five are summarized in Table 5.1.

Within the context of a Buddhist ritual, if it is an Observance or similar rite, the priest addresses the participants as pupils (*śiṣya*, usually pronounced *sikhi*); and, as noted above (§2.6), a Vajrācārya priest is addressed by his patrons, and often politely by others, as *guruju*, reverend teacher, *guru* being the term always coupled with *śiṣya*. This is quite a different sort of vocabulary from that of priest and patron. Although *guru* may (and usually does) denote one's *purohit*, and *śiṣya* denotes, *inter alia*, one's *jajmān*s, the two sets of terms are not interchangeable: the terms 'teacher' and 'pupil' cannot be used to describe the social and hereditary relationship of priest and patron.

A third type of vocabulary is also, though more rarely, used. This alone is distinctively and uniquely Buddhist. In this Śākyas and Vajrācāryas are monks (*bhikṣu*). This is usually only implied, though very strongly implied, by the context, rather than actually stated. Consequently it is rare to hear the correlative term, *upāsak*, layman, though it is used to justify the position of the Tulādhar *et al.* as high-caste Buddhists ranking just below the Śākyas and Vajrācāryas, and it is sometimes given as the origin of their caste name 'Urāy'. In other contexts *bhikṣu* is sometimes contrasted with *gṛhasthī*, householder (often pronounced *gristi*). In rites such as Pañcadān and Samyak, Śākyas and Vajrācāryas are both monks (receiving *dān*) and householders (giving it). Often those who give *dān* or make offerings are referred to simply as devotees (*bhaktajan*).

Two other types of vocabulary are not specifically Buddhist, but need to be mentioned since Buddhists fill both kinds of role. The first has to do with temple worship. Guardians of a temple or monastic complex, are called *dyaḥpāḥlāḥ*, as we have seen above (§3.1). Both Vajrācāryas and Śākyas are god-guardians of monasteries, but only Vajrācāryas may be family priests (*purohit*). Those who come to offer at a temple are not always inferior in social status. Indeed, at a Mother Goddess shrine outside the city, where the guardians are Untouchables, almost all the devotees who visit it will be superior in social status. Nonetheless, there is a sense in which the guardian is closer to the deity than the casual devotee, and although the schema is slightly forced, the devotees are marked down as the inferior role in Table 5.1.

The second type of non-Buddhist vocabulary is the medical. There are many healers of different kinds all going under the name of *vaidya*. Some of these are traditional doctors following the Āyurveda system, some are Vajrācāryas practising a mixture of this and Tantric healing, and others are folk healers (§11.4).

Part of the time I have followed accepted anthropological usage and translated *jajmān* as 'patron'. This is not ideal as one is not dealing here with patron-client relations of the sort discussed by students of politics. Many observers in Nepal and India have found it more natural to refer to the *jajmān* as the client of the Vajrācārya or Brahman priest, since the latter is superior in status.[6] In the Hindu case *jajmān* refers back to classical Vedic theory, in which the King is the paradigmatic patron who sacrifices by means of his Brahman priests. As is well known, this is the model for the Indian *jajmānī* system, that is, the sacrificially and religiously defined division of labour underlying the caste system. In the present case, as Table 5.1 shows, the Hindu vocabulary of *jajmān* and *purohit* is an outer layer, albeit a necessary one, which is replaced, in religious contexts, by the vocabulary of preceptor and disciple. Consequently, I have not stuck rigidly to the translation 'patron': in the context of the rite I have often translated 'sponsor' and on other occasions I have translated 'parishioner', which brings out the responsibility a Vajrācārya priest has for his patrons' spiritual welfare.

There are other terms which are difficult to translate without misleading or unwanted overtones. One such is *dān*, which I have variously translated as alms-giving, donations, gifts, and charity depending on context (it refers both to the gift and the giving). Southwold (1983: 214–18) argues, controversially for the Sri Lankan context, that 'priest' is a better translation of *bhikṣu* than 'monk', which he reserves for that tiny minority of virtuosi who live in the jungle and meditate. He would presumably argue that *a fortiori* Śākyas should be called priests, not monks, that *bare chuyegu* should be called Caste Initiation, not Monastic Initiation, and that it is a travesty to translate *vihāra* in the Nepalese context as 'monastery' rather than 'temple'. In these cases, however, I prefer the translation which emphasizes monasticism in every case, because it brings out the claim being made – ritually and socially – by the use of these terms.[7]

5.2 Religious and liturgical typologies of ritual and ritual action

5.2.1 A Newar Buddhist typology

We have already seen one way in which the doctrine of Ways (*yāna*) is used by knowledgeable Newar Buddhists to order the different types of god they worship (Table 4.1 above). Underlying the Three Ways is a very basic opposition, already referred to (§4.2), between the exoteric and the esoteric. The elements of this opposition are summarized in Table 5.2.

These differences are very clear to those Newars who have taken Tantric Initiation. Even those who have not are aware that substances required in one context are forbidden in another. All are aware of the distinction between exoteric (*bāhya*) and esoteric (*guhya*) which, as M.R. Allen (1975: 56) and Vergati (1979: 127) have observed, is fundamental to the religion and society of the Newars. Those who do not know these Sanskritic terms

Table 5.2 *Ideal-typical contrasts between Śrāvakayāna rites on the one hand and Vajrayāna rites on the other.*

Rites of the Disciples' Way	*Rites of the Diamond Way*
Worship only using pure substances	Worship must include impure substances, in particular meat and alcohol
Dance and song forbidden	Dance and song essential parts of worship
Chastity required	Sexual imagery central
Calmness required: hostility to possession	Controlled possession by deity required of women, permitted for men
Worship (*pūjā*)	Yogic Visualization (*sādhana*)
Aim: merit and blessing of deity	Aim: power, liberation through identification with deity
Access open to all clean castes	Access only to the initiated, initiation only for high castes and specified others

Note: In practice Newar Buddhist exoteric rites are Śrāvakayāna during the rites themselves, but bracketed by an unoffensive exoteric version of the Vajrayāna (cf. §9.1). In practice esoteric rites are Vajrayānist from start to finish but incorporate certain values of the Śrāvakayāna (worship, pursuit of merit).

express the opposition simply as that between what one may see ('swaye jyū') and what one may not see ('swaye ma jyū'). Often indeed it is the middle and lower castes, who may not receive Tantric Initiation, who seem to exclude outsiders most fiercely. Perhaps it is because they do not have a more strictly religious sphere in which to practise the exoteric/esoteric distinction that they insist all the more strongly on keeping non-members out of their *guthi* feasts (cf. §11.1).

There are inevitably certain overlaps to the oppositions outlined in Table 5.2. The distinction between the two types of rite is not absolute. Many esoteric rites are undertaken for merit. Both exoteric and esoteric rites contain both Worship and Visualization; what differs is the emphasis each receives. The line between the esoteric and the exoteric is laid down slightly differently by different groups and in different contexts.

Most ordinary exoteric rites of Newar Buddhism combine elements of both Disciples' Way and Diamond Way. For the duration of the rite the rules of the Disciples' Way hold force. At its end elements – certain elements only – of the Diamond Way are obligatory. There is an exoteric form of the (esoteric) Diamond Way in which Tantric deities appear openly, but without their female partner (this is explained below, §9.1). In an Observance participants must eat only pure food, refrain from sex, and so on. On the final day, to mark the Observance's end, they consume a feast with meat and alcohol, which is considered the blessing (*prasād*) of the goddess. In exoteric contexts like this only these elements of the Diamond

Way (meat, alcohol, disguised use of Visualization by the priest alone) are permitted. Dance, song, and sexual symbolism belong to the purely esoteric sphere. This tradition – observing Disciples' Way practices within a limited context and framed by Diamond Way ones – is, as a whole, characterized as the Great Way.

Following the analysis given here it is possible to see what place Newar Buddhism gives to the values of Theravāda Buddhism. One cannot be a pure follower of the Śrāvakayāna in Newar Buddhism: the Disciples' Way is always followed only within the context of a given ritual and is always brought to an end by a rite with Diamond Way implications. In fact, as explained below (§10.2), it also cannot begin without the Tantric ministrations of a Vajrācārya priest. This applies even to rites such as Monastic Initiation, and even, at the limit, to the daily ritual of a monastery deity. In this broader sense there are only two kinds of rite: exoteric rites, i.e. rites of the Great Way which bracket practices of the Disciples' Way in a Diamond Way framework; and esoteric rites which are Vajrayānist from start to finish, but which are often carried out in the devotional and merit-making spirit characteristic of exoteric rites. Thus the oppositions outlined in Table 5.2 define two ideal types. In reality, when exoteric and esoteric rites are compared in terms of these distinctions, the difference is one of emphasis and attitude.

Michael Allen (1973: 13) characterizes Tantric logic, i.e. the ritual logic of the esoteric Diamond Way, as based on inversions of monastic, i.e. Disciples' Way, rules. It is perhaps more exact to say that it is based on infractions of a taboo. They are precisely controlled infractions. Newar Buddhists, like all Buddhists, are hostile to licentiousness (cf. below, §9.2, 10.4). Esoteric rites, although using substances forbidden in the exoteric sphere, are governed by rules as strict in their way.

5.2.2 A local Hindu typology

The above account in terms of the purely Buddhist concepts of the Three Ways can be contrasted with a more worldly or Hindu classification. R.P. Pradhan (1986), on the basis of material from the Hindu Newars of Kathmandu, divides rituals into life-cycle rites and 'cosmic' rituals (i.e. public festivals). Following Das (1982), Pradhan (1986: 60–70) shows how Newar life-cycle rites can be analysed in terms of two oppositions: pure/impure and auspicious/inauspicious. First Rice-Feeding, Loincloth Worship, Mock Marriage, and Marriage are both auspicious and pure. Birth Purification and Confinement are auspicious but impure. Ancestor Worship is pure but inauspicious. The rituals immediately following a death are both impure and inauspicious. Pure rites begin with purifications ('nisī yāyegu') and, when auspicious, end with the consumption of the good-luck foods (*sagã*). Impure rites, by contrast, begin with the event incurring impurity and end with purifications called *bẽkegu*.

Public rituals, Pradhan argues, are orientated not by axes of purity/impurity or auspiciousness/inauspiciousness but by the opposition of the good and bad sacred. He distinguishes six types: calendrical festivals, chariot and palanquin festivals, fairs, pilgrimages, Observances, and recitations of scriptures. These are often combined: many Observances are performed in the context of a pilgrimage (*tīrtha yātrā*); other Observances occur as a calendrical festival, as do many chariot festivals.

The basic distinction underlying Pradhan's analysis, between life-cycle rituals (*saṃskāra*) and public festivals (*varṣakriyā, nakhaḥ cakhaḥ*), is certainly built in to both Buddhism and Hinduism as practised by the Newars. His other analytical distinctions, though not explicitly articulated by Newars themselves, are also valid for both Buddhists and Hindus.

5.2.3 A Tibetan Tantric Buddhist typology

Another typology is possible, derived from the different uses to which Tantric (esoteric) Buddhist ritual is put. Here I follow Beyer (1973: 255–7ff.), while adapting his vocabulary.[8] Beyer's typology reproduces the terms Tibetans evolved to describe the rituals they inherited from India. Such a systematic terminology does not exist among the Newars, but since their ritual is essentially of the same type the typology can be applied to them also, as illustrated in Table 5.3. Many rituals fulfil 'functions' of several types, but they can be classified according to the function which is predominant.

This categorization of Tantric Buddhist ritual functions corresponds to the types of religion outlined above (§1.1, 2.7). The 'ritual' function of ritual (category II) predominates in social religion: that is, where rites are performed according to a regular calendar for no other reason than that they always are performed at those particular times. The function of 'magical empowerment' (III) is one of the ways that Vajrācārya priests perform instrumental rites on behalf of their parishioners when they have a particular need. The 'freelance, non-liturgical' function (IV) corresponds to the similar, instrumental use of ritual by self-chosen healers and mediums.

Such a framework analyses ritual from the point of view of the advanced Tantric practitioner. Exoteric ritual only fits into this framework to the extent that it is effected by esoteric means. The recurrent rituals performed by Vajrācāryas fit well into category II because they depend on the priest's

Table 5.3 *A typology of Tantric Buddhist rituals according to predominant 'function', adapted from Beyer 1973: 257.*

Type of ritual	*Locus of power*	*How mantras are viewed*	*Examples*
I SOTERIO-LOGICAL	self	as contemplative and purificatory	daily worship, supererogatory practices such as *puraścaraṇ cwanegu*
II RECURRENT RITUAL	'in front' i.e. worship of an image	as effective in evoking deities	Regular worship of important deities, life-cycle rites
III MAGICAL EMPOWERMENT	in objects (or persons) to be permanently empowered	as effective and useful	initiations, consecrations of deities, empowerment of thread (*pasūkā*)
IV FREELANCE NON-LITURGICAL USE	aspects of profane world	as effective and useful	use of ritual for healing, black or white magic, alchemy

use of esoteric powers. Rites such as Observances (*vrata*) are from the lay participants' point of view wholly non-Tantric expressions of devotion. They cannot easily be ascribed to one or other of these categories. They are soteriological (although often performed with some worldly end in mind), but are carried on at a lower level where there is no intimation of self-divinization. This self-divinization is a crucial part of Tantric practice (§10.2) and is implied by saying that the locus of power is one's 'self'.

5.2.4 A typology of ritual acts

In spite of the fundamental distinction between esoteric and exoteric, all rites are built up in a very similar way out of units that I shall call 'elements'. One could define an element as the smallest meaningful unit of a complex ritual.[9] These elements can be divided into two types, which would probably be recognized by most Newar Buddhists (though they might well wonder what was to be gained by such an exercise). The first type consists in the worshipper offering a given substance (e.g. rice grains, water, vermilion) while the priest recites the appropriate verse and/or mantra and, where necessary, displays the appropriate hand gesture (*mudrā*). It is worth noting that it is the mantra which is believed to be crucial and must be correct, whereas there is greater variability in the hand gestures. Sound is more fundamental than 'form' in the Tantric Buddhist worldview. The mantra is crucial for evoking the deity, and is often considered to *be* the deity.

Buddhist liturgical tradition recognizes several different types of the mantras relating to a given deity. The two most important types are the 'heart-seed' or 'seed' (*hṛdbīja* or *bīja*) mantra, and the 'heart' (*hṛdaya*) mantra. The former is a single syllable used to generate the deity, the mandala, and indeed the whole universe (see §10.2); the latter is longer, usually made up of several syllables beginning with OṀ and ending with HŪṀ, PHAṬ, or SVĀHĀ. The heart mantra corresponds to what in other Tantric traditions is known as the 'root' (*mūla*) mantra (but, confusingly, Vajrayāna texts, in some cases at least, specify a root mantra distinct from the heart mantra). Sometimes only the main deity of a mandala has both seed and heart mantras, and the deities of his or her retinue or mandala have only heart mantras. In other cases both the main deity and the others have both kinds of mantra. A third important type of mantra is the 'all-purpose' (*sārvakarmika*) mantra: this is the mantra which should be recited when no other mantra has been specified. Usually a principal deity's all-purpose mantra is the heart mantra of one of the divinities from his or her retinue. For instance, the all-purpose mantra of the esoteric divinity Cakrasaṃvara is that of the *ḍākinī* Khaṇḍarohā.[10]

The second type of ritual element is a kind of prayer (*binti*) where the worshipper sits with palms together, holding rice grains between the palms, while the priest recites several verses; only at the end does the worshipper offer the rice. While I refer to this as 'prayer', it should be borne in mind that the worshipper does not conduct an inner dialogue with a divine person, but simply sits while the priest recites. Ideally the worshipper should concentrate respectfully on the deity. In practice his or her mind is often quite blank, if facial expression is anything to go by. Nonetheless the translation 'prayer' is apposite. *Binti* in fact means 'request' or 'entreaty', deriving, according to Turner (1980: s.v.), from the Sanskrit *vijñaptiḥ* with the same meaning. A *bintipatra* is a written request for help or intervention submitted to the ruler or other powerful person by a group of subjects, a practice still common in Nepal.

Within these two basic kinds of ritual element, further distinctions can be made. These are suggested by the ritual handbooks used by priests and by the uses to which different offerings are put. They arc illustrated in Figure

Figure 16. An analysis of different types of 'element' which make up a complex ritual.

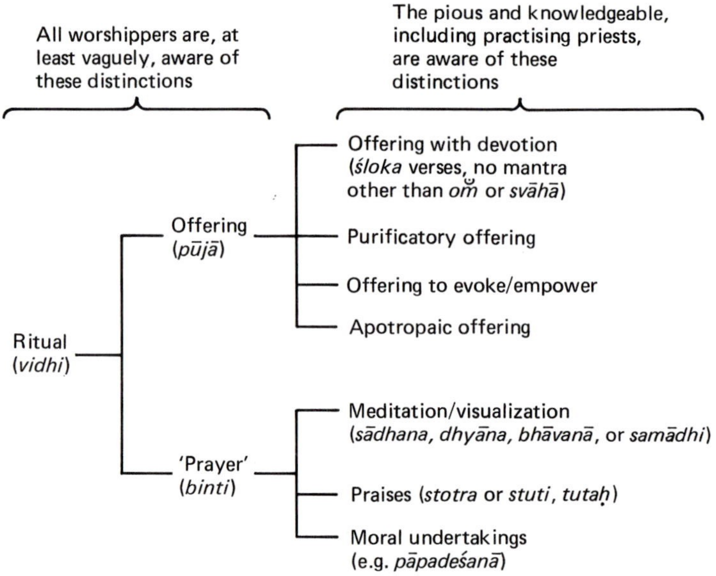

16. The different types of 'prayer' shown there are based on terms found in the ritual handbooks themselves. The distinctions are supported by an analysis of the Sanskrit utterances. By contrast, the distinctions between types of offering are my own. They are not found in the handbooks, but they are based on explanations given by priests (e.g. 'This purifies the worshipper'; 'this makes Vajrasattva present'; 'this prevents obstacles'). The categories are not necessarily exclusive (they are, once again, ideal types): a ritual act can purify by making a deity present; the meditation on a deity includes praises, and is also meant to make the deity present.

5.3 Basic rituals of Newar Buddhism

Having presented broad categories of ritual (sociological, Buddhological, Hindu), of ritual roles, and of types of ritual action, it remains to discuss the basic named rituals of Newar Buddhism. The three most important are the offering of the *guru maṇḍala*, Flask Worship (*kalaśa pūjā*), and Fire Sacrifice (*homa*).[11] It is from these basic rituals that others, such as Observances, life-cycle rituals, or Tantric Initiation, are built up.

All complex rites begin with the *guru maṇḍala*. The sponsor performs it under the direction of his priest. The priest is present in order to make the ritual happen on behalf of his parishioner. His responsibility for doing so is marked by the sponsor handing to him the Worship Plate (*pujābhaḥ*) immediately after the priest has located the ritual in time and space using the 'Adya Mahādāna' utterance described below (§7.1). By a kind of Chinese box arrangement, the *guru maṇḍala* ritual acts as a framework within which the rest of the ritual occurs: all of it except the final dismissal is performed at the beginning, and the final sections [(ix) and (x) below] are repeated with the dismissal (*visarjana*) at the end of the whole complex rite. However, there is a puzzle here. As Witzel (n.d.) has pointed out, rather than putting the dismissal of the *guru maṇḍala* at the very end, it comes before the dismissals of the Flask (*kalaśa-visarjana*) and of the Spirit-Offering (*bali-visarjana*). In other words, the dismissals occur in the same order as the original worship, and not in reverse order as one would expect with a true framing device.

What is here called Spirit-Offering (*bali*) refers in a Hindu context and generally in colloquial Newari to an animal sacrifice to a major deity. In strictly Buddhist ritual no such animal sacrifice occurs (although, as noted above, Vajrācārya priests do indeed oversee them). Thus in a Buddhist liturgical context *bali* refers to the apotropaic offerings made to ghosts or other spirits who might cause problems for the ritual (who are at a lower level of the pantheon than the Hindu divinities receiving *bali*). In a simple ritual such as the *guru maṇḍala* the *bali* is a small cone made of ground rice and water called *gwaḥjā*. It tends to be thought of both as the offering and the recipient of the offering at once. In large and complex rites a special Spirit-Offering including blood, alcohol, buffalo entrails, and beaten rice is made. Such offerings are also made by Hindus, and they are called *bau* (etymologically the same word as *bali*). Similar offerings are made outside the framework of organized rituals when someone has been 'attacked' ('punāḥ haḥgu') by the *chwāsā* god, causing sudden stomach pains. It is significant that while Spirit-Offerings are never made to Buddhas or other high, pure divinities, they are made to Tantric gods such as Cakrasaṃvara and Vajravārāhī. As fierce gods, they can receive such offerings, which are not acceptable to Buddhas.

The *guru maṇḍala* ritual is, then, the most common and basic Newar Buddhist ritual. It is performed by some pious Śākyas and Vajrācāryas as part of their personal daily ritual, and by all practising Vajrācārya priests. It is performed by husband and wife together onto a single mandala as part of the wedding ceremony (they share the mandala as they share polluted food, and as they are believed to share religious merit). All *buddhamārgī* Newars perform it, or have it performed for them, as part of life-cycle rituals. All those who participate in Buddhist Observances perform it as a preliminary to other worship. The *guru* in question is Vajrasattva, who is both the *guru* of Vajrācārya priests and an exoteric deity who is a kind of representation of the absolute in Vajrayāna Buddhism. The ritual can be broken down in the following sections:

(i) purification of the body, statement of intention (*saṃkalpa*), and obeisance to Vajrasattva and the Three Jewels;
(ii) worship of the conch;
(iii) lustration of mandala, further purification, and protective rites;
(iv) meditation on moral and worldly benefits of worship, worship of the sun and moon, purification of the hand;
(v) Visualization of Vajrasattva, worship of Vajrasattva;
(vi) building up of the Mount Meru mandala and offering it to Vajrasattva;
(vii) worship of the sixteen worship goddesses (*ṣoḍaśa lāsyā*);
(viii) obeisance to Vajrasattva and the Three Jewels, confession of sins, rejoicing in merit, *bodhisattva* vow, fuller confession of sins;
(ix) three Spirit-Offerings;
(x) recitation of the hundred-syllabled mantra (*śatākṣara*) of Vajrasattva as a request for forgiveness (for mistakes in the ritual);
(xi) dismissal.

There are both fuller and more compressed versions of the ritual. In some versions sections (v) and (vii) are omitted, and the verses recited in (viii), and the offerings made in (ix), are much abbreviated.

It will be seen that the ritual contains the moral undertakings of Mahāyāna Buddhism (iv, viii), but has placed them firmly within a ritualistic Vajrayānist framework. The Visualization of Tantric deities occurs, however, in a very simplified form. The full form of such Visualization, enacted in the *trisamādhi* ritual which prefaces both Flask Worship and Fire Sacrifice, is described below (§10.2). The way in which Mahāyānist goals are ritualized can be illustrated with verses recited in section (iv) which expound the Six Perfections:

Dānaṃ gomayam ambunā ca sahitaṃ
Śīlaṃ ca saṃmārjanaṃ
Kṣāntiḥ kṣudrapipīlakāpanayanaṃ
Vīryaṃ kriyotthāpanaṃ
Dhyānaṃ tatkṣaṇam ekacittakaraṇaṃ
Prajñā surekhojjvalā
Etāḥ pāramitāḥ ṣaḍ eva labhate
Kṛtvā muner maṇḍalam.

Charity is [purifying with] cowdung and water,
Moral conduct is sweeping,
Patience is removing tiny ants,
Heroism is carrying through the rite,
Trance is onepointedness of mind at that moment,
Wisdom is [drawing] splendid clear lines.
Whoever worships the mandala of the Buddha
Obtains all six of these moral perfections.[12]

By contrast, in the *bodhisattva* vow of section (viii) of the *guru maṇḍala* no such ritualized interpretation occurs. It is only ritualized in the practice of it, in that in most cases the priest reads out the verses in an incomprehensible mumble. Nonetheless these verses are known to, understood, and recited by pious Newar Buddhists.[13]

At all complex life-cycle rites at which a Vajrācārya is invited to officiate (except for Ancestor Worship), the minimum required performance is a Flask Worship. The Fire Sacrifice is rarer: a Fire Sacrifice includes Flask Worship, but not vice versa. Flask Worship is therefore the simpler, and cheaper, rite. The main object of worship in Flask Worship is, unsurprisingly, the Flask or holy waterpot, into which the Five Buddhas are summoned.[14] In more complex versions of the rite there are several flasks, of which one is designated the main Flask (*mū kalaś*). In secret rituals worship is directed to the Alcohol Pot (*thāpī*) filled with red beer, not water. This is the worship of Māmakī. The Alcohol Pot, though differently shaped, and differently named in Newari, is also called a flask, the 'secret flask' (*guhya kalaś*).

On either side of the main Flask the priest establishes various ritual implements, known collectively as *thāpā̃*.[15] These various implements are known to all by their Newari names; and it is known that they represent deities which the sponsor of the rite worships under the direction of the priest. The correspondences are shown in Table 5.4. Also often included is a Spirit-Offering container (*balipau*). Most lay people are unaware which gods the implements are supposed to represent, though they may have a vague idea about the Five Buddhas being in the Flask, and Guhyeśvarī in the Alcohol Pot. The same implements (except the Alcohol Pot) are also made use of by Newar Brahmans, though they worship them as different deities.

The implements are established in a space which has been purified with cowdung. Rice powder is used to draw swastikas and other designs in the places where the implements will be put. On top of these a 'throne' (*āsan*) of unhusked rice is strewn.[16] The implements are placed on top of this. The mouth of the Flask has a small clay saucer with unbroken husked rice, an

Figure 17. The worship implements (*thāpā̃*) as established for a Buddhist Kumārī Pūjā. Sketch by Carolyn Clarke.

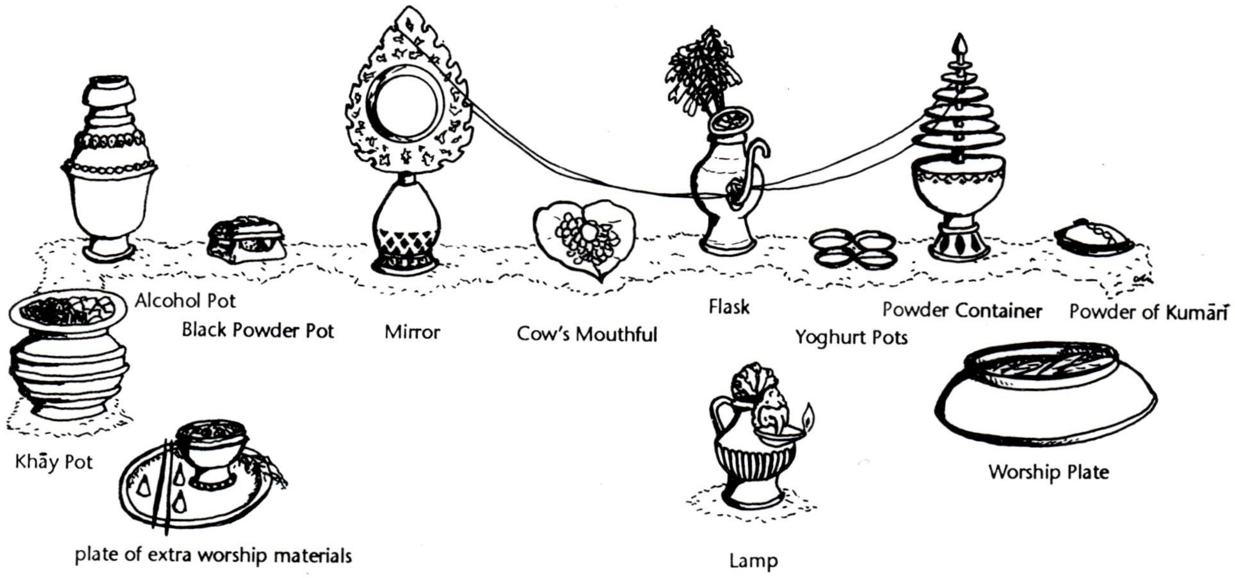

areca nut, and a coin (collectively called *kisalī*, 'rice saucer') on it. Around the implements five-coloured thread (*pañcasūtrakā*, *pasūkā*; *kā* = Nw. thread) is hung, the ball being balanced on the spout of the Flask. In front of the implements are placed rice cones (*gwaḥjā*). The rice cones represent Gaṇeś, the Eight Mothers, and Bhairava, protective deities who receive the offerings of meat and alcohol. The Vajrācārya priest sits facing the line of implements, with the sponsor on his left. The priest places his *vajra* immediately in front of him, and the bell to its left. (When this rite is performed in monasteries there is usually a small portable mandala to rest the *vajra* on.) Near this, established separately on a pile of rice, is the oil lamp (*sukundā*). Also established separately in front of him is a small clay saucer with the Five Products of a Cow (*pañcagavya*) and a sprig of *situ* (Skt. *durvā*) grass for sprinkling it. On the priest's right is placed the Worship Plate (*pujābhaḥ*) and near it the conch shell (*śaṅkha*) on a tripod.

The implements which represent Tantric deities, the Alcohol Pot and *Khāy* Pot, are established by Kwā Bāhāḥ Vajrācāryas in a continuous line with the other implements, but at an angle, forming an L-shape. Vajrācāryas from Bu Bāhāḥ are said to establish them separately. In some rituals, for instance the First Rice-Feeding, two further implements are included: two clay saucers, one upside down on top of the other, containing orange powder (*bhuyū sinhaḥ*); and an upturned clay saucer balanced on a kind of clay tripod with a burning wick beneath it to collect lampblack (*mwahanīsinhaḥ*). During First Rice-Feeding three feast shares to be taken to a shrine of Kumārī (*kumārībhū*) are also established, i.e. divinized, in the same way. At the purification on the fourth day after birth, none of these is needed, but instead a *kuli*-measure with broken rice is included. This is supposed to stand for the goddess Hārītī, under whose special protection the child is deemed to be in the first days after birth; it is poured away at the *chwāsā* deity. In the rite the *kuli*-measure is addressed as Ugracaṇḍī, which is the Tantric and liturgical Buddhist identity of the *chwāsā*.

Once the various ritual implements have been set out, the Flask Worship is accomplished in the following steps:

(i) declaration of intention (*saṃkalpa*) by the sponsor;
(ii) establishment of the powder;
(iii) performance of *guru maṇḍala* by sponsor;
(iv) performance of the Threefold Meditation (*trisamādhi*) by the priest;
(v) Visualization, purification, and worship of the Flask and other implements;
(vi) Visualization and worship of the Tantric implements;
(vii) Visualization and worship of any other objects of worship;
(viii) rites specific to the occasion;
(ix) concluding rites.

Table 5.4 *Worship implements (*thāpā*) used in Newar Buddhist rituals, with both Buddhist and Hindu divine identifications.*

English	*Newari*	*Sanskrit*	*Buddhist identity*	*Hindu identity*
Powder of Kumārī	*kumārīsinhaḥ*	*kumārī-candana*	Kumārī (i.e. Vajravārāhī)	Kumārī
Powder Container	*sinhamū*	*sindūra-bhāṇḍa* or *-kumbha*	Lakṣmī or Vasundharā	Gaurī
Four Yoghurt Pots	*sagã dhaupatti*	*saptavṛddhi-maṅgala-bhāṇḍa*	Four Brahmā Vihāras or Vasundharā[a]	Eight Cīrañjīvas
Flask	*kalaśa*	*amṛtaghaṭa*	Five Buddhas in form of seven oceans	Trimūrti (i.e. Brahmā, Viṣṇu, Maheśvara)
Cow's Mouthful	*gãlāybã*[b]	*gogrāsa*	Cow or Five Gomātā	Five Gomātā
Mirror[c]	*jwalā-nhāykã*	*darpaṇa-bhāṇḍa*	Lakṣmī	Sarasvatī
Black Powder Pot	*mwahanī sinhathala*	*mohany-ākarṣaṇa prajñopāya-sindūra*	Cakrasaṃvara	Śaktirūpa
Alcohol[d] Pot	*thāpī*	*guhya-kalaśa*	Guhyeśvarī or Vāruṇī/Māmakī	—
Khāy[e] Pot	*khāythala*	*sahaja-sukhabhāṇḍa*	Bhairava (= *upāya* = Hevajra)	Bhairavī
Lamp	*sukundā*	*dīpakuṇḍa*	Agni-vaiśvānara or Sūrya	Gaṇeś

Sources: Buddhist identifications and Sanskrit names were provided by Asha Kaji Vajracharya, Hindu identifications by Bharat Kanta Sharma. Other informants gave slightly varying identifications: for example, a less learned Vajrācārya priest identified the Cow's Mouthful as the earth and the *Khāy* Pot as Vajranairātmyā. For some of the verses used in worshipping these implements, see the appendix to this chapter.

Notes:

[a] Alternatively identified as the seven 'increases' (*vṛddhi*) 'which are the fruit of [fulfilling] the four Brahmā-states'. Tantrically the yoghurt stands for *bodhicitta*, the thought of enlightenment or semen (cf. Locke 1980: 97). A.V. Vajracharya (1976a: 2, 5) indicates that at different points the yoghurt is to be regarded as the moon, as the asterisms (*nakṣatra*), and as the seven 'increases'.

[b] In Kathmandu this is replaced by the *nāgpã*, a clay pot in which Vāsuki, king of the *nāga*s and ruling serpent of the Kathmandu Valley, is worshipped (Locke 1980: 97–8). The *gãlāybã* used in Lalitpur consists of beaten rice, (rock-) salt, and ginger, placed on a leaf. After the ritual it is offered by Hindus to Nārāyaṇa or to a cow, and by Buddhists to Amoghasiddhi on a *caitya*. (In theory Buddhists may also offer it to a cow, but I have never known this to happen.) In secret rituals the *gãlāybã* is replaced by the *pātra*, a 'skull-bowl' fashioned from brass or silver sitting on a tripod, which contains alcohol.

Notes to Table 5.4 (*cont.*)

[c] The Mirror may be called *jwalā* because it is a pair (Nw. *jwa lāye*, 'to be a pair/identical') with the Powder Container (a girl receives both in her dowry; Sarasvatī and Vasundharā hold them in each hand). *Jwalā* could also mean 'symmetrical', though this would be an unnecessary epithet. A third possibility, implied at S.M. Joshi 1987: 209b, is that it is a Newarization of *jwālā*, 'flames', since moulded flames, a Buddhist symbol of impermanence like the mirror itself, surround the central mirror part. Against this last, tempting etymology are the facts that the word would be an unusual Skt.-Nw. hybrid and that Sanskritically inclined priestly handbooks never seem to spell it *jwālā-*.
[d] What I have called the Alcohol Pot is filled with spirits (*aylāḥ*) or rice beer (*thwã*). In this context it is known as nectar (*amṛta*). If some priests say that Guhyeśvarī is summoned into the *kalaśa* (Locke 1980: 101) it is presumably this 'secret' Flask which is intended. Vajrayānist textual prescriptions of the goddess Māmakī's form (e.g. Saṃvarodaya Tantra 26.2–7) show evidence of being borrowed from Śaivite sources on the goddesses Surādevī and Aghoreśvarī (A. Sanderson, personal communication). Since the goddess Guhyeśvarī in Mṛgasthalī is generally considered by Buddhists to be Nairātmyā, not Māmakī, the popular identification of the Alcohol Pot with Guhyeśvarī is probably due to its name (*guhya-kalaśa*).
[e] The *Khāy* Pot contains *khāy*, diluted yoghurt with oil and turmeric, with, balanced on top of it, a saucer containing pieces of buffalo meat and boiled duck egg. In Kathmandu the *Khāy* Pot is called *khāykuri* (Manandhar 1986: s.v.; G.S. Nepali 1965: 392, 437, wrongly reports it as containing liquor).

Steps (i) and (iii) have been mentioned above. Steps (ii) and (v) through (vii) are all similar: they consist each in the summoning (Skt. *ākarṣaṇa* or *āvāhana*) and worship of the deity or deities supposed to be present in the implement in question. Normally the Double-Headed Powder Pot (*khāybha*) is worshipped also (step (ii) above): in one 'head' it has red powder (vermilion), in the other yellow (made from sandalwood mixed with perfume). It is identified with Vajravārāhī. Once worship has been performed the sponsor takes up the pot and flicks powder towards the line of implements twelve times. On these occasions, when orange powder and lampblack are included with the other ritual implements, worship of them takes place at this point.

The fourth step is the Threefold Meditation by the priest. This rite is examined below (§10.2). The sponsor of the ritual has no part to play here. It consists in the priest summoning and worshipping his own tutelary Tantric deity, and most importantly, identifying himself with the deity. The priest empowers his own body, his *vajra* and bell, and the offerings to be used in the ritual. Once he has summoned and worshipped the deity and his retinue, the priest consecrates himself by touching his head in each cardinal direction.

The next stage is summoning the deities into the Flask and the other non-Tantric implements. Here the sponsor helps the priest, who remains seated, by taking the Five-Coloured Thread from the spout of thc Flask, passing it to the priest, and removing the *kisalī* placed over the top of the Flask; in place of the *kisalī* he puts the priest's conch shell, and, balanced on the spout in place of the thread, the priest's *vajra*. The priest holds the ball of thread and a stick of incense in his left hand, while manipulating his rosary out of sight (under his coat or in a special glove). Once he has summoned the deities, the conch shell is removed from the mouth of the Flask, water is poured from the former into the latter three times, and the *kisalī* is replaced, likewise the *vajra* and thread.

The second stage of the worship of the Flask is a series of apotropaic rites. This is known as 'nīrājan' or 'nirañjan yāyegu'.[17] A small clay saucer with burning coals is brought: a lighted wick, mustard seeds, a flower, and rice are offered to it, it is touched to the Flask and taken out of the house and placed at the threshold (*pikhālakhu*). The invocations which accompany this rite request Khaṇḍarohā and Vajrasattva to remove sins and obstacles.[18] Finally to complete this stage, the Flask and other implements are worshipped with 'footwater' and the Five Offerings.

Once the Visualization, purification, and worship of the Flask have been performed, the same process is repeated, first for the Tantric implements (*Khāy* Pot and Alcohol Pot), and secondly for any other additional item required by the overall rite. An example of the latter would be the feast shares to be sent to the family's traditional Kumārī shrine, after the rite of First Rice-Feeding. These too have to be visualized as deities and worshipped. In this case, however, and in the case of the Visualization of the Tantric implements, no removal of obstacles (*nīrājan*) is performed.[19] The worship of the Tantric implements, the Alcohol Pot and the *Khāy* Pot, is called in the handbooks *kumbhapūjā* or *vāruṇīpūjā*. Vāruṇī is another name of the goddess Māmakī who is supposed to reside in the alcohol.

These rites complete the Flask Worship. On most occasions there will be other rites, specific to the occasion, which follow immediately. A comparison of this account of Flask Worship with Locke's (1980: 95–103) reveals several differences which may be due to regional variation in the performance of the rituals, of the sort already alluded to.[20]

The *nīrājan* rite occurs at many points in complex rituals. It is often combined with others which equally seem to be aimed at avoiding obstacles and increasing auspiciousness: showing light in a wooden volume measure (*pha*), pouring fruits and flowers over the head with the volume measure, and touching with an old key on shoulder and head three times.[21] A ritual similar to *nīrājan*, which is nonetheless kept distinct, is that of 'bali piyegu'. In both 'nīrājan yāyegu' and 'bali piyegu' mustard seeds are used to remove sins and avoid obstacles, although the simplest form of 'bali piyegu' consists in pouring pure water in front of a person who is being led over a significant threshold (e.g. of house or monastery). As for the difference between the two rituals, 'nīrājan yāyegu' is used during a complex ritual, whereas 'bali piyegu' is used for unelaborated rites of entering a house or a ritual area or on returning from a cremation ground.[22] V.P.P. Joshi (1956: s.v.) glosses 'bali piyegu' with Np. 'bhūt panchāune', pushing away spooks. *Piyegu* is therefore being used in its sense of 'push aside'; *bali*, usually used to denote an offering to low spirits or ghosts, would seem here to denote the spirits themselves.

The second basic rite of Newar Buddhism is the Fire Sacrifice. Normally in texts this is referred to as *homa* or *yajña*. The latter is pronounced *jagya*, *jog*, or even *jogi* in colloquial Newari. The rite is always preceded by the Flask Worship. It can be performed very briefly and cheaply, when the thirty-two types of grain ideally present are replaced by far fewer, or it may be performed strictly and elaborately. There are esoteric versions of the Fire Sacrifice which include offerings of buffalo meat. There are also bigger and more conspicuous exoteric versions, such as the Fire Sacrifice of a Hundred Thousand Oblations (*lakṣāhuti homa*).[23] This rite, occasionally sponsored by very rich members of Kwā Bāhāḥ to celebrate the wedding of their sons or daughters, lasts about seventeen hours, beginning in the middle of the night. Along with the Fire Sacrifice, 108 Vajrācāryas are invited to read the text, the Perfection of Wisdom in twenty-five thousands lines (Pañcaviṃśati-prajñāpāramitā). The potlatch quality of this version of the rite is emphasized by the fact that, at the point when cloth, usually represented by a single circle of thread, is offered into the fire, each woman of the sponsor's family is expected to offer into the fire a truly valuable garment, such as a gold-embroidered shawl received at her wedding.

The following are the main steps of Fire Sacrifice as performed in Lalitpur:[24]

(i) preliminary rites;
(ii) summoning of Agni (the firegod), including purification of the ghee;
(iii) First Oblation (*prathamāhuti*);
(iv) Oblation to the Convention-Deity (*samayāhuti*);
(v) Oblation to the Knowledge-Deity (*jñānāhuti*);
(vi) Oblation to the principal deity (*devatāhuti*);
(vii) Full Oblation (*pūrṇāhuti*);
(viii) consecration of the Spirit-Offering (*bali hāykegu*), followed by ritual stipend and blessing of the king;
(ix) Oblation of the Remainder (*śeṣāhuti*);
(x) Dismissal of the deities.

The terms Convention-Deity and Knowledge-Deity relate to different stages of Visualization: the former refers to the deity as first visualized emerging from the priest's own being, the latter to the deity-as-absolute, summoned from heaven, and fused with the Convention-Deity. As Locke observes (1980: 108 fn. 58), Newar priests cannot explain these terms correctly. However I would not conclude from this that they do not understand the idea which the terms express. The question of how far Newar priests understand the process of Visualization is taken up below (§10.2).

The principal deity is the deity for whom the Fire Sacrifice is being performed. After each Oblation (except for the Oblation to the Convention-deity) good-fortune verses (*svastivākya*) are read which mention the sponsor's name and the reason for the rite, and then the deity to whom the oblation was made is worshipped and given water (*tarpaṇa*). The ghee which is offered as the First Oblation is first worshipped as the Five Buddhas. The Oblation to the Convention-Deity consists in the offering of the woods and grains that have been brought: it is preceded by their being purified and worshipped as Cakrasaṃvara. At the end of the Oblation to the Knowledge-Deity the ladle (*sulupā*) is made to touch the Flask; at the end of the Oblation to the principal deity, it is made to touch the deity.

One of the fruits offered into the fire at the end of the rite is a coconut. This is widely believed to represent the head of the sponsor, to be a substitute for his offering his own head. In the elaborate Fire Sacrifice of a Hundred Thousand Oblations it is made up with eyes, a mouth, and a nose. One of the onlookers, who had himself sponsored this rite, told me that in the old days the sponsor himself jumped into the fire; and that in those days Vajrācārya priests were learned enough to enter fire and come out alive. On another occasion, Jog Maya favoured me with the following (unprompted) thoughts:

> You know, it seems to me that when our body is burnt at the cremation ground [after death] this is meant to be a Fire Sacrifice, so that we'll be saved. In an ordinary Fire Sacrifice the coconut offered represents the head [of the sponsor]. In the Hundred Thousand Oblation Fire Sacrifice, the face is actually painted on. Many previous Buddhas did this, lighting oneself up as a great lamp (*mahādīp*), Dīpaṅkara for instance. And others sacrificed their body too.

In likening cremation of the dead to the ultimate oblation, i.e. offering oneself to the gods, Jog Maya had worked out for herself an idea common in Hindu religious thought.[25] The expression I have translated as 'meant to be a Fire Sacrifice' was literally: this is in the *pramāṇ* of a Fire Sacrifice. *Pramāṇ* means proof or authority. One can ask, and the anthropologist frequently does ask, 'In the *pramāṇ* of what is X done?' The answer that a ritual action or symbol X is in *pramāṇ* of Y implies that Y legitimizes the use of X, and that X accomplishes Y by other means.

Newar Buddhist rituals do indeed conform in structure to Hindu ones. Ordinary Newars are therefore encouraged to see them in a Hindu way. The learned often deny the obvious meanings ascribed to rituals and give more Buddhist interpretations. Thus *paṇḍit* Asha Kaji Vajracharya told me that the coconut used in Fire Sacrifice is not the sponsor's head, but is actually supposed to be a ball of sin (*pāp*) which is then destroyed in the fire.[26] Another learned gloss is given by Locke (1980: 111): when, during the Fire Sacrifice, the priest ties a red shawl under his right arm and over his left shoulder, he should see himself as fire, and this offering of himself into the fire is equivalent to his dissolution into the void (*śūnyatā*).

At the lowest level of interpretation Newar Buddhist rituals seem Hindu because they are meant to seem Hindu. It is no surprise that observers who have written about Newar Buddhism after superficial acquaintance should describe Newar Buddhist rituals as highly Hinduized. The theory which underlies them is sophisticated, however. Locke (1980: 105–21) quite rightly emphasizes that one cannot understand the rituals of Newar Buddhism without considering the Visualization of deities (*sādhana*) by which they are effected, and that, although the form of the rite was borrowed from Hinduism, the content is thoroughly Buddhist.

Locke (1980: 121) further says that 'the rituals of the Vajrācāryas can only be understood if one realizes their original purpose in the acting out in ritual of the *sadhana*'. This is true of soteriological uses of the rites, but in other cases it is, if anything, the other way around. It is the Visualization which is used for ritual, and via the ritual for thisworldly purposes, not ritual which is used to enact the Visualization. Thus the editor of the published handbook which Locke used, Amogha Vajra Vajracharya (1976a), wrote in the preface:

> The Fire Sacrifice not only has the result for living beings of worldly enjoyment and liberation (*bhukti-mukti*), it also brings peace if the country is afflicted by calamities. Furthermore, all the rites from the ten sacraments of men up to the consecration rituals of gods and goddesses are fulfilled by means of the Fire Sacrifice . . . [T]he main purpose of the Fire Sacrifice is the causing of plenty (*subhikṣa*) in the whole world. The authority for this is found in the twenty-third chapter of the Saṃvarodaya Tantra, and indeed in every Tantra.[27]

The Tantric Buddhist scriptures divide Fire Sacrifices into four main types for pacifying, causing to prosper, overpowering and destroying respectively (Snellgrove 1957: 112, 258–9). It is the first which is the principal and basic type, though aspects of each of these functions are found in every complex ritual.[28]

Appendix: Some verses used in Newar Buddhist ritual

The following are some of the verses which are used to worship the implements presented in Table 5.4 and Figure 17. The grammar is not always correct in these versions, and the translation is therefore approximate.

Conch

Oṁ Nāgapāśātmako nityaṃ jalarājo mahābala
Nirvikalpeti vikhyāto varuṇāya namo 'stu te.

OṂ Obeisance to you Varuṇa, who permanently takes the form of a serpent noose, king of waters, possessing great strength, famous for your indeterminate form.

This is the verse used to worship the conch during the *guru maṇḍala* ritual. Tantrically, as noted elsewhere, the *ḍākinī* Khaṇḍarohā is invoked when using water from the conch, and she has a special link with Cakrasaṃvara.

Powder Container

Natvā śrī-vajravārāhīṃ mantramūrtiṃ jineśvarīm
Atyantavaradāṃ bhīmāṃ laghubinduniväsinīm.

Having performed obeisance to the blessed Vajravārāhī, who takes the form of mantras, mistress of the Buddhas, bestower of infinite boons, fearsome (in form), residing in the tiny point (of the *candrabindu* of the mantra HŪṂ).

(U.V. Vajracharya 1968: 5).

Yoghurt Pots

Āyuvṛddhir yaśovṛddhir vṛddhividyā sukhas tathā
Ārogyaṃ dhana-santānau saptavṛddhiṃ namāmy aham.

I worship the seven 'increases', namely increase of life, fame, knowledge, happiness, health, wealth, and offspring.

(A.V. Vajracharya 1976a: 2; U.V. Vajracharya 1968:

5 has a slightly variant reading as has A.V. Vajracharya 1983 II: 497; see below, p. 188.)

Mirror

Pratibimbasamā dharmā acchāḥ śuddhā hy anāvilāḥ
Agrāhyā anabhilāpyāś ca hetukarmasamudbhavāḥ.

All things are like reflections in a mirror, transparent, pure, and uncontaminated. They are ungraspable, inexpressible, and arise from causes and actions.

This is also used in the daily worship of a monastery: see Gellner 1991c.

Alcohol Pot

**Nīlamāṃkārajāṃ nīlām* akṣobhyasaṃgasaṃginī*
Bhaktyāhaṃ tvāṃ mahāvīrāṃ akṣayāṃ bhava-māmakīm.

I worship you with devotion Māmakī, you who are black, and arise from a black MĀṂ (in the heart), consort of Akṣobhya, great heroine, indestructible.
(U.V. Vajracharya 1968: 6).

The actual reading of the first *pāda* is *Nīlanīlāṃja-nīlābhā.* I owe the suggested amendment to Alexis Sanderson.

Khāy *Pot*

Ānandaṃ paramānandaṃ viramānanda-rūpinīṃ
Caturānanda-bhāvena sahajānandaṃ ca rūpinī.
(Asha Kaji Vajracharya, personal communication).

Ānandaṃ viramānandaṃ paramānandaṃ namo 'stu te
Sahajānandaṃ vīravīreśvarāya namo 'stu tu.

Obeisance to Bliss, the Bliss of Cessation, and the Ultimate Bliss. Obeisance to the Innate Bliss and to the lord of heroes. (U.V. Vajracharya 1968: 6).

Lamp

Rū-je-saṃ-bījasaṃjātaṃ vaiśvavarṇa-mahojvalaṃ
Vaiśvānaram ahaṃ vande sarvasampati-dāyakaṃ.

I worship Vaiśvānara [an epithet of Agni, god of fire] who arises from the seed mantras RŪ, JE, and SAṂ, who blazes up in all colours, and grants all wealth.
(U.V. Vajracharya 1968: 6).

This is the reading common in Lalitpur (though one often sees *vaiśravarṇa* or even *vaiśravaṇa* for *vaiśvavarṇa-*). A.V. Vajracharya (1976a: 5) gives *suviśuddhaṃ* for *vaiśvavarṇa-* and *sarvasiddhipradāyakam* for the last *pāda*.

6

The Disciples' Way: the monastic ideal in Newar Buddhism

We ourselves are monks.

A Vajrācārya priest on being asked if he had ever invited Theravāda monks to his home.

Paul Mus has pointed out that in ancient India the notion of inheritance should be considered primarily as taking over one's father's position and identity, rather than the taking over of possessions. As he put it in his succinct manner: 'One does not inherit *from* one's father; instead, one inherits *one's* father.' We should not hesitate to apply this notion to the filiation of Buddhist monks. As 'sons of Śākyamuni' (Śākyaputra) and 'heirs of the Dhamma' (*dharmadāyāda*), Buddhist monks (or at least some of them) were more than Buddhists; they were also, in a sense, Buddhas.

John S. Strong, *The Legend of King Aśoka*, p. 82.

6.1 Śākyas and Vajrācāryas as hereditary monks

I have attempted to describe the context of Newar Buddhism and to outline some of its basic concepts and rituals. It is now time to turn to a systematic exposition of the Three Ways introduced above (§4.2). The first Way, the Disciples' Way, focuses on the monastic ideal and it has already been indicated (§2.4) how important this is for Śākya and Vajrācārya identity. The claim of Vajrācāryas and Śākyas to be monks is in fact a crucial part of traditional Newar Buddhism. Of course, they are more than monks: they are householders and, in the case of Vajrācāryas, priests as well. Their claim to be monks was traditionally accepted by others, for example, when kings gave them gifts as *bhikṣus*.[1] It is Vajrācāryas' and Śākyas' own, as well as others', doubts about this status which are now undermining traditional Newar Buddhism.

Every Śākya and Vajrācārya male must be a member of a Monastic Community (*saṃgha, sā̃*) based on a monastery (*bāhāḥ* or *bahī*; Skt. *vihāra*). He becomes a member by going through Monastic Initiation in that monastery. These institutions are defined in the culture as monasteries (as is discussed further below). Thus, as Locke (1989: 106) has pointed out, it is incorrect to refer to them, as outsiders often do, as 'former monasteries'. Furthermore, in the historical sense intended, it is incorrect in another way: very few of the Newar monasteries of today ever housed celibate monks; most were founded after the present system had already emerged.

Initiation in a monastery gives a Śākya or Vajrācārya boy membership, that is, the right and duty to participate in the monastery's recurrent functions. He has to take his turn as guardian of the principal deity (*kwābāju, kwāpāḥdyaḥ*). As with many posts in an Oxford college, duties pass down the list from senior to junior. Eventually, by seniority reckoned from time of initiation, a Śākya or Vajrācārya man may become one of the five or ten elders of the monastery, for which it is necessary to have taken Tantric Initiation (*dīkṣā*).[2] These elders are known as *sthavira*, an ancient (Sanskrit) Buddhist term, and colloquially as *āju* (grandfather). In Kathmandu, and occasionally in Lalitpur, they are also called *thāypā*. The elders are responsible for the regular worship of the monastery's Tantric deities, and have various other ceremonial functions (see Plate 1). Elders are often invited to receive gifts (*pañcadān*) on auspicious occasions, particularly at weddings. The idea here (though it usually remains implicit) is that they stand for the whole Monastic Community (who would in many monasteries be too numerous to invite).

The Monastic Initiation ritual preserves many features of the ancient Buddhist ordination rite, but it places them in a Mahāyāna and Vajrayāna framework which changes their import. I have described the ritual at length elsewhere,[3] and will here make only a few remarks. The ritual is the Śākya and Vajrācārya equivalent of Loincloth Worship performed by other castes. Different monasteries perform Monastic Initiation differently. Those, such as Bu Bāhāḥ, which are largely Vajrācārya have the largest overlay of Tantric (Diamond Way) elements; the *bahī* and (it seems) monasteries in Kathmandu have the least. In all monasteries the main emphasis is on incorporation into the religion of the Buddhist householder: on the fourth day the neophyte lays down his robes and is made to announce his intention of keeping the Five Precepts. In all monasteries, the central initiating ritual is monastic: the five most senior elders pour the consecrating waters over the new member;[4] for this, and on certain other occasions, the elders bare their right shoulder in monastic fashion.

The monastic part of Vajrācārya and Śākya identity revolves, as might be expected, around the monastery and its principal deity, who is usually Śākyamuni Buddha.[5] Only Śākyas and Vajrācāryas may perform the daily worship (*nitya pūjā*) of such monastery deities. Members of other castes occasionally found a small monastery but either they turn it over entirely to Śākyas and/or Vajrācāryas, or they have them come to perform the required daily ritual.

The high status of Śākyas and Vajrācāryas is in the first place the consequence of their control of monasteries and their monopoly of monastic ritual. The position of Vajrācāryas as priests and preceptors of other castes is a consequence and elaboration of their monastic identity. They cannot be priests for other castes unless they are first fully initiated members of a Monastic Community. This is in contrast to Brahmans, whose primary entitlement is to fill the role of family priest. If they also act as temple priests (the equivalent of the Buddhists' monastery god-guardianship) this is an optional extra. A further difference from Brahmans is that, in justifying their position Vajrācāryas put emphasis far less on descent and concentrate rather on ritual legitimizations and the relationship to Buddhist deities which goes with them. Certainly the right to become a Vajrācārya is hereditary, but Newar Buddhist tradition provides no obvious justification for this. At least where the monastic status of Śākyas is concerned, there is the apologetic myth about Śaṅkara Ācārya as well as the tradition that they are descended from Śākyamuni's kinsmen (§2.4). Until recently most Śākyas and Vajrācāryas themselves accepted the fact of recruitment by descent and did not question it, because it was their tradition.

In the past, during the period when celibate monks had already died out, it seems likely that the position of Vajrācārya was open to Śākyas as well. Any member of a monastery who wished to, could take the Consecration of a Vajra-Master and become a Vajrācārya. If he did not, he remained a Śākya. If this interpretation is incorrect, it was certainly open to any Śākya who was remembered to have had a Vajrācārya in the family at some point in the past (cf. Rosser 1966: 126–7). Thus a birch-bark document of 1507 records the sale of land to a Śākyabhikṣu of Nyākhācuk in which his lineage brother (*sagotra*), a Vajrācārya, was the witness.[6] Today, by contrast, only the sons of Vajrācāryas may be consecrated as a Vajra-Master and all of them invariably are so consecrated, whether destined for the priesthood or not. Even the single exception I know of, the writer and translator Dunda Bahadur Vajracharya, who has declined to go through the ritual, still uses the title as a surname. Thus it is now impossible for one of two agnatically related men to be a Śākya and the other a Vajrācārya. This is notwithstanding the fact that Śākyas and Vajrācāryas recognize the theoretical possibility that a Vajrācārya who fails to take the Consecration of a Vajra-Master falls to the status of a Śākya.

This theoretical proposition was put into practice in the Malla period, as noted. Still further in the past it was possible to be a Śākya and a Vajrācārya simultaneously. Both the titles *śākyabhikṣu-vajrācārya*, used in a document of 1142 (Kölver and Śākya 1985: 115–16), and *vajrācārya-bhikṣu*, from 1153 (D.R. Regmi 1965 I: 654), would nowadays be considered a contradiction in terms.

There have been other, more recent changes. About thirty or forty years ago all Śākyas changed their surname from various longer forms. Whereas Vajrācāryas all shared the same surname, several different titles were traditionally used by Śākyas. These were (with non-honorific equivalents in parentheses):

(i) Śākyavaṃśa (Bare): 'of the Śākya lineage';
(ii) Śākyabhikṣu (Bare): 'Buddhist monk';
(iii) Brahmacarya Bhikṣu (Bhikhu Bare): 'celibate monk';
(iv) Bauddhācārya/Buddhācārya (Bare): 'Buddhist preceptor';
(v) Cailaka Bhikṣu (Cībhāḥ Bare): '*caitya* monk'.

Of these 'Śākyabhikṣu' (often, in inscriptions at least, appearing simply as 'Bhikṣu') predominated in Kathmandu. After about 1615 'Śākyavaṃśa' seems to have been the most common surname in Lalitpur for members of the *bāhāḥ*.[7] From the nineteenth century, members of Lalitpur *bahī* called themselves 'Brahmacarya Bhikṣu'. All of these now call themselves 'Śākya'.

'Cailaka Bhikṣu' is interpreted by Newars today to mean what its non-honorific equivalent does mean, namely '*caitya* monk' (in fact 'Cailaka' derives from Skt. *cela*, referring to a monk's robe). The epithet 'Cībhāḥ Bare' is used of half-caste boys – sons of Śākya or Vajrācārya fathers by lower-caste mothers – who are initiated not in a monastery but at a *caitya*. Thus they do not gain membership of the Monastic Community with its rights, duties, and public confirmation of caste status. There is another category of Śākyas whose traditional title was 'Cailaka Bhikṣu/Cībhāḥ Bare': the members of Michu Bāhāḥ, Lalitpur. Although no one believes them to be half-castes, and they have no difficulty intermarrying with other Śākyas and Vajrācāryas, in formal contexts they seem to have used the surname 'Śākya' even traditionally, presumably in order to avoid being taken for half-castes. Nonetheless, they continue to be known as 'Cailaka Bhikṣu' in liturgy, i.e. in the recitation of the 'Adya Mahādāna', just as other Śākyas' traditional titles are so used. The final title, Bauddhācārya, was, and still is, used by many Śākyas in Bhaktapur, Sankhu, and Panauti, as well as by the members of Syangu Bāhāḥ and Makhã Bahī in Kathmandu.[8]

Thus of the various titles used by Śākyas traditionally, some were monastic while one, Śākyavaṃśa – the most common in Lalitpur – emphasized descent from the kin of the Buddha. These different titles coexisted with a number of different, and prima-facie conflicting, myths of origin (see above, §2.4). Inscriptional evidence reveals that from the late Malla period onwards Śākyas often used no title at all; this suggests that even in the 'traditional' past – and not just in the last forty years – Śākyas felt considerable ambivalence about their title. This, I submit, was and is the result of a dilemma facing Śākyas: they form a caste but have no place in the scheme of the four *varṇa*s; they are monks but recruit only sons by pure mothers as members. These contradictions are partly, but only partly, overcome by the doctrine of levels which explains monasticism as the lowest and most exoteric identity of the Śākyas. It is significant that the Vajrācāryas seem to have less of a problem than the Śākyas over this: Śākyas are denied, in the popular imagination, if not in point of fact, full access to the Vajrayāna. That is, they may take Tantric Initiation as individuals, but as a group their identity is not Vajrayānist but Mahāyānist: they are householder monks. Vajrācāryas, on the other hand, seem to escape this dilemma to some extent by their close association with the Vajrayāna: their primary identity is as Tantric priests who must be married.

The Newar Buddhist attitude to caste and descent is expressed well in a short text which Hodgson had his *paṇḍit*s translate: 'the distinctions between Brahmans, Kshatriyas, Vaisyas and Súdras are founded merely on the observance of divers rites, and the practice of different professions'.[9] When caste was supported by the force of law, Buddhists accepted it in practice while retaining reservations about it in myth and ideology. Now that caste is officially frowned upon, no longer has the direct support of law, and is known to be scandalous to foreigners, both Śākyas and Vajrācāryas find themselves in an increasingly awkward position.[10] The fact that in the distant past any (clean-caste) man could join a Buddhist monastery, but now it is hereditary, was a frequent topic of conversation among Buddhists I knew. Some argued that they ought again to open their doors to all comers, or at least to the sons of Vajrācārya and Śākya fathers by lower-caste wives, in order to stop the continual decline of the Buddhist percentage in the decennial national census.[11] In Kathmandu, in a compromise between this and tradition, a new monastery has been established for such boys.[12] By this action the Buddhist view of caste is asserted against, without annihilating, the claims of tradition. Although meetings have been called (in 1989) to discuss proposals for a similar step in Lalitpur, so far no action has been taken there.

6.2 Ritual in the monastery: Kwā Bāhāḥ as an example

The place in which monasticism is most continuously and visibly kept up is the shrine of the principal deity of a monastery. Here the ancient rules are most clearly preserved. The Newar Buddhist monastery has evolved from a classical model: a two-storeyed building around a square courtyard set back from the road, with the principal Buddha shrine opposite the main entrance. The old model can best be seen in the *bahī* class of monastery: until recently the members of the *bahī* consciously kept up a kind of conservative and purist Buddhist ideology.[13] They claimed descent from the last laicized monks, and supported this claim by the title they traditionally used in Lalitpur, Brahmacarya Bhikṣu, or 'celibate monk' (see above, §6.1). This was notwithstanding the fact that they were, like Śākyas in *bāhāḥ* monasteries, married householders. Nonetheless, they maintained that there was a difference, and retained many ritual markers of a more Śrāvakayānist accent to Newar Buddhism (for instance, not performing the Fire Sacrifice as part of Monastic Initiation). Retaining as far as possible the old architectural style was no doubt part of the same claim to represent an older, purer Buddhism abandoned by the majority attached to the *bāhāḥ*.

In the *bahī* the four sides of the courtyard are usually only partially enclosed, and it is possible to walk around the back of the main Śākyamuni shrine in a special circumambulatory passage.[14] Most of the *bahī* have been preserved from the encroachment by members which has converted part of the courtyard of many small *bāhāḥ* monasteries into private housing. With their long open halls not put to any regular use, many Lalitpur *bahī* are used in the daytime as primary schools. Another in Puco, on top of a small hill overlooking Lalitpur, has been wholly rebuilt as a Buddhist study and meditation centre, an impressive and expensive affirmation of Buddhist modernism.

The *bahī* consciously and deliberately remained austere and simple, adding to the traditional *caitya* in the centre of the courtyard, and the main Buddha shrine behind it, only the simplest of Tantric shrines on the upper floor (usually immediately above the Buddha shrine). This addition seems to have been made only after the mid-seventeenth century whereas the *bāhāḥ* had certainly by then incorporated Tantric Buddhism very fully into both their ritual and their architecture.

Newari usage recognizes two types of *bāhāḥ*: the main (*mū*) *bāhāḥ*, and the branch (*kacā*) *bāhāḥ*. A system of main monasteries with limited ritual functions was established in Lalitpur by Siddhi Narasiṃha in the seventeenth century, probably building on an older convention. The vast majority of the Śākyas and Vajrācāryas of Lalitpur belong to these main monasteries (there is a similar system in Kathmandu). Branch monasteries include: (a) those few monasteries with an initiated membership which fall outside the system of main monasteries; and (b) those monasteries established, usually by a Śākya or Vajrācārya, as an act of merit and which have no initiated membership. The latter are run as a kind of *guthi* and I call them lineage monasteries. Within Lalitpur city there are eighteen main monasteries (known confusingly as 'the fifteen *bāhāḥ*'), twenty-five *bahī*, nine branch monasteries with initiated members, and 114 lineage monasteries (Locke 1985: 513–14). Not only are there more lineage monasteries in Lalitpur than in Kathmandu (and vastly more than in Bhaktapur), all monasteries are in a better state of repair, and less encroached upon by houses and businesses. Nowhere in Lalitpur is far from a Buddhist courtyard, and in many parts of the city every courtyard seems either to be a monastery or at least to have a *caitya* in it.

From the strictly religious point of view, all *bāhāḥ* and *bahī* are equally monasteries (*vihāra*) and all of them must have at least a *caitya*, a main shrine (normally to Śākyamuni), and a Tantric shrine (*āgã̊*). However, most main *bāhāḥ* are more ornate than this. There seems to have been no ideological inhibition, as there was in the *bahī*, preventing them from making the courtyard ever more elaborate. This is most evident in the courtyard of Kwā Bāhāḥ, the largest Newar Buddhist monastery in the Valley (see Figures 18 and 19, and Table 6.1). Here there have been numerous gifts over the centuries, and many spectacular donations of gold-washed copper roofs in the last 100 years or so. Kwā Bāhāḥ is a shrine of city-wide importance. In addition to its regular Newar devotees, it is visited by many Tibetan Buddhist pilgrims. Nowadays there are also many tourists who come in the middle of the day. They spend most of their time taking photographs, and show no interest in making offerings, having *darśan* (literally 'vision') of the gods, or in receiving the gods' material blessings. Consequently, they constitute a new and non-religious category of visitor.

As already suggested above (§4.2), ritual differs in different parts of the monastery. In this section the Śrāvakayānist daily ritual offered to the main image of Śākyamuni will be described. Other exoteric deities receive a liturgy modelled on that offered to him. The Amoghapāśa Lokeśvara shrine in Kwā Bāhāḥ is nowadays tended by Newar monks in the Tibetan tradition; the long hall housing the shrine is thus known as the *gumbā* (from

Figure 18. The ground floor of Kwā Bāhāḥ (Hiraṇyavarṇa-mahāvihāra or the 'Golden Temple'), Lalitpur. Groundplan scale 1:100. Drawing by Gyanendra Joshi, April 1989.

Key:

1 Main shrine of Kwābāju, i.e. Śākyamuni.
2 Verandah where the god-guardian and his family sit to pass offerings to the two priests (*bāphā*) inside the shrine.
3 Steps where the two priests wash themselves before entering the shrine.
4 Storeroom and sleeping space for the god-guardian's family.
5 Shrine of Vajrasattva.
6 Kitchen called *nīgaḥ* ('pure place') where the woman designated as *nīkulimha* prepares food for the god and for the priests.
7 Shrine of Nāmasaṃgīti, established in 1985.
8 Receptionist, Bhai Ratna Vajracharya.
9 Main entrance called *bhairadwār* ('the door of Bhairava').
10 Shelter (*phalcā*).
11 Disused water tank.
12 Small shrine to Gaṇeś, Mahākāla, and Guhyeśvarī.
13 Stone carved as a thousand petalled lotus (*sahasradala paleswã*) where holy water 'of the four oceans' is used to consecrate boys going through Monastic Initiation.
14 *Kṣetrapāl* where leftovers from feasts in the *gumbā* are thrown.
15 *Kṣetrapāl* where leftovers from the Tantric shrine and from offerings to Kwābāju are thrown.
16 Stone identified as a 'Gayā-stone' (*gayālhwã*) where, on very rare occasions, riceballs from Ancestor Worship are thrown.
17 Shrine to Tārā.
18 Storeroom, renovated in September 1989.
19 Small shrine in wall to Hanumān.
20 Back entrance (from Ilā Nani).
21 Small monastery known as Vaidya Bāhāḥ (cf. Locke 1985: 52).
22 Small stone mandala for making peace (*śānti*) offerings in case of 'obstacles' (*vighna*) in the monastery.
23 Fire pit (*yajñaśālā*).
24 Shrine to the lineage deity, *digu dyaḥ*, i.e. Svayambhū.
25 Spout receiving liquid offerings (basically milk) poured over *digu dyaḥ*.

Beneath it is a stone identified as Vāsuki (*nāgarāja*).

Note: The main deity of Kwā Bāhāḥ is thought of as east-facing although it is a long way from true east. The whole city of Lalitpur is laid out in a north–south, east–west grid pattern with the same degree of deviation.

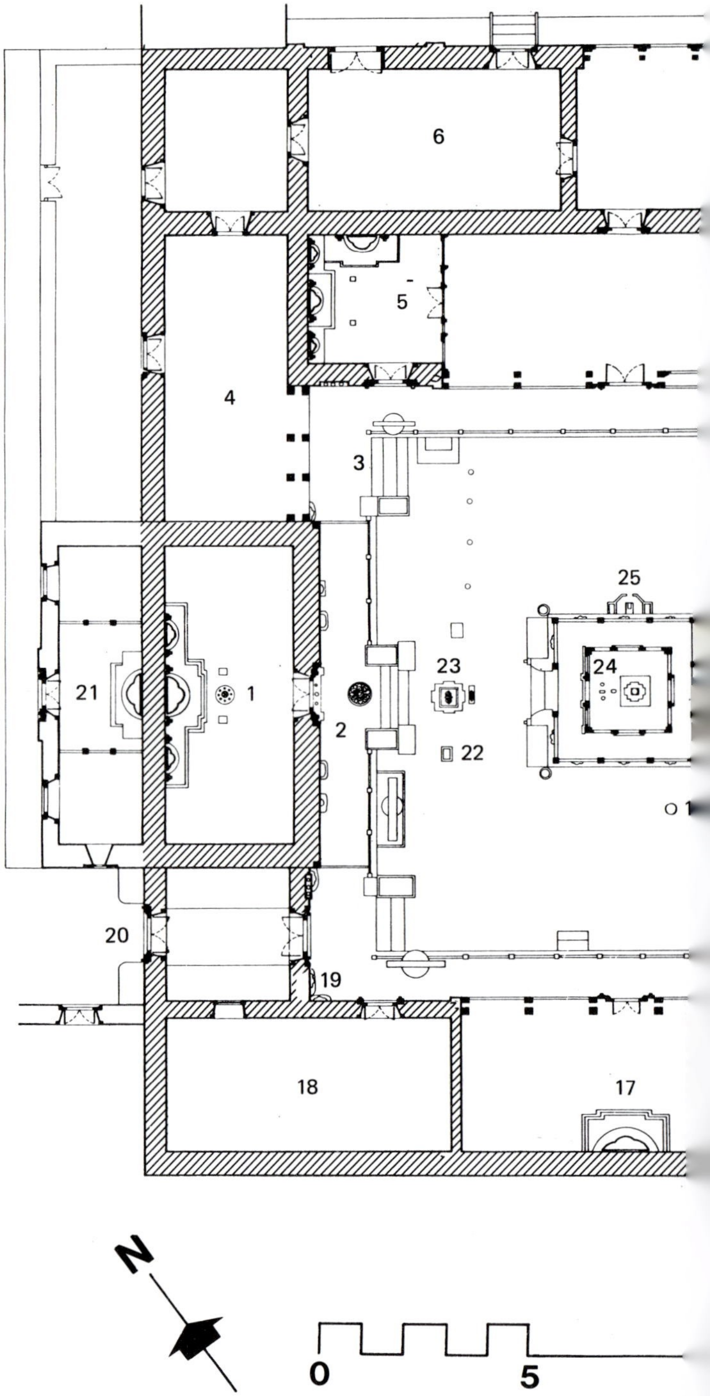
6
5
4
3
2
1
21
25
24
23
22
20
19
18
17
N
0
5

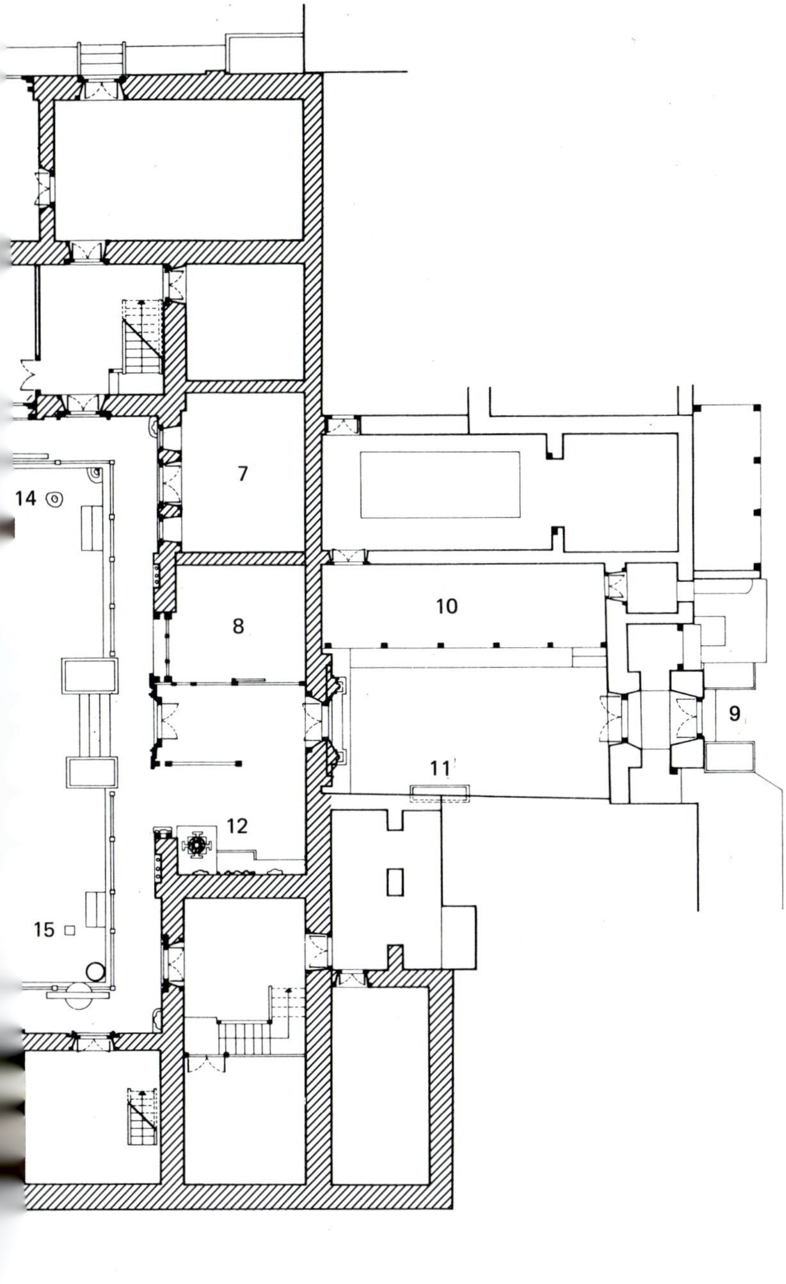

KWĀ BĀHĀḤ, LALITPUR

GROUND FLOOR

Drawing: Gyanendra Joshi

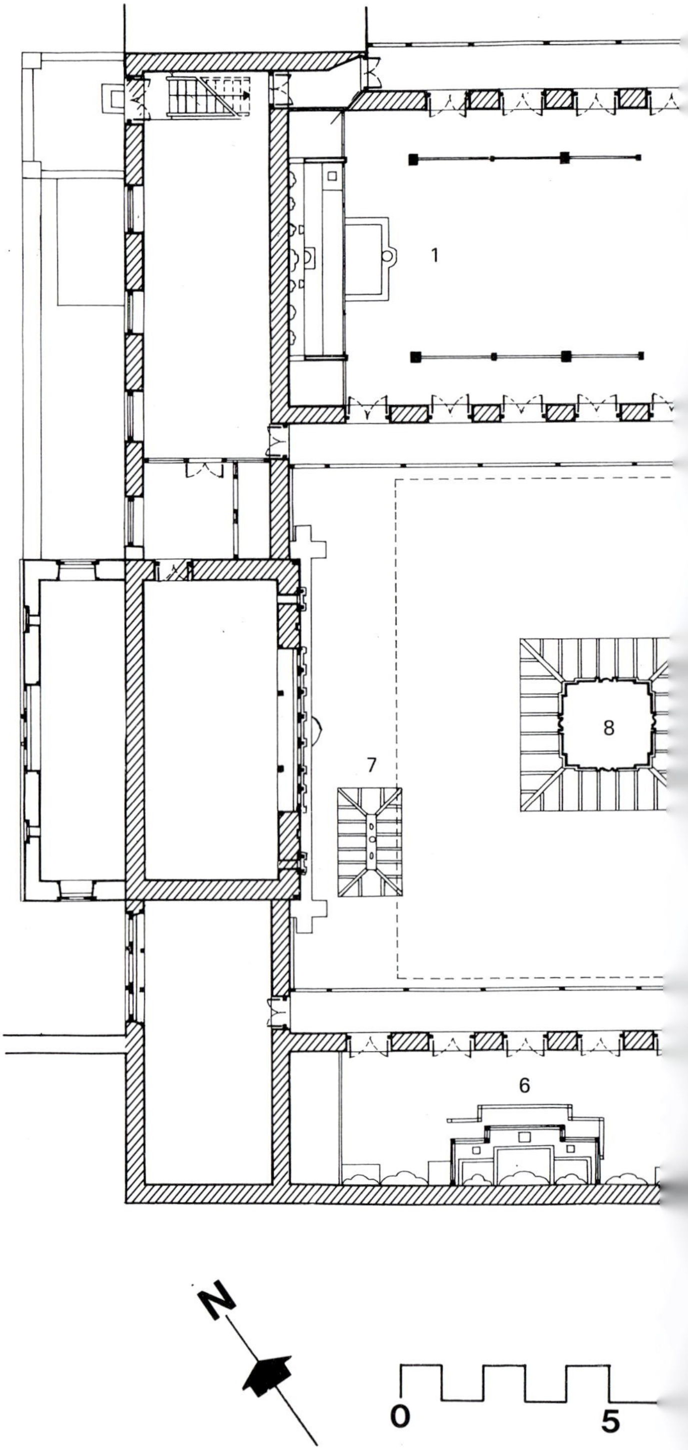
1
8
7
6
N
0
5

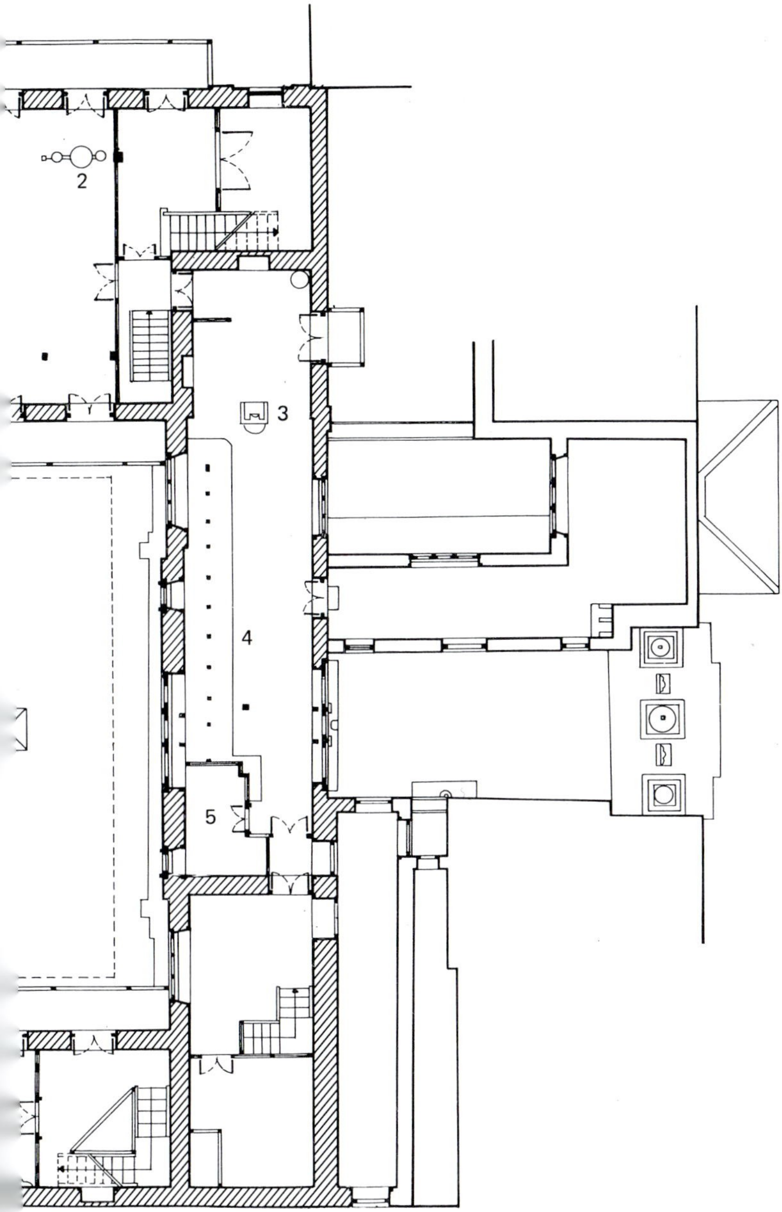

10 M

UPPER FLOOR Drawing: Gyanendra Joshi

Figure 19. The upper floor of Kwā Bāhāḥ (Hiraṇyavarṇa-mahāvihāra or the 'Golden Temple'), Lalitpur. Groundplan scale 1:100. Drawing by Gyanendra Joshi, April 1989.
Key:

1 The shrine of Amoghapāśa Lokeśvara, known as *gumbā* (from the Tibetan for monastery).
2 Large prayer wheel (*māne*).
3 Goddess, exoterically known as Vasundharā; esoterically she is probably Vajrayoginī.
4 Seats for the ten elders in the foyer to the Tantric shrine, known as *āgå*, *digī*, or *wotātalay* (see note below).
5 Shrine of the Tantric deity, Yogāmbara, entered only by the Cakreśvara/Casalāju.
6 Shrine of Amitābha.
7 Roof over the 'big bell'.
8 Roof of lineage deity (Svayambhū).
9 Small roof over *vajradhātumaṇḍala.*

Note on Kwā Bāhāḥ's Tantric shrines:
Probably because of its unusually large membership, Kwā Bāhāḥ has a second Tantric shrine, outside the main complex. Worship there is the responsibility of a subsidiary set of twenty elders. This second Tantric shrine is housed in a long two-storeyed building known as the *digī*, situated on the far (west) side of Ilā Nani. The deity is Cakrasaṃvara with his consort Vajravārāhī. The main Tantric deity in Kwā Bāhāḥ itself is Yogāmbara, whose consort is Jñānaḍākinī. The long room outside Yogāmbara's shrine that takes up the eastern side of the monastery courtyard is also sometimes known as the *digī*, since this is where the *digī* normally is in other monasteries (see Gellner 1987b). Usually however, to avoid confusion, the latter is known as the *āgå* or as 'Wotalay', short for *wotātalay*. *Talay*/*tale* seems to be a Nw. term for a Tantric shrine (and the very name of the royal tutelary goddess, Taleju, may at some level be related to this). For example, an inscription of 1960 calls the shrine of Cakrasaṃvara *guhya*-[secret] *tale*; the shrine of Taleju in the royal palace was frequently called *degu*-[lineage deity] *tale*. *Wota* perhaps derives from the old Nw. *wãtā*, east.

the Tibetan for 'monastery'). The Tibetan-style monks perform their regular rituals there, assisted by Newar laymen who have adopted the Tibetan tradition. This includes a monthly taking of Precepts and three times a year the Observance of Silence (*mauna vrata*, also known by its Tibetan name, Nyungne).[15] On these occasions considerable numbers of Newar women also attend. Similar Observances in the Newar tradition, overseen by the Kwā Bāhāḥ Betāju (Rituals Officer) are also held in the *gumbā*, though less often (see below, §7.5).

The Tantric shrine to Yogāmbara is the preserve of the seniormost Vajrācārya elder, the Cakreśvara or Casalāju. He performs the daily ritual.

Table 6.1 *Shrines in Kwā Bāhāḥ, Lalitpur.*

Deity	*Founded*	*Other deities present*	*God-guardian*	*Length of service*
Śākyamuni	ancient	numerous, 'Balabhadra' in front	all of Saṃgha, by turns	1 month
Vajrasattva	ancient	Vairocana, Vasundharā, Karuṇāmaya, Mañjuśrī	all Vajrācāryas of Kwā Bāhāḥ (c. 300)	2 weeks
Svayambhū (*digu dyaḥ*)	ancient	—	10 elders	1 month
Nāmasaṃgīti	1985	Tārā, Maitrī	15 members of Nāmasaṃgīti group	1 month
Tārā	1958	—	53 members of Tāremām Saṃgha	2 weeks
Amoghapāśa Lokeśvara	renovated in present form in 1940s	numerous; hall painted in Tibetan style	monks in Tibetan tradition	no formal system
Amitābha	1953	numerous; include Indra and Dīpaṅkaras	20 subsidiary elders of Kwā Bāhāḥ	1 month
Yogāmbara	ancient	—	Casalāju	permanent

Note: Kwā Bāhāḥ is said by tradition to have been founded in the time of King Bhāskaradeva and this is probably the Bhāskaradeva who ruled 1045–8. The ancient shrines are presumed to date from that time, except that locals believe that the enshrined Svayambhū *caitya* in the centre of the courtyard, which is the Lineage Deity of Kwā Bāhāḥ members, predates the monastery itself.

All elders meet for the monthly worship which in Kwā Bāhāḥ is, unusually, on the full-moon day (*punhī*). In other monasteries it occurs on the tenth of either the dark or the light fortnight, on the new-moon day (*amāy*), or on the dark fourteenth (*cahre*) (the day before the new-moon day). In addition to the monthly worship there are various annual rituals, either part of the monastery's own workings, or the consequence of a *guthi* established by devotees, which require the elders to be present. These *guthi*s include several established by high-caste Hindus (e.g. the Jośīs of Patuko), or by *buddhamārgī* Śreṣṭhas. In the case of Kwā Bāhāḥ the elders are very old, and often many of them have to send sons or grandsons to substitute for them, at the feasts which follow the ritual. The ritual performed on these occasions is an elaborate form of that described below (§10.1–2).

Access to the divinity is ever more restricted the more one moves up towards the Tantric shrine. By tradition Untouchables may not enter the courtyard. 'Clean' castes only may enter the long Mahāyānist *gumbā* dedicated to Amoghapāśa Lokeśvara on the upper floor. Some elders have at times wished to exclude foreigners from the *gumbā* by locking it during the day, though in the morning it is in effect open to all those who wish to make offerings. The long foyer before the Tantric shrine is open only to those of Maharjan status and above, and in fact no one enters unless they have to be present for a ritual. My own knowledge of what goes on there is therefore all at second hand.

Few monasteries are large and important like Kwā Bāhāḥ. In most monasteries the daily ritual (*nitya pūjā*) is performed as quickly and perfunctorily as possible. There are no spectators and no offerings by outsiders. But in main monasteries women from the households of members come with offerings as part of their morning round of worship. People of all castes come from all over Lalitpur in great numbers to Kwā Bāhāḥ, to Tanga Bāhāḥ (the home of Cākwādyaḥ-Mīnnāth), and to Ta Bāhāḥ (home of Karuṇāmaya-Matsyendranāth). In Kwā Bāhāḥ locals explain the greater ritual elaboration, and the larger number of purity rules, compared to other monasteries, by citing the presence of the Perfection of Wisdom (Prajñā Pāramitā), the goddess-cum-text mentioned above (§4.3.5).

Performance of the daily ritual inside the main shrine is the responsibility of the current god-guardian. Length of service in this post varies from monastery to monastery. In some Lalitpur monasteries (e.g. Ta Bāhāḥ, Bhīchẽ Bāhāḥ, Cikã Bahī) it lasts only a week, in others a fortnight (e.g. Tanga Bāhāḥ, Ha Bāhāḥ, Dau Bāhāḥ, Uku Bāhāḥ, Guji Bāhāḥ) and in yet others it is a month in duration (Kwā Bāhāḥ, Dhum Bāhāḥ, Si Bāhāḥ). All those monasteries with an extant association have a list system for determining who will be god-guardian: turns pass down the list of members in order of seniority. Kwā Bāhāḥ has so many members that one's turn comes once a lifetime.[16] Elsewhere it recurs over a regular period.

The most important regular ritual of any deity is performed in the morning. After that, the next most important is the offering of light (*ārati*) in the evening. As one would expect, the ritual for the main deity of a monastery is most elaborate in the larger monasteries. At Kwā Bāhāḥ, Bu Bāhāḥ, Ha Bāhāḥ, Uku Bāhāḥ, and Guji Bāhāḥ it is done four times a day. In Lalitpur's other main monasteries the principal deity is worshipped only three times or twice a day, and in small lineage monasteries once only, in the morning. The ritual consists of bathing the image, cleaning the shrine, and reciting various verses. The recitation of hymns is itself a long and elaborate practice in Kwā Bāhāḥ: in principle it is open to all comers everywhere, but only here, at Tangaḥ Bāhāḥ, Ta Bāhāḥ, and at the chariot of Karuṇāmaya-Matsyendranāth during his festival, do large numbers actually participate every morning. In fact these three – Karuṇāmaya (whether on his chariot or in Ta Bāhāḥ), Cākwādyaḥ (whether on his chariot or in Tanga Bāhāḥ), and Kwābāju of Kwā Bāhāḥ – are the three most popular divinities of Lalitpur. Their liturgies seem to be coordinated so that devotees have time to receive holy water (*jal*) at Karuṇāmaya and Cākwādyaḥ, and then cross town to receive it also at Kwā Bāhāḥ.[17]

In Kwā Bāhāḥ the god-guardian appoints two priests called *bāphā* who actually carry out the ritual.[18] Some other large monasteries, such as Bu Bāhāḥ and Uku Bāhāḥ, have a single such temple priest. Elsewhere the god-guardian himself performs the ritual. In Kathmandu it seems to be common for there to be one man or one family which specializes in performing the ritual and, for a small fee, they do it on behalf of all other members. In Lalitpur such solutions have not yet been adopted. But in Kwā Bāhāḥ, at least, many members decline to take their turn because of the heavy responsibilities involved, and because subsequently they will have to help organize the annual monastery feast, a task which may cost them 2–3,000 rupees. Those who decline their turn in this way are considered by some to be 'out of the Monastic Community'.

In taking on the duty for a month, the god-guardian of Kwā Bāhāḥ may, if he wishes, or if he cannot get anyone else to do it, himself take on the role of the 'big' or elder *bāphā*. The 'little' or younger *bāphā*, who is reckoned to be the principal attendant of the god, is supposed to be under twelve years old, but must also, like the god-guardian and the other *bāphā*, be an initiated member of Kwā Bāhāḥ. Because of the organization involved in being god-guardian, and because the *bāphā*s have to remain inside the monastery for the whole month, most god-guardians appoint sons or nephews as both *bāphā*s. They themselves remain outside to help and coordinate matters.

Each day the back entrance to Kwā Bāhāḥ is opened first, long before dawn, so that members of the group (*khalaḥ*) which recites the Nāmasaṃgīti every morning may assemble. The elder *bāphā* enters the shrine first and sweeps the floor. Then he fetches pure water from the well in Ilā Nani, the courtyard behind Kwā Bāhāḥ, and with it he washes the worship materials in the shrine. Outside, once four or five men have assembled, they sit cross-legged on straw mats and begin chanting the Nāmasaṃgīti. Gradually they are joined by others, including a few women. Some men chant while repeatedly circumambulating the central shrine to Svayambhū and operating the prayer wheels at its corners. The elder *bāphā* grinds yellow powder and places food offerings in the shrine. All the while more and more people arrive. The morning liturgy in each of the other shrines – to Vajrasattva, Nāmasaṃgīti, Tārā, and Svayambhū – goes on simultaneously. Devotees visit each shrine in turn. The women usually carry a small tray or raffia basket of offerings; as they circulate they collect blessed leaves or flowers and red and yellow paste which will be taken home for other members of their household. Once they have visited all the shrines of the monastery they return to the main one, and either sit with the Nāmasaṃgīti group, or stand behind them.

If the Nāmasaṃgīti is finished before the younger *bāphā* is ready, they chant various *dhāraṇī* again and again: the Aparamitā, the Durgatipariśodhana, Tārā's. A metal chain is put up along the front of the verandah to prevent devotees approaching too close and touching the younger *bāphā*. Once he has swept the verandah and washed himself on the steps in the north-west corner, the younger *bāphā* enters the shrine and puts on the bell he rings daily. All chanting stops. Then the courtyard becomes a cacophany of sound as devotees join the two *bāphā*s and ring all the numerous bells donated to the monastery over the years. Once that is over the younger *bāphā* shows the mirror in which the god's face has been washed. This is the moment everyone has been waiting for, and everyone cranes to see it. There is an audible sigh, and grains of rice and coins are thrown towards the main shrine over the backs of the assembled crowd. Almost immediately the elder *bāphā* comes out with the holy water and throws it vigorously to left and right. Some men shout 'Over here' if they have not received any spots of water. Then the two *bāphā*s come out and beat a long wooden gong (a hollow log) and a member of the Nāmasaṃgīti group sounds a conch shell. All movement stops for the 108 strokes of the gong. After this the crowd, already beginning to depart, disperses rapidly, but only after they have received yellow powder from the main shrine and red powder from the Svayambhū shrine, a spot of both placed carefully on the forehead. As people leave the two *bāphā*s wave yaktails on either side of Kwābāju (Śākyamuni) as the final part of the morning liturgy. By now it is only shortly after daybreak and a steady stream of devotees continues to arrive until about 8.30 a.m., or even later on the full moon or other holy days.

This is how the morning liturgy appears to the outsider and devotee. More detail, from the point of view of the practitioner, has been given elsewhere (Gellner 1991c), along with an account of the whole daily round in Kwā Bāhāḥ. Twice during the day the younger *bāphā* goes out of the monastery ringing a bell. The ringing of the bell by the younger *bāphā* is the only time that he is permitted to leave the monastery compound during his month of service. He visits several places where the inhabitants are mostly members of Kwā Bāhāḥ: Nhū Bāhāḥ, Nyākhācuk, Nāg Bāhāḥ, and Sarasvatī Nani.[19] In the morning this is referred to as 'mājhã wanegu', in the evening as 'sã wanegu'. The former at least seems to be a signal that the time of worship is over and that one may eat: I was told that certain Śreṣṭhas of Kwāchẽ used to be 'so attached to Kwābāju [the main deity of Kwā Bāhāḥ] that they never used to eat in the morning until they heard the sound of the younger *bāphā*'s bell'.

The evening liturgy is much simpler. A few members of the Nāmasaṃgīti group come and recite hymns: usually the 'Buddhaṃ trailokyanāthaṃ',[20] 'Snigdhanīla' (usually pronounced 'Sanidhani'), 'Dīpajvālā', and one other optional one. Light (*ārati*) is offered to the main image, and at the end the participants 'take light' ('mata kāye') by holding the palms of their hands over the burning wicks and then, without actually touching, passing them over their eyes and head.

It should not come as a surprise to learn that the finer details of the morning liturgy differ from monastery to monastery. There is no body or institution capable of imposing uniformity. I did not conduct a survey of these details over many monasteries, but information from Cikã Bahī, and Hemraj Sakya's published account of the daily liturgy in Bhĩchẽ Bāhāḥ, both suggest that elsewhere various elements from the *guru maṇḍala* ritual have made their way into the morning liturgy.[21] In short, the daily worship of a Buddha-image, which is supposed to be the sphere of the Disciples' Way, is in fact partially colonized by ritual and ideas coming from the Great Way and the Diamond Way.

At the same time, the daily ritual of the monastery does indeed preserve elements with ancient monastic, i.e. Śrāvakayāna, associations. The ringing of the bell around the monastery's courtyards has already been mentioned. It is performed in all eighteen of the main monasteries of Lalitpur (several of them, as noted above, have, like Kwā Bāhāḥ, a 'younger *bāphā*' to do this). Beating the wooden gong is also a very ancient custom, kept up in all but three or four of the main monasteries. Nowadays it is believed that everyone must stand still while the beating is going on and it is usually interpreted in devotional terms: the gong tells the god that he may leave or should enter ('līn juye') his image. In the past it surely marked out the divisions of the monastic day.[22] Interestingly, neither of these ritual practices is thought appropriate in lineage monasteries.

Bathing the deity, waving the yaktail, ringing the bell, and offering light and water were probably common devotional acts performed to Buddha images in large monasteries even before the rise of the Mahāyāna. Certainly these ritual acts, and offerings similar to those found in Nepal, make up the ritual performed to Buddha-images in monasteries with royal associations in Sri Lanka (Evers 1972: chapter 4). Although in Nepal this kind of ritual has certainly been influenced by the Vajrayānist ritual which dominates the rest of Newar Buddhism, it has not been thoroughly reworked. As far as I know there are no ritual handbooks laying down the prescribed daily ritual in a monastery. Unlike every other area of ritual activity in Newar Buddhism, and influenced though it is by the Great Way and the Diamond Way, the daily monastic liturgy seems to have escaped priestly codification.

6.3 The cult of Dīpaṅkara: Śākyas and Vajrācāryas as the recipients of alms

In a large monastery like Kwā Bāhāḥ (which has over 2,000 members) few can become elders. This no doubt explains why Kwā Bāhāḥ has a second subsidiary group of twenty elders responsible for the worship in a second Tantric shrine in Ilā Nani. As elders of a monastery they often have to fulfil monastic roles, in particular receiving alms from others, e.g. after Ancestor Worship for a recently deceased parent or at a wedding. Sometimes at weddings a rich donor may invite not just the elders of his own monastery but the elders of all the main monasteries of Lalitpur and all their current god-guardians, a total of nearly 200.[23] The seniors of the monastery here act as monks. In a different way they also act as monks in the regular monthly ceremonies they perform in secret in the Tantric shrines. This is symbolized by the fact that the family priest of the elder whose turn it is to organize the worship sits below, and not above, the elders, since this is 'the monastery's work'. By contrast, if the elders are invited to a family rite, such as marriage, then the family priest sits at the head, above the monastery elders.

Receiving alms as a monk is not the exclusive prerogative of monastery elders however. Every Śākya and Vajrācārya receives alms once or twice a year during the festival of Pañcadān (see Plate 10). For clarity of exposition I will call the festival Pañcadān, and the alms offered (which are given on other occasions too) *pañcadān*.[24] In fact there are four occasions when ordinary Śākyas and Vajrācāryas may receive *pañcadān*; these are numbered (ii) to (v) below (and see Table 6.2).

(i) Celebratory *pañcadān*: inviting monastery elders on an auspicious or funerary occasion, giving them *pañcadān* gifts and feasting them.

(ii) Regular Pañcadān: this festival occurs every year in Lalitpur on Śrāvaṇ śukla 8 and in Kathmandu and elsewhere on Bhādra kṛṣṇa 13.[25]

Table 6.2 *Types of alms-giving ceremony.*

	(i) Celebratory *pañcadān*	(ii) Regular Pañcadān	(iii) Optional Pañcadān (*nadā̃*)	(iv) Regular Samyak	(v) Optional Samyak
Gifts of husked and unhusked rice	√	√	√	√	√
Gifts of monastic requisites	√	×	√	×	×
Gifts of rice pudding (*kṣīra, khīr*) to men	×	sometimes	√	×	√
Gifts of rice pudding to gods	×	√	√	√	√
Organized by *guthis*	×	√	×	√	×
All Śākyas & Vajrācāryas invited	Specified elders only	√	√	√	√
Place held	Donor's house	All over city	Donor's house	Nāg Bāhāḥ	Lagan-khel
Date	On (optional) occasions	Every year in Gũlā	As for Regular Pañcadān	Phāguṇ śukla 3	Ghyaḥ Cāku Sãnhū
Last performance in Lalitpur	Several times a year	Every year	1982	Every 5 years[a] (1988)	1927[b] (in Kathmandu 1951)

Notes: √ indicates that the characteristic in question is present, × that it is absent.

[a] In Kathmandu it is performed every twelve years, and was last performed in 1979. In Bhaktapur it is performed every year on Ghyaḥ Cāku Sãnhū (Makar Saṃkrānti).

[b] Dharma Aditya Dharmacharyya seems to have held a kind of Samyak in Cyāsaḥ, Lalitpur, in the 1940s and donated an image which is brought to Samyak in Nāg Bāhāḥ; as the most recent image it is placed at the end of the line.

(iii) Optional Pañcadān: this is called *nadā̃ in Lalitpur and nyā pañcadān* in Kathmandu and occurs on the same day as (ii), whenever a rich donor chooses to perform it.

(iv) Samyak (from Skt. *samyak*, 'correct', viz. correct charity): this festival occurs every five years in Lalitpur, in Nāg Bāhāḥ, and once every twelve years in Kathmandu, in the open field (Bhuikhya) below Svayambhū.

(v) Optional Samyak: this is performed by a rich donor, but is so expensive that it has not been performed since 1927 in Lalitpur or 1951 in Kathmandu (H. Sakya 1979: 57; Rosser 1966: 128).

These five ceremonies are basically variations on the same theme, and in his book, *Samyak Mahādān Guthi* ('The Religious Association [for the performance] of the Correct Great Gift Ceremony') Hemraj Sakya, though concentrating mainly on the regular Samyak of Kathmandu, in fact discusses all the above five types of ceremony. All of them focus on the

Buddha Dīpaṅkara. In all of them, even the giving of *pañcadān* to monastery elders, the recipients begin by intoning 'OṀ obeisance to Dīpaṅkara' (H. Sakya 1979: 75).

In all types of alms-giving the main gift is *saruwā*, a mixture of husked and unhusked rice (usually more of the latter since it takes less of it to fill up any given measure). To this is sometimes added rice boiled in milk, *khīr* or *chīr* (from Skt. *kṣīra*). That uncooked rice is meant as a substitute for the more truly monastic gift of cooked rice is suggested by the etymology of the word *pañcadān*. It does not come from *pañca*, 'five' (a meaning it has come to have in the minds of many, no doubt because of the importance of the number five in Tantric Buddhism), but from *puṇya-jā* (merit-boiled-rice), *piṇḍa-jā* (balls of boiled rice), or *paṇḍāju-jā* (Buddhist priest-rice).[26] In recognition of this, *pañcadān* is often, and perhaps more correctly, written *pãjadān* or *pãjādān*. The various occasions when cooked rice is offered are shown in Table 6.2. Usually it resembles rice pudding, being cooked in molasses with pieces of coconut mixed in. This is much less susceptible to impurity than the ordinary boiled rice consumed every day.

Optional Pañcadān is called *nadā̃* from *navadāna*, 'nine gifts'. The significance of 'nine' remains unclear.[27] In practice the number of gifts is nearer twenty. Ratna Kaji Vajracharya (1980: 101) gives a list of sixteen items which he reproduces from a ritual handbook dated 1897 as follows:

uncooked rice	mustard oil	[writing] chalk
needle	thread	broom
string	black lentils	black soyabeans
rice pudding (*chīr*)		myrobalan and other fruits
salt	molasses-juice	medicine (*gulaḥ*)
beaten-rice prestation (*nislāḥ*)		toothpick

To this should be added a ritual gift of money (*dakṣiṇā*). I have observed the rite of Optional Pañcadān twice, once in Lalitpur (in 1982, the first time for fifty-five years) and once in Kathmandu (in 1984, where it had been performed almost every year by one donor after another for the previous five or six years). In both cases the list above was almost exactly what was given[28] though in both cases the following were also given: unhusked wheatgrains, peas, and two types of pastry.

When *pañcadān* is offered to the elders of a monastery in what has been called here Celebratory *pañcadān* the same items are given, though somewhat reduced in number. This is a list of offerings, in the order they were given before a Śākya wedding feast in Ilā Nani, Lalitpur:

napkin	sesame	peas
black lentil	husked rice	wheatgrains
unhusked rice	salt	chalk
broomstring	exercise book	pencil
two rupees		

The gifts given are clearly meant to be monastic requisites. They do not correspond to the simple list of eight monastic requisites (three robes, belt, razor, filtering cloth, needle and thread, and alms bowl) of the early Vinaya tradition but the idea is, I think, the same. One Kathmandu Vajrācārya explained to me that Pañcadān means 'gifts of the five elements (*pañcatattva*), i.e. of everything that one might need'. Around the simple act of alms-giving, however, there has grown up, as in the case of the Monastic Initiation already considered, an enormous amount of Mahāyānist and Vajrayānist ritual, especially in the case of Optional Pañcadān (*nadã̄*).[29] The preparations for Optional Pañcadān go on for many days beforehand; numerous friends and relatives have to be involved in order to prepare and actually give the *pañcadān*; the total cost runs into many tens of thousands of rupees.[30]

The accretion of Mahāyānist and Vajrayānist ritual is even more true in the case of Samyak. The principal difference between this and the various types of Pañcadān is that it centres on the larger-than-life cast statues of Dīpaṅkara which are brought to Nāg Bāhāḥ (in Kathmandu to Svayambhū) and are the centre of the laity's devotion. Śākyas and Vajrācāryas do receive gifts of rice also but they are secondary to the Dīpaṅkara images. In Lalitpur, where I observed the festival in 1983, there are two types of Dīpaṅkara deity. Firstly there are those from each of the main monasteries, who are in fact meant to represent the main deity (*kwābāju* or *kwāḥpāḥdyaḥ*) of each monastery (who is normally Śākyamuni): iconographically they are indistinguishable from the others. Secondly there are the Dīpaṅkara deities which were commissioned by individuals performing Optional Samyak and now belong to particular families, lineages, or clans descended from the original donor. Along with the Dīpaṅkara deities come numerous others, in most cases a small accompanying Tārā. At the head of the line of deities as they are arranged in Nāg Bāhāḥ come various deities: Vasundharā from Tanga Bāhāḥ, Cākwādyaḥ (Mīnnāth), Karuṇāmaya (Matsyendranāth), and five small Buddhas representing the southern 'Aśokan' *stūpa* (Lagã Thūr) since that is where Optional Samyak used to be held, on the land now occupied by the army camp.

The Tārā who accompanies each Optional Samyak deity is known as 'grandmother goddess' (*ajidyaḥ*) and is popularly taken to represent the original donor's wife. The Dīpaṅkara himself is known, among other names, as 'grandfather god' (*ājudyaḥ*) and is taken to be the donor himself.[31] These popular notions fit rather well with the Tantric ones, since one of the ideas behind Tantric ritual is the identification of the worshipper with the godhead. Dīpaṅkara, like Svayambhū, is often addressed as 'Ādibuddha', original Buddha. In Mahāyāna Buddhism this is given a theological interpretation on top of the merely chronological sense in which, for Theravāda Buddhism, Dīpaṅkara is the first Buddha to predict the future Buddhahood of Śākyamuni. According to Hemraj Sakya (1979: 77) the light both of Svayambhū and of Dīpaṅkara is the *dharmakāya*, 'religion body'; this is the ultimate essence of the Buddha in Mahāyāna Buddhism, and in effect the Buddhist Absolute. These private Dīpaṅkara deities or 'Samyak gods' have annual reconsecration ceremonies which include long rites, some of them held in the Tantric shrine. This identity of the Dīpaṅkara deity, the founder of the rite, and the esoteric divinity of the Tantric shrine – all of them in some way consubstantial with the Absolute or *nirvāṇa* – is no doubt indicated symbolically in that context.

The role of Dīpaṅkara is, however, more precise than that of standing for the Buddhist Absolute, a role which in general is performed in Newar Buddhism by the Svayambhū *stūpa*. Rather, Dīpaṅkara has come to be associated with the virtues of Buddhist alms-giving. The principal scripture related to him in Nepal is called the Kapiśāvadāna.[32] It is this collection of stories that is important in Nepal and not the Pali Nidānakathā. The latter relates how Sumedha, a young Brahman, lay down in the mud for Dīpaṅkara to pass over it, and Dīpaṅkara then predicted that Sumedha would be a Buddha called Gautama in a future life. Rather than devotion, the Kapiśāvadāna stresses the importance of feeding and giving alms to the Monastic Community, but then makes the same connection between doing this and future Buddhahood. In imitating King Sarvānanda, the main protagonist of the Kapiśāvadāna, with their devotion to Dīpaṅkara and the Monastic Community, Newar Buddhists are implicitly starting on the same path to Buddhahood themselves.

The Kapiśāvadāna begins with the self-contained story of the monkey Jñānākara ('Mine of Knowledge') who is devoted to Dīpaṅkara.[33] Next comes the story of the child Dharmaśrī, who has nothing to offer Dīpaṅkara but a pile of dust he has been playing with. Because he offers it with such a pure mind, it turns into gold. Dīpaṅkara predicts that he will be reborn in a royal family in the city of Dīpāvatī. After a disquisition by Dīpaṅkara on alms-giving, in which he emphasizes that the value of the gift depends on the purity of the intention with which it is given, there follows the story of King Sarvānanda. Although the connection is not made by Newars, as far as I know, the story of the gift of dust or earth must surely derive from the tradition that Aśoka as a small boy made the same gift. It is tempting, though rather more speculative, to connect the five-yearly Samyak festival of Lalitpur to the practice, supposedly initiated by Aśoka and imitated by subsequent Buddhist monarchs, of a quinquennial festival in which the whole kingdom is offered to the Monastic Community and then redeemed with a vast amount of money.[34]

The local stories that have grown up around King Sarvānanda are an interesting example of the construction of tradition. The Sanskrit versions of the Kapiśāvadāna simply describe King Sarvānanda carrying out an exemplary alms-giving (including feast) for Dīpaṅkara and his monks (R.L. Mitra 1971: 98). The local story is rather more interesting.[35] It identifies King Sarvānanda's city as the Lalitpur locality, Guita. Dīpaṅkara goes first to receive the few grains of rice an old woman of Guita offers him, before attending King Sarvānanda's alms-giving. The King, somewhat offended, asks why and Dīpaṅkara explains that the old woman's alms were earned by hard work, whereas the King's were not. The King goes off and apprentices himself to a blacksmith, earns much money, and returns to give a large amount of alms. Lalitpur's Pañcadān is observed on the anniversary of his gift.[36] A small statue of the old woman is displayed every year in Guita Bahī which Sarvānanda is supposed to have founded. Karunakar Vaidya (1986: 82–3) points out the 'historical paradox' (which locals seem not to notice) that the city of Sarvānanda was supposedly built in the first or Satya world era, at a time when, according to another universally accepted local tradition, the Valley was still a lake.

One of the morals which may be drawn from the story of the old widow is that of the widow's mite.[37] In Dīpaṅkara's sermon, after the story of Dharmaśrī, the boy whose gift of dust turns to gold, the moral is explicitly drawn that it is the intention which counts (A.K. Vajracharya 1983 II: 445–6). This preserves the ancient Buddhist morality of intention. Newar Buddhists sometimes say that religious works done for show are not meritorious. At the same time, it is King Sarvānanda who is to be the future Buddha. This also fits with what Newar Buddhists feel, that religion and making merit is easier for the rich, and that there is more merit in bigger and more expensive demonstrations of piety.[38] And it is in imitation of King Sarvānanda that Pañcadān is given. Thus Siddhi Raj Shakya, the donor of the optional Pañcadān in Lalitpur of 1982, mentioned above, wrote in the preface to the book of 'gift-verses' (*dānavākya*) which was also given to all comers, as follows:

In the time of Dīpaṃkara Buddha, King Sarvānanda held *pañjadān* in the city of Dīpāvatī, by giving alms of a meal etc. to Dīpaṃkara Buddha and his following of monks, with the intention of bringing about the happiness of all beings. Today, Pañja Eighth of 1982, *pañjadān* is taking place with the intention of (bringing about) the happiness of all living beings. This little book of 'gift-verses' is being offered with the hope that by means of the merit of this alms-giving all living beings will be freed from suffering.

(A.K. Vajracharya 1982)

In a short article on the Nepalese cult of Dīpaṅkara, Vergati (1982b) makes two important points. First, all the evidence for it is from the late Malla period, i.e. seventeenth century and later. Second, there is a triad formed by Dīpaṅkara (the first Buddha), Śākyamuni (the Buddha of this age), and Maitreya (the future Buddha).[39] This triad is surely intended in the three monasteries (*bahī*) of Guita. The smallest and oldest has a north-facing Maitrī Bodhisattva (Maitreya) as main deity, the next-door Guita Bahī has an east-facing Śākyamuni, and the larger Tadhā̃ Bahī has a north-facing Dīpaṅkara. That the cult of Dīpaṅkara is late is indeed very probable. The cult brings the supremely Buddhist act of alms-giving to the Monastic Community into association with a previous Buddha. Alms are offered to Dīpaṅkara in imitation of Śākyamuni himself in one of his previous lives. The implication is therefore that the ordinary devotee of today is also, by giving alms, setting out on the path to complete enlightenment as a Buddha.

The way in which this Śrāvakayāna activity has been put in a Mahāyānist framework is typical of Newar Buddhism. The same is true of Observances discussed below (§7.5), and it is also true of the iconography of the Śrāvakayāna part of the monastery: the shrine of the main deity, who explicitly stands for the Śrāvakayāna part of Newar Buddhism, is usually decorated with paintings and statues of Tārā, Avalokiteśvara, and other Mahāyānist deities. In addition there are frequently symbols which may be given a Diamond Way interpretation; and the struts often display many-armed Tantric forms of the five Buddhas, or the Five Protections (Pañcarakṣā). But the struts are on the upper part of the building, and there we are already in the sphere of the Great Way, and that is the subject of the next two chapters.

Appendix: Some important alms- or gift-receiving verses

When Śākyas and Vajrācāryas receive alms they are meant to recite the verses appropriate to that gift (and in the case of most middle-aged or elderly recipients they do so recite). The verses for different gifts have been published by Asha Kaji Vajracharya (A.K. Vajracharya 1982; this pamphlet, given during Siddhi Raj Shakya's 1982 Optional Pañcadān in Lalitpur mentioned above, appears expanded in A.K. Vajracharya 1983 II: 465–97). What follows is a small selection of the different verses.

When the feet are being washed (receiving *pādyārgha*, *licāykegu*):

Yaḥ[40] *kiṃ cid uṣṇodaka-pādyam eva ca*
Suśītalaṃ svacchaṃ sugandhikaṃ tathā
Karoti pādau sugatasya śraddhayā
Tataḥ kuberatvam upaity asau naraḥ.

That man who offers faithfully to the feet of a Buddha lukewarm foot-water which is cooling, clear, and sweet-smelling, will become as rich as Kubera [god of wealth].

When offering powder on the forehead:

Śrīkhaṇḍa-kuṃkuma-suśobhita-candanāni
Kurvantu ye[41] *satilakān sahabuddhasaṃghe*
Te prāpnuvanti jagati tilakopamatvaṃ
Saundarya-rūpa-pṛthu-divya-viśāla-vaṃśam.

Those who offer (a powder spot of) sandalwood, beautified with (the fragrance of) *śrīkhaṇḍa* or saffron, on the forehead of the Monastic Community along with the Buddha(s), becomes like a decorative spot on the forehead of the world (which consists of having) beauty, looks, and a great, divine, and famous aristocratic lineage.

When receiving rice or paddy (this verse is supposed to be recited by a Śākya or Vajrācārya boy for the first time when he receives a begging bowl with rice in it during Monastic Initiation: Gellner 1988a: 57–8):

Sauvarṇarūpya-vividhadhātuja-mṛnmayaṃ vā
Śālyodanaiḥ suparipūrṇa-supiṇḍapātraṃ
Bhaktyā dadanti satataṃ jinasaṅghikebhyaḥ
Syāt tasya puṇyaṃ asamaṃ phalam aprameyam.

Be it of gold, silver, other metal, or even of clay, if a begging bowl is filled with cooked and uncooked rice, and given always with devotion to the followers of the Conqueror [the Buddha], may the donor gain unparalleled merit and immeasurable good results.

When receiving gifts of money (*dakṣiṇā*):

Yathānulabhyate dravyaṃ dakṣiṇāya prayacchati
Dharmārthaṃ kāmaṃ mokṣaṃ ca prāpnoti bhaktimānasaḥ.

He of devoted mind who offers as *dakṣiṇā* whatever goods he receives will attain [all four ends of man, viz.:] *dharma*, wealth/power, pleasure, and liberation.[42]

Once all the gifts have been presented, he or they should recite as a blessing (*āśirvād*):

Dānaṃ vibhūṣaṇaṃ loke dānaṃ durgati-nivāraṇaṃ
Dānaṃ svargasya sopānaṃ dānaṃ śāntikaraṃ śubham.

Charity [religious gift-giving] is the decoration of the world, charity prevents a bad rebirth, charity is the stairway to heaven, charity is the auspicious bringer of peace.

Then both donor(s) and recipient(s) recite together:

Atha khalu rājā sabhāpayitvā[43] *bhagavantam etad avocat:*
Adya me saphalaṃ janma saphalaṃ jīvitaṃ ca me
Adya buddhakule jāto buddhaputro 'smi sāṃpratam.

Then the king [Sarvānanda] addressed the Lord [Dīpaṅkara] as follows: Now this birth of mine is successful, now my life is successful, now I have been born into the Buddha's family, now I am a son of the Buddha.

This verse goes back at least to the Bodhicaryāvatāra (3.25) of Śāntideva (probably seventh century). It is used in other contexts too; for example, it is put in the mouths of the neophytes towards the end of Tantric Initiation.

Finally a second blessing is recited:

Āyuvṛddhir yaśovṛddhir vṛddhiprajñā sukhas tathā
Ārogyaṃ dhanaṃ santānaṃ santu te sapta vṛddhayaḥ.[44]

The increase of life, the increase of fame, the increase of wisdom, happiness, health, wealth, offspring – may you obtain the seven increases.

7

The Great Way (Part I): the Buddhist householder, his duties and religion

A man cannot fulfil his *saṃskāradharma* [religion or duty of sacraments] without going through the Ten Sacraments. In accordance with this rule the prince Siddhārtha [the future Buddha] first married Yaśodharā and only then did he renounce the homely life and go off to obtain complete enlightenment . . . Without a *śakti* [a wife] no rite such as Observances (*vrata*) and so on can be complete.

The Wedding Dialogue (*vivāhayā khȁ*)

7.1 Merit-making through local pilgrimage

The practices which make up the religion of Śākyas and Vajrācāryas and other Buddhist Newars take place in a sacred setting. This is equally true of Hindus, who have an alternative set of sacred identifications for the different points of the Kathmandu Valley. For Hindus, however, the local sacredness is perhaps more often a reflection of still holier sites in India, whereas for Buddhists, though they too accept the holiness of the Ganges, and go on pilgrimage to both Buddhist and Hindu sites in India, the sacredness of the Kathmandu Valley is something unique. A folk etymology cited equally by Buddhists and by Hindus derives the name 'Nepal' from 'niyam pāl', 'keeping the rules'. The gods have descended to Nepal (i.e. the Kathmandu Valley), it is believed, because the people there keep the rules of religion; and as they gradually abandon those rules, so the gods decline to grant their favours.

Michael Allen (in press) has recently drawn a useful contrast between two types of pilgrimage. First there is that undertaken at long distance in which pilgrims leave their own region and enter what would in the past have been another region, subject to another King. Contrasted with this is the local pilgrimage, which can usually be accomplished without staying overnight away from home. In any case, it does not involve leaving one's own region. Some of these local pilgrimages are optional; others, such as Matayā, occur as part of the annual cycle of festivals. Such festivals which take the form of a local pilgrimage play a crucial role in legitimizing this view of the Kathmandu Valley as a sacred space. Many local pilgrimages trace out a clockwise movement around a centre and, as will be seen below, in some cases learned interpretation sees this explicitly as marking out the framework of a mandala.

In line with this image of the Valley as a mandala, Mary Slusser called her cultural history *Nepal Mandala*. Riccardi has attacked this title as a linguistic hybrid and as historically inexact, since the phrase is only used 'once or twice' in Licchavi inscriptions.[1] These criticisms miss the point that the Valley is indeed conceptualized in the rituals and inscriptions of both Buddhists and Hindus as a mandala and that the mandala model serves to structure space in a host of other contexts as well (as discussed above, §2.1). Because the perception of the Valley as a mandala is never explicitly analysed by Slusser, the fact that at a given historical period the mandala model became pervasive is not brought to the fore. Instead the main thesis of Slusser's book is that the culture of the Valley is continuous and unbroken from Licchavi times down to the present. This means that religious changes do not get the discussion they deserve. In short, Riccardi may be right that the term 'Nepal mandala' is anachronistic for Licchavi Nepal. He is wrong to dismiss it altogether: it is accurate and informative for the Malla period and for what counts as traditional Newar religion today.[2]

A mandala is an arrangement of deities conceived of in sets (of four, eight, sixty-four or more) laid out along the axes of the cardinal points around a centre. Most basically the mandala model is used by priests in complex rituals to arrange patterns of coloured powder and representations of divinities. This is what most ordinary Newars understand by the word 'mandala'.[3]

At the same time the mandala is the model for all religious activities which can be represented spatially. Thus N. Gutschow and M. Bajracharya (1977) describe three concentric sets of eight Mother Goddesses forming three circles of increasing size around the city of Kathmandu; they are visited in turn during the course of Power-Place Worship. The three pilgrimage circles are interpreted as standing for the circles (*cakra*) of body, speech, and thought (*kāya*, *vāk*, *citta*), a common trilogy. A correspondence is also made with the three bodies (*trikāya*) of the Buddha, his corporeal, divine, and ultimate forms (*nirmāṇa-*, *saṃbhoga-*, and *dharma-*

kāya).[4] In completing the pilgrimage circuit one is deemed also to have experienced these aspects of the Buddha.

Such practices as these make clear that the mandala model applies equally to the universe as a whole, to the country (*deśa*) Nepal, to each city, to each temple and shrine, and, Tantrically, to the worshipper's own body. The realization of one's own identity with these larger designs is the attainment of salvation, a process discussed below (§9.3, 10.2). The works of Gutschow and Kölver (1975) and Barré *et al.* (1981) have established beyond doubt that the mandala design was the basis of town planning in early Malla Nepal.

In spite of the architectural and anthropological interest which these themes have rightly aroused, the significance of the specifically Buddhist sacred schema built into every complex Buddhist ritual has not been appreciated.[5] At the beginning of every ritual performed on behalf of a parishioner the Vajrācārya priest recites in Sanskrit what is called 'And now the great gift' ('Adya mahādāna'), while the parishioner touches the Worship Plate. This is known as 'doing the intention (*saṃkalpa*) (of the rite)'. It runs as follows:[6]

OṂ, now in the period of the Attained One, Lion of the Śākyas [i.e. the Buddha], in the auspicious time, in the world system called Sahā, in the Manu-age called Sun-born (*vaivasvata*), in the Kali world era that comes after the Satya, Tretā, and Dvāpara world eras, in its first section, in the northern Pañcāla country of the Bharata continent, in the Himālayas, in the region of Vāsuki [the *nāga* or holy serpent], in the Power-Place (*pīṭha*) called Upachandoha, in the holy land of South Asia (*āryavarta*), in the home of Karkoṭaka, king of serpents, in the great lake called 'dwelling of the holy serpents', in the place of the *caitya* Śrī Svayambhū, which is presided over (*adhiṣṭhita*) by Śrī Guhyeśvarī Prajñā Pāramitā, in the land presided over by Śrī Mañjuśrī, in the land (or mandala) of Nepal, which has the form of the mandala of Śrī Saṃvara [i.e. Cakrasaṃvara, the main Buddhist Tantric deity], which is the same as the land of Sudurjayā, adorned with the Eight Passionless Ones, [namely] Maṇiliṅgeśvara, Gokarṇeśvara, Kīleśvara, Kumbheśvara, Garteśvara, Phaṇikeśvara, Gandheśvara, and Vikrameśvara, flowing with the four great rivers, [namely] Bāgmatī, Keśavatī, Maṇirohinī, and Prabhāvatī, adorned with the twelve holy Bathing-places, [namely] Puṇya Tīrtha, Śānta Tīrtha, Śaṅkara Tīrtha, Rāja Tīrtha, Manoratha Tīrtha, Nirmala Tīrtha, Nidhāna Tīrtha, Jñāna Tīrtha, Cintāmaṇi Tīrtha, Pramoda Tīrtha, Sulakṣaṇa Tīrtha, and Jaya Tīrtha, surrounded by the mountains Jātamātra Height, Śaṅkha Height, Phūla Height, and Dhyāna Height, adorned with Vajrayoginī, with the Eight Mothers, the Eight Bhairavas, Siṃhinī, Vyāghriṇī, Gaṇeśa, Kumāra, Mahākāla, Hārītī, Hanumān, and the troupe of the Ten Wrathful Ones; on the south bank of the Bāgmatī, on the east bank of the Keśavatī, on the west bank of the Maṇirohinī, on the north bank of the Prabhāvatī,[7] here, within Nepāl Maṇḍala, in the city of Lalitapaṭṭana, in the kingdom (*vijaya rājya*) of Āryāvalokiteśvara [i.e. Karuṇāmaya-Matsyendranāth].

There follows a detailed formula giving the season, month, day, and other astrological information, and then the name of the sponsor, stating his city, quarter of the city (or monastery if he is a Vajrācārya or Śākya), caste, *gotra*,[8] and name, and then the purpose of the ritual.[9]

This 'Adya mahādāna' recitation locates Nepal mandala within the Bharata-continent of Āryavarta, the land of the noble or civilized. Traditionally, in the ancient Indian conception, this meant north India. (Nowadays Bhārat, from Bharata, has been adopted as the name of the modern Indian Republic.) This reflects the fact that culturally the Kathmandu Valley (far more than the Nepalese hills) has been a full and integral part of South Asia for nearly two millennia, and that the differences between the Kathmandu Valley and the Gangetic plains to the south are of the same order as the differences between any two different regions of India. They seem greater at first sight simply because Buddhism has survived there (a proper parallel would be with the way Jainism has survived in Gujerat, Maharashtra, and Karnataka though extinct in its birthplace, the Gangetic plain).[10] Although minor details differ, the 'Adya mahādāna' scheme is shared equally by Hindus, who also describe the Valley as the region of Vāsuki and invoke the presence of Guhyeśvarī. For them, however, Paśupati replaces Svayambhū. The Newar Hindu version of this was taken over by Parbatiyās too, and even given official status by Jang Bahadur Rana (Burghart 1984: 116).

The places described in the 'Adya mahādāna' recitation are shown on the map (Figure 20). The mythical visits to the Valley by Buddhist saints, an integral part of the sacralization of the Valley, are summarized in Table 7.1. Most of the deities mentioned in the recitation can be found in Figure 12 (§3.1 above). The Valley is called Nepal Mandala twice, and also Upachandoha Power-Place (*pīṭha*).[11] That is, it is identified as one of the system of Tantric Power-Places spread around South Asia (particularly famous ones were located in Assam and in Oḍḍiyāna, usually identified as the Swat Valley, now in Pakistan). The Kathmandu Valley is explicitly stated to have the form of a mandala of Saṃvara (= Cakrasaṃvara), the most important Buddhist esoteric deity. Then the various deities are listed, including the Eight Passionless Ones, four great rivers (often in fact no more than muddy streams in the dry season), twelve holy Bathing-Places, and the four holy mountains.

The system of worship, ritual practice, and pilgrimage that goes with the deities and sacred space here described probably dates in this form from the fifteenth century. The Svayambhū Purāṇa, a Sanskrit text existing in various recensions of different lengths, gives the origin myths associated

Table 7.1 *The seven Attained Buddhas (*tathāgata*) plus Mañjuśrī who visited the Nepal Valley and their associations with different peaks and fairs (*melā*).*

Name of Buddha	World era	Came from	Main action in Nepal	Stayed at mountain called (Nw./Skt./Np.)	Date of fair
VIPAŚVĪ	S	Bandumatī	Sowed the seed of Svayambhū	Jāmacwa/ Jātamātrocca/ Nāgārjun	Lhuti Punhī
ŚIKHĪ	S	Aruṇpurī/ Aruṇākṣa	Absorbed into Svayambhū	Dhemacwa/ Dhyānocca/ Campadevī	Khai Sãnhū
VIŚVABHŪ	T	Anuparam/ Anupam	Offered flowers to Svayambhū	Phūcwa/ Phūlocca/ Phūlcoki	Khai Sãnhū and Bhādra kṛṣṇa 3
MAÑJUŚRĪ	T	Mahācīna (China)	Drained lake and settled followers	Mañjuśrīthān/ Mahāmaṇḍapa/ Mañjuśrīthān	Śrī pañcamī
KRAKUCHANDA	T	Kṣemavatī	Created Bāgmatī and Viṣṇumatī rivers, and initiated monks	Śiphūca (Śiuca)/ Siddhiphūlocca[a]/ Śivapurī	Khai Sãnhū[b]
KANAKAMUNI	D	Śobhavatī	Visited Svayambhū	Svayambhū (Śẽgu)/ Vajrakūṭaparvata[c]/ Svayambhūnāth	—
KĀŚYAPA	D	Vārāṇasī (Benares)	Taught Pracaṇḍa Dev = Śānta Śrī Vajrācārya	Svayambhū (Śẽgu)/ Gośṛṅgaparvata[c]/ Svayambunāth	—
ŚĀKYAMUNI	K	Kapila-vastu	Proselytized, visited Guhyeśvarī and Namobuddha	Svayambhū (Śẽgu)/ Gopuccagiriparvata[c]/ Svayambhūnāth	—

Sources: The information derives ultimately from the Svayambhū Purāṇa. Before that the tradition of the seven Attained Ones goes back to the earliest stratum of Buddhist scripture (see Mahāpadāna Sutta, Dīgha Nikāya II). The Svayambhū Purāṇa traditions can be found in Wright (1972: 77–84), BV (1r–7r, 37r–38r). Similar tables with further information can be found at A.K. Vajracharya (1977: 5–6), H. Sakya (1977: 772; and pp. 3ff.), and B.R. Bajracharya (1986: 7–14).

Notes:

[a] H. Sakya (1977: 22) gives Śaṃkhocca as the Skt. name, Wright (1972: 81) gives Phulocca, R.L. Mitra (1971: 247) gives Śaṅkhagiri. In the case of the first three Buddhas at least, the name of the mountain refers to the Buddha's actions (sowing seed, meditating, and offering flowers respectively).

[b] The fair actually takes place at Bāgh Duwār, the source of the Viṣṇumatī, not on the peak. H. Sakya (1977: 21) derives the name from *vāk-dvāra* (= Bāgmatī), the reference being to Krakuchanda's creating the Viṣṇumatī and Bāgmatī with the hair of the monks he had initiated.

[c] These Skt. names are the ones given by H. Sakya 1977: 772. According to the Svayambhū Purāṇa these alternative names apply to Svayambhū in different ages: Padmagiri in the Satya, Gośṛṅga in the Dvāpara, Vajrakūṭa in the Tretā, and Gopuccha in the Kali Yuga (R.L. Mitra 1971: 246).

Under 'world era', S = Satya, T = Tretā, D = Dvāpara, K = Kali Yuga.

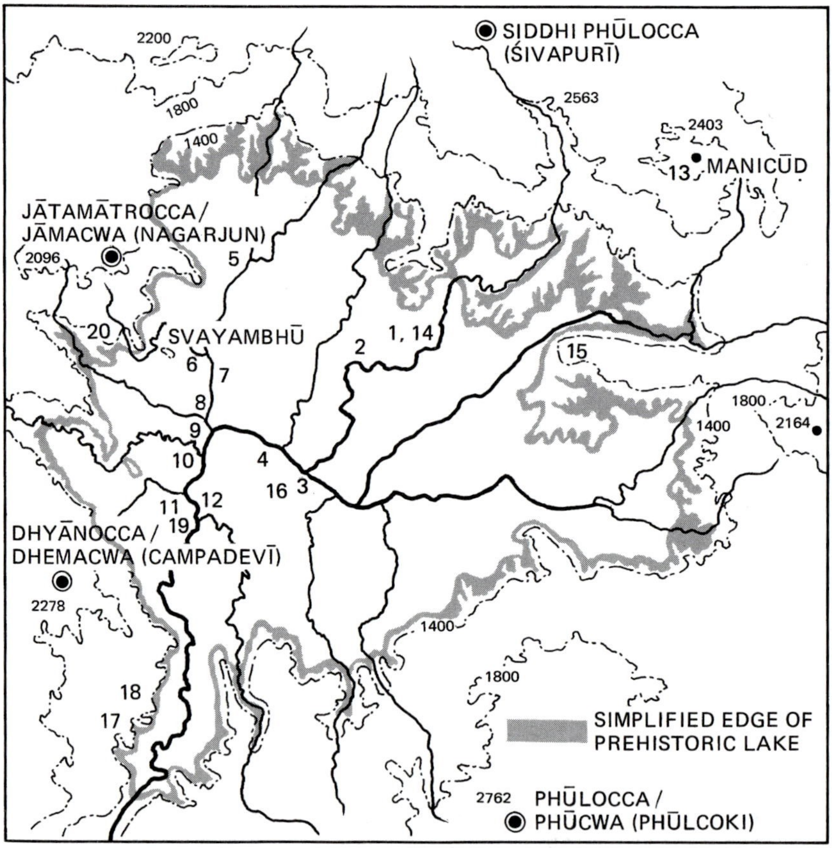

Map: N. Gutschow

Figure 20. Map of the Kathmandu Valley showing the four holy mountains (see Table 7.1), the sacred rivers and Bathing-Places, and the sites of the Eight Passionless Ones. The names of all these places are recited during the 'Adya mahādāna'. Map: N. Gutschow.
Key:

BATHING-PLACES

Name of Tīrtha	Place	Sanskritic names of joining river and main river	
1 Puṇya	Gokarṇa	Amoghaphaladāyaṇī	Bāgmatī
2 Śānta	Guhyeśvarī	Māradāyiṇī	Bāgmatī
3 Śaṅkara	Śaṅkhamūl	Maṇirohiṇī	Bāgmatī
4 Rāja	Dhātilā (Vārāhī)	Rājamañjarī[d]	Bāgmatī
5 Manoratha	Khusikhya[a]	Vimalāvatī	Keśavatī[e]
6 Nirmala	Bhacā Khusi[b]	Kusumāvatī[f]	Keśavatī

7 Nidhāna	Lakha/Lakhutīrtha[c]	Suvarṇavatī	Keśavatī
8 Jñāna	Kara/Kanhakhusi	Pāpanāśinī	Keśavatī
9 Cintāmaṇi	Tyekhu Dobān	Keśavatī	Bāgmatī
10 Pramoda	Dānigā	Ratnavatī	Bāgmatī
11 Sulakṣaṇa	Bhājāgā	Cārumatī	Bāgmatī
12 Jaya	Nyekhuhwā̃	Prabhāvatī	Bāgmatī

THE EIGHT PASSIONLESS ONES (*aṣṭavaitarāga*)

Name	Object worshipped according to A.K. Vajracharya (1981a)	Place	Buddhist identity
13 Maṇiliṅgeśvara	*caitya*	Maṇicūḍ	Maitrī
14 Gokarṇeśvara	Mahādeva[g]	Gokarṇa	Gaganagañja
15 Kīleśvara	*caitya*	Cā̃gu Nārāyaṇa	Samantabhadra
16 Kumbheśvara	Mahādeva	Konti	Vajrapāṇi
17 Garteśvara	Mahādeva	Behind Phampi	Mañjughoṣa[i]
18 Phaṇikeśvara	Mahādeva	Śeṣanārāyaṇa, Phampi	Sarvanivaraṇa-viṣkambhin
19 Gandheśvara	Mahādeva	Cobhar[h]	Kṣitigarbha
20 Vikrameśvara	Mahādeva	Icangu Nārāyaṇa	Khagarbha

Notes to key:

The indications given in Locke (1987), based on different (though cognate) sources, agree almost entirely with the above. It will be seen from the notes below that there is no universal agreement on the Sanskrit appellations of the more obscure streams. The order of the Eight Passionless Ones is, roughly, a clockwise circumambulation of the Valley, starting in the north-east. Kumbheśvara is also known as Sarveśvara, Garteśvara as Gopāleśvara, Gandheśvara as Garṇeśvara, and Vikrameśvara as Ādīśvara.

a Near Manmaiju. R.K. Vajracharya (1980: 121, 127) identifies this as Tyekhu Dobān which would reduplicate number 9 and ruin the order.
b A.K. Vajracharya (1981a: 7): Vilāsaḥ.
c A.K. Vajracharya (1981a: 8): 'Kā̃gu Khusi, below Svayambhū'.
d =Rudramatī.
e =Viṣṇumatī.
f R.K. Vajracharya (1980: 121]: Puṣpāvatī. H. Sakya (1977: 774): Bhadramatī.
g I.e. a *śivaliṅga*.
h R.K. Vajracharya (1980: 124) cites this as 'Kwenā', but it is definitely inside the monastery of Co Bāhāḥ (Locke 1985: 142b).
i According to A.K. Vajracharya 1981a. R.K. Vajracharya (1980: 123) gives this as Khagarbha.

with all these places and deities, and the earliest text is dated 1557 (Malla 1982: 41). Many other cults, such as that of Dīpaṅkara and of the goddess Svasthānī, seem to have their origin in the same period. Naturally this creative synthesis built on much that was there already, but at the present stage of knowledge, or rather ignorance, about the Ṭhakurī period, it is impossible to say exactly what existed before the fifteenth-century cultural renaissance.

Sylvain Lévi called the Svayambhū Purāṇa 'a *māhātmya* for Buddhists'. Māhātmyas are Hindu pilgrimage texts describing holy sites and giving the myths and stories explaining their sacredness.[12] The Svayambhū Purāṇa does not belong to the very first rank of Buddhist sacred texts. It does not encapsulate the highest soteriological values like the Prajñā Pāramitā (Perfection of Wisdom), it does not describe the life of the Buddha or his previous lives, nor does it give the secret instructions and teachings associated with the systematic worship of an esoteric deity as do the various Tantras. What the Svayambhū Purāṇa does do is describe and legitimize the sacred historical and geographical framework within which Newar Buddhists live and which is articulated in the 'Adya Mahādāna' recitation given above. As such its contents have filtered down into many other texts (e.g. the chronicle translated as Wright's 'History of Nepal') and contexts (e.g. the cycle of Observances to the Eight Passionless Ones). Its stories are therefore better known to ordinary Buddhists than the contents of other scriptures.

A useful summary of the Svayambhū Purāṇa's teachings about pilgrimage sites in the Valley can be found in Kölver 1986. The most important of these teachings is the list of Twelve Bathing-Places (*dvādaśa tīrtha*) (Kölver 1986: 147–51). With each Bathing-Place the text associates a reward (*phala*), an evil to be abandoned and a state of mind to be cultivated, a holy text, a gift and so on. Newar Buddhist *paṇḍit*s have produced similar lists inspired by or based on the various different recensions of the Svayambhū Purāṇa: these include a holy serpent (*nāga*), type of incense, a jewel, a colour, a stipend (*dakṣiṇā*), for each Bathing-Place. The lists agree on the order of the Bathing-Places and on the names of the serpents, but on the other items they differ. In practice it is the Vajrācārya priests in charge of the visiting pilgrimage group who decide which associations to make. Thus R.K. Vajracharya (1980: 120) protests that although *śāstra* and *grantha* (scripture) on which the rites are based are one, every priest has his own list of the gifts (*dān*) appropriate to each Bathing-Place. He continues:

In this rite of bathing and gift-giving (*snān dān*) at the twelve Bathing-Places each Vajrācārya has alms given according to his own idea. I believe that, if this were done away with and a single formula were adopted, the position (*astītva* [sic]) of priests (*guruju*) would improve because then parishioners would have faith that their priests (were acting) all on a single (scriptural) basis. At the moment one priest has one kind of prestation given, the next a different one. In my experience priests agree on what has to be given down to Manoratha Tīrtha (Tyekhu Dobān) but below there they do it each in their own way.

(R.K. Vajracharya 1980: 122)

In contrast to the gifts given at each Bathing-Place, the stories which are read at each site appear to be relatively fixed and derive from the Svayambhū Purāṇa. I have seen a modern printed Newari version by Badri Ratna Bajracharya (1983) being used by a Kathmandu Vajrācārya at the Kumbheśvara temple in Lalitpur (identified as the *bodhisattva* Vajrapāṇi).[13]

The Svayambhū Purāṇa also has a second set of eight, as opposed to twelve, Bathing-Places (Kölver 1986: 152–9). These are associated each with a Mother Goddess, a Power-Place (*pīṭha*), a Bhairava, a cremation ground, a Worship Goddess (*lāsyā*), a corpse, a Realized One (*siddha*), a river, a cloud, a type of Tantric food, a form of Śiva, and so on. What we have here is a Tantric set of pilgrimage sites in which the Kathmandu Valley is visualized as the mandala of Cakrasaṃvara, as stated in the 'Adya Mahādāna' recitation above. The same mandala is met in Tantric Initiation (§9.3.3). The set of twelve Bathing-Places is, by contrast, an exoteric, Mahāyānist practice.[14] Thus the set of twelve is better known and is the set followed in the popular cycle of Observances to Lokeśvara.

7.2 Buddhism and life-cycle rites[15]

Buddhism was not at first a religion of life-in-the-world, and in Theravāda Buddhism today there are usually only two specifically Buddhist life-cycle rituals: the local equivalent of Monastic Initiation, i.e. temporary ordination, and death rituals.[16] In so far as Buddhist monks in Theravāda countries are involved in other life-cycle rituals it is only in order to receive alms or recite protective formulae, that is, to carry out religious acts which are appropriate to any occasion, and not specifically designed for the rite in question. It is not surprising therefore that the life-cycle rites of Buddhist householders, when they came to be cast in a specifically Buddhist form, took a parallel course to Hindu life-cycle rites. The Newar Buddhist 'Wedding Dialogue' translated in the appendix below assumes unselfconsciously that the life-cycle rites of a householder, as the Buddha was before he renounced to seek enlightenment, are the same as those of a Hindu householder.

In order to demonstrate the similarity between Hindu and Buddhist life-cycle rites among the Newars, the standard sixteen Hindu sacraments are included in Table 7.2. This list was the outcome of a long historical evolution and even now the same sixteen are not always cited; there is even more diversity in ancient texts (Pandey 1969: 19–21). I have included two scholarly lists by Vajrācāryas. One, a list quoted by a modern Newar *paṇḍit*, is clearly a copy of the Hindu schema, reduced to ten sacraments. The other, of thirteen sacraments, is a more truly descriptive list, compiled by Hodgson's informant, Amṛtānanda. Only three of the Hindu list, those to do with Vedic study, are completely irrelevant to the Buddhist case.

Of the three 'pre-natal' sacraments Newar Buddhists say (C. Vajracharya 1984: 46), just as Pandey himself said of Indian Hindus (1969: 279), that they had all been performed in the past, but have, in these bad times, fallen into disuse.[17] This is a pious myth. Most ordinary people perform as few rituals as is compatible with their caste status. Higher castes perform more rituals than lower castes and the rich do them more elaborately than the poor. It is unlikely that the sacred texts describe a state of affairs once general but now abandoned; it is more probable that the texts and the *paṇḍits*' schemas describe an ideal which those of high status (particularly kings) might enact in full, but which were never wholly practised by the vast majority.

Another context in which Newars come across the sacraments is the 'ten rituals' (*daśakarma*) used to consecrate or reconsecrate a holy image. They are shown in Table 7.2. These sacraments are also used in the special old-age ritual, or rather set of three (or four) rituals performed at different ages, called *burā jā̃kwa*: ordinary Newars know that in this rite the 'ten sacraments' are performed on the old person, thus rendering them divine. (Strictly it is only the third and fourth Old-Age Initiations which are supposed to do this, but popularly all such rites are credited with it.) These rites of old age are not usually included in the sets of sacraments; rather, the set of sacraments is recapitulated within Old-Age Initiation.[18]

As to the life-cycle rites of clean-caste Newars, the thirteen listed by Amṛtānanda are a better description than the other schemas, but his list includes customs of widely differing order: some, like 'going to the maternal uncle's', are not rituals to the Newar way of thinking, but merely customs. Some, such as 'cutting the umbilical cord', are merely ritualized actions occurring in the course of a life-cycle ritual properly speaking. As shown in Table 7.3, of the ten or thirteen scriptural sacraments, only five (or six for some Newars) are real life-cycle rituals. It is worth noting that many of the small ritual specialist castes, such as the Nāpit, Taṇḍukār, Mānandhar, and Khaḍgī, follow the practice of high-caste Hindus and observe the First

Table 7.2 *The sacraments according to different sources.*

	Sixteen Brahmanical sacraments (Pandey 1969)	The ten sacraments acc. to B.R.Bajracharya (1986: 62ff.)	The ten sacraments administered to divinize an image (Locke 1980: 210–18)	The thirteen Buddhist sacraments and the time performed acc. to Hodgson's *paṇḍit* Amṛtānanda (Brough 1948)		Current Newari where relevant	Time after birth performed	English (capitals show that it is performed by Newars, underlining that it is a main ritual)
Pre-natal rites	Garbhādāna	Garbhādāna[c]						Conception[c]
	Puṃsavana	Puṃsavana[d]						Quickening of male[d]
	Simāntonnayana	Simāntonayana[d]						Hair-parting[d]
Rites of childhood				Bāladarśana	1st day			Viewing child
				Nābhikṣedana	3rd day	pī dhenegu	4th day	CUTTING UMBILICAL CORD
	Jātakarma	Jātakarma	1 Jātakarma	Jātaśuddhi	6th day	macābū bẽkegu	4th, 6th or 10th day	BIRTH PURIFICATION
	Nāmakaraṇa	Nāmakaraṇa	2 Nāmakaraṇa	Nāmakaraṇa	11th or 12th day	nā̃ chuyegu	4th, 6th or 10th day	NAME GIVING[e]
	Niṣkramana			Niḥkāsana	c. 1st month	pājuyā thāy wanegu	1 month	GOING TO MB'S HOUSE
	Karṇavedha			Karṇavedha	2nd or 3rd month	nhāypāpwā khanegu		EAR PIERCING[f]
			3 Phalaprāśana					Feeding fruits
	Annaprāśana	Annaprāśana	4 Annaprāśana	Annaprāśana	6th or 8th month	(macā) jākwa	6 or 8 months[g]	FIRST RICE-FEEDING
	Cūḍākaraṇa	Cūḍākaraṇa	6 Cūḍākaraṇa	Cūḍākaraṇa	3rd, 5th, or 7th year	busā khāyegu[h]	5 years[h]	FIRST HEAD-SHAVING
Educational rites	Vidyārambha	Vratādeśa/ Śīlapradāna	7 Vratādeśa	Vidyārambha	5th year			Beginning learning
	Upanayana[a]		5 Upanayana	Mekhalābandha	10th year[i]	kaytā pūjā/ bare chuyegu[k]	5,7,9, or 11 years	LOINCLOTH WORSHIP/ MONASTIC INITIATION
	Samāvartana[b]	Vratamokṣaṇa	8 Vratamokṣaṇa			cīvar kwakāyegu[k]		REMOVING MONK'S ROBE
Adult rites	Vivāha	Pāṇigrahaṇa	9 Pāṇigrahaṇa (+10 Prāṇapratiṣṭhā)	Vivāha	14th or 16th year	bihā yāyegu		MARRIAGE
			11: 8 abhiṣekas[j]			ācā luyegu	5–20 years	CONSECRATION OF VAJRA-MASTER
				Dīkṣā		dekhā kāyegu		TANTRIC INITIATION
	Antyeṣṭi			Mṛtyusaṃskāra		dāha saṃskār, śī uyegu		CREMATION AFTER DEATH

Notes:

[a] The Vedic *upanayana* followed the twelfth and thirteenth sacraments, *vedārambha* (beginning Vedic study) and *keśānta* (shaving the beard).

[b] The Vedic *samāvartana* or *snāna* (end of studentship) is assimilated here to the end of Monastic Initiation.

[c] B.R. Bajracharya (1983: *ka*; 1986: 52–4) glosses this as Confinement. Similarly he glosses the Vedic rite of beginning study as *śīlapradāna*, the giving of vows in Monastic Initiation.

[d] Both of these are explained by B.R. Bajracharya (1986: 54) as 'feeding the pregnant woman food as per her wish', with a worship of a *caitya*. In other words, these are not Newar Buddhist rites, and the terms are made to fit the practice willy-nilly.

[e] Initial letter chosen then, but name only chosen and used after the First Rice-Feeding.

[f] Done after birth at First Rice-Feeding but not ritualized.

[g] Or for a girl: five or seven months.

[h] Or *busākhā*. Castes with Buddhist priests usually perform this at the same time as Loincloth Worship.

[i] Amṛtānanda specifies the fifth or seventh year for girls, i.e. for Mock Marriage (*ihi*).

[j] These eight consecrations are the same as in the Consecration of a Vajra-master (Locke 1980: 219–20).

[k] Monastic Initiation performed by Śākyas and Vajrācāryas only. Interestingly Amṛtānanda's list does not mention Monastic Initiation, but if anything his description of *cūḍākaraṇa* (hair to be cut by *sthavira*, invite the *sthavira*s of the monastery to a feast) seems to fit it.

Table 7.3 *The main life-cycle rites for three categories of Newar male.*

High-caste Hindus plus some others	Śākyas and Vajrācāryas	Maharjans and most other *buddhamārgīs*
Birth Purification	Birth Purification	Birth Purification
First Rice-Feeding	First Rice-Feeding	First Rice-Feeding
First Head-Shaving		
Loincloth Worship	Monastic Initiation	Loincloth Worship
Marriage	Marriage	Marriage
Death	Death	Death

Head-Shaving as a separate ritual.[19] This is not true, however, of Lohākār/ Nakarmī (Kau), of Citrakār, or of Mālākār (Mālī, Gathu).

Each caste, and indeed each local clan, has its own traditional ways of performing these rites. Ordinary Newars, particularly Maharjans, carry out Birth Purification themselves, without calling a priest. Śākyas and Vajrācāryas call a priest only for the First Rice-Feeding of the first child: subsequent children receive their first rice not from the priest, but from the Maharjan midwife (*didi aji*). The girls' equivalent of Loincloth Worship, i.e. the rite which marks their passage to the status of adults, is *ihi*, Mock Marriage to the *bel* fruit.[20] However, Maharjans in outlying villages, and Khaḍgī and other low castes everywhere, do not perform Mock Marriage; they have only the subsequent rite of Confinement (*bārāy tayegu*).[21] For them it performs the same social function, that of marking the onset of adulthood, as Mock Marriage does in the cities (Toffin 1984: 141).

Life-cycle rites mark progress to adulthood in two ways. Firstly, each new status requires a different mode of cremation and increasing degrees of death pollution to be observed by relatives (this is shown in Table 7.6). Secondly, the rites bring about an increasing incorporation into one's caste. In particular, after the 'puberty' ceremonies that mark the threshold of adulthood, one is expected to observe the purity taboos surrounding the consumption of food and drink like an adult. It is popularly (though incorrectly) supposed that *jāt* in *jātakarma* (Birth Purification) refers to *jāt* meaning 'caste': this folk etymology is invoked to justify the custom whereby a child whose umbilical cord has not been cut can be adopted by anyone because it 'has no caste'. Even after this caste is a matter of degree: young children are not expected to bother about eating polluted (*cipa*) food, although they are taught not to put inedible things into their mouths, not to eat with the left hand, and so on. At this time too they are sometimes said 'to have no caste'. After Monastic Initiation/Loincloth Worship for boys and Mock Marriage for girls they then have caste and must obey the rules like an adult.

The way in which the life-cycle rites are remodelled in a Buddhist form can be seen from the example of Loincloth Worship. The rite of Monastic Initiation, through which Śākyas and Vajrācāryas pass, has been discussed above (§6.1). Other *buddhamārgī* castes count as laity and not as monks and may not undergo this ceremony: their boys pass instead through Loincloth Worship (*vratabandha, kaytā pūjā*; Np. *bartamān*).[22] In fact during Monastic Initiation Śākyas and Vajrācāryas pass briefly through the same rite, having a symbolic loincloth tied and removed, as a sign of the householder status they leave behind in becoming monks. In the case of other Newars with Vajrācārya priests, the ritual follows instead a Hindu model, and is similar to the rite performed by Brahmans for their patrons who are not entitled to the sacred thread. (Taking the sacred thread is confined among Newars to Brahmans, Jośīs, and a few other Chatharīya Śreṣṭhas.)

In Loincloth Worship the boy dresses as an ascetic with bow and arrow, antelope skin, waterpot, and begging bowl, and prepares to leave for the forest. When he 'attempts to leave' his maternal uncle must hold him back. (Among Maharjans it sometimes happens as a joke that instead the uncle or others abduct him until his parents pay a fine.) In the case of those with Buddhist priests the boy is made to take refuge in the Buddha, Dharma, and Saṃgha, and told to avoid the Ten Unproductive Sins. Then he is instructed to 'leave home, go to the wilderness (*jaṅgal*), sit on an antelope skin, recite mantras (*jap*), do meditation (*dhyān*), and perform devotional service (*sevā*) of Śākyasiṃha Tathāgat [the Buddha]'.[23] As in Monastic Initiation and in Observances, this explanation is ritualized, that is, the priest reads it out on the boy's behalf. Later he receives alms from his mother and paternal aunts. Originally a Hindu rite, Loincloth Worship has here been put in the idiom of Buddhist lay householderhood.

The Van Gennepian scheme of separation, liminal stage, and reintegration fits these male initiation rites, both Buddhist and Hindu, particularly well. The symbolism of liminality is striking and obvious. It is also clear in the girls' rite of Confinement with its twelve-day period of seclusion. By contrast, the theme of liminality plays a less prominent role in the symbolism of either Mock Marriage or Marriage proper.

Carrying out life-cycle rites for one's family represents the fulfilment of one's duty as a Mahāyāna Buddhist householder. As parents this means that Newar men and women consider it a religious duty to see that their children go through the various life-cycle rituals up to marriage. Young and middle-aged women, whose time and effort is devoted to running the household and caring for young and unmarried children, regard the fulfilment of such tasks as a religious duty; the active piety of visiting temples and performing numerous rituals is considered both more appropriate and more attainable when old. Looking after aged parents while they are alive, and performing rituals (whether Ancestor Worship or other rites) on their behalf after they are dead, is likewise considered one's religious duty. Not to perform this is to be 'without *dharma*'.

Important duties are also owed by the mother's brother (MB, *pāju*) to his sisters' children and by married women to their brothers' children. The paradigm case of ritual duties is at First Head-Shaving or Loincloth Worship (for castes other than Śākyas and Vajrācāryas): notionally, it is the MB who cuts the hair (although in fact he only pretends to and the Barber finishes the job); it is the child's father's sister (FZ, *nini*) who has to catch the hair in a ritual plate on a tripod (*thāybhū*) and dispose of it afterwards in a sacred river (in Lalitpur, the Bāgmatī). The role of the FZ is identical in the Śākyas' and Vajrācāryas' Monastic Initiation ritual, but the MB does not pretend to cut the hair (although his presence is required, simply to accompany the boy). The Barber shaves the boy's head except for the topknot. The topknot, the symbol of householder status, is cut off either by the seniormost monastery elder or by the boy's father's sister's husband (FZH); different monasteries follow one or the other tradition in this matter.

Thus the Monastic Initiation ritual indicates an equivalence between venerated monastery elder and FZH which complements the equivalence of MB and Barber implied by the parallel rites of other castes. The choice of the FZH is determined, no doubt, as Greenwold (1974b: 140) has pointed out, by north Indian hypergamous logic. One must remember, however, that the Newars' marriage pattern is fundamentally isogamous (Quigley 1986). Although an elaborate version of the Wedding Dialogue reproduced below (Appendix 2, pp. 228–30) refers to the 'gift of a virgin', the actual ritual of *kanyādān* occurs only in Mock Marriage and not in traditional weddings to human husbands. The north Indian religious ideology of hypergamy, in which one makes of one's daughter an unreciprocated, meritorious gift to a superior, is found only in this ritual context, and it does not affect marriage patterns or relations between affines.

The duty of the FZ to accept the hair is recompensed by a gift of cloth placed on the ritual plate. The duties of the MB are not recompensed at all, and they are onerous, as Newar men often complain. At all life-cycle rituals numerous prestations flow from wife-givers to their married-out daughters (*mhyāy masta*) and to the daughters' children (*bhinna masta* or *bhincāpī*). Usually a set of clothes has to be given to the child, and often to the mother and father as well. When a young woman gets married a considerable part of her dowry comes from her MB.[24] The provision of all these prestations is viewed as a religious duty.[25] The same applies to the support and festival invitations a married-out daughter receives (involving frequent visits to her natal home where her brothers' wives do all the work). These duties are justified by appeals to fairness: daughters do not inherit any of their parents' assets, so they are owed all this instead. In fact daughters also have to make prestations to their brothers' children, for instance bringing paddy to offer to nephews going through Loincloth Worship/Monastic Initiation and to nieces going through Mock Marriage or Confinement ('badã chuyegu'). But these prestations, as well as the help that daughters provide after a death in their natal home, are very minor in financial terms. Both MB and FZ provide ritual services (and FZH in the case of Śākyas and Vajrācāryas, as we have seen), but only the MB's duties are a serious drain on his material resources.

The course of events during life-cycle rituals is usually supervised by the senior woman of the household, who is likely to be the person who remembers best the numerous details of what has to be done. The ritual, in the narrow sense, is directed and largely performed by the family priest. Thanks to his Tantric powers, i.e. his Vajrayānist qualifications, the householder's priest is able to summon up the deities for his parishioner and perform the required ritual on his behalf. (Most lay people usually show relatively little interest in how the priest accomplishes this – that is 'his work'.) At each of these life-cycle rites, except Ancestor Worship after death, a Flask Worship is performed. Other rites are sometimes included (e.g. the Fire Sacrifice in Loincloth Worship and Monastic Initiation), but Flask Worship is the most basic rite.

Different life-cycle rites require different special arrangements of the ritual implements. At Birth Purification an extra wooden pot (*kulīcā*) is established, containing old beaten rice (*cwaki*), mustard oil, and clarified butter. It represents Hārītī, the Buddhist goddess of smallpox, who has power over young children; after the ritual it is thrown at the nearest *chwāsā*. At marriage, there is particular symbolism involving the ritual Mirror and the Powder Container: the bride receives the former from her father and the latter from her mother as part of her dowry.[26] Later, at the groom's home, in the central rite of Causing to Join (*hwākegu*), bride and groom put their heads together over the Mirror while water from the Flask is poured over their heads.

It is clear from this ritual, and from the lists of sacraments given above, that marriage is indeed a sacred tie for the Newars, contrary to what numerous authors have asserted.[27] They have been misled by the exaggerated accounts of Oldfield and others which claimed that a Newar woman was free to terminate her marriage at will by returning the areca nuts given to seal the marriage contract. In fact this occurs only when the husband dies and the bride is still young (a fact which Fürer-Haimendorf himself records), or if the husband sends the wife away ('ma-yaḥkāḥ chwaye') and does not recall her. Among most Newars widow remarriage is rare and disapproved of when the woman is middle-aged or old. Frequent remarriage without stigma for either men or women is found only in a few outlying Newar villages (e.g. Pyangaon or the nearby Bulu).[28]

At the beginning of each life-cycle ritual the sponsor performs the *guru maṇḍala* rite. At First Rice-Feeding the mother performs it for her newborn child. At Loincloth Worship and Monastic Initiation young boys perform it. At marriage husband and wife perform it together to the same mandala, indicating that henceforth their religious merit is in common. In this way a ritual framework expressing the soteriological aims of the Great Way, using the means of the Diamond Way, is provided for all of the life-cycle rites of the Newar Buddhist householder.

7.3 Buddhist death rituals

Newar Buddhist death rituals are both parallel to Hindu rites, just as we have seen for other life-cycle rites, and at the same time express a difference of values from Hinduism. Buddhists are, as it were, pulled in two directions. On the one hand Vajrācāryas need to be able to provide all the ritual services which lay Buddhist castes desire, and above all, they want to perform Ancestor Worship (*śrāddha*). Moreover, Buddhists' and *buddhamārgī*s' involvement in the *jajmānī* system is primarily a question of specialists required at death: the Barber and the Kāpālī.[29] On the other hand it is at death that Buddhism, as a soteriological system distinct from Hinduism, comes into its own.

The outcome of these different pressures is that Śākyas and Vajrācāryas do perform Ancestor Worship as required up until the Two-Year Rite (see Table 7.8). Thereafter they prefer to mark the anniversary of death in other ways. The men (and in the absence of men, the women) of other castes often perform Ancestor Worship annually for their dead parents (either together or separately) for as long as they live. Often they also perform an apotropaic Ancestor Worship[30] before any big life-cycle ritual, so that no deaths in the family can prevent its completion. Further, many families perform an annual Sixteen Ancestor Worship (*sohra śrāddha*) on behalf of all ancestors.[31] Few Śākyas or Vajrācāryas do any of this today, unless they have a *guthi* which obliges them to. Instead they prefer to patronize Buddhist monks, either Theravāda or Tibetan Mahāyāna, or else to perform a Tantric worship in the dead person's name.

The basic terms which describe the traditional and, for the most part, obligatory mourning-cum-death pollution observed by Newars, as used by the Buddhists of Lalitpur, are given in Table 7.4. I say 'for the most part' for two reasons: the most general term, 'bāre yaye', meaning to observe restrictions, is active: a man may choose to observe restrictions as a mark of respect, for his father-in-law, or a member of the royal family, where it is not obligatory. Conversely families can refuse to do so as a sign that they no longer wish to be considered related to kin with whom there has been a quarrel.[32] Second, although all the other terms are passive, that is, refer to states which befall a person, there is in fact considerable latitude in how strictly one observes them, at least among castes other than high-caste Hindus. The terms themselves and their interpretation vary considerably from one Newar settlement to another. It is in any case a personal matter. If, for example, a farmer's parent should die during the rice-transplanting season, he will not be able to follow the rule about remaining at home until the release from death pollution. Buddhists are in general less strict than high-caste Hindus. A Buddhist who is 'observing restrictions' may enter a monastery compound or approach the temple of a god and get someone else to make offerings for him or her; Hindus refrain even from this.

Concepts of mourning and of death pollution are not distinguished. Underlying the rituals is the idea of pollution but the degree to which those affected by death pollution have a real sense of uncleanness is highly variable: high castes more than low, Hindus more than Buddhists, and women more than men. Some will not take water from those 'observing restrictions', assimilating them thereby to 'unclean' castes; others consider this extreme. There is strong social pressure to conform outwardly to the requirements of mourning; what goes on in the privacy of one's own home is, to some extent, one's own affair.

Leaving aside all these considerations of caste, religion, and personal disposition, the degree of mourning varies along two axes: the closeness of one's relation to the deceased person and their age (strictly: degree of adulthood in ritual terms). The types of mourning required for different categories of relative are shown in Table 7.5. Normally the amount of mourning is roughly proportional to the closeness of the relation. Indeed Newars often use the amount of mourning required as a way of expressing

Table 7.4 *Mourning and death pollution vocabulary as used by Lalitpur Śākyas and Vajrācāryas.*

Newari Term	*bāray yāye*	*dukhā̃ cwane*	*du māle*	*barkhi cwane*	*śokā̃ cwane/ juye*
English	to observe restrictions	to remain in sorrow	to have to observe death pollution	to remain in year-long (mourning)	to remain/to be in grief
Derivation	Np. *bārnu* to enclose, to limit (Turner 1980: 436)	Skt. *duḥkha*, 'pain', 'suffering'	Nw. *dukhā̃ cwane māle*	Skt. *varṣa* 'year' (cf. Turner 1980: 421)	Skt. *śoka*, 'grief'
Denotation	The most general term	Death pollution of household and close relatives for 7 days (other castes: 13 days)		Mourning by sons for parents, by wives for husbands	Mourning by sons for parents, by wives for husbands, by husbands for wives, by brothers for each other.
Connotation	Avoid meat, onions, garlic, tomatoes, beans, etc.; avoid beautification; avoid gods' shrines and accepting *prasād*; avoid leather or wearing cap	Stay in house observing *bāray yāye*; for first 4 days no cooked rice, thereafter rice cooked by married daughters		As *bāray yāye* plus: wear white, sleep on floor; if mother's death, avoid milk, if father's, avoid curds	Either in sense of *barkhi cwane* or in sense of *bāray yāye* by close relatives
Ended by	Bathing, nails touched; (for males:) head shaved	Bath, etc., plus house purification by fire sacrifice		Bath, etc., plus one-year *śrāddha*	Bath, etc., plus 45-day *śrāddha*
Newari term used to refer to end	*bāray yāye kwacāla/ siddhala* ('Observing restrictions is over')	*du bẽkegu* ('to end death pollution')		*śokā̃/barkhi phenegu* ('to be released from grief/ mourning')	

Table 7.5 *Periods of mourning for a deceased adult observed by Śākyas and Vajrācāryas (for meaning of terms see Table 7.4).*

Category of relative	Degree of mourning/pollution
Distant lineage (*tāpā phuki*)[a]	Observe restrictions till cremation
Allies (married daughters, their husbands if desired; mother's brothers and household)	Observe restrictions for four days
Lineage (*phuki*)	Observe restrictions for 7 (other castes: 13) days
'Bone marrow' lineage (*syāphuki*) (households of brothers; husband for wife)	Remain in sorrow/observe death pollution for 7 (other castes: 13) days, observe restrictions for 45 days[b]
Sons and wife of deceased	Remain in sorrow/observe death pollution for 7 (other castes: 13) days; remain at home for 45 days; remain in year-long mourning/grief for rest of year[b]

Notes:
[a] Distant *phuki* are those with whom a patrilineal connection is remembered which is no longer considered important. Lineage members are those, other than 'bone marrow' lineage, with whom one celebrates Lineage Deity Worship.
[b] At the close of the ritual marking the end of these periods the Vajrācārya priest hands a new cap to the men and puts mustard oil in the parting of the women who are released from impurity. This indicates that they may now beautify (*bā̃lāke*) themselves.

the closeness or otherwise of an agnatic relative. In extreme cases where there has been an irrevocable breakdown of relations after some family quarrel, the two sides may show this, as already mentioned, by no longer observing death pollution for each other.

The second axis is the adulthood of the dead person. This is shown in Table 7.6. As one might expect from the discussion of other life-cycle rituals, the more such rites a person has been through, the more nearly the mourning and other ritual approximate to that of an adult.

There is no distinction in the vocabulary used to describe Buddhist and Hindu mourning, nor, as far as I know, in the classes of kin affected, other than those slight differences which are normal between any two castes or localities. The crucial difference between Buddhist and Hindu death rites lies in the number of specialists employed, and the prominence given to Ancestor Worship. Hindus make use of many more specialists, as discussed elsewhere (§2.5, 11.2). The Buddhist specialists, and the death prestations received by them, are summarized in Table 7.7. Hindus employ both Nāpit and Kāpālī, and, instead of a Vajrācārya, a Ghaḥsū Karmācārya (Ghaḥsū Ācā) (though many in Lalitpur and Kathmandu, where practising Karmācāryas are now rare, use Vajrācāryas).[33] In addition they employ a

Table 7.6 *Type of death rite and length of mourning according to the status of the deceased, among Śākyas and Vajrācāryas.*

Age of deceased	Death rite	Mourning period
<4 days	Buried anywhere	None
4 days<3 months	Buried in children's graveyard (*macāgā*)	Family observe restrictions till burial
3 months<time of Monastic Initiation (for girls: Mock Marriage)	Cremation: carried in arms (not bier); House Purification on 4th day; no Ancestor Worship	Family 'have to observe death pollution' for four days; lineage observes restrictions for four days
After Monastic Initiation/ Mock Marriage	Cremation; carried on bier; 7th day (other castes: 13th day) House Purification; regular Ancestor Worship till Two-Year Rite.	=Adult: see Table 7.5

Karamjit (Bhāḥ), occasionally referred to as a Mahābrāhmaṇ ('Great Brahman'), as in India. He consumes ten bowls of rice said to be mixed with a portion of the dead person's brain on the tenth day. The point of this, as Parry remarks on the basis of Indian data, is to make the Mahābrāhmaṇ '*consubstantial* with the deceased'; this is also, though less graphically, the aim of rituals performed by the Kāpālī for all clean-caste Newars.[34] Finally, high-caste Hindus also, later, at the time of Ancestor Worship, require the services of a Karmācārya and a Jośī at the same time as the Brahman family priest.[35] Traditionally both Buddhist and Hindu high castes employed Maharjan cremation specialists called Gwā̃ to burn the body, but, as discussed below (§8.2.6), many have now begun to do it themselves instead.

Jajmānī relations are maintained with only a few of these specialists. From Śākyas, Vajrācāryas, and Maharjans, the only specialist who receives an annual prestation of grain, a share of the harvest (*bāli*), in return for services rendered is the Barber (he gets 2 *phaḥ*, Np. *pāthī*, about 9 litres, of paddy). High-caste Hindus also give *bāli* to the Karamjit (Toffin 1984: 297). In Kathmandu I have heard of the Maharjan cremation specialist, Gwā̃, claiming *bāli* from a Tulādhar patron.[36] Priests do not receive *bāli* but only a ritual payment (*dakṣiṇā*) on each occasion they carry out a ritual, and also a yearly offering (*nislāḥ*) on behalf of dead parents. The Kāpālī receives a share of feast food at each major festival. It is evident, then, that among the Newars the *jajmānī* system seems to be rather less elaborate than in north India, with many fewer specialist castes being paid with an annual offering of harvest grain.[37]

Table 7.7 *Ritual specialists at the death of a Śākya or Vajrācārya of Lalitpur and prestations received.*

Specialist	Clothing	Food in dead person's name	Feast share
Kāpālī (Jogi)	Dead person's clothes left at *chwāsā*[a]	Receives dead person's share of beaten rice and pastries and spirits every morning for 7 days, once a week till 45th day, once a month for a year	On 7th day (and at all big feasts, *nakhaḥ*)
Nāpit (Nau)	Clothes worn during 7 days of *dumā* by those who have to observe year-long mourning	None	On 7th day
Vajrācārya (Gubhāju)	New clothes at 45th-day Rite plus bedding, utensils, and (uncooked) food	Beaten rice, ginger, and pastries (*nislāḥ*) at every death anniversary when Ancestor Worship not done, as well as at every Ancestor Worship	After every ritual performed

Note:
[a] In many cases Dyaḥlā now take the dead person's clothing from the *chwāsā* because the Kāpālī no longer wish to do so. According to Toffin (1984: 293) the Nāpit also receives clothes at the One-Year Rite.

A second crucial distinction, this time between Śākyas and Vajrācāryas on the one hand and other clean castes on the other, is that the former observe death pollution only for seven days after death, and not for thirteen days. This is usually expressed by saying 'they finish off the Seventh-Day Rite, Ending [Death] Impurity, and House Purification all on the same day'.[38] This difference between Śākyas and Vajrācāryas and other clean castes is surely due to their Buddhist and monastic identity, since it contravenes the local convention that higher castes tend to have a slightly longer period of mourning, or, to be more precise, that only a few low castes have shorter mourning periods than the twelve-day high-caste norm.[39] This local convention inverts the scriptural norm of Hinduism, according to which death pollution and periods of impurity in general are supposed to get progressively longer as one descends the *varṇa* hierarchy (Orenstein 1968; Dumont 1980: 70). In fact such schemes have only rarely been put into practice in South Asia; the normal pattern, as with the Newars, is for low castes to have shorter death pollution periods, a deviance from scripture which at least some versions of the Garuḍa Purāṇa ascribe to the degeneracy of the present Kali world era (Evison 1989).

Another difference between Hindus and Buddhists relates to the way and frequency with which they perform Ancestor Worship. Table 7.8 gives the compulsory death observances of Śākyas and Vajrācāryas and shows that the first time they perform Ancestor Worship is at the 45th-Day Rite. High-caste Hindus by contrast perform a special kind of Ancestor Worship called 'the ten riceballs' (*daśapiṇḍa*) on each of the ten days following the death. The principal mourner lives at home on the ground floor and cooks for himself. Each day he goes to the riverside (*ghāt*) and 'makes' one limb of the dead person's body by offering a riceball.[40] The (Buddhist) Tulādhars of Kathmandu still perform this rite of making 'ten riceballs' but they do it all in one go on the thirteenth day (Lewis 1984: 323), an abbreviation which sometimes occurs in India also (Parry 1980: 108 n. 10). Whether in this form or otherwise, Vajrācārya priests can certainly direct this rite for those of their parishioners who want it. Śākyas and Vajrācāryas of Lalitpur do not perform it now, but may have performed it in an abbreviated way, like the Tulādhars, in the past.

Such abbreviations by Buddhists of what most conceive of as essentially Hindu rites occur also with ordinary Ancestor Worship as performed from the 45th-Day Rite onwards. That is to say, Buddhists perform *śrāddha* less frequently than Hindus. To sum up these differences between Hindus and Buddhists, the seclusion of the principal mourner is extreme in the Hindu case, virtually non-existent among Buddhists. The Buddhist rite of Ancestor Worship is performed less often, but is longer and more elaborate than the Hindu rite on which it is based; it includes worship of the Three Jewels and also Tantric offerings (meat, alcohol) excluded from the Hindu rite.

In spite of these differences the basic purport of Ancestor Worship is the same in both religions. This can be illustrated by the verse read by the Vajrācārya priest for his patron who, just before beginning his 'gift of riceballs' (*piṇḍadāna*), holds the bowl with ingredients and faces south:

Oṁ tilā durgativṛddhāś ca kuśena cakṣuśrotayoḥ
Madhunā nāsikābāhūṃ kṣīrodasyāghṛtodaram.
Dadhiś ca katijānūbhyāṃ toyena hastapādayoḥ
Annādau sarvagātrāś ca jāyate bodhivīryavān.

OṀ, by offering sesame a bad rebirth is avoided, by *kuśa* grass (he will have) eyes and ears.

Table 7.8 *Timetable of the compulsory death rites performed by Lalitpur Śākyas and Vajrācāryas.*

Time after death	Rite	Newari	State of deceased	Corresponding ritual representation
day 1	Cremation	*śī uyegu*		
			Returns every night	Food put out every night
7th day	Seventh-Day Rite, House Purification, and Ending Death Impurity	*nhaynhūmā, ghaḥsū*, and *du bẽkegu*		
			Period as wandering spirit	General merit making
45th day	45th-Day ('month and a half') Rite[a]	*latyā*	Becomes an ancestor (*pitṛ*)	Dead person's riceball mixed with three ancestors' balls; gifts to priest; '*dīkṣā* returned'[b]
6 months	Six-Month Rite	*khulā*	Crosses Vaitaraṇī river	Wooden shoes and staff to priest; paper boat in rite
1 year	One-Year Rite	*dakilā*		
2 years	Two-Year Rite	*nidā tithi*		

Notes:

[a] Sometimes Śākyas and Vajrācāryas perform this rite twice, once on the thirteenth day and again on the forty-fifth day. In this way the sons of the deceased person may leave the house and live elsewhere if that is necessary for their work. It may also be necessary to do this if someone in the household dies with less than forty-five days to go before the One-Year or Two-Year Rite of another household member: in order to allow the latter to go ahead the more recently deceased person's 45th-Day Rite will have to be done on the thirteenth day.

[b] This rite, performed in the family's Tantric shrine (*āgå*), is popularly understood as 'returning the Tantric Initiation' of the dead person (to the deity). This idea was ridiculed by *paṇḍit* Asha Kaji Vajracharya: 'How can a dead person return Tantric Initiation?' He said that in fact the priest is merely receiving the dead person's worship materials. The idea seems to be pervasive, however, both among Hindu Newars (Toffin 1984: 561) and in India (Fuller 1985a: 131 n. 12).

By honey (are) nose and arms (made), by rice pudding and clarified butter is the stomach.
For his loins and thighs yoghurt, the water is his hands and legs.
Food etc. are all limbs; he will be born wise and strong.

The verse is ambiguous: the worship may be thought (i) to be on behalf of the dead person or (ii) to be a worship of the dead person him- or herself. The Sanskrit sometimes says 'by this offering he will have X', and at other times 'this offering is his X'. In support of the latter interpretation, small crosses of *kuśa* grass in a kind of effigy are laid on top of the riceballs before the items mentioned in the verse are offered. However, Asha Kaji Vajracharya explained it to me in the former way, as an altruistic and therefore meritorious practice on behalf of the dead person. Interpreting a rite with an apparently literal meaning in terms of the worshipper's intentions, and the benefits these good intentions bring, is a hermeneutic technique that is no doubt so much a stock-in-trade of Buddhist *paṇḍit*s as to be more or less unconscious.

The basic difference between the practices of the high-caste Hindus and those of the Śākyas and Vajrācāryas is that the death rites of the former take the underlying logic of death pollution and Ancestor Worship – the idea that death involves physical pollution and that dead relatives must be fed – and elaborates it. Buddhist rites are cast in the same form, but the emphasis is more on making merit to transfer to ancestors: they do not perform the 'ten riceballs' Ancestor Worship, most do not nowadays perform Ancestor Worship beyond the Two-year Rite, and, it is my impression, they are much less particular in observing minor details of death pollution.[41] Vajrācāryas are more likely than Śākyas to continue Ancestor Worship for a long time (up to twelve years or more): in this case however it is often a secret Tantric 'otherworldly' (*lokottara*) Ancestor Worship accompanied by a worship of the Tantric deity (*āgằ pūjā*). The 'blessings' from the Tantric worship are offered to the riceballs used in the Ancestor Worship (and therefore to the ancestor).

Optional rites surrounding death are concentrated as far as possible in the period between the seventh and the forty-fifth day, when the dead soul is supposed to be between births and most in need of merit to ensure a good rebirth.[42] Buddhists light lamps at important Buddhist shrines: Karuṇāmaya (Matsyendranāth), Cākwādyaḥ (Mīnnāth), Svayambhū, Cobhādyaḥ (Ādināth), Khāsti (Bauddha). These are all either *stūpa*s or powerful *bodhisattva*s.[43] When the festival of Matayā comes round, at least one person from each bereaved family will participate. During the chariot festival of Karuṇāmaya-Matsyendranāth families light lamps in front of the chariot, either on the night that, had there not been a death, the family would be observing the festival, or when the chariot stops at Jawalakhel. Theravāda and/or Tibetan Mahāyāna monks are also invited to perform rites on behalf of the dead person.

In the seven days after death food is put out every day; thereafter it is put out every week, and after the 45th-Day Rite only every month. It is given to the Kāpālī in the dead person's name. In the Nepali language both polluted food and the state of a person in mourning are referred to as *juṭho*. Newari does not make a direct connection between the two states in this way. Nonetheless, clothes which have been worn either for the seven or thirteen days after death (depending on caste), or for the four days (or sometimes ten days) after birth, and must be changed and washed, are referred to as *cipa*. This is exactly the word used to refer to polluted food. In general it is recognized that similar states of pollution occur at birth and death, as well as for a girl during her Confinement; but death is clearly the most severe and has its own terminology (given above).[44]

In the days after death, and on anniversaries thereafter, members of the family are on the look out in case 'the dead person has come'. The main sign they look for is whether any of the food left out overnight appears to have been taken. After the 45th-Day Rite the dead person is supposedly reborn. His or her joining the ancestors is graphically demonstrated by the merging of the deceased's riceball, divided into three, with those of the three immediate ancestors, a pan-Indian Brahmanical practice.[45] From this point on, however, Newar ideas on the afterlife are not very precise. As discussed above (§4.4), there is no general agreement on whether or not Ancestor Worship and other meritorious acts must necessarily benefit the deceased wherever he or she may be.

Rebirth cannot be guaranteed. Some souls remain and haunt their homes, particularly those who have died an early or violent death. The case of girls dying during Confinement was noted above (§4.3.11). Others may fail to be reborn and exist as an *agati*, 'one without rebirth'. An old Tulādhar man whose father had died over forty years previously had long since given up performing Ancestor Worship; one day he dreamt that his father was still wandering without rebirth and performed an especially elaborate Ancestor Worship to ensure that his father would finally be reborn.

7.4 Buddhism and calendrical festivals

A sociological distinction can be made between two kinds of festival that occur once a year, and there are Buddhist and Hindu versions of both: the local festival and the calendrical festival. The local festival is the annual festival of a local deity. The date on which it falls is determined by local custom and the festival is celebrated only by locals.[46] On a few days each year there are local festivals in numerous places at once, but in general there seems to be a principle that adjacent villages celebrate the festival of their main local divinities at different times. This is shown by Toffin's table of the main local festivals (*deś jātrā*) at twenty-four different cities, towns, and villages of the Kathmandu and Banepa Valleys (Toffin 1984: 502). The best-known Buddhist local festivals are the chariot festivals of the various Karuṇāmaya-Matsyendranāths. In outlying villages, festivals are usually devoted to some form of Mother Goddess.

Calendrical festivals proper are those which are observed by all Newars, and, in many cases, by all Nepalese too. There is, however, a certain overlap between the two categories of festival, either because certain local festivals have come to be celebrated throughout the Valley as a calendrical festival, or because a given calendrical festival is particularly associated with, and paradigmatically celebrated in, one locality. Examples of basically local festivals are Yẽnyāḥ (Indra Jātrā), which is fundamentally a Kathmandu festival,[47] or the Karuṇāmaya-Matsyendra Jātrā of Lalitpur. In the latter only the final day (the 'showing of the vest') is a festival for the whole Valley.

An example of the second tendency, for basically calendrical festivals to have an archetypal epicentre, is the Gathā̃ Mugaḥ (Skt. & Np. Ghaṇṭā-karṇa, 'Bell Ears') festival associated with purification and the expulsion of demons after the transplanting of rice seedlings. It is celebrated with the most panache and with the most elaborate ritual in Naradevī (Nyata) in Kathmandu. It seems unlikely that this was in origin a local festival because of its close connection to the agricultural calendar, which is everywhere the same. It is more probable in this case that one locality has come to be recognized as the centre for the festival's celebration.

The three biggest festivals of the year in Lalitpur are Mohanī (Np. Dasaĩ), Swanti (Np. Tihār), and 'The Festival' (*jātrā*), i.e. the chariot festival of Karuṇāmaya-Matsyendranāth. A fairly complete list of calendrical festivals observed in Lalitpur is given in Table 7.9. Karuṇāmaya's chariot festival is particularly associated with the city of Lalitpur and its district, but is big enough and important enough to have spawned smaller imitation shrines and festivals in Kathmandu, Thimi, Nala, and Dolakha.[48] It is a local festival which has spread. The other two big festivals, Mohanī and Swanti, are pan-Nepalese, and indeed pan-Hindu, and are calendrical festivals proper.

Gaborieau (1982b) has recently advanced a neat interpretation or schematization of the Hindu festival cycle, and Newar calendrical festivals fit the pattern he outlines. Main calendrical festivals fall in the period of 'four months' (*caturmāsa*) from Śrāvaṇ to Kārttik when Viṣṇu is asleep. This is a time of disorder when demons are particularly threatening. It is also the time of the rains, and of the hardest agricultural work (rice planting and weeding). It is the time of year when people fall ill with fevers and stomach complaints. Newar Buddhists sometimes say that the Buddhist

Table 7.9 *Calendrical festivals observed in Lalitpur, with indications of the level of Buddhist observance.*

	Date	Newari name	Description of rite	Remarks
	Vaiśākh (April–May)			
	kṛṣṇa 1	Nhawa	Bathing Karuṇāmaya and Cākwādyaḥ	
	varies	Khai Sãnhū	Drinking peasoup, raising poles (*yaḥśī*)	
	kṛṣṇa 15	Mãyā Khwā Swayegu	Sweets to mother, *śrāddha* or prestation to priest if dead	
N*	śukla 1	Būga Yā/Jātrā	Beginning of Karuṇāmaya's chariot festival	Lalitpur's biggest
B	*Swãyā Punhī*	Buddha Jayantī	Celebrates Buddha's birth, enlightenment, and death	Theravādin, since 1926
	Jyeṣṭh (May–June)			
	śukla 6 *Jyā Punhī*	Sithi Nakhaḥ	Final day to W. lineage deity	Beg. of heavy agricultural season
	Āṣādh (June–July)			
	Dillā Punhī	Guru Punhī	W. and gifts to *guru*	
	Śrāvaṇ (July–Aug)			
n	kṛṣṇa 14	Gathā̃ Mugaḥ	Purifying house, scapegoat dragged out of city	End of rice transplanting
B	śukla 1	Gũlā Dharma	Begin fasting, text reading	
	śukla 5	Nāg Pañcamī	Worship of holy serpents	
B	śukla 8	Yala Pañcadān	Alms to Śākyas and Vajrācāryas	
B	śukla 12	Bahidyaḥ Bwayegu	Displaying deities in monasteries	Minor now due to thefts
H	*Gũ Punhī*	Gũ Punhī	Tying protective threads, festival at Kumbheśvara	
	Bhādra (Aug–Sept)	Gũlā		
H	kṛṣṇa 1	Sā Pāru	Procession with cows for dead	
	kṛṣṇa 2	Matayā	Procession to *caityas* of city for dead	
H	kṛṣṇa 4	Narasiṃha Jātrā	Narasiṃha around main route of city	

Table 7.9 (*cont.*)

	Date	Newari name	Description of rite	Remarks
H	kṛṣṇa 9	Kṛṣṇa Jātrā	Procession to Kṛṣṇa shrines	
	kṛṣṇa 9	Bhīmsen Jātrā	Procession to Bhīmsen shrines	
B	kṛṣṇa 13	Ye Pañcadān	Alms to Śākyas and Vajrācāryas	In Kathmandu only
	kṛṣṇa 15	Bāyā Khwā Swayegu	Gifts to father, prestation or *śrāddha* if dead	
B	śukla 1	Gū̃lā Pāru	Feasts mark end of Gū̃lā	
n	śukla 8	Kāyāṣṭamī	Beginning of observances for Mohanī	
n	śukla 13 *Yẽnyāḥ Punhī*	Yẽnyāḥ	W. of Indra, Mahākāla, and Gaṇeś	Lasts four days, one quarter of city per day
	Āśvin (Sept–Oct)			
B	kṛṣṇa 3	Gātilā	Observance of Vasundharā	Celebrates rice harvest
	śukla 1	Naḥlā swane	Plant barley shoots in *āgā̇*	
N	śukla 10	Mohanī	Main day of Mohanī	Nepal's biggest festival
B	*Kati Punhī*		Reconsecration of *caitya*s	
	Kārttik (Oct–Nov)			
	kṛṣṇa 13	Khwa Pūjā (Swanti)	W. of crows,	Includes W. of self and others for long life
	kṛṣṇa 14	Khicā Pūjā (Swanti)	W. of dogs,	
	kṛṣṇa 15	Lakṣmī Pūjā (Swanti)	W. of goddess of wealth,	
	śukla 1	Mhā̃ Pūjā (Swanti)	W. of own body,	
N	śukla 2	Kijā Pūjā (Swanti)	W. of younger brothers	
B	śukla 8	Mukhaḥ Aṣṭamī	Main 8th Day Observance of year	Buddhists fast
	Sakimilā Punhī		Feasting, display grain drawings for end of *kārttik sevā*	Harvest festival
	Mārga (Nov–Dec)			
	Thilā Punhī	Yaḥmari Punhī	Eating rice-flour pastries; Farmers' Lineage Deity W.	Harvest festival
	Pauṣ (Dec–Jan)			
B	kṛṣṇa 10	Disī Pūjā	W. of Cakrasaṃvara	Winter solstice
	varies	Ghyaḥ Cāku Sā̃hū	Bathing; eat ghee, molasses and sesame	End of Pauṣ (inauspicious month)

Table 7.9 (*cont.*)

	Date	Newari name	Description of rite	Remarks
H	*Milā Punhī*		Beginning of Svasthānī Observance	
	Māgh (Jan–Feb)			
	śukla 5	Śrī Pañcamī	W. Mañjuśrī/ Sarasvatī for skill and learning	Beginning of spring
	Si Punhī			
	Phāgun (Feb–March)			
	kṛṣṇa 14	Śivarātrī	Big festival at Paśupati, elsewhere bonfires	
	Holi Punhī	Holi	Throwing water/ red powder	Minor in Lalitpur
	Caitra (Mar–April)			
n	kṛṣṇa 13	Pāsā Cahre	Śiva worshipped as Luku ('hiding') Mahādyaḥ	Minor in Lalitpur
	kṛṣṇa 14	Ghoḍe Jātrā	Festival of Bāl Kumārī, Kwāchẽ, drunken horse made to gallop	
H	śukla 9	Rām Navamī	W. of Rāma	Hindus only
	śukla 10	Cait Dasaĩ	W. of Power-Places	
	Lhuti Punhī		Pilgrimage to Jāmacwa	

Notes:
*The exact day this festival is observed varies from year to year.
(i) W. = Worship. 'kṛṣṇa' refers to the dark fortnight of the month, 'śukla' to the bright half, i.e. the waning and waxing moon respectively. 'B' and 'H' indicate respectively festivals which are Buddhist to the exclusion of high-caste Hindus and Hindu to the exclusion of Śākyas and Vajrācāryas (and usually of ordinary Newars also). Since Lalitpur is a predominantly Buddhist city, middle and lower castes tend to celebrate festivals marked 'B' (except Disī Pūjā) with more fervour and a greater level of participation than those marked 'H'. In Bhaktapur, which is strongly Hindu, it would be the other way round.
(ii) 'N' indicates *nakhaḥ*, those festivals where a feast must be consumed and prescribed relatives (married daughters and their children) invited. 'n' indicates those festivals next in importance which were observed as full feasts in the past, and still are by conservative middle-ranking castes.
(iii) Only the most important chariot festivals have been indicated. None from outside Lalitpur has been included.
(iv) All twelve full-moon days (*pūrṇimā*, *punhī*) have been marked. In some cases their names derive from the old Newari names for the months (see appendix 2 to Chapter 1).

holy month of Gũlā is such a terrible time that none of the gods wanted to have anything to do with it, so the Buddha adopted it as his out of compassion for suffering humanity.[49] This period of disorder is brought to an end, according to Gaborieau, by the two great festivals of Mohanī and Swanti (Dasaĩ and Tihār in Nepali).

It is certainly true that the majority of calendrical festivals, big and small, fall during this four-month period. Festivals outside this period are either small calendrical festivals or what I have called local festivals. It is consistent with this view of the calendar that the period of festivals is inauspicious for movable life-cycle rituals such as Loincloth Worship, Monastic Initiation, and Marriage. The auspicious days for these events, which Newars know about by consulting astrologers or astrologers' almanacs, always fall outside this four-month period, whether in the cold period, or in the hot 'summer' before the monsoon. Marriages tend to be held in winter, when it is feasible to make the jellied buffalo meat (*taḥkhā*) which is an essential item of feast food in that season. Thus, as Newars experience it, there is a broad contrast between the monsoon and immediately after, when feasts are occasioned by festivals, and are mostly indoors, and the dry season, when large marriage feasts and other celebrations are held outside.

Buddhists justify their participation in festivals in different ways, the justification becoming increasingly problematic the more obviously Hindu the festival is. In Theravāda Buddhism calendar festivals celebrate events in the life of the Buddha or essential turning-points in the monastic year. These are now celebrated by some Newars too, that minority which supports Theravāda Buddhism. In Newar Buddhism, by contrast, festivals are observed simply because they are traditional and because it is meritorious to do so. But in answer to the question, 'Why on this date?' a commemorative rationale, like that of the Theravādins, may also be given. As we have had occasion to observe already (§3.6), the traditional date for observing the Buddha's attainment of enlightenment is that of the festival of Matayā, and not Swãyā Punhī (Buddha Jayantī). Since this is Mahāyāna Buddhism, in justifying festivals less stress is put on Śākyamuni Buddha alone: visits by previous Buddhas also play a part (see above, Table 7.1). The ritual surrounding the chariot festivals of Karuṇāmaya-Matsyendranāth recapitulates the circumstances of his arrival in the Valley.[50] Two of the purely Buddhist festivals listed above also have mythical legitimizations of this sort. Disī Pūjā falls on the day when, so it is said, Mañjuśrī had a vision of Cakrasaṃvara and his consort during his visit to the Valley; and the Observance of Lokeśvara on Mukhaḥ Aṣṭamī celebrates the day that

Paśupati was protected by Karuṇāmaya's helmet from the wrath of Virūpākṣa.

In other festivals there is no very strong Buddhist justification. The myth may be given a slight Buddhist tinge, but it could otherwise be used quite happily by a Hindu. For instance, Yẽnyāḥ (Indra Jātrā) celebrates the capture of Indra, who had descended to the Valley in order to collect flowers for his mother. The images of Indra displayed at crossroads show him tied up with splayed arms, a similarity to the Christian cross that Newar artisans in Tibet, commissioned by the Jesuit d'Andrade to produce crosses in 1628, impressed upon him (Slusser 1982: 268). In Kathmandu, in particular, Yẽnyāḥ is for Buddhists a festival of the dead. Kathmandu has no festival of Matayā as in Lalitpur. In both cities (and in Bhaktapur where it is the most spectacular of all) Hindus take part in Sā Pāru (Gai Jātrā) on behalf of the dead in their families. Instead of either of these practices, on the evening of the fourth day of Yẽnyāḥ (Bhādra śukla 14: R.P. Pradhan 1986: 387) Kathmandu Buddhists participate in two circumambulations of the city. First, in 'upākhu wanegu', encircling the city walls offering light; secondly, they follow a Farmer man dressed as 'Dāgĩ' who leads them around the city's processional route and finally out to the west.[51]

Although this procession does not exist there, in Lalitpur also Yẽnyāḥ is the only festival (*nakhaḥ*) that may legitimately be observed with feasting during the year after there has been a death in the family. Thus it is called 'the dead people's festival' ('sīpinigu nakhaḥ'). The presence of the Dāgĩ or Ḍākinī in Kathmandu is also a tantalizing hint of further Buddhist connections. The normal Dāgĩ is, as noted, a man of the Farmer caste wearing a white mask, who is given five *ropanī*s of land to cultivate for his pains. But in addition anyone who has performed Optional Pañcadān that year has the right to circle the city as a Dāgĩ with a red mask; people say that he has reached heaven, that he has 'become Indra'.[52]

The most extreme case of an essentially Hindu festival which is simultaneously very important for Buddhists is Mohanī. Even more than Yẽnyāḥ, which itself has crucial royal elements, Mohanī is a festival of the king, of Kṣatriyas, of royal power, and of the solidarity of the patrilineage. Buffalo sacrifices to Taleju take place at the royal palaces and there are masked dances of the Mother Goddesses. Male members of high-caste Hindu lineages assemble at their Tantric god-house, if they have one. They each take an ancient sword from the shrine and outside in the open air line up to take turns in slashing a pumpkin.

In Lalitpur Śākya and Vajrācārya families perform a similar rite in private, sacrificing rather a stalk of sugarcane and a ginger plant, using a curved Nepalese knife (*khukuri*). In all cases the barley shoots, planted in the shrine room ten days previously, are taken as 'blessing'. Traditional Newar Buddhists also celebrate Mohanī with Tantric rituals of the kind mentioned below in discussing worship of the lineage deity (§8.2.4) (though such rituals are on the decline). Modernist Buddhists say 'I am a Buddhist, I don't celebrate Mohanī'; and at the same time they reinterpret the name of Mohanī's main day, 'Victory Tenth' (*vijaya-daśamī*), to mean 'Aśoka's Victory Tenth', the day when Aśoka defeated the Kalingans, repented, gave up violence, and became a Buddhist. In Kathmandu there is a Buddhist practice called *navarath melā* (probably from *navarātrī*, for the nine nights of Mohanī). It celebrates Mohanī by visiting ten holy Bathing-Places each morning for the ten days of the festival (R.K. Vajracharya 1980: 124–6). This is not observed in Lalitpur.

7.5 The religious Observance (*vrata*): asceticism for the laity

In an article comparing Buddhism and Jainism, which asks the question why Buddhism died out in its land of origin but Jainism survived, P.S. Jaini (1980) concludes that one of the crucial factors was the relative absence in Buddhism of specifically Buddhist observances for the laity to perform.[53] Jainism by contrast developed very early the practice of ascetic observances by the laity. An anthropologist working on Śvetāmbara Jains in Jaipur reports that there is 'a huge array of different fasts' for the laity to perform (Reynell 1985: 27). One of the earliest Buddhist scriptures ridiculed the Jaina laity for 'becoming a monk for a day' (Aṅguttara Nikāya I, 206, quoted at Jaini 1979: 223), and to this day Theravāda Buddhism lacks the Observances which are present both in Jainism and in Mahāyāna Buddhism.

The only occasional practice which ancient Buddhism provided for the laity was the temporary assumption on holy days of the Eight Precepts.[54] A lay person normally only keeps the Five Precepts, so taking the Eight is half way towards the Ten Precepts which make one equivalent to a novice monk or nun. The Eight Precepts are the Five Precepts (undertakings not to take life, not to steal, not to commit sexual misconduct, not to tell lies, and not to intoxicate oneself) plus three others: not to eat at the wrong time (i.e. after midday); not to watch dancing, singing, music shows, not to wear perfumes and finery; and not to sleep on high or big beds. Furthermore, in the context of the Eight Precepts, the third is interpreted as a complete ban on sex. The most usual days for taking these precepts are the full moon and new moon days, though they are also sometimes taken on the eighth day of the month.

The Śākyas and Vajrācāryas of Nepal do not have a monastic code since they do not practise permanent celibate monasticism, but they have preserved the taking of the Eight Precepts. Technically this is known as *upoṣadha vrata*; popularly, since it is most commonly performed on the eighth day of the bright half of the month, it is known as the Observance of the Eighth Day (*aṣṭamī vrata*) or in full, and most formally, as 'the Noble Observance of Eight-Limbed [=with Eight Precepts] *upoṣadha*' (*āryāṣṭ-āṅga upoṣadha vrata*). In Newari 'to fast' is 'apasã cwane' and it may well be that *apasã* derives from *upoṣodha* (or its Pali equivalent, *uposatha*).[55] Fasting is, however, only one part of a *vrata*, which is why I translate it as 'Observance'. In colloquial Newari performing an Observance is called 'dhalã dane'. This derives from 'dharma dane' (a connection not evident to all Newars today) and the phrase means 'to observe or fulfil the *dharma* [of a specific deity]'. It may be specified, if the context does not make it clear, whose religious practice is being performed: thus, 'aṣṭamī vrata dhalã danegu' means 'to perform the Eighth Day Observance (of Amoghapāśa Lokeśvara)'.

Although the Newar Buddhist Observance is descended historically from the practice of taking the Eight Precepts, still preserved by Theravāda Buddhism, there are certain important differences. First, unlike the Theravāda custom, in Newar Buddhism the precepts are not chanted by the participants but simply recited by the priest as part of the 'explanation' (*khå̃*) of the rite to which the participants listen passively. The participants know that they must keep strict rules but are often ignorant of the fact that these are the moral undertakings known as the Eight Precepts. Secondly, the Newar Buddhist Observance is primarily a ritual of devotion to the *bodhisattva* Amoghapāśa Lokeśvara.

Amoghapāśa Lokeśvara is a particular form of Avalokiteśvara (Karuṇā-maya) associated with this Observance and the Eight Precepts. Many larger Newar monasteries have a shrine to him and a long chamber for performing his Observance on the upper floor, as we have seen to be the case with Kwā Bāhāḥ (§6.2). The ritualization of the Newar practice is greater than that of the Tibetans. Newar Buddhists who are monks in the Tibetan tradition direct the Taking of the Eight Precepts on every eighth day of the bright half of the month in Kwā Bāhāḥ. The Tibetan practice of this ritual is, like the Newar practice, expressed in terms of devotion to the Three Jewels and to Amoghapāśa Lokeśvara, but at the same time, the taking of the Eight Precepts is carried out explicitly, and cognitive assent to them receives great emphasis.

Locke (1980: 188–202; 1987) has given a detailed description of the performance of the Observance of Lokeśvara. There are, as in any ritual, differences of detail from place to place, but these need not concern us here. Essentially the rite consists in the worship of the Three Jewels (Buddha, Dharma, and Saṃgha) and then of Amoghapāśa Lokeśvara. Each is worshipped in a mandala, that is to say, surrounded by a circle of attendant deities. Since the central deity is Amoghapāśa Lokeśvara his mandala is worshipped more elaborately and with various subsidiary circles of deities. The set of deities for the Buddha Mandala are the Five Buddhas and the four Tārās,[56] the Saṃgha Mandala is made up of the Nine Bodhisattvas, and the Dharma Mandala of the Nine Sacred Texts (*navagrantha*) (see Locke 1980: 191; 1987: 168).

At the end of the worship of each mandala, but before the mandala is finally offered up as a whole, the priest reads out an explanation (*khȁ*) of the mandala in question in slightly archaic (but easily comprehensible) Newari. Locke (1980: 193) writes that he has never seen this done, but I have and it is worth reproducing one such text:[57]

'Oh lord, Oh *guru*, as long as we live, putting our name forward, while this circular Buddha Mandala remains whole, we all take refuge in this Buddha Mandala so that all our sins of this and other rebirths, whether committed knowingly or unknowingly, may be destroyed. Oh *guru*, we wish to hear the account of the greatness (*mahimā*) of this Buddha Mandala. Show pity, love, and compassion for us and speak.' Thus the pupils (*śiṣya*) petitioned. The blessed spiritual *guru* (*sadguru*) looked in the faces of his pupils and said, 'How is he of the Buddha Mandala? He is blue like the sky, he is called Śrī Akṣobhya Tathāgata. He is present as long as the circular "wisdom pavilion" (*bodhimaṇḍapa*) [i.e. the mandala each devotee has before him or her] is not broken and remains [in place]. On the lotus petal in front of Akṣobhya is Vailocana [sic] who is white, on the lotus petal to his right is Ratnasambhava who is yellow, at the top lotus petal is Amitābha who is red, on the left lotus petal is Amoghatathāgata [who is green]. On the right lower lotus petal is the goddess Māmakī, on the right upper lotus petal is the goddess Locanī [sic], on the left upper lotus petal is the goddess Pā̃ḍurā, and the left lower petal is the goddess Tārā. All these deities being extremely happy to see the worshipful attitude (*pūjābhāva*) of all these devotees, gave their blessing. "Oh devotees, may the wish (*icchā*) you have in mind quickly be fulfilled, may you overcome the dangers of disease, sorrow, poverty, and affliction (*saṃtāpa*), may you not suffer from various diseases, pains, difficulties, or burdens." Do all of you take refuge in the Lord Buddha who blesses thus.' Thus did the blessed spiritual *guru* speak.

The same formula is used, changing the names, both for the Dharma Mandala (the central deity being Prajñā Pāramitā) and for the Saṃgha Mandala (central deity: Avalokiteśvara). These ritualized exchanges take place with the priest speaking both parts. It is a notable feature of such 'explanations' that they have been set in a mythic past in the manner of Hindu Purāṇas. They recount the original ectype of which the present performance is a well-intentioned, but inevitably imperfect, imitation.[58]

The explanation of the Amoghapāśa Lokeśvara Mandala is longer. Having begun in the same way, and described all the different deities in three concentric circles, and the iconography of Amoghapāśa himself, it continues:

'This Karuṇāmaya ['embodiment of compassion'] shows compassion towards the devoted, causes religious stories to be told concerning past, present, and future; he causes the four ends of man – worldly advantage, religious merit, physical pleasures, and liberation – to be fulfilled, and destroys the Ten Unproductive Sins. Now when you are performing the Observance of Amoghapāśa Lokeśvara who is as explained, you must abandon all the things you like to have and so on. Furthermore you must give up the playing of instruments, singing songs, dancing, putting on beautiful flower garlands, combing your hair in front of the mirror, and putting on beautiful jewellery and clothing. If you do this and show respect to Amoghapāśa Lokeśvara, and worship him with flowers, incense, light, vermilion, foodstuffs, and so on, Lord Karuṇāmaya will be pleased, and at the end [of life] Śrī Amoghapāśa Lokeśvara will carry you across to the attainment of liberation (*mokṣa*), to such an Amoghapāśa go in refuge!' Thus spake the blessed spiritual *guru.*[59]

It will be seen that the seventh of the Eight Precepts (to avoid shows and beautification) has been incorporated here and slightly elaborated. Since normally most of the participants are women the elaboration is quite appropriate. The other precepts are all also observed: on the night following the rite participants sleep on a mat on the floor and abstain from touching members of the opposite sex. The precept not to eat at the wrong times is not observed in the Theravādin way as a prohibition on eating after midday but, like it, it is understood to mean that one should eat only one meal. Furthermore it must be of pure food (*pālã*), i.e. rice cooked in milk, without vegetables or spices: sweets and fruits are therefore consumed. The participants fast while doing the ritual and it normally ends about two or three in the afternoon. The prohibitions are then kept until the following morning. While actually performing the ritual the participants are in a state of extreme purity, having bathed at the beginning, and fasting: no one who has eaten may touch them or enter the purified area of the ritual. Once it is over, these taboos are less important.[60] Men normally shave their heads before participating but women do not.

Before the end of the ritual the participants all sit holding the Observance thread (*bartakā*; Skt. *vratasūtra*) which has been unwound from the central Flask and passed around, while the priest reads out a story associated with the Observance. Which story is read depends on the site and the occasion. At a single performance the story may be omitted, but when the Observance is part of a set the story appropriate to each site in the set is read. The most popular way to perform the Observance is in a group based on a locality, sponsored by one or more rich men, who undertake to pay for the meals.

Once a month for a period of just over two years, beginning usually on Mukhaḥ Aṣṭamī (R.K. Vajracharya 1980: 79), the group visits each of the twelve holy Bathing-Places, each of the Eight Passionless Ones, and the five Buddha shrines.[61]

The Observance of the Eighth Day is the main such Observance in Newar Buddhism, but it is by no means the only one. The second most important Observance is that of Vasundharā, the Buddhist goddess of wealth. This occurs usually only once a year on the third day of the dark fortnight of the month of Āśvin (Bhādra by the old reckoning). In many places where there are Śākyas and Vajrācāryas there are *guthi*s to ensure an annual performance, and there is a saying that 'it is forbidden (*ma tyaḥ*) to live in a place where Vasundharā's Observance is not performed'. As with the Eighth-Day Observance any (clean-caste) person may attend, though it is usually done in small groups in a *guthi*-member's home (see Plate 12). The form of the worship is very similar to the Eighth-Day Observance. Another different Observance is that of the Hundred Thousand *Caitya*s (*lakṣa-caitya-vrata*) known in Newari as 'luchidyaḥ' or simply as 'dyaḥ thāyegu', making gods (from clay) (see Vaidya 1986: chapter 16). For the whole month of Gũlā devotees make small clay *caitya*s every day (see Plate 4); on the final two days (*amāy* and *pāru*) they fast and worship them, and finally take them off to be thrown in the river. There are often *guthi*s for this too, though it is less common than the Observance of Vasundharā.

Other Observances of this sort are sometimes performed to Tārā and to Svayambhū. R.K. Vajracharya (1980: 84–5) points out that they may indeed be performed for any deity and gives as an example the Observance of the Fourteenth Day (*caturdaśī vrata*) which was performed every month for a year to the Mother Goddess Bhadrakālī in Kathmandu in 1954. Such cases are, however, relatively rare. For Tārā it is more common to perform a form of the *satwa pūjā*.[62] This is sometimes performed in front of the chariot of Karuṇāmaya-Matsyendranāth.

It is important to note how devotional rituals aimed at a particular deity (*dharma* and *pūjā*) have become in many ways indistinguishable from Observances (*vrata*), which centre on the keeping of precepts, even though the vocabulary which marks this distinction has been maintained. If a family decides to perform a *satwa pūjā* in front of Karuṇāmaya's chariot they will all (except children) observe purity rules and fast until the ritual is over. These rules are the same as the precepts of the Observances. From the other end, so to speak, Observances are like Worship because they are directed at a particular *bodhisattva*, who responds by blessing the devotees and expressing the hope that their wishes will be granted. The similarity is made all the closer because, as noted, unlike the Tibetan version of the same rite, the participants in a Newar Buddhist Observance do not verbally undertake the Eight Precepts; they are simply built into the rite.

For all that the two types of rite – complex Worship (*pūjāvidhi*) and Observances (*vrata*) – are behaviourally identical (in terms of the rules followed), they do nonetheless remain conceptually distinct. Observances, unlike devotional rites, are brought to an end by a Kumārī Worship: once this has been performed the precepts associated with the Observance need no longer be kept. A Kumārī Worship is also performed, for the same reason, after a Monastic Initiation or Loincloth Worship. Practising Vajrācārya priests explain that the Kumārī Worship marks the transition to the Great and Diamond Ways after the restrictions and rules of the Disciples' Way. Asha Kaji Vajracharya (1972: *ca*) describes the place of Kumārī Worship under the heading 'The scriptural basis (*pramāṇa*) for the worship etc. involved in Buddhist Observances':

Matsyaṃ māṃsaṃ madyapānaṃ strīṇāṃ saṃgaṃ vivarjayet
Upoṣadhe 'pi saddharme samāptaṃ pratipālayet.

[He avoids fish, meat, drinking alcohol, contact with women, And in the true practice of the *upoṣadha* Observance he keeps the rules till the end.]

In the Eighth-Day Observance consisting of devotion to Karuṇāmaya, in the *caitya* Observance of Wālā, the Observance of Vasundharā, the Observance of Tārā, and also in any other Observances, in Pañcadān, in the worship of Dīpaṅkara, in Samyak and so on, one must keep the Eight Precepts of true religious conduct in the Great Way, viz. abstaining from meat-foods such as fish, meat, eggs, and also from drinking alcohol and from sexual activity etc. If one follows these restrictions from the beginning up to the Diamond or Tantric Way (which is called Kumārī Worship), thereby carrying out the Observance properly, one's particular desire, whatever it may be, is fulfilled, and one obtains [the four ends of man] religious merit, worldly advantage, physical pleasures, and liberation.[63]

Fasting is a part of all these rites, but it can also constitute a practice in itself. The most common form this takes is a five-day fast on the last five days of the month of Kārttik. The *bodhisattva* at Cobhār, Ādināth Lokeśvara (worshipped by Hindus as Nārāyaṇa), is a popular place for this. The husbands of women who have fasted and stayed in the temple for five days are supposed to come and fetch them with a band playing, and take them home in triumph. The same applies if a woman undertakes a month-long fast during Gũlā, drinking only the holy water (*jal*) in which the deity has been 'bathed'. This is sometimes performed in Kwā Bāhāḥ, and the woman or women sit around the central temple to Svayambhū.[64]

Certain of the Mahāyānist deities in whose names Observances are performed are very broadly associated with the granting of certain favours.

Fasting in general, but particularly the Observance of Amoghapāśa Lokeśvara, is supposed to cause a son to be born (cf. Locke 1980: 184, 203). At a time of great danger to oneself or one's family prayers are directed either to Karuṇāmaya or to Tārā. Thus R.K. Vajracharya (1980: 63) writes that the merit from performing the *tārā dharma* to Tārā 'frees one from illness, disease, pain, and untimely death'. Alternatively one may make a vow to perform the worship of Hārītī, goddess of smallpox, or of Kwā Bāhāḥ's text-cum-goddess, the Perfection of Wisdom (Prajñā Pāramitā), if a particular danger or challenge is overcome. Such promises (known as 'phyānāḥ tayegu' or, using the Nepali, 'bhākal yāyegu') may be made when ill, before an exam, when travelling abroad, or when establishing a new business.[65]

In extreme illness certain powerful Tantric deities may be worshipped: Caṇḍamahāroṣaṇa (also known as Pālāḥdyaḥ) or Mahākāla. Vasundharā is rarely worshipped outside the context of her Observance which falls at the time of the harvest: this, her name ('Wealth-Bearer' or simply 'the Earth'), and the fact that she holds a ripe rice-stalk in one of her hands, associate her with wealth. Thus she is identified with the Hindu goddess of wealth, Lakṣmī, worshipped during the festival of Swanti. Yet even the story which goes with Vasundharā's Observance (R.L. Mitra 1971: 266; A.K. Vajracharya 1981b) promises sons as the fruit of fulfilling it, as well as wealth and bountiful harvests.[66] Karuṇāmaya (Matsyendranāth/Avalokiteśvara) is also associated with the harvest: he was brought to Nepal in order to end a twelve-year drought and famine, and is believed to bring every year the rains on which the rice harvest depends.

In sum, it is broadly correct to say that the 'great *caitya*' of Svayambhū represents the Buddhist Absolute, that Karuṇāmaya and Tārā are saviour figures, and that Vasundharā is associated with wealth. It would be wrong, however, to apply these identifications in a rigid fashion. That would be to go quite against the spirit of a system which indulges in extremes of hyperbole in order to encourage the laity to worship at the approved Buddhist shrines and in the approved Buddhist ways. If questioned, this hyperbole is justified by the doctrines that ultimately all the objects of worship are one, that the differences between them are conventional, that piety in whatever form is good for you, and that any conceptual means are justified in order to induce it. By contrast, clear delimited functions *are* found in the case of the lower deities worshipped for some precise worldly end: for the relief of toothache, earache, or finding lost objects. These lower deities are not particularly Buddhist: the last two are associated in Lalitpur with Gaṇeś shrines, in Kopundol and Capa respectively.

We have seen how Observances are ritualizations of the Eight Precepts, and how, since they are directed at different deities, they are, to a limited extent, functionally differentiated. What of the participants? Observers of traditional Theravāda Buddhism point out that those who take the Eight Precepts on holy days are usually female or old, and often both (Gombrich 1971: 274). An inscription dated 1900 from Nyākhācuk, Lalitpur, lists the participants in a cycle of Eighth-Day Observances: there were seventy-eight women and eighteen men, which parallels Gombrich's figure of four women to one man for Sri Lanka. I suspect, however, that there is one difference due to the worldly benefits promised by the Mahāyāna practice but not in Theravāda Buddhism: young and middle-aged women are also keen to perform Observances in Nepal.

These Observances are very important in the mobilization of the Buddhist laity. Large groups performing Observances at different holy sites around the Valley are not a prominent feature of Newar Hinduism, although there are equivalent rites (particularly the *satya nārāyaṇ pūjā*) performed privately in the home.[67] Without these elaborate Observances Newar Buddhism would appear – at least to those lay castes debarred from Tantric Initiation – merely as an alternative to the Hindu set of rites and festivals. If one can show that these Observances evolved in India in the first millennium of the common era, it might then be necessary to qualify the judgement with which I began this section. Jainism survived not just because it provided an ethic for the laity but because it made lay participation in regular Observances mandatory, as Buddhism did not.

Appendix: The Wedding Dialogue

Newar weddings consist of a complex series of presentations and counter-presentations, visits and counter-visits by the two families involved.[68] The most important procession, called *janti*, occurs when the groom's family and relations go to fetch the bride. When they finally leave her house, taking her away, some members of her family, and her family priest, accompany her as far as the nearest Gaṇeś temple. There a ritualized exchange takes place between the priests of the two families. Normally it is relatively short and consists in the request and the promise to take care of the young girl in her new life. Hridaya (1970: 252–4) published a more elaborate version which is worth reproducing in translation because it reflects faithfully the attitude of Newar Buddhists to marriage and the householder life.[69] I have left the Sanskrit as it is in the original.

The Wedding Dialogue

The following is said by the bride's side:

'In this world it is only humans who practise ten types of sacramental religious duty (*saṃskāra dharma*), from conception (*garbhādhāna* [sic]) up to marriage. A man cannot fulfil his sacramental religious duty without going through the Ten Sacraments. In accordance with this rule the prince Siddhārtha [the future Buddha] first married Yaśodharā and only then did he renounce the homely life and go forth to obtain complete enlightenment.

Furthermore, as a householder one can experience neither worldly nor otherworldly fruits (*bhukti mukti phala*) without practising the family *dharma*. And in order to practise the family *dharma*:

Śaktivinā na siddheyu vratāni sarvakarmasu
Tasmāc chaktiṃ samādāya kuladharmaṃ samācara.

[In other words:] Without a *śakti* [a wife] no rite such as Observances (*vrata*) and so on can be complete. Therefore one must practise the family *dharma* along with a *śakti*. Since these are the words of the Lord [Buddha], be a man ever so full of all good qualities, yet without a *śakti* or *prajñā* he will not be able to make his family *dharma* stable. In treatises on advantageous conduct (*nīti śāstra*) also it is said:

Putraḥ prayojanaṃ bhāryā putraḥ piṇḍaprayojanam.

[In other words:] Marry a wife for the sake of sons; in order to receive Ancestor Worship one needs a son. For this reason, in order to make your family permanent, you have graciously requested the gift of a virgin of our daughter for your son. Now our daughter is full of all good qualities. From childhood she has followed the teaching and instructions of her parents. She does not think of her own desires; the only emotion she feels is the desire to serve her mother and father. How can we give such a virgin away? We have given much thought to the matter. In this world there is no *dharma* greater than charity (*dān*). It is only by beginning with this *dharma* of charity that complete enlightenment is obtained.[70] And it is written in scripture:

Dānaṃ vibhūṣaṇaṃ loke dānaṃ durgatinivāraṇaṃ
Dānaṃ svargasya sopānaṃ dānaṃ śāntikaraṃ śubham.

[Charity is the decoration of the world, charity prevents a bad rebirth, charity is the stairway to heaven, charity is the auspicious bringer of peace.]

Remembering wisdom such as this, although we have cherished her as equal to our own life-breath, on this day, not wanting to deride your request, considering the son of your pure family a true vessel (*satpātra*), we are giving our daughter in the gift of a virgin. Now our daughter knows nothing yet of worldly wisdom (*vyavahāra*). She still eats and drinks as she wishes and plays.[71] Therefore do you please teach and explain to her whatever is required and take care of her like a daughter, not like a servant.'

The following is said by the groom's side:

'Good sir, most excellent sir, be pleased to listen:[72] In our pure and good family a son has been born who is full of all good qualities, accomplished in numerous sciences (*vidyā*). We have looked everywhere for a suitable virgin daughter as his bride. And in your family:

Kulaṃ ca śīlaṃ ca guṇaṃ ca tulyaṃ sarvān militvā iti tāṃ payācet.

[In other words:] We have requested your daughter because she is right in the following respects: she matches our family, her family has the right behaviour, and she has the right qualities. By this, as you have said, a daughter's sacraments will be fulfilled. Furthermore women have many faults, but only three virtues:

Strīṇāṃ doṣa-sahasrāni guṇāni trīṇi eva ca
Kulācāra sutotpatti maraṇe patinā saha.

Which is to say, women have three main virtues only, and without a husband these virtues cannot be attained: carrying on family life, giving birth to sons, going along with her husband at death. It is impossible to acquire these virtues without a husband. For this reason, and for you to attain the wisdom of enlightenment which begins with the perfection of charity, and – [since, like your daughter,] our son is not addicted to satisfying his own desires – for the sake of purifying both families (it is said, 'ubhayo kula-śuddhyārtham') we have requested [your daughter] in the gift of a virgin. You, not taking our request badly, on this day have made the gift of a virgin. We have respectfully accepted your gift. As to your daughter being innocent of worldly wisdom, there is this saying:

Kiś [sic] *cit śaṃkā na kartavya putrivat pālayāmi vai.*

[In other words:] Please do not feel any anxiety or worry. Where she has to be taught we shall teach her, where she has to be told, we shall tell her. We shall look after her not as a servant but as if she were one of our own daughters, good sir.'

8

The Great Way (Part II): *guthi*s

Guṭhi is a mode of ostensible alienation in *pius usus* whereby the Newars contrive to secure their lands, to indulge in piety and love for social merry making. Feasts in honour of the gods are continually going on in every pleasant nook of the Valley, the costs of which are discharged in rotation by the Guṭhiyas or holders of the *Guṭhi* lands. The Guṭhiyas are tenants in common who cannot alienate the *Guṭhi* though the gods are satisfied with a pepper corn rent or nominal service. *Guṭhi* cannot be confiscated even by the State for high treason. It cannot be sold or even impledged.

B.H. Hodgson, marginal note (Hasrat 1970: 64 fn. 1).

In this enchanted Valley where religion has not completely ceased to be a continual round of public festivals, each caste has to compete to play its part in the festivities; the *gatti* [*guthi*] determines in rotation which families will fulfil the necessary tasks on each occasion and it oversees their execution.

Sylvain Lévi, *Le Népal*, vol. I, p. 246–7.

8.1 Basic principles of the *guthi*

The socio-religious association called *guthi* (Np. *guṭhi*) is one of the fundamental bases of Newar social organization and has deservedly attracted considerable attention from anthropologists. When qualified with other words to give the name of a particular type of *guthi*, it is often shortened to *gu*: e.g. *ācā gu*, short for *ācārya guthi* ('*Guthi* of Vajrācāryas'). *Guthi* derives from the Sanskrit *goṣṭhi*, association. Inscriptions from the Licchavi period attest various such *goṣṭhi*, for worshipping deities, ensuring the maintenance of irrigation canals, and so on. According to a recent and plausible interpretation, the medieval and modern Newar *guthi* is the direct descendant of these Licchavi *goṣṭhi* (Sharma 1983).

Toffin, introducing his discussion of *guthi*s, suggests that they are a unique and distinctively Newar principle of social organization:

> Anthropologists have usually distinguished three levels in the social structure of Indian and Nepalese villages: the family (and by extension the lineage and the clan), the caste and territory (or the locality). In studying Newar society a fourth level has to be distinguished, that of the *guthi*. These are religious associations with very close ties to clans, castes, and territory, but they cannot be reduced to any of them.
>
> (Toffin 1984: 177)

Quigley, on the other hand, stresses the interconnection of *guthi*s and the territorial principle. For all Newars two *guthi*s are of particular importance: the Lineage Deity *guthi* and the death *guthi*. Thus Quigley writes, of *guthi*s in Dhulikhel:

> It is these [two] associations which pre-eminently provide the residential element of Newar social organisation and which ensure that identity is not simply a matter of affiliation to lineage and caste. Lineage and caste are themselves defined in terms of a ritual attachment to a locality.
>
> (Quigley 1985b: 11)

The three principles which underlie the operation of *guthi*s were listed thirty years ago by Fürer-Haimendorf (1956: 36), who correctly described them as basic features of Newar social structure as such: (i) the role of territory; (ii) the rule of seniority within the group; (iii) 'the allocation of public duties according to a rigid system of rotation'. The degree to which locality plays a determining role in *guthi*s varies, though it is significant in nearly all of them; all alike are based on respect for seniority and the rotation of duties. There is a Newar ritual, often performed at *guthi* feasts, in which the head of the sacrificed buffalo, goat, sheep, or chicken is divided up, the different parts going in order to the eight most senior members.[1] The same sacramental logic appears in intercaste contexts also: in public festivals, such as Mohanī, which are associated with the royal palace, the whole body of the sacrificed animal is divided and distributed to those with specified roles in the ritual in a way that reflects the caste hierarchy. Thus the Brahman and Karmācārya priests receive each a thigh, whereas the tail, entrails, and hooves go to the Khaḍgī butchers (Toffin 1981a: 73).

Nearly all *guthi*s have at least one, and often more than one, annual feast. The organization of the feast is the responsibility of the current 'turn-holder' (*pāḥlāḥmha*) or 'turn-holders' (*pāḥlāḥpī*). He may make use of any income which the *guthi* has, donated by the founder or previous members. Traditionally this was in the form of land; nowadays *guthi*s often have other assets: buildings on rent or bank deposits. Where there is no income – and this is usually the case with death *guthi*s – the *guthi*-members have to make an annual contribution. If there is a shortfall the turn-holder may have to make it up himself. In certain cases he is allowed to defray some of it by collecting a contribution (*lhāpā̃*) from those who attend the feast. Women may not be members of a *guthi.* If a member cannot attend himself he may send a substitute, but if possible this should be a male member of the family. Women do nonetheless play a prominent part in *guthi* activities, preparing items for worship, and cooking and serving food.

Since *guthi*s play such an important role in Newar social life there is a highly developed vocabulary to describe their functioning. The senior of a *guthi* is called *thakāli* and his wife (who takes charge of those ceremonial functions that must be performed by a woman) is the *thakāli nakī̃. Thakāli* means simply 'senior', and its opposite is *kwakāli*, 'junior'. The terms derive from the Newari for 'up' and 'down' and are also used to mean 'older' and 'younger'. Although these terms can be used for 'elder brother' and 'younger brother', it should be noted that Newari does not have kin terms for this and has to borrow from Nepali/Hindi the terms *jethā/māhilā/sȧilā* etc. ('first-born' etc.). The second most senior member of a *guthi* is called the *naku*, 'number two', and there are other terms, also derived from numerals, up to 'eighth-placed', though they are not as often used.

To take one's turn in the *guthi* is referred to by several expressions: 'pāḥ kāyegu' (to take a turn), 'pāḥ phāykegu' (to promise, to undertake one's turn), 'tā [or tācā] kāyegu' (to take the key). The last mentioned expression is used metonymically as well as literally. Often, when the responsibilities of the *guthi* include daily worship at a shrine which has to be locked, or the guarding of valuables, a key is indeed handed over: this occasion has come also to stand for the whole act of handing over a *guthi*'s duties. The new turn-holder signifies acceptance of his duties by taking a plate of food called *pābwa*; its contents vary from *guthi* to *guthi. Wāla* refers to a group or individual whose turn will come next after the present one (cf. Srestha-charya 1976: 12–13, 107).

In most *guthi*s, and especially in death *guthi*s, attendance on certain occasions is compulsory, and failure to come oneself or to send a substitute (*palesā*) incurs payment of a fine (*bā̃*).[2] Responsibilities are usually handed over at a special meeting the day after the main feast of the year: the accounts are done ('lyāḥ swayegu'), the valuables checked in the presence of the seniors, and the leftovers eaten. In *guthi*s founded by an individual for the benefit of his own lineage, it was customary to introduce one member from outside known as *nā̃wā*, literally 'speaker', whose role (though otherwise a normal member of the *guthi*) is supposed to be that of witness, to prevent brothers and lineage brothers falling out, as so often happens, over the *guthi*'s duties, income, and property. (This last term seems to be confined to Lalitpur.)

The most important form of wealth in Nepal, now as traditionally, is land. The *guthi* institution of the Newars has given its name to a form of land tenure, whose 'tenurial characteristics may be defined as permanence and irrevocability of *Guthi* land endowments, relinquishment of individual title to the lands endowed, a ban on alienation, and tax exemption' (M.C. Regmi 1976: 63). It is therefore 'virtually synonymous with the *Debutter* land tenure of the Hindus in India, the *waaqf* system of the Muslim communities in India and the Middle East countries, and the tenure of church and monastic lands in Medieval Europe' (ibid.: 46). While *guthi* land is found throughout the present kingdom of Nepal, the *guthi* institution which I have described is virtually unique to the Newars.[3] The link between them is that the land held by *guthi*s of the Malla period (and no doubt earlier too) was tax free, as it is today, and this form of tenure provided the name for religious land throughout the modern kingdom of Nepal after 1769.

In theory *guthi* land cannot be sold or alienated, but should ensure the performance of the *guthi*'s duties in perpetuity. In practice of course the temptation and the danger of embezzlement or expropriation were ever present. Thus most inscriptions donating *guthi* land end with dire imprecations threatening the perpetrators of the sin of taking the deity's land with the curse (*kudṛṣṭi*) of the gods concerned. Kings who have felt powerful enough have resumed *guthi* land: much was taken in 1806 and although Jang Bahadur condemned this on his assumption of power in 1846 he did nothing to return it. Of the three cities of the Valley Kathmandu seems to have escaped with relatively little appropriated; Lalitpur and Bhaktapur both suffered badly (M.C. Regmi 1978: 698).

In the last twenty years, with land values rocketing in the Kathmandu Valley, many quarrelsome and/or apathetic *guthi*s have had their land registered by the tenant, or embezzled by one of their number, and rapidly sold. Much *guthi* land has been lost to the building of new roads or other projects, particularly the ring road, with scant compensation. On the other hand, cohesive *guthi*s with active leaders have in some cases become very rich because land they owned happened to be in what had become an urban area: by selling it (from one quarter to one third of the selling price goes by law to the tenant) and banking the proceeds the *guthi* has ensured itself a regular income to hold its rituals and feasts.

From the point of view of land tenure and the state there are, in effect, three sorts of *guthi*:[4] private *guthi*s which are self-regulating, whose duties and land are not registered with the government Guṭhi Corporation (*guṭhi saṃsthān*); *chūṭ guthi*s, which are so registered but which are run by private individuals (the fact of registration makes embezzlement much harder); and *rājguthi*s which are administered by the Guṭhi Corporation. Originally *rājguthi* referred to *guthi*s founded by members of the royal family (M.C. Regmi 1976: 58). It came to have its present meaning as *guthi*s founded by others were resumed by the state, after bankruptcy or voluntary abandonment (ibid.: 89). Then in 1920 Chandra Shamsher Rana seized many private *guthi*s' land and established the ancestor of the present Guṭhi Corporation.[5] Much of the surplus, after the religious duties had been fulfilled, accrued now to the state instead of to the descendants of the original owner. During the Rana regime, granting lucrative *guthi* land was a favoured way of rewarding a relative or client (M.C. Regmi 1978: 222).

All the land supporting the cult of Karuṇāmaya-Red Matsyendranāth is held as *rājguthi*. There is a small office of the Guṭhi Corporation in Ta Bāhāḥ, where the deity's Lalitpur temple is sited. It is this office which ensures that all the many and complex rituals associated with the cult of the deity, and in particular those of the chariot festival (which may last up to three months), are paid for and carried out.

Subarna Man Tuladhar put the following paradox to me. Chandra Shamsher's reforms were motivated primarily by a desire to siphon off untapped revenue, and so only well-endowed *guthi*s were nationalized: at the time this represented an attack on Newar *guthi*s and an attack on religion. Yet, by making these *guthi*s official it has in fact preserved them, whereas many private *guthi*s have disappeared with the decline in piety and the concomitant unwillingness of *guthi*-members to finance deficits themselves. The establishment of the Guṭhi Corporation should perhaps be seen as an aspect of increasing centralization; it ensures that really important cults continue, while the cults of more local divinities are left to decline.

8.2 Types and examples of *guthi*s

Having considered the organizational principles of Newar *guthi*s and their economic basis, it is time to answer the question of what they do for Newars, and in particular for Newar Buddhists. Toffin (1984: 179) lists six different types of *guthi*: death *guthi*s, *guthi*s to ensure the worship of a particular deity, Lineage Deity *guthi*s, caste council *guthi*s, economic *guthi*s, and *guthi*s which function as youth clubs. The last seem to be a peculiarity of Pyangaon and so need not be considered here. One other type, the public utility *guthi*, needs to be added to the list. Each type will be considered in turn, leaving till last the three most important, the Lineage Deity *guthi*, the *guthi* for the worship of a specific deity, and the death *guthi*.

8.2.1 Economic **guthis**

Economic *guthi*s are confined, it seems, to oil-pressers (Mānandhars in Kathmandu, and Maharjans in Khwanā [= Np. Khoknā] and Theco); they are a kind of cooperative. Toffin (1976a) has described their working and it is clear that they do indeed have characteristic *guthi* features: fixed (though voluntary) membership, the seniority system, rotation of duties, an annual feast, and the cult of a patron deity. However, the significant fact about Newar culture is not the existence of such *guthi*s but their relative rarity. With the one exception of oil-pressers, Newars never use their sophisticated and powerfully binding socio-religious traditions for economic ends. Thus Quigley (1985a: 40) refers to

> the most striking fact about Dhulikhel's economy – its fragmentary nature, the way in which each household stands as an independent 'corporation' in comparison with other households. This is striking because it is in complete opposition to the moral collectivism embodied in the ways that *guṭhi*, caste and kinship all operate.

Newar farmers do share labour in working their fields, but these work groups (*bwalā*) are informal and do not persist over time and cannot be considered *guthi*s.[6] Newar artisans seem never to form cooperative groups at all, though friends sometimes work in each other's company. Where groups of artisans work together it is either in the context of the joint family, as master and apprentice, or as employer and employee, or some combination of these. With the one exception cited, Newar *guthi*s do not have economic aims. A few *guthi*s do occasionally give loans to their members, but this is simply a way of managing their capital and it is not their main, or even a normal, function.[7]

8.2.2 Public utility **guthis**

These are *guthi*s founded to ensure the upkeep of wayside shelters or temples, to keep water fountains (*hitī*) in good repair, to put out plank bridges over rivers during the winter when they run low, and so on. Some of them still function as intended, in others the income is sufficient only to cover the cost of the annual feast, and others have been disbanded. The temptation to convert wayside shelters (*phalcā*) into shops, especially when they are sited at strategic crossroads in the middle of the bazaar, has often proved irresistible. Even traditionally, most public utilities were probably maintained by *ad hoc* cooperation at the level of the locality. Nowadays this continues but with larger and larger subventions from local government.

8.2.3 Caste council guthi*s*

Caste council *guthi*s are relatively rare. According to Toffin (1984: 179) they are found among Brahmans, Mānandhars (Oil-pressers), Citrakārs (Painters), and Rañjitkārs (Dyers). All these castes are very small and urban, and the caste-*guthi* brings together all members of the caste within one area. The Citrakārs' caste *guthi*s are called *deślā guthi*, i.e. locality *guthi*. They function to preserve caste rules, and to regulate economic competition by enforcing rules for the assignment of government contracts (Toffin 1984: 214–15). Toffin also claims that Śākyas and Vajrācāryas have caste council *guthi*s, but in this he is wrong, or at least oversimplifies.

The council in question is the Ācā Gu or Ācārya Guthi of Kathmandu, that is, the *guthi* of all the Vajrācāryas of Kathmandu which meets once a year at the Tantric shrine called Śāntipur behind Svayambhū. It is supposed to regulate relations between priests and parishioners, and also to oversee ritual and maintain its uniformity (Locke 1980: 24–5; 1985: 253–7). There is no single Vajrācārya *guthi* for Lalitpur or Bhaktapur, though there is a separate one in each of the larger monasteries with Vajrācārya members. Like the single Kathmandu *guthi*, these are supposed to oversee the performance of ritual. The Kwā Bāhāḥ Ācārya Guthi is also responsible for the worship of the monastery's shrine of Vajrasattva. In practice, overseeing ritual is an impossible task in the absence of a bureaucratic church-like organization. It may be true that the rituals of Kathmandu Vajrācāryas are more uniform than those of Lalitpur or Bhaktapur, as Locke's informants claimed, but in order to achieve this the Vajrācārya *guthi*s must rely on the goodwill and cooperation of their members.

The inability of the Kathmandu Ācārya Guthi to impose its will on its members was graphically illustrated by the twenty-year Vajrācārya versus Tulādhar *et al.* dispute ('gubhāju-urāy-yā lwāpu') described by Rosser (1966: 107–34) and Greenwold (1981: 94–101). The question at issue was the relative caste status of Vajrācāryas and Tulādhar *et al.*: the latter accepted, and accept, the ritual superiority of the former, but refused to accept the innovation which the Vajrācārya *guthi* tried to impose, that Vajrācāryas should refuse cooked rice in the houses of their Tulādhar parishioners. One of the factors in the defeat of the Vajrācārya *guthi* was that most of the Śākyas, who form one caste with the Vajrācāryas, as well as a minority of practising Vajrācārya priests themselves, sided with the Tulādhar *et al.*

The Vajrācārya *guthi* of Kathmandu tried to behave like a caste council, but it was defeated. Part of this must have been due to the large size and diverse backgrounds of the Vajrācārya status group: castes with caste council *guthi*s are all small and need each other as marriage partners. The main function of the Vajrācārya *guthi*, which it still fulfils, is to group together the priests of Kathmandu, and to ensure the worship of the Tantric shrines attached to Svayambhū. In Lalitpur, where marriage between Śākyas and Vajrācāryas occurs more frequently, it is even more evident that the Vajrācārya *guthi*s of the various monasteries are concerned with priesthood and not with caste.

8.2.4 Lineage Deity guthis

Traditionally, and indeed for all Newars until about thirty years ago, the *digu dyaḥ* (Lineage Deity) *guthi* was of paramount importance. Hence, it is claimed, the Malla kings took a form of their tutelary deity Taleju, calling her Degutale, as their Lineage Deity, so as to conform to the practice of their subjects in this respect (Manandhar 1983: 35). In his pioneering study of the Newars G.S. Nepali wrote:

> While the caste or sub-caste sets the limit to the general status-position of a person in the total society, his ritual and social life is regulated and controlled through these 'guthi' institutions . . . While the manifest function of such guthis is the fulfilment of some secular or religious interests, they have the latent function of preserving the norms and values of the community . . . In the event of sanctions imposed by any of these 'guthis', the social living of a defaulting household becomes quite miserable. Of these guthis, the principal ones whose sanctions are most dreaded by the Newars are the 'Sana-guthi' [= death *guthi*] and the 'Dewali' or 'Deya' [i.e. Lineage Deity] guthi.
>
> (Nepali 1965: 191–2)

The importance of the Lineage Deity *guthi* derives from the power of the lineage to control its members. Among the farming castes of the cities and villages of the Valley, as well as among some peripheral groups such as the Śreṣṭhas of Dhulikhel, the role of the lineage is as yet undiminished (see Plate 5). Quigley writes of Dhulikhel:

> *Deo pujā* [*digu pūjā*, the annual worship of the Lineage Deity] is the major occasion for demonstrating the solidarity of the lineage overtly. If a household is not represented other members of the lineage will neither attend the funerals of that house nor observe death pollution . . . Membership in the *deo pujā guṭhi* and *śī* [death] *guthi*, because they are residential units and not just based on kinship, is the acid test of caste pedigree. Without this membership one has no lineage and therefore no caste status. In Newar terms this amounts to losing any meaningful ritual identity.[8]
>
> (Quigley 1985b: 58–9)

What is true of Dhulikhel Śreṣṭhas and of Farmers in the big cities is no longer true of high-caste Newars, whether Hindu or Buddhist. For them – with one or two exceptions – the incentives to remain in a large Lineage Deity *guthi* have evidently disappeared.[9] (It remains true that membership of a death *guthi* is an acid test, as Quigley calls it, of caste status.) They observe Lineage Deity Worship (*digu* or *degu pūjā*) in single families or groups of two or three very closely related ones. Where once it lasted up to five days with various rituals and feasts, it now lasts two days at most. In this way considerable expense is spared and quarrels avoided. Even though related families no longer form a Lineage Deity *guthi* they may still observe death pollution for each other. Toffin, writing about Panauti (1984: 494), goes so far as to say that 'one sometimes feels as if the festival of Lineage Deity worship is on the way to becoming extinct and that it will have disappeared completely in several years, at least among high-caste Hindus'. Some high-caste families in Panauti have abandoned regular Lineage Deity Worship altogether and take offerings to their *digu dyaḥ* only as a part of Mock Marriage and Loincloth Worship rites for their children (ibid.: 499).

The decline has not been so extreme among the Śākyas and Vajrācāryas of Lalitpur. A few cohesive lineages still perform Lineage Deity Worship together. Some, like the Dhakhwa clan which comprises more than fifty households, have *guthi* investments to finance it, but others do not. One lineage from Nāg Bāhāḥ, of about fifteen households half of whom now live in the new residential suburbs of Lalitpur, decided in 1984 to observe Lineage Deity Worship together again after a lapse of twenty-five years 'because the young people no longer knew each other'. To pay for it ten rupees was levied from each male member who had completed Monastic Initiation and from each female who had completed Mock Marriage. All those who observe Lineage Deity Worship together must observe death pollution for each other. Those who do not perform it together have the option of observing death pollution and will do so if relations are close and remain amicable.

There is a presumption that those who share the same Lineage Deity are related even if no relationship is remembered. Thus I heard a man of the Khaḍgī caste arguing to a young Vajrācārya from Kwā Bāhāḥ that it was wrong for members of Kwā Bāhāḥ to marry each other, since they all share the same Lineage Deity. In fact among many Newar castes it sometimes happens that unrelated families share the same Lineage Deity. The most likely reason is that one or both groups migrated and adopted a local deity; in theory this should not happen, so that normally no explanation is given for the anomaly. In most cases, however, worship of Lineage Deities is very conservative: many families of all castes have Lineage Deities a long way from where they live. The normal solution to this is to 'pull' ('sālāḥ taye') the deity to a nearby site. Henceforth the original faraway site of the god need only be visited once every few years, on special occasions.

It is possible to use data on Lineage Deities to trace migration. Locke has done this systematically for all the Śākyas and Vajrācāryas of the Valley. His data show that more than half of the Śākyas and some of the Vajrācāryas of Bhaktapur originated in Lalitpur, as their Lineage Deity is Yogāmbara brought from Kwā Bāhāḥ (Locke 1985: 517). Many Kathmandu Śākyas and Vajrācāryas have the enshrined *caitya* at Vajrayoginī, Sankhu, as their Lineage Deity: this is very suggestive of a historical and ritual link going back to the Licchavi period, when one of the biggest monasteries of the Valley was at the site of Vajrayoginī.[10]

Worship of the Lineage Deity performs the same functions for Śākyas and Vajrācāryas as it does for other Newars, but there is an important difference between them and others in the siting of the Lineage Deity and the form that its worship takes. Other Newars worship a group of stones – anything from two to twelve – and these are sited somewhere outside the town.[11] Maharjan lineages sometimes use stones taken from the river for the occasion by the senior of the *guthi*; normally a group of stones is put together permanently and though aniconic they have a *garuḍa* bird or *kīrtimukha* (*chepu*) devouring serpents (*nāga*) carved over them, as are normally found on the top of tympana above the doors in Newar temples. Of these stones at least one is vegetarian and identified as Nārāyaṇa or Mahādeva but the rest are 'blood-drinking' and are worshipped with animal sacrifices if there is a *guthi*, or with an egg as a substitute if there is not. A few Śākyas and Vajrācāryas conform to this practice of worshipping at aniconic Lineage Deity shrines outside the city boundaries. Others have open, aniconic shrines inside the city and near the monastery (e.g. Guji Bāhāḥ). But the majority worship either a *caitya* or a Tantric deity in a secret Tantric shrine as their Lineage Deity.[12]

In fact, as we shall see below, the ritual of Lineage Deity Worship in Kwā Bāhāḥ is directed both to the *caitya* and to the Tantric deity (here, Yogāmbara), and implies an identity between them. This explains why many of those Śākyas and Vajrācāryas who have migrated from Kwā Bāhāḥ to Bhaktapur, Thimi, or Kirtipur say that their Lineage Deity is Yogāmbara, whereas those who are still members of Kwā Bāhāḥ always mean the enshrined *caitya* when they say *digu dyaḥ*. In more formal contexts the Kwā Bāhāḥ *caitya* is identified as Ādibuddha Svayambhū and is said to have 'been there from the beginning', before the main deity (Śākyamuni) was brought to that spot.

Here we have a case then of some 500 families, the members of Kwā Bāhāḥ, who all share the same Lineage Deity and yet regularly intermarry. This occurs more often with Śākyas and Vajrācāryas than with other castes; in this case it is considered that only those whose Lineage Deity Worship falls on the same day are related, and all those whose day is different are legitimate marriage partners. The symbolism of the *caitya* as Lineage Deity is appropriate, since it continues old Buddhist metaphors which call the Monastic Community the monk's family. Once again (as we have seen in the case of Monastic Initiation) Buddhist monastic symbols serve to differentiate Śākyas and Vajrācāryas from other Newars. Since they worship a *caitya*, no blood sacrifice is ever made,[13] whereas it is essential at the Lineage Deity Worship of other castes (when performed by a *guthi*).

Farmer castes and those similar to them refer to their Lineage Deity as *digu dyaḥ* and attempting to elicit from them a Sanskritic name for it is usually a waste of time (§3.2). One of the reasons why high castes and others who have a Tantric deity are more inclined to provide the questioner with a Sanskritic name for their Lineage Deity is that the latter is identified in some contexts with the Tantric deity (*āgǎ dyaḥ*), who always has a Sanskritic identity. Vergati, in a stimulating article on the cult of the Lineage Deity, insists that the Lineage Deity and the Tantric deity are one, the worship of the former beginning always with the invocation of the latter. She points out the parallel with the cult of the Mother Goddesses who have a Tantric shrine-house (*āgǎ chẽ*) inside the city and an aniconic shrine or Power-Place (*pīṭha*), served by Untouchables, outside it (Vergati 1979: 124, 127).

Toffin, in contrast, denies that Lineage Deity and Tantric deity are identical and lists four points on which they have to be distinguished:

> 1 – Firstly Āgã dya (or Āgama devatā) are Tantric deities who may only be approached and worshipped by initiates whereas Digu dya are honoured equally by everyone, initiated or not;
> 2 – in principle Āgã dya never leave their shrine whereas Digu dya [that is, the head-dress, *kikimpā*, worshipped at home for the rest of the year] are carried out of the city once a year;
> 3 – agamic [Tantric] deities are not divided up between the descendants of a lineage or family, and they are never moved;
> 4 – apart from certain Karmācāryas the cult of the Āgama devatā is wholly masculine: only men may see and make offerings to the deity whereas women play an important role in worship of the Digu dya.
>
> (Toffin 1984: 558)

These points are well taken, except the last (we shall see in the next chapter that female participation is also important in the worship of the Tantric gods). It is true that enshrined Tantric deities seem never to be 'pulled', i.e. moved, from one secret shrine to another. This expression is generally reserved for small, public, aniconic shrines, such as those of Lineage Deities. However, because Śākyas and Vajrācāryas often identify their Lineage Deity with their Tantric god, this expression is used when a god, like the Yogāmbara of Kwā Bāhāḥ, a classical Tantric deity kept in a secret shrine, is 'pulled' to another, more convenient place.

The contexts in which the Lineage Deity and the Tantric deity are worshipped do indeed vary, as Toffin claims. The Tantric shrine is worshipped on occasions not connected with Lineage Deity Worship. Middle- and low-ranking castes may not have their own Tantric shrines but they all have Lineage Deities. In short, the sociology of the two cults is not the same. Yet for high castes who have both kinds of deity the two are identified both implicitly and explicitly by the ritual; exoterically, however, they differ and the correspondence is only made by those interested in such things.

Lineage Deity Worship in Kwā Bāhāḥ proceeds as follows. The menfolk of the lineage and some of the women come to the monastery, make offerings to all the shrines on the ground floor, and proceed up to the hall before the Tantric shrine on the upper floor of the east side of the monastery. If the lineage is large and cohesive the older men sometimes recite hymns before the principal deity downstairs. Each household brings a worship basket (*kalaḥ*) of offerings: these are made principally to the Tantric deity, Yogāmbara, by the Casalāju (senior Vajrācārya of Kwā Bāhāḥ) on their behalf. The members of the lineage eat a special snack there in the hall and a feast at home. This snack is not called as normal, *samay*, but 'wisdom plate' (*prajñābhū*, usually pronounced *pariyābhū*). It consists of the usual *samay* foods (§10.5) but they are placed on two rice-flour pancakes (*catāmari*) which serve as a plate, a practice which occurs also in Tantric Initiation (§9.3.6).[14]

Traditionally, and still by cohesive lineages such as the Dhakhwas, a special rite is performed called 'taking the skull-bowl' ('pātra kāyegu'). All male members of the lineage sit in order of seniority; all female members are excluded except the most senior unwidowed woman, the *nakĩ*.[15] She trembles, possessed by the deity, and proceeds down the line, giving to each in turn a fish and an egg, and the skull-bowl of beer to sip from. She also blows mantras on their heads. The fish and the egg are normal good-luck foods (*sagã*). The ritual is clearly one of lineage solidarity since – a point emphasized by informants – all share others' pollution (*cipa*) by sipping from the same bowl. It should be noted, though, that since the bowl passes from senior to junior it also emphasizes rank: juniors share seniors' pollution but not vice versa. The procedure differed slightly in another account of this ritual (no doubt because of lack of space): the senior woman was enthroned in the small Tantric shrine of the lineage and the Goddess was invoked in her by the family priest. Then the male members of the lineage who had taken Tantric Initiation entered one by one to receive the skull-bowl. This ritual of taking the skull-bowl is also performed at other times when the Tantric deity is worshipped, not just on the occasion of Lineage Deity Worship: at Mohanī, Disī Pūjā, and at other *guthi* meetings which bring together the whole lineage.

8.2.5 **Guthi***s for the worship of a particular deity*

Under this heading come a vast number of different *guthi*s. We have already met some of them, for example the many *guthi*s established to ensure an annual performance of the Vasundharā Observance. The Lineage Deity *guthi* is a special and rather complex type of this sort of *guthi*. Indeed all *guthi*s, to be defined as such, require a presiding or patron deity who is honoured before the annual feast, and in whose name several shares (*dyaḥbhū*) are laid out at the head of the line of eaters. Nonetheless a clear conceptual distinction can be made, and would be recognized by Newars, between *guthi*s whose primary aim is worship and *guthi*s established for some other reason.

Some *guthi*s are joined and left more or less at will; they are an expression of individual piety. Even in this sort of *guthi*, when a *guthiyār* dies, one of his sons may well inherit his father's place, but there is little disapproval if he refuses. Unlike all other *guthi*s, this sort often brings together people of different castes.[16] The two main types under this heading are *sā̃nhū* or *sā̃lhū guthi*s, *guthi*s for the worship of Karuṇāmaya (Matsyendranāth) on the first day of the month according to the solar calendar, and *Yẽnyāḥ guthi*s (*guthi*s for worship at Yẽnyāḥ or Indra Jātrā). In *sā̃nhū guthi*s the member whose turn it is for the month visits the shrine of Karuṇāmaya (who from July or August to December is in Bũga, Np. Bũgamati, three and a half miles from Lalitpur) and worships the deity. He then returns with blessings in the form of leaves, flowers, and food-offerings for all the members of the *guthi*, which are presented before the feast or meal; after it, he hands over to the next *guthiyār*. One *sā̃nhū guthi* based in Tangaḥ, Lalitpur, which is kept going solely by the contributions of its members, has the following different castes among its twelve members: Śākya, Vajrācārya, Śreṣṭha, Maharjan, Citrakār. *Yẽnyāḥ guthi*s put up images of Indra (*Yẽnyāḥdyaḥ*) at crossroads for the four days of Yẽnyāḥ in Lalitpur and distribute *samay baji* on the day on which it is celebrated in that section of the city.

Often it happens that a particular lineage has in effect a single *guthi* with multiple obligations, and one person is responsible for them all (including Lineage Deity Worship) in a single year. Such a *guthi*, belonging to a single lineage and combining manifold obligations, is known as a *gharsā guthi*, from Np. *ghar*, house. As an example we can take the Dhakhwa clan, who are proud of the fact that, although they have more than fifty separate households and count nine generations from apical ancestor to youngest members, they still all observe seven days' death pollution for each other. Less than half of them still live in the maze of small courtyards (*cuk*) that lead one into the other from the north-western corner of Nāg Bāhāḥ; the rest have moved out, buying houses elsewhere in Nāg Bāhāḥ, in Lalitpur, or outside, in the new suburbs of Lalitpur and Kathmandu.

All Dhakhwas are descended from five brothers who became rich trading in Tibet.[17] In 1878 they performed Optional Samyak. A brother of their apical ancestor, called Cakasĩ (Cakra Siṃha), died childless and, as well as donating land to Kwā Bāhāḥ, gave land for the annual performance of a Tantric rite (*dau pūjā*) to Yogāmbara in Kwā Bāhāḥ. Nowadays the Dhakhwa *guthi* is funded largely by bank deposits derived from the sale of strategically placed *guthi* land: the yearly interest is said to be as much as 16,000 rupees. Each year the 'main turn-holder' (*mū pāḥlāḥmha*) has to organize the following rites:

- two Tantric rites (*sinhaḥ pūjā*) for the anniversaries of the death of Grandfather Cakasĩ and his brother;
- Samyak Anniversary (*samyak tithi*), celebrating the performance of the 1878 Samyak;
- displaying the Dīpaṅkara from this Samyak at Pañcadān and in Kwā Bāhāḥ during *bahidyaḥ bwayegu*, and at regular Samyaks;
- two reconsecrations of *caitya*s belonging to the Dhakhwas (*cībhāḥ busādā̃*);
- the distribution of beaten rice (*baji*) and yoghurt to all the members of Kwā Bāhāḥ at the annual Kwā Bāhāḥ feast (*sambhway*);
- Lineage Deity Worship.

One Dhakhwa from each household plus the ten elders of Kwā Bāhāḥ are invited to the Samyak Anniversary feast; previously the whole of every family plus all married daughters and their children used to be invited. On the other occasions all members of the clan used to be invited. This was then reduced to one representative of each of the five sub-lineages. Now no one at all is invited except the senior of the lineage, the turn-holder, and the priest. Still today, however, every member of the Dhakhwa clan, male and female, is invited to the Lineage Deity feast. This is referred to as inviting 'the whole household (*bhwachi*)'. At all these rites, although organized by the 'main turn-holder', the senior of the lineage acts as the sponsor (*jaymā*).

This is not the end of the Dhakhwas' *guthi*s. The descendants of the five brothers stayed together, trading in Lhasa, Shigatse, and Kuti, until 1905. At this point the descendants of the eldest and of the youngest brothers split off from the joint family. It was the descendants of the three middle brothers, who stayed together, who prospered. In 1918 they performed a second Optional Samyak at which time, according to the inscription recording the event put up in Kwā Bāhāḥ, the household numbered forty-nine persons. This second Samyak created a second *guthi*, the 'three brothers' *guthi* (*tin bhai guthi*), with a separate Samyak Anniversary to celebrate and a separate image to be displayed at Pañcadān. Only the descendants of the three brothers belong to this *guthi* and responsibility for organizing it rotates only among them.

There are other large and cohesive lineages which also have a large number of *guthi*s like the Dhakhwas. It is interesting to note that few practising priests have a large number of *guthi*s of their own: they worship deities so often on behalf of their parishioners that they feel little need to demonstrate piety on their own account.

Some other examples of *guthi*s for the worship of particular deities are as follows:

Tāremām Saṁgha. Established in 1939, and based on the Nāg Bāhāḥ area, this was the first of the modern-style hymn groups (*bhajan khalaḥ*), i.e. the first with accordion accompaniment singing hymns in modern Newari.[18] It meets on holy days in the shrine of Tārā, Kwā Bāhāḥ, in which its members take two-weekly turns to be god-guardian. It plays every day during the month of Gũlā and has its annual feast at the end of it on Gũlā Pāru (formerly a second feast was held in the spring). It has around forty-five members.

Prajñā Pāramitā Guthi. This *guthi* has seventeen members, all Śākyas, and is in charge of the 'Perfection of Wisdom' text which is frequently read as an act of faith or as the fulfilment of a vow in Kwā Bāhāḥ. Seven Vajrācārya families inherit rights to read the text, but the *guthi* for sealing the box in which it is kept is wholly in the hands of Śākyas, an illustration perhaps of their primarily devotional monastic role subordinate to the Vajrācāryas. Two members of the *guthi* take a turn at any one time, one to take the text out of the shrine, the other to ensure it is returned properly, tasks for which they must be in a pure state, i.e. fasting. They receive the same fee (*dakṣiṇā*) that is due to the text-readers, as do the current god-guardian, the Casalāju, and the wife of the main Vajrācārya (*gurumā̃*).[19]

The Wednesday Guthi. This *guthi*, with about ten members, comes to chant hymns (*stotra, tutaḥ*) in Kwā Bāhāḥ every Wednesday. During the month of Gũlā they also visit the shrine of Karuṇāmaya in Bũga.

8.2.6 Death guthis

Of all *guthi*s this type is the most important. Every Newar man of the Valley, and most of those outside it, even many of those otherwise strongly influenced by Parbatiyā culture, belongs to a death *guthi*, even if it is his only *guthi*. In Lalitpur they are called *sanā* (from *snāna*, holy bath) *guthi*, in Kathmandu *sī* (death) *guthi*. As so often, local variations in terminology can be confusing: there is a second type of *guthi* associated with death which is called *bicā guthi* in Lalitpur and *sanā guthi* in Kathmandu. This is an optional *guthi* for those who can afford it, though in some Kathmandu *guthi*s it is combined with the normal death *guthi*. Its members go to pay their respects to the families of its members after a death for up to four days in a row.

Death *guthi*s ensure the cremation of their members. Nowadays there is an important distinction between those *guthi*s which make use of Maharjan cremation specialists, Gwā̃ or Gwā̃t, and those which do not. Traditionally all high castes made use of them:[20] *guthi*-members or their substitutes had to accompany the corpse to the burning ground (*dīpa* or *śmaśāna*, pronounced *samsān* or *masān*); once there, they left and the cremation specialists disposed of the body. The Gwā̃ inspire some fear because of their traditional specialism. One Śākya informant compared them to demons (*rākṣasa*) and recalled that people used to be afraid to meet them in the street. According to Asha Kaji Vajracharya, in Lalitpur they are given an initiation of Bhairava by a Vajrācārya priest. Others say simply that 'they have Bhairava' ('imike bhairav du'), i.e. they have something of Bhairava's power.

In some cases the death *guthi* coincides with a maximal lineage, and this is thought vaguely desirable. In most cases, however, *guthi*s are based on a particular locality and any head of household of the right caste may join if he moves there and is willing to pay the annual contributions and take his turn as organizer in his first year as member. In Nāg Bāhāḥ there used to be a very large *guthi* including both Śākyas and Vajrācāryas. After a dispute because the cremation specialists came late, the *guthi* split in two. The majority were in favour of giving up Gwā̃ and formed a new *guthi* which would cremate its own dead; as the majority they kept the original image of Vajravīra Mahākāla and the original date for the annual feast. This *guthi* is known as the *gwā̃ mwāḥpĩ*, 'those who don't need Gwā̃'. The minority continue to make use of Gwā̃, have a new image, and hold their feast a month later: this *guthi* is known as the *gwā̃ māḥpĩ*, 'those who need Gwā̃'.

The former have to cremate their dead down by the river (*ghāt*) since the burning area is reserved for the Gwã. Those who no longer use cremation specialists frequently assert that it is better: it is cheaper (the Gwã now require 400 rupees per corpse), more reliable, and the corpse is treated better. The very frequency with which they assert this is evidence perhaps of an uneasy conscience at going against tradition, though in doing so they are in a majority, not just in Nāg Bāhāḥ, but among high castes throughout the Valley (cf. Toffin 1984: 291).

In large death *guthi*s, there is a division into sections, *kawaḥ*, of around twenty-six members each. In Nāg Bāhāḥ the *guthi* not using Gwã has six such sections; the one which uses Gwã has four. The sections rotate duties so that only one section need turn up for any one death. Within the section duties also rotate, half staying to cremate the body, half being allowed to leave. The senior of the section takes a register at the house of the dead person and at the place of cremation. Fines have to be paid by absentees. Responsibility for bringing wood, straw, the shroud (*dewã*) to cover the corpse, and palanquin to carry it on, is also rotated within the section.

In general, as noted, women are never members of any *guthi*. They participate only as wives, daughters, or mothers of members. In death *guthi*s the exclusion of women goes further since they are forbidden to enter the room where the annual feast takes place. Unlike other *guthi*s they may not serve food at a death *guthi* feast, although they may help in its preparation.[21] On the other hand, if a man dies without sons, his *guthi* will still come to cremate his widow and any unmarried daughters, even though they can take no part in *guthi* activities.

Most Newars take their death *guthi* for granted. The idea that life might be possible without one does not occur to them. If a young man separates from his father's family or from his brothers, he applies to join immediately so that should there be a death in his household the *guthi* will come; in some *guthi*s there is a 'period of grace', e.g. of three years after separation, in which they will come regardless. A Śreṣṭha shopkeeper in Kathmandu, whose family originally came from Bhaktapur, and who shares a death *guthi* with thirty-five others, also ex-Bhaktapur Śreṣṭhas, told me: 'If someone has only this death *guthi*, then he has no troubles. He doesn't need his relatives (*dāju-kijā*) or anyone else.' On the other hand a Dãgol of Lalitpur told me that the most important *guthi* is the Lineage Deity *guthi*: outsiders may join any other *guthi*; only the Lineage Deity *guthi* is reserved exclusively for relatives. This remark illustrates the greater kin-orientation of conservative peasants as compared to high castes, especially mobile, high-caste Hindus.

8.3 The Buddhist monastery as a *guthi*; *guthi*s and Buddhism

We have seen that the *guthi* functions on three basic principles: seniority, rotation, and territory. The first two principles can be reduced, I would argue, to a single principle: equality. It is the equal status of the *guthi*'s members that requires them to take turns in strict rotation. Likewise, the rule of seniority is the most democratic way of determining roles of authority, since each member has only to wait (and live) to fill them. These basic principles – equality and territory (attachment to a given place) – are equally the basis of the institution of the Newar monastery. The Newar Buddhist monastery can be regarded with some considerable justification as a kind of *guthi* whose point is to run a monastic complex.

As noted above (§6.2), there are three basic types of Newar monastery: the main monastery, the *bahī*, and the lineage monastery. Main monasteries and *bahī* have initiated members and a Monastic Community (*saṃgha*, *sã*) made up of them. Lineage monasteries are founded as a supererogatory act of merit and have no initiated members or *saṃgha*; rather, they 'belong to' a lineage or family, the descendants of the founder.

The lineage monastery institution is a kind of *guthi* for the worship of a particular deity. Its duties may be overseen by the Lineage Deity *guthi* if there is one. The shrine and its income, if any, are treated just like any other inherited *guthi*. As in other *guthi*s inherited by kin groups, duties are determined in rotation through lineages (*kawaḥ*). In modern times, as *guthi* income declines or disappears, duties become a burden, rather than a jealously guarded privilege. In this situation the system is often changed and duties are made to pass through households rather than lineages, since otherwise households in lineages with few households have to take a turn of duty far more frequently than households in lineages with many member households.

In main monasteries and *bahī* duties are determined not by kin groups but by rotation through individuals. The monastery has a list of initiated members and turns of service as god-guardian pass down the list in turn. The term for god-guardian, literally 'he to whom the turn (for worshipping and guarding) the god has come' (*dyaḥpāḥlāḥ*) is very close to that for the turn-holder (*pāḥlāḥmha*) of a *guthi*. Other monastery duties, such as organizing various rituals and feasts and filling the role of elder, are also assumed in order of seniority. The only exception is that, in monasteries with both Śākya and Vajrācārya members, the Casalāju/Cakreśvara, in charge of the daily ritual to the Tantric deity, must be a Vajrācārya. The territorial principle is maintained in that duties focus on the monastery and initiation must take place there. Before 1951 Śākyas and Vajrācāryas who had migrated out of the Valley trekked for many days to have their boys initiated in the monastery of their forefathers, and many still come from afar today. With the monastic complex as a focus, the monastery can unite enormous numbers into one super-*guthi*. Kwā Bāhāḥ in Lalitpur, the largest Newar Buddhist monastery, has over 2000 initiated members.

In most *guthi*s only adult men, heads of households, are members. In death *guthi*s it is particularly clear that they represent the whole of their household; this is probably the correct way to regard other *guthi*s as well. Only when the head of the household dies or the joint family separates does the possibility arise of anyone else in the family joining the *guthi*. In short, the unit of membership is the household. In monasteries, however, and in Lineage Deity *guthi*s, this is not so. In monasteries every initiated male is equally and individually a member. In Lineage Deity *guthi*s all men who have been through Monastic Initiation (for Śākyas and Vajrācāryas) or Loincloth Worship (in other castes) are members, as are unmarried women who have had Mock Marriage and wives of members who have been ritually 'made to belong' (*dukāyegu*). Unlike monasteries, however, organizational duties in Lineage Deity *guthi*s often pass through households, not down the list of individual members.

In several main monasteries of Kathmandu, instead of the individualist principle for determining the god-guardian, the household or lineage system is used.[22] Here a main monastery is being run like a lineage monastery, in other words like a *guthi*. Is it possible that there has been influence in the other direction, from monastery to *guthi*?

At the present stage of research such questions of historical causation are difficult even to pose, let alone answer. All the same, it is tempting to assume that the organization of Newar *guthi*s has been influenced by the organization of Buddhist monasteries in ancient India. The emphasis on territory is strictly Newar, but the rule of seniority as the only hierarchical principle lies at the very basis of Buddhist monastic organization as described in the Vinaya texts which date from a hundred years after the Buddha's death at the latest. The lack of a hierarchy within the Buddhist Order explains why Buddhism split into numerous sects and why versions, as well as interpretations, of scripture varied from place to place. Church-like hierarchies only developed later, encouraged by Buddhist kings in Thailand, Sri Lanka, Tibet, and elsewhere.

Another factor which has to be considered is the influence of 'tribal' – i.e. peripheral or pre-Hindu – practices. The Buddha himself clearly admired the so-called republican tribes of his day, rather than the hierarchical monarchies which were emerging and would shortly sweep all before them. Thus the Buddha seems to have modelled the organization of the Buddhist Monastic Community on tribal political organization; he unequivocally rejected the idea of a king-like leader to take his place after his death.[23] Just as the organization of the Monastic Community may have been originally inspired by the model of a tribal assembly, so at a later period the Newars' *guthi*s may have owed something to the Monastic Community.

In any case, it is clear that, even though caste provides a strongly hierarchical context, the principle of equality is the basis of the *guthi*s which permeate Newar life. Toffin (1984: chapter 8) has shown how intimately *guthi* organization structures the whole social life of Theco, a village of 528 households. Of these 435 are Maharjan and 82 of the only slightly inferior caste of Mālī (Gardener). Every household belongs to one of two *guthi*s devoted to the worship of the two Mother Goddesses which define the upper and lower halves of the settlement. The sub-groups which make up these *guthi*s may have grown out of kin groups, but now they are structured only by the *guthi* principle. Although membership is usually inherited patrilineally, it does not have to be, and *guthi*s are not exogamous.

In Theco, *guthi*s have an even more dominant role than elsewhere because it is virtually a monocaste village, yet it is too large for kinship to determine all social relationships. The *guthi*s preserve a rich socio-religious life and exclude all those who are not of equal status and resident in the village. Sylvain Lévi (1905 I: 33) was basically right when, in comparing Hinduism and Buddhism in South Asian history, he said that the 'rigid and uniform discipline [of Buddhism] applied only to monks; lay society was too diverse and too supple and escaped their influence'. Nonetheless, it is a hypothesis worth considering that Buddhism did have some influence on lay life and that the pervasiveness of *guthi* organization among the Newars owes something to the importance of Buddhism in their history. Kinship, the example of the Monastic Community, and perhaps also a tribal heritage now irrevocably lost in prehistory, may have come together to produce one of the most basic and pervasive features of Newar social life.

9

The Diamond Way (Part I): priesthood and initiation

Vajrayana is essentially a set of techniques.

G. Samuel, 'Tibet as a Stateless Society', p. 218.

9.1 Two types of Vajrayāna, the exoteric and the esoteric

As explained above (§4.2), the Vajrayāna or Diamond Way is considered to be a special path within the Great Way. It involves meditation and elaborate ritual using forbidden substances. It thus presents dangerous temptations, but if used successfully it is thought to lead to enlightenment in one life. For example, Hemraj Sakya, describing the Newar Buddhist monastery, writes:

> Secret rites for which one needs Tantric Initiation are carried out in the Tantric shrine (*āgå digi*). According to the teachings of the Diamond Way, which is beyond the Disciples' Way and the Great Way, by practising these rites the glorious *dharma*-body of Buddhahood is attained in one life.
>
> (H. Sakya 1979: 4)

The origins and development of Vajrayāna Buddhism are still imperfectly understood. On the internal evidence of the Tantras, the scriptures of the Diamond Way, there was a long and continuous development of new cults and new liturgies over hundreds of years. For the understanding of modern Newar Buddhism two stages in this history are particularly important: first, the emergence of the Five Buddhas and, second, the appearance of the esoteric deities, such as Cakrasaṃvara. If one were writing the history of Tantric Buddhism, many other stages would have to be discerned. For instance, several early Tantras now classified as Kriyā Tantras (see below), such as the Mañjuśrīmūlakalpa, predate the rise of the Five Buddha system.

The first stage in the history of the Diamond Way which needs to be considered for present purposes is the establishment of the set of Five Buddhas (*pañcabuddha*).[1] In early Mahāyāna Buddhism only two of the five had an independent existence: Akṣobhya ('Imperturbable', a representation of Śākyamuni calling the earth to witness that he had attained enlightenment) and Amitābha ('Unbounded Light', who presides over the western heaven, Sukhāvatī, in which Mahāyāna Buddhists hope to be reborn after death). Three other Buddhas, Amoghasiddhi, Ratnasambhava, and Vairocana, were added by the early Vajrayāna, and the philosophic categories of Buddhism were subjected to a systematic pentadic analysis, each of the Five Buddhas heading a different category and being assigned to a different spatial direction.[2] The characteristic pattern of the first four Buddhas was established: one on each side of the *caitya*, each being identified with a particular direction. On an early Nepalese *caitya* in Oṁ Bāhāḥ, Lalitpur, Vairocana is found above each of the four (Slusser 1982: 272–3), but subsequently he was usually considered to be inside the *caitya* since he, or Vajrasattva (another of his forms), was considered the central and ultimate deity in this form of the Diamond Way. Still today Vairocana is usually not represented on *caitya*s. The later, more esoteric, schema in which Akṣobhya replaces Vairocana at the centre of the mandala, appears in some Newar Buddhist ritual contexts,[3] but seems never to be expressed in the iconography of the *caitya*, which remains an expression of this early, more exoteric form of Vajrayāna.

Roughly two hundred years after the establishment of the pentadic system the second important type of Vajrayāna Buddhism came to prominence.[4] The texts of this later Vajrayāna introduced a series of fierce esoteric deities – Cakrasaṃvara, Hevajra, Yogāmbara, Caṇḍamahāroṣaṇa, and others – who are normally worshipped along with their consort or *yoginī*. They also elaborated and made explicit references to sexual rites, putting them at the centre of the cult. In the earliest Vajrayānist scriptures (the Kriyā and Caryā Tantras) such rites had been absent.[5]

Both these two main types of Diamond Way Buddhism were based on holy scriptures called Tantra and both types contain an amalgam of gnostic teachings, ritual instructions, mantras, and magic. I use the terms 'Vajrayāna' and 'The Diamond Way' to refer to the type of Buddhism legitimized by these texts; many Newars understand 'Vajrayāna' (*bajrayān*) in an imprecise way to mean simply 'what Vajrācāryas do'. I use 'Tantric Buddhism' as a synonym for 'Vajrayāna Buddhism', since this usage is so well established in Western sources. As with the term 'Vajrayāna' most Newars tend to understand by the word *tantra* something different from, though related to, learned usage: they are often not aware that the scriptures of Vajrayāna Buddhism are called Tantras; for them *tantra* means *tantra-mantra*, magical spells (cf. Turner 1980: 272). A practising Vajrācārya priest explained Tantrayāna to me as the ability to cure someone at a distance, for instance to cure a sick person in England by performing rites in Nepal. Newars relate many stories of the magical powers of Tantric adepts. On the other hand, Asha Kaji Vajracharya reproduces a traditional 'etymology' or gloss which emphasizes the fundamentally soteriological focus of the Tantras: '"taratīti taṃtra": in other words, that knowledge which saves from the cycle of rebirth is called Tantra' (A.K. Vajracharya 1986: *ṭha*).

Indian Buddhist commentators on the Tantric scriptures soon established a hierarchy of different types of Tantra. The origin of the schema they elaborated lay in the chronological difference between earlier and later Tantras, and the different deities to whom the texts were addressed: the later ones were considered higher and more profound than the earlier. Since traditional Buddhist scholars were not interested in dating as such – as far as they were concerned, all Tantras went back to the Buddha himself – but in theological differences, it may well be that the classification preserved in Tibet, and briefly illustrated in Table 9.1, does not reflect in every case a straightforward chronological sequence. Though the classification is intended to explain what was in fact a historical development, it is quite possible, even probable, that not all the texts assigned to a lower Tantra class were composed before those assigned a higher rank.

The Tibetans called the last two categories 'Father' and 'Mother' Tantras respectively, and the definition of the two classes was evidently of considerable importance to them and the object of much learned debate. Newar Buddhists are not concerned with these scholastic details because they lack the highly educated monk class for whom alone they have much meaning. However they do share the underlying presupposition that certain types of teaching are more esoteric and more fundamental than others and that such distinctions can be made even within the body of material expounded in the Tantras.

The fact that the threefold distinction between Disciples' Way, Great Way, and Diamond Way is used to classify gods and spheres of worship within the monastery has already been mentioned (§4.2). However, certain deities play an intermediate role between the Great Way and the Diamond Way. That is, they may be displayed outside and worshipped by all comers like the typical Great Way deities, the *bodhisattva*s, while at the same time they would be recognized as belonging to the Diamond Way. The most obvious example here is Vajrasattva, clearly identified by Newars as the

Table 9.1 *The hierarchy of Tantras, with the lowest given first, and examples of texts falling into each category.*

Tantra type	English		Examples
I Kriyā Tantra	Ritual Tantras		Vasudhārānāma-Dhāraṇī, Pañcarakṣā
II Caryā Tantra	Practice Tantras		Mahāvairocana Tantra
III Yoga Tantra	Yoga Tantras		Tattvasaṃgraha, Sarvadurgatipariśodhana
IV Yogottara Tantra	Higher Yoga Tantras	(Tibetan: 'Father' Tantras)	Guhyasamāja Tantra and ancillary Tantras (Vajramālā, Sandhivyākaraṇa etc.), Kṛṣṇayamāri Tantra, Vajrabhairava Tantra
V Yogānuttara Tantra	Ultimate Yoga Tantras	(Tibetan: 'Mother' Tantras)	Cakrasaṃvara Tantras (Laghusaṃvara, Abhidhānottara, Saṃvarodaya, Vajraḍāka, Ḍākārṇava Tantras), Hevajra Tantra, Catuṣpīṭha Tantra (of Yogāmbara), Caṇḍamahāroṣaṇa Tantra
		(Tibetan: 'Non-dual' Tantras)	Kālacakra Tantra, Nāmasaṃgīti

Note:
These five types are listed by Kāṇha in his commentary on the Hevajra Tantra, except that he calls the last type Yoganiruttara (Snellgrove 1959a II: 156). The fourth and fifth types are together known as the Anuttara Tantras. For the Tibetan classifications, see Lessing and Wayman 1978: chapter 7. For a detailed analysis of the Tibetan Tantric canon on these lines by Bu-ston, see Wayman 1973: 234–9. The Nāmasaṃgīti, recited every morning in Kwā Bāhāḥ and elsewhere, belongs properly in the Yoga Tantra class, but was also interpreted in a Yogānuttara manner as part of the Kālacakra cycle (Wayman 1973: 234 n. 7). According to Snellgrove (1987: 279), all Buddhism based on the Tantras is called Mantrayāna, whereas strictly speaking (and in contrast to the usage I have followed) 'Vajrayāna' refers only to the Yoga Tantra level and above.

ectypal *guru* and Vajrācārya. Thus Hemraj Sakya (1971: 1) writes of Vajrasattva: 'Vajrayāna's main *guru*, also known as Vajradhara, he is worshipped as Ādibuddha Svayambhū.' Quite apart from his name, Vajrasattva would be classed as a Vajrayāna rather than a Mahāyāna god because, as noted above, many Newar Buddhists understand 'Vajrayāna' to mean 'the religion of the Vajrācāryas'.

In Kwā Bāhāḥ, where there is a separate shrine of Vajrasattva, it is run by the *ācārya guthi*, the *guthi* of all Vajrācārya members of the monastery. Vajrasattva is worshipped frequently by every Newar Buddhist in the *guru maṇḍala* rite and with the 100-syllabled mantra of Vajrasattva. Thus the worship of Vajrasattva may be performed externally and by those without

Tantric Initiation, but, as with the chanting of the Nāmasaṃgīti text, the full meaning of the texts recited may not be expounded openly.

Another form of Vajrasattva is Vajradhara (instead of *vajra* and bell he holds two *vajra*s crossed at his chest). He represents the sixth Buddha, above and subsuming the Five Buddhas headed by Vairocana. A Tantric form of the *bodhisattva* Mañjuśrī is also connected to Vajrasattva. He is known to Newars as Mañjuvajra; the form most often seen is called canonically Mañjuśrī Dharmadhātu-vāgīśvara (Mañjuśrī Lord of Speech and of the Dharma-realm/the Dharma). The ambivalent word *dharma* means both (ultimate) thing (or constituent of the universe) and the Dharma, i.e. the Buddhist teaching. *Dharmadhātu* means literally 'the sphere of *dharma*', and it refers to 'the universe seen correctly, the quicksilver universe of the visionary perspective wherein all is empty and therefore is seen as a flow lacking hard edges' (Williams 1989: 123).

Like Vajrasattva, Mañjuśrī Dharmadhātu-vāgīśvara belongs to the exoteric level of the Diamond Way; that is, he may be displayed in public. It is to Mañjuśrī Dharmadhātu-vāgīśvara that is dedicated the most common Buddhist cult object after the *caitya*, viz. the *dharmadhātu* (called *vajradhātu* if there is a *vajra* on top). Lévi (1905 II: 19) was told that *dharmadhātu* are dedicated to Mañjuśrī and *vajradhātu* to Vairocana. In fact it seems that both are dedicated to this single deity who is a combination of the two and whose mandala is given in detail in the Niṣpannayogāvalī (Locke 1985: 486 n. 22). Van Kooij (1977) has made a detailed study of the iconography of Chusya Bāhāḥ, Kathmandu. As in many Buddhist monasteries, the main tympanum there displays Mañjuśrī Dharmadhātu-vāgīśvara. Van Kooij concludes, following Bareau and de Mallman, that 'in Tantric Buddhism a kind of unification had taken place between the transcendent Buddhas [= the Five Buddhas] and certain great Bodhisattvas, in this case between Vajrasattva/Vairocana and Mañjuśrī' (Van Kooij 1977: 77).

The epithets given to Mañjuśrī in the Niṣpannayogāvalī (Bhattacharya 1972: 65) are indeed found in an inscription on a *dharmadhātu* established in 1856 in Cikã Bahī. It reads:

Oṁ namo śrī-dharmmadhātu-vāgīśvarāya.
Mañjughoṣaṃ mahācīnaṃ mahāvairocanātmakaṃ
Pravṛttaṃ dharmmabījaṃ taṃ dharmmadhātuṃ namāmy aham.

OṀ obeisance to the blessed Lord of Speech and the Dharma-sphere! I do obeisance to the Dharma-sphere, Sweet-voiced [an epithet of Mañjuśrī], from Great China, having Vairocana as his essence, The seed of things/Dharma, active in this world.

Caityas, and in particular Svayambhū, are also addressed as Lord of Speech and of the Dharma-sphere in liturgical contexts, but it is the cult object specifically dedicated to Mañjuśrī which is known popularly as *dharmadhātu*.

Another Tantric deity who forms a kind of bridge between the Great and the Diamond Ways as experienced by Newar Buddhists is Caṇḍamahāroṣaṇa.[6] Unlike other Tantric deities he may, in a two-armed form, be worshipped externally: in Kwā Bāhāḥ under the shrine of Cakrasaṃvara (see Plate 6); in Guji Bāhāḥ in the wall of the main courtyard; and in Te Bāhāḥ, Kathmandu, in a special shrine house. In the public shrines he is referred to, and labelled as, Saṃkaṭā, an epithet of Bhairava, but Buddhists of any sophistication refer to him as Caṇḍamahāroṣaṇa or as Pālāḥdyaḥ, 'protector deity'. In this external form he is indeed a protective deity, and the liturgy indicates that he is identified with the nail hammered in to the lintel to keep out ghosts and spooks both when a house is constructed and at the House Purification ritual after a death. Where, on the other hand, he is the main Tantric deity of an esoteric shrine, as he is according to Asha Kaji Vajracharya of one lineage of Bu Bāhāḥ, he appears, no doubt, with many arms and with a consort.

In all these cases we have equivalents of the Kriyā, Caryā, and Yoga Tantra levels: gods who point to the ultimate Tantric deities (i.e. to Cakrasaṃvara, Yogāmbara, Hevajra and their consorts) but who, unlike the latter, may be displayed and worshipped exoterically. The breakdown of this distinction between two types of Vajrayāna, as when the multi-armed esoteric gods embracing their consorts are displayed openly in shop windows, dismays and angers Buddhists of the older generation.

It is more difficult to place Newar Buddhist female divinities precisely within the categories Mahāyāna, exoteric Vajrayāna, and esoteric Vajrayāna. But Vajrayoginī seems, like the male deities considered, to play a role in uniting exoteric deities, such as Tārā or Kumārī and the Eight Mothers, with the consorts of the secret Tantric deities, viz. Vajravārāhī (consort of Cakrasaṃvara), Jñānaḍākinī (consort of Yogāmbara), and Nairātmyā (consort of Hevajra).[7] This is particularly clear in the town of Sankhu of which Vajrayoginī is the tutelary deity. She is simultaneously identified with Prajñā Pāramitā, the Tantric goddess Ugratārā, and Durgā (Zanen 1986).

On the level of texts, the division into two types of Diamond Way can be discerned in the ritual of Newar Buddhism. The Guhyasamāja is the only Tantra to be included in the list of nine canonical works (*nava grantha*) which make up the Dharma Mandala worshipped during the *guru maṇḍala*, and is therefore the only Tantra whose name is uttered frequently in exoteric contexts. As the main Tantra of the Yogottara level (one level below the highest) it might seem appropriate that the Guhyasamāja should play this role. In fact, however, this is very probably the result of a mistaken identity. Originally the name Tathāgataguhyaka, as one of the nine scriptures, almost certainly referred to the Sūtra of that name, not to the Guhyasamāja Tantra.[8]

In complex esoteric rituals three terms are used: outer (*bāhira*), secret (*guhya*), and inner (*abhyantara*). Typically the last refers to the inner shrine to which access is restricted, e.g. the principal Tantric shrine of Kwā Bāhāḥ, or the mandala of Cakrasaṃvara in Tantric Initiation, which is revealed to the neophytes only after long preparatory rituals. The distinction between the secret and the inner is another form taken by the two levels of the Diamond Way.

Two types of Vajrayāna were also distinguished in the following explanation of the different Ways of Newar Buddhism given by *paṇḍit* Asha Kaji Vajracharya:

> Śrāvakayāna [the Disciples' Way] refers to monastic practice (*bhikṣucaryā*), and this was preached by Lord Buddha at Sārnāth.
> Pratyekabuddhayāna [the Solitary Buddha's Way] is that practised alone.
> Mahāyāna [the Great Way] teaches the practice of the *bodhisattvas*: Lord Buddha preached this on Gṛdhakūṭa hill.
> And on Vajrakūṭa hill he brought to light Vajrayāna [the Diamond Way]. There are two types of Vajrayāna. The first is onefold (*ekākār*): this is for one who does not marry and lives alone. The second is twofold (*dvārākār*): this is what is known as Tantrayāna [the Tantric Way] or Sahajayāna [the Way of Innate (Bliss)], in which a couple (*strīpuruṣ*) eat from the same plate. It is called Sahajayāna because they are united ('saṃjog juye') and eat each other's polluted food. The practice of Sahaja is Tantric Initiation; that is why those who come to take it on their own are sent away.[9]

Here the distinction is between a kind of Diamond Way that involves sex (the esoteric) and that which does not (the exoteric). The iconography of Tantric deities in Newar Buddhism does indeed conform with this. Only the esoteric deities are shown in sexual union. The 'bridging' Vajrayāna deities so far discussed are all displayed on their own.

The view of Asha Kaji Vajracharya represents a sophisticated and learned Newar view.[10] Ordinary Newars are unlikely to be able to expound distinctions between types of Vajrayāna. The common 'popular' view is that Vajrayāna is for Vajrācāryas. Thus a lively seventy-year-old Śākya artisan, who had taken Tantric Initiation at the age of twenty and had therefore been practising Tantric Buddhism all his life, contradicted his son who had claimed that the sacred syllable OṀ 'is' Śiva-Mahādeva and is found in Buddhism only through the influence of Brahmans. Not so, he replied, the three syllables OṀ ĀḤ HŪṀ are body, speech, and mind (*kāya, vāk, citta*). He was in fact giving a Tantric teaching[11] and yet he went on to say:

There are four Ways, Śrāvakayāna, Pratyekayāna, Mahāyāna, and Vajrayāna, but I don't know Vajrayāna. Vajrācāryas have a special initiation for this [he meant, I think, the Consecration of a Vajra-Master]. Vajrayāna is the highest but what I practise is Mahāyāna.

On the other hand, an old Vajrācārya, an active priest and an elder of Kwā Bāhāḥ, told me that he practised all Three Ways (as explained above, §4.2, the Solitary Buddhas' Way is excluded by definition). That is why, he continued, he eats meat only when it is (gods') blessed food (*prasād*), and does not smoke. He meant that he observes Śrāvakayāna rules in ordinary life and only breaks them in a proper Mahāyāna or Vajrayāna religious context, when the food or drink in question is 'purified' ('śodhan yānāḥ taḥgu'). In the same way, other pious Buddhists often told me that they only drink alcohol when it is 'blessed food'.

In short, as far as ordinary usage is concerned, 'Vajrayāna' means 'what Vajrācāryas do'. There is some justification for this usage: without the Vajrācāryas Vajrayāna could certainly not survive. Only they may perform its crucial rites. Traditionally many of those who are entitled to Tantric Initiation (Śākyas, Śreṣṭhas; in Kathmandu, Śākyas, Tulādhar *et al.*) were very knowledgeable, capable of singing Tantric songs and performing Tantric rituals; they were often invited along to make up the numbers. But they could not replace the Vajrācāryas as the principal priests, a privilege Vajrācāryas have jealously and successfully guarded.[12] Nowadays there are few who covet it; even to Vajrācāryas it has come to seem more like a burden.

9.2 Vajrācāryas as a status group

The distinction between a caste and a caste sub-group has been outlined above (§2.1). It was explained in that context why Śākyas and Vajrācāryas should be considered two caste sub-groups forming one caste. Even in the dispute between Vajrācāryas and Tulādhar *et al.* in Kathmandu, the Vajrācāryas never claimed openly to be of a different caste from the Śākyas. Although one consequence of that dispute was that status differences between Śākyas and Vajrācāryas in Kathmandu were exacerbated, and intermarriage became less frequent than in Lalitpur, there was not then, nor has there even been, any question of Vajrācāryas refusing to eat boiled rice cooked by Śākyas.

All the same, even in Lalitpur, it is clear that Vajrācāryas consider themselves a separate group with a separate identity.[13] This can be measured effectively by intermarriage since marriages are only arranged after a great deal of thought, and many enquiries, about the compatibility of the two families involved. Out of 430 Śākya and Vajrācārya arranged marriages recorded in ward 15 of Lalitpur, 61% were between Śākya and Śākya, 17.9% between Vajrācārya and Vajrācārya, 16.7% between Śākya men and Vajrācārya women, and only 4.4% between Vajrācārya men and Śākya women. Thus it seems that Vajrācārya women are slightly more likely to be given in marriage to Vajrācārya men than to Śākyas. Vajrācārya men, for their part, are roughly four times as likely to take a Vajrācārya as a Śākya bride.

This bears out what informants say, that for several reasons Vajrācāryas do not like to accept Śākya brides. Parishioners prefer to have a Vajrācārya woman as the priest's wife (*gurumā̃*) to whom half her husband's stipend (*dakṣiṇā*) is due; a Śākya girl is less likely to be well acquainted with rituals; if a Vajrācārya is ever to give Tantric Initiation his wife must be a Vajrācārya. In fact, the only parishioners likely to object strongly to a priest's wife being a Śākya are Vajrācāryas themselves, and possibly also very traditional and pious Śākyas. Lower castes, as has been seen (§2.5), tend to run Śākyas and Vajrācāryas together as one caste and do not concern themselves with differences between them.

In order to describe the basis of Vajrācārya socio-religious identity it is worth recapitulating the findings of two previous students of Newar Buddhism, Steven Greenwold and Michael Allen. The main points of Greenwold's article (1974a), 'Buddhist Brahmans' – a description of Vajrācāryas going back to Lévi (1905 I: 226) – can be listed as follows:

(i) The ideal Vajrācārya is a Realized One (*siddha*) who lives in the world, not a monk who renounces caste and family.[14]
(ii) The ritual of Monastic Initiation is used to maintain control of monasteries and exclude outsiders: 'the very basis of the Newar priesthood is prior ordination as a monk' (Greenwold 1974a: 110).
(iii) Since only Vajrācāryas may perform the Fire Sacrifice for Buddhists, they alone may act as family priests for parishioners.
(iv) Only 28% of Greenwold's sample of working Vajrācāryas in Kathmandu served as priests and only 11.9% had no other job but the priesthood. It is the ritual status of priest, not the actual practice of priesthood, which is essential to being a Vajrācārya.
(v) There is a close parallel with the position of Brahmans whose high status in a hierarchy of purity, and whose ability to act as priests for others, depend on their incarnating ascetic values.

Some of these points were also made in another of Greenwold's articles. However, this second paper (1974b), the very title of which ('Monkhood versus Priesthood') suggested a contradictory opposition, gave an oversimplified picture of Tantric Buddhist ideology. In a somewhat later article (1981), Greenwold went even further in presenting the position of the Vajrācāryas as an unlegitimized and desperate contradiction.

Thus, to these five points made by Greenwold, three others need to be added. They were first made, in the Newar context, by Michael Allen, in his article (1973), 'Buddhism without Monks' (this title has already been criticized, §2.4):

(vi) The Three Ways of Buddhism represent a hierarchy through which the Buddhist neophyte ascends, thereby recapitulating the history of Buddhism itself.

(vii) The highest, Tantric Way is based on inversions of the first, monastic one: 'sex in place of celibacy, long hair instead of shaven pates, indulgence instead of abstinence, drunkenness instead of sobriety' (Allen 1973: 13).

(viii) A crucial factor in the preservation of the income and identity of Buddhist priests has been the development of popular cults, such as that of Karuṇāmaya-Matsyendranāth, which appeal equally to all Newars.

Material amplifying these points has since been published by others, particularly by Locke.[15]

Greenwold's analysis of Newar Buddhism has the great merit that it avoids the hostile and dismissive tone of so many other observers. Nonetheless, in spite of its greater attention to detail, and avoidance of value judgements, at a deeper level Greenwold's account reproduced the errors of the previous observers whom he criticized. His simple opposition of monk and priest can be faulted on several grounds. Firstly, it runs together Śākyas, who are married monks but not priests, and Vajrācāryas, who are both married monks and priests. Secondly, monasticism was not a cynical 'cover-up' or a blatant contradiction, but a status acted out, believed in, and accepted by others also (see above, §2.4, and chapter 6). Finally, the statuses of monk, householder, and priest were integrated into a single hierarchical system. Vergati (1975) criticized Greenwold for ignoring this: his framework was both too schematic and unhistorical in straightforwardly and bluntly opposing the monk to the 'magician' (*siddha*). Point vi above and, in a more detailed way, the structure of this book, are intended as responses to this criticism. Traditional Newar

Table 9.2 *Soteriological ideals and social roles of the Three Ways.*

Religious level	Soteriological ideal	Social role
Disciples' Way	*arhat* (noble one)	Monk (e.g. during Monastic Initiation)
Great Way	*bodhisattva* (wisdom-being)	Pious Mahāyāna Buddhist practitioners; Vajrācāryas in their exoteric aspect
Diamond Way	*siddha* (Realized One)	Vajrācārya

Buddhism managed to combine apparently opposed models of spiritual excellence into a coherent whole. In other words, it was an ideological and ritual system which functioned, and was accepted, with minimal, if any, coercion, for a long period of time. This type of Buddhism now appears less coherent, but that is due to a changed intellectual climate discussed below (§11.5).

Greenwold exaggerated and distorted the opposition of the priest to the monk partly because he followed La Vallée Poussin in translating *siddha* as 'magician', rather than as 'Realized One', which is much closer to the word's meaning. Furthermore, in so far as he opposed the monk and the 'magician', as Vergati charged, he was not comparing like with like. He should have compared monks to Vajrācāryas and *arhat*s (Noble Ones) to *siddha*s (Realized Ones) (see Table 9.2). In the Disciples' Way the ideal is the *arhat* who has attained enlightenment by following the teaching of the Buddha. In the Great Way, the ideal is the *bodhisattva*, who could become an *arhat* but takes a vow to attain complete Buddhahood for the sake of all beings. In the Diamond Way the ideal is the *siddha* who manages to combine both the above and attain enlightenment in a single lifetime, by using antinomian symbols which are at once the sign and the means of grace. In practice, as pointed out above (§4.2) and discussed further below, the infraction of the rules is highly controlled; antinomianism is, with very rare exceptions, strongly disapproved of.

It is important to distinguish the ideal from the social role. The monk is to the *arhat* as the Vajrācārya is to the *siddha*: that is to say, both monk and Vajrācārya are ritualized social roles which are modelled on a specific soteriological ideal. Everyone knows that it is the rare monk who is an *arhat* and a rare Vajrācārya who is a true *siddha*. Newars frequently remark that the Vajrācāryas of today lack the *siddhi* (attainments) their forebears had.

Unlike *arhat* and *siddha*, there is no clearly defined role in Newar society which corresponds to the *bodhisattva* ideal of the Great Way, though one could say that every practising Buddhist is supposed to aspire to it, and the rhetoric of altruistic striving is an important part of all Newar Buddhism. The fulfilment of one's duties as a householder, as we have seen in chapters 7 and 8, is both seen as part of the Mahāyāna and justified in terms of altruism. Furthermore, there is no requirement that a *bodhisattva* not be a householder. Nonetheless, Newars do not specifically define the householder's duties in terms of the *bodhisattva*. These duties are too mundane for that. Vajrācāryas, on the other hand, frequently stress their altruistic service to others as a legitimization of their priestly role, and in this context the *bodhisattva* concept is often invoked. A good example occurs in a recent description of Vajrācāryas by Ratna Kaji Vajracharya:

> On the one hand, the Svayambhū Purāṇa relates that Vajrācāryas are the descendants of [lit. 'flow from'] the tradition of Śāntikar Ācārya. On the other hand, according to the Vajrācāryas' [own] tradition, it is also said that they take the form of *guru* Vajrasattva's 'created body' (*nirmāṇakāya*). These Vajrācāryas have taken to heart the scriptural teaching about acting in all ways for the benefit of the people ('sarvaprakāraṃ jagato hitāya') and have become experts in 'powerful utterance' (*tantra-mantra*) and have attained in full the sixty-four types of knowledge (*vidyā*). This is why Vajrācāryas draw up horoscopes, practise healing by blowing, act as healers (*vaidya*) etc., and especially why they carry out acts of worship and ritual [for others]. In this way they are continuously fulfilling the conduct, or following the path, of the *bodhisattva*.
>
> (R.K. Vajracharya 1989: 5)

Each level of this spiritual hierarchy includes within itself, and does not merely replace, the levels before it. Thus Vajrācāryas are supposed to fulfil the ideals of all Three Ways at once. All three of these ideals, the *arhat* of the Disciples' Way, the *bodhisattva* of the Great Way, and the *siddha* of the Diamond Way are soteriological ideals, and all three, because of their advanced spiritual state, are deemed to possess magical powers. Only the *arhat* is forbidden to use them. Of the other two, it is the *siddha* whose magical power has a greater hold on the imagination of the laity; this is perhaps encouraged by the antinomianism which underlies the *siddha* ideal. It explains why La Vallée Poussin translated *siddha* as 'magician'. All the same, the translation is misleading as it voids the term of its primary soteriological content.

From a sociological point of view, the function of these three ideals is not identical (for all that, religiously, the Vajrācārya is supposed to fulfil all three). The *arhat* ideal preserves Vajrācāryas' (and Śākyas') control of monastic institutions, along with popular cults based within them. Although enacted in the ways described above (chapter 6), Vajrācāryas' monastic status does not receive much mythic elaboration, probably because it is seen as opposed to the ideal and values of the Diamond Way.

The *bodhisattva* ideal is used, as shown above, by Vajrācāryas themselves to legitimize the priestly services they provide for others. By contrast, it is the *siddha* ideal which motivates those others to have recourse to Vajrācāryas when they are ill, or when they wish for some powerful intervention in the world. It is interesting, and no doubt not a coincidence, that the myths of Karuṇāmaya-Matsyendranāth view him as both *bodhisattva* and *siddha*.[16]

Although the values of the Disciples' Way are reversed in the Diamond Way, it is a controlled and limited reversal. Contrary to what Allen implied (point vii, above), drunkenness is never enjoined and practising Newar Buddhists often assert that they only drink alcohol in ritual contexts. Possession takes place during Tantric Initiation, as described below, but it is a relatively decorous sort of possession, and it is women who are more often possessed than men (cf. §8.2.4). Śākya and Vajrācārya men do not grow their hair but regularly shave it off, whenever an important ritual requires it. Sex is enjoined, but strictly within marriage and in private; the ritual copulation of the texts has been symbolically reinterpreted (see below, §9.3.5, 9.3.9). Vajrācāryas are admired for their strict adherence to the rules of religion, not for indulgence. Charges of indulgence are heard precisely when Vajrācāryas are being compared unfavourably with Brahmans or with Theravāda monks.

The Vajrācāryas' prime identity is, then, as Tantric priests. Few of them, however, are able to live from this alone (and very few now aspire to). As Greenwold (1974a: 113–14) pointed out, the very small number of Newar Brahmans means that their services as priests are in high demand, so that a high proportion of them live from this. By contrast, even in former times, most Vajrācāryas must have had to follow some other occupation; only a minority can have been supported by full-time priesthood. Thus, unlike Brahmans, many Vajrācāryas have become artisans. Like Śākyas, they often follow trades which Hindus would consider low caste. Table 9.3 shows figures for the occupations of Vajrācāryas and Śākyas of ward 15 compared to Greenwold's figures for Kathmandu.

The figures for Śākyas in Kathmandu and Lalitpur are fairly similar given that over half the Śākya-run shops in Lalitpur sell curios – i.e. images and souvenirs – to tourists. With Vajrācāryas, however, there is a sharp contrast. Most Lalitpur Vajrācāryas are artisans, like Śākyas, whereas Kathmandu Vajrācāryas are clearly more educated and have a high number of government and professional jobs. Kathmandu Vajrācāryas evidently lack the prejudice against government service which has only recently disappeared among Lalitpur Buddhists. The contrast between Vajrācārya and Śākya employment in Kathmandu, a contrast which does

Table 9.3 *Occupations of Vajrācāryas, in Lalitpur and Kathmandu, compared with Śākyas (Kathmandu figures from Greenwold 1974a: 113–5).*

	Vajrācāryas		*Śākyas*	
	Lalitpur ward 15	Kathmandu	Lalitpur ward 15	Kathmandu
	(N=114)	(N=201)	(N=404)	(N=182)
Artisans[a]	59.6%	9.0%	62.9%	71.4%
Trade[b]	14.9%	15.9%	32.2%	11.0%
'Service'[c]	21.1%	56.2%	12.6%	16.5%
Professions[d]	/	7.0%	/	1.1%
Priesthood alone	4.4%	11.9%	/	/
	100%	100%	107.7%[e]	100%
Priesthood with other work	22%	28%	/	/

Notes:

[a] Includes tailors.

[b] Includes retail and wholesale, the former, often on a very small scale, being the most common.

[c] I.e. *jāgir*: this includes government service (by far the most common) as well as those working for private corporations and those doing paid work for private individuals.

[d] Includes doctors, lawyers, and traditional medical practitioners (*vaidya*).

[e] This figure is over 100% because of the common practice of Śākya artisans combining their craft with a shop selling its products, or, more rarely, with holding a government post.

not exist in Lalitpur, may be another reason for the sharper cleavage between the two groups there. Nonetheless, although most Vajrācāryas and most Śākyas in Lalitpur are artisans, and though there is much overlap, there do seem to be certain specializations, at least within ward 15: Vajrācāryas are far more likely to be tailors or plasterers, while Śākyas predominate in the making of curios and gods.

The greater number of practising priests, and the greater number of priests living from that alone, in Kathmandu compared to Lalitpur shown in Table 9.3 is probably due simply to the passing of time. The data on Lalitpur were collected in 1984, Greenwold's data on Kathmandu over ten years earlier. Vajrācāryas themselves assert that it is no longer possible to live from the priesthood, however many parishioners one may have; people perform fewer rituals than in the past and continue to give the same stipend as they did years ago. All Vajrācāryas are therefore obliged to have some other occupation, and they dream of their sons becoming doctors and engineers.

Plate 10. The members of an Āwāle *guthi* in Bhelāchē̃, Lalitpur, worship and make *pañcadān* offerings to Vajrācāryas and Śākyas every year on the occasion of Pañcadān.

Plate 11. Two young Vajrācārya boys perform their first Fire Sacrifice in Kwā Bāhāḥ under the direction of their family priest and their mother as part of the Consecration of a Vajra-Master.

Plate 12. Śākya women perform the Observance of the goddess Vasundharā in a private home, which is a member of the *guthi* that organizes it every year. At the head of the line is Jog Maya Shakya who here acted as *jaymā*.

There is no explicit prohibition on Vajrācāryas (or Śākyas) farming and in some villages or outlying city areas they are said sometimes to do so. When I suggested that there might be such a prohibition Jog Maya retorted that on the contrary, it was honourable work, that the Buddha's father, King Śuddhodana, had himself worked in the fields. Nonetheless, there is, I think, a feeling that it is inappropriate to the social status of Śākyas or Vajrācāryas, even if there is no religious bar on it. Traditionally, Śākyas affirm, shopkeeping was considered demeaning. This did not apply, however, to large-scale wholesale trade, or to setting up shop in Tibet. Artisans by contrast have always been respected. The prejudice against shopkeeping has now vanished, although certain types of shop are despised: selling vegetables is a low-caste occupation, as is keeping a restaurant.

Certain occupations, in particular certain types of artisan work, tend, not surprisingly, to be passed down in certain families and localities, and therefore to be regionally concentrated. In this context it is worth reproducing a list given by the local scholar Hemraj Sakya:

> metalwork and god-making: Uku Bāhāḥ;
> artwork [i.e. curios] and scholarship (*śāstra-vidyā*): Mahābuddha;
> woodcarving: Guji Bāhāḥ and Si Bāhāḥ;
> desired rites (*iṣṭakalā*): Dhum Bāhāḥ and Hyan Bāhāḥ;
> Tantric knowledge: Cuka Bāhāḥ, Dau Bāhāḥ, and Bu Bāhāḥ;
> ayurvedic medicine: Cikā̃ Bahī;
> trade: Kwā Bāhāḥ and Nāg Bāhāḥ;
> plasterwork: Nyākhācuk and Ikhāchẽ Bāhāḥ;
> goldsmithing and refining gold-dust (*dhūsaḥ*): Ha Bāhāḥ, Oṁ Bāhāḥ;
> casting: Na Bāhāḥ;
> stonemasonry: Bhĩchẽ Bāhāḥ.
>
> (H. Sakya 1973: 57)

This gives a good idea of the specializations for which different monasteries or areas of the city are well known, though it is a rather idealized list, giving only one or two occupations for each. For instance, there are, it is true, more rich traders in Nāg Bāhāḥ than elsewhere, but the majority there are not rich and not traders, but curio-makers and god-makers.

In spite of this variety of occupations, the identity of Vajrācāryas – in their own, as in others', eyes – centres on the priesthood. Those few Vajrācāryas who practise their religion with commitment are spoken of with awe: their rituals 'really work'. They are often also healers, curing with mantras and various rites involving blowing ('phūphā yāye') or brushing with a broom ('jhārphuk yāye') (see below, §11.4), and in this role a reputation for piety certainly helps. Other Vajrācāryas are often spoken of slightingly though not to their face. The respect in which Vajrācāryas are held as a class has undoubtedly declined. Traditionally one might, at certain publicly permitted times such as Sā Pāru and Matayā, make fun of priests as of other authority figures (except the King). But such satire took place in a context in which priestly status was not in danger.

Nowadays genuinely anticlerical feelings are on the increase. In Kathmandu, bitterness still persists from the days of the Vajrācārya/Tulādhar *et al.* dispute, already mentioned several times, which pitched the Vajrācāryas against the castes who otherwise would have been their strongest supporters, Śākyas and Tulādhar *et al.* In Kathmandu, unlike Lalitpur, it is not uncommon to hear impassioned denunciations of Vajrācāryas as lazy, greedy, ignorant, proud, and so on. The Young Men's Buddhist Association of Kathmandu (whose members are defined by their modern education rather than their youth) is then in the paradoxical situation of wishing to study Mahāyāna Buddhism without recourse to precisely those in a position to instruct them in it. Instead – and this will come as no surprise to those acquainted with the *déraciné* intellectuals of other Third World cultures – they seek enlightenment from those who are educated in English and in Western scholarship about Buddhism.

9.3 Entering the Diamond Way: Tantric Initiation and the Consecration of a Vajra-Master

We have seen that for Newars 'Vajrayāna' refers both to the cult of secret esoteric deities and to the religion of the Vajrācāryas. Access to the former is determined by Tantric Initiation (*dīkṣā*), and to the latter, i.e. to the status of Vajrācārya, by the Consecration of a (Vajra-)Master. In Newari this is called *ācā luyegu* and in Sanskrit *ācārya* – i.e. *vajrācārya* – *abhiṣeka*; Nw. *luyegu*, to pour, is a direct translation of Skt. *seka/abhiṣeka*, consecration or lustration. As Locke (1980: 50, 53–5) has pointed out, the Consecration of a Vajra-Master is in fact an abbreviated form of Tantric Initiation, but nonetheless the two rites are not considered equivalent. Only the sons of Vajrācāryas may be consecrated as a Vajra-Master, and thus only they may perform the Fire Sacrifice, act as priests, and have parishioners. Other high castes may receive Tantric Initiation, but this does not entitle them to act as priests.

Evidence was presented above (§6.1) which suggests that at the beginning of the sixteenth century it may still have been possible for any Śākya to become a Vajrācārya. By the time of King Siddhi Narasiṃha (second quarter of the seventeenth century) and perhaps as a consequence of his reforms, this seems no longer to have been so. The fact that the 'monastic association priest' (*sā̃ gubhāju*) of the *bahī* class of monastery does not perform Fire Sacrifice, seems to imply that by this time the Vajrācāryas had become a closed descent group. It is this sociological fact, rather than any doctrinal reason, which explains why many Newar Buddhists who are not Vajrācāryas tend to think of the Diamond Way not as an aspect or level of their own religious practices, but as the religion of the Vajrācāryas.

Locke (1975: 14–17) has provided a summary of the Consecration of a Vajra-Master and it seems from his description that in Kathmandu the rite normally takes place immediately after Monastic Initiation. In Lalitpur, by contrast, it is often celebrated separately, and in certain monasteries (notably Bu Bāhāḥ) it is usually performed only after one has married. Given the close relationship between the Consecration of a Vajra-Master and Tantric Initiation, it is not surprising that in some quarters it should be felt better to go through both only after marriage. In Kwā Bāhāḥ, however, the majority of Vajrācāryas take even Tantric Initiation before marriage, effectively turning it, like the Consecration of a Vajra-Master, into a rite of passage (cf. Table 7.2).

The Consecration of a Vajra-Master, though embedded like other rites of passage in a large number of framing rituals, consists in principle of 'five consecrations' (*pañcābhiṣeka*).[17] Within each of these five main consecrations, others are also sometimes performed or added on, so the number five should not be taken too literally. The same five consecrations are the first stage of Tantric Initiation (see below, §9.3.5) and are also used in the establishment of a new image, which likewise receives all the consecrations of Tantric Initiation.[18] At the same time, in the numerous liturgical schemes of the various Tantras and commentaries, the Consecration of a Vajra-Master is itself considered to be a separate sixth consecration received after the five, both separate from them and simultaneously acting as their summation. It will be seen that the same is also true of the Newars' Consecration of a Vajra-Master. Taken together, all of that which falls under the Consecration of a Vajra-Master forms the first step of Tantric Initiation, which is itself divided into four 'macro' consecrations (Master, Secret, Wisdom, and Fourth Consecrations respectively).[19]

It seems that at the time when the Kriyā Samuccaya was written, the Consecration of a Vajra-Master in the narrow sense, i.e. as a specific consecration and not the name of the first part of Tantric Initiation, was given only to those who wished to practise as ritualists for others. Those who did not wish so to practise, but intended to practise for themselves only, omitted it.[20] In Newar Buddhism this distinction has been preserved, but with two important differences. There are now two distinct rituals performed on separate occasions, rather than having the Consecration of a Vajra-Master as an optional extra during Tantric Initiation. Secondly, access to the ritualist's role has been made hereditary.

The main part of the Newar Buddhist Consecration of a Vajra-Master takes place in the foyer before the Tantric shrine of the monastery. The rituals here are overseen by the monastery's officiants: the senior Vajrācārya (the Cakreśvara) and the Rituals Officer (Betāju). The boy's family priest takes over later, outside in the monastery courtyard, for the performance of the boy's first Fire Sacrifice (see Plate 11). During the main part of the ritual the following consecrations are given.[21]

(i) Flask Consecration: sprinkling with water from the main Flask;
(ii) Crown Consecration: the neophyte is given a Vajrācārya's ceremonial crown (*mukuṭa, mukhaḥ*);
(iii) Vajra Consecration: a Vajrācārya's *vajra* is placed in the neophyte's right hand;
(iv) Bell Consecration: the neophyte receives the Vajrācārya's bell (*ghaṇṭā, gā̃*) into his left hand;
(v) Name Consecration: he receives a new name;
(vi) Consecration of the Vajra-Master: this consists of performing the *āliṅganā mudrā*, i.e. holding the bell and *vajra* with fingers splayed and wrists crossed as if embracing a consort.

In some versions still further consecrations are given.

(vii) Headband Consecration: a fillet or headband is put around the neophyte's forehead and he receives a rosary;
(viii) Lampblack Consecration: lampblack is placed on the neophyte's eyes with the tip of the *guru*'s *vajra*;
(ix) Mirror Consecration: the neophyte receives the yoghurt-and-oil mix on his eyes by means of which he is supposed to perceive the ultimate emptiness of things.

It will be seen below how these consecrations are shared with Tantric Initiation, but before proceeding to a detailed exposition of the latter ritual some sociological generalities need to be laid out.

For Newar Buddhists, Tantric Initiation (*dīkṣā*) means primarily the initiation of Cakrasaṃvara and his consort Vajravārāhī. In Kathmandu, Vajrācāryas, Śākyas, and Tulādhar *et al.* may take it. In Lalitpur, Vajrācāryas, Śākyas, and Śreṣṭhas may take it. The Lalitpur caste, the Tāmrakār *et al.*, may also take it, according to Asha Kaji Vajracharya, but because they are initiated into the two-armed, and not the twelve-armed, form of the deity, they may not receive it with other castes. Citrakārs may receive the initiation of Mañjuvajra, and certain Maharjans may receive initiations of Mahākāla or Bhairava for specific purposes.[22]

At present in ward 15, Lalitpur, about one third of all Vajrācāryas have taken Tantric Initiation, and about one sixth of all Śākyas, but these figures conceal considerable variation in different age groups.[23] Only three Śreṣṭhas surveyed (1.9%) had taken the Initiation of Cakrasaṃvara, two of them forty, the other twenty-two, years previously. Nine Vajrācāryas (including two couples) and three Śākyas (including one couple) had the Initiation of Caṇḍamahāroṣaṇa. Two Śākyas had taken Tantric Initiation only with Tibetan lamas; three Vajrācāryas (who had taken both Cakrasaṃvara and Caṇḍamahāroṣaṇa Initiations in the Newar tradition) had also taken the Tibetan Initiation. Out of eighteen Jośī families and three Amātya families, only two Jośīs had taken Hindu Tantric Initiation. Certain Dãgols living in Na Bahī have Initiation but are unable (or unwilling) to say of what kind. According to Asha Kaji Vajracharya they take an Initiation of Mahākāla, since they are *ñawā* (who climb up the chariot of Karuṇāmaya-Matsyendranāth) and this prevents them from falling down. Only the senior of the lineage receives the mantra and he performs the daily worship on behalf of everyone else. Likewise the 'brake-men' (*ghaḥkū*) who brake the chariot with wooden blocks receive an initiation of Bhairava (the wheels of the chariot are identified with four Bhairavas).

According to my survey, two thirds of all Vajrācārya, and 40% of all Śākya, household heads had taken Tantric Initiation (cf. Table 9.4). Riley-Smith (1982: 59), working in Uku Bāhāḥ, found similar figures for the Śākyas there: 17.5% of all men, and 20.3% of women, had taken Tantric Initiation, but this rose to 39.2% and 39.4% respectively among the married population. It might be thought that, although those taking Tantric Initiation are in a minority overall, a majority of Vajrācāryas and a substantial number of Śākyas do eventually take it later in life. This proves not to be so. An analysis of different age groups shows that there has been a sharp decline in the number of Śākyas and Vajrācāryas taking Tantric Initiation since the 1950s, a change I would attribute to the coming of 'democracy' (*prajātantra*) in 1951 and the consequent decline of traditional observances. In Kathmandu, Lewis reports (1984: 239), fewer than 10% of Asan Tulādhars have Tantric Initiation, whereas the majority did so fifty years ago.

The sharp difference between over-55 and under-55 age-groups cannot

Table 9.4 *Percentage of Vajrācārya and Śākya men of ward 15, Lalitpur, having taken Tantric Initiation for given age-groups.*

	Vajrācāryas			Śākyas		
Age	*w/dīkṣā*	*Total*	*%w/dīkṣā*	*w/dīkṣā*	*Total*	*%w/dīkṣā*
15–35	8	78	10.3%	1	269	0.4%
36–55	18	46	39.1%	17	154	11.0%
56<	25	26	96.2%	63	91	69.2%

Note: These figures exclude those under the age of fifteen, and refer to a survey of the families of Lalitpur's ward 15: sixty-six Vajrācārya families (150 men, 136 women) and 211 Śākya families (514 men, 507 women).

be accounted for by the age at which Initiation is taken: the average for taking it with the over-55s was twenty-five, for the under-55s thirty-two, a rise of only seven years. The difference can only be explained by assuming that since 1951 taking Tantric Initiation is no longer a matter of course for Vajrācāryas, and has become a minority interest with Śākyas. Conversely though, the figures show that in the past taking Tantric Initiation was virtually universal among Vajrācāryas and normal among Śākyas. The only alternative explanation of the figures given in Table 9.4 – one which might tempt some Newar Buddhists themselves – is that those who have taken Tantric Initiation live longer.

As far as the age at which Tantric Initiation is taken is concerned, two distinct patterns emerge, depending on whether it was taken with one's spouse or not (the latter usually meaning: before marriage). This is shown in Table 9.5. The figures show clearly that Śākyas – whether men or women – are slightly more likely to take Tantric Initiation after marriage and with their spouse, whereas Vajrācāryas, particularly Vajrācārya men, are considerably more likely to take it young and before marriage. This is somewhat paradoxical since Vajrācāryas are thought to embody the values of the Diamond Way, and Tantric Initiation is, preferably, taken with one's spouse. The paradox is easily explained. Vajrācārya men are often required to act as priests in Tantric worship at a very young age. For this they need Tantric Initiation. The table also shows that the average age for women who take Tantric Initiation alone is higher, both among Śākyas and among Vajrācāryas, than for men. Where Vajrācārya women are concerned the explanation is probably simple: they take Tantric Initiation on their own because their husband took it before they were married. In the case of Śākya women the explanation may have more to do with a woman's life-cycle.

Table 9.5 *Average age, now and at taking of Tantric Initiation, by caste, sex, and whether or not taken with spouse; frequency of taking with spouse. (Information available for 84% of those with Initiation. Percentages rounded to nearest full digit.)*

		Men				Women			
	dīkṣā taken:	*average age at dīkṣā*	*No.*	*%*	*ave. age now*	*ave. age at dīkṣā*	*No.*	*%*	*ave. age now*
Vajrācārya	*separately*	14	31	67	44	20	22	60	48
	w/spouse	37	15	33	54	33	15	40	51
Śākya	*separately*	20	31	44	57	25	34	46	50
	w/spouse	33	39	56	62	27	40	54	58

Young women, when first married into their husband's household, have no status or independence. By their mid-twenties they have usually borne children and are sufficiently well established in their new family to be able to take Tantric Initiation even though their husband is not taking it with them.

There are other Tantric initiations, such as those of Caṇḍamahāroṣaṇa (*acala dīkṣā*), of Yogāmbara, and of Kālacakra, but these are much rarer, just as Tantric shrines to them are much less common than those to Cakrasaṃvara and Vajravārāhī. The initiation of Caṇḍamahāroṣaṇa is sometimes taken by Vajrācāryas who practise as Tantric healers (see below, §11.4), because it is supposed to help in acquiring the powers necessary for this.[24] The initiations of Yogāmbara and Kālacakra are not nowadays taken in Lalitpur as far as I have been able to establish. The senior Vajrācārya of Kwā Bāhāḥ, the Casalāju, ought to have the initiation of Yogāmbara to tend the shrine of Yogāmbara which is the monastery's main *āgǎ̇*. But the last Casalāju to have it died about sixty years ago without giving it to anyone else. According to Asha Kaji Vajracharya, a divination ritual was performed ('yaḥ/ma yaḥ kaykegu') to find out if the god would permit worship by those with only Cakrasaṃvara Initiation, and the answer was positive. Consequently Yogāmbara Initiation is preserved only in Kathmandu, in Tachẽ Bāhāḥ. Presumably also, the Tantric Initiation of Hevajra must have been given in Kathmandu in the past, even if it no longer survives today, since the Tantric deity of Yatkhā Bāhāḥ is Hevajra (H. Sakya 1978b: 18).

There is another kind of initiation, which is non-Tantric. It is known as

Eighth-Day Initiation (*aṣṭamī* or *asti dekhā*), that is, Initiation of Amoghapāśa Lokeśvara. It is also sometimes called 'small initiation' (*cīdhãgu dekhā*). As explained below, it is included in the rite of Tantric Initiation, but it may be taken separately. Sometimes a family may organize it at home, in which case the rite lasts two days. Many people take it after performing a series of Observances to Lokeśvara. It involves the obligation to say the six-syllabled mantra of Avalokiteśvara (OṂ MAṆI PADME HŪṂ) every day, and to recite other verses, a five- or ten-minute task. As with the more onerous initiations of the high Tantric divinities, it may not be given to those of the Farmer caste and below. This is justified on the grounds that they would be unable to perform the daily worship required because of their work. They may receive it from Tibetans or from Newar monks in the Tibetan tradition, since Tibetan Buddhism is less fastidious in this respect. Since it is a non-Tantric initiation there is no presumption that it is better to take it with one's spouse: only 23% of those for whom the information was available had done so. The relative rarity of taking Eighth-Day Initiation on its own (and not in the context of Tantric Initiation) is illustrated by the fact that in the sample of ward 15 only 6.7% of Vajrācārya men, 3.7% of Vajrācārya women, 4.5% of Śākya men, and 7.3% of Śākya women had done so.

Tantric Initiation is a long and expensive collocation of rituals which take eight or more full days to perform, and these may be spread out over two weeks or a month. What follows is an outline summary, based on a description provided by Asha Kaji Vajracharya, who had himself recently acted as principal *guru*. Whereas I had discussed and examined other rituals with him on the basis of written priestly handbooks, he dictated this account from memory over eight meetings. Asha Kaji's account has an integrity of its own, and is worth reproducing in this way. There is certainly room, however, for a longer study based on detailed consultation of ritual handbooks and the scriptural sources they rely on. For the main part of the initiation, focusing on Cakrasaṃvara, the handbooks follow the Kriyā Samuccaya; for the subsequent section, focusing on his consort, Vajravārāhī, some material is taken from the Saṃvarodaya Tantra, but it has not been possible (as yet) to identify the main source.

Tantric Initiation is secret and held in secret. This contrasts with the Tibetan practice of allowing it to be held in public, and of not restricting access to Tantric divinities (Snellgrove 1987: 146, 323). Nonetheless, in spite of the Newar stress on secrecy, I believe that the statistics given in Tables 9.4 and 9.5 are broadly accurate. While the content, and above all the mantras are secret, the bare fact that someone has Tantric Initiation is not. Indeed it could hardly be kept secret since all the members of the family know that those who have initiations have to disappear into the god-room before they eat every day.

Learning about the content of Tantric Initiation was problematic. Receiving initiation myself was out of the question; even if it had not been, there would have been the practical difficulties of understanding what is going on, and genuinely combining observation with full participation, which Evans-Pritchard points out (1937: 150–1) in a comparable situation among the Azande. Nor could I have had someone else initiated, as he did, in order to relay information to me. Initiations are held at irregular intervals, often years apart. Initiates are sworn to secrecy (at least towards non-initiates) and fear the dire misfortunes widely believed to result either from talking to others or from not practising the rituals as promised. In any case, a non-specialist is unlikely to grasp, and be able to remember and communicate, the details of the ritual. The only recourse, then, was to a *paṇḍit* such as Asha Kaji.

9.3.1 Preliminaries to Tantric Initiation

One to three months before the Initiation begins a Worship of Vajrasattva is performed at the house where the events will take place, and arrangements are made. The various roles are determined: principal teacher (*guru*), assistant teacher (*upādhyāya*), four male helpers (*kalyāṇa mitra*, 'good friends [on the Buddhist path]'), and four female helpers (*subinī*), and finally the group of (male) singers of Tantric songs (*caryā gīti*, *cācā me*). The singers are known as the *cācāpā* and there must be at least eight of them. There may also be a Vajrācārya appointed solely to follow along in the ritual handbook and ensure that everything is being done as it should. He is called the *karmācārya*; this term is used by Buddhists only in this way, i.e. in the context of elaborate Tantric rituals.[25] According to a Śākya woman who had taken Initiation, the main *guru* must not only be married but must not have been married more than once.

Day 1: Offering Areca Nuts ('gwaydā̃ tayegu')

On this day areca nuts and coins are offered as in other rites in earnest of one's intention to go through with Tantric Initiation.[26] Blue cloth has to be given to the main *guru*, red to his wife, by all the candidates (*dhaḥmū*). It is explained to them that by this means they will be saved ('taray yāye') and achieve liberation (*mokṣa*), and that it is too late to go back now. Then they proceed to a Power-Place to perform Power-Place Worship; the main action here is the offering of a large Spirit-Offering of rice, egg, fish, and buffalo blood and lungs to Bhairava. It is explained that the Bhairava of the Power-Places teaches the way to Cakrasaṃvara, that the Realized Ones performed asceticism in cremation grounds (which are always associated with a nearby Power-Place), and that they show the way.

*Day 2: Observance of the Eighth Day (*aṣṭamī vrata*)*
On this day, which may follow immediately on Day 1 or may fall some time later, an Observance of Lokeśvara is performed in the normal way, with a meatless meal. The candidates are given the six-syllabled mantra (*ṣaḍakṣarī* – pronounced *khadakṣarī* – mantra) and the fact that each syllable 'purifies' (i.e. liberates from) one of the six rebirths (*gati*) is explained (cf. §4.3.11). The assistant priest explains the qualities of the *guru* and the disciple (*śiṣya*). The *guru*'s qualities are accomplishments (*siddhi*), knowledge, and good conduct; the disciple's are devotion to the *guru* and observance of the moral precepts (*śīl*).

*Day 3: Preparation rites (*pūrvāṇga vidhi*)*
The ritual arrangement (*thāpā̃*) is set up. From this day only beaten rice, not cooked rice, may be eaten.

*9.3.2 Day 4: The rite of nailing down (*kīlana vidhi*)*

This day begins with a long worship of the Ten Wrathful Ones (*daśakrodha pūjā*). Then the candidates perform a mandala worship (*dhalā̃ danegu*) of the Three Jewels in their Tantric form, the Buddha being worshipped as Vajrasattva, the Dharma as Vajradevī, and the Saṃgha as Lokeśvara of the Six Syllables (Ṣaḍakṣarī Lokeśvara). The *guru* dances as Vajrasattva, and then as Heruka, and gives the candidates the mantra of Vajrasattva. Vasundharā is worshipped and the thread, Flask, coloured powder, *vajra*, and bell to be used in the next day's ritual receive Preliminary Empowerment (*sūtra-*, *kalaśa-*, *raṅga-*, *vajra-*, and *ghaṇṭādhivāsana*).[27]

*9.3.3 Day 5: Preliminary Empowerment of the mandala (*maṇḍalādhivāsana*)*

On this day, after various introductory rituals, including a worship of Cakrasaṃvara, his statue is placed in the middle of where his mandala is to be made up, and the Vajrācāryas begin to make it with coloured powder, each wearing a handkerchief over the mouth to prevent polluting saliva falling on it. This takes all day. In the centre is Cakrasaṃvara, and he is surrounded in the four directions by sets of four of the Sixteen Worship Goddesses (*ṣoḍaśa lāsyā*) and by the four Guardian Kings of the directions.

Working outwards there are three circles of lotuses, *vajra*s, and flames. Then there are representations of the eight cremation grounds, each with their own Realized One, each with a *caitya*, *śivaliṅga*, a tree with three birds, a bull, a tiger, a dog, a vulture, a crow, a river, and various spirits (*kawã*, *khyāḥ*, *bhūt*, *pret*). Finally outside this is a circle of skulls. And the whole is protected by the Ten Wrathful Ones.[28]

*9.3.4 Day 6: Establishment of the mandala (***maṇḍalapratiṣṭhā***) and preparation of the pupils (***śiṣyādhivāsana***)*

After worshipping all the deities of the mandala (which takes about three hours) the various priests dance. The main *guru* dressed in white dances as Vajrasattva, his wife in red as Vajradevī, the Assistant in yellow as Mañjuvajra, his wife in orange as Keśinīvajra, and the others as different Wrathful Ones according to the colour of their costume. The candidates are not present for this. Instead they wait in an outer room where they perform the *guru maṇḍala* rite. Then they are led inside, but only into the antechamber to the main room, not into the main room itself. In this antechamber there is a statue (*pratimā*) or a painting (*paubhāḥ*) of Caṇḍamahāroṣaṇa.[29] They are then told that the *guru* is Vajrasattva, his wife is Vajradevī, and so on: they must be respected as such. The candidates are given a protective amulet (*jantra*) to wear around their necks. Those who have not come as (married) couples are paired off, men with women. They are given the mantra of Svayambhū. They are told to make ready to go into the inner chamber (*abhyantara*) of Cakrasaṃvara. Their offerings are presented to Caṇḍamahāroṣaṇa.

*9.3.5 Day 7: Heroic Conduct (***vīryacaryā***)*[30]

On this day the candidates are told to bathe in the river Bāgmatī and to come at around 4 p.m. wearing blue (for men) or red (for women). Many friends and relatives who have already taken Tantric Initiation are also likely to be present to watch the proceedings. The candidates must each bring a silver model jewel-mandala, which is offered to the *guru* by each candidate as he or she performs the *guru maṇḍala*. The candidates wear string headbands and cloth to cover the eyes: the men's are blue, the women's red. Some ash from inside is smeared on their heads.

Then, with their eyes covered, the pairs line up, women first, and are led inside. Dancing, the main *guru* leads the way and his wife takes the hand of the first woman. The singers of Tantric songs line up half on either side as the candidates enter the main room, and they sing. The candidates' blindfolds are lifted up: first of the wife then of the husband, in the order in which they entered the room. They are warned not to look too soon, for even great *bodhisattvas* have been blinded by Cakrasaṃvara's mandala. Tantric fivefold nectar (*pañcāmṛta*), consisting of partridge, deer meat, and alcohol, is placed on the candidates' tongues. The various parts of the mandala are explained to them, starting from the outside and working inwards. Many of the women candidates are likely to be shaking, possessed by the goddess. The Tantric singers will stop them by touching their hands and reciting a verse from the *guru maṇḍala* rite, and if this does not work, by sprinkling them with water and reciting the hundred-syllabled mantra of Vajrasattva.[31]

Now the candidates are ready for the series of fourteen consecrations. The first five recapitulate what we have already seen for the Consecration of a Vajra-Master: they are, in order, Consecrations of the Flask, Vajra, Bell, Crown, and Name. The ritual continues as follows.

*Mantra Consecration (*mantrābhiṣeka*)*
The candidates place their rosaries on a plate and worship them. The *guru* tells them the mantra of Vajrasattva, his wife that of Tārā.[32] It is explained to them that by these mantras Vajrasattva becomes Cakrasaṃvara, and Tārā becomes Vajradevī.

*Headband Consecration (*paṭākābhiṣeka*)*
They receive a headband of five-coloured threads, as in one version of the Consecration of a Vajra-Master.

*Consecration of Shooting an Arrow (*śarakṣepābhiṣeka*)*
The candidates come in pairs and shoot a white jasmine with a bow onto the mandala. It lands on a cloth which has been stretched over the mandala to protect it. It is explained that the jasmine stands for the mind (*citta*) of the candidates which has come to pay obeisance to the feet of Cakrasaṃvara.[33]

*Consecration of the Secret Flask (*guhyakalaśābhiṣeka*)*
Here the candidates are offered the contents of the flask used in Secret Flask Worship, that is, five types of beer mixed. This, they are told, is the means of purifying one's body, speech, and mind. It is the blessing of Cakrasaṃvara.

*Lampblack Consecration (*añjanābhiṣeka*)*
The wife of the main *guru* gives each candidate orange powder with her left thumb: a spot for the men, along the hair parting of the women. The *guru* follows putting a silver streak through the middle of the orange powder and

putting lampblack (*mwahanīsinhaḥ*) on the forehead and eyelids. The assistant *guru* explains that now evil spirits (*bhūt-pret*) will not be able to see them, and they will be free from eye disease.

*Mirror Consecration (*darpaṇābhiṣeka*)*

The seniormost of the assistant women shows each candidate a ritual Mirror and a light, and the assistant or the main *guru* explains the meaning of emptiness (*śūnyatā*):

If you can see your face, is it you or not? If it is, how come it can't talk? How is it that it disappears when you put the mirror down? If it is not, what is your face doing there? This is the meaning of emptiness. In reality our body is nothing at all. (And so on at greater length.)

*Wisdom Consecration (*prajñābhiṣeka*)*

Here all the participants eat two round rice-flour pancakes (*catāmari*) with eggs, milk, sweets, and tea brought from home. It is explained that the pancakes are round like the mandalas of sun and moon.

*Knowledge Consecration (*jñānābhiṣeka*)*[34]

Those candidates who came alone (who came 'without *śakti*', i.e. not as a married couple) now have to leave. The couples sit side by side and lean together so that their heads are touching. A shawl is placed over their heads. The man's right hand is put in the woman's left hand. They sit silently like this while a long Tantric song is sung. Finally the shawl is removed and the single candidates are allowed to return to the room. It is explained to them that this is Sahajayāna [the Way of Innate (Bliss)], a couple being together: this is the *dharma* of householders. Then they all eat, the couples eating a shared meal (*sahabhojana*) off one plate. All the remains are worshipped and sent off. It may be 2 or 3 a.m. by this time.

*Secret Consecration (*guhyābhiṣeka*)*

For this the couples come in turn and dress in bone ornaments (*hāḍābharaṇa, hāl tissā*) of Cakrasaṃvara and Vajradevī. They hold a skull-bowl (*pātra*) of alcohol in their left hand and a double-headed drum (*ḍamaru*) in their right hand. The *guru* and his wife, who have been dancing as Cakrasaṃvara and Vajradevī, circumambulate the couple and drink from their own and each other's skull-bowls. Then the two neophytes also drink from their own skull-bowls, exchange them, and drink each from the other's. Now they are possessed by Cakrasaṃvara and Vajradevī and the woman begins to shake. It is explained to the candidates that there is no 'I' or 'you', no pure or impure; there are in reality no differences of caste. When they have circled the mandala they remove the bone-ornaments and it is the turn of the next couple. When all this is over offerings (*pañcadān*) and ritual stipends (*dakṣiṇā*) are given to the various priests. The candidates return home. It will be morning by this time.

*9.3.6 Day 8: Rite of the Main Flower (***mūlaswā̃yā vidhi***)*

The pupils return around 1 or 2 p.m. The priests have meanwhile drawn the mandala of Vajradevī (i.e. Vajravārāhī). They sing twelve Tantric songs and perform a Worship of Cakrasaṃvara. Outside the pupils assemble, perform the *guru maṇḍala* rite, and the two senior Tantric song singers give them directions: they worship with water (*argha*) the *guru* and his wife and again offer them silver jewel-mandalas. Today, they are told, you will see the mandala of Vajradevī and hear her mantra. After various good-luck rites, they are led in, blindfolded as before, and shown the mandala.

In the centre is Vajradevī in an equilateral triangle surrounded by the first twelve vowels of the (Sanskritic) alphabet. In another circle, working outwards, are the fifty letters of the alphabet. They are arranged anti-clockwise, since this is left(-handed) (*vāma*) practice. Next is a six-pointed star with the six *yoginī*s, and in between them six of the eight auspicious signs. This is enclosed by a square with the moon and the sun in the top corners, and the other two auspicious signs in the lower corners. The whole is enclosed with circles of lotuses, *vajra*s, and flames. Around the outside there are no cremation grounds, as in the mandala of Cakrasaṃvara, but there are eight Power-Places.[35]

The *guru* and his wife dress with bone ornaments as Cakrasaṃvara and Vajradevī, and dance. They hand over the staff (*khaṭvāṅga*) in turn to each neophyte, the *guru* to the men, his wife to the women: they place it for a moment under the arm. Then the *guru* and his wife hand to them the bowl and chopper in turn, and each neophyte holds it in the flicking posture (*bindu-mudrā*). There follows a series of consecrations.

*Secret Skull-Bowl Consecration (*guhyapātrābhiṣeka*)*

The candidates offer money (*dakṣiṇā*) into the skull-bowl, take the Five Nectars out with the left hand and place it on their eyes, and flick it into their mouth with the ring finger of the left hand.

Secret Flask Consecration (*guhyakalaśābhiṣeka*), Powder Consecration (*sindūrābhiṣeka*),[36] and Lampblack Consecration (*añjanābhiṣeka*) follow as before. Then:

*Mantra Consecration (*mantrābhiṣeka*)*
The couples approach the *guru* and his wife in pairs, and receive the mantra of Vajradevī in the left ear (Cakrasaṃvara's was given into the right ear).

*(Main) Secret Skull-Bowl Consecration (*guhyapātrābhiṣeka*)*
The *guru*'s wife hands to each pupil the main skull-bowl which she has been using and they each drink from it.[37] The Assistant's wife fills it up as she goes.

*Wisdom Consecration (*prajñābhiṣeka*)*
They eat rice-flour pancakes and the spectators join them in this. Then there is a feast, and, as before, couples eat from the same plate.

*Parasol Consecration (*chattrābhiṣeka*)*
The Tantric song singers hold a parasol over the couples in turn, and it is explained to them that they have now attained the parasol of the Buddhas and *bodhisattvas*. By this time it is morning and they all return home to sleep. It is still forbidden to bathe, and forbidden to eat cooked or beaten rice.

*9.3.7 Day 9: Raising the mandala (*maṇḍalaropaṇavidhi*)*

Around 3 p.m. the same day the pupils return. A Fire Sacrifice is performed to the accompaniment of Tantric songs. It is a speciality of this Fire Sacrifice that meat (*māṃsāhuti*) has to be offered; normally this is 108 bits of buffalo lung.[38] Then they offer a large coconut, decorated to look like a head with eyes, nose, and ears, into the fire. Now the *guru*'s wife, the sponsor's wife, and the next four most senior women pupils come dressed as the six *yoginīs* and sit around the fire. Each is given a skull-bowl with a different Tantric mixture (four types of rice beer, spirits with egg, and so on). Their husbands stand behind them holding alcohol flasks. The women close their eyes and shake, possessed. They flick the alcohol with the ring finger of the left hand into the fire 108 times. Finally all return to their own places for the normal concluding rites. Tantric songs are sung while the dust of the mandala is swept up. To conclude, a Kumārī Worship is performed, and the Kumārī offering is offered before the painting of Cakrasaṃvara. The day ends with a feast.

*9.3.8 Day 10: Consigning the powder (to the river) (*rajaḥpravāha*)*

Next day in the morning the powder from the mandala is swept up and placed in Flasks. All the participants go in procession to the river carrying the Flasks. After worshipping a holy serpent at the confluence, all the pupils sit in a row, overturn their Flask, and throw the powder in the river. They bathe, remove all the blessed thread which has accumulated around their neck, put on a new set of clothes, sit down, and make a *caitya* out of sand. They worship it and, for the first time, perform their regular daily worship. They return home and can now eat cooked rice.

Later they return to the house where the initiation was held. They sit in line for the 'establishment of the candidates' ('dhaḥmū swāyegu'). Seven Tantric songs are sung, and each candidate receives a Flask painted with a blue *vajra* and a red skull-bowl which is kept at home in their Tantric shrine and placed by their head when they die. They hold the Flask in their lap while they receive good-luck food (*sagã*). Then after giving ritual stipends to all the priests, they eat a feast and return home.

9.3.9 Remarks on the symbolism of Tantric Initiation

It will be clear that central to Tantric Initiation are sexual imagery and also reversals of normal values, that is, of values upheld outside in everyday life, and that these two go hand in hand. During Tantric Initiation the woman enters first and sits on her husband's right, whereas in normal life she always walks behind him and keeps him to her right. Tantric Initiation takes place at night, other religious rites during the day. In the rite from which single candidates are excluded the couples hold hands. This is strictly taboo outside and serves as a substitute (which only just remains implicit) for the ritual copulation enjoined by the Tantric scriptures. The order of the rites implies that, esoterically, the female is higher, since the initiation proceeds from lower to higher and ends with the mandala and mantra of Vajradevī. In secret, high-caste people who would normally regard spirit-possession as undignified themselves show signs of possession.

Female is identified with left and male with right (this remains constant between internal and external ritual), and the Tantric ritual, particularly the final stage, the worship of the goddess Vajradevī, is said to be the 'left-hand' path. The ultimate wisdom (*prajñā*) which is the aim of Buddhists is female; male is only the means (*upāya*) to that wisdom. However, this female predominance is largely implicit. Tantric Buddhists do not seem to go as far as Śākta Hindus in asserting loudly the preeminence of the female divinity.[39] Rather they stress the importance of both male *and* female, means *and* wisdom, moon *and* sun.

The symbolism of Tantric Initiation makes full use of a series of dualistic correspondences given in Table 9.6. These correspondences are found in the Tantric songs which accompany the rituals (Kvaerne 1977: 32), in

Table 9.6 *Corresponding oppositions in Tantric Buddhist symbolism.*

wisdom	night	woman	left	moon	lotus (*padma*)
means	day	man	right	sun	*vajra*

iconography, and in ritual. It is these sexual, mystic, and antinomian symbols which are central to Tantric Initiation. Political symbols of royalty or overlordship are less important: Snellgrove (1959b) discusses the evolution of such ideas in Buddhist Tantric literature and concludes that although they were important in one of the earliest Buddhist Tantric texts, the Mañjuśrīmūlakalpa, subsequently 'kingship or crown-princeship is merely an associated idea' (ibid.: 214).

Although I have not heard them express it exactly in these terms, traditional Newar Buddhists would agree with the sentiment which the Saṃvarodaya Tantra (18.34–5; Tsuda 1974: 128, 298–9) ascribes to the neophyte who has received all the different consecrations of Tantric Initiation:

Adya me saphalaṃ janma saphalaṃ jīvitaṃ ca me,
Adya buddhakule jāto buddhaputro 'smi sāmpratam.

Now my birth is fruitful; and my life is fruitful too,
Now I am born in the family of the Buddha: now I am a son of the Buddha.[40]

Indeed this very verse is put into the mouth of candidates after they have taken Tantric Initiation, according to some priestly handbooks.[41] For traditional high-caste Newar Buddhists, Tantric Initiation represents the culmination of their religious career, all other, exoteric, practices being merely a preparation for it.

10

The Diamond Way (Part II): the regular cult

. . . the mandala, although imagined (*bhāvita*), exists on a higher plane of reality than the phenomenal world it represents. Likewise the idealized representation of the body [and] . . . the divine forms. They are not pure symbol as we might interpret them . . . The Buddhists . . . regard them as real in the beginning, more real than flesh and blood . . . Nor is any real distinction to be made between an esoteric and exoteric interpretation, between the few who know all these things are symbols, and the many who place faithful trust in them . . . A distinction is made, it is true, between an inner (*adhyātmika*) and an outer (*bāhya*) interpretation with regard to actual rites, but they remain rites none the less, and the distinction arises from no embarrassment with regard to them, or a desire to explain them away. On the contrary, the outer sense is usually commended as necessary to lead men to the inner, which is precisely their use . . . Those Buddhists believed, and it was necessary for their whole scheme of 'release' that they should believe, in those gods and magical practices for their own sakes, before they began to use them as means. There was no short-cutting of this way, or the means would have been completely ineffective; nor indeed were they inclined to believe otherwise.

David Snellgrove, *The Hevajra Tantra*, Part I, pp. 33–4, fn. 3
(Reproduced by permission of Oxford University Press.)

10.1 The cult of Tantric deities

Every high-caste family, every monastery, and many lineages possess their own Tantric shrines, called *āgă̊* (see Plate 7). The degree of secrecy surrounding them varies. In many families the *āgă̊* is primarily just a 'god-room' (*dyaḥkwathā*, *dyaḥkū*): the principal deity is non-Tantric and access is not restricted to those with Tantric Initiation. In this case there are likely to be several small images of Tantric deities one of whom – unidentified to others – is the tutelary deity of those in the family who have taken Tantric Initiation. In other families access is strictly controlled, at least while Tantric rites are being performed: one young Śākya man knew very well the seniormost woman of the lineage became possessed (literally 'shaking', *khāye*) and said that if anyone, such as himself, who did not have Tantric Initiation were present, it would be impossible to end the possession.

It is in this 'god room' or *āgȧ̆* that those members of the family who have Tantric Initiation perform their personal daily ritual. Others who wish to perform daily prayers also do so here. For instance, Jog Maya's daughter-in-law, who has taken the 'small initiation' of Amoghapāśa Lokeśvara told me that she recites the following every morning before eating: (i) the 'Ākāśadhātu' verses; (ii) verses describing Amoghapāśa and his iconographic attributes; (iii) verses in praise of the Buddha; (iv) the *dhāraṇī* of Vairocana. Then she repeats ('jap yāye') the mantra of Lokeśvara, OṀ MAṆI PADME HŪṀ. This much is required by the initiation she has taken. Then she recites verses from the Theravāda *paritrāṇ* (in Pali), and ends with sixty-two verses of the Bhadracarī (in Sanskrit once again). This eclecticism is typical of the non-partisan, devotional nature of Śākya piety in Lalitpur.

For those with Tantric Initiation the ritual is longer and more complex. Ideally the process of rising and carrying out one's ablutions should also be accompanied by mantras and the offering of libations to the Three Jewels, to Sūrya, and to one's ancestors.[1] This is followed by a short worship of Cakrasaṃvara and Vajravārāhī, including recitation of their mantras, inserted in a performance of the *guru maṇḍala*.

As with family god-rooms, there is some variation in the degree of strictness with which rules of exclusion are applied to the Tantric shrines of monasteries. In Kwā Bāhāḥ only one man, the Casalāju (Cakreśvara), may enter the shrine of the principal Tantric deity, Yogāmbara. Access to the foyer before it is restricted to those of the status of Maharjan and above. Elsewhere, in Uku Bāhāḥ, I was struck by how reluctant a Śākya man from Kwā Bāhāḥ was to enter even the foyer of a Tantric deity which was not his own when he had not been invited to do so and had no pressing reason to be there. Where lineages possess their own Tantric shrine, whether in a special room in the origin-house (*mūlchẽ*) of the lineage, or (as is the case with some prestigious and wealthy Śreṣṭha lineages) in a special Tantric god-house (*āgȧ̆ chẽ*), access is *a fortiori* restricted to members of the lineage, their married daughters on occasions determined by tradition, and invited priests. Some Śākya and Vajrācārya lineages which have founded a lineage monastery have their Tantric shrine as part of it. As discussed above (§8.2.4), the Tantric deity of a lineage is identified in certain contexts with its Lineage Deity: this is not surprising given the fact that Tantric deities are supposed to be the secret 'inner' identity of exoteric deities.

Many stories are told illustrating the power of Tantric deities and the folly of disregarding the taboos surrounding them. Those who look on them without the authority to do so are believed to become blind or go mad. One old Śākya man commented that the Tantric deity in his house was extremely 'naughty' or 'badly behaved' (*harā̃* – the word is most often used of children): when the house was being rebuilt one of the Maharjan workmen got a very bad eyeache. He consulted a traditional doctor (*vaidya*) who said he had incurred the punishment (*doṣ*, literally 'fault') of an important god (*taḥdhā̃gu dyaḥ*). They then questioned him and he finally admitted that he had looked behind the curtain over the door of the Tantric shrine. They made him offer a rice-saucer (*kisalī*) to the deity and he recovered immediately. A similar story is told, sometimes of Mukunda Sena (who invaded the Valley in the early sixteenth century), sometimes of Jang Bahadur Rana: he forced his way into Yogāmbara's shrine in Kwā Bāhāḥ, but a green field opened up in front of him, and however far he walked it was just the same. Realizing his fault, he begged the deity's forgiveness (*kṣamā*) by offering a headdress to him.

Those who are responsible for the regular worship of a Tantric deity often ascribe any subsequent misfortunes they experience to the god's punishment, *doṣ*, for mistakes or omissions.[2] In the same vein I have heard Śākya women discuss dreams they had had which clearly reflected anxiety about keeping the rules properly. Such anxiety is more frequent where Tantric gods are concerned because their worship is more elaborate, and the gods themselves more ambivalent: they are not benign and compassionate like Śākyamuni Buddha or the *bodhisattva*s, but angry and fierce.

In households the household head, in lineages the oldest male member, and in monasteries the senior Vajrācārya is responsible for regular worship of the Tantric deity. Lay castes with Tantric shrines (Śreṣṭha, Tāmrakār *et al.*, in Kathmandu Tulādhar *et al.*) often arrange for a Vajrācārya to perform the regular worship of their lineage Tantric deity for them. In shrines of any importance more elaborate rituals, requiring the presence of more than one priest, are performed once a month: the most usual days are the tenth, fourteenth, and new-moon days of the fortnight of the waning moon. In Kwā Bāhāḥ the regular worship of Yogāmbara occurs on the full-moon day and that of the second Tantric shrine, to Cakrasaṃvara, on the new-moon day. Special rites are performed in most Tantric shrines at Mohanī (Vijayadaśamī) and Disī Pūjā. In addition every lineage Tantric shrine is likely to have at least one elaborate rite once a year to celebrate its foundation. Although rituals are secret, outsiders know that they are taking place, from the beating of the double-headed drum (*ḍamaru*) and the unmistakeable Tantric songs, half chant, half song, which can be heard in the street or courtyard outside. The shrines in which such rites take place are usually identifiable from the characteristic lattice windows.

The basis of the cult of Tantric deities is the use of songs, dance, alcohol, and meat to worship them in their mandalas, that is, worshipping at the same time the Eight Mother Goddesses, the Bhairavas, the various door-guardians, and making a number of Spirit-Offerings, culminating in the worship of the central deity him- or herself. One of the most popular ways to do this is the *kolāsyā pūjā* ('Sow-Face Worship'), i.e. worship of Vajravārāhī, the Adamantine Sow. It is also known in Newari as *tāhā sinhaḥ pūjā*, the translation of Skt. *dīrgha-sindūrārcana-vidhi* (the long rite of offering vermilion), or as Skt. *rahasya-guhya-pūjā* (secret secret worship).

Michael Allen (1975: 56–8) has provided a brief description of this rite. Two powder mandalas are constructed, though both are to Vajradevī, one inside (*abhyantara*) and one in an outer room where the living goddess Kumārī will be placed. In Kathmandu (whence Allen's description comes) there is a special Vajrācārya Kumārī, as opposed to the royal Kumārī (who in Kathmandu is always a Śākya). It is the Vajrācārya Kumārī who is invited for such rituals. Allen's informant stressed that the highest blessing (*prasād*) of Vajradevī was to have her crown (*mukuṭa*), which had been worshipped on the inner mandala and then on the head of the young Kumārī, placed on one's head. Consultation of a ritual handbook for the *kolāsyā pūjā* (NGMPP E 1104/14) confirms the general outline of Allen's account. It also makes clear that it is not just the living Kumārī who is Vajradevī in this rite. The wife of the principal priest, referred to as 'mother' (*mātrā*), is also worshipped thus, and at two points it is specified that she should become possessed (*āveśa*). As in the giving of Tantric Initiation, the *guru*, her husband, dances at these (as well as at other) points of the ritual (dance is more acceptable than direct possession in a Buddhist male of high status). This worship of Vajradevī is certainly performed in Lalitpur, though perhaps less often than in Kathmandu. It is possible to perform it without calling the living Kumārī, though, as Allen's informant implied, this is considered to be particularly meritorious.

Another, even more elaborate and more rarely performed rite is the Worship of the Thirty-Six Saṃvaras (*mahāsambar chattisāmat* – from *ṣaṭtriṃśat – pūjā*). A report published by the Vijayeśvarí Vihār Samiti (Mahāsambar 1982) on a performance of this rite over one week, March–April 1982, gives some idea of its scale. A total of 141,945 rupees were contributed by 155 donors, thirty-two of them contributing 1,000 rupees or more, the largest single donation being of 19,300 rupees. Eighty-two donors also gave 5,381 rupees to put a brass canopy (*jhallar*) around the lower roof of the goddess' shrine. A total of 317 people participated in various capacities, all of them apparently from Kathmandu:[3] 57% were Vajrācāryas, 28% Śākyas, and the remainder (15%) were Tulādhar *et al.* Śreṣṭhas in Kathmandu may not take Tantric Initiation and could not therefore be involved, though four Śreṣṭhas contributed to expenses. The position of the Vajrācāryas as ritual specialists, and of the Tulādhar *et al.* (the foremost Buddhist lay caste in Kathmandu) as their principal sponsors, is clearly shown in Table 10.3 (this, along with further details on participants and costs, is given in the appendix to this chapter).

These two types of Tantric rite, the Long Vermilion Worship and the Thirty-Six Saṃvara Worship, are two of the more spectacular esoteric rituals of Newar Buddhism. And it seems that these two are, along with Tantric Initiation, the main kinds of elaborate Tantric Buddhist rite. According to Asha Kaji Vajracharya there are two kinds of *āgā̊* or *guhya pūjā*: the ordinary (*sādhāraṇa*) in which it is not necessary to sing Tantric songs; and the special (*viśeṣa guhya pūjā*), also called *rahasya* (secret) *pūjā*, which require Tantric songs. Of the special rites he listed twelve kinds, as follows:

(i) *kūś pūjā*, with a minimum of seven songs, the most abbreviated form; *kūś* is short for *pañcākūśa*, i.e. five pieces of buffalo meat, the goddess' blessed food;
(ii) *sinhaḥ pūjā* = *sindūrārcana pūjā*; at least fourteen songs;
(iii) *tāhā sinhaḥ pūjā* = *dīrghasindūrārcana pūjā*; at least twenty-eight songs;
(iv) *māṃsāhuti pūjā* [Fire Sacrifice with an oblation of meat; cf. §9.3.7];
(v) *śirāhuti pūjā* [Fire Sacrifice with an oblation of a 'head'; cf. p. 158, 9.3.7];
(vi) *sinhāmat pūjā*, a Fire Sacrifice combining (iv) and (v);
(vii) *trayodaśa-samvata* [sic, for *-saṃvara*] *pūjā* [Worship of Thirteen Saṃvaras];
(viii) *chatrisamvata* [sic] *pūjā* [Worship of Thirty-Six Saṃvaras];
(ix) *acala-dīkṣā-pūjā* [Tantric Initiation of Caṇḍamahāroṣaṇa];
(x) *herukasaṃvara-dīkṣā-pūjā* [Tantric Initiation of Cakrasaṃvara];
(xi) *hevajra-dīkṣā-pūjā* [Tantric Initiation of Hevajra];

(xii) *yogāmbara-dīkṣā-pūjā* [Tantric Initiation of Yogāmbara].

Asha Kaji then added a thirteenth type:

(xiii) *ahorātrī pūjā* = *dwaru pūjā*, combining various of the above; it is performed a year after a big Tantric rite as an anniversary.

The simplest Tantric rites, performed by a single practitioner without songs, combine worship and Visualization (*sādhana*). The same elements form the essential framework of complex rites as well. What is meant by *sādhana* is examined in the next section.

10.2 Basic principles of Tantric worship

Both Mahāyāna and Vajrayāna rites are based on worship (*pūjā*) carried out with devotion to a given deity. In both types of worship strict rules have to be followed and devotion is expressed through the recitation ('jap yāye') of mantras. In neither is blood sacrifice permitted. There are, however, important differences between ritual of the two types which can be represented as a set of oppositions. Table 5.2 (above, §5.2.1) illustrates this. Even the most unlearned Newars know that there is an opposition between secret and public rites.

We have noted above (§9.1) that the esoteric deities also appear externally in a non-sexual form. In a similar manner, exoteric rites are given a Vajrayāna frame. It has already been mentioned (§7.5) how all Observances, which enact the values of the Disciples' Way and express devotion to a divinity of the Great Way, are completed with a Kumārī Worship. This Kumārī Worship is classified as belonging to the Diamond Way: meat and alcohol are essential. Thus some offerings characteristic of the Diamond Way are frequently made externally. Other offerings – overt sexual symbolism, possession, dance, and song – are made only in secret. These elements mark the boundary between the esoteric and the exoteric Vajrayāna.

In Table 5.2 yogic Visualization (*sādhana*) was listed as characteristic of Vajrayāna rites, and so it is. But like offerings of meat and alcohol it appears in exoteric rites also. Furthermore it is more pervasive and essential than these offerings. It is yogic Visualization which provides the frame of all rites, of all kinds. In all complex rituals the priest has to visualize and make present the deity whom the laity will worship. As Amogha Vajra Vajracharya (1976a: i) wrote:

> The main aim of the Flask Worship Rite is to make the deity who has been summoned present in the Flask by means of a *sādhana*, then to receive [oneself] and give [to others] the consecration (*abhiṣeka*) of that waterpot so as to reach even to *nirvāṇa*.

This basic division between Worship (*pūjā*) and Visualization (*sādhana*), both being essential for Accomplishment (*siddhi*), is shared equally by Tibetan Buddhism and by Tantric Hinduism.[4]

Sādhana is related etymologically to *siddha*, Realized One: it is the means of attaining *siddhi*, literally accomplishments or success, which are the attributes of a *siddha*. Snellgrove (1959a I: 138) explains *siddhi* as '"Attainment" in the sense of "Perfection" when referring to the highest religious striving; in the sense of "Success" when referring to meaner objectives'. Thisworldly kinds of supernatural accomplishment (Snellgrove's 'meaner objectives') have always been believed to accompany advanced spiritual states in South Asia. In Mahāyāna and Vajrayāna Buddhism they are positively valued, as aids in helping other beings. As Samuel observes for Tibet (1978: 51): 'While the powers are strictly speaking irrelevant from the point of view of obtaining Enlightenment (they may be justified as helping to relieve the sufferings of living beings) they are at the basis of the lama's importance for the lay population of Tibet.' In Theravāda Buddhism, though admitted to exist, they were and are frowned upon as a distraction from the pursuit of salvation and evidence of pride on the part of the virtuoso who practises them. The Vajrācārya, by contrast, in performing rituals for others, is continually making use of his power to evoke the requisite deity. In particular, the Threefold Meditation (*trisamādhi*) or brief version of the full worship of the priest's tutelary Tantric deity, is performed before each complex rite. At the crucial points of the Threefold Meditation the priest mutters the mantras silently and performs his hand gestures under his coat or in a special pocket which hides them from the view of the uninitiated.

A summary of the liturgy of Cakrasaṃvara should make clear how this yogic Visualization works.[5] There are four, progressively higher and more esoteric, Visualizations of and identifications with the deity (corresponding to stages 1 through 4 of the liturgy given below). The four Visualizations are: (i) identification with the two-armed Cakrasaṃvara; (ii) generation of the six-armed Cakrasaṃvara, the Convention-Deity, and its fusion with the Knowledge-Deity (Cakrasaṃvara in heaven); (iii) Visualization of the whole mandala of the twelve-armed Cakrasaṃvara and his consort, and its fusion with the Knowledge-Deity; (iv) Visualization of the mandala being breathed out by the worshipper and then gradually re-absorbed into the body again, until the whole universe and the mandala are one, ending with the emission of the mandala again 'for the good of all beings'. In the brief form of Cakrasaṃvara Worship, i.e. the Threefold Meditation, the fourth Visualization is omitted, whence presumably its name.[6] The liturgy of the full Cakrasaṃvara Worship, divided into seven stages, runs as follows:

1. Identification
With the white two-armed Saṃvara without consort.

*2. Preliminary yoga (*ādiyoga*)*
After a series of purifications and empowerments, the worshipper generates in front of himself the black six-armed Saṃvara, without consort or attendants; this is the Convention-Deity (*samayadevatā*). After various protective rites, he ascends to the Akaniṣṭha heaven and, using rays from the syllable HŪṂ in his heart, he draws down the mandala of the Knowledge-Deity (*jñānadevatā*)[7] and fuses him with the Convention-Deity already visualized. Offerings are made to the deity in the mandala. He visualizes his hand as a mandala of Vajravārāhī. He concludes with a brief confession of sins, followed by rejoicing in merit, Dedication of Merit, Triple Refuge, and raising the thought of enlightenment.

*3. Initial worship of the mandala (*maṇḍalādiyoga*)*
The worshipper contemplates the four Brahmic states and the universe as 'mind only' and as emptiness. Then piece by piece he visualizes the mandala of Cakrasaṃvara, culminating in the deity himself, as black, four-faced, twelve-armed, and in union with his red, two-armed, one-faced consort. They trample on Bhairava and Kālarātrī.[8] This is the Knowledge-Deity and it is fused in the mandala and in the deity himself. He then consecrates the deity and himself with the Five Consecrations, makes offerings, and recites praises.

*4. Subtle yoga (*sūkṣmayoga*)*
The worshipper breathes out through his right nostril all the deities represented by the vowels and the consonants, and then breathes Cakrasaṃvara, Vajravārāhī, and the *yoginī*s in through his left nostril. He then meditates on the union of Sahaja-Saṃvara [Saṃvara in Innate Bliss] with his consort, a bliss which gradually absorbs the whole universe: the world dissolves into the cremation grounds, the cremation grounds into the mandala, the outer circles of the mandala into the inner, until this culminates in the mystic syllable HŪṂ, which itself is absorbed into the dot which symbolizes the Great Bliss. Then suddenly, for the benefit of all beings, the mandala is re-emitted, and worship is offered to it.

*5. The yoga of recitation (*jāpayoga*)*
He recites the mantras of the deities.

*6. Meditation on the Spirit-Offering (*balibhāvanā*)*
After a complex Visualization of the offering it is offered first to

Cakrasaṃvara and his consort, then outwards through the mandala, ending with the demons of the cremation grounds and beyond. He worships the twenty-four Power-Places and ends with a benediction and the hundred-syllabled mantra.

*7. Dismissal (*visarjana*)*
By snapping his fingers he causes the deities to return to their abodes.

This fourfold pattern of yogic Visualization = initial identification with two-armed form, Visualization of six-armed form, Visualization of the twelve-armed form with mandala, Visualization of the universe and the mandala as one – reappears again and again in Newar Buddhist ritual. From Locke's analysis (1980: 107–11) it is clear that it underlies the Buddhist Fire Sacrifice also, as well as a complex ritual such as the reconsecration of the image of Lokeśvara (ibid.: 217).

Locke (1980: 96, 115–21) has rightly emphasized that yogic Visualization is central to all the rituals of Newar Buddhism. Without it lay Newar Buddhists would not be able to worship deities in images or ritual implements. The only complex ritual from which Visualization is absent is the regular worship of a monastery deity. Even here it is possible to argue that 'any ritual of offering (even without explicit self-generation) is always the delayed second half of a full-scale evocation [= Visualization]' (Beyer 1973: 257). In other words, it would not be possible to make even daily offerings to a Buddha-statue without a prior Tantric Visualization, which is the central act of the 'establishment' of the image. In both scriptural and local stories which encourage lay devotion, such worship of unconsecrated images occurs; but in the actual practice of Newar Buddhism there is no worship without prior Tantric Visualization, by someone, however far in the past. Without the motor of Visualization the whole religion would grind to a halt.

To what extent do Vajrācāryas actually visualize the deity as described above (i.e. as described in the Sanskrit they recite while performing the ritual)? Locke (1980: 121) is right to tax the Vajrācāryas of the Kathmandu Valley with a lack of scholarship: one can count the number of Vajrācāryas alive today who have a knowledge of Sanskrit on the fingers of one, or at most two, hand(s). The Sanskrit verses which give the prescribed form of these Visualizations are known to all practising Vajrācārya priests, but few could analyse them with any accuracy. However, it is not so easy to conclude that they have 'no mastery of yogic techniques and meditation'. In the first place, what has to be done is passed on through oral instruction (in Newari), and practitioners are likely to be acquainted with different forms of the esoteric divinities by simply seeing them as icons or paintings in Tantric shrines. Secondly, one must remember that what counts as yogic success often seems to depend on the ideological outlook of the judge; among traditional Newars it is more a matter of public reputation and hearsay than of any objective criterion.

Fuller (1984: 141–2) discusses criticism of Ādiśaiva priests of Madurai which follows similar lines. He concludes that 'it would be logically impossible for an external observer to test whether rituals were in accordance with Agamic stipulation, even if they appeared to be, because of the central role given to the worshipper's mental powers'. This is where the believer parts company with the anthropologist. Newar Buddhists believe, as Tibetan Buddhists do, that 'Fake progress may deceive and impress others, but never an accomplished Lama' (Blofeld 1974: 92). Furthermore, a Buddha can see directly what another person's mental powers are. In other words, from the Buddhist point of view, it is not *logically* impossible (as Fuller puts it), but contingently impossible – since we are not enlightened – to judge whether or not a priest is 'really' visualizing correctly. For this reason pious Buddhists do refrain from making judgements about priests; but many other, less pious Newars do not hesitate to make negative judgements about the capabilities of Vajrācārya priests.

In short, even though Vajrācāryas may not be able to explain the most abstruse concepts of their tradition, they may nonetheless have a grasp of them in a more intuitive form. For example, practising Vajrācāryas are indeed unable to explain the terms 'Knowledge-Deity' and 'Convention-Deity'.[10] Nonetheless few of them can fail to understand that they are identifying with Cakrasaṃvara in performing the ritual; indeed after taking Tantric Initiation they could hardly not be aware of this (see above, §9.3.5).

Ordinary Newars, on the other hand, are not directly and immediately aware of the identity between god and practitioner (here: the Vajrācārya priest) implied by the process of Visualization. Some of them know and use the expression 'sādhan yāye', 'to do *sādhana*', and know that this is what the priest is doing when he holds the Five-Coloured Thread which is wound around the Flask and other ritual implements (described above, §5.3). But they understand 'sādhan yāye' to mean the same as 'sālāḥ taye', 'to pull down'. In other words, this understanding omits the identification with the deity and emphasizes instead the priest's technical proficiency: his ability to manipulate deities by uttering the right mantras and performing the right rituals.

This way of viewing Tantric practitioners as magical manipulators belongs to the lowest level of interpretation.[11] It ignores the esoteric theory at the heart of Visualization which is built into the rituals. At a higher level, identity with the deity, and the liberation-in-this-life which is implied by it, is the most characteristic feature of the Diamond Way. In the Disciples' Way one follows the teachings of the Buddha, becomes a monk, and 'guards the rule of celibacy'. In the Great Way one vows to become a Buddha and save all beings, a task requiring many thousands of lifetimes to reach fruition. There is a vast gap between the *bodhisattva*-as-god and the mortals who take the vow to become *bodhisattva*. This gap is bridged in one life by the Diamond Way. One can identify oneself with the highest deities here and now. Arguably, it is only through the existence of the Diamond Way that it is possible, for example, for high lamas of Tibet to be worshipped as *bodhisattvas*. Certainly, it is only through the means of the Diamond Way that selected young girls, the living Kumārīs, can be worshipped as a Buddhist divine symbol of ultimate wisdom.

It will be noted how, within the esoteric ritual, the popular 'pulling down' view is replicated: the Knowledge-Deity is pulled down and fused with the Convention-Deity which has already been visualized as emitted from the practitioner's own self. It is only in the final stage – omitted in the brief and most commonly performed version (the Triple Meditation) – that the practitioner's unity with the whole universe is visualized. There is a modern apologist's view, which sees Vajrayāna divinities as mere useful fictions, and it posits a sharp gap between the 'popular' (mis-)understanding and the true inner teaching of a therapeutic meditation. Such a view fails to do justice to the way in which esoteric doctrine is both a transformation of the so-called popular view and, simultaneously, serves popular ends. Even for most of the Newars who take Tantric Initiation, whatever other, higher interpretations may be held concurrently, Tantric practice remains a question of devotion to a god 'out there', and of unequal exchange between devotee and god. This is illustrated by the custom, referred to above (Table 7.8), of 'returning one's Tantric Initiation' after death.

10.3 The hierarchy of symbols

As has been briefly indicated above (§4.2, 6.2), the three levels of Newar Buddhism, the Disciples' Way, the Great Way, and the Diamond Way, are symbolically and practically represented in the organization of the Newar monastery. On the ground floor, the principal deity of the monastery is held to represent the Disciples' Way. The *bodhisattva* Amoghapāśa Lokeśvara, in whose name the Observance of the Eighth Day is performed on the upper-floor wing of the monastery, represents the Great Way. The Tantric deity, situated over the main deity, or over the entrance to the monastery, represents the Diamond Way. As argued above (§9.1), two levels can be discerned within the Diamond Way representing different types of Tantra, one being more exoteric than the other, and functioning as the external representation of the more esoteric form.

It is not merely that there is a hierarchy of levels, but *the gods at the different levels are considered to be forms of each other*. The *bodhisattva*s of the Mahāyāna are representatives or emanations of the Five Buddhas; popularly they are said to be their sons.[12] The Five Buddhas belong to the more exoteric form of Vajrayāna. The relationship of this sort best known to Newars is that between the *bodhisattva* Lokeśvara or Karuṇāmaya and the Buddha Amitābha who is always present on his crown. This relationship is concisely expressed in BV (66r–v) in thoughts put into the mind of the Realized One, Gorakhnāth:

> In this universe, Ādibuddha, who had form and thoughts, but was without blemish, in order to create the universe caused the five elements to arise. These then took on form and shape and were called and appeared as the Five Buddhas. The fourth Buddha was called Amitābha and from him arose his mind-born son (*mānasīputra*), called Padmapāṇi Bodhisattva, who practised the meditation called 'world-creating' (*lokasaṃsarjana*). Ādibuddha gave Padmapāṇi Bodhisattva the name Lokeśvara ('lord of the world') . . .[13]

We have seen the same kind of relationship between the *bodhisattva* Mañjuśrī and the Buddha Vairocana in a verse carved on a *dharmadhātu* (above, §9.1).

In order to have a single account explaining the relationship of Buddhas to *bodhisattva*s, and in addition to explain the role of the Buddha-as-man Śākyamuni, Mahāyāna Buddhism developed the 'three body' (*trikāya*) doctrine: the Created Body (*nirmāṇakāya*) is the Śākyamuni Buddha, appearing as man, the Enjoyment Body (*saṃbhogakāya*) is the Buddha as he appears in heaven, and the Dharma Body (*dharmakāya*) is the Buddha as identical with the absolute, which is *nirvāṇa*.[14] *Stūpa*s, *caitya*s, and *dharmadhātu* are representations of the Dharma Body; statues of Śākyamuni or representations of his life as Sarvārthasiddha are of the Created Body; principally, however, it is the Enjoyment Body which is represented iconographically. To these Three Bodies the higher, secret form of Tantric Buddhism added a fourth called variously the Innate Body (*sahajakāya*), the Body of Great Bliss (*mahāsukhakāya*), or the Self-Existent Body (*svābhāvikakāya*). This reflected the idea that the secret Tantric deities are the real inner essence of all three previous levels.[15] Furthermore, since the Vajrayāna is a system of yoga as well as of identification with the ultimate,

Table 10.1 *The Three Jewels at different levels of interpretation.*[a]

Śrāvakayāna (Disciples' Way)	Śākyamuni Buddha	The Dharma (doctrine)	The Saṃgha (Monastic Community)
Mahāyāna (Great Way)	Svayambhū	Prajñā Pāramitā (goddess and text, The Perfection of Wisdom)	Amoghapāśa Lokeśvara (*bodhisattva*)
Vajrayāna (Diamond Way)	Vajrasattva	Vajrayoginī	Ṣaḍakṣarī Lokeśvara[b]

Notes:
[a] Asha Kaji Vajracharya (1972: 1), for example, explains the first triad in terms of the second at the outset of a Mahāyānist work encouraging devotion to Karuṇāmaya.
[b] He may be represented here not in his usual four-armed form holding lotus and rosary but as Padmanarteśvara who is identified with Nāsadyaḥ (the Newars' god of music and dance). Padmanarteśvara is also called Dharmarāj, i.e. Yama, and identified with Cākwāḥdyaḥ-Mīnnāth.

these different bodies of the Buddha are placed in relation to parts of the body or *cakra*, starting with the Created Body in the navel and ending with the Body of Great Bliss in the head.[16]

So far we have considered how the Buddha appears in a hierarchy of different forms. In the same way the Three Jewels, displayed on numerous tympana over monastery doorways and shrines, can be explained at three levels as shown in Table 10.1. In this way all the symbols of Buddhism can be given an interpretation depending on context, or, to use the idiom of the religion itself, depending on the ability and entitlement of the listener.

A concise statement of this hierarchy of levels is given in the Hevajra Tantra in reply to the question 'How are those who are obdurate to be brought within the rules?':

First the Eight Precepts should be given, then the Ten. Then he should teach the Vaibhāṣya, then the Sautrāntika. After that he should teach the Yogācāra, then the Madhyamaka. After he knows all [the levels of] the Way of the Mantras, then he should begin on Hevajra. The pupil who lays hold with zeal will succeed, there is no doubt.[17]

(Snellgrove 1959a II: 90)

Kāṇha's commentary on this passage interprets this even more emphatically as a process of moving from exoteric to esoteric teachings.[18] In the Newar Buddhism of today there is no question of so many different levels being consciously distinguished, but the underlying structure and the spirit of Newar Buddhism are exactly as the Hevajra Tantra prescribes (and

Vajrācāryas of any learning would recognize immediately the references made both in the scriptural passage and in the commentary).

It is the organization of these different teachings into a hierarchy which prevents the lower teachings being contradicted by the higher. The Kriyā Samuccaya begins (KSc: 3^2ff.) with a long discussion of whether or not the Vajrācārya should or should not be a monk (*bhikṣu*).[19] Its conclusion, heavily supported with Tantric scriptural references, is that in order to receive initiation the Vajrācārya should (a) be a monk but (b) not be merely a monk, i.e. he should have abandoned the monk's garb and shaven head. In other words the Tantric initiate should have started as a monk, but should have left that stage behind (like Śākyas and Vajrācāryas in Nepal, but unlike other castes entitled to Tantric Initiation). The Kriyā Samuccaya then asks the question:

> [In taking Tantric Initiation] will he not then be guilty of abandoning his earlier vows [of celibacy]? No, for each subsequent observance transcends the preceding, just as the lay devotee becomes a novice and the novice a monk. When a person has become a monk is there the absence of the vows he took as a lay devotee etc.? [of course not].
>
> (KSc: 6^{3-5})

In becoming a Vajrācārya, therefore, a man is still the monk he used to be. From the Theravāda point of view this is a false analogy. The discipline of the monk does not contradict that of the layman because it follows the same rules but with greater strictness, whereas the rules of the Vajrācārya *reverse* the rules of monk. In the Tantric scriptures, however, this reversal is precisely the point: by means of it the aims of the monk (non-attachment and therefore liberation) are fulfilled more quickly and effectively. For the traditional Newar Buddhist these different values are not thought to be in contradiction because they apply to different contexts; the discipline of the Śrāvakayāna is good in its way, but fails to reach to the heart of the matter.

The existence of a hierarchy of teachings has an effect which deserves to be noted. Since the highest level is the closest to the ultimate, the most real, its way of viewing things tends to permeate downwards, providing unifying principles which tie all three levels together. One example, itself part of a general Vajrayānist preference for pentads, is the way in which the giving of the robe, staff, begging bowl, shoulder-piece, and new name are said to constitute the Five Consecrations (*pañcābhiṣeka*) of the Monastic Initiation ritual. Here a Vajrayāna terminology is used to describe a Śrāvakayāna rite. Vajrayānist ritual in fact permeates Monastic Initiation and only in the daily worship of the Śrāvakayāna image is the influence limited (as noted above, §6.2). *A fortiori* many Mahāyāna rituals are given a Vajrayāna frame, ending as they do with a Kumārī Worship. In fact, any ritual requiring the services of a Vajrācārya priest is bound to have numerous Vajrayāna elements (a point in favour of the common understanding of 'Vajrayāna'). Two rites which end most rituals, the consumption of *pācāku* and *samay* (see below, §10.5), are both Vajrayānist symbolic acts, though the symbolism is known to few who are not Vajrācāryas.

In addition to the hierarchy of the Three Ways, expressed in ritual, there is another hierarchy, of attitudes, in Newar Buddhism. At the lowest level there is a literal way of approaching Buddhist divinities which takes them as real, no different in nature from Hindu gods. This attitude is essentially polytheistic: gods are independent powers each with his or her own sphere of influence. Above this, there is a more subtle interpretation which sees connections between divinities. Regular rites are viewed as training the mind, as expressive rather than as immediately effective. Exoteric worship is a preliminary to esoteric worship. All worship is conceived as a soteriological exercise. Thus it is perhaps wrong to speak of 'the true meaning of the ritual' (Locke 1980: 96); one should rather say, 'on the "higher" level of interpretation, the ritual means . . .'. A naive understanding of the rite is not wholly and simply invalid; it merely has less validity than the higher interpretation from the ultimate point of view.[20] Furthermore, many Newars hold 'lower' and 'higher' interpretations, simultaneously or according to context, and they do not always distinguish clearly between them.

Both kinds of hierarchy – of attitudes to the gods and of the Three Ways – were expressed by Guna Ratna Shakya, a disciple of the famous *paṇḍit* Ratna Bahadur Vajracharya, in answer to my question 'What is the difference between Mahāyāna and Vajrayāna?':

There are four ways of doing *pūjā*:
(i) focused on gods (*devatātmak*);
(ii) focused on the Five Constituents (*pañcaskandhātmak*);
(iii) focused on emptiness (*śūnyātmak*);
(iv) focused on yoga (*yogātmak*).
The first is the approach of those who believe gods are responsible for everything, bringing rain, causing illness, and they also act from fear of the god's punishment (*doṣ*). The second is the approach of [adherents of] the Theravāda, who do not worship gods but only the Five Constituents. The third is the approach which asserts that nothing exists, there are no gods; it is completely nihilistic (*nāstik*). The fourth is the approach which combines Śrāvakayāna and Mahāyāna, which combines (i), (ii), and (iii). It puts gods in front, analyses all things as the Five Constituents, and realizes that all is void (*śūnya*). This, combining emptiness and compassion (*karuṇā*), is the yogic way of worship and is called Vajrayāna.

Initially Guna Ratna had given a more light-hearted answer to my question which had puzzled both me and the others present. In the light of the above it should be easier to understand:

The Disciples' Way is like making noodles from flour. The Solitary Buddha's Way is making *capātis*. The Great Way is like the repeated kneadings necessary to make *lakhāmari* [the magnificent and gigantic Newar wedding pastries]. The Diamond Way is like going into a sweetshop, mixing all the pastries they have, crushing them, eating them all, using everything, and leaving nothing.

10.4 The routinization of Tantric Buddhism

Much work remains to be done on the Buddhist Tantric scriptures, but it is clear, even in the present state of knowledge, that they originated in a milieu which was on the very edge of polite and sophisticated society, whether Buddhist or Hindu. This is obvious from the type of Sanskrit in which the Tantras are written as well as from the practices enjoined. Subsequently, in a process yet to be explained, they were taken over by (sections of) the monastic establishment, commented on, refined, and worked up into ritual and yogic systems of great complexity. It is an interesting question how far these systems were 'routinized', to use Weber's term, at this time. Tantric Buddhism had become a complex system practised by ritual specialists, members of a religious organization with established economic interests; such specialists are unlikely to have favoured open displays of antinomian behaviour.

While routinization must surely have been occurring, the virtuosi continued to have religious experiences which were recorded as Visualizations for others to practise. While it is likely that most would accept only a symbolic interpretation of the antinomianism implied by Tantric ritual, it also seems certain that some took it literally.[21] The Kriyā Samuccaya, upon which much of the Newars' own Tantric tradition is based, provides clear evidence that at least some sections of the twelfth-century monastic hierarchy favoured sexual practices during Tantric Initiation (i.e. in secret).[22] Such practices would certainly be regarded as abhorrent by Buddhist Newars today, although they understand the sexual imagery and implications of Tantric Initiation. According to the Kriyā Samuccaya, 'that sacramental circle (*gaṇacakra*) which is without [sex with] a female partner (*prajñā*) is a [mere] meeting of rice scum'.[23] For Newar Buddhists, however, as for Tibetan Buddhists, the *gaṇacakra* is a sacramental meal after a Tantric ritual.

Routinization can always be reversed. In Theravāda Buddhism there were, from time to time, movements back to the forest and to meditation, an attempt to reverse the 'natural tendency for the Sangha to become domesticated' (Carrithers 1983: 141). In the same way there surely were in Buddhist India, in Tibet, and in Nepal individuals who tried to follow the Tantric Buddhist scriptures to the letter in the hope, and with the faith, of really obtaining the prizes – especially the magical powers – promised therein.

Nepal has certainly had many deeply pious Buddhists who have sought to follow the exact teachings of other types of Buddhism in defiance of the routinized forms of Newar Buddhism. Many have become Tibetan or Theravāda monks or nuns. A Vajrācārya called Yog Ratna (1904–67) became a celibate renouncer unordained in any tradition (except his own as a boy) and practised a kind of Tantric yoga. He spent much time doing yoga in remote places near the Valley. Sometimes he acted as a Tantric healer of the sick or gave Buddhist teachings. Evidently he had a considerable number of devotees (A. Pradhan 1968). However his teachings seem to have remained on the exoteric level and there is no hint of his having tried to follow the Tantras literally.

The only case I know of a conscious attempt to enact the Tantras is a man known as Dharma Guruju.[24] Born in Lalitpur, he spent some time as a monk in Tibet. He now lives in Kindol, Svayambhū, with his two female partners (*śakti*). He wears blue and is liable to become possessed when performing rituals. His religious practice is based on a Newari translation of the Ekallavīra or Caṇḍamahāroṣaṇa Tantra by Ratna Bahadur Vajracharya. Newar lay people are happy that their priests and healers should have Tantric powers and they come to Dharma Guruju for cures. However, he seems to have only foreigners as disciples; the reason seems to be that he insists that his disciples follow his belief that sex is the path to enlightenment and consume the sexual fluids of their *śakti*. Openly prescribing this kind of thing is enough to brand him as mad in the eyes of most Newars.[25]

Dharma Guruju is an unusual case. Asha Kaji Vajracharya (1977: 16) writes (and he repeated it to me in person):

> In the Tantras, if one follows the literal meaning of the Sanskrit text and ignores the intended meaning of the 'intentional' language [see below, §10.5] not only will one's rite be unsuccessful, afterwards one will become mad.

This represents the normal view of the learned minority acquainted with the Tantric scriptures. (All others are simply unaware of their antinomian contents.) Consequently, the study of Newar Tantric Buddhism is, necessarily, the study of its routinized forms. These represent, and surely for most if not all of its history have represented, either most or the whole of its practice, so that need be no disadvantage. Probably the routinized forms visible today are not very different from those established a millennium ago.

The *yogin*, that is to say the enlightened and realized man of the Tantras, is characterized by his being above all worldly distinctions. Thus the Hevajra Tantra (2.3.41–5) describes him as follows:

> The Lord said: 'Food and drink must be just as it comes. One should not avoid things, wondering whether they are suitable or unsuitable. One should not perform special ablutions or purifications, nor avoid sexual intercourse.[26] The wise man does not utter *mantras*, nor devote himself to meditation; he does not abandon sleep, nor restrain his senses. He should eat all meat and associate with all manner of men. He keeps the company of all women, his mind quite free of trepidation. He should have no love for friend, nor hatred for any enemy. Those gods he should not honour, which are made of wood and stone and clay. For the yogin should always be consubstantiated with the form of his own divinity. Men of all castes he may touch as readily as his own body . . .'
>
> (Snellgrove 1959a I: 98)

The high-caste man, brought up to observe manifold ritual, social, and moral distinctions, is enjoined to obtain mystic detachment and identity with the ultimate, by discarding them. There are many other similar passages:[27] such ideals are still recognized in the great Realized Ones of the past, but to give up distinctions of caste and purity, to give up mantras and religious practices – as opposed to simply being told in the context of Tantric Initiation that such things ultimately do not exist – is not a practical ideal for Newar Buddhists.

The Tantras also contain other passages, which tend to show that already at the time of their composition, the *yogin* ideal had been to some extent routinized. Thus, the Saṃvarodaya Tantra (17.1–6) describes the characteristics of the Vajra-Master who should give initiations:

> Now I will explain (the characteristics of the *ācārya* and other things). (A man described as follows) is considered to be a *vajrācārya*: a man who has subdued (his passions), whose appearance is tranquil, who gives safety to all living beings, who knows the practice of mantras and tantras, who is compassionate and who is learned in treatises, who talks sweetly to everybody, who treats all living beings as his own son, who always takes pleasure in almsgiving and is engaged in yoga and *dhyāna*-meditation, who speaks the truth, who does not injure living things, and whose mind is compassionate and intent upon benefiting others. Sameness (*samatā*) is the emblem (*mudrā*) of his mind; he is the protector of living beings; he knows the various intentions of living beings and is (regarded as) the kinsman by those who have no protector. His body is complete as to sense-organs; he is beautiful and

agreeable to see. He knows the true meaning of consecration (*abhiṣeka*). His speech is clear; he is an ocean of merits; (and) he always and continuously resorts to *pīṭha* [Power-Places]; he is called an *ācārya* (teacher).

(Tsuda 1974: 294)

This is much closer to the actual practice of Newar Buddhism: far from having abandoned mantras and scripture, or religious practices such as alms-giving, yoga, meditation, and restraint of the senses, the ideal Vajrācārya is expected to be devoted to all of them. Although he is supposed to treat all beings as his children, and to have 'sameness as the emblem of his mind', he is not said to discard purity or caste distinctions.

Clearly then, the Tantric scriptures possess two models: the liberated *yogin* for whom all worldly distinctions are meaningless and the teacher who realizes this but continues to act as if he accepts those distinctions out of compassion for all beings. This latter model is crucial for understanding how an apparently antinomian doctrine can constitute the highest and most revered teachings of a whole Great Tradition.

Confirmation of this view comes from a work of Advayavajra, also known as Avadhūtipā, who flourished according to Bhattacharya (1928: xci) at the end of the tenth and the beginning of the eleventh century. In the first work of the Advayavajrasaṃgraha (Shastri 1927: 1–12), the Kudṛṣṭi-nirghātanam (Refutation of Wrong Views), Advayavajra sets out to show that even those who are beyond teachings (*aśaikṣa*) and enlightened like Śākyamuni himself, and even those who perform the Observance of the Madman (*unmattavrata*), will continue to perform and carry out beginners' rites and observances (*ādikarma*), i.e. they will continue to observe and respect the ritual and rules of less advanced practitioners. In outlining what these 'beginners' rites' are, Advayavajra refers to the householder-*bodhisattva* (*gṛhapatibodhisattva*) and gives detailed rules for his daily religious practice (ibid.: 4–10). Some of these correspond strikingly to current Newar practice: for instance, the injunction to read the Nāmasaṃgīti and the prescription of various other Mahāyānist verses still in use. More important than points of detail, however, is the fact that the general structure and spirit are exactly the same as that of Newar Buddhism today, showing that the Tantric scriptural ideal was adapted and routinized for the use of householder *bodhisattva*s a very long time ago.

10.5 Routinization, 'intentional' language, and food symbolism

The routinization of Tantric Buddhism also required a reinterpretation of the more extreme statements of the Tantric scriptures, and this too began at an early stage. We have already seen, in describing Tantric Initiation, how sexual acts prescribed not only by the scriptures but also in subsequent authoritative codifications of them such as the Kriyā Samuccaya, are followed only symbolically (§9.3.5, 9.3.9, 10.4). A practising Vajrācārya priest told me that the reason why Farmers and others are not allowed to take Tantric Initiation is that they would wrongly assume that *saṃbhoga-kāya* (the Enjoyment Body of the Buddha) referred to *saṃbhog*, the sexual act.

There are two ways in which statements of the Tantric texts are made to mean something other than what they might seem to mean: euphemism and 'intentional' or 'non-literal' language (*saṃdhā-bhāṣā*). Through a pervasive scribal error, this term has become 'twilight' (*saṃdhyā*) language in the Nepalese tradition. Bharati (1965: 173) distinguishes two types of this intentional language. In 'afferent' *saṃdhā*-terminology a word normally referring to the absolute 'intends' something concrete (one of the most frequent examples is the use of *bodhicitta*, the thought of enlightenment, to mean 'semen'). In 'efferent' *saṃdhā*-terminology, the more frequent type, a word normally referring to something concrete 'intends' the absolute.

These semantic subtleties, while important for the analysis of Tantric texts and commentaries, need not detain us here. In a passage on this question Asha Kaji Vajracharya (1977: 14–19) makes a straightforward contrast between the intended or definite meaning (*niścita artha*) on the one hand, and the unintended, indefinite (*aniścita*) or contrary Sanskrit (*viparīta saṃskṛta*) meaning on the other.[28] He quotes a verse from the Guhyasamāja Tantra in which the Five Nectars (*pañcāmṛta*) are said to consist of excrement, urine, phlegm, blood, and semen: the intended meaning is curds, milk, sugar, honey, and ghee, i.e. the Five Nectars as used in exoteric Buddhist ritual. Taking another verse, from the Saṃvarodaya Tantra, which explains the Five Lamps (*pañcapradīpa*) as the meat of a cow, a horse, an elephant, a man, and a dog respectively, he gives the intended meaning as milk, curd, ghee, honey, and sugar, i.e. the Five Nectars once again. In longer versions of the *guru maṇḍala* ritual the Five Nectars are to be visualized as the Five Lamps as part of the Spirit-Offering.[29]

Asha Kaji insists, as already noted in the previous section, that if one were to act on the unintended meaning of the text, not only would the rite be unsuccessful, but one would certainly become mad. In introducing the whole subject he writes: '(Where the various texts say) Saṃvara or some other god gave a vision (*darśan*) of himself with [i.e. in coitus with] the goddess, this is all merely the magical display of Vajrasattva and nothing else' (1977: 14). I do not think that this insistence on the 'intended', i.e. unoffensive, meaning is merely for exoteric consumption; it represents the feelings of other Vajrācāryas also. Although other Vajrācāryas are not happy about Asha Kaji's willingness to discuss these subjects, in their interpretation of these matters they do not differ, I believe, to any significant extent.

In this way, then, scriptural references to the Five Lamps are explained, or explained away, as referring to the Five Nectars. All Newars are familiar with the Five Nectars: they are used in all Newar Buddhist rituals, often being represented by ghee mixed with beaten rice and molasses. The term 'the Five Lamps' by contrast is known only to the very learned. Indirectly, however, it has influence on regular, routinized practice. During Newar Buddhist rituals one must fast. At the end of the rite (unless it is the main day of an Observance or other rite requiring abstention from meat foods) the first food consumed is *pãcāku*, known as *nyākū* in Kathmandu. (It is given the pseudo-Sanskrit equivalent *pañcākūśa*.) Both terms mean 'five pieces', i.e. five pieces of buffalo meat, although in practice it is not thought necessary to include exactly five pieces. The chunks of meat are mixed with a little *khāy* from the *Khāy* Pot; once the pieces of meat have been transferred to the left hand, the saucer is filled with liquor (*aylāḥ*) from the Alcohol Pot (see Plate 8).

Like any pentad the 'five pieces' can be interpreted in numerous ways. A pious Maharjan with a preference for the Theravāda told me that it is symbolic of the Five Precepts like the Five-Coloured Thread of Tantric rituals. A Jośī said that it represented the five M's of Hindu Tantrism (sex, meat, fish, alcohol, and beans – all begin with 'm' in Sanskrit). Another informant said that *pãcāku*, as a type of *prasād*, is a symbol (*pratīk*) of the god just worshipped (quoted above, §4.1). All of these are possible interpretations. The scriptural Tantric Buddhist explanation is that this sacramental food is the Five Lamps. The five pieces of buffalo meat stand for five types of meat: not those given above, according to Asha Kaji Vajracharya, but partridge, deer, fish, egg, and the dregs of rice-beer (*ajikaḥ*). These are respectively a sky-borne (*khecara*), earth-borne (*bhūcara*), water-borne (*jalacara*), egg-born (*aṇḍaja*), and ?fermented (?*giri*) form of life. The *khāy* served at the bottom of the clay saucer, as part of *pãcāku*, is a substitute for the dregs of rice-beer.

The routinization of Tantric symbolism involves the development not only of a purely exoteric interpretation of Tantric doctrine, but also of an acceptable esoteric interpretation. The term 'Five Nectars' refers to two different sets of substances in esoteric and exoteric rituals. *Pãcāku*, on the other hand, is the same in both kinds of rite. This is illustrated in Table 10.2.

Another Tantric sacramental food is *samay* or *samay baji*. This is eaten

Table 10.2 *Different levels of Tantric symbols.*

Scriptural definition	Routinized definitions	
	Esoteric	Exoteric
Five Lamps (*pañcapradīpa*) (meat of a cow, a dog, a horse, an elephant, and a man: *gokudahana* for short)	*pācāku* (five pieces of buffalo meat)*	*pācāku* (five pieces of buffalo meat)
Five Nectars (*pañcāmṛta*) as excrement, urine, phlegm (or human flesh), blood, and semen	Five Nectars as five types of rice-beer*	Five Nectars as milk, curds, ghee, honey, and sugar

*Partridge meat, deer meat, fish, egg, and alcohol, are substituted in some esoteric contexts.

after *pācāku* at the end of a ritual. It in turn is followed later by a full feast; it can also be a substitute for a full feast. *Samay* is the same word as *samaya*, Skt. vow or sacrament.[30] It consists of beaten rice with buffalo meat, black soyabeans, black-eye beans, ginger, puffed rice, and a green vegetable. Sometimes a lentil cake is added. (Optionally potatoes, egg, and sweet pastries are often also served.) These, according to Asha Kaji Vajracharya, represent the six tastes (*ṣaḍrasa*): sweet, bitter, sour, salty, spicy, and astringent.[31] (It is not possible to establish an item by item correspondence with the ingredients of *samay*.) A Tantric feast is known as a *gaṇacakra*, and includes the singing of Tantric songs. At the end the leftovers are collected up and worshipped by the senior priest present as Dhūmāṅgārī/Ugracaṇḍī, and then taken out and deposited at the appropriate Remains Deity.

Similar food symbolism is also characteristic of Newar Hinduism. A Newar Brahman told me that *samay* represents the nine grains (*nava caru*) offered in a Fire Sacrifice. Thus *samay* should contain beaten rice, puffed rice, meat, fish, egg, lentil cake, ginger, black lentils, and one green vegetable. Other Hindus often say that the constituents of *samay* are a substitute for animal sacrifice. According to S. Shrestha there are five basic items representing the five elements: beaten rice, black soyabeans, ginger, buffalo meat, and liquor.[32] Some say that lentil cake, fish, and egg should also be included; any other items are just for show. He claims that the equivalence with animal sacrifice is shown in the practice of placing a piece of a sacrificed goat's neck on the plate of *samay* offered to the gods.[33]

There are many competing explanations of these sacramental foods. An exploration of them all would take us far afield. Most Newars do not worry about them, and indeed would be shocked to be told of some of them.[34] For them *pãcāku* and *samay* are blessed food, and they function to define who is a participant in the rite. Where the rite is that of a distinct social group, they serve to exclude outsiders. A Śreṣṭha informant from Kathmandu recounted how one member of his death *guthi* was made to offer a goat as a fine for having offered a share of *samay* to the Parbatiyā servant of the *guthi* 'who was not one of us'. Thus the routinization of Tantric symbolism requires not only the development of different levels of interpretation but also of social functions of those same symbols. Some of the most important of these functions are examined in the next chapter.

Appendix: details of a Tantric worship in 1982

A Thirty-Six Saṃvara Worship, held in Bījeśvarī (Vijayeśvarī), Kathmandu, was discussed briefly above (§10.1). Some further details will give an idea of the scale of the ritual. Fifty-two Vajrācāryas and their wives carried out the priestly functions and there were thirty-eight other couples participating in the worship (five Vajrācārya, thirteen Śākya, and twenty Tulādhar *et al.*, of whom ten were Tulādhar, four Kaṃsakār, four Tāmrakār, and two Sthāpit). In addition there were fifty-five Vajrācāryas singing Tantric songs, thirty Śākyas playing horns (*pañcatāl, pẙytāḥ*), twenty-nine Śākyas looking after the food (seven of them women), eleven Vajrācārya women in charge of worship items, nine men (five Tulādhar, two Śākya, one Vajrācārya, and one Tāmrakār) in charge of the storeroom and three general overseers (two Śākyas, one Vajrācārya). The caste of participants and donors is shown in Table 10.3.

Table 10.3 *Caste of participants in and donors to a Thirty-Six Saṃvara Worship (percentages rounded to nearest full digit) (Mahāsambar 1982: 1–7).*

	Participants (N=317)	All donors (N=125)[b]	Over 1,000 r. (N=31)	Under 1,000 r. (N=94)
Vajrācārya	57%	11%	7%	13%
Śākya	28%	22%	19%	22%
Tulādhar *et al.*	15%	59%	61%	59%
Śreṣṭha	/	5%	7%	4%
Other[a]	/	3%	6%	2%
	100%	100%	100%	100%

Notes:
[a] This included four individuals: two Mānandhars, one Nakarmī, and one Prajāpati.
[b] For thirty donors (mostly women, presumed widowed) caste is not given.

Organizing the material side of things for such a large ritual is a considerable feat. Fifty-three metal images of Cakrasaṃvara were made specially for it by a Śākya god-maker of Uku Bāhāḥ, Lalitpur. The breakdown of different expenses is given in Table 10.4.

Table 10.4 *Expenses of performing a Thirty-Six Saṃvara Worship (Mahāsambar 1982: 17–18).*

Worship materials	10,329.50
Gods, masks, jewel mandalas etc.	26,371.00
Repairs to the room for storing gods, masks etc.	5,948.29
Worship-clothes, wages	11,919.80
Ritual stipends (*dachinā*)	2,969.75
Pots and pans	2,682.50
Cost of teaching horns, Tantric songs, dances	2,500.00
Feasts	42,172.40
Electricity, kerosene	457.00
Printing invitations	287.50
Rent, wages	523.60
Other	3,520.40
Cost of installing banisters (on entrance stairway)	2,160.00
Wages for making and engraving roof canopy	2,100.00
Placed in bank in name of Vijayeśvarī Vihār Sudhār Samiti	34,000.00
Remaining	96.03
	Rupees 149,034.77

Note: The difference between the total given here and the total of donations (see §10.1) is accounted for by the sale of certain leftovers at the end of the ritual. The grand total should read 148,037.77.

11

The uses of Tantra

A Buddhism of social bonding and communal solidarity seems a contradiction in terms. And yet . . . much of Southeast Asia has developed, in contrast to the Sherpas, precisely such a social, communal Buddhism.

Sherry Ortner, *Sherpas through their Rituals*, p. 157.

In any activity seeking the origins of a human activity there lurks the same danger of confusing ancestry with explanation.

Marc Bloch, 'The Idol of Origins', *The Historian's Craft*, p. 32.

11.1 Tantra, social closure, and types of power

We have seen the place of Tantra, i.e. the Diamond Way, within Newar Buddhism. It has been shown how the Diamond Way legitimizes a priesthood (§9.2), and how it is essential for all the practices which fall under the head of the other Ways (§10.2). We have also seen how the Diamond Way provides a soteriology for the individual through initiation; and we have mentioned how it plays a role in the alleviation of worldly sufferings through the activities of Tantric healers (§9.2 and below, §11.4).

Tantric Buddhism also has certain social functions, of which, unlike magic and healing, one gets little hint in the scriptures. These social functions can best be summarized by saying that Tantric Buddhism permits the introduction of a significant degree of particularism – that is, local, kin, and caste-based exclusivity – into a universalistic doctrine. At the level of the Disciples' Way, the restriction of Monastic Initiation to the sons of previously initiated Śākyas and Vajrācāryas is uneasily justified by tradition and putative descent from the Buddha. There is also a caste-based relativism, described above (§3.5), which can be used to exclude outsiders ('we have our religion and you have yours'); but this is not a Buddhist doctrine, and reflective Buddhists know it. The cult of Tantric deities, on the other hand, with its stress on secrecy and exclusion of the uninitiated, provides a much readier Buddhist means of sanctifying the kin or *guthi* group, and excluding outsiders.

Many observers have remarked on how exclusive Newars are towards those they define as outsiders. Michael Allen (1975: 55) noted that 'group membership is commonly defined by ritual initiation and social boundaries are maintained by secrecy and closure'. Todd Lewis (1984: 14), working in Asan, Kathmandu, wrote: 'Most of the dynamics in social life emphasize in-group/out-group exclusiveness and encourage the growth of factions.' Declan Quigley (1984: 213–16) has described the problems and tensions generated by his presence at a death-*guthi* feast.

Any anthropologist who has worked with Newars is likely to have had experiences like these. Most of the time the Śākyas and Vajrācāryas I worked among were extremely open and welcoming. Young and old alike approved of the fact that I was studying Buddhism. Nonetheless there were occasions when I unwittingly crossed a boundary. At the annual Kwā Bāhāḥ feast an old man, thinking I was about to sit down and eat too, said angrily to the young Śākyas I was with: 'This is *our* feast, you must not invite him to eat.' On another occasion a friend and I stumbled across a Maharjan feast by the northern Aśokan *stūpa* of Lalitpur and were politely, but firmly, told to leave. I knew that I was not permitted to enter the foyer to the Tantric shrine of Kwā Bāhāḥ and never did so. The shrine to Amoghapāśa Lokeśvara, also on the upper floor, was always open to outsiders and tourists during the time of my fieldwork. Seniors of Kwā Bāhāḥ differed, however, on whether outsiders should be allowed in during rituals. On one occasion one of the elders told me to leave, although on others no objection was made to my presence. On a return trip in 1986, the situation had changed. A new elder of the monastery had imposed a new rule: tourists are now excluded from this part of the monastery altogether.

The high castes of the cities have probably always been more open, at least on first acquaintance, than other castes. This tendency has been increased by the fact that they are the most westernized of Newars. Just how exclusive marginal low or middle castes can be is described by Gérard Toffin (1984: 17–21). He relates the extreme difficulty he experienced in acquiring any information at all about the small monocaste village of Pyangaon, where he first worked on Newars. At first he had to content himself with a study of its material culture (Toffin 1977). It was only thanks to one member of the village, who had worked as a labourer in Calcutta airport, that Toffin was able to gather any information on social and religious matters. His informant was nearly expelled from his clan for having divulged too many 'secrets' about the village and its past. Adopted by one of the two factions into which the village was divided, Toffin had to face continual hostility and suspicion from the other faction. The inhabitants of Pyangaon have their own dialect, unknown to outsiders. They either refused to teach it to Toffin, or would divulge their name for something only if he told them the French word for it: 'they even claimed (to frighten me?) that the first outsider who spoke their dialect would die on the spot'. Later, when he felt the need to study other Newar settlements, the inhabitants of Pyangaon accepted this with very bad grace: 'By the very fact of living in Pyangaon I was implicitly committed to conforming to the values of its inhabitants and sharing their hostility to the world outside.' The contrast was startling when Toffin began to work in Panauti, a small multi-caste town just outside the Kathmandu Valley. 'I was rapidly adopted by the locals and encountered no opposition. Even the religious specialists, who were very reticent at first, came ultimately to trust me and permitted me to be present at certain rituals which were supposed to be forbidden to outsiders.'

Should one say, then, that hostility to outsiders and severe control of insiders is limited to small peasant communities, particularly where there is only one caste represented in the settlement? This conclusion would be a mistake. The concern to exclude outsiders, to keep them ignorant of what goes on inside, to frighten them away, which Toffin describes so well for Pyangaon, is equally to be found in the big cities of the Valley, and equally among all Newar castes. The same type of caste, *guthi*, and kin organization is found everywhere, and the same exclusivity is pervasive. What differs is the subtlety with which boundaries are maintained. In monocaste or near-monocaste settlements, such as Pyangaon or Dhulikhel, both of which have deep-seated insecurities because their putative status (Maharjan and Śreṣṭha respectively) is not accepted by others, suspicion and exclusion of outsiders are particularly crude and direct. Elsewhere there may be superficial openness but outsiders are kept out, and insiders in, by what are fundamentally the same methods. Outsiders are made welcome, but only so long as they do not enter too far, and only in certain contexts.

One measure of openness is exogamy: Pyangaon and Dhulikhel are almost entirely endogamous. By stark contrast, in Panauti 83% of all marriages are contracted with partners from outside Panauti (Toffin 1984: 406–7). Only the Maharjan, Mānandhar, and Untouchable Dyaḥlā have figures markedly lower than this, and only among the Dyaḥlā are more than a third of all marriages contracted inside Panauti. However, as a measure of exogamy in urban Newar settlements these figures are very misleading. Although Panauti is multi-caste, most castes are present only in small numbers, so that the rules of kin exogamy force them to look outside. The only large groups are the Chatharīya and Pãctharīya Śreṣṭhas, who tend, in any case, to marry over long distances.

Just how different Panauti is from the three large cities of the Valley, can be seen by considering my figures for Lalitpur. In ward 15 only 13% of Śākya and 28% of Vajrācārya men marry brides from outside Lalitpur. Of forty-two Śreṣṭha marriages in ward 15 only sixteen (38%) were with spouses from outside Lalitpur. Of seventy-one marriages recorded from two Maharjan lineages in Gaḥchẽ, Lalitpur, only five (7%) were with spouses from outside Lalitpur.[1]

The marriage pattern in Panauti is in fact typical, not of the cities, but of a large number of Newar towns and villages in and near the Kathmandu Valley. Ishii has shown that in Satungal, a village to the west of the Valley, there are similar levels of settlement exogamy: 83% for Maharjans and 84% for Śreṣṭhas.[2] Thus, rather than a simple city-village dichotomy, the marriage patterns of the Newars require one to posit a model of at least three parts: the cities, with a high rate of settlement endogamy for large castes; smaller towns and villages in which there is a high rate of exogamy for all castes; and peripheral, inward-turned settlements, such as Pyangaon and Dhulikhel, in which, for lack of acceptable marriage partners elsewhere, there is a very high degree of endogamy.

Even allowing for these varying rates of exogamy, however, it remains true that all Newars, whatever kind of settlement they inhabit, put a high value on their place of origin. One's status is given not just by one's caste, but by being an X from a given, well-known place. This leads to a marked territorial introversion, which Toffin explains as follows:

> In Newar society each localized fragment of caste tends to become strongly individualized and autonomous in relation to the overall caste hierarchy. Pyangaon . . . illustrates this so well that it is virtually a caricature of it . . . Admittedly, it is possible that the preeminent role of territory was accentuated by the extreme political divisions which existed in the Kathmandu Valley during the whole of the Middle Ages [the later Malla period] . . . But, in my opinion, the introversion of Newar society and the development of tiny territorial units turned in on themselves are above all the expression of an old tribal substrate, a cultural inheritance which is totally distinct from that of Hindu civilization.[3]
>
> (Toffin 1984: 216)

I have outlined elsewhere (Gellner 1986: 113–18; 1991a) my reasons for rejecting naive classifications which place the Newars in the same category as the tribes of the Nepalese hills. To confound the two on the basis of race or language is to ignore completely both the social structure and the culture of Newar society. This is not the basis of my disagreement with Toffin, who is, of course, well aware of the difference between Newars and hill tribes. He wishes rather to connect the two historically. For him the hill tribes represent the Newars' past and he believes that, among the Newars today, it is the Maharjans who are closest to the tribes in social structure.

There are two issues here. Can one explain crucial features of contemporary social organization as survivals of a past system no longer in existence? Secondly, if so, can one say that the Newars' territorial introversion is inherited from a tribal past? Probably few today would agree with the dogmatic negative response to the first question (and therefore by implication to the second) given by traditional British structural-functionalism. Nonetheless, the insight which lay behind that response – that social systems are explained better by contemporary pressures than by a hypothetical and distant past – remains valid. At the same time, social systems do have histories, and do change, far more than structural-functionalism seemed to allow. Indeed, far from social change being the principal theoretical challenge, it is long-term stability, so often taken as unproblematic, which requires explanation.

What, at any rate, seems clear is that some things are likely to survive much more easily than others. Certain isolated cultural elements, and in particular language use, can surely be explained as survivals. For example, K.P. Malla (1981, 1983) demonstrates that there are many old Newari elements in the place-names of the Sanskrit inscriptions of the Licchavi period. It is also likely that the equivalence in Newari kinship terminology MB = FZH, and also, in Pyangaon, FZ = MBW, can be explained as historical leftovers.[4] On the other hand I suggest that the simple invocation of very long-term historical factors is not sufficient to explain contemporary Newar social structure. Even if one were willing to accept explanations in terms of an atavistic 'tribal substrate', one would need to show that the tribes from which the Newars evolved in the distant past were as territorially minded as the Newars are today. For this, there is no evidence one way or the other, and probably never will be.

In contrast to Toffin, I see the extreme introversion of some marginal Newar groups as a *result* of the caste hierarchy, and not as predating it. Introversion springs from the desire to maintain a caste status and from a concern to differentiate oneself from the hill tribes, that is, from the groups seen as 'primitive' (*jaṅgalī*).[5] The extreme exclusiveness of Pyangaon and Dhulikhel are the result not of their closeness to a putative tribal origin, but of their insecurity in the caste hierarchy. As marginal sub-castes, they are obliged to follow the rules of caste society, as they understand them, more strictly than those whose status is more generally accepted. They have to exclude outsiders in order to maintain their own purity and status, not because they have inherited from a distant tribal past an obsession with territory. It is right to invoke history to explain this, but it should not be a remote and unprovable past as a tribe that we look to, but rather the immediate past (under the Ranas) when caste was backed by all the power of the state.

An important contribution here has been made by Quigley in his article 'Introversion and Isogamy: Marriage Patterns of the Newars of Nepal'. He argues, to my mind convincingly, that the Newars' marriage pattern is fundamentally isogamous.[6] This isogamy is part and parcel of the Newar caste hierarchy. Membership of important *guthi*s, particularly Lineage Deity and death *guthi*s, publicly guarantees a Newar's status. With these bona fides, potential affines will accept him as a marriage partner. To belong to these *guthi*s one must be resident, on important ritual occasions at least, in the *guthi*'s locality and be accepted as an equal by other *guthi* members. Only through the *guthi* and its territoriality can equality of status be defined. Without them, one cannot marry and this explains the Newars' great attachment to these fundamental *guthi*s. Quigley concludes:

> Paradoxically, the Newar system is much less blurred than that of north India and resembles that of south India in its proliferation of endogamous units . . . The ideology of hierarchy among Newars is consistent and incontrovertible and operates primarily through isogamous marriages. Unambiguous affiliation to a locality, rather than the south Indian alternative of kinship, provides the means by which the status of one's affines may be guaranteed and, most importantly, publicly demonstrated.
>
> (Quigley 1986: 94)

In pointing out how *guthi* membership, an isogamous marriage pattern, and territoriality, mutually reinforce each other, and how together they produce the 'sense of introversion which is the hallmark of Newar settlements' (1984: 274), Quigley has made a significant advance in the sociological understanding of Newar culture.

High-caste Newars add one more element to the triad of *guthi*, isogamy, and territoriality: Tantric religion. Since only they may take Tantric Initiation, this serves to emphasize their status *vis-à-vis* middle and low castes. And with its subtle combination of exoteric and esoteric religion it enables them to include or exclude outsiders as required. Maharjans' collective rites and feasts take place in the open air, and they simply have to ask outsiders to keep away. High castes have Tantric god-houses (*āgå chẽ*) or Tantric shrines within monasteries, which outsiders cannot even enter unless they have been specifically invited. In theory most Tantric shrines can be entered by anyone who has taken Tantric Initiation. But in practice the details of the rules of entry vary from shrine to shrine. The same kind of scare stories with which Toffin was threatened in Pyangaon are told about people who have disregarded the prohibition and looked on Tantric deities they were not entitled to see. Consequently no one will enter a Tantric shrine unless pressed to do so by the owner or other person in charge. There is a close parallel here with the rules about entry into the kitchen, the highest and most private room in the house. As noted above (§1.3), members of middle castes disagree on whether or not higher castes are allowed into their kitchens. In the same way, they often say that, apart from members of their own caste, only 'their Gubhāju' priest may enter their Tantric shrine, and no one else.

One important function of Tantric deities is to define and reinforce the identity of lineage or clan (non-Tantric deities, other than the Lineage Deity, generally define larger groups than this). The Tantric rite of Taking the Skull-Bowl (§8.2.4) represents graphically the unity of the male members of the lineage as they share the same skull-bowl of liquor handed to them by the senior woman of the lineage while she is possessed by Vajradevī. In the past many lineages performed this rite several times a year at different festivals. Toffin remarks in discussing the peasant village of Theco:

> It all looks as if the various segments of the society sought to place themselves in opposition to each other by worshipping different gods. From a sociological point of view the pantheon works to separate groups just as much as it maintains – through a system of equivalences – their identity and cohesion.
>
> (Toffin 1984: 203)

With Tantric deities, groups can be opposed to each other *even though the deity is the same*, because of the secrecy which surrounds the cult and the shrine.[7] It is not necessary to evolve a local name and identity to differentiate a Tantric deity from other images of the same deity. Superficially there is a paradox in that it is the potentially irascible, antisocial Tantric god who symbolizes group solidarity (or for lower castes, a fierce exoteric god such as a Bhairava or a Mother Goddess). The paradox is easily resolved when one remembers that it is precisely the fierce qualities of the Tantric god which serve to exclude and frighten off outsiders. Buddhas and *bodhisattvas*, who are benign and compassionate by nature, are much less suited to play such a role.

Tantrism expressed and reinforced the solidarity of the lineage in much the same way for Śreṣṭhas as it did for Śākyas and Vajrācāryas. However, in another way Tantric religion has served them somewhat differently. Such differences are a reflection of their traditional positions as ruling political caste and sacerdotal caste respectively. For Śreṣṭhas it was important to demonstrate publicly their position as patrons of religious works. This, however, was better achieved by sponsoring non-Tantric religious acts. Śreṣṭhas were probably interested in Tantric religion mostly as a means of acquiring divine power for military purposes.[8] Thus the Tantric shrines of Śreṣṭhas are commonly full of swords and shields; and at Mohanī the swords are empowered by the goddess and used by male members of the lineage to 'sacrifice' a pumpkin. According to S. Shrestha,[9] some still perform this Sword Festival (*khaḍgajātrā*, *pāyāḥ* or *pāyā̃*) wearing chain shirts and metal helmets as if going to war. The ritual is supposed to ensure success with the sword (*khaḍgasiddhi*) against enemies and demons; some still say 'May you attain success with the sword' (*khaḍgasiddhir astu*).

S. Shrestha's analysis of the Tantric symbolism of *khẽ sagā̃*, good-luck food, also highlights the Hindu, Kṣatriya view of Tantra. The emphasis is on animal sacrifice: the three bites with which one eats the food represent the spurting of sacrificial blood, the offering of life, and the offering of meat (Juju and Shrestha 1985: 25). We have seen a similar analysis of the sacramental food, *samay*, above (§10.5). In Buddhist Tantric exegesis, by contrast, although meat is required, and although Realized Ones may, under duress, harm their enemies by magical means, animal sacrifice is abhorred and would never be used as a legitimizing and explanatory device.

The traditional importance of Tantric religion to Vajrācāryas and Śākyas follows not just from their being Buddhists, but also from their position as a holy order. The Śrāvakayāna and Mahāyāna aspects of their religion encourage all comers to worship Buddhist deities, and to support them, the Buddhist Saṃgha. This is particularly true of rites such as Pañcadān and Buddhist Observances. Although admission to the Monastic Community is restricted, in other ways these facets of Newar Buddhism are universalistic. Tantric Buddhism, and the gods of the Diamond Way, have a crucial role to play in mitigating this: they help to exclude others and to legitimize the Vajrācāryas' monopoly of control. The image of the Realized One who can perform magical rites and control deities (discussed above, §9.2, 10.4) is their legitimizing ideal. These powers may be used for military purposes, but it is not the priests themselves who fight. A Vajrācārya from Kwā Bāhāḥ told me that thanks to the lampblack blessing (*mwahanīsinhaḥ*) of Bāl Kumārī the Nepalese army was able to defeat the Tibetans: 'The Vajrācāryas and Karmācāryas of Lalitpur explained [to them] that the blessing of the Parbatiyā Brahmans was ineffective.'[10]

The Tantric powers of the Vajrācārya priest, unlike those sought by Śreṣṭhas, are not military, even if they may be put to military use.[11] They are rather all-purpose magical and spiritual powers, to be used for the good of others, and in particular those others who are his patrons. These opposing conceptions of Tantric power reflect the social reality of different caste values, as does the 'pervasive contrast in Newar religion' identified by M. Allen (1975: 59–60) 'between a belief in a basic earthy kind of power embodied in such themes as fertility, sexuality and maternity, and in a more rarified power of an intellectual kind'.

There are some forms of Tantric worship controlled by Vajrācāryas and Śākyas which are not exclusive. They reflect the attempt to use Tantric power for others, and they encourage worship from all comers. One of these is Kumārī Worship. The Kumārī shrines used by a very wide range of Lalitpur Newars (including some high-caste Hindus) are located in Buddhist monasteries or in the homes of Vajrācāryas (or occasionally of Śākyas). A similar case is the main Tantric deity of Kwā Bāhāḥ, Lalitpur, where there are many endowed annual acts of worship (*dau pūjā*) performed by non-member lineages, including lineages which, even traditionally, would have called themselves Hindu (i.e. *śivamārgī*). In cases such as these, those offering worship may not see the deity. They bring offerings and receive blessings, but may not enter the shrine (nor, indeed, may any member of Kwā Bāhāḥ itself, save only the Cakreśvara). In these cases, the Tantric deity is not being used to define a lineage, clan, or patrilineally recruited group. Śākya and Vajrācārya control of the cult is legitimized, as with exoteric deities, in terms of heredity, caste, and sacerdotal life-style.

Fuller (1985b: 40) has argued for an ideal–typical distinction between Durkheimian lesser deities and universalist great gods within Hinduism. The former are those 'whose realm is bounded, and around whom a group of worshippers generate in ritual an ideal social structure of their group, whose axis is the deity itself'. The latter are those 'whose realm is ritually shown to be unbounded and around whom no group of worshippers can generate an ideal social structure'. One type of universalist deity is, Fuller suggests, the principal deity of a royal capital city.

I have suggested above (§3.1) that Karuṇāmaya, the principal deity of Lalitpur, should be seen as a universalist deity, even though caste rank is thought by some – those closely connected to the cult – to reflect, in a Durkheimian way, relationship to the god. In the examples given above – Kumārī and Kwā Bāhāḥ's Yogāmbara – one can see Tantric deities taking on a universalist form, in line with their theological attributes of being coextensive with the universe or being the universe. These very same deities, however, by making use of exclusions based on secrecy and initiation, can, and for the most part do, appear as paradigmatic Durkheimian sacred forms.

Tantric religion does not just lend itself, with equal adaptability, to soteriology, social religion, and instrumental religion. It also straddles what are otherwise opposed styles of religion. This has been noted, for Tantric Hinduism, by Toffin (1984: 555): 'It is one of the numerous contradictions of tantrism to be at once an extremely popular religion, having close contacts with the cult of goddesses and with blood sacrifice, and an esoteric religion to the highest forms of which only a limited group has access.'[12]

The groups whose social needs are served by Tantric shrines are not all high caste. Even though low castes are debarred from Tantric Initiation they may have Tantric shrines served for them by Vajrācāryas. Furthermore, Hinduism seems to permit Tantric Initiation further down the social scale than Buddhism, at least to certain individuals for defined priestly functions. There is a class of peasant Karmācāryas (Jyāpu Ācā) who serve their fellow Maharjans as priests in certain areas.[13] Thus for Śreṣṭhas and Maharjans it is possible to have life-cycle rites performed by a Tantrically qualified Hindu priest who is of the same social status. This is not possible for them in Newar Buddhism. Although a Buddhist Tantric Initiation (not that of Cakrasaṃvara) is given to selected Maharjans, this is only in order for them to carry out a specific religious role (e.g. riding on Karuṇāmaya's chariot). Low castes often surround non-Tantric rituals with a Tantric degree of secrecy, and thereby obtain the same social result. For instance, the death *guthi*s of the Khaḍgīs are their most important social organizations. The cult of their death *guthi* god is enclosed in great secrecy and they even refer to it as their *āgȧ dyaḥ*.

The thrust of the present argument has been to look at how Tantrism is used. The main theory of Tantrism in Indology, by contrast, explains it in terms of its origins. Thus Kvaerne remarks, in a survey of Buddhist Tantric Initiation:

> One of the most striking features of the Buddhist tantras is the role played by the female partners of gods and men . . . This particular feature has been interpreted as an aspect of a general resurgence of non-Aryan religious sub-stratum.
>
> (Kvaerne 1975: 106)

This Kvaerne characterizes as a 'plausible explanation'. (The other 'well-spring' of the Tantras he believes to have been the Upaniṣads.)

Unfortunately Indology is bedevilled by pseudo-analyses which seek to disentangle Aryan from non-Aryan elements. This has some plausibility in dealing strictly with language. As a model for social and cultural phenomena it has disastrous results; in the hands of South Asians it often reflects political concerns.[14] The Tantras rose to prominence over two thousand years after the arrival of the Aryans in India. By that time 'Aryan' referred not to an ethnic group distinct from others, but to the values and practices of the elite of all South Asia. To say that Tantra is non-Aryan is therefore a misleading way of saying that it offended the sensibilities of the ruling elite. This in fact is untrue: it offended certain sections of the Brahmanical elite, the degree and manner in which it did so varying considerably according to time and place.

It should be clear from the present study that Tantrism, far from being 'tribal', 'non-Aryan', 'non-Sanskritic', or 'popular', is an essentially urban, learned, sophisticated, and esoteric movement. It is passed on by literate high-caste priests and is exclusive towards low castes. It is based on a learned soteriology. It is, or is part of, what anthropologists call a Great Tradition. This significant sociological fact about how it works and has worked for most of its history has been ignored. Too often analysis has focused exclusively on Tantrism's incorporation of magic and elements of possession.

Explaining how a religious movement functions and what its significance is in its heyday and, on the other hand, investigating its origins, are two very different things. In the kind of analysis I am attacking they are run together and not distinguished. In explaining the origins of Tantrism (as opposed to explaining how it functions), its provenance from the fringes of polite society, that is, among antinomian renouncers, is far more relevant as an explanation than the hackneyed invocations 'non-Aryan' and 'tribal'.[15] As for the appearance of Tantrism within Buddhism, Gombrich and Obeyesekere's work on new religious trends in Sri Lanka shows how severe social, economic, and political disruption may lead to startlingly new forms of Buddhism, influenced by a variety of Hindu types of religiosity. They themselves (1988: 462) draw a parallel with the rise of Tantric Buddhism.

11.2 The place of Tantra in Buddhism and Hinduism compared

High-caste Newar Hindus employ more religious specialists than Buddhists do. As we have had occasion to note above (§7.3), they employ more specialists at death; they also have diverse specialists of a priestly sort who should be called on auspicious occasions as well (§2.5). Where Buddhists need call only their Vajrācārya, Hindus must call Brahman, Karmācārya (Śaiva Tantric priest), and Jośī (astrologer). High-caste Buddhists, specifically Śākyas and Vajrācāryas, diverge only slightly from this pattern of 'high status = more rules and more rituals'. The Buddhists base their claim to higher status not on the number of specialists employed but on the amount of religious devotion they display themselves. Unlike in Tamil

Nadu, devotion is not here opposed to ritual, but is precisely expressed through ritual.[16] It is my impression that the amount of ritual of all types performed by Śākyas and Vajrācāryas exceeds markedly that performed by Chatharīya Śreṣṭhas, both today and in the past. Where Śreṣṭhas are paradigmatically patrons of others, Śākyas and Vajrācāryas are typically religious specialists themselves.

The difference in the number of priests used by Hindus and Buddhists is not just a function of their different social and religious aspirations, however. It has also to do with the doctrines of the two religions, or rather the structure in which the doctrines are arranged. The hierarchy of the Three Ways which make up Newar Buddhism has been outlined above (§4.2). In Newar Hinduism there is a similar triad which equally reflects three types of scripture: the Vedic, the Puranic (relating to the *purāṇa*s, purportedly historical accounts of the gods' actions), and the Tantric.[17] One might be tempted to see this triad as corresponding to the Buddhist one. The Vedic tradition in Hinduism is after all the oldest, as is the Disciples' Way in Newar Buddhism. The Tantric tradition is clearly equivalent to the Diamond Way (Tantric Hinduism and Tantric Buddhism share – as is quite clear to Newars themselves – many rites, practices, and concepts).[18] Hodgson (1972 I: 144 fn.) was evidently aware of the parallels. When describing Monastic Initiation he borrowed the Hindu term and contrasted 'the Pauranik exoteric and purely Buddhist ritual' with 'the Tantrik esoteric, and not purely Buddhist ritual'.[19]

Such a correspondence between Hindu and Buddhist triads is very superficial however, mainly because the Hindu triad does not represent a unitary hierarchy. As a boy the high-caste Hindu male assumes the sacred thread (Vedic), as a householder he practises and sponsors devotional Observances (*vrata*) and other rites (Puranic), and sooner or later he may take Tantric Initiation (Tantric). The similarity to the Three Ways of Newar Buddhism is, as stressed, purely superficial. The Puranic tradition is not a superior, more genuine, and more altruistic summation of the Vedic tradition, in the way that, from the traditional Newar point of view (as for all Mahāyāna Buddhists), the Mahāyāna is of the Śrāvakayāna. Rather, the Puranic is the inferior type of Hinduism suited to women and lower castes who are not entitled to Vedic initiation.

Furthermore, the Hindu triad is most often heard reduced to a binary opposition between the Vedic and the Tantric. The Tantric is not unequivocally superior to the Vedic, as the Vajrayāna is to both Mahāyāna and Śrāvakayāna in Newar Buddhism. Newar Brahmans tend to stress their Vedic entitlements to express their superiority to the Karmācārya priests, but their Tantric qualifications to demonstrate their superiority to Parbatiyā Brahmans (Toffin 1984: 562). In fact the Vedic is generally recognized as superior and this is only denied in particular contexts or by particular interested groups (Karmācāryas). This is shown by the social superiority, universally acknowledged except by Karmācāryas, of Brahmans to Karmācāryas, and also by the frequent habit of Nepalese kings of importing purer Brahmans from India who would not be so involved with Tantric practices.[20] Recent work by Toffin (1989), mentioned above (§2.5), describes the institutionalized superiority of the *guru* (who gives to his patrons both the Gāyatrī and Tantric mantras) over the *purohit* (who carries out exoteric life-cycle rites). This is a tantalizing hint that perhaps the superiority of the Vedic over the Tantric was not so clear or so universally acknowledged in the past.

However this may be, evidence from India supports the same conclusions, that the different traditions of Hinduism tend to be juxtaposed rather than inextricably combined, and that the Vedic always remained the touchstone of purity and superior status for the society as a whole. Sanderson writes of the Kaula Śaivite philosophy which arose in Kashmir, that it integrated

> the antagonistic paths of purity and power. Thus one could be 'internally a Kaula, externally a Śaiva [a worshipper of Svacchandabhairava in the Kashmirian context] while remaining Vedic in one's social practice'.
>
> (Sanderson 1985: 205)

In practice these three identities remained separate in spite of the sophisticated philosophical synthesis evolved to justify their concurrent practice. To take another example, from south India, the temple priests of Mīnākṣī, in Madurai, described by Fuller (1984) are an equivalent of the Karmācāryas of Nepal. In contrast to the latter, however, they have succeeded in getting themselves accepted as a form of Brahman, albeit low status, non-Vedic Brahmans. Also, unlike the Karmācāryas, they act only as temple priests and do not perform rituals in patrons' homes. However, like them, they are *ācārya* whose position is justified by appeal to the Āgamas: like them, they claim superiority to purely Vedic Brahmans, a claim recognized by no one but themselves. Other Tamils may receive the initiation of Lord Śiva but only they, as descendants of Śiva himself, may perform worship for others in public temples (Fuller 1984: 28).

The Newar Buddhist case is interestingly parallel and significantly different from the Mīnākṣī priests. Śākyas and Vajrācāryas as 'sons of the Buddha' are alone entitled to be members of Buddhist monasteries, and to serve as temple priests in the public temples there. But Vajrācāryas alone may serve as priests for worship in others' homes. Buddhism evolved a Tantric *purohit* (family priest) as a subset of the temple priest. By contrast, in Hinduism the Tantric temple priest was always in competition with the non-Tantric Brahman. This follows from the fact that Vedism, and the Puranic rituals evolved for others but administered by Brahmans, were and remained autonomous ritual systems. The Śrāvakayāna within Buddhism was never, in the same way, a system of ritual. Consequently the Three Ways are tightly integrated into one system. In Hinduism, even when Vedic, Puranic, and Tantric rituals are carried on by the same person, they remain juxtaposed, rather than fully integrated. And in practice they are often associated with different people. Witzel (1986), for instance, compares the permanent Fire Sacrifice of the Newar Brahmans, carried on at the Agnimaṭha, Lalitpur, with that of the Parbatiyā Brahmans in Paśupati. Both are supposed to protect the kingdom, but the former, dating from the Malla period, incorporates numerous Tantric elements, whereas the latter, introduced by Prithvi Narayan Shah, is almost entirely Vedic.

Thus, however important Tantric practices, rituals, and symbols are and have been in Hinduism, it is still possible to carry on Vedic and Puranic traditions without them. In a study of Newar Brahmans, Toffin (1989: 32) also emphasizes how Vedism and Tantrism, though practised concurrently, are kept distinct. He notes that the exoteric rituals which Rājopādhyāyas perform for their patrons do not contain esoteric elements, as those of the Vajrācāryas do. He concludes: 'Contrary to what has happened in Newar Buddhism, in which *dīkṣā* is the central and culminating point of the religious life, Tantrism remains for the Rājopādhyāya Brahmans a relatively distinct and problematic tendency (*courant*).' In short, the Vedic, the Puranic, and the Tantric have not been worked into a single ritual system. I claim that this is so for Nepal, and I advance the hypothesis that it has generally been so in India. (That they remain in practice separable systems does not preclude them being viewed as aspects of a single, greater whole, as in the Kaula philosophy described by Sanderson.)

The same is not true of Newar Buddhism. All Three Ways require Vajrācārya priests to perform rituals, in which they invoke Tantric deities secretly. This is true for all but the most clearly and unequivocally Śrāvakayāna practices, Pañcadān and Samyak, in which Śākyas and Vajrācāras receive alms in their capacity as monks. Even Samyak involves various Tantric rituals, as do complex forms of Pañcadān. The rite of initiation as a monk is set in a ritual frame which is clearly Mahāyāna and Vajrayāna. This applies *a fortiori* to all other rites. Traditionally, everything in Newar Buddhism points towards the highest way, towards

Tantric Initiation and the practices associated with it. Today some intellectuals educated in the Western style are trying to study Mahāyāna texts without any ritual context and without any reference to the Vajrayāna. In the past too, a few intellectuals knew and studied texts such as the Bodhicaryāvatāra, but they carried on their ritual obligations just the same. The modern study groups bring out books and organize meetings but they do not look likely to institutionalize a specifically Mahāyāna non-Tantric form of Buddhism. In short, a Buddhist priesthood requires a Tantric justification and wherever there are complex forms of worship there are thoroughgoing Tantric elements.

In Hinduism there are alternative sets of priests, with separate scriptures, each legitimizing a different ritual system. In Buddhism, although there are alternative scriptures, there is only one ritual system. In this system the values and inheritance of the Śrāvakayāna on the one hand, and the aspirations and devotionalism of the Mahāyāna on the other, have both been integrated within the frame of Vajrayāna ritual. While Hinduism has permitted only the accretion of systems kept separate, Buddhism has integrated them and produced a new system.

It seems, then, that Tantrism had a more profound effect on Buddhism than on Hinduism; this point will be discussed further below (§11.3). That this judgement is consistent with the perceptions of Newars themselves is shown by the association of Vajrācāryas with Tantrism in the popular imagination. It is also implicit in the structure of the pantheon, as shown above (Figure 12). That such an association is not confined to Nepal, but may well reflect the state of religion in late medieval South Asia, is at least suggested by the fact that in Bali Śiva is considered less Tantric than the Buddha (Pott 1966: 120–1).

11.3 Theravāda Buddhism and Tantrism

At first sight Tantrism appears as the rejection of everything Theravāda, or Śrāvakayāna, Buddhism stands for. I have already quoted M. Allen's (1973: 13) pithy characterization of the Diamond Way as 'based on a simple inversion of orthodox monastic Buddhism – sex in place of celibacy, long hair instead of shaven pates, indulgence instead of abstinence, drunkenness instead of sobriety'.[21] He could have added: elaborate ritualism in place of simple memorials, provision of magical means and thisworldly rites instead of disdain for worldly religion, a complex pantheon instead of a single-minded focus on the Buddha alone, and a hereditary priesthood instead of an open monastic order.

It is hardly surprising that Vajrācārya priests are rarely well disposed to

Table 11.1 *Caste origin of Nepalese Theravāda monks (*bhikkhu*), (male) novices (*sāmaṇera*), and nuns (*anāgārikā*).*

	1978–82		1989		
	monks (N=c. 60)	nuns (N=c. 65)	monks (N=59)	novices (N=72)	nuns (N=70)
Śākya	38.4	42.6	39.0	27.8	35.7
Maharjan (incl. Āwāle)	22.7	12.6	13.6	31.9	15.7
Tulādhar *et al.*	14.0	14.2	13.6	/	11.5
Vajrācārya	7.0	7.1	8.4	1.4	11.5
Śreṣṭha	7.0	7.1	8.4	9.7	11.5
Mānandhar	?	10.6	3.4	5.5	7.1
Others (incl. non-Newars)	?	5.8	13.6	23.7	7.0
	100%	100%	100%	100%	100%

Sources: The source of the 1978–82 figures is Tewari 1983: 75–6. The figures for 1989 are based on information kindly provided by John Locke and Uwe Hartmann.

the Theravāda movement which has established itself in the Kathmandu Valley since the 1930s. This is not the place to discuss its history.[22] Suffice it to say that it has become a major challenge to traditional Newar Buddhism. The factors which facilitate the rise of Theravāda Buddhism and underlie the decline of traditional Newar Buddhism are discussed below. Although it is these factors which are the underlying causes, many Vajrācāryas blame the Theravāda monks. Vajrācārya priests often blame the sermons of Theravāda monks for the decline in their parishioners' performance of Ancestor Worship. Other rituals, both esoteric and exoteric, are also very much on the decline. There is a growing tendency for Vajrācārya priests to be called only when they have to be called; at other times, Theravāda or Tibetan monks are patronized. Not surprisingly, practising Vajrācārya priests are sometimes bitter about this.

The Śākyas' response to Theravāda Buddhism, while not universally so, is much more often enthusiastic than that of the Vajrācāryas. This is shown clearly by the figures given in Table 11.1 (although in interpreting them it must be remembered that there are roughly twice as many Śākyas as Vajrācāryas). The table also shows that there has been a considerable upsurge in Maharjan support for Theravāda Buddhism in recent years. All the novices joined the Monastic Community in the years since 1979. By contrast, there is at present only a single novice from a Vajrācārya background. Vajrācārya participation in Theravāda lay activities is equally low. Out of sixty-six Vajrācārya families in ward 15, Lalitpur, only five (8%) had ever invited Theravāda monks to the house, and none had done so more than once. Of the 211 Śākya families 24% had invited monks once, a further 7% had invited them more than once, and a further 14% were regular supporters. This still leaves more than half of the Śākyas who had never invited Theravāda monks. Nonetheless the contrast is sharp. Furthermore, among the five Vajrācārya families who had invited Theravāda monks there were no practising priests. There is at least one wealthy Vajrācārya family in Lalitpur (not inhabiting ward 15) which supports Theravāda Buddhism enthusiastically; but they come from Ha Bāhāḥ, none of whose members are practising priests.

The veiled hostility of Vajrācārya priests to the Theravāda is not just a question of professional competition, though that is indeed involved. The Tantric scriptures contain slighting references to the Lesser Way (*hīnayāna*), and forbid certain teachings to its followers.[23] Other Tantric texts, evidently written by monks or by those more favourably inclined to them, argued that the highest Tantric Initiations could equally well be taken by monks. The Tantric way is based *both* on rejection *and* on incorporation of the values of the Disciples' Way, as argued above (§10.3). (That is why it does not represent licentiousness as might be suggested by the quotation above from M. Allen.)

Theravāda Buddhism, equally, has good cause to be hostile to Vajrayāna, which, in its eyes, represents a capitulation to Hinduism. Taranatha's history of Buddhism records that in the reign of Dharmapāla (c. 770–810) Śrāvakas (i.e. Theravāda monks) from Sri Lanka, who were the predominant group at the temple of Vajrāsana, Bodh Gaya, where the Buddha attained enlightenment, burnt Vajrayāna books, saying that they were composed by Māra ('the Killer', or Evil One). They also smashed a silver Heruka (Cakrasaṃvara) and told pilgrims not to follow the Mahāyāna (Chattopadhyaya 1970: 279; D. Mitra 1971: 19). Dharmasvāmin met similar hostility to the Mahāyāna on the part of the Sri Lankan Theravādins in Bodh Gaya, when he visited it in 1235, in the very last days of Indian Buddhism (Roerich 1959: 73–5).

Today in Nepal the Theravāda monks are careful not to attack Vajrayāna Buddhism outright like this, since many of its followers are not ready to abandon their traditional rites. But they do attack it by implication in their preaching and by such practices as referring to their own form of Buddhism simply as 'Buddhism'.[24] Thus followers of the Theravāda will say 'I don't observe Mohanī, because I'm a Buddhist', with the implication that those Newar Buddhists who do observe it (all but the strictest

Theravādins) are not really Buddhists. The Theravāda monks of modern Nepal are not openly hostile to traditional Newar Buddhism. They do not need to be. They feel that history is on their side and they have only to wait.

The attitude of the laity, with the exception of the minority of Theravāda enthusiasts, is different. They often say that it is all Buddhism and in practice they often patronize all three forms of Buddhism locally available. Of the forty-four (all Śākya) families from ward 15 who have more than once invited Theravāda monks to their home only seven were regular supporters who never called Tibetan monks and had never sponsored a reading of the Mahāyāna scripture 'The Perfection of Wisdom' in Kwā Bāhāḥ. In fact family members often differ in their preferences; only when the household head is a determined supporter of the Theravāda movement does the whole pattern of the family's religiosity fall into line. It is not uncommon for Śākyas to be regular supporters of Theravāda monks and to support Tibetan Mahāyāna monks as well. The pious are more likely to be ecumenical between types of Buddhism than they are to be exclusively attached to one type.

At an abstract level of sociological analysis one can find some justification for these Newars' ecumenical views. There is an important continuity between pre-Mahāyāna Buddhism and Tantric Buddhism in spite of the fact that Tantric Buddhism causes the spiritual hierarchy of monk and layman to be superseded by those of master and disciple, initiated and uninitiated. Toffin (1984: 565) put his finger on this continuity when he wrote that 'as far as Buddhism is concerned it would certainly be possible to find affinities between the religion of renunciation and individual affirmation advanced by the Buddha, and the superhuman exploits of Buddhist Tantrics which ascribe an independent moral value to the individual'. This focus on the individual is also part of what is implied by Snellgrove's (1959a I: vii) reference to 'the essential continuity underlying the development of Buddhism, a continuity achieved by devotion to a single ideal, which was ever seeking better means of realization and expression'.

In theory, both in Theravāda and in Vajrayāna Buddhism, the highest spiritual roles are open to anyone. Although in fact the position of Vajrācārya is hereditary, people know that Realized Ones of the past are supposed to have come from many different backgrounds including the lowest. Today as well, Untouchables are often thought to possess Tantric powers acquired in the cremation ground. The hereditary nature of Vajrācārya status can therefore only be justified in Hindu terms and in terms of tradition. The Vajrayāna hierarchy of *guru* and disciple is no closer than the Theravāda hierarchy of monk and layman to the Hindu priest/patron model (cf. Table 5.1, above). In practice, however, the Diamond Way lends itself to the legitimization of hereditary roles far better than the Theravāda, if only because of its emphasis on secrecy and on the need for a sexual partner.

From the fact that both Theravāda and Tantric Buddhism stress the value of the individual, Toffin concludes that Tantrism had more influence on Hinduism than on Buddhism. He sees the significance of Tantrism for Hinduism (a) in its overcoming, or at least mitigating, the strict Brahmanical division between the religious power of the Brahman and the secular power of the king; and (b), concomitantly, in Tantrism's denial of the preeminence of the Brahman. Since Buddhism already denied these two Brahmanical theories, the addition of Tantrism to Mahāyāna Buddhism did not, Toffin claims, introduce new values in the same way.

There are several qualifications to be made to these conclusions (which, to be fair, Toffin advances only with the greatest caution). First, and least importantly for present purposes, it is not strictly true to say that Buddhism already denied a division between the religious order and the holders of secular power. On the contrary, it upheld the distinction between the ordained and the unordained. The King might be considered a *bodhisattva* but he remained inferior to the most junior monk. Second, and more importantly, Toffin approached the question of the impact on Buddhism of Tantrism from the perspective of its impact on Hinduism. Certainly Buddhism did not need Tantra in order to deny the preeminence of the Brahman or to emphasize the importance of the individual. The importance of Tantrism was quite different for Buddhism, as, I hope, the discussion above (§11.1, 11.2) has shown. Tantra was required for Buddhism to deny explicitly the preeminence of the monk, and replace the monk–layman dichotomy with the *guru*–disciple dichotomy. It was needed to legitimize a priesthood. And it was needed to effect a convergence with, or rather to construct parallels to, Hindu life-cycle rites, while yet remaining opposed to Brahmanism (although this last development occurred, it seems, only in Nepal). In all these ways Tantrism had a profound effect on Buddhism. Hinduism, by contrast, had no need of Tantra to justify a priesthood or life-cycle rites; it had them already. Thus I would invert Toffin's conclusion and say that Tantrism had a greater impact on Buddhism than on Hinduism. It could have this impact precisely because of its emphasis on the individual, so that Tantric teachings could be incorporated at every level of Buddhism.[25]

There is a third point in Toffin's conclusion requiring qualification, namely his characterization of Tantrism as thoroughly opposed to the 'holism of the world of caste' (Toffin 1984: 564). Toffin (ibid.: 566 n. 9) himself points out that Tantric priesthood in Pyangaon is 'a question neither of choice, nor of a freely acquired proficiency; it is based entirely on heredity'. He ascribes this to 'an interesting deformation of Tantric theology, due to the strength of clan ties in the village'. He is right to see this as contrary to Tantric ideology, but wrong to think that it is confined to the village. Priesthood among Karmācāryas in the city is also hereditary, as it is among Vajrācāryas. As in so many cases in South Asia (cf. Dumont 1980: 187–91), an individualistic soteriology is in fact used to define another hereditary group. Tantrism combined mysticism and ritual to great effect: it gave value to the individual and the search for salvation through initiation. Yet at the same time, with its emphasis on secrecy, the necessity of a *guru*, and the importance of a sexual partner and therefore of marriage, Tantrism also provided a Sanskritic idiom for the religion of the group. Although the Tantric scriptures do not directly justify this development, it is nonetheless based on elements which are scriptural.

If we move on from the values of Buddhist Tantrism and compare its ritual practice to Theravāda Buddhism, in this sphere too it is possible to discern continuities beneath the obvious differences. From the Tantric Buddhist point of view the Triple Refuge formula of Theravāda Buddhism is a mantra (Govinda 1960: 32; Bharati 1965: 104, 123). The recitation of praises of the deity (*stotra*) and of the deity's mantra (*japa* or *jāpa*) is considered to be, and is called, meditation (*dhyāna*), as in the Theravāda tradition. Many ancient verses shared with Theravāda Buddhism are recited as part of the *guru maṇḍala* rite and in Monastic Initiation. The protective recitation of the Pañcarakṣā goddesses was evolved from the Pali verses recited in the *paritrāṇ* (protection) ceremony performed by Theravāda monks, according to Newar *paṇḍit* Dibya Vajra Vajracharya. The Pañcarakṣā used to be recited frequently, and it was so important to Newar Buddhism that, when in court, Buddhists were sworn in on a copy of it (Hodgson 1880: 226). Nowadays it is rarely heard. Instead many Newar Buddhists recite Pali *paritrāṇ* verses from one of many easily available printed pamphlets as part of their morning worship.

The roots of the Diamond Way can be seen if we look at the claims made on behalf of the Theravāda Protection Ceremony. In a short article entitled 'The Importance of the Protection (*Paritrāṇ*) Ceremony' Bhikṣu Buddhaghosha lists twelve 'protection' scriptures (*sūtra*) and the protections provided by each:

By the recitation of the Āvāhana Sūtra the gods are summoned; a deep relationship is established with them: thus they will give us whatever help they can. By reading the Maṅgala Sūtra, one will have good luck. By reading the Ratana Sūtra illness, dangers, and obstacles are removed. By reading the Maitri Sūtra nothing will be done to one that one does not want. By reading the Khandha Sūtra one will not be harmed by poisonous snakes, scorpions etc. By reading the Mora Sūtra one will be saved from accidents. By reading the Vatta Sūtra one will be saved from danger by fire. By reading the Dhajagga Sūtra one will be saved from the fear of danger. By reading the Āṭānāṭiya Sūtra one will be saved from the attacks of spooks, ghosts, and so on. By reading the Aṅgulīmāla [sic] Sūtra women who cannot have children will be saved from barrenness. By reading the Bojjhaṅga Sūtra the danger of disease will be appeased . . . By reading the Pubbaṇha Sūtra the effects of bad omens, bad luck, inauspicious cries of birds, bad conjunctions of stars, and bad dreams will all be avoided.

(Buddhaghosha 1982: 3)

Similar interpretations are made in Thailand, Burma, and Sri Lanka.[26]

The reference to summoning deities with the Āvāhana Sūtra might sound like the Vajrayāna ritual described above (§10.2). Buddhaghosha makes it clear, however, that the gods may or may not come; if they do not (and only a Buddha can tell if they are present), at least one has done one's duty and given them an opportunity to hear the Doctrine being taught. Bhikṣu Sudarshan (1982: 15–16) describes and lists even more fully all the scriptural passages recited in the Theravāda protection ceremony. He divides them into four types: the first three are those which, in wishing for good fortune (*maṅgala*), recall, respectively, the qualities of the Three Jewels, of the Buddha, and of the Doctrine. The final type includes only the Āṭānāṭiya Sūtra, which is the last to be recited. In it the Buddha wins round the bloodthirsty and harmful spirits and prevents them from doing harm; Vaiśravaṇa offers his protection. Sudarshan comments: 'Some say that this Āṭānāṭiya Sūtra is the seed of mantra in Buddhist philosophy.' Since the Āṭānāṭiya Sūtra is recited last, I would see its presence rather as illustrating the most basic ritual structure – worship of the principal deity followed by appeasement of the lower protective spirits with a Spirit-Offering – which we have seen also in the *guru maṇḍala* rite. Furthermore, it seems that traditionally, in Sri Lanka, a young woman in the audience hearing such protection verses often became possessed when the Āṭānāṭiya Sūtra was recited (Gombrich and Obeyesekere 1988: 52).

These underlying homologies of practice and value do not mean that there are not very important differences between Theravāda and Vajrayāna Buddhism. Ritual in the former is simple and plain (and cheap, as Newars point out[27]). Ritual in Vajrayāna Buddhism is long and deliberately complex. Theravāda Buddhism adopted certain symbols such as the Flask and the protective thread. It therefore permits tacitly an affective belief in the instrumental and magical power of the rite, but cognitively always denies such an interpretation. If spirit-possession occurs, it is considered of no spiritual value. What Theravāda Buddhism turns a blind eye to, Vajrayāna Buddhism encourages either openly or in secret. But even here there is a continuity: the cognitive doctrine of the Theravāda (that if worship of the Buddha or reciting prayers have a result this is due only to the good intentions thus generated) survives at a higher level of interpretation embedded within the assertion of the magical power of words.

11.4 Tantrism, healers, mediums, and witches

One of the ways in which Vajrācāryas make use of Tantric powers outside the purely ritual sphere is as healers. In this capacity they are known as *vaidya*, a term which also applies to ayurvedic doctors. To distinguish them from the latter they are often known as *jhārphuke vaidya*. *Jhārphuk*, a word of Hindi origin, refers to 'brushing' with a broom, and 'blowing' mantras on the body of the afflicted person (see Plate 9). Depending on the diagnosis they make, Tantric healers combine this with the prescription of ayurvedic medicine, and with astrological predictions. In many cases they decide that the problem is caused by witch attack, in which case ritual techniques are used to reverse it ('ultā yāye'). Clients usually receive some empowered water to drink before departing.

Healers of this sort may come from any caste, but Vajrācāryas are very numerous. Durkin-Longley (1982: 193) exaggerates when she says: 'In the past most or all gubhajus [Vajrācāryas] may have engaged in healing.' Still, it is true that more people resort to Vajrācāryas in this capacity than in any other, and they come from a very wide variety of backgrounds, far wider than those Newar castes who use Vajrācāryas as family priests, and wider too than those (mainly Newars) who frequent cults (such as that of Karuṇāmaya-Matsyendranāth) controlled by them. It is also true that among such healers, Vajrācāryas form the biggest single caste group.[28] Among neighbouring non-Newar groups (Tamangs, Parbatiyās) Vajrācāryas have a high reputation as healers and magicians. Members of other castes who practise in the same way have often had a Vajrācārya as their *guru*.

The basis of this kind of healing is religious and, more precisely, Tantric. Astrological charts are usually drawn; ayurvedic medicines are often prescribed. But the level of astrological or ayurvedic expertise displayed is often not such as to account for the reputation of the healer. An educated person who suspects that their problem has astrological causes is probably more likely to go to an astrologer pure and simple; and for a complaint which they think may respond to ayurvedic treatment they are more likely to go to a specialist who deals in Āyurveda alone. Others, however, bring any complaint to Tantric healers.

The source of Tantric healers' power is the possession of powerful, and *ipso facto* dangerous, mantras. As indicated above (§9.2), the practitioners often see themselves as providing a selfless service to others. They have no fixed fees. As with a priest's *dakṣiṇā*, they take whatever is offered (though they can specify prices if they prescribe a medicine). They compare this with the expensive fees of western-style doctors and 'compounders' (medical suppliers). Tantric healers see themselves as, and are called by others, 'the doctors of the poor'.

The techniques of these healers are open in the normal run of things only to men. Midwives (usually Maharjans) often know how to perform *jhārphuk*, but they usually only use it on pregnant women or for their own immediate family. Many women do, however, often become possessed, and heal as mediums. Most typically they are possessed by the goddess Hārītī, Buddhist goddess of smallpox, whose main temple is on the north-west side of the Svayambhū *stūpa*. Being possessed, and frequently also illiterate, they cannot use the astrological methods of the healers. But they use identical brushing and blowing techniques. They receive the same range of cases as healers: chronic illnesses which allopathic medicine has not been able to cure, minor ailments not considered important enough to see a doctor about, problems thought to be due to curses or witchcraft, and family problems such as an intransigent mother-in-law, a husband suspected of having a mistress, or a child who refuses to study. Men do sometimes become mediums but they are vastly outnumbered by women.[29]

Many people say that mediums (*dyaḥ waipĩ*, literally 'those to whom gods come') are on the increase. Fifty years ago, it is said, although possession was certainly known, mediums did not set themselves up with daily sessions. It is very probably true that the numbers of such mediums are increasing. But one must be sceptical about whether it is an entirely new phenomenon. A farce written by Jagat Prakāśa Malla, King of Bhaktapur in the middle of the seventeenth century, features a female Buddhist *siddhayoginī*, very likely a medium, who is portrayed as giving charms to people having trouble with their spouses and as having the power to know what is happening in Tibet (Brinkhaus 1987b: 111–17).

As well as the techniques of brushing, blowing, and empowering water using a Buddhist Tantric dagger, mediums, in a more extended sense, share with healers the very technique of possession. It has been shown how this is part of Tantric Initiation. Mediums use the same method, but make it public and routine. Often indeed, though the main possessing and healing deity is Hārītī Ajimā̃, Vajrayoginī, an exoteric form of Vajravārāhī, also appears in the medium's body.

I. Lewis (1971) has distinguished central from peripheral possession. A central possession cult exists when possession is a part of the dominant religion and possession is the preserve of those of high status; typically the possessing spirits are highly moral. Peripheral possession is possession by amoral spirits (e.g. demons or witches), and the spirits are frequently perceived to come from outside. The victims of such possession are typically those of low status, and are mostly, but not exclusively, women. Peripheral possession is a kind of protest at, or compensation for, lack of power and status. Lewis (1971: 44) admits that these two ideal types are 'opposite extremes on a single continuum'.

The Newar material does by and large fit Lewis' framework. Women curers frequently begin on the peripheral end of the spectrum. A very common pattern seems to be for them to suffer repeated possession by a witch or witches when a young woman, and for the witches to be banished only when she undertakes to be possessed regularly by the goddess (usually Hārītī). Once they set themselves up as regular mediums (shamans, in Lewis' terminology), they attempt to move themselves as far as they can towards the 'central' end of the spectrum. Thus they intersperse their healing sessions with religious, and often highly moral, homilies. They advise their clients to observe religious taboos carefully, and generally show themselves to be religiously conservative.

Yet, by the very fact of their being predominantly women, mediums have low status, and people are often sceptical about them. They cannot attain the status of a central cult. *Public* possession remains incompatible with high status. Women are debarred from becoming Tantric healers, since this requires a course of study; it is a career, where the only career open to women is, in the first place, as wife and mother. Thus a woman cannot cure except by becoming a medium; becoming a medium is conceptualized as the god choosing the woman, rather than the woman choosing a career. Still, the increase in their numbers can be seen as a reflection of a slow democratization, whereby it is increasingly possible for those of low status at least to imitate the religious technology of the priestly castes.

To an extent it would be correct to see the possession which takes place during Tantric Initiation as what Lewis would call a central possession cult, since it is reserved to high castes. Yet even here, it is women who get possessed more frequently than men; and the stress on secrecy, and the fact that what goes on in secret is a reversal of public values, can be seen, paradoxically, to strengthen the marginality of public possession.

In perhaps a third of the cases brought to both healers and mediums, the diagnosis involves some kind of harm caused by other people. Those who cause such harm intentionally are known as *bwaksi*, usually translated as 'witch'. (Newar data do not warrant the sharp distinction, made famous by Evans-Pritchard's work on the Azande, between witches, who cause harm involuntarily, and sorcerers, who harm consciously through the use of spells.) The term *bwaksi*, like the English 'witch', is usually presumed to refer to a female. Those individuals who are in practice suspected of witchcraft are invariably women (and normally middle-aged or old as well). Grammatically *bwaksi* is a feminine form. Most people admit that there can be male *bwaksi*s, i.e. *bwaksā*, but the term is in practice an empty category. One explanation given why witches are normally women is that Pārvatī fell asleep while Mahādeva was recounting all the wisdom of the world. She woke up with a start, however, when he reached the section on black magic (*kuvidyā*). Others (both men and women) say simply that women, being weak, are more likely to feel the need to acquire such knowledge, and are more likely not to be able to resist the temptation to use it.

The gender opposition was put very starkly by a young Maharjan *vaidya* who said: we men worship Bhairava, a frightening male god, in order to repair the damage women do as witches and mediums through their worship of Hārītī, a female god. For him mediums were as bad as witches. While others do not go so far, the manner in which many women become mediums (being possessed first by witches) may encourage a conflation with witchcraft. The same association of mediumship and femaleness occurs among the Tamangs, though there more mediums (or 'shamans') are men; in the same way, it is a vocation which begins in suffering (Holmberg 1989: 147). Newars also make a connection between male healers and witches. It is often said that the knowledge which healers must have is the same, only stronger, than the witches'; healers must know both how to cause the harm, and how to undo it. The basic knowledge is the same. Whether it is good knowledge (*suvidyā*) or bad, i.e. black magic (*kuvidyā*), depends on how it is used. Thus healers (*vaidya*) have to be witches; and, being only human, they may succumb to the temptation to use their knowledge harmfully.

Clients or patients of the healers and mediums often suspect witchcraft, and this is frequently diagnosed. It is not necessary to name the witch or to take other than ritual action against a person suspected of witchcraft, although throwing a brick through the suspect's window (whether it has glass in it or not) seems to be a common response. Fear of repeated witchcraft does, however, often make people avoid or cut off relations, if possible. In the past it is clear that aggressive action – beating, chasing out of town – was used against some of those accused of being witches, since the Law Code of 1854 attempted to regulate this and subject it to objective tests (Macdonald 1976). The diagnosis 'someone has caused harm' ('syākāḥ taḥgu') suggests that steps were taken deliberately, typically the use of a mantra. In other cases, illness or mishap may be caused simply by someone's seeing the food one eats, and feeling desire or jealousy: literally, one's 'eye goes' ('mikhā wãgu'), i.e. the evil eye. Opinions differ on how easily this can happen. Some deny it can happen at all without the knowledge of mantras. Others say that a child who has eaten his or her own excrement through the parents' inattention will be able to cause harm simply by looking at something. Others believe that anyone can do it.

In counteracting all these forms of affliction, the Tantric Buddhism of Vajrācārya healers has played a significant role. Nowadays its methods are more widely available to healers and mediums of all castes. At the same time there is increased competition from allopathic medicine. Furthermore, Vajrācāryas are also on the defensive as guardians of a soteriological and social tradition. This is examined in the next section.

11.5 The decline of Tantric Buddhism

Since 1951 there has been rapid social change in the Kathmandu Valley. One consequence of this is that Vajrācāryas, and the kind of religion they represent, have suffered a rapid decline in prestige, which is evident to all. In the city of Kathmandu itself this has been exacerbated by the famous dispute between Vajrācāryas and their most important lay supporters. The Vajrācāryas were clearly motivated by caste feelings and even now, more than sixty years after the events which began the dispute, one can still hear in Kathmandu impassioned denunciations of Vajrācāryas' venality and pride contrasted with the true spirituality of Theravāda and/or Tibetan monks. (In other contexts one may be told that in fact the monks are not as untarnished as they might be.)

Regardless of this dispute, which did not affect Lalitpur, there are less adventitious reasons why the position of the Vajrācāryas is in decline. In the first place there has been an overall decline in religiosity among the high castes from which the strongest supporters of Buddhism come. Members of middle and low castes are often better off than they were, and some of their new-found wealth goes into religion. However, this is no substitute for the numerous and highly complex Tantric rites that high-caste Buddhists used to hold regularly but now perform much more rarely. Secondly, Vajrācāryas now have to compete with the very active and successful Theravāda movement. In the past century or more there has been considerable support for Tibetan Buddhism; this continues but is not obviously expanding. Furthermore, the similarity of Tibetan and Newar forms of Buddhism, and the fact that Newar followers of Tibetan Buddhism seem to have none of the Theravādins' proselytizing spirit, make Tibetan Buddhism less of a threat. Theravāda Buddhism could in theory replace the rites of traditional Newar Buddhism if there was no one left to perform them. Theravāda Buddhism receives much that in former times would have gone into traditional religion: daily devotion, organizational ability, and large donations from rich lay people. The difference can be illustrated by the man (a Śākya) who wanted to sell me his old hand-written copy of the *dhāraṇī* of Vajravārāhī and use the proceeds to print a book written by a Theravāda monk.

It is interesting that Śākyas have not suffered the same obvious and dramatic decline in prestige. One reason for this is that most other castes do not much concern themselves with the difference between Vajrācāryas and Śākyas: for them a Śākya is simply a kind of Vajrācārya who does not have the hereditary right to serve others as family priest.[30] Since they do not serve as family priests, Sākyas are not as closely identified with traditional Newar Buddhism as Vajrācāryas are. One of their first responses to modernity has been to drop the second half of their surname, which in Kathmandu emphasized their monastic role (see above, §6.1). Śākyas are among the most prominent supporters of Theravāda and Tibetan forms of Buddhism; they are also among the most active in attempts to 'revive', i.e. to modernize, traditional Newar Buddhism.

Vajrācāryas themselves perceive and regret the decline in their status. But in their role as sponsor of rites they themselves are not immune to the trends affecting Newar society as a whole: they too perform fewer rites than they did in the past. And as the prestige of the priestly identity has fallen, fewer and fewer know how to perform rites for others. In the past only a few Vajrācāryas could live from the priesthood alone. Most have always practised some other profession as well (§9.2). But all of them used to take pride in the priesthood. Even Vajrācāryas who had no personal patrons or parishioners of their own took care to learn rituals so that they could assist and take part when invited.

Nowadays even the sons of practising priests with numerous patrons sometimes refuse to learn the rites because, they say, others will laugh at them. ('Come on Guruju, ring your bell!' teenagers tease their Vajrācārya friends.) If the family cannot afford to give up the income to someone else, then only, after their father's death, do young Vajrācāryas reluctantly learn the rituals. The income has not in fact kept pace with inflation. As one son of a practising Vajrācārya who keeps a photography shop said to me: 'A priest cannot set the price of his services as I can the cost of my photographs: he must take whatever the patron offers as *dakṣiṇā*.'

Vajrācāryas often complained to me (in a tone of resigned bitterness) that patrons, especially Farmers who do not understand about money, give the same one rupee emolument that they did years ago. They have to learn vast texts by heart, fast all day while performing the rite, and receive scant respect and derisory payment. Is it surprising (they continue) that they should prefer their sons to acquire a secular education and the security of a government job? One gets more money, more security, and a much less arduous life-style with less study. If only the rich men (*sāhu*) cared about supporting Buddhism, by setting up a school for young Vajrācāryas and giving them scholarships for instance, instead of using their money for showy feasts, there might be some hope for the future.

What Durkin-Longley reports of 'gubhaju [Vajrācārya] healers' in Kathmandu reflects feelings that Vajrācāryas have in general about the decline of traditional Newar Buddhism:

> Conceding that the 'tantric age' has recently been replaced by the 'age of science' they reported having encouraged their own children to pursue 'modern' careers. They added that the decline in tantric healing has come about in part as a result of declining popular demand and belief (replaced by demand for allopathic medicine) and in part because the distractions of modernization in Nepal preclude successful wielding of tantric power . . . One gubhaju explained that certain accompaniments of modernization, such as radios, the need to work outside the monastery during office hours and the pressure he feels to be financially successful, have made it increasingly difficult for him to achieve the concentration needed to make his mantras effective and succeed in healing.
>
> (Durkin-Longley 1982: 193–4)

On their side other (non-priestly) Newar Buddhists often deplore the decline in the Vajrācāryas' learning and religious vocation. They are greedy, one is often told, making a 'sour face' if the emolument is not large enough. They are ignorant: they cannot explain the rituals they do (unlike the Theravāda monks) and they use the doctrine of secrecy to cover up their ignorance. They refuse to adapt to the modern world and teach those who want to learn regardless of caste; because of this narrow-minded attitude their teachings are about to become extinct. They won't come when you call them, but out of greed insist on doing three rituals in one day rather than send a substitute to one of them: so they keep their parishioners waiting and fasting. They cannot understand their texts and no longer come to read holy scriptures for their patrons during the holy month of Gũlā as they used to. They no longer maintain a strict, rule-governed, and devoted religious life-style.

The reproaches that lay Buddhists make today reveal the reasons why Vajrācāryas were respected in the past: for their mastery of ritual (for most lay people a good priest is one who knows the text by heart and finishes quickly), for their holy life-style (bathing and worshipping every day), and for their literacy. In traditional Newar Buddhism the Vajrācāryas had a monopoly on the recitation of holy texts for others. This was and is supposed to be meritorious regardless of whether the reader or anyone else understands what is being read. Traditionally such readings would have been despised only by the occasional learned *paṇḍit* and even he would certainly not have recommended anything else for ordinary Buddhists. The introduction of modern education is changing all this, and is an extremely important factor in the decline of the prestige accorded to the traditional learning of the Vajrācāryas. The claim that all Three Ways of Newar Buddhism were equally taught by the Lord Buddha is getting harder to maintain in the face of Theravādins drawing upon modern historical scholarship. *Paṇḍit* Dibya Vajra Vajracharya nonetheless argues forcefully that both Śrāvakayāna or Theravāda and Mahāyāna are equally the Buddha's teaching: 'There is no original or early Buddhism and no later or developed Buddhism' (D.V. Vajracharya 1986: 18). In the absence of effective institutions of learning such denials are powerless to convince the new generation educated in the Western style.

In short, traditional Newar Buddhism was well adapted to a stable, strongly traditional, and hierarchical society, but unlike the Theravāda or Tibetan Buddhism, it seems to be incapable of modernizing itself. Partly this is due to the small numbers involved; partly it is due to the difficulty of becoming learned in Mahāyāna or Vajrayāna Buddhism. Young modernists cannot find sufficient Mahāyāna and Vajrayāna scriptural sources in English, Nepali, or Hindi, the languages they are educated in, whereas the whole of the Theravāda canon and much else besides is available in English and is published assiduously, translated into Nepali or Newari, in Buddhist magazines and pamphlets. Unlike with the Tibetans, there are no well-organized monastic teaching institutions which have added a knowledge of the modern world and English to their traditional methods. In Kathmandu Badri Ratna Vajracharya has started a school for young Vajrācārya boys where they learn ritual and something of its justifications. Nothing similar has appeared elsewhere. (Buddhism may have a higher profile in Lalitpur than in Kathmandu, and its Buddhist community may be far less riven than that of Kathmandu by aggressive preferences for different types of Buddhism, but by the same token it produces fewer specifically Vajrayānist initiatives.)

There are still some learned Newar *paṇḍits*, and there is a demand from young Newar Buddhists for a modernized version of Newar Buddhism. But the young will not listen to a teacher who cannot express himself in a modern way and there are as yet no Vajrācāryas who combine a modern education with traditional learning. If such an individual appears he will probably be a product of Badri Ratna's school. Even if he did emerge, it is hard to imagine how he could establish the principle that either the Monastic Community or the priesthood should be open to all comers. Without this the tradition is unlikely to regain the deepest allegiance of its own adherents. Only a revival which combined traditional learning with modern methods could reverse the trend for the Vajrācāryas' rituals to be considered as mere local and family custom, devoid of any serious soteriological interest.

12

Social and religious hierarchies

It would be a grave error, and reveal an insufficient understanding of the special nature of Tibetan Buddhism, if one were to disregard the soteriological goals permeating and dominating it.

G. Tucci, *The Religions of Tibet*, p. 93. (Reproduced by permission of Penguin Books Ltd.)

The main aim of this work has been to describe and analyse Buddhism as practised by the Newars. Several themes have emerged from the material and have been used to organize it. They can be listed as follows.

(i) In terms of anthropological comparison (and ignoring questions of historical provenance for reasons outlined above, §1.1) Newar Buddhism stands somewhere between Theravāda Buddhism and Hinduism; but it is significantly different from both.

(ii) The hierarchy of the Three Ways provides a framework which integrates and makes sense of the diverse practices which make up Newar Buddhism.

(iii) There are different, hierarchically ordered levels of interpretation of the same rite.

(iv) Newar data support an analytical distinction between three hierarchically ordered types of religion, a distinction which may indeed be universally valid: between soteriology and worldly religion, in the first place, and within the latter between social religion and instrumental religion (see Figure 1, p. 6). These themes interlock and each supports the others.

It is the doctrine of the Three Ways which Newar Buddhists themselves use to explain the relation of their religion to Theravāda Buddhism and also to explain the structure of their own rites and practices. In comparative terms Theravāda Buddhism provides for amazingly little social religion and permits instrumental religion only on very restrictive terms. Newar Buddhism, by contrast, has expanded to include all types of social religion and to supply enthusiastically any instrumental needs the laity may have, while yet remaining fundamentally a soteriology.

Carrithers (1984) has suggested that the history of the (Theravāda) Monastic Community in Sri Lanka could be written in terms of three adaptations and a response: it has adapted to roles as ceremonial specialist, landlord, and political actor respectively; it has responded by preserving the ideal, and among a minority the role, of meditating forest monk. The Vajrācāryas and Śākyas of Nepal adapted in very similar ways. They also became landlords, but in this case it was not monastery servants who were the crucial adaptive mechanism for administering the land, but the *guthi* which indeed may have originally been inspired by the example of monastic organization (§8.3). Vajrācāryas and Śākyas did not have a political role like that of the Theravāda Saṃgha in Sri Lanka, since Buddhism was never the official national religion; the closest they came was the relatively unimportant position of *rājguru*, the chief Vajrācārya who advised the king on Buddhist affairs in the Malla period. Surprising though it may seem, the Newars also preserved the forest monk ideal: it was the underlying rationale of the *bahī* class of monasteries (see §6.2; Gellner 1987b). The *bahī* may be compared to the 'forest monks' of the Asgiri segment of the Siyam Nikaya in Sri Lanka, who inherited the position of a 'forest' monk movement but have now come to live in villages exactly as the 'village' monks do. Although the Newars have preserved traces of this ideal it has been marginalized, at least as a permanent role. With the development of the Great Way and the Diamond Way, other ideals (those of the *bodhisattva* and *siddha*) superseded it. Within the Diamond Way there is, rather, the practice of temporary retreats known as 'puraścaraṇ cwanegu' which Vajrācāryas used to perform near or in a temple of Vajrayoginī.

Finally, and most obviously, like the Theravāda monks of Sri Lanka, Vajrācāryas have adapted to, and indeed become identified with, the role of religious specialist. Carrithers writes that the Theravādin laity could accrue merit for three purposes:

> It could be stored up by oneself for a better rebirth; it could be given to dead relatives for their future welfare; or it could be given to gods so that they would help one in some worldly aim. These correspond very roughly to the three chief services provided for the laity by the monks in Sri Lanka today, and probably since the

earliest days: preaching, presiding at funerals, and chanting *pirit*, texts designed to improve one's material and psychical[1] state.

(Carrithers 1984: 134)

In a different form all three of these services are provided by Vajrācāryas. Preaching occurs, but has a lesser place, and is less frequent than in the Theravāda; the texts are often Rebirth stories, or the life of the Buddha according to the Lalitavistara. At funerals a whole series of rituals are provided for the Buddhist laity, and in particular a reworking in a Buddhist idiom of Hindu Ancestor Worship (often interpreted as feeding the ancestors). Like both Theravāda monks and Brahmans, the Vajrācārya priest receives gifts on behalf of the dead person. Protective texts are also provided. In the Newar case, the Pañcarakṣā was traditionally the most common, the laity themselves being able to recite various *dhāraṇī* according to the affliction in question. Alongside these continuities with and adaptations of the original pre-Mahāyāna adaptations, there are others going far beyond what the Theravādins accepted: the provision of life-cycle rites, regular festivals, and manifold objects and methods of devotion. 'Theravādins only have to worship the Buddha', say Śākyas and Vajrācāryas, 'our householder *dharma* is much more demanding.' They see what scholars often represent as an indulgence to lay needs, as a higher, more onerous path.

The scholars of the past have tended to judge Newar Buddhism by the canons of Theravāda Buddhism and to find it wanting. They have also tended to assimilate it to Hinduism. There are two problems here. Very rarely do people stop to consider what kind of Hinduism they are referring to. Where it is a question of Hindu influence on Newar Buddhism, I have tried to specify in each case what the influence is: of Brahmanical values, of Tantric Śaivism, or of a caste environment. The second point is that, quite simply, Newar Buddhism did retain a strong self-identity. It is unthinkable for Vajrācāryas, Śākyas, or Tulādhar *et al.* to be anything other than Buddhist. Certainly Newar Buddhism *appears* Hindu in many respects: rites are parallel, yet distinct, so that similarity or difference can be stressed according to context. Newar Buddhists naturally fall into a Hindu way of speaking when explaining to outsiders what they are about. Most observers relying on interpreters or speaking in Nepali have taken this preliminary explanation as the whole story.

To see Mahāyāna and Vajrayāna Buddhism of the Newars as Hinduized Buddhism is not wrong, but it corresponds to only one way in which Newar Buddhists themselves see their religion. The same objection can be made to

Greenwold's (1974a: 122) description of it, following La Vallée Poussin, as 'the "buddhized" aspect of contemporaneous Nepalese Hinduism'. Neither of these views takes into account Newar Buddhists' belief in the superiority of their religion to Hinduism. That a full Buddhist identity is retained by them can be seen by a comparison with the caste of married Śaivite renouncers (*saṃnyāsī*) living in the Nepalese hills, described by Véronique Bouillier. They perform only initiation and death rites differently from (Parbatiyā) Chetris, with whom they intermarry to a certain degree. Marriage, birth rites, and calendrical festivals are all identical. They accept the services of and the superiority of Brahmans. Their renouncer identity gives to their life 'in the world' 'a certain ascetic "coloration"; this "coloration" is not enough to call into question their integration into the [social] system, but does allow them to be distinguished from other castes' (Bouillier 1979: 212). The position of Newar Buddhism goes far beyond this: it exists in a Hindu environment, but it does not need that environment. Newar Buddhists do not accept the superiority of Brahmans and do not require their presence; Newar Buddhism has not become a mere sect of Hinduism. Rather, it has preserved a complex ritual and ideological vision. Even within Hinduism it is an oversimplification to reduce all renunciatory traditions to an opposition between the man-in-the-world and the renouncer. As Burghart argues:

> [T]he only general statement which one can make concerning asceticism in the religious traditions of South Asia is that all ascetics see themselves as followers of some path which releases them from the transient world (*not* the social world) and that all ascetics distinguish themselves from non-ascetics who do not seek such release. The criteria must be specified in each case, for one sect does not necessarily accept the criteria of other sects.
>
> (Burghart 1983: 643; italics in the original)

Since this is so of Hindu sects, it is *a fortiori* simplistic to see Newar Buddhists merely as Hinduized, or as monks who have abandoned the Buddhist path.

The position of Buddhism in Bali presents an instructive contrast. The number of Buddhist priests in Bali is very small indeed, thus inverting the position in the Kathmandu Valley where Brahmans are few and Vajrācāryas many. The daily ritual of Balinese Buddhist priests, recited in Sanskrit, is remarkably similar to that of the Vajrācāryas' tradition, and contains many verses also found in the Newars' *guru maṇḍala* ritual (Lévi 1933: 79, 82; Hooykas 1973: 103, 114). At the same time it includes the placing of various forms of Śiva on the body, and invocations to Śiva, in a way which would never be found in a Buddhist ritual in Nepal (Hooykas 1973: 65, 87).

Further, it seems that the distinction between Śaiva and Buddhist priests is of little consequence to the vast majority of ordinary Balinese. It is therefore probably fair to view the Buddhist priests of Bali, like the married ascetics of the Nepalese hills, as a sectarian tradition within Hinduism.

It is Tibetan Buddhism which is closest, in terms of scripture and liturgy, to Newar Buddhism. Tantric Buddhism exists also in Japan, and the techniques of visualization appear to be very similar, if not identical, to those outlined above (Yokoyama 1983: 71; Yamasaki 1988: 154–9). But the Japanese lack the highest level (Yogānuttara) deities (Cakrasaṃvara and the rest). Tibetan Buddhism, unlike Newar Buddhism, came to dominate the whole of Tibetan culture. Tibetan Buddhist monks reached a very high degree of intellectual sophistication and were able to analyse, organize, and extend the vast Tantric (and other) scriptural corpus in ways the Newars could not. Monastic institutions became increasingly important and monastic personnel, as is well known, came to fill the highest offices of state. Among the Newars, by contrast, the position of Buddhism was very different: celibate monasticism as a corporate way of life died out, and Buddhism became a minority religion under Hindu kings. The Newars lacked the powerful monastic institutions both of Tibet and of the Theravāda countries. Thus the Newars cannot validly be included along with the 'Buddhist States' of the Theravāda countries, as is done in Samuel's otherwise suggestive article which contrasts Tibet with such Buddhist states, and likens it instead to decentralized Muslim polities (Samuel 1982). Samuel is right, however, that the Newars, living in a settled, rice-growing society, with a relatively strong (though small) state, have strong kin institutions and have developed a communal form of Buddhism. Had the Malla kings of Nepal favoured Buddhism, substantial monastic institutions might have been encouraged under their sponsorship. In fact it seems rather, as suggested above (§2.3), that the Mallas preferred to keep Buddhism as the religion of their low-status subjects, reserving the full range of Brahmanical services for themselves and their immediate followers.

On the face of it, Tibetan religion is more individualistic, and less communal, than the Buddhism of the Newars (Ortner 1978, 1989), at least if the Sherpas are as typical of Tibet as Samuel (1978) suggests. Tibetans seem not to have evolved the social, communal uses of Tantra, discussed above (§11.1), at least to the same degree; their communal rituals seem to be more a question of individuals pooling their effort, rather than groups expressing their solidarity. Nonetheless, there is in Tibet a small stratum of hereditary priestly lineages, of which the most famous is that of the Sa-kya lamas; there are also numerous commoner hereditary religious specialists (*ser-ky'im*).[2] It is possible that Tantric justifications of their position, or even just of the clan rituals of lay groups, may be, or may have been, more common than has hitherto been appreciated.

Another difference between Tibetan and Newar Buddhism – probably unrelated to the question of individual versus communal forms of action – has to do with the general flavour and tenor of that part of the ritual directed at lower powers. Tibetan Buddhist rituals seem to lay greater stress on the aggressive expulsion or killing of scapegoats (Ortner 1978: chapter 5), which occurs occasionally, or on the regular sacrifice to the Buddhas of Rudra (Śiva) understood as a symbol of all one's moral obstacles (*kleśa*).[3] In Newar Buddhist ritual there is only the unmarked and unemotional offering to lower spirits, the Spirit-Offering. A parallel to the Tibetan scapegoat sacrifice would be rather the *Hindu* sacrifice of a pumpkin or other vegetable substitute at Mohanī (§7.4).

Although it is less dominant in the society as a whole than Theravāda Buddhism is in south-east Asia or Sri Lanka, Newar Buddhism is less restricted, at least where Śākyas, Vajrācāryas, and Tulādhar *et al.*, are concerned, in its application to individuals' lives. For Tambiah's (1970: 376) villagers in north-east Thailand, Buddhism is incorporated into the life-cycle. Buddhism is something men do (a) in youth (as an initiation into adulthood), and (b) in old age. As with W. Christian's northern Spanish villagers 'activity and religiosity are incompatible' (Christian 1989: 158). Piety is for old age or for those not actively involved in the struggles and compromises of earning a living. To a degree Newars do share this view. But there is much less sense that life in the world is incompatible with piety. Religion gives a place to male camaraderie in hymn-singing (*bhajan*) and (more staidly) hymn-chanting (*tutaḥ*) groups, and women of all ages are keen temple-goers and participants in Observances.

In Thailand the village ritualist (*paahm* from '*brāhmaṇ*') must have passed through temporary ordination as a monk, but is junior to all monks, whatever their respective ages (Tambiah 1970: 256). In the same way the Vajrācārya must have been ordained as a monk, but since this is Vajrayāna Buddhism, he has the highest status, above monks. Not only does the Vajrācārya incorporate within himself the status of monk, he goes further even than most Tibetan ritual practitioners (who are equally Vajrayānists) in incorporating opposed religious specialisms. Thus even among the Tamangs, who live around the Kathmandu Valley and would be viewed as unorthodox by many other Tibetan Buddhists, their (married) lamas do not take on sacrificial functions and do not oversee animal sacrifices (Holmberg

1989), as Vajrācāryas do. There remains among the Newars, as in all Buddhist societies, an opposition between the Buddhist ritual specialist on the one hand, and the shaman, medium, or psychopomp on the other (§11.4).

The hierarchy of the Three Ways enables Newar Buddhism to be extraordinarily flexible. As we have noted, it allows Newar Buddhists to locate themselves in relation to the Theravāda, and to explain how their tradition is both a continuation of it and yet superior. The structure of the exposition (chapters 6 to 10) is intended to illustrate this. At the same time the Three Ways also place Newar Buddhism in relation to Hinduism. While all Three Ways are distinct from Hinduism it is clear to Newars that the Diamond Way is closest to Tantric Śaivism. Tantrism, as Toffin (1984: 566 n. 8) points out, provides a common idiom for the two religions. The Disciples' Way on the other hand, with its symbols of monasticism, plays a crucial role in keeping Buddhism and Hinduism distinct. It is perhaps ironic that from the point of view of Hindu outsiders it is this specifically Buddhist (Śrāvakayāna) identity which is 'secret', whereas the common (public) symbols of Tantrism and common ritual practices make the Vajrācāryas seem like a kind of Hindu practitioner. Where Newar Buddhism's own lay adherents are concerned, by contrast, it is the combination of Śrāvakayāna Monastic Initiation and control of the Diamond Way which keeps *them* apart from the sacerdotal caste, serving to legitimize the latter's hereditary prerogative (§9.2, 11.1). Meanwhile the Great Way provides a devotion-orientated and altruistic idiom of salvation for all (§6.3, 7.5).

Like all forms of traditional Buddhism, Newar Buddhism recognizes spiritual hierarchy. It is true that all Buddhism presupposes spiritual equality of opportunity over the long run. But the long run means many hundreds of lifetimes, so that at any given moment some are always more advanced than others. Consequently Buddhism is inherently elitist (cf. Samuel 1978: 52). Newar Buddhists also recognize a social hierarchy, which they tend to justify in terms of the spiritual hierarchy. Corresponding to this are various levels of interpretation (§4.4, 10.3). It is considered natural that there should be different levels of understanding. Deference to Vajrācāryas is an important factor ensuring that different interpretations and diverse rites are all considered to be aspects of one path. Vajrācāryas are not only ritual experts but guardians of the knowledge on which the rituals are based. Anyone attempting to solicit the opinions of ordinary Newar Buddhists is frequently told to go and ask a Vajrācārya for the answer.

These levels of explanation do not correspond exactly to the Three Ways. The doctrine of the Three Ways is, after all, a scriptural theory, albeit one which has been built into the ritual and organization of Newar Buddhism. But one part of the hierarchy of explanations can on one local interpretation be read in terms of the difference between the Great Way and the Diamond Way. At the lowest level are non-Buddhist explanations in terms of tradition and magic. These, for want of a better expression, I have called 'folk religion'. They are the practices which are neither clearly Buddhist nor Hindu, although they are done by people who in other contexts are Buddhists or Hindus or both. Above this comes the first level of Buddhist explanation: in terms of devotion, protection, and exchange, which Weber (1968: 424) called the '*do ut des* [I give so that you will give] . . . [which] clings to the routine and the mass religious behavior of all people at all times and in all religions'. To call this 'popular Buddhism' and imply thereby that it is not really Buddhist is misleading at best: as Gombrich (1971: 319) points out, such practices have always been a part of Buddhism. Newar Buddhists recognize them as authentically Buddhist, while also believing that there are other, more spiritually advanced practices and other, more advanced ways of regarding the same practices (§10.3). The most readily available of the more advanced practices are those of the Diamond Way.

The notion of hierarchy used here is that familiar from the work of Louis Dumont.[4] Hierarchy for Dumont is based on the repeated application of a polar opposition in which one pole is superior to the other. At one level the two poles are set in opposition to each other. At a higher level the unmarked pole 'encompasses' the marked pole. That is, at the higher level the superior pole stands for the whole which is made up of the two poles taken together. For Dumont the caste system is based on the opposition of the pure to the impure and its corollary, the separation of status from power. Whether or not Dumont's framework is the most adequate for the analysis of caste and traditional South Asian society – a question on which there is a burgeoning literature[5] – the concept of hierarchy Dumont proposes is, I would suggest, important and fruitful. The hierarchy in question here is not, like the Hindu caste hierarchy, primarily social. Newar Buddhism does indeed accept the caste hierarchy of pure and impure but it does not give it the highest value. Salvation and the knowledge or insight which saves, the ritual means to which are the monopoly of Vajrācāryas, are placed highest. Soteriology 'encompasses', in Dumont's terms, the thisworldly religion which is opposed to it at a lower level. In a similar way, instrumental religion is opposed to, but subsumed within, other-directed forms of religious action, whether social or soteriological. The hierarchy of the Three Ways can be regarded in the same way. The Śrāvakayāna is opposed to the Mahāyāna at one level, but subsumed within it at a higher level. The same is true of the relation of the Mahāyāna to the Vajrayāna. Here, however, the whole made up of the Mahāyāna-plus-Vajrayāna tends to be called 'Mahāyāna' because of the esoteric associations of the Vajrayāna (see Figure 13).

The fourth theme, the distinction between soteriology, social religion, and instrumental religion, is crucial for understanding the difference between Theravāda Buddhism on the one hand, and on the other the Mahāyāna and Vajrayāna of the Newars. Theravāda Buddhism is a soteriology which tolerates limited instrumental use of its resources on condition that the cognitively orthodox explanation is retained. Newar Buddhism is a soteriology which *positively encourages* social and instrumental ritual and belief, provided that they remain within a framework which gives salvation the highest value. Although the highest Way, Vajrayāna, is used to legitimize and symbolize group boundaries, its primary focus remains on the individual. In spite of the altruistic emphasis of the Mahāyāna, the reform of this world – punishing evildoers, attacking witches – is not the business of Buddhas.[6] The Vajrācāryas who do use Tantric means to these ends find it a double-edged sword. Though Newars may fear their displeasure, the healers' spiritual superiority is often doubted. The belief that, in the nature of things, sin is automatically punished sooner or later is still a fundamental part of Newar Buddhism.

The distinction between soteriology and thisworldly religion is fundamental to all traditional scriptural religions of South Asia.[7] Mandelbaum (1966) labelled these the 'transcendental' and 'pragmatic' aspects of religion respectively. Babb (1975: 212) has criticized this terminology on the grounds that transcendental religion contains much that is in fact pragmatic. Concepts are indeed tidier than reality. The opposition is expressed 'on the ground' as the difference between types of religious specialists. Looked at in this way, the opposition is between the transcendental-plus-pragmatic (in which power used for instrumental and social purposes is derived from soteriological sources) versus the purely pragmatic. In Mandelbaum's terms all Three Ways of Newar Buddhism are transcendental systems, adapted in different ways to social and instrumental interests, the Diamond Way doing so with the most enthusiasm and fewest caveats. The advantage of the terminology used here is that it distinguishes – within 'pragmatic' religion – social religion (the religion of the group) from instrumental religion (which is, paradigmatically, self-interested action by an individual).

I offer a final contrast with the medieval English church as characterized by Keith Thomas (1978: 52ff.). According to Thomas it was basically salvation orientated, but tolerated magic in the form of miracles and holy sites on the grounds that they increased devotion and encouraged conversion. It was hostile, however, to what it categorized as superstition, which effectively meant magic not controlled by the Church (ibid.: 55). Mahāyāna Buddhism equally accepts miracles, holy sites, and magical acts in order to draw as much lay religious activity as possible into the Buddhist sphere, but it lacks the negative and condemnatory concept of superstition in the sense of 'false and heretical belief about the empirical world'.[8] There is no religious duty to combat and suppress erroneous expectations. Rather, there is an important, ideologically central, scriptural charter for encouraging faith in the Buddha, Dharma, and Saṃgha, by whatever means necessary, including making promises and assumptions which are true only in that they lead eventually to salvation. This is the doctrine of 'skill in means', exemplified by the scriptural stories in which Karuṇāmaya assumes whatever form is required, including that of Hindu gods, to lead people onto the right path. Vajrācāryas often regard mediums with scepticism and even dismiss the claims of any given specialist as wholly false, but they do not regard other priestly specialists or other paths to salvation in the same way, nor do they – or can they – dismiss the possibility of spirit-possession altogether. Other paths are ranked lower than the Buddhist way, but are considered valid for their traditional adherents. In a religiously plural situation of this sort there can be no question of claiming a monopoly of access to the sacred or the supernatural. Rather, the adherents of one religion claim that their own way subsumes or 'encompasses' the others. If one looks for a more radical rejection of others' claims, one finds only the teaching, accepted on trust by Newar Buddhists, that all beliefs about the empirical world are illusory when seen in the light of the ultimate salvific gnosis.

Notes

Notes to chapter 1

1 It is necessary to call this the 'South Asian cultural environment' rather than the 'Indian cultural environment' because 'India' refers to a recently created political unit, a point about which the Nepalese are understandably sensitive.

2 I have briefly surveyed the anthropology of Theravāda Buddhism, and suggested some reasons for the relative neglect of Mahāyāna Buddhism, in a separate paper (Gellner 1990).

3 Lienhard (1978: 243) makes the same point. It seems that there are, even now, some survivals of Tantric Buddhism in Bangladesh, but only at a 'folk' level, that is, without a specialist class of ritual and religious experts to maintain a distinctive Great Tradition.

4 The tiny Risshū sect in Nara, Japan, whose monks claim that they base their practice entirely on one of the pre-Mahāyāna codes (Richard Gombrich, personal communication), is a small, and arguably partial, exception to this generalization.

5 *Nibbāna* is the same word as *nirvāṇa*, *kamma* the same as *karma*. The former is Pali, the latter Sanskrit, in each case.

6 A brief and simplified overview of this sort is Gellner 1988c. A rather different approach is taken by Lienhard 1978. Toffin (1984) is a massive and very important attempt at such a synthesis, but has minimal information on Buddhism.

7 I have discussed these types of religion at greater length elsewhere (Gellner 1988b).

8 Spiro (1982: 208) brings out what these two types of religion have in common by calling them both instrumental: the difference, which I think it essential to capture in one's terminology, is that the result aimed at by soteriology lies in the next life.

9 Partly as a response to this need, a volume edited by Declan Quigley and me, provisionally titled *Newar Society*, is currently in preparation. In this six anthropologists of the Newars attempt to pool their different knowledge of Newar social organization.

10 It is possible that *Mesocosm* (University of California Press), Robert Levy's long-awaited work on Bhaktapur, will be a monograph of this sort.

11 There are said to be some Maharjans in Kirtipur and the west of the Valley who claim descent from the Gopālas.

12 See Lévi 1905 II: 80; K.P Malla 1985b: vi.

13 The best summary in English of the history of Licchavi, Ṭhakurī, and Malla periods is in Slusser 1982. On recent politics and the political history of Nepal, see Joshi and Rose 1966; Gaborieau 1982a; Burghart 1984; and Shaha 1982 (which was effectively, though informally, banned for naming the eighteen most powerful people around the King). An excellent introduction on the anthropology of Nepal, including the politics of modern Nepal up to the mid-1970s, is Gaborieau 1978. A good survey of Nepal's ecological and economic problems is Blaikie *et al.* 1980.

14 On the history of Nepali, see Hutt 1988.

15 I have gone into this question in greater depth, and attacked the simple two-part Hindu-tribal model often used to explain Nepalese social history in two separate articles (Gellner 1986, 1991a).

16 On language politics in the Tarai, and over the border among Indian Maithils, see Gaige 1975: chapter 6, and Brass 1974 respectively. On early publishing in Nepali, see Hutt 1988: chapter 9.

17 I have examined the Newars' cultural nationalism, and its relationship both to Newar identity and to the Theravāda Buddhist movement, in a separate article (Gellner 1986).

18 Gaige 1975: 162; cf. Shaha 1982: 96. For figures showing Brahman, Chetri, and Newar representation in administrative positions, in the intelligentsia, and elsewhere, see Gaige 1975: 147, 164–7; Malla 1979b: 200; Höfer 1979: 208 fn. 33; Gellner 1986: 142. Newar representation in the army has always been low, since in the early Shah and Rana periods they were barred from it.

19 See Burghart (1984) for a discussion of the process of redefinition and reconceptualization which was involved in this.

20 On the Newars' urban life-style, even when they inhabit villages, see Quigley (1984: chapters 1 and 7) and references given at Toffin 1984: 57 n. 22.

21 This theme is illustrated for Panauti in Barré *et al.* 1981.

22 These types are outlined in greater detail in Gellner 1986. One should perhaps add to this typology bazaar towns in the Tarai, such as Biratnagar, where there are large numbers of Nepali-speaking Newars, and also a number of Tarai peasant villages said to describe themselves as Newar.

23 See M.C. Regmi 1976: 221, and Joshi and Rose 1966: 465–7. The decline in the landlord's share of the harvest is a matter of frequent complaint by high-caste Newars. It has been offset for some by spectacular increases in land values in the Valley.

24 'Kathmandu, Your Kathmandu' (Malla 1979b: 212).

25 Cf. Slusser 1982: 59b. There are chronicles attributing similar if not identical regulations to other Malla kings, namely Siddhi Narasiṃha and Viṣṇu Malla, in Hodgson's papers (vols. 51:176ff. and 59:93ff. respectively).

26 Cf. Toffin 1984: 589–90.

27 See M.A. Stein 1900: 74; Locke 1985: 482.

28 Locke 1986: 66. See Sakya and Vaidya (1970: 29–31) for the inscription; for summaries of it, see Locke 1980: 42 fn. 44, or 1985: 489 n. 50.

29 On the *bahī* see §6.2 below, and more particularly Gellner 1987b and Locke 1985.

30 See the references given on p. 350, n. 7.

31 For a Spanish example of the same sentiment, see Christian 1989: 22.

32 On Newar kinship terminology, see Toffin 1975, 1984: 167–72, and Quigley 1984: 175–82.

33 As for the causes of division, one could apply equally to the Newars Parry's (1979: 193–4) distinction between the underlying cause (the tension between a man's loyalty to the joint family and his loyalty to his own wife and children), the predisposing cause (the fact that because of inequalities of income, separation becomes advantageous to one or other party at a specific time), and the immediate cause (usually a quarrel, often blamed on women).

34 In Dhulikhel, Quigley (1985a) reports, generation takes precedence over age where these conflict. According to my information from Lalitpur, this does not always happen. Toffin (n.d.) relates a serious dispute within the Kathmandu Rājopādhyāya community occasioned by a conflict over precedence between a man and his uncle who was younger than him.

35 Toffin (1984: 398) recorded only 3% matrilocal unions in Panauti. As Nepali (1965: 235) notes, a man who lives with his wife's family is a butt of jokes and contempt. He heard of two cases in the village of Panga and found no cases at all in 224 marriages in Kathmandu.

36 Macdonald and Vergati Stahl 1979: 115–18; Slusser 1982: 130–4; Shepard 1985. In particular one should consult Barré *et al.* 1981: 97–162, and Gutschow *et al.* 1987: 134–8. Barré *et al.* discuss the different and changing styles of house.

37 On these, see the references given on p. 371, n. 6.

Notes to chapter 2

1 On these distinctions in the Law Code of 1854, see Höfer 1979: 45. The verb *jiye* in the first expression means 'to be permitted/right' and the verb *juye* in the second expression is the auxiliary verb 'to be' used with Indo-European loan verbs. They are not the same. The abbreviated expression *majupī̃* refers to the larger grouping, i.e. all unclean castes.

2 For a general analysis of how these rules work see Stevenson 1954. On the Newars, see Toffin 1984: 279–86.

3 Kölver and Śākya (1985: 46) seem to be surprised that this superiority of Śākya and Vajrācāryas is invariably expressed in Malla-period land documents, and put forward the unconvincing hypothesis that only scribes accepted their superiority.

4 It may look as if *kujāt* actually means 'bad' or 'evil' caste, but in fact *kujāt* is a contraction of *kwahā̃ wāgu jāt* ('caste gone low', i.e. low caste) or *kwajāt*.

5 Fürer-Haimendorf (1956: 34) recorded the Nepali expresssion 'si̊ḍhī caḍnu', 'to climb the ladder', used to describe the social climbing of Śreṣṭha or would-be Śreṣṭha Newars. I did not hear it used spontaneously but the term was recognized by some informants.

6 See Snellgrove (1987: 198–213) for an analysis of the mandala in Tantric Buddhism. Understood primarily as a 'sacred enclosure' it 'becomes the most potent expression of pantheistic realization that has ever been devised'. See also

§10.2 below for a brief summary of how this is achieved. On the mandala in Tantric Hinduism, see Sanderson 1986 and Gupta 1989.

7 On this theme see Gutschow and Kölver 1975, Barré *et al.* 1981, Toffin 1981b, Gutschow 1982, and Gellner 1984. Kölver (1976) discusses a fifty-year-old painting-cum-map which represents the city of Bhaktapur as a mandala.

8 See Gutschow (1982) for maps of Lalitpur showing all these various divisions (except that for Yẽnyāḥ). The division into twenty-four localities is reflected roughly by twenty-four stopping places for processions around the main festival route (Gutschow's Figures 170 and 188).

9 Barré *et al.* 1981: 91. The only attempt to test quantitatively how far Newars really do perceive their surroundings in terms of the mandala model is that of Stoddard 1979. Although the testing was evidently superficial and liable to error, one plausible conclusion to emerge was that Newars perceive shrines in their immediate vicinity in this way more readily than the more distant sets of four Gaṇeś or four Nārāyaṇa in the Valley as a whole.

10 On Nepal, see Burghart 1984.

11 According to Toffin (1989) the total community of Rājopādhyāyas, men, women, and children, numbers only 1500.

12 Both Jośī and Karmācārya groups within the Śreṣṭhas admit to being Kṣatriyas now (cf. Höfer 1979: 140 fn. 31), but claim a Brahman origin in line with their sacerdotal functions. For a Newar Brahman arguing that some Śreṣṭhas are 'really' Brahmans, others Vaiśyas, and only certain of them 'really' Kṣatriya, see Greenwold 1975: 69. This sort of argument is based on current occupations and on a reluctance to concede Kṣatriya status to the lower Pā̃ctharīya Śreṣṭhas.

13 The meaning of the term *thar*, as it is used today, is discussed at length below (§2.6). In the time of Prithvi Narayan Shah there were in Gorkha thirty-six 'high-class' (*tharghar*) clans, Brahman and Kṣatriya, who monopolized state positions, of whom the top six were called *chatra* (Lévi 1905 I: 286). Hodgson (Papers 18: 85, reproduced at Hasrat 1970: 71 fn. 2 and 85 fn. 2) gives *khumopama*, i.e. *khumha paḥmã/paḥmāy* (the six Pradhāns), as the Newari for *tharghar*. According to Baburam Acharya (1979: 14) these Newar Śreṣṭhas adopted the Nepali name 'Chatharīya' from the Gorkhalis, and 'Pā̃ctharīya' was a 'meaningless name' derived for those of lower rank on the model of 'Chatharīya'. One often hears the folk etymology which derives 'Chatharīya' from 'Chetri', i.e. Kṣatriya.

14 It is these hill Śreṣṭhas who are being thought of when non-Newars assert that Newars are Vaiśyas (merchants) (Bista 1972: 30; Sharma 1977: 284 n. 18), since they fit into this position just below the Parbatiyā Chetris (Kṣatriyas). Nonetheless the Law Code of the Ranas classified them as Śūdras (menials), not as Vaiśyas, because they drink alcohol (Höfer 1979: 117).

15 For further details on the Maharjans of Lalitpur and Kathmandu, see Gellner and Pradhan n.d.

16 According to G.S. Nepali (1965: 163, 295) the Lalitpur Tāmrakārs say that they migrated to Nepal from Mathura, and this, if true, and of recent date, might account for their strong Hindu leanings. Deriving valid historical explanations from traditions like these, which are intimately tied in with a caste's self-image and public face, is a tricky business.

17 See Vaidya (1986), pp. 132–6 for the fast and p. 135 for this incident. He claims that the woman was a Tāmrakār, but in view of their preference for Hinduism, Jog Maya's memory that she was a Śilpakār is more plausible. See Shepard (1985) for further details on the Tāmrakār *et al.* She refers to the whole caste as Pā̃cthare, but this, I believe, is a mistake: this name is always understood as referring to low Śreṣṭhas, as described above.

18 Cf. Toffin 1984: 233. For further details see Gellner and Pradhan n.d.

19 See the excellent maps in Gutschow (1982: 49, 119, 162) which show how in each of the three cities of the Valley the Dyaḥlā live outside the city gates and the Khaḍgī just inside them. A few further details on the Khaḍgī of Bhaktapur are to be found in Wegner 1988.

20 Gaborieau (1982a: 285) points out that much of this is rhetoric, and he argues that in practice Hinduism plays a smaller role in the official ideology of modern Nepal than Islam does in Pakistan.

21 Tibetan Buddhists' pilgrimage routes take in all the above (Dowman 1981; cf. Lévi 1905 II: 355, on Paśupati). Untouchables were forbidden to enter Paśupati by a law of 1924 (Höfer 1979: 102 fn. 26); this no doubt restated pre-existing convention.

22 Höfer 1979: 160. Höfer suggests that *yantradīkṣā* might mean 'marriage rites', but it clearly refers to Buddhist Tantric Initiation, which indeed *buddhamārgī* Śreṣṭhas, and even some *śivamārgī* ones, were traditionally entitled to take.

23 On the basis of this it is tempting, but quite possibly misguided, to argue by extrapolation that in pre-Malla Nepal, i.e. before 1200, most of the population were Buddhist. Licchavi Nepal had, side by side, important Buddhist monasteries and large Hindu temples. We cannot say which, if either, religion was favoured by the majority (Riccardi 1980: 266).

24 See Locke 1980: 335, 338; D.R. Regmi 1965 II: 258; Burleigh 1976: 21.

25 Buddhist informants recalled that in the old days Jośī daughters given in marriage to Śreṣṭha families had to bathe and fast for a day before being re-admitted to the kitchen of their natal home.

26 On Bu Bāhāḥ, see Locke 1985: 156–8. In the case of Michu Bāhāḥ the claim is based on the myth that they carried the deity of Kwā Bāhāḥ to Lalitpur in their basket (see Gellner 1987b). Lok Bahadur Shakya (1984: 27) writes that members of Bhĩchẽ Bāhāḥ are supposed to be Nāpit in origin, members of Dhum Bāhāḥ Nakarmī, and members of Cikã Bahī Karamjit-Mānandhar (sic: *bhāḥsāymi*). These informal identifications are not, it will be observed, consistent. They grow up, I suspect, out of associations with other castes who happen to live in the locality of the monastery in question. Their main use, as far as Śākyas and Vajrācāryas are concerned, is for making fun of their caste fellows (often affines) living in another locality. It would be a mistake to use such associations as a basis for the reconstruction of the history of Newar Buddhism, although the Bu Bāhāḥ traditions may well have some basis in fact (see below p. 355, n. 27).

27 See p. 63 for a translation of BV (Wright 1972: 185) on this point. This is to assume that BV, written in the nineteenth century, is correct, on this point at least, in recording events of the late fourteenth century.

28 Buddhist modernists evidently do this everywhere. Houtman (1984: 67–8) reports it for village Burma. A particularly virulent example occurred in a

Nepalese Buddhist magazine, *Ananda-Bhoomi*, 11 (7) (Nov. 1983), when it published an article entitled 'Lamaism is not Buddhism but a copy of Hinduism.' The modernist, and usually Theravāda, view, coincides therefore with the official Hindu one.

29 See Gombrich 1971: 321–7. Theravāda Buddhists in Nepal recognize this too. See, for example, the article 'Buddhism and Householder Happiness' by J. Shakya, in *Ananda-Bhoomi*, 11 (2) (June 1983), which makes precisely this point, that Buddhism is not just for monks.

30 On the distinction between *guru* and *purohit* among Newar Brahmans, see Toffin 1989, and on Hindu death specialists Toffin 1979b, 1987.

31 Though Newars do not use the adjective *jajmānī*, they frequently use the terms *jajmān* and *jaymā* for the patron who employs a specialist: see below, §5.1, for their use in ritual. Only priests (Brahmans, Vajrācāryas, and Karmācāryas) and Jośīs receive *dakṣiṇā*; the payment given to Barbers and other low-status specialists is not so designated.

32 See below §11.2. Cf. Toffin 1979a: 77; Gupta and Gombrich 1986: 132ff.

33 *Tāremāṃ* is often understood to be a short form of *tāre māṃ śaraṇa*, and this is glossed as 'Oh Tārā, my refuge', which is intuitively plausible but grammatically incorrect (genitive for accusative is normal, but not vice versa). According to Asha Kaji Vajracharya the phrase originates in the verse: *Buddhaṃ dharmaṃ ca saṃghaṃ ca bhajāmi ṣarvadā tu 'ham/ Tārām jineśvarīṃ caiva māṃ tāraya iti smṛtaḥ* (I worship always the Buddha, the Dharma and the Saṃgha, as well as Tārā, empress of the Buddhas; I think always 'Save me').

34 An exception here is the fact that some low castes follow the Śreṣṭha pattern of observing a young boy's first tonsure (*busākhā*) as a separate life-cycle ritual (see below §7.2).

35 Tibetan Buddhist influence was confined either to individuals or to relatively superficial borrowings (e.g. prayer wheels). Although contact was continuous (Lewis and Jamspal 1988), Vajrācārya priests seem never to have incorporated Tibetan practice into the Newar tradition.

36 The only exception to this generalization of which I am aware is the cult of Chwāskāminī, a Tibetan Buddhist goddess, in Khāsti (Bauddha). That Newar artisans and shopkeepers there, many of whom once traded in Tibet and all of whom cater to a Tibetan Buddhist clientele, should carry on such a cult is not surprising.

37 On the fundamentally isogamous nature of Newar marriage, see Quigley 1986.

38 BV: 108^{2-4}. Here is a case in which Wright's (1972: 185) translation is very misleading, implying as it does that Vajrācāryas and Śākyas were classified by Sthiti Malla's *paṇḍits* as Brahmans or Kṣatriyas.

39 On the Vajrācārya preference for Vajrācārya wives, see below, §9.2. Lewis (n.d.) reports a slight preference for caste sub-group endogamy on the part of the nine sub-groups which make up the Tulādhar *et al.* in Kathmandu. Among Parbatiyās, whose *thar* do not so much resemble castes, there is, by contrast, a slight preference for marrying *out* (Bennett 1983: 18).

40 This would explain V.P.P. Joshi's (1956: 34) gloss of *kunā̃* (nickname) with *thar*.

41 Some try to derive *gubhāju* from *guru-bhāju*, 'teacher gentleman' (C. Vajracharya 1983: 7; S.M. Joshi 1987: s.v.) or from *guthi* plus *bhāju* (*Ināp* II, 22: 4).

The correct etymology seems to be *guru-bhaṭṭāraka-ju* via *guru-bharāda-ju*, whereas *bhāju* comes from Skt. *bhadraloka* (Manandhar 1986: s.v.).

42 For the concept of essentially contested concepts, which seems particularly apt in attempting to explain the diverse designations of castes in the Newar context, see Gallie 1964: chapter 8.

43 However, there are some articulate Maharjans who display considerable subtlety in arguing that they are Hindus. They may say, 'We are *śivamat* but not exclusive: we don't say "we'll just do that one"'; or they may argue, using the canons of the Theravāda and of Hindu inclusivism, that since they drink alcohol, worship Gaṇeś, and perform animal sacrifice, they must be Hindus. On the other hand, an eighty-year-old Maharjan contradicted his grandson and grandson's friend in my presence, saying 'No, we're *buddhamat*: look at our customs, we don't honour Mahādyaḥ [Śiva].'

44 I have discussed the double-edged relationship of Buddhism to the cultural nationalism of the Newari language movement in Gellner 1986.

45 John Locke has cited to me the case of a Vajrācārya who is a high-level civil servant, married to a Darjeeling Gurung, who uses Parbatiyā Brahman priests and sponsors the Hindu *satya nārāyaṇ pūjā* regularly; and there is, it seems, a Śākya family who are converts to Islam. Both of these cases are very unusual.

46 Lewis (1984: 546–7) describes the case of a Tulādhar man who was pious towards different forms of Buddhism *and* towards Hindu ascetics, but he had clearly been influenced by modern neo-Hindu ecumenism.

Notes to chapter 3

1 This scheme amalgamates and adapts two apparently separate scholarly traditions: one runs from Wadley 1975: 115, 137–8, 145 to Moffat 1979: 231–3 and L. Caplan 1985: 24; the other includes Campbell 1976: 24 and Bennett 1982: 47–50. On the Sinhalese Buddhist pantheon, quite similar in many ways to the Buddhist perspective on the Newars' pantheon (Hindu gods also regarded as *bodhisattvas*), see Obeyesekere 1963, 1966, 1984: 50ff.; Ames 1966; and Gombrich 1971. On the Tibetan pantheon, of which the same is true, see Samuel 1978: 56–7.

2 The *khyāḥ* and the *kawã* are frequently represented on the walls of Newar temples and they seem to symbolize the female and male contributions to conception (soft flesh and blood versus hard bones), an interpretation made by some Newars (R.P. Pradhan 1986: 96).

3 'Tantric' here means esoteric. In Buddhism, Tantrism refers to the third of the three principal Ways, the Diamond Way (Vajrayāna), which is explained below (§4.2, chapters 9 and 10).

4 This is Dumont's theory of hierarchy. For references, see p. 380, n. 4.

5 Literally *dyaḥpāḥlāḥ* means 'those whose turn of the god it is', i.e. the person who is responsible for the worship and safekeeping of the icon. There has no doubt been a conflation with the Sanskritic *devapāla(ka)*, 'guardian of the god'.

6 Bījeśvarī (whose Sanskritic identity is actually Vidyādharī: see H. Sakya 1978a) in Kathmandu and Vajrayoginī (alias Khaḍgayoginī) in Sankhu (Nw. Sakhwa) are evidently of this sort (on the latter, see Zanen 1986). In Lalitpur Cāmuṇḍā (Sikabahīdyaḥ) must once, from her informal Newari name, have been so too,

though now she is one of the Eight Mothers around Lalitpur and, apart from the name, has no monastic associations at all (cf. Locke 1985: 234). She has therefore moved from category C to the bottom section of D.

7 Several authors have written about the importance of the Eight Mother Goddesses who ring the city: Kölver 1976; Gutschow and Kölver 1975; Macdonald and Vergati Stahl 1979; Barré *et al.* 1981; Gutschow 1982.

8 Ortner (1978: 103) suggests that among the Sherpas 'there is a fairly neat correlation between the supernatural and the social hierarchy'.

9 The *caturmāsa* (Skt. four months) is the period from Āṣāḍh śukla 11 to Kārttik śukla 11, when Nārāyaṇa is supposed to be in cosmic sleep. It corresponds to the ancient Indian rainy season.

10 Sanjukta Gupta has inspected some of the inscriptions inside the Guhyeśvarī temple and informs me that they are addressed to Kubjikā. There are other indications that she is also worshipped as Guhyakālī (Kirkpatrick 1975: 191; Lienhard 1978: 258; Slusser 1982: 327b). D.R. Regmi (1965 II: 585) reckons that Kubjikā was less popular after the fifteenth century.

11 On the possible etymology of this term, see Locke 1985: 8 and Gellner 1987b: 368.

12 Unlike Herdick (1987: 247) in Kirtipur, I found no evidence of a distinction between 'good' *chwāsā* for birth and 'bad' *chwāsā* for death.

13 *Buddhamārgī* Maharjans often call him Karuṇāmaya, though their pronunciation led Toffin (1984: 550) to record the name as *kornama.*

14 In addition he has many other, less common epithets. There are also many other icons of the same deity. They are all known as Karuṇāmaya and Matsyendranāth, but their colloquial name is unique, deriving from their location: e.g. Janbādyaḥ in Jana Bāhāḥ, Kathmandu.

15 'Violence' here refers to animal sacrifice. Although meat offerings are required, it is not strictly true that Buddhist Tantric deities receive blood sacrifice.

16 From the old Newari, *su*, mustard oil, and Skt. *kuṇḍa*, vessel/holy spring (H. Sakya 1970: 62).

17 It is interesting to note that Locke's first book (1973) on the subject was entitled *Rato Matsyendranath*, but the second (1980), the result of much deeper, first-hand research, was called *Karunamaya: The Cult of Avalokitesvara-Matsyendranath in the Valley of Nepal.* On this cult one should also see Owens 1989.

18 In fact many of the artisan professions practised by Śākyas and Vajrācāryas, such as goldsmithing, carpentry, and casting are not generally associated with untouchability in the subcontinent. The reason why Śākyas and Vajrācāryas believe that they are is that among Parbatiyās, whose caste system is not very complex, these services are performed by Untouchables (Gaborieau 1978: 219).

19 Occasionally Śākyas also have such shrines in their houses. Members of Cikã Bahī take the plate (*kumārībhū*) to the Tantric deity of the monastery; except that, when the Observance of Vasundharā is performed in the monastery, they take it to the Power-Place of Bāl Kumārī. This latter practice, taking it to a Power-Place, seems to be followed by high-caste Hindus in Kathmandu.

20 See Locke 1980. Vergati (1985) describes a Newar painting of 1712 which depicts the myth associated with Bũgadyaḥ's festival: Karuṇāmaya is not identified with Matsyendranāth, although his companion deity, Cākwādyaḥ, another form of Avalokiteśvara, *is* called Mīnnāth.

21 Not to be confused with the festival of lights called Diwālī in India (Skt. Dīpāvalī). This is known as Tihār in Nepali and Swanti in Newari, and is equally important to Buddhists and Hindus. On Matayā see Vaidya 1986: chapter 6. Similar circuits of *caitya*s are undertaken by *buddhamārgī* peasants in villages to the south of Lalitpur (Toffin 1984: 550; Owens 1989).
22 The spirit of this kind of relativism is perfectly expressed in a passage from Bernier's *Voyages* quoted by Dumont 1980: 402–3. It was also noted by the Abbé Dubois 1897: 18. It was written into Hindu law texts because of radical differences between north and south Indian customs, in particular in regard to cross-cousin marriage. See Trautmann 1981: 302–3, 445–6.
23 Local tradition claims that they first came to live in the Kathmandu Valley at the end of the fifteenth century, but documentary evidence dates only from the eighteenth (Gaborieau 1977: 31–6).
24 The Law Code of 1854 codified this view of things, defining Islam, Christianity, and the Kabirpanth sect as foreign religions opposed to *dharma* (*vidharmī videśī mata*) (Höfer 1979: 160; cf. Gaborieau 1977: 203).
25 This is beautifully illustrated by the long exchange between anthropologist and *paṇḍit* given at Greenwold 1974a: 121. Asked why Buddhist priests could not initiate everyone and abolish social hierarchy the Vajrācārya *paṇḍit* replied among other things, that 'Only the Vajracharya and Bare [Śākya] have the time and the desire to devote their lives to the *dharma*.'
26 Interestingly, Turner (1980: s.v.) seems to have been told that the two were equivalent, as he records in his dictionary: 'Sunār, s. Goldsmith (= bā̃rā).' Riley-Smith (1982: 28) was told that Sthiti Malla forced the Śākyas to marry Sunār women.
27 Michael Witzel, who has conducted research on the Agnimaṭha, informs me that genealogical and inscriptional evidence suggests that there really were two such brothers in the seventeenth century.
28 Cf. Oldfield (1981 II: 138), who wrote that young Brahman boys were occasionally taken in and brought up by Vajrācāryas and Śākyas because 'their spiritual rank is recognised by the Banhras'. As far as I know, this never happens today, but I would not rule it out for the past. A few Vajrācārya faces struck me as characteristic of hill Brahmans, a physiognomy easily distinguishable from that of most Newars.
29 On the Zone of Peace initiative, see Shaha 1982: chapter 9.
30 *Ināp*, 2, 21 (1983) p. 3, letter to the editor from Madan Mohan Mishra. Asked in an interview (*Śānti Vijaya* 13: 54) whether he ever visited Kwā Bāhāḥ (where it is said Brahmans never go), Mishra replied, 'Yes, I have been there, not just once, many times. There is not one sun just for Buddhists and another just for the followers of Śiva's way, rising to the west. The sun rises for everyone in the east.'
31 Williams 1989: 133. According to Pal 1974: 35, the matted locks, rosary, and vase of Maitreya, as portrayed in Licchavi sculpture, are in imitation of Brahmā.
32 Thus an image of Halāhala Lokeśvara in Bhuvaneshwar is believed by locals to be Brahmā and Sarasvatī (de Mallman 1961), and in Kadri, Karnataka, two images of Avalokiteśvara are worshipped as Brahmā and Nārāyaṇa, and an image which is probably the Buddha is identified as Vyāsa (Nagaraju 1969: 67).
33 On this form, see Brinkhaus 1985. He reckons that it may well have been developed in Nepal and entered the Sādhanamālā from there.

34 This is also the Theravādin view (Gombrich 1971: 46), but the man could equally have derived the notion from Mahāyāna sources.

35 For songs, see Lienhard 1974: 37; for the same scene transposed to Bũgadyaḥ's arrival in the Valley, see Wright 1972: 146. In 1980 members of Uku Bāhāḥ dressed up as the Buddha and all the Hindu gods worshipping him for the Buddha Jayantī procession of that year (R.J. Shakya 1980: 22–5).

36 No one seems to notice the inconsistency of celebrating it also on Swãyā Punhī (Buddha Jayantī) some months earlier, an imported tradition going back only to 1942. The older tradition is recorded by A.K. Vajracharya (1980: 64) and is still current. See also Vaidya 1986: 57.

37 Subarna Man Tuladhar has pointed out to me that this is an adaptation of the proverb 'to see your enemy, look in your brother's face'.

38 See, for instance, Gonda 1970: chapter 5. Brinkhaus (1987a) produces textual evidence for competition between Vaiṣṇavism and Śaivism in his very detailed analyses of the Hindu *purāṇas* relating to the Kathmandu Valley. The earliest complete Newari play, by Jagat Prakāśa, King of Bhaktapur in the mid-seventeenth century, contains a debate between the great gods of Hinduism, but ends with Brahmā giving the judgement that all are one (Brinkhaus 1987b).

39 Greenwold (1947b: 129–31) has quoted passages in this vein from Hodgson, Lévi, Oldfield, and Snellgrove. To these one could now add several from Slusser 1982: chapter 10.

40 Carrithers (1979a, 1979b, 1984) has discussed this for Theravāda Buddhism in Sri Lanka, as has Tambiah (1976, 1984) for Thailand. For an excellent general discussion, see Strenski 1983.

41 Thus I find Greenwold's analysis (1974a, 1974b, 1981) too simple (Gellner 1989a). The claim that Newar Buddhism became 'secularized' (Slusser 1982: chapter 10) is correct only in the narrow sense that Śākyas and Vajrācāryas are not celibate. Newar Buddhist monasteries certainly are considered to be holy places and the Vajrācāryas' rituals are most certainly considered to be sacred. Lienhard's (1978: 269) use of the term 'laicization' to describe Newar Buddhist history is unfortunate for the same reason.

42 Herbert (1967: 46) describes how Buddhist and Shinto divinities were considered forms of each other in Japan, until the attempt to purify Shintoism in the nineteenth century.

43 A good example is a story from India, preserved in Tibet by Taranatha's history of Buddhism (D. Chattopadhyaya 1970: 100). It records how two Brahmans of Magadha were converted to Buddhism when Mahādeva himself told them, 'Only the path of the Buddha leads to salvation, which is not to be found anywhere else.'

Notes to chapter 4

1 Cf. Durkheim's remark that 'respect is the religious sentiment par excellence' (quoted in Lukes 1973: 188).

2 Locke (1980: 76–8) describes this in detail and gives the verse for each following Amogha Vajra Vajracharya 1972: 14–17.

3 These verses, the full title of which is Bhadracarī-praṇidhāna-gāthāḥ, Prayer verses concerning the Pious Life, are usually found appended to the Gaṇḍa-vyūha (Winternitz 1972: 326), which is one of the nine holy texts (*nava grantha*)

of Newar Buddhism. The Bhadracarī goes back to the fourth century and is very important in Tibetan and Japanese Buddhism also. 'Its popularity is such that many Tibetans, lay and monastic, know it by heart' (Tatz 1977: 153; cf. Beyer 1973: 188–9).

4 This is verse twelve of the text as published by Nagendra Raj Vajracharya (1975) which lacks the interpolated seventh verse of some versions (Tatz 1977: 157). I have followed his text without attempting to amend it, except to add a missing *ṣa* in *adhyeṣaṇa*. The text has been published in various places by modern scholars. For bibliography, translation, and analysis, see Tatz 1977. Idumi (1930) produced a text and translation.

5 The ritual is known Sanskritically as *sapta vidhāna pūjā*. In his list Ratna Kaji Vajracharya (1980: 61) substitutes Raising the Thought of Enlightenment (*bodhicittotpāda*) for Entreating (*yācanā*). Asha Kaji Vajracharya (1983 II: 240) lists the seven (with Newari glosses) but with Raising the Thought of Enlightenment instead of the Dedication of Merit as the seventh. In another book (1985: 12–13) he also has Triple Refuge (*tri-śaraṇa-gamana*) for Summoning. As summarized by Dayal (1970: 54–8), Taking the Triple Refuge is the second, and Requesting Teaching and Entreating are combined as the sixth. For references to similar variations in the Tibetan sources, see Beyer 1973: 478 n. 66.

6 Tatz (1977: 159) translates *puṭa* as herbs, and Idumi (1930: 235) as incense. Beyer (1973: 188) also translates it as powders.

7 In a recent paper Gombrich (1990) has argued that the widespread use of literacy was a necessary condition of the emergence of Mahāyāna Buddhism. Before then the Buddhist canon was preserved orally and monks chanted its texts together regularly in order to preserve the true teachings and to prevent the emergence of false ones.

8 This is expressed as the difference between teaching the non-self (essencelessness) of all elements (*dharma-nairātyma*) and the non-self of individuals (*pudgala-nairātmya*) respectively. Non-self is here a synonym of emptiness (*śūnyatā*). Strictly, Mahāyānists were reacting against what they saw as the innovatory doctrine of the systemizing Abhidharma (philosphical analysis) schools of the pre-Mahāyāna, which taught that there were ultimately existing elements (*dharmas*) (Williams 1989: 46–7).

9 For the *bodhisattva* vow as part of the *guru maṇḍala* rite, see Gellner (1991b: 182). The common claim in Western books on Buddhism that the *bodhisattva* postpones enlightenment, i.e. becoming a Buddha, until all other beings have been brought to enlightenment, is a misunderstanding (Williams 1989: 52–4).

10 E.g. A.K. Vajracharya 1977: 76–7, and J.M. Vajracharya 1979: 4.

11 J.M. Vajracharya 1979: 5–6. The charge that pre- and non-Mahāyāna Buddhism is selfish, i.e. does not believe in altruism, is in fact unfair (Gombrich 1971: 321).

12 Riley-Smith 1982: 122. For *pāp* as the opposite of *dharma*, see below, §4.3.1.

13 There are stories of the Buddha as an Untouchable or as an animal in the most ancient of Rebirth stories. In Sri Lanka the story of his rebirth as a woman dates only from the fourteenth century. Most Newar Buddhists are aware that the Buddha was reborn once as a woman (the story has been published by M.R. Vajracharya 1977).

14 H. Sakya (1979: 104–7) argues that the Buddhist view of the monarch as both a god (*deva*) and a *bodhisattva* is particularly relevant to his role in the twelve-

yearly festival of Samyak in Kathmandu. On the King as a *bodhisattva* in Theravāda countries, see Tambiah 1976.

15 On the translation of 'Sahaja' as Innate, see Snellgrove 1987: 245.

16 See Locke 1980: 23–9 and 1985: 254–7. On the (inglorious) role of the Kathmandu Ācārya Guthi in the twenty-year dispute between Vajrācāryas and Tulādhar *et al.*, see Rosser 1966: 116ff.

17 In Gellner (1988a) I discuss variants between Kathmandu and Lalitpur in the way that Monastic Initiation is performed, and translate a pamphlet written 'to bring about uniformity of rituals'. See also the quotation from R.K. Vajracharya given on pp. 196–7.

18 This is less true of some adherents of the new Theravāda movement who ascribe much greater importance to holding the right belief.

19 Adi Vajra Vajracharya (1980: 66) glosses *dharma* as 'sadācāra, puṇyakarma': right behaviour, meritorious action.

20 I owe to Alexis Sanderson the point that *dharma* is used in the sense of 'the result of a ritual' in orthodox Brahmanical Mīmāṃsā philosophy.

21 Thus Adi Vajra Vajracharya (1980: 67) glosses *pāpī*, sinful, as 'pātakī, aparādhī, adharmī': sinful, guilty of an offense, lacking *dharma*; cf. S.M. Joshi 1987: s.v.

22 In Newari *māyā* denotes a combination of love, affection, and compassion; it does not mean 'delusion', as in the Advaita Vedānta, or 'magical trick', as in early Hinduism. Another Vajrācārya explained to me that *māyā* means being attached to one's family.

23 A model of it is displayed in Guita Bahī, Lalitpur, once a year. 'This water fountain represents the imaginary one installed in the nether world – where the departed souls are to find water' (Vaidya 1986: 36). The name, Dālāy Hitī, probably means 'once-a-year water spout'.

24 By 1989 this model was no longer being displayed.

25 *Samay baji* is the sacramental food shared after a ritual, either before, or instead of, a feast. See §10.5.

26 For citations by Newar Buddhist *paṇḍit*s see A.V. Vajracharya 1963: 17, and A.K. Vajracharya 1977: 62–3; 1983 II: 425. Cf. Dayal 1970: 199–204 and Snellgrove 1987: 76.

27 On the Five, Eight, and Ten Precepts in Theravāda Buddhism, see Gombrich 1971: 64–5.

28 'Thaḥgu karmay cwayāḥ taḥgu' or 'thaḥ thaḥgu karmabhog'. According to Lewis (1984: 524) *karma* is also sometimes thought to be written on one's hand or in one's heart (*man*).

29 This absence of fatalism is just what Srinivas (1980: 290) reports for Karnataka.

30 In fact, in many outlying Newar settlements Maharjans *do* plough; and in most of those parts of the Valley where it is taboo, there are considerable advantages to using the hand-plough (*kū*) instead. On this whole question, Webster's (1981) fascinating article is essential reading.

31 See Dayal 1970: chapter 5. The term *pāramitā* was known to pre-Mahāyāna Buddhism but the list is a creation of the Mahāyāna. Theravāda Buddhism has a different list of Ten Good Deeds (Gombrich 1971: 74). Significantly it too begins with giving and morality, the two Buddhist virtues thought particularly appropriate for the laity.

32 A Newari version and English translation of this latter story have been

published by Lienhard 1963.

33 *Dakṣiṇā*, by contrast, is usually a payment of money for ritual services and is not so stigmatizing. Occasionally, however, *dakṣiṇā* can refer to a *dān* of money (see pp. 182, 188).

34 R.P. Pradhan (1986: 225ff.), in his excellent analysis of Newar death rituals, criticizes Parry for running together Brahmans and Mahābrāhmaṇs: the latter may be primarily absorbers of sin, but the former are not.

35 See A.K. Vajracharya (1977: 23), where the verse is said to come from the Citraviṃśati Avadāna, and (1981a: 79; 1983 III: *cha*), which give the Caitya-puṃgava Avadāna as the source. At the latter place, the writer interprets the second and fourth *pāda*s of the verse as meaning that one obtains the highest rebirth by the practice of *ahiṃsā*.

36 In arguing for vegetarianism the monk Sakyananda ('Why eating meat is wrong', 1977) ignores this doctrine and has to rely on modern scientific and on Hindu arguments (Yudhiṣṭhira's teaching in the Mahābhārata and the three *guṇa* theory). The only Buddhist support he can find is a verse from the Laṅkāvatāra Sūtra to the effect that the killer of beings and the buyer of meat both go to the Raurava hell.

37 S. Shrestha in Juju and Shrestha 1985: 48.

38 On these in the Tibetan context, see Beyer 1973: 229ff.

39 The seven days of the week, beginning with Sunday, are Vasudhārā (Vasundharā), Vajravidāraṇī, Gaṇapatihṛdayā, Uṣṇīṣavijayā, Parṇaśabarī (and/or Prajñāpāramitā), Mārīcī, and Grahamātṛkā (van Kooij 1977: 60ff.; A.V. Vajracharya 1976b). The Five Protective Goddesses are Pratisarā, Sāhasrapramardiṇī, Mantrāṇusaraṇī, Mahāmāyurī, and Sītavatī. Few Newars today would be able to list all these.

40 This is discussed at greater length, and the mistaken use of Hodgson as an authority on this point demonstrated, in Gellner 1989b.

41 Doing *cākari* has been described well by Lionel Caplan 1975: 36–8.

42 This is probably by conflation with *nirmāṇakāya*, the 'created' body of the Buddha, and *nirmāṇacakra*, a Tantric term which relates the former, one of the series of 'bodies' of the Buddha, to the yogic structure of the practitioner's own body (see §10.3).

43 *Asura*, literally 'antigod', is considered equivalent to *daitya*.

44 Asha Kaji Vajracharya (1983 II: 436–7) characterizes the six rebirths (in a speech put into the mouth of Āryaputra, disciple of Dīpaṅkara) as follows: (i) gods are pure in mind and body, and eat vegetarian food; (ii) demons are irreligious, greedy, and addicted to meat, wine, and blood; (iii) men think only of almsgiving and merit, are devoted to parents, scriptures, monks, ascetics, and learned men, and do not like meat or wine [sic!]; (iv) animals ignore the learned, like smelly things, have difficulty in being devoted to gods, teachers, or scriptures; (v) ghosts are always angry and like rotten food; (vi) the denizens of hell are always hungry however much they eat, are addicted to black magic, and cannot bear the sight of wisdom.

Notes to chapter 5

1 Turner 1980: s.v. Interestingly, the same word seems to have come to mean the exact opposite in western Uttar Pradesh, India, where it is used to denote the

'appropriate obligation' of ritual specialists (Raheja 1988a).

2 The period of kite flying lasts from Yẽnyāḥ (Np. Indra Jātrā) to Mohanī (about three weeks).

3 The expression I have translated as 'optional', namely 'pharmās yāye', is used, to be absolutely precise, for soteriological reasons. Where a particular ritual is clearly and openly being done for instrumental ends, e.g. because of a sudden and unexpected illness, the search for the cure is liable to be given as the reason for the ritual. In such a case, although having the ritual performed is strictly optional, to call it a *pharmās* would make it sound too light-hearted and not sufficiently urgent. Where, on the other hand, the ritual is performed ostensibly for soteriological reasons, there may in fact be some rather specific worldly benefit which is being hoped for by the sponsor.

4 I owe to Alexis Sanderson the point that this latter is the interpretation of Jayaratha commenting on Abhinava Gupta's Tantrāloka 28.1–9.

5 Diehl's (1956) interesting study of south Indian ritual rightly insists on the importance of purpose in distinguishing types of ritual, but, like the learned schemas, he sticks rigidly to the perspective of the individual.

6 E.g. Fürer-Haimendorf 1956: 18; Rosser 1966: 118; A.P. Caplan 1972: 1, 31, 60; Singer 1972: 89; M. Allen 1973: 11; Locke 1980: 471; Greenwold 1981: 95; Slusser 1982: 217a, 420a; Good 1982: 29; Manandhar 1986: s.v.; Toffin 1984: 287, 290; 1989: 22.

7 Newars themselves are, not surprisingly, confused in their use of English. Kwā Bāhāḥ is widely referred to in English as 'the Golden Temple', and locals are happy to use this designation. The signs in Kwā Bāhaḥ say 'Please give a donation for the monastery', which leads tourists to ask where the monastery is.

8 For example, Beyer refers to 'ordinary' or common-sense reality as 'nonreality', and what I have called 'freelance, non-liturgical' use of ritual he calls 'general function'. I have tried to choose a vocabulary which does not presuppose a Buddhist orientation on the part of the reader.

9 It would be misleading, at least for the Newars, to call the smallest meaningful unit of ritual a symbol (V.W. Turner 1977: 189). The smallest meaningful unit of ritual is itself a ritual *act*.

10 I am indebted to Alexis Sanderson for making these distinctions clear to me. For a general survey of mantras see Bharati 1965: chapter 5.

11 For more detail one should consult Locke (1980: 74–121) who has given blow-by-blow accounts of all three following the printed handbooks of Amogha Vajra Vajracharya 1972, 1976a. I have attempted to synthesize different mss. and performance traditions of the *guru maṇḍala* in Gellner 1991b.

12 This verse seems to be referred to in the Bhāvanākrama, attributed to Kamalaśīla (eighth century), where it is denied that one attains the Six Perfections by the practice of the *gomaya-maṇḍala* (Tucci 1958: 26).

13 For these verses some of which may be found in the Sādhanamālā, others in the Bodhicaryāvatāra, see Gellner 1991b: 180–3.

14 On the whole question of summoning, and how this is supposed to be done, see §10.2. Ideally the Flask contains various sets of five (for a long and impractical list, see Hodgson 1972 I: 139). Normally the Flask contains pure water (*nīlaḥ*) with the Five Nectars (*pañcāmṛta*), and sometimes the Five Leaves (*pañcapallava*).

15 This derives, one presumes, from Skt. *sthāpanā*, 'establishing' or 'that which is established'. Manandhar (1986: s.v.) gives a variant *thāpĩ jwalā̃*, 'materials for worship'. More rarely, and more Sanskritically, the implements may be called *devagaṇa*, 'group of gods'.

16 Strictly this should be mixed husked and unhusked rice (*saruwā*), but since it requires much less unhusked rice to provide the required volume, husked rice is rarely included.

17 The latter form, or variants of it, is usual in handbooks I have seen. It might be thought to derive from Skt. *nirañjana*, 'spotless', and there may well be semantic contamination from this source. However A.V. Vajracharya (1976a: 4), a careful author, uses the form *nīrājana*, Skt. 'making bright'; this is probably the correct form in view of the *nīrājana* light-offering described by Kane 1941 III: 230; V: 334.

18 The conch shell is often worshipped as Varuṇa, king of serpents, and this is the identification likely to be known by lay people. Here, however, and in all Tantric contexts, it is the *ḍākinī* Khaṇḍarohā who is invoked when the conch shell's water is used. As noted above, Khaṇḍarohā's mantra is in fact the all-purpose mantra of Cakrasaṃvara, so that indirectly it is he who is being invoked. According to Locke (1980: 100–1) this part of the rite is understood as directed to the eight cremation grounds. This is not implied by the mantras used (A.V. Vajracharya 1976a: 4–5), which are approximately the same in Kathmandu as in Lalitpur.

19 In the most abbreviated account available to me this is omitted even in the case of the worship of the Flask.

20 First, there is a difference of order: in Lalitpur the removal of obstacles (*nīrājan*) takes places during section (v), not after section (vi), as implied in Locke's source (A.V. Vajracharya 1976a: 4); in Locke's account it seems that summoning the deity occurs twice (1980: 99, 101; A.V. Vajracharya 1976a: 3, 5) which is possible (for rites consist of different layers) but requires explanation. Second, worship of the Tantric implements is certainly often included in exoteric rites, contrary to what Locke implies (1980: 99). Third, there are minor differences in interpretation, for example the reference to the eight cremation grounds which seems to be absent in Lalitpur. Further research might well reveal other such variations.

21 These are called 'metapha kenegu', 'sipha luyegu', and 'tācā̃ thikegu' respectively. They are part of the auspicious welcoming ritual ('lasakus yāyegu') and appear also in Body Worship and Younger Brother Worship, as well as many other places.

22 On returning from the cremation ground, cf. Nepali 1965: 131. In Panauti 'bali piyegu' seems to be known as 'lā̃ suyegu' (Toffin 1979b: 246; 1984: 294, 305, 499).

23 Colloquially this is referred to as *samsā jog*. I am not sure what this comes from; possibly from *sahasrāhuti yajña* ('Fire Sacrifice of a Thousand Oblations'); probably not from *saṃsāra yajña*.

24 Unfortunately I have not made an in-depth and comparative study of the Fire Sacrifice ritual. Consequently this summary is based on a single priestly handbook. The account of A.V. Vajracharya (1976a), followed by Locke (1980), inverts steps (vii) and (viii). This is perhaps a Kathmandu convention.

25 See, for example, Parry (1982: 77–88), and the references given by him on p. 101 n. 9.

26 For the process of breathing out all sins as part of daily worship, see Gellner 1987a: 429; n.d.b.

27 Amogha Vajra is correct to cite the twenty-third chapter of the Saṃvarodaya Tantra (see Tsuda 1974: 144, 313), though it does not explicitly promise the various benefits of the Fire Sacrifice (wealth, prosperity etc.) to the whole world.

28 KSc (380, 385) seems to substitute either summoning (*ākarṣaṇa*) or magic (*abhicāra*) for destroying in this list. B.R. Bajracharya (1986: 48) gives the first two of the standard list, the least offensive of the four. The Saṃvarodaya Tantra 23.12–15, on the other hand, lists eleven different types of Fire Sacrifice by function (Tsuda 1974: 138).

Notes to chapter 6

1 See, for example, Slusser 1982: 201b, for Siddhi Narasiṃha's gifts in 1627 when establishing the Viśveśvara temple in Maṅgal Bazaar, Lalitpur; and H. Sakya (1979: 40–1, relying on D.R. Regmi 1965 III, part 2: 6) for Nṛpendra Malla's participation in gift-giving at Pañcadān in the name of his dead elder sister.

2 Exceptionally, in Kwā Bāhāḥ there are thirty elders. Some Kathmandu monasteries, rather than using the list system for the determination of duties and the recruitment of elders, are divided into sections (*kawaḥ*) based on descent. In Lalitpur this system is used only in lineage monasteries (defined below).

3 See Gellner 1988a. For briefer descriptions of the rite, see Locke 1975 and Hodgson 1972 I: 139ff.

4 The rule that five senior members must be present to initiate a new monk goes back to the time of the Buddha himself or shortly after (Frauwallner 1956: 90–1). Local tradition takes the initiation ritual back to the mythical time of Krakucchanda Buddha (Wright 1972: 80; cf. §7.1).

5 Locke (1985) is the standard survey of Newar Buddhist monasteries. I have analysed the architectural features of the Newar Buddhist monastery and distinguished different types of monastery – *bāhāḥ*, *bahī*, independent branch monastery, and lineage monastery (the latter two both types of *kacā bāhāḥ*) – in Gellner 1987b. These distinctions are outlined briefly in the main text (§6.2).

6 I am indebted to Dhana Vajra Vajracharya for reading the document (of which I have a photograph) and pointing this out to me. Chunda Vajracharya (1983: 9) writes that the Śākyas of six main monasteries in Kathmandu (Jana Bāhāḥ, Itum Bāhāḥ, Sikhamu Bāhāḥ, Oṁ Bāhāḥ, Makhā̃ Bāhāḥ, and Lagan Bāhāḥ) are believed to be the descendants of Vajrācāryas who at some point omitted to take the Consecration of a Vajra-Master and therefore fell to the status of Śākyas.

7 The inscriptional evidence for this historical claim, and for others advanced here, is presented in Gellner 1989c.

8 For all these monasteries, see the relevant entries in Locke 1985.

9 Hodgson 1972 I: 132. This text, the Vajrasūcī, is attributed to Aśvaghoṣa but this is unlikely to be historically accurate (Winternitz 1972: 266).

10 The word for caste (*jāt*) is taboo in the official ideology. The Skt. term *varga*, 'group', is used as a euphemism for it (Höfer 1979: 121 fn. 8, 203), though it also covers such things as the corporate organizations (*saṃgaṭhan*) of peasants, women, ex-servicemen, and workers which have separate representation under the present Partyless Democracy (Gaborieau 1982a: 264 and 279–80; Joshi and Rose 1966: 406–10).

11 Riley-Smith (1982: 39), working in Uku Bāhāḥ, heard the same argument. L. Shakya (1984: 27–8) has argued the point in print.

12 For details see C. Vajracharya 1983: 10–11, and Gellner 1989c.

13 Much of the data supporting the conclusions presented in this and the following paragraphs can be found in Gellner 1987b; see also Locke 1985. I pointed out in that article that there is in fact no historical evidence to support the traditional claim of the *bahī* to be older than the *bāhāḥ*; rather than being viewed as a survival (as Westerners have tended to regard them), the *bahī* should be seen as exemplifying in their ritual and architectural practice the renunciatory pole of an ever-present Buddhist tension between compromising and mixing with the world on the one hand and retreating from it on the other. On lineage monasteries, see further, §8.3.

14 This is indeed an archaic feature of Buddhist monasteries. See D. Mitra 1971: chapter 2, for illustrations of the early '*caitya* houses', temples in which a *caitya* that could be circumambulated was the main cult object.

15 On Nyungne among the Sherpas, see Ortner 1978.

16 Kwā Bāhāḥ used to have a system by which each year the six members next on the list received turns in that year. But instead of having a single turn of two months, they each received two one-month turns six months apart. This system was abolished some years back as a way of reducing the time that members had to wait for their turn. Now twelve members take a turn each year, each for one month.

17 Owens (1989) records a popular belief – which would probably be rejected as too narrow by Kwā Bāhāḥ members themselves – that Karuṇāmaya provides food, Cākwādyaḥ (who is identified with Dharmarāj or Yama) takes care of the afterlife, and Kwābāju of Kwā Bāhāḥ gives wealth.

18 *Bāphā* could mean 'half-turner' or 'monastery-turner' (from *bāhāḥ* + *pāḥ-lāḥmha*). The small or younger *bāphā* is known as *bāphācā*, *-cā* being the diminutive suffix in Newari. Joshi (1987: s.v.) records the form *bāphaḥcā*, but defines it much too loosely as a 'pure-minded devotee (*dharmasevaka*)'.

19 On two successive days at the beginning of the month of Kārttik he visits other places, the independent branch monasteries attached to Kwā Bāhāḥ. See Gellner 1987b.

20 For the 'Buddhaṃ trailokyanāthaṃ' see Gellner 1988a: 83.

21 The Bhĩchẽ Bāhāḥ liturgy, given in Newari by H. Sakya (1973: 61–4), is translated in Locke 1985: 489–91; 1989: 83 fn. 16; and Gellner 1987a: 559–61. For details of the differences between the different monasteries, see Gellner 1987a: 288; 1991c.

22 A few notes on the wooden gong are given in Gellner 1987a: 561–2.

23 See the picture in Gutschow and Sakya 1980: 170.

24 Interestingly, Tamang (married) lamas also circulate once a year begging grain (Holmberg 1984: 700).

25 The Kathmandu date by the old (*amānta*) reckoning is Śrāvaṇ kṛṣṇa 13; both fall within the Buddhist holy month of Gũlā, which is the Nw. name for Śrāvaṇ (by the old reckoning).

26 For the first two etymologies, see H. Sakya 1979: 98–9. For the third, see Lienhard 1989: 595.

27 Hemraj Sakya (1979: 98) relates this to a very scholastic list of nine types of gift

given in the text, the Bodhisattvabhūmi (cf. Dayal 1970: 173).

28 In Lalitpur water was given instead of molasses-juice and there was no beaten-rice prestation. The mendicants were each given a copy of a pamphlet by Asha Kaji Vajracharya (= Vajracharya 1982) listing the 'gift-verses' (*dānavākya*) to be recited on the reception of different gifts (perhaps a rather pointed gift considering the inability of most young Śākyas and non-priestly Vajrācāryas to recite these verses). At the Kathmandu performance no chalk was given.

29 Some idea of the extent of these rituals, associated with bringing a special Pañcadān deity (Dīpaṅkara) from Svayambhū and other preparatory rites, can be got from consulting R.K. Vajracharya 1980: 88–101.

30 The conspicuous display involved in this ceremony can be compared to some Burmese *kaṭhin* offerings made to monks at the end of the rainy season (Spiro 1982: 227).

31 As noted above (§3.2), Dīpaṅkara deities are also commonly known as 'Samyak god' (*samedyaḥ*) and 'carried grandfather' (*kwiyampāju* from *kwabiyāḥ haḥmha āju*).

32 Another alternative explanation for the festival of Pañcadān is found in the Hinduized Varṣa Kriyā ('Yearly Festivals') literature. In this tradition Brahmā offered his middle head (severed by Śiva) to Dīpaṅkara on Śrāvaṇ śukla 8, and hence Lalitpur Pañcadān falls on that day (P.R. Vajracharya 1979: 44; Varṣa Kriyā: 9r). Asha Kaji Vajracharya (1956: 35–6) quotes three verses of the Piṇḍapātrāvadāna which cite the examples of both Brahmā and King Sarvānanda. Interestingly, in a 1987 reissue of that work Asha Kaji cites a different verse from the same source mentioning only Sarvānanda (A.K. Vajracharya 1987: 51–2).

33 Of the four monkey lampstands in each corner of the courtyard of Kwā Bāhāḥ, the one in the south-west corner represents Jñānākara offering a jackfruit to Dīpaṇkara, according to the inscription on its base.

34 On the gift of dirt by Aśoka see Strong 1983: 56ff., who gives a subtle analysis of its symbolic meaning, and on Aśoka's quinquennial festival, ibid. 91–7.

35 It has been incorporated into Asha Kaji Vajracharya's 'translation' of the Kapiśāvadāna into Newari (1983 II: 421–97). It is summarized by Hemraj Sakya (1979: 8–10) and K. Vaidya (1986: 74–5), and occurs in Wright's *History of Nepal* (Wright 1972: 87–9). I have retranslated BV's version in Gellner 1987a: 563–4.

36 The date of Kathmandu Pañcadān, by contrast, is one of the four days during the year which are supposed to mark the beginning of the four world eras. The four 'Aśokan' *stūpa*s in Lalitpur are believed to have been founded on these four days also (cf. Wright 1972: 116). All four days are good for giving *pañcadān* (Wright 1972: 88; Brough 1948: 673) and Hemraj Sakya (1979: 48–9) cites an inscription showing that a Kathmandu Tāmrakār actually did so in 1863, while in the process of founding a monastery.

37 On a more local level one might say that it legitimizes Śākyas and Vajrācāryas working as artisans, but I have never heard the story of Sarvānanda cited in this way, and Blacksmiths are in fact rather low, though not unclean, by caste.

38 Here too Newar Buddhists do not differ from Buddhists in other times and places (Gombrich 1971: 250; Tambiah 1970: 147; Spiro 1982: 107, 454; Ortner 1978: 112–13).

39 Another contention Vergati advances is that Dīpaṅkara ('Causing light') is still associated in Newar Buddhist minds with the gift of light; she further conjectures that Matayā is connected with him. It is true that the connection with light is made by Newar Buddhist scriptures, and the name of the city, Dīpāvatī ('Having light'), is explained by the connection (A.K. Vajracharya 1983 II: 464). Nonetheless, though giving light is indeed a typically Buddhist offering, it is not, and therefore Matayā is not, especially connected to Dīpaṅkara in the minds of ordinary Newar Buddhists. He is rather, as I have described, associated with gifts of rice and with the spectacular piety of Samyak and Optional Pañcadān.

40 Following Richard Gombrich's suggestion of *Yaḥ* for *Na*. One would also expect the dual *padbhyām* rather than *pādau* in the third line.

41 Correcting *te* to *ye*.

42 In the later book (1983 II: 474) Asha Kaji Vajracharya gives a different verse (perhaps because the four ends of man seemed too Hindu): *Sauvarṇaṃ rūpyaṃ tāmraṃ vā mudrā nirmitadakṣiṇāḥ/Saṃghebhya yat prayacchati tasyādhikaphalaṃ labhet* (He who offers money of gold, silver, or copper to the Monastic Community will attain a very great reward).

43 This is the reading of A.K. Vajracharya 1982: 15; 1983 II: 494, reads *saṃbhā sayitvā*. In neither place is it translated.

44 An oral account from Dharma Ratna Shakya added another line at the beginning of this verse (which I give as recited): *Para bhavantu sadā sukhī āyu ārogya sampadam*. His version of the final line reads: *Āyu ārogya dhanajana guṇa santānaṃ santute saptavṛddhi astu*. This gives some idea of the variations which occur when these verses are learned by heart.

Notes to chapter 7

1 See Riccardi 1985. The title *Nepal Mandala* is, he says, 'either to be considered incorrect or a curious Anglo-Sanskritic or Anglo-Nepali hybrid form'. Surely 'Nepal Mandala' is acceptable English and is preferable to the Sanskrit, Nepali, or Newari alternatives: 'Nepālamaṇḍala', 'Nepāl Maṇḍal', and 'Nepāḥ Mandaḥ'.

2 It is a pity that Slusser did not use some local painting or map (such as that of Bhaktapur analysed in Kölver 1976) as a frontispiece. The use of an invented design does rather suggest that her title has been forced onto the facts, which is not so.

3 It is often pronounced *manda* in Newari and there is also a confusion in the popular mind between 'mandala' and *maṇḍapa* (Skt. pavilion).

4 On these three 'bodies' of the Buddha, see §10.3. Blacker (1965) describes a Japanese case where pilgrimage traces out a cosmic mandala.

5 Wilson (1862: 32–3) translated part of a handbook for the performance of the Observance of Amoghapāśa Lokeśvara which included the recitation.

6 This is a translation of the text as given in A.V. Vajracharya 1963: 1–2; see also Gellner 1987a: 567–8.

7 The position of the rivers is given as for Lalitpur. For other cities the necessary adjustments are made.

8 The *gotra* is a Brahmanical institution. All Brahmans belong to a *gotra* named after an ancient Indian sage, and they may not marry members of their own

gotra. Other castes, including all Newars except the Rājopādhyāyas, have adopted this in name only: all, or nearly all, members of the caste have the same *gotra* and it has no bearing whatever on rules of exogamy. Śākyas and Vajrācāryas nearly all belong to the Gautama *gotra*, as Śākyamuni himself is presumed to have done. For further details, see Gellner 1989c.

9 Very abbreviated versions of the 'Adya Mahādāna' recitation occur in inscriptions, followed by astrological information (e.g. Regmi 1965 II: 385; cf. Rajvamshi 1983: 93–4). They often add *paśupati-sannidhāne*, 'in the region of Paśupati', since Paśupati has for Hindus the same defining importance as Svayambhū for Buddhists.

10 I discuss the South Asian character of Newar culture, and the local and scholarly attempts to deny it, in Gellner 1986 and 1991a.

11 The Himālaya is called an *upachandoha-pīṭha* in the Saṃvarodaya Tantra (Tsuda 1974: 104, 272). In other words this is a class of Power-Place, not the name of one particular Power-Place, as, I believe, the Nepalese often understand it.

12 Research by Horst Brinkhaus has shown that the earliest versions of the Svayambhū Purāṇa did not in fact call themselves *purāṇa* in the manner of Hindu pilgrimage texts, but *uddeśa*, a more strictly Buddhist term meaning 'teaching'.

13 Locke (1987) provides a summary of these stories.

14 Kölver characterizes the second set as 'markedly Hindu in its overall appearance, with but few traits specifically Buddhist' (Kölver 1986: 152). This is to ignore the fact that both are considered Buddhist by the Svayambhū Purāṇa itself: they refer to different levels within what Newar Buddhists consider to be one religion.

15 The most detailed analysis of Newar life-cycle rituals available in English, based on those of Kathmandu Hindus, is to be found in R.P. Pradhan 1986: chapters 2–6.

16 On temporary ordination in Southeast Asia see Tambiah 1970: chapter 7; Bunnag 1973: 165–78; Spiro 1982: 234–7; and Houtman 1984.

17 B.R. Bajracharya (1986: 52) ingeniously tries to explain the first, *garbhādāna*, as the Newar girls' puberty rite, Confinement. R.P. Pradhan (1986: 59) follows him with a question mark.

18 A few notes on Old-Age Initiation are included in Gellner 1987a: 569.

19 See R.K. Vajracharya's (1989) excellent recent summary of Kathmandu Newars' life-cycle rituals. For notes on other sources on Newar life-cycle rituals, see Gellner 1987a: 317–18.

20 *Bel* is Np. and Skt.; Nw. *byā*; botanical name *Aegle marmelos*.

21 On these two girls' puberty rituals see M. Allen 1982: Vergati 1982a; Toffin 1984: 401–5; B.R. Bajracharya 1986: 52–4; and R.P. Pradhan 1986: 110–42. Various etymologies have been suggested for the term *bārāy* (also spelt *bāhrāḥ* or *bādhāḥ*: S.M. Joshi 1987: 425b). That from *bādhā*, barrier, seems most plausible to me (cf. Turner 1980: 433b).

22 Lienhard (1986: 130) derives *kaytā* from Skt. *kaupīna*. Turner (1980: s.v.) derived *bartamān* from *vratabandha*, but this is doubtful.

23 This is from the explanation (*khā̌*) of Loincloth Worship read out by the

presiding Vajrācārya at a performance, taking place at the same time as an Old-Age Initiation ceremony in a Lalitpur Maharjan household.

24 For a summary of such prestations in the village of Pyangaon, see Toffin 1984: 164.

25 Good (1982: 26) writes that in Tamil Nadu the fulfilment by the MB of his ritual duties is considered a scriptural duty, the same term (*sastiram*) being used here as for caste-specific religious duties.

26 It may well be that the Powder Container is identified with the mother of the bride because it is designed with levels to look like the spire of a *stūpa*, i.e. as a representation of the ultimate wisdom, *prajñā*, which is feminine, while the Mirror is identified with the father because it symbolizes the impermanent world which is the means, *upāya* (a male noun), for reaching the ultimate.

27 E.g. Fürer-Haimendorf 1956: 34; Nepali 1965: 198; Toffin 1984: 404. R.P. Pradhan (1986: 167) argues that the marriage tie 'almost seems contractual'. I have discussed this question at greater length in Gellner 1991a.

28 For Pyangaon see Toffin 1984: 120, and on Bulu, B. Pradhan 1981: 71, 74.

29 The Barber, it is true, is required on many other occasions as well, but death is probably that on which it would be most unthinkable to do without him and his wife.

30 Asha Kaji Vajracharya gave the term *aprapakṣa piṇḍa śrāddha* for this. R.P. Pradhan (1986: 64, 71 n. 4) records the terms *vṛddhi-* and *maṅgalaśrāddha*: unlike ordinary Ancestor Worship, which is pure but inauspicious, this kind is both pure and auspicious. This sort of Ancestor Worship is found also in India (Stevenson 1971: 62).

31 This is performed either on one day during the fortnight preceding the beginning of the Mohanī festival or on every day during that fortnight. Counting an extra day at the end makes sixteen days, hence the name.

32 For an example of a dispute over caste which led to lineages splitting and refusing to observe death pollution for each other, see Quigley 1984: 219–23. I heard of several similar cases. The same manipulation of purity rules occurs among Parbatiyās (A.P. Caplan 1972: 79; Blustain 1977: 57; Bennett 1983: 21).

33 In Bhaktapur the Ghaḥsū Karmācarya is known as a Śivācārya (and colloquially as Tinī).

34 Parry 1980: 93 (italics in the original). For the Kāpālī see Toffin 1984: 148. According to Asha Kaji Vajracharya, there was a dispute between the Kāpālīs and the Dyaḥlā during the Rana period over who should be entitled to the dead person's clothes thrown at the *chwāsā*. The Kāpālī won on the grounds that 'they were the Buddhists' Mahābrāhmaṇ.' Since Hindus make use of both Kāpālī and Mahābrāhmaṇ, this shows how their rites undergo reduplication. This is further indicated by the nature of the rituals they perform: the Kāpālī consumes seven portions of rice on the seventh day (and also sometimes, in Bhaktapur, five on the fifth); the Karamjit or Mahābrāhmaṇ consumes ten on the tenth.

35 For further details on the ritual division of labour at the death of high-caste Hindu Newars, see Toffin 1979b and 1987.

36 Interestingly this was so even though he no longer carried out the service.

37 Some landlords seem to have given *bāli* to Blacksmiths (Nakarmī) in the past. Tamang lamas circulate annually and collect grain from agriculturalists in

return for rituals which prevent hail from damaging the crops. For two different critiques of approaches which use '*jajmānī* system' as a pan-South Asian analytic category, see Good 1982 and Fuller 1989.

38 These three rites, *nhaynhūmā*, *bĕkegu*, and *ghaḥsū* respectively, have been described by Nepali 1965: chapter 5; Toffin 1979b and 1984; 144–50; Lewis 1984: 318–26; and R.P. Pradhan 1986.

39 This principle is noted in passing by D.R. Regmi 1965 I: 643–4, and by Toffin 1984: 228. It is also evident in the list of Newar castes, which specifies periods of mourning for each, given by the nineteenth-century chronicle, the Bhāṣā Vaṃśāvalī, a system it attributes to Sthiti Malla (Paudel and Lamshal 1963 II: 45–50).

40 See Toffin 1979b; 1984: 291–2; and R.P. Pradhan 1986: 200. For the same rites as practised by Parbatiyās, see Bennett 1983: 101–4.

41 In the past they used to perform an Ancestor Worship actually at the cremation ground, before the body was burnt (Tulādhars still do: Lewis 1984: 314), and they would often perform Ancestor Worship for many years after the death of their parents. According to G.S. Nepali (1965: 128) this offering of Ancestor Worship at the cremation ground is uniquely Newar.

42 An exception is the traditional optional rite known as 'asthi kāyegu', 'taking the bone-relic'. For details, see Gellner 1987a: 338 fn. 33.

43 Cākwāḥdyaḥ (var. Cākupātadyaḥ, Cākubādyaḥ) has a particular role here: he is also known as Dharmarāj and is identified as Yama, king of the dead. Behind his temple is a Power-Place called *yamadwār*, 'the gate of Yama [Lord of the dead]', which is supposed to be open on the days of Sāpāru and Matayā (see Plate 2). The connection with Yama is further emphasized by the myths of origin of Cākwāḥdyaḥ which have King Vṛṣadeva dying and being taken down to the kingdom of Yama; Avalokiteśvara (the formal exoteric identity of Cākwāḥdyaḥ is Jaṭādhārī Lokeśvara, one of Avalokiteśvara's forms) then tells Yama that such a religious man ought not to have been taken so early and sends him back (Wright 1972: 117; A.V. Vajracharya 1979: 192; Locke 1980: 378).

44 Pollution at birth is called *jaybili* (in Lalitpur: *jabyā*). From the south of the Valley Toffin (1984: 154) reports *jabuli* for birth pollution, and *khaybuli* for the Confinement pollution. In Lalitpur *jabyā-khabyā* is a reduplicated term used for all pollution and *khabyā* is not understood to refer to Confinement pollution; for the latter the general term 'bāray yāye' is used.

45 In the case of a married woman this means her husband's mother, husband's father's mother, and husband's father's father's mother. The incorporation of a woman into her husband's lineage could hardly be expressed more clearly. On the same theme, there is a Newari saying that for woman 'one's own [people] become other, others become one's own'.

46 There are also annual festivals celebrated only by families, lineages, castes, or sub-castes. These are *a fortiori* of local significance only.

47 The name 'Yẽnyāḥ' is connected by some to the Newari name of Kathmandu, Ye, so 'Yẽnyāḥ' would mean 'the Kathmandu festival'. The true etymology seems to be Indrayātrā > Endayāta > Yẽnyāḥ (G.V. Vajracharya 1976: 172 fn. 3).

48 See Locke (1980) for details.

49 The observance of Gũlā by Buddhists goes back no doubt to the monastic rain retreat still practised by Theravāda monks (Locke 1980: 233), but Newar Buddhists today do not explicitly make this connection. As during the Burmese rain retreat (Spiro 1982: 222), Gũlā is not an auspicious time for weddings.

50 At all the Karuṇāmaya-Matsyendranāth shrines of the Valley, before the annual reconsecration, the god is 'fetched' from a river. In the case of Lalitpur Karuṇāmaya this is done from Kotwal, to recapitulate his arrival from Assam (Owens 1989).

51 For the myth justifying this practice see Anderson 1977: 136. For a translation of a Nepali language version, see Gellner 1987a: 573.

52 For details of the many other rites and customs, both Hindu and Buddhist, going to make up Yẽnyāḥ, see Nepali 1965: 358–69; G.V. Vajracharya 1976: 169–81; and R.P. Pradhan 1986: chapter 10.

53 The other factor Jaini emphasizes is the Buddha's silence when faced with ultimate theological questions. Since this could be interpreted in different ways it permitted Buddhism to draw closer to Hinduism. Jaini dismisses other theories which have been advanced to explain the demise of Buddhism in India: the withdrawal of royal patronage, the Muslim invasion, Brahmanical persecution, and internal sect divisions. All of these factors applied equally, if not indeed more fully, in the case of Jainism. For a different survey of such theories, see Ling 1980: 22–46. Although it survived in Karnataka, Jainism, like Buddhism, died out in Tamil Nadu (B. Stein 1980: 79–86).

54 Ancient Buddhism did not even allow temporary ordination, a practice which has emerged in Theravāda Burma and Thailand. On the recent (1982–3) attempt to introduce temporary ordination in Sri Lanka, a move denounced by traditionalists as encouraging hypocrisy, see Gombrich 1984.

55 If not, it derives from *upavāsa*, Skt. fast, a synonym of *upoṣadha/uposatha*. *Māsopavāsa*, Skt. 'month-long fast', becomes *māy apasã* in Newari.

56 Since nine are needed (one central and eight for the directions), the consort of Vairocana is omitted. Locke's text makes Vairocana the centre of the Buddha Mandala. The modern text cited below puts Akṣobhya in this position and displaces Vairocana to the eastern direction. This transposition is no doubt due to the fact that Akṣobhya is the exoteric representation of, among others, the most important Tantric deity in Nepal, Cakrasaṃvara (Snellgrove 1957: 206); thus we have here an exoteric mandala influenced by the esoteric.

57 The text is translated from a modern priestly handbook copied in Kathmandu's Naka Bahī of which I obtained a photocopy. I have heard such explanations read out on three occasions.

58 The same thing occurs in Monastic Initiation which has come to be modelled on, and called, an Observance (Gellner 1988a: 52).

59 The explanation cited by Locke (1987: 173–4) is similar to this, though slightly longer. It lists the Ten Unproductive Sins and their karmic consequences (theft leads to poverty, and so on).

60 When I watched the rite in a private house, the head of the household, who had acted as senior participant (*dhaḥmū thakāli*) and sponsor (*jaymā*) of the rite, untied the Observance thread from his wrist, after the meal had been eaten and the priest left, in order to smoke a cigarette.

61 See Figure 20 and key. The five Buddha shrines are Svayambhū, Khāsti (Bauddha), a *caitya* at Baregã (in the south of the Valley), Namura (Namobuddha, near Panauti), and the ancient Dhanado *caitya* in Cābahīl (see D.R. Regmi 1965 II: 571; A.K. Vajracharya 1981a: 19, lists four of the five, omitting Dhanado).

62 Further details on this ritual can be found in R.K. Vajracharya 1980: 63, and in K. Vaidya 1986: 140–1. For translations of texts relating to the Observances of Tārā and Mahākāla, see Lewis 1989.

63 The same 'ends of man' are promised in the recitation from the rite of the Eighth Day, given above. Asha Kaji Vajracharya quotes the same Sanskrit verse in another work (1981b: *cha*) and also gives references to the Karavīra Tantra and Kālacakra Tantra showing the necessity of keeping the Eight Precepts.

64 See Vaidya 1986: chapter 17. After a gap of some years a Maharjan woman from Satungal performed this fast in 1989. For the Śvetāmbara Jains of Jaipur a month-long fast is the most important of all their different fasts (Reynell 1985: 28–9). For Newar Buddhist women, by contrast, it is a rare supererogatory action (often performed by those who fear they have been abandoned by their husband for good and wish to shame him into recalling them from their natal home).

65 Vaidya (1986: 234) mentions the rite of reciting the Kwā Bāhāḥ Prajñā Pāramitā. I have described the ritual in a separate paper (Gellner in press) and have attempted to analyse the reasons people gave for having the text read. The single most important reason was illness, cited explicitly by 30% of a sample of 114.

66 When I watched the Observance of Vasundharā the explanation of the mandala, read out by the priest and 'originally explained in ancient times by Vajradhara', claimed that the 'mother of the world' Vasundharā would fulfil all the desires of those who practised her Observance one-pointedly. 'The childless will give birth to sons. The poor will obtain riches. By the merit of the Observance many illnesses will be destroyed. You will be freed of all sin. In order to observe this *vrata* you must abandon the Ten Unproductive Sins . . .' R.K. Vajracharya (1980: 81) explicitly identifies Vasundharā with the earth and as the giver of all kinds of plenty.

67 Lewis (1984: 248) records that approximately 35% of Tulādhar families in Asan, Kathmandu, had a member who had performed *satya nārāyaṇ pūjā*, and that they felt no embarrassment at admitting it. This contrasts with Śākyas and Vajrācāryas who, being Buddhist clergy, would never call a Brahman for this purpose.

68 The two descriptions which bring this out best are Toffin 1984: 408–18, and R.P. Pradhan 1986: chapter 5, especially pp. 176–7. Other useful accounts of Newar marriage can be found in P.H. Bajracharya 1959; Nepali 1965: chapter 5; Quigley 1984: 253–61; and Lewis 1984: 281–95.

69 For a different text of the wedding dialogue, see R.K. Vajracharya 1980: 25–8.

70 This is a reference to the fact that *dān* is the first of the Ten Perfections, and the point is taken up in the reply below.

71 One should remember here that marriages were conducted at a very young age, both for boys and for girls, until forty or fifty years ago. Even so, this seems to be

in direct contradiction of what has already been said about her thinking of nothing but serving her parents!

72 The text reads 'mahā dayā mahā tawadhanagu dayā prasanna juyāwa bijyāta'. I presume that 'mahā daya' is an incorrect (deliberate?) analysis of *mahodaya*, Skt. 'good sir'.

Notes to chapter 8

1 This is called *sīkāḥ bhū* and has been described in Toffin 1976b and 1984: 104–5 (he gives the variant form *sīkā bhway*). Toffin notes the similarity to the famous Puruṣa Sūkta from the Ṛg Veda in which the parts of the body represent the hierarchically arranged castes. In the Newar ritual there is great variation in the sequence in which the pieces of the sacrificed animal's head are distributed: in some *guthi*s the cheeks are given first, in others the eyes; in some the snout and tongue come last, in others they come before the cheeks. Everywhere, however, right ranks above left and everywhere the basic principle is that seniors rank above juniors. Siegfried Lienhard (personal communication) derives the term *sīkāḥ* from 'śiras kāye', 'taking the head'.

2 One of the death *guthi*s of Nāg Bāhāḥ has three types of fine: *pākhābā̃* (eave fine), paid by members who fail to appear at the dead person's house; *khusibā̃* (river fine), paid by those who fail to appear for the cremation at the river; and *dābā̃* (?cheap fine), a fine of one paisa for each death paid by women on their own (*yāka misā*) who cannot attend, but still need the services of the *guthi*.

3 K.B. Bista (1972: 94) cites the case of a Chetri lineage which established a *guthi* at the end of the nineteenth century for the worship of their lineage deity. This was in imitation of the Newar institution, as indeed is the cult of the Lineage Deity among Parbatiyās of the Valley (ibid.: 129–30). Quigley (1985b: 5–9) lays great stress on the need to distinguish the institution from the form of land tenure, and M.C. Regmi (1976: 48) goes so far as to say 'it is obvious that [the *guthi*] institution has no relationship with the land tenure system'. This clearly overstates the case, as his own materials show.

4 The best introduction to the whole question of land tenure is M.C. Regmi 1976. M.C. Regmi (1978) contains much more detail and documentation and is the standard work on the subject. In its present form the Guṭhi Corporation was set up in 1964.

5 M.C. Regmi 1978: 702–3; cf. Landon 1976 II: 173. As M.C. Regmi (1978: 701–2) points out, this was not unprecedented. The Malla kings had on occasion seized *guthi* revenue. Jang Bahadur introduced a contract system on *guthi* land. Chandra Shamsher was, however, the first to contemplate detailed bureaucratic direction of *guthi* revenue and activities.

6 On cooperative agricultural work groups, see Toffin 1977: 92; Ishii 1980: 170–1; Quigley 1985a: 35–7; and Webster 1987.

7 Quigley (1985b: 53–9) discusses the oft-made comparison between *guthi*s and the rotating credit associations found elsewhere in the Himalayas. He shows convincingly, as ought to be evident from the present discussion, that *guthi*s are fundamentally different in nature.

8 Vergati (1979: 127) makes a similar point for Bhaktapur and claims that those without a lineage deity at all are considered 'without status': no one will marry

them for fear of unwittingly committing incest. On the persisting strength of the patrilineal joint household in Dhulikhel, see Quigley 1985a.

9 The Lineage Deity continues to be worshipped on birthdays and in case of illness even when the *guthi* is no longer important. Most Newars would agree with the Chetri who told K.B. Bista (1972: 59): 'If one worships one's lineage deity, the lineage will survive and have enough to eat.'

10 It was called Gum Vihāra, presumably from Nw. *gũ*, 'mountain' or 'hill', and the site is still known locally as Gum Bāhāḥ. Aṃśuvarman donated land to it in CE 608 (Slusser 1982: 165–6; Locke 1985: 469).

11 With the growth of Kathmandu, and to a lesser extent Lalitpur, many Newars' Lineage Deities are now in the middle of buildings. Many lineages from Kathmandu had to move their Lineage Deities in the nineteenth century to permit the creation of the parade ground (Tundhikhel). Some of these can be seen at the Bhadrakālī temple.

12 For a complete list of Śākya and Vajrācārya Lineage Deities, see Locke 1985: 516–20.

13 As always, cooked meat and alcohol are offered to the Tantric deity.

14 For details on how other castes observe Lineage Deity Worship see Nepali 1965: 390–7; Toffin 1984: 491–4; and Quigley 1985b: 12–30. Bista (1972) describes Lineage Deity Worship among the Chetris of the Kathmandu Valley: for the ritual see pp. 71–91.

15 The Tulādhar *et al.* of Kathmandu perform a Tantric rite with the same social functions, which they call 'nyāgaḥ swanegu' ('establishing the five [skull-bowls]'). From this, female members of the family are not excluded, but are, on the contrary, essential, since a female partner is required in order to present the goddess' blessing.

16 An exception here – a *guthi* for a practical purpose which also has multi-caste membership – is the Temple (*degaḥ*) *guthi* of Kwā Bāhāḥ, which was originally supposed to be in charge of repairs to the monastery. Its income is nowadays sufficient only to pay for the annual ritual and feast, so that in effect it has passed from being a public utility *guthi* to the status of a simple deity-worship *guthi*. Its membership has always been multi-caste, including Jośīs, Śreṣṭhas, and Śākyas.

17 I am indebted to Michael Allen for sending me an account of how the Dhakhwa fortune started. Their ancestor was a goldsmith in Lhasa and some Tibetans brought him gold to gold-plate a lama's throne. He only needed half what was given. With the rest he started retailing cloth and other goods brought from Calcutta.

18 Traditional hymn groups, which nowadays meet more rarely, tend to sing hymns in what they call 'Hindi', i.e. presumably old Maithilī, or in old Newari.

19 On this ritual, see Gellner, in press.

20 While all high castes were served by Gwā̃ in this way, in some localities Farmers also received, and still receive, the same service. According to Toffin (1984: 146, 196), in Pyangaon and the upper half of Theco older men act as Gwā̃ to the rest of the community for religious merit and without payment.

21 This exclusion seems to be confined to high castes. Some Newar women in Kirtipur must accompany the funeral procession and bathe while the corpse is being burned (Herdick 1987: 268–9). Maharjan women of Kathmandu also accompany the corpse to the river (Lewis 1984: 315 fn. 1).

22 For details see Locke (1985) under Jana Bāhāḥ, Iku Bāhāḥ, Musya Bāhāḥ, Itum Bāhāḥ.

23 The evidence is in the Mahāparinibbāna Sutta. It describes the Buddha's last days, his instructions on what the Monastic Community should do in order to flourish, and his rejection of his followers' appeals to appoint a successor (Dutt 1978: 63–4; Gombrich 1988: 50, 109).

Notes to chapter 9

1 The Five Buddhas are also known as the Five Attained Ones (*pañcatathāgata*). Hodgson introduced the term 'Dhyāni Buddha' which has become current in Western writings. It is entirely without scriptural justification, nor did I ever hear the term used by Newar Buddhists. Locke (1980: 127 fn. 7) writes that it is used by Newars and some Newars do claim to recognize it (and H. Sakya 1973: 1, has written it), but I suspect this is only because they have seen it in Western sources.

2 See Dasgupta (1974: 87) and Snellgrove (1959a I: 129) for tables of correspondences. Some idea of the extreme complexity which results may be had from Wayman 1973: chapters 4 and 15.

3 See, for example, p. 369 n. 56.

4 This may have been around the beginning of the ninth century CE, but, like most issues of absolute (as opposed to relative) dating, this is a controversial question on which only tentative hypotheses are possible in the present state of scholarship.

5 In the Yoga Tantras (principally the Tattvasaṃgraha), a class of Tantras intermediate between the two main types of Vajrayāna described here, veiled and peripheral references to sexual rites do occur (see, e.g., the fifth chapter of the Tattvasaṃgraha: Chandra and Snellgrove, 1981).

6 See below, on Tantric Initiation (§9.3.4), for example. Interestingly, Caṇḍamahāroṣaṇa is also the patron deity of the death *guthi*s of the Citrakārs, the painter caste (Toffin 1984: 211).

7 An example of a Newar making a connection of this sort, between Bāl Kumārī (a Mother Goddess), Kumārī (exoteric Vajrayāna), and a Tantric goddess (esoteric Vajrayāna), was given above (§3.2, p. 82).

8 The confusion probably arose because the colophons of the Guhyasamāja contain the phrase: *sarvatathāgatakāyavākcittarahasyātirahasya guhyasamāje mahāguhyatantrarāje* (Alexis Sanderson, personal communication).

9 They are sent away for one consecration. See §9.3.5.

10 For the 'three turnings of the wheel' as conceived by Tibetan Buddhists, see Snellgrove 1987: 94–5, 119 fn. 4.

11 See Hevajra Ṭantra 1.1.10 (Snellgrove 1959a I: 51; II: 6). The artisan's son was right that OṂ has its origin in Hinduism, wrong in implying that it had been taken over thoughtlessly and without being worked into a new system.

12 Locke (1980: 54 fn. 62) mentions the unsuccessful attempt of a Śākya of Kwā Bāhāḥ to attain Vajrācārya status. None of the Śākyas I knew aspired to it, and they would have been mocked by other Śākyas had they done so.

13 For the monastic identity of the Śākyas, shared but overlaid with a priestly identity by Vajrācāryas, see §6.1.

14 In this connection it is interesting to note that in the Newar tradition the

personal name of Śākyamuni Buddha was not Siddhārtha, 'he whose aim has been achieved' (as in Theravāda Buddhism), but Sarvārthasiddha, 'he who has achieved all aims'. However, for an exception, see chapter 7: epigram and appendix.

15 Locke 1975, 1980, 1985, 1989. In particular, on point (i), see Locke 1980: 65,115ff.; on (ii), 1980: 13; 1989: 92; on (iii), 1980: 20; on (vi), 1975: 18; 1989: 91.

16 The name 'Karuṇāmaya' is an epithet of the *bodhisattva* Avalokiteśvara, while 'Matsyendra' is the name of a famous *siddha*. There is a long, complex, and fascinating history behind their conflation. See Locke 1980, and Owens 1989: chapter 5.

17 Skt. *abhiṣeka* is pronounced in Newari as *abhiṣek*, *abhiṣeś*, or *abhikhek*. Kvaerne (1975: 93) gives a table correlating seven different canonical texts showing that details of the schema of different consecrations vary from one to the other. The five given here (Flask through Name) seem to be the most standard list. Asha Kaji Vajracharya (1983 II: 354–6) lists the five as here, except that the Crown Consecration comes last.

18 Locke 1980: 219–20; KSc: 295–9.

19 See, e.g., Snellgrove 1959a I: 131–2; 1987: 243.

20 KSc: 326^{5-6}, 329^{8}–330^{1}, 347^{3}.

21 For further detail on the liturgy used in the Consecration of a Vajra-Master, see Gellner 1987a: 439–45 (further refined in n.d.a).

22 Unfortunately I do not know which version or which mandala of these deities is involved here. It seems likely that the Mañjuvajra initiation is that of the form of Mañjuśrī called Mañjughoṣa, mentioned at §9.1, in view of the importance of the cult of the *dharmadhātu*.

23 My survey included sixty-six Vajrācārya families (150 men, 136 women) and 211 Śākya families (514 men, 507 women). Those under fifteen were excluded from the figures for calculating the numbers with Tantric Initiation, since they would normally be considered too young to take it.

24 Since the Citrakārs' death-*guthi* god is Caṇḍamahāroṣaṇa (Toffin 1984: 211), some Citrakārs may be entitled to this initiation also.

25 In the Kriyā Samuccaya this ritual specialist is known as the *karmavajrin*.

26 S.K. Tuladhar (1979) has described this ritual as it is performed at the beginning of the preparations for Kathmandu Samyak.

27 Skt. *adhivāsana* means literally 'causing to dwell in'. It is a technical term of ritual referring to the preliminary setting up, after which a ritual object is treated with respect even though its full empowerment (*pratiṣṭhā*) or consecration (*abhiṣeka*) has yet to be performed. It could equally be derived from the root *vās*, to perfume, and would mean in that case that the things established were being 'fragranced' with the divine during the night. Tibetan translators sometimes preferred this interpretation (Tsuda 1974: 296 fn. 1).

28 This is the esoteric mandala arrangement in terms of which the Svayambhū Purāṇa describes the Kathmandu Valley (see §7.1).

29 Caṇḍamahāroṣaṇa seems to perform the function of a kind of exoteric substitute for Cakrasaṃvara. He is treated, in this form at least, as belonging to the exoteric level of the Vajrayāna (§9.1).

30 This is a reference to the heroes (*vīra*) of Tantrism who achieve enlightenment by consorting with female *yoginīs* and become Realized Ones.

31 It is likely that in fact the esoteric version of this, in which Heruka is substituted for Vajrasattva, is used (cf. Finot 1934: 58). In the *guru maṇḍala* the hundred-syllabled mantra is used as a request for forgiveness of mistakes (*kṣamāpaṇa*). Here it is used for pacifying, though of a non-evil influence.

32 Note this duplication of the giving of the Vajrasattva mantra (see above §9.3.2).

33 This would seem to be a reworking of a rite found frequently in canonical texts (e.g. the Sekoddeśaṭīkā: Carelli 1941: 17, 19; KSc: 336) by which the candidates, while still blindfolded, cast a flower onto the mandala in order to determine which of the Five Buddha families (*kula*) they belong to. I found no evidence that these Buddha families have any ritual significance in Newar Buddhism, though they certainly have iconographic import (e.g. Lokeśvara is generally known to belong to the family of Amitābha). Fairly recent handbooks on Tantric Initiation prescribe the prediction of the type of success (*siddhi*) the neophyte will attain on the basis of where the flower falls, a rite also performed, according to these texts, in the second part of the ritual devoted to Vajravārāhī. They also say that if the flower falls outside the mandala the candidate will attain no *siddhi* and should be sent away, either after seeing the mandala only for a short time (Bubi 80: 149r), or without seeing mandala at all (Babi 45: 87v).

34 Here, what is, in the scriptural texts such as KSc, a single consecration, the *prajñājñānābhiṣeka*, has been split into two. The rituals which Asha Kaji here classifies as the Knowledge Consecration come under the head of the Secret Consecration in the handbook NGMPP E 1093/5. Furthermore, the handbook, sticking more closely to KSc, has a Fourth Consecration in which the meaning of the previous consecrations is given (principally explanations of the Four Blisses). What is given by Asha Kaji as the Secret Consecration is there, as in KSc, the Vow of Practice (*caryāvrata*), undertaken *after* all the consecrations have been received.

35 For a study of one version of the mandala of Vajravārāhī, see Meisezahl 1967.

36 Here the putting of orange powder in the parting (included above within the Lampblack Consecration) is listed as a separate consecration.

37 This is no doubt the same rite as that used in Lineage Deity Worship (§8.2.4). The eating of rice-flour pancakes which follows is another indication of this.

38 A Tantric Fire Sacrifice of this sort is also sometimes performed in exoteric contexts. Asha Kaji Vajracharya is keen to emphasize that the meat offered should properly consist of 108 balls of mixed musk, camphor, and two types of incense, since these are what is referred to in the Tantric song, Kāṇhapā Ācārya's 'Kolāīre', used in the ritual (A.K. Vajracharya 1977: 15). (See Hevajra Tantra 2.4.6ff. and Wayman 1973: 134, for the text of the song, which bears out Asha Kaji's interpretation.) Likewise he says that the coconut symbolizes a ball of sin (*pāp*), not the main sponsor's head as is commonly thought (pp. 158–9).

39 Such statements are found in strictly esoteric contexts. Thus the Caṇḍamahāroṣaṇa Tantra 8.27 (George 1974: 23) says that 'women are heaven, women are the *dharma*, women are the ultimate asceticism, women are the Buddha, women are the Saṃgha, women are the Perfection of Wisdom'.

40 This verse also occurs in the Bodhicaryāvatāra 3.25 (no doubt the original source) with the variant *sulabdho mānuṣobhavaḥ* for *saphalaṃ jīvitaṃ ca me*. The first line also appears in A.V. Vajracharya 1972: 15.

41 E.g. NGMPP E1093/5 (=Bubi 23): 75v; Babi 47: 144.

Notes to chapter 10

1 On this see Gellner 1987a: 423–7; revised and improved in n.d.b.

2 M. Allen (1975: 30) records this worry on the part of a family whose daughter had been the royal Kumārī of Lalitpur.

3 Eight of the donors however (5.1%) were from outside Kathmandu.

4 On Tibet, see Beyer 1973: 66; also Blofeld 1974: 91: 'Tantrists combine worship and meditation in one by means of the sadhanas.' In describing Tantric Hinduism, Gupta (1979) uses a slightly variant terminology: *sādhanā* (fem.) (means for accomplishment) dividing into *pūjā* (worship) and *yoga*. Bharati (1965: chapter 9) also uses the feminine *sādhanā*. In classical Tantric texts it seems always to be neuter.

5 What follows is an abbreviation of a summary prepared by Alexis Sanderson of the Cakrasaṃvara-pūjā-vidhi (NGMPP D 35/28, a text dated 1855) and the Saṃkṣipta-trisamādhi-pūjā (Takaoka 1981: DH 372, undated). The following paragraph simply summarizes his work. For the same ritual in Tibet, the Process of Generation (*utpattikrama*) followed by the Process of Perfection (*utpanna-krama*), see Beyer 1973: 100–43, esp. pp. 112–14 and 130.

6 The other main difference is that in the Threefold Meditation stage 3 is greatly reduced in length and there is no Visualization of the twelve-armed form. The Knowledge-Deity is fused directly with the six-armed form of Cakrasaṃvara generated in the second stage.

7 The text calls this mandala the *jñānacakra*, the wisdom circle or sphere.

8 These are two of the principal deities of esoteric Śaivism; see Sanderson 1988.

9 This is also known as the Process of Perfection (*utpannakrama*, *niṣpannakrama*, or *niṣpattikrama*) of the Preliminary yoga (stage 2); that is, it is the realization of the ultimate Knowledge-Deity as opposed to the Convention-Deity.

10 Locke 1980: 108 fn. 58. These terms denote two of the 'most difficult' ideas in Tantric Buddhist literature (Lessing and Wayman 1978: 162 fn. 17). Tucci (1980: 95) translates Knowledge-Deity as deity created 'out of transcendent consciousness' and Convention-Deity as 'being resulting from the vow', which is perhaps clearer though less succinct.

11 Within the different types of Tantra distinguished above (§9.1) it is characteristic of the Kriyā and Caryā Tantras. These lack the explicit self-divinization of the later and higher Tantras (Snellgrove 1987: 240), although many Tibetan Tantric exegetes argued that Kriyā and Caryā Tantras must possess such 'self-generation', both on scriptural grounds and because without it there could be no *siddhi* (Lessing and Wayman 1978: 163–71).

12 For an illustration of the relationships between Buddhas and *bodhisattvas*, see Wright 1972: 43; Wiesner 1976: 26–7; Hodgson 1972 I: 49.

13 There follows the account of how Lokeśvara, as Sṛṣṭikartṛ-lokeśvara, emitted all the Hindu gods. This passage is a re-translation of Wright 1972: 140.

14 See Dayal (1970: 26–8) for early variants of these terms. Strong (1979) shows how a simple twofold opposition between the physical body and the Dharma-body of the Buddha, which was the origin of the threefold division, related in the Avadāna literature to acts of alms-giving (*dān*).

15 Snellgrove (1959b: 213) points out that the four floors of the famous Mahābuddha monastery in Lalitpur, containing in ascending order Śākyamuni

Buddha, Amitābha, a *caitya*, and a *vajradhātu* mandala, must have been intended to represent the four Bodies. According to H. Sakya (1988: 31–3), there are in fact six levels, with a *dharmadhātu* above the (Svayambhū) *caitya*, a *vajradhātu* above that, and on the final level another small gold *caitya* surmounted by a Vajrācārya's or Buddha's crown. Nonetheless, Snellgrove's interpretation is probably still sound.

16 See Snellgrove 1959a I: 37–8, 105. It has been noted above how a pilgrimage to the Power-Places surrounding Kathmandu city is brought into relation with the system of yoga and the Buddha's bodies (§7.1).

17 I have adapted Snellgrove's translation. A similar passage occurs in the Caṇḍamahāroṣaṇa Tantra (George 1974: 21, 52).

18 See Snellgrove 1959a II: 156 and Warder 1980: 503.

19 I am indebted to Alexis Sanderson both for bringing this passage to my attention and for providing me with his draft translation, quoted here.

20 It is presumably to accustom the reader to this ultimate point of view that Beyer (1973) calls what one might naively designate ordinary reality 'nonreality'.

21 Snellgrove (1987: 512) regards the existence of conflict in the eleventh and twelfth centuries between 'the free-roving tantric yogin', on the one hand, and the Monastic Community, on the other, as evidence that Tantric ritual had not yet been fully absorbed (i.e. routinized) into monastic ceremonial.

22 See KSc: 352–5. The fifteenth-century Tibetan text translated by Lessing and Wayman (1978: 323) indicates that the female partner is to be imagined.

23 KSc 411[3]: *Prajñāhīnaṃ yac cakraṃ tac cakraṃ maṇḍamelakam.*

24 Unfortunately I never interviewed Dharma Guruju myself and he died in 1991. The informants I have relied on knew him well.

25 One wonders whether the devotees of the flamboyantly antinomian Aghoris described by Parry (1982) would remain devotees for long if they had to carry out the same antinomian practices as their *guru*.

26 Snellgrove translates *grāmyadharmam* as 'affairs of the town'. The correct translation was pointed out to me by Richard Gombrich.

27 Hevajra Tantra 1.6.18f, 1.7.24–6, Saṃvarodaya Tantra 21.3f. Kvaerne (1975: 132–3) translates verses from the Pañcakrama to the same effect. The Caṇḍamahāroṣaṇa Tantra which, judging by the number of manuscripts, has always been popular in Nepal, makes the antinomian implications of this doctrine quite explicit: the liberated yogin 'although he may kill a hundred Brahmans . . . will not be stained by sin . . . The same terrible action which leads people to hell, undoubtedly leads them to Release if it is done together with Method' (George 1974: 79).

28 Asha Kaji equates the definite or intended meaning with the *saṃdhā bhāṣā*. This, it seems, was also Tsong kha pa's position, although it is the opposite of what some modern scholars have assumed (Katz 1983: 120).

29 Gellner 1991b: 184. For other references to these esoteric interpretations see Snellgrove 1959a I: 86 fn. 2; 1987: 163; Wayman 1973: 34, 116; and KSc: 401. In the first list, human flesh seems normally to take the place of phlegm. Snellgrove (1959a I: 43) comments that 'to consume [the Five Lamps] in the accepted Buddhist sense, means to consume the Five Buddhas and thus to purify (*viśuddh*) the Five Evils'.

30 Jayabhadra, commenting on the Laghusaṃvara Tantra in his Cakrasaṃvara-pañjikā, explains in several places that there are two types of *samaya*: those to be kept (*rakṣaṇīya*), i.e. vows, and those to be eaten (*bhakṣaṇīya*), i.e. sacraments (NGMPP B 30/41: $5r^1$, $5v^7$, $8v^{2-3}$) (I owe these references to Alexis Sanderson). Cf. Snellgrove 1987: 165–6.

31 In Newari they are respectively *cāku*, *khāyu* (Lalitpur: *khāyi*), *pāũ*, *cisawāḥ*, *pālu*, and *phāku*, and in Sanskrit *madhu*, *tiktaka*, *amla*, *lavaṇa*, *kaṭuka*, and *kaṣāya*. This set of six tastes is given at Hevajra Tantra 2.3.46b. KSc (395^4) indicates that a religious feast (*bhojana*) ought to encompass all six tastes.

32 Juju and Shrestha 1985: 12. He spells *samay* '*samhay*', an archaic spelling also preferred by S.M. Joshi 1987.

33 Juju and Shrestha 1985: 18. Asha Kaji Vajracharya (1981c: 79) obtained the following list from a Brahman. In the *paṃcabali* offered to Bhairava, pumpkin stands for a buffalo, sugarcane for a goat, cucumber for a sheep, ginger for a duck, and snakegourd (*toriyā*) for a fish.

34 A similar case is the *śivaliṅga*. The vast majority of Newars would be surprised and shocked to learn what Westerners and western-educated South Asians often glibly take for granted, that it is a phallic symbol. As far as Newars are concerned, it is Mahādeva's (Śiva's) visible form.

Notes to chapter 11

1 Khaḍgīs, on the other hand, typically marry over long distances. Of 100 same-caste brides of a high-status Khaḍgī lineage, only twenty-one were from Lalitpur, fifty-eight coming from Kathmandu, and the remaining twenty-one from other settlements, such as Thimi, Bhaktapur, Panauti, and Dakṣiṇkālī. Of fifty-eight daughters of the same lineage, fully thirty-nine were married to husbands in Kathmandu.

2 See Ishii n.d. There is however a big difference between Maharjans and Śreṣṭhas in that whereas nearly all Maharjan men find brides in villages near Satungal, only 3% going further afield, only 27% of Śreṣṭhas marry women from nearby villages, fully 57% of them bringing in brides from further afield.

3 I find it hard to reconcile what Toffin says here with his lucid demonstration a few pages later (pp. 221–2), in criticism of Dumont, of the thoroughly Indian nature of the Newar caste system.

4 See Toffin 1984: 63–4, and Quigley 1984: 179–82.

5 In the past Newars were keen to differentiate themselves from Parbatiyās also. Nowadays their mutual relations are very complex. I have tried to sort out the different attitudes taken by different Newar groups towards Parbatiyās in Gellner 1986.

6 Many observers had thought it was hypergamous on the basis of very scant and unreliable data. See references in Quigley (1986), as well as the discussion in Quigley (1984), particularly the conclusion 'Newar urbanism and cohesion'.

7 As with Lineage Deities (*digu dyaḥ*) – a category, not a proper name – Tantric deities are frequently just called *āgǎ dyaḥ*, also a category. However, unlike the Lineage Deity, there always is a specifiable Sanskritic name as well.

8 This is not to deny that elderly Śreṣṭhas must also have regarded Tantric Initiation in a soteriological way. Nowadays very few take it.

9 Juju and Shrestha 1985: 51, 53. Juju also has a chapter on the sword as a symbol

of protection (*surakṣā*) (ibid.: 38–47). G.V. Vajracharya (1976: 185) points out that for the Malla kings the Sword Festival was the central event of Mohanī. See Gupta and Gombrich (1986) for a general discussion of the influence of Hindu Tantrism on the concept of political power in India.

10 Presumably he meant the war of 1854–6.

11 Newar Buddhism does provide a *dhāraṇī* for success in warfare (Mitra 1971: 280), but it is a very obscure one.

12 Cf. Dumont 1980: 282.

13 For Pyangaon, see Toffin 1984: 155–6. Brahmans and Karmācāryas are called from outside the village only at death. Peasant Karmācāryas are important in Bhaktapur, and also, I suspect, in Tokhā. In Theco it seems that family rituals are performed by Vajrācāryas, but some Maharjans are given initiation by a Karmācārya in order to carry on the duties of god-guardian to Bāl Kumārī (Toffin 1984: 184, 204 n. 8).

14 I have discussed these in the context of Newar identity in Gellner 1986. Cf. Dumont (1957: 15) and Singer (1972: 401–2) on Tamil Nadu.

15 Cf. Snellgrove's (1959a I: 5, 17) criticisms of Dasgupta's view that Tantric method was introduced 'for the sake of the common run of people'. On the origins of Śaiva Tantra, which in turn influenced Buddhist Tantra, see Sanderson 1988; in press.

16 On Tamil Nadu, see Fuller 1984: 16–17, 141–2. Van der Veer (1987) has rightly emphasized that *bhakti* is interpreted in very different ways, even within the confines of a single sectarian order.

17 Some prefer to use 'Āgamic' for non-Vedic traditions for whom Śiva and not the goddess is the highest divinity. Here I use the term 'Tantric' to denote all types of Hinduism based on non-Vedic esoteric scriptures, be they Tantras or Āgamas. This is the way Dumont (1980: 281–2) used it in his influential essay on world renunciation, and it can, I think, be regarded as standard scholarly usage.

18 The exact relationship of Hindu and Buddhist Tantric traditions is a complex question. There were borrowings in both directions. As far as the scriptures themselves go, many parts of some Buddhist Tantras, even though usually reworked, seem to have been modelled on Hindu Tantras, and in some cases lifted wholesale from them (Sanderson 1985: 214 n.106, 216 n. 134; in press).

19 By the latter he meant the Spirit-Offering (*bali*).

20 A recent article by Michaels (1989) deals with the paradox that the Brahmans of Paśupati derive their status from not being involved with the locality.

21 See §4.2, 9.2, 10.3–4 for qualifications to this judgement.

22 See Kloppenberg 1977; Tewari 1983; Bechert and Hartmann 1987. I have also discussed the movement briefly, in the context of Newar ethnic identity (Gellner 1986: 128–37).

23 Thus the Svayambhū Purāṇa says that the twelve-syllabled mantra is not to be explained to monks or other ascetics (Kölver 1986: 164).

24 See, for example, the article referred to in n. 28, p. 352.

25 Veena Das (1982: 56) has also noted an affinity between the heterodoxies (i.e. Buddhism and Jainism) and Tantrism, in that they all reject Hinduism's 'grammar of structural relations'.

26 See Tambiah 1970: 210–4; Spiro 1982: 266–71; Gombrich 1971: 202. Gombrich found only one of these sets of verses actually being used for a specialized

purpose, namely the Aṅgulimāla to ease the pains of childbirth. Spiro's description implies that in Burma a wide variety of specialized recitations are found. In Nepal, as far as I know, such specialized uses are, as yet, entirely theoretical.

27 This is one aspect of the success of Buddhist modernism everywhere. According to Houtman (1984: 61) the modernist version of a Burmese boy's ordination ceremony costs one third of the traditional ceremony.

28 In fact Durkin-Longley (1982: 162) distinguishes *jhārphuke vaidya*s from 'Gubhaju/Guruama'; there were apparently an estimated twenty-six of the former, and sixteen of the latter in Kathmandu in 1980–1. But the only real ground of distinction between the two categories seems to be caste, and the greater prestige of the Vajrācāryas, and I consider them as one category.

29 Two recent descriptions of female mediums, one from Kathmandu, the other from Lalitpur, are Dougherty 1986 and Coon 1989.

30 I have heard this expressed jocularly by saying that Śākyas are Vajrācāryas who do not have the right to ring the bell.

Notes to chapter 12

1 This reads 'physical' but should have been 'psychical' according to a personal communication from the author.

2 See Aziz 1978: chapter 3. On the Sherpas' married lamas, see Kunwar 1989: 205, 208–9.

3 The sacrifice of Rudra-Śiva to the Buddhas is a pervasive theme of Nying-ma ritual. I am indebted here to discussions with Rob Mayer, SOAS, who is working on this. His research shows that some Nying-ma Mahāyoga ritual is based on a conscious and aggressive inversion of Śaivite ritual. This contrasts with the later Tantras taken up by the other Tibetan schools, and with Nepal, where hostility to Hinduism is much more subtle and restrained. On Nying-ma ritual, see Cantwell 1989.

4 See Dumont 1980: 239ff.; Houseman 1984; N.J. Allen 1985.

5 Raheja 1988b is a useful survey of this debate; Burghart 1978 is an early challenge to Dumont.

6 See Hodgson (1972 I: 50) for Amṛtānanda's indignant rejection of the idea that the Buddha might have anything to do with punishing the wicked. My suggestion that he might do away with witches received a similar response from Jog Maya's daughter-in-law.

7 Mīmāṃsā, the Brahmanical school of Vedic ritual exegesis, might be seen as an exception here. Although philosophically influential, it has not had a separate institutional existence for many hundreds of years.

8 There is the traditional concept of *mithyā dṛṣṭi*, false views, but it is applied primarily to doctrine. Buddhist modernists have borrowed from neo-Hinduism the neologism *andhaviśvās*, literally 'blind faith', to translate the negative force of 'superstition'.

Bibliographies

Works in Newari and Nepali

Acharya, Baburam 1979. *Newāḥ, Newāḥbhāy wa Saṃskṛti*. Swayambu Lal Shrestha (tr.) Lalitpur: Sāhityā Mūlukhā. (First published in Nepali in *Nepāl Saṃskṛtik Pariṣad Patrikā* 1 (1) (1953): 1–16; tr. in English in *RRS* 2 (1) (1970): 1–15.)

Bajracharya, Badri Ratna 1983. *Śrī Svayambhū Mahāpurāṇa*. Kathmandu: Sanu Maya Tuladhar. (1103 N.S.)

Buddhaghosha, Bhikṣu 1982. 'Paritrāṇyā Mahattva' *Dharmodaya* 5 (37): 2–3.

Hridaya Ch. 1970. *Nepāl Bhāṣā Sāhityāyā Jātaḥ*. Kathmandu: Nepāl Bhāṣā Pariṣad. (1091 N.S.).

Joshi, Satya Mohan 1987 (ed.) *Baḥcādãgu Newāḥ Khǎgwaḥ Dhukū (A Concise Dictionary of the Newar Language)*. Kathmandu: Baikuntha Prasad Lacoul, Lacoul-Publications. (1107 N.S.)

Joshi, Vaidya Panna Prasad 1956. *Saṃkṣipta Nepāl Bhāṣā Śabda-koś*. (2012 V.S.)

Juju, Bal Dev and Surendra Man Shrestha 1985. *Nepālyā Tāntrik Dyaḥ wa Tāntrik Pūjā*. Kathmandu: self-published. (1105 N.S.)

Kayastha, Chattra Bahadur 1980. *Śrī Gaṇeś Brat Kathā (Cathā kunhu kanigu bākhã)*. Lalitpur: Sāhityāyā Mūlukhā. (1100 N.S.)

Mahāsambar 1982. *Mahāsambar Chattisāmat Pūjāyā Riporṭ*. Kathmandu: Vijayeśvarī Bihār Sudhār Samiti. (1102 N.S.)

Malla, Kamal Prakash 1979a. *Nepāl Bhāṣāyā Dhwānā Saphuyā Dhalaḥ, N.S. 1020–1097*. Kel Tol, Kathmandu: Laytā Dabu.

1984a. *Nepāl Bhāṣāyā Dhwānā Saphuyā Dhalaḥ – 2, N.S. 1098–1104*. Bhotahiti, Kathmandu: Pāsā Munā.

Manandhar, Thakur Lal 1983. 'Jhī "Digu Pujā"' in Indra Mali (ed.) *Nepāl Bhāṣā Nibandha Pucaḥ*. Kathmandu: Pāsā Munā.

Paudel, Nayanath and Devi Prasad Lamshal (eds.) 1963. *Bhāṣā Vaṃśāvalī*. Kathmandu: Rāṣṭriya Pustakālaya. 2 vols. (2020 and 2023 V.S.)

Pokharel, B. *et al.* (eds.) 1983. *Nepālī Bṛhat Śabdakoś*. Kathmandu: Royal Nepal Academy. (2040 V.S.)

Pradhan, Amar Man 1968. *Yogābhyāsī Yog Ratna (N.S. 1024–1087)*. Svayambhu, Kathmandu: Śānti Niketan Surakṣā tathā Saṃrakṣan Samiti.

Rajvamshi, Shankar Man 1983. *Bhūmisambandhi Tamasūk Tāḍpattra, Bhāg 1.* Kathmandu: Rāṣṭriya Abhilekhālaya. (2040 V.S.)

Sakya, Hemraj 1970. *Nepāl Saṃskṛtiyā Mūlukhā.* Lalitpur: Candralaksmi Devi Shakya. (1089 N.S.)

1971. *Sthirobhava-vākya (Chyẽ Paniṣṭhā yāibale bwanīgu vākya).* Lalitpur: Surya Man Vajracharya.

1973. *Mayūrvarṇa Mahāvihāryā Saṃkṣipta Itihās.* Lalitpur: Bhĩchẽ Bāhāyā Sarvasaṃgha. (2517 B.S.)

1977. *Srī Svayambhū Mahācaitya.* Kathmandu: Svayambhu Vikās Mandal. (1098 N.S.)

1978a. *Śrīvidyādharī-Vijayeśvarīsthān Saṃkṣipta-Paricay.* Kathmandu: Vijayeśvarī Mahāvihār-Sudhār Samiti. (1098 N.S.)

1978b. *Śrī Bhāskarakīrti Mahāvihār Yeṭkhā Bāhāḥ Chagu Adhyayan.* Yaṭkhā Bāhāḥ, Kathmandu: Āryanāmasaṃgīti Guṭhī. (2522 B.S.)

1979. *Samyak Mahādān Guthi.* Kathmandu: Jagat Dhar Tuladhar. (1100 N.S.)

1988. *Bodhimaṇḍap Kūṭāgār Mahābuddha-Mandir Saṃkṣipta-Itihās.* Lalitpur: Chakra Raj Shakya *et al.*

Sakyananda, Bhikṣu 1977. *Māsu Kina Khāna Hůdaina.* Tansen: Vishnu Maya Vajracharya (1097 N.S.)

Shakya, Lok Bahadur 1984. *Prajñāpāramitā Mhasīkegu Jñānayā Khå Munā.* Lalitpur: Prajñāpāramitā Caryā Guthi.

Sudarshan, Bhikṣu 1982. *Mahāparitrāṇ (Nepāl Bhāṣāy artha sahit).* Gaṇa Mahāvihāra, Kathmandu.

Vajracharya, Adi Vajra 1963. *Mahāyāni Nityacāra Vidhiḥ.* Lalitpur: Hiraṇyavarṇa-mahāvihārayā Bajrācārya Guṭhi. (2020 V.S.)

1980. *Nigūgu Paryāyavācī Koś.* Asan Tol, Kathmandu: Basanta Raj Tuladhar. (1100 N.S.)

Vajracharya, Amogha Vajra 1972. *Gurumaṇḍalārcana-pustakam.* Kathmandu: De Ācāryya Guthī. (1092 N.S.)

1976a. *Kalaśārcanādi-homavidhāna-pustakam.* Kathmandu: De Ācāryya Guthī. (1096 N.S.)

1976b. *Saptabārapāṭha Pustakam.* Kathmandu: self-published. (1096 N.S.)

1979. *Lokeśvarayā Paricay.* Kathmandu: Lokeśvara Saṃgha. (1099 N.S.)

Vajracharya, Asha Kaji 1956. *Nepāl Varṣakriyā (Nakhaḥcakhaḥ Parvakāl).* Atha Nani, Lalitpur: self-published. (1077 N.S.) Reissued, revised 1987.

1972. *Sānhūguṭhiyā Mahimā, Suradatta Kathā.* Self-published. (1092 N.S.)

1977. *Mahāyān Bauddha Dharma Darśan.* Self-published. (1097 N.S.)

1980. *Bũgadyo Nepāle Haḥgu Khå.* Self-published. (Fourth impression 2037 V.S.)

1981a. *Mahāyān Buddhadharma (Svayambhū Purāṇayā chagu aṃśa): Nepāl Dvādaśa Tīrtha Brata.* Lalitpur: Sthavir Buddha Raj Shakya. (1101 N.S.)

1981b. *Sūryodaya Rājayā Bākhå (Ślok tathā Nepāl Bhāṣā).* Atha Bāhāḥ, Lalitpur: self-published. (Second impression 2038 V.S.)

1981c. *Bṛṣā Janma Vadān.* Bhaktapur: Maṃgal Dharmadvīp Vihār. (Second impression 1101 N.S.)

1982. *Pājadān Vidhi.* Lalitpur: Siddhi Raj Shakya and family. (1102 N.S.)

1983. *Bodhisattvāvadānamālā.* Kathmandu: NBP. 3 vols. (1103, 1103, and 1105 N.S.)

1985. *Mahāyān Buddha Dharma Caryyā*. Lalitpur: Prem Bahadur Shakya *et al.* (1105 N.S.)
1986. *Tārā Pārājikā, Mūl wa Nepāl Bhāṣā artha sahit*. Self-published. (1106 N.S.)
1987. See 1956.
Vajracharya, Chunda 1983. 'Newāh Samājay Vajrācārya wa Śākyayā chũ Paricay' *Jhī* 196: 7–11. (Kachala 1104 N.S.) Revised 1989 in *Smārikā* 1: 12–15.
1984. *Mallakālyā chũ Saṃskṛti*. Kathmandu: Kashinath Tamot. (1105 N.S.)
Vajracharya, Dhana Vajra 1980. 'Madhyakālik Nepālkā ek prakhyāt Rājā Śivadev' *CNS* 8 (1): 207–22.
Vajracharya, Gautam Vajra 1976. *Hanumān Ḍhokā Rājdārbār*. Kathmandu: CNAS. (2033 V.S.)
Vajracharya, Jog Muni 1979. *Samyaksambuddha Nirbāṇ Mārg (Jīvan Saphal)*. Self-published. (1099 N.S.)
Vajracharya, Mohan Raj 1977. *Rūpāvatyāvadāna: Bhagavān Buddha misā juyā janma jūgu*. Bhĩchẽ Bāhāḥ, Lalitpur: self-published. (1097 N.S.)
Vajracharya, Nagendra Raj 1975. *Āryya Bhadracarī, Mahāpraṇidhāna Ratnarāja Stotra*. Oṁ Bāhāḥ, Lalitpur: self-published. (1095 N.S.)
Vajracharya, Punya Ratna 1979. *Hāmro Cāḍ-parva*. Kathmandu: Ratna Pustak Bhandar. (Fourth impression 2036 V.S.)
Vajracharya, Ratna Bahadur 1972. *Bauddha Prathama Śikṣā*. Lalitpur: Guna Ratna Shakya. (1092 N.S.)
Vajracharya, Ratna Kaji 1980. *Yẽ Deyā Bauddha Pūjā Kriyāyā Halãjwalã*. Kathmandu: NBP. (2524 B.S.)
1989. *Newāḥ Saṃskāra Saṃskṛtiyā Tāḥcā (Cultural Heritage of the Newara)*. Kathmandu: Vajracharya Prakashan.
Vajracharya, Ushnisha Vajra 1968. *Totrārcana Pustaka*. Bu Bāhāḥ, Lalitpur: self-published. (2025 V.S.)

Bibliography of works in other languages

Allen, M.R. 1973. 'Buddhism without Monks: The Vajrayana Religion of the Newars of the Kathmandu Valley' *South Asia* 2: 1–14.
1975. *The Cult of Kumari: Virgin Worship in Nepal*. Tribhuvan University, Kathmandu: INAS. (Reissued 1987 by Madhab Lal Maharjan, Himalayan Booksellers, Kathmandu.)
1982 'Girls' Pre-puberty Rites among the Newars of the Kathmandu Valley' in M. Allen and S.N. Mukherjee (eds.) *Women in India and Nepal*, Australian National University Monographs on S. Asia No. 8. (Included as chapter 5 of 1987 reprint of 1975 above.)
in press. 'Procession and Pilgrimage in Newar Religion' in S. Lienhard (ed.) *Change and Continuity in the Nepalese Culture of the Kathmandu Valley*. Turin: CESMEO.
Allen, N.J. 1985. 'Hierarchical Opposition and Some Other Types of Relation' in R.H. Barnes, D. de Coppet and R. Parkin (eds.) *Contexts and Levels: Anthropological Essays on Hierarchy*. Oxford: Journal of the Anthropological Society of Oxford.
Ames, M.M. 1966. 'Ritual Prestations and the Structure of the Sinhalese Pantheon' in M. Nash (ed.) *Anthropological Studies in Theravada Buddhism*. Yale

University Southeast Asia Studies No. 13.
Anderson, M.M. 1977. *The Festivals of Nepal.* Calcutta: Rupa. (First published 1971.)
Aziz, B.N. 1978. *Tibetan Frontier Families.* Delhi: Vikas.
Babb, L.A. 1975. *The Divine Hierarchy: Popular Hinduism in Central India.* New York: Columbia University Press.
Bachnik, J. 1983. 'Recruitment Strategies for Household Succession: Rethinking Japanese Household Organisation' *Man* (N.S.) 18 (4): 160–82.
Bajracharya, B.R. 1986. *Buddhism of Nepal* G.M. Bajracharya (tr.). Kathmandu: Ananda Kuti Vihara Trust.
Bajracharya, P.H. 1959. 'Newar Marriage Customs and Festivals' *South-Western Journal of Anthropology* 15: 418–28.
Barré, V., P. Berger, L. Feveile, and G. Toffin 1981. *Panuti: une ville au Népal.* (Collection Architectures.) Paris: Berger-Levrault.
Bechert, H. (ed.) 1978. *Buddhism in Ceylon and Studies on Religious Syncretism in Buddhist Countries.* Göttingen: Vandenhoeck and Ruprecht.
1989. 'Aspects of Theravāda Buddhism in Sri Lanka and Southeast Asia' in Skorupski (ed.).
Bechert, H. and R.F. Gombrich (eds.) 1984. *The World of Buddhism: Buddhist Monks and Nuns in Society and Culture.* London: Thames and Hudson.
Bechert, H. and J.-U. Hartmann 1987. 'Observations on the Reform of Buddhism in Nepal' *JNRC* 8: 1–30.
Bennett, L. 1979. *Tradition and Change in the Legal Status of Nepalese Women.* (*The Status of Women in Nepal* Vol. I, Part 2.) Kathmandu: CEDA, Tribhuvan University.
1983. *Dangerous Wives and Sacred Sisters: Social and Symbolic Roles of High-Caste Women in Nepal.* New York: Columbia University Press.
Beyer, S. 1973. *The Cult of Tārā: Magic and Ritual in Tibet.* Berkeley and Los Angeles: University of California Press.
Bharati, A. 1965. *The Tantric Tradition.* London: Rider.
Bhattacharya, B. 1925, 1928. *Sādhanamālā,* Vols. I and II. Baroda: GOS 26 and 41.
1972. *Niṣpannayogāvalī of Mahāpaṇḍita Abhayākaragupta.* Baroda: GOS 109.
Bista, K.B. 1972. *Le Culte du Kuldevata au Nepal en particulier chez certains Ksatri de la vallée de Kathmandu.* Paris: CNRS.
Blacker, C. 1965. 'Initiation in the Shugendo: The Passage through the Ten States of Existence' in C.J. Bleeker (ed.) *Initiation* (Supplements to *Numen* 10). Leiden: E.J. Brill.
Blaikie, P., J. Cameron, and D. Seddon 1980. *Nepal in Crisis.* Delhi: Oxford University Press.
Bloch, Marc. 1954. *The Historian's Craft* P. Putnam (tr.). Manchester: Manchester University Press.
Blofeld, J. 1974. *The Tantric Mysticism of Tibet: A Practical Guide.* New York: Causeway Books. (Published as *The Way of Power*, 1970, London: George Allen and Unwin.)
Blustain, H.S. 1977. 'Power and Ideology in a Nepalese Village' Ph.D., Yale University. UMI 7815710.
Bouillier, V. 1979. *Naître renonçant: une caste de Sannyāsi villageois au Népal central.* Nanterre: Laboratoire d'Ethnologie.

Bouillier, V. and G. Toffin (eds.) 1989. *Prêtrise, pouvoirs et autorité en Himalaya* (*Puruṣārtha* 12). Paris: Editions de l'EHESS.

Brass, P.R. 1974. *Language, Religion and Politics in North India.* Cambridge: Cambridge University Press.

Brinkhaus, H. 1980.'References to Buddhism in the Nepāla-māhātmya' *JNRC* 4: 274–86.

1985. 'Harihariharivāhana Lokeśvara in Nepal' *Zeitschrift der Deutschen Morgenländischen Gesellschaft Supplement VI*: 422–9.

1987a. *The Pradyumna-Prabhāvatī Legend in Nepal: A Study of the Hindu Myth of the Draining of the Nepal Valley.* (Alt- und Neu-Indische Studien 32.) Stuttgart: Franz Steiner.

1987b. *Jagatprakāśamallas Mūladevaśaśidevavyākhyānanāṭaka: Das älteste bekannte vollständig überlieferte Newari-Drama.* (Alt- und Neu-Indische Studien 36.) Stuttgart: Franz Steiner.

Brough, J. 1948. 'Nepalese Buddhist Rituals' *BSOAS* 12: 668–76.

Bunnag, J. 1973. *Buddhist Monk, Buddhist Layman: A Study of Urban Monastic Organization in Central Thailand.* Cambridge: Cambridge University Press.

Burghart, R. 1978. 'Hierarchical Models of the Hindu Social System' *Man* (N.S.) 13: 519–36.

1983. 'Renunciation in the Religious Traditions of South Asia' *Man* (N.S.) 18: 635–53.

1984. 'The Formation of the Concept of Nation-State in Nepal' *JAS* 44 (1): 101–25.

Burleigh, P. 1976. 'A Chronology of the Later Kings of Patan' *Kailash* 4 (1): 21–71.

Campbell, J.G. 1976. *Saints and Householders: A Study of Hindu Ritual and Myth among the Kangra Rajputs.* (Bibliotheca Himalayica III.6.) Kathmandu: Ratna Pustak Bhandar.

Cantlie, A. 1984. *The Assamese: Religion, Caste and Sect in an Indian Village.* (London Studies on South Asia 3.) London: Curzon Press.

Cantwell, C.M. 1989. 'An Ethnographic Account of the Religious Practice in a Tibetan Buddhist Refugee Monastery in Northern India' Ph.D., University of Kent.

Caplan, A.P. 1972. *Priests and Cobblers: A Study of Social Change in a Hindu Village in Western Nepal.* London: Intertext Books.

Caplan, L. 1975. *Administration and Politics in a Nepalese Town.* London: Oxford University Press.

1985. 'The Popular Culture of Evil in Urban South India' in D. Parkin (ed.) *The Anthropology of Evil.* Oxford: Blackwell.

Carelli, M. 1941. *Sekoddeśaṭīkā.* Baroda: GOS 90.

Carrithers, M.B. 1979a. 'The Modern Ascetics of Lanka and the Pattern of Change in Buddhism' *Man* (N.S.) 14: 294–310.

1979b. 'The Social Organisation of the Sinhalese Sangha in an Historical Perspective' in G. Krishna (ed.) *Contributions to South Asian Studies* Vol. I. Delhi: Oxford University Press.

1983. *The Forest Monks of Sri Lanka: An Anthropological and Historical Study.* Delhi: Oxford University Press.

1984. '"They will be Lords upon the Island": Buddhism in Sri Lanka' in H. Bechert and R.F. Gombrich (eds.)

Chandra,L. (ed.) 1977. *Kriyā-samuccaya.* (Śatapiṭaka Series 237.) Delhi: S. Rani.

Chandra, L. and D.L. Snellgrove (eds.) 1981. *Sarva-tathāgata-tattva-saṅgraha.* (Śatapiṭaka Series 269.) Delhi: S. Rani.

Chattopadhyay, K.P. 1980. *An Essay on the History of Newar Culture.* Kathmandu: Educational Enterprises. (Reprinted from *Journal of the Asiatic Society of Bengal* 19 (10) (1923): 465–560.)

Chattopadhyaya, D. (ed.) 1970. *Tāranātha's History of Buddhism in India,* Lama Chimpa and Alaka Chattopadhyaya (tr.). Simla: Indian Institute of Advanced Studies.

Christian, W.A. 1989. *Person and God in a Spanish Valley.* Princeton, NJ: Princeton University Press. (First published 1972.)

Collins, S. 1982. *Selfless Persons: Imagery and Thought in Theravāda Buddhism.* Cambridge: Cambridge University Press.

Cone, M. and R.F. Gombrich 1977. *The Perfect Generosity of Prince Vessantara: A Buddhist Epic.* Oxford: Oxford University Press.

Conze, E. 1960. *Buddhism: Its Essence and Development.* Oxford: Bruno Cassirer. (First published 1951.)

Coon, E. 1989. 'Possessing Power: Ajima and her Medium' *Himalayan Research Bulletin* 9 (1): 1–9.

Das, V. 1982. *Structure and Cognition: Aspects of Hindu Caste and Ritual.* Delhi: Oxford University Press. (2nd ed.)

Dasgupta, S.B. 1974. *An Introduction to Tantric Buddhism.* Berkeley and London: Shambala. (First published 1958.)

Dayal, H. 1970. *The Bodhisattva Doctrine in Buddhist Sanskrit Literature.* New Delhi: Motilal Banarsidass. (First published 1932.)

Dhargyey, Geshey N. 1974. *Tibetan Tradition of Mental Development.* Dharmasala: Library of Tibetan Works and Archives.

Diehl, C.G. 1956. *Instrument and Purpose: Studies on Rites and Rituals in South India.* Lund: CWK Gleerup.

Dirks, N.B. 1987. *The Hollow Crown: Ethnohistory of an Indian Kingdom.* Cambridge: Cambridge University Press.

Dougherty, L.M. 1986. 'Sita and the Goddess: A Case Study of a Woman Healer in Nepal' *CNS* 14 (1): 25–36.

Dowman, K. 1981. 'A Buddhist Guide to the Power Places of the Kathmandu Valley' *Kailash* 8 (3–4): 183–291.

Dubois, Abbé J.A. 1897. *Hindu Manners, Customs and Ceremonies* H.K. Beauchamp (tr.). Oxford: Oxford University Press.

Dumont, L. 1957. 'For a Sociology of India' *CIS* 1: 7–22.

1980. *Homo Hierarchicus: The Caste System and Its Implications* M. Sainsbury, L. Dumont, and B. Gulati (tr.). Chicago and London: Chicago University Press.

Durkheim, E. 1965. *The Elementary Forms of the Religious Life* J.W. Swain (tr.). New York: The Free Press. (First published 1915.)

Durkin-Longley, M.S. 1982. 'Ayurveda in Nepal: A Medical Belief System in Action' Ph.D., University of Wisconsin. UMI 8224034.

Dutt, S. 1978. *The Buddha and Five After-Centuries.* Calcutta: Sahitya Samsad. (First published 1957.)

Ensink, J. 1978. 'Śiva-Buddhism in Java and Bali' in H. Bechert (ed.).

Evans-Pritchard, E.E. 1937. *Witchcraft, Oracles and Magic among the Azande.* Oxford: Clarendon Press.

1956. *Nuer Religion.* Oxford: Clarendon Press.

Evers, H. 1972. *Monks, Priests and Peasants: A Study of Buddhism and Social Structure in Central Ceylon.* Leiden: E.J. Brill.

Evison, G. 1989. 'Indian Death Rituals: Ambivalence in Action' D.Phil., University of Oxford.

Finot, L. 1934. 'Manuscrits Sanskrits de Sādhana's retrouvés en Chine' *Journal Asiatique* (Juillet-Septembre): 1–86.

Frauwallner, E. 1956. *The Earliest Vinaya and the Beginnings of Buddhist Literature.* (Serie Orientale Roma 8.) Rome: ISMEO.

Fuller, C.J. 1979. 'Gods, Priests and Purity: On the Relation between Hinduism and the Caste System' *Man* (N.S.) 14: 459–78.

1984. *Servants of the Goddess: The Priests of a South Indian Temple.* Cambridge: Cambridge University Press.

1985a. 'Initiation and Consecration: Priestly Rituals in a south Indian temple' in R. Burghart and A. Cantlie (eds.) *Indian Religion.* (SOAS Collected Papers on South Asia 7.) London: Curzon Press.

1985b. 'Royal Divinity and Human Kingship in the Festivals of a South Indian Temple' *South Asian Social Scientist* 1 (1): 3–43.

1988. 'The Hindu Pantheon and the Legitimation of Hierarchy' *Man* (N.S.) 23: 19–39.

1989. 'Misconceiving the Grain Heap: A Critique of the Concept of the Indian Jajmani System' in J. Parry and M. Bloch (eds.) *Money and the Morality of Exchange.* Cambridge: Cambridge University Press.

Fürer-Haimendorf, C. von 1956. 'Elements of Newar Social Structure' *JRAI* 86 (2): 15–38.

Gaborieau, M. 1972. 'Muslims in the Hindu Kingdom of Nepal' *CIS* (N.S.) 6: 84–105.

1977. *Minorités musulmanes dans le royaume hindou du Népal.* Nanterre: Laboratoire d'Ethnologie.

1978. *Le Népal et ses populations.* (Editions Complexe.) Paris: Presses Universitaires de France.

1982a.'Les Rapports de classe dans l'idéologie officielle du Népal' *Puruṣārtha* 6: 251–290.

1982b. 'Les Fêtes, le temps et l'éspace: structure du calendrier hindou dans sa version indo-népalais' *L'Homme* 22 (3): 11–30.

1985.'From Al-Beruni to Jinnah: Idiom, Ritual and Ideology of the Hindu-Muslim Confrontation in South Asia' *Anthropology Today* 1 (3): 7–14.

Gaige, F.H. 1975. *Regionalism and National Unity in Nepal.* Berkeley and Los Angeles: University of California Press.

Gallie, W.B. 1964. *Philosophy and the Historical Understanding.* London: Chatto and Windus.

Geertz, C. 1960. *The Religion of Java.* Berkeley and Los Angeles: University of California Press.

Gellner, D.N. 1982. 'Max Weber, Capitalism and the Religion of India' *Sociology* 16 (4): 526–43.

1984. 'Cities and Mandalas (Review of Barré *et al.* 1982)' *CNS* 12 (1): 115–26.

1986. 'Language, Caste, Religion and Territory: Newar Identity Ancient and Modern' *EJS* 27: 102–48.

1987a. 'Monk, Householder and Priest: Newar Buddhism and Its Hierarchy of Ritual' D.Phil., University of Oxford.

1987b. 'The Newar Buddhist Monastery: An Anthropological and Historical Typology' in Gutschow and Michaels (eds.).

1988a. 'Monastic Initiation in Newar Buddhism' in R.F. Gombrich (ed.) *Indian Ritual and its Exegesis*. (Oxford University Papers on India 2.1.) Delhi: Oxford University Press.

1988b. 'Priesthood and Possession: Newar Religion in the Light of some Weberian Concepts' *PV* 29 (2): 119–43.

1988c. 'Buddhism and Hinduism in the Nepal Valley' in S. Sutherland, L. Houlden, P. Clarke, and F. Hardy (eds.) *The World's Religions*. Boston: G.K. Hall; London: Routledge.

1989a. 'Monkhood and Priesthood in Newar Buddhism' in V. Bouillier and G. Toffin (eds.).

1989b. 'Hodgson's Blind Alley? On the So-Called Schools of Nepalese Buddhism' *JIABS* 12 (1): 7–19.

1989c. 'Buddhist Monks or Kinsmen of the Buddha? Reflections on the Titles Traditionally Used by Śākyas in the Kathmandu Valley' *Kailash* 15 (1–2): 5–20.

1990. 'Introduction: What is the Anthropology of Buddhism About?' *Journal of the Anthropological Society of Oxford* 21 (2): ~~1–18~~. 95–112.

1991a. 'Hinduism, Tribalism, and the Position of Women: The Problem of Newar Identity' *Man* (N.S.) 26: 105–25.

1991b. 'Ritualized Devotion, Altruism, and Meditation: The Offering of the *Guru Maṇḍala* in Newar Buddhism' *Indo-Iranian Journal* 34: 161–97.

1991c. 'A Newar Buddhist Liturgy: Śrāvakayānist Ritual in Kwā Bāhāḥ, Lalitpur, Nepal' *JIABS* 14(2).

in press. '"The Perfection of Wisdom": A Text and its Uses in Kwā Bahā, Lalitpur' in S. Lienhard (ed.) *Change and Continuity in the Nepalese Culture of the Kathmandu Valley*. Turin: CESMEO.

n.d.a. 'The Consecration of a Vajra-Master in Newar Buddhism'.

n.d.b. 'Personal Daily Ritual in Newar Buddhism'.

Gellner, D.N. and R.P. Pradhan n.d. 'Urban Peasants: The Maharjans of Kathmandu and Lalitpur' (chapter of forthcoming volume, D.N. Gellner and D. Quigley (eds.), provisionally entitled *Newar Society*).

George, C.S. 1974. *The Caṇḍamahāroṣaṇa Tantra, Chs. I-VIII: A Critical Edition and English Translation*. (American Oriental Series 56.) New Haven, CT: American Oriental Society.

Gombrich, R.F. 1971. *Precept and Practice: Traditional Buddhism in the Rural Highlands of Ceylon*. Oxford: Oxford University Press.

1972. 'Buddhism and Society (Review of Spiro 1982 [1970])' *Modern Asian Studies* 6 (4): 483–96.

1983. 'From Monastery to Meditation Centre: Lay Meditation in Modern Sri Lanka' in P. Denwood and A. Piatigorsky (eds.) *Buddhist Studies: Ancient and Modern*. (SOAS Collected Papers on South Asia 4.) London: Curzon Press.

1984. 'Temporary Ordination in Sri Lanka' *JIABS* 7 (2): 41–65.

1988. *Theravāda Buddhism: A Social History from Ancient Benares to Modern Colombo.* London and New York: Routledge and Kegan Paul.
1990. 'How the Mahayana Began' *Buddhist Forum* 1: 21–30. First published in *Journal of Pali and Buddhist Studies* 1 (Nagoya, March 1988): 29–46.
Gombrich, R.F. and G. Obeyesekere 1988. *Buddhism Transformed: Religious Change in Sri Lanka.* Princeton, NJ: Princeton University Press.
Gonda, J. 1970. *Viṣṇuism and Śivaism: A Comparison.* London: Athlone.
Good, A. 1982. 'The Actor and the Act: Categories of Prestation in South India' *Man* (N.S.) 17: 23–41.
Govinda, Lama Anagarika 1960. *Foundations of Tibetan Mysticism.* London: Rider.
Greenwold, S. 1974a. 'Buddhist Brahmans' *EJS* 15: 101–23. Reprinted as 'The Role of the Priest in Newar Society' in Fisher (ed.) *Himalayan Anthropology* 1978. The Hague and Paris: Mouton.
1974b. 'Monkhood versus Priesthood in Newar Buddhism' in C. von Fürer-Haimendorf (ed.) *The Anthropology of Nepal.* Warminster: Aris and Phillips.
1975. 'Kingship and Caste' *EJS* 16 (1): 49–75.
1981. 'Caste: A Moral Structure and a Social System of Control' in A.C. Mayer (ed.) *Culture and Morality: Essays in Honour of Christoph von Fürer-Haimendorf.* Delhi: Oxford University Press.
Gupta, S. 1979. 'Modes of Worship and Meditation' in *Hindu Tantrism.* (Handbuch der Orientalistik 4.2.) Leiden/Cologne: E.J. Brill.
1988. 'The Maṇḍala as an Image of Man' in R.F. Gombrich (ed.) *Indian Ritual and its Exegesis.* (Oxford University Papers on India 2.1.) Delhi: Oxford University Press.
Gupta, S. and R.F. Gombrich 1986. 'Kings, Power and the Goddess' *South Asia Research* 6 (2): 123–38.
Gutschow, N. 1982. *Stadtraum und Ritual der Newarischen Städte im Kathmandu-Tal: Eine architektur-anthropologische Untersuchung.* Stuttgart: Kohlhammer.
Gutschow, N. and M.V. Bajracharya 1977. 'Ritual as a Mediator of Space in Kathmandu' *JNRC* 1: 1–10.
Gutschow, N. and B. Kölver 1975. *Ordered Space, Concepts and Functions in a Town in Nepal.* Wiesbaden: Franz Steiner.
Gutschow, N., B. Kölver, and I. Shresthacarya 1987. *Newar Towns and Buildings: An Illustrated Dictionary, Newārī-English.* (Nepalica 3.) Sankt Augustin: VGH Wissenschaftsverlag.
Gutschow, N. and A. Michaels (eds.) 1987. *Heritage of the Kathmandu Valley.* (Nepalica 4.) Sankt Augustin: VGH Wissenschaftsverlag.
Gutschow, N. and Hemraj Sakya 1980. 'The Monasteries (Bāhā and Bahī) of Patan: A contribution towards the cultural topography of a Newar Town' *JNRC* 4: 161–74.
Hale, A. 1986. 'User's Guide to the Newari Dictionary' in Manandhar 1986.
Harrison, P. 1987. 'Who Gets to Ride in the Great Vehicle? Self-Image and Identity among the Followers of Early Mahāyāna' *JIABS* 10 (1): 67–89.
Hasrat, B.J. 1970. *History of Nepal, As Told by Its Own and Contemporary Chroniclers.* Hoshiarpur, Punjab: V.V. Research Institute Book Agency.
Herbert, J. 1967. *Shintô: At the Fountainhead of Japan.* London: George Allen and Unwin.

Herdick, R. 1987. 'Death Ritual in Kīrtipur in relation to Urban Space' in Gutschow and Michaels (eds.)

HMG 1975. *Population Census – 1971: Selected Locality Tables, Major Urban* [sic] *Vol. V*. Kathmandu: Central Bureau of Statistics.

1984. *Population Census – 1981: Urban Areas. Tables, Vol. III*. Kathmandu: Central Bureau of Statistics.

1988. *Statistical Pocket Book, Nepal*. Kathmandu: Central Bureau of Statistics.

Hodgson, B.H. 1880. *Miscellaneous Essays Relating to Indian Subjects*. 2 vols. London: Trübner and Co.

1972. *Essays on the Languages, Literature and Religion of Nepal and Tibet*. (Bibliotheca Himalayica 2.7.) Delhi: Mañjuśrī Publishing House. (First published 1874.)

Höfer, A. 1979. *The Caste Hierarchy and the State in Nepal: A Study of the Muluki Ain of 1854*. (Khumbu Himal series 13 (2): 25–240.) Innsbruck: Universitätsverlag Wagner.

Holmberg, D. 1984. 'Ritual Paradoxes in Nepal: Comparative Perspectives on Tamang Religion' *JAS* 53 (4): 697–722.

1989. *Order in Paradox: Myth, Ritual, and Exchange among Nepal's Tamang*. Ithaca and London: Cornell University Press.

Hooykas, C. 1973. *Balinese Bauddha Brahmans*. Amsterdam and London: North Holland Publishing Co.

Houseman, M. 1984. 'La Rélation hiérarchique: idéologie particulière ou modèle générale?' in J-C. Galey (ed.) *Différences, valeurs, hiérarchie: textes offerts à Louis Dumont*. Paris: Editions de l'EHESS.

Houtman, G. 1984. 'The Novitiation Ceremonial in Theravada Buddhist Burma: A "received" and an "interpreted" version' *South Asia Research* 4 (1): 50–76.

Hutt, M.J. 1988. *Nepali: A National Language and Its Literature*. London: SOAS; Delhi: Sterling.

Idumi, H. 1930. 'The Hymn on the Life and Vows of Samantabhadra, with the Sanskrit Text, Bhadracarīpraṇidhāna' *The Eastern Buddhist* 5 (2–3): 226–47.

Iltis, L. 1985. 'The Swasthani Vrata: Newar Women and Ritual in Nepal' Ph.D., University of Wisconsin. UMI 8528426.

Ishii, H. 1980. 'Recent Economic Changes in a Newar village' *CNS* 8 (1): 157–80.

n.d. 'Caste and Kinship in a Newar Village' in Gellner and Quigley (eds.) (see Gellner and Pradhan above).

Jaini, P.S. 1979. *The Jaina Path of Purification*. New Delhi: Motilal Banarsidass; Berkeley and Los Angeles: University of California Press.

1980. 'The Disappearance of Buddhism and the Survival of Jainism: A Study in Contrast' in A.K. Narain (ed.).

Joshi, B.L. and L.E. Rose 1966. *Democratic Innovations in Nepal: A Case Study of Political Acculturation*. Berkeley and Los Angeles: University of California Press.

Kane, P.V. 1941. *History of Dharmaśāstra*. 5 vols. Poona: Bhandarkar Oriental Research Institute.

Katz, N. 1983. 'Tibetan Hermeneutics and the *Yāna* Controversy' in E. Steinkellner and H. Tauscher (eds.) *Contributions on Tibetan and Buddhist Religion and Philosophy*, Vol. II. Vienna: Arbeitskreis für Tibetische und Buddhistische Studien, Universität Wien.

Kirkpatrick, Col. 1975. *An Account of the Kingdom of Nepal*. Delhi: Asian Publication Series. (First published 1811.)
Kloppenberg, R. 1977. 'Theravada Buddhism in Nepal' *Kailash* 5 (4): 301–21.
Kölver, B. 1976. 'A Ritual Map from Nepal' *Folia Rara* 65: 68–80.
1986. 'Stages in the Evolution of a World Picture' *Numen* 32 (2): 131–68.
Kölver, B. and S. Lienhard (eds.) 1986. *Formen Kulturellen Wandels und andere Beiträge zur Erforschung des Himālaya*. (Nepalica 2.) Sankt Augustin: VGH Wissenschaftsverlag.
Kölver, B. and H. Śākya 1985. *Documents from the Rudravarṇa-Mahāvihara, Pāṭan 1. Sales and Mortgages*. (Nepalica 1.) Sankt Augustin: VGH Wissenschaftsverlag.
Kunwar, R.R. 1989. *Fire of Himal: An Anthropological Study of the Sherpas of Nepal Himalayan Region*. Jaipur and New Delhi: Nirala.
Kvaerne, P. 1975. 'On the Concept of Sahaja in Indian Buddhist Tantric Literature' *Temenos* 11: 88–135.
1977. *An Anthology of Buddhist Tantric Songs: A Study of the Caryāgīti*. Oslo: Universitetsforlaget.
1984. 'Tibet: The Rise and Fall of a Monastic Tradition' in Bechert and Gombrich (eds.).
Landon, P. 1976. *Nepal*. (Bibliotheca Himalayica 16.) Kathmandu: Ratna Pustak Bhandar. (First published 1928.)
Leach, E. 1982. *Social Anthropology*. Fontana.
Lessing, F.D. and A. Wayman 1978. *Introduction to the Buddhist Tantric Systems*. New Delhi: Motilal Banarsidass. (First published 1968.)
Lévi, S. 1905. *Le Népal: étude historique d'un royaume hindou*. 3 vols. Paris: Leroux. Reissued 1986, Kathmandu and Paris: Raj de Condappa, Le Toit du Monde, and Editions Errance.
1933. *Sanskrit Texts from Bali*. Baroda: GOS 67.
Lewis, I. 1971. *Ecstatic Religion: An Anthropological Study of Spirit Possession and Shamanism*. Harmondsworth: Penguin.
Lewis, T.T. 1984. 'The Tuladhars of Kathmandu: A Study of Buddhist Tradition in a Newar Merchant Community' Ph.D., Columbia University. UMI 8506008.
1989. 'Mahāyāna *Vratas* in Newar Buddhism' *JIABS* 12 (1): 109–38.
n.d. 'The Tulādhars of Asan' (see Gellner and Pradhan).
Lewis, T.T. and L. Jamspal 1988. 'Newars and Tibetans in the Kathmandu Valley: Three New Translations from Tibetan Sources' *Journal of Asian and African Studies* 36: 187–221.
Lienhard, S. 1963. *Maṇicūḍāvadānoddhṛta: A Buddhist Re-birth Story in the Nevārī Language*. Stockholm: Alquist and Wiksell.
1974. *Nevārigītimañjarī: Religious and Secular Poetry of the Nevars of the Kathmandu Valley*. Stockholm: Alquist and Wiksell. (Reissued 1984 as *Songs of Nepal*. Hawaii: University of Hawaii Press.)
1978. 'Problèmes du Syncrétisme Religieux au Népal' *BEFEO* 65: 239–70. Also published in German in Bechert (ed.).
1980. *Die Legende vom Prinzen Viśvantara: Eine Nepalische Bilderrolle*. Berlin: Museum of Indian Art.
1984. 'Nepal: The Survival of Indian Buddhism in a Himalayan Kingdom' in Bechert and Gombrich (eds.).

1986. 'Dreimal Unreinheit: Riten und Gebrauchen der Nevars bei Geburt, Menstruation und Tod' in B. Kölver and S. Lienhard (eds.).

1989. 'The Monastery and the Secular World: Saṅgha-Buddhism and Caste-Buddhism' *Journal of the American Oriental Society* 110 (4): 593–6.

Ling, T. 1980. *Buddhist Revival in India: Aspects of the Sociology of Buddhism*. London: MacMillan.

Locke, J.K. 1973. *Rato Matsyendranath of Patan and Bungamati*, Kathmandu: INAS Historical series 5.

1975. 'Newar Buddhist Initiation Rites' *CNS* 2: 1–23.

1980. *Karunamaya: The Cult of Avalokitesvara-Matsyendranath in the Valley of Nepal*. Kathmandu: Sahayogi.

1985. *The Buddhist Monasteries of Nepal: A Survey of the Bāhās and Bahīs of the Kathmandu Valley*. Kathmandu: Sahayogi.

1986. 'The Vajrayana Buddhism in the Kathmandu Valley' in Locke (ed.).

1986. (ed.). *The Buddhist Heritage of Nepal* (Souvenir of the 15th General Conference of the World Fellowship of Buddhists.) Kathmandu: Dharmodaya Sabha.

1987. 'The Upoṣadha Vrata of Amoghapāśa Lokésvara in Nepal' *L'Ethnographie* 83 (100–1): 159–89.

1989. 'The Unique Features of Newar Buddhism' in T. Skorupski (ed.).

Lukes, S. 1973. *Emile Durkheim: His Life and Work*. London: Allen Lane.

Macdonald, A.W. 1976. 'Sorcery in the Nepalese Code of 1853' in J.T. Hitchcock and R.L. Jones (eds.) *Spirit Possession in the Nepal Himalayas*. Warminster: Aris and Phillips.

Macdonald, A.W. and A. Vergati Stahl 1979. *Newar Art: Nepalese Art During the Malla Period*. Warminster: Aris and Phillips.

Malla, K.P. 1979b. *The Road to Nowhere*. Kathmandu: Sajha.

1981. 'Linguistic Archaeology of the Nepal Valley: Preliminary Report' *Kailash* 8 (1–2): 5–23.

1982. *Classical Newari Literature: A Sketch*. Kathmandu: Educational Enterprises.

1983. 'River-Names of the Nepal Valley: A Study in Cultural Annexation' *CNS* 10 (1–2): 57–68.

1984b. 'Nepala: Archaeology of the Word' *PATA Conference Souvenir*: 63–9.

1985a. *The Newari Language: A Working Outline*. (Monumentica Serindica 14.) Tokyo: Institute for the Study of Languages and Cultures of Asia and Africa.

1985b. 'Introduction' in D.V. Vajrācārya and K.P. Malla *The Gopālarājavaṃśāvalī*. (Nepal Research Centre Publications 9.) Wiesbaden: Franz Steiner.

Mallman, M.T. de 1961. 'Un Aspect méconnu d'Avalokiteśvara II' *Arts Asiatiques* 8 (3): 203–10.

1975. *Introduction à l'iconographie du Tantrisme bouddhique*. Paris: CNRS.

Manandhar, T.L. 1986. *Newari-English Dictionary* A. Vergati (ed.). Delhi: Ecole Française d'Extrême Orient and Agam Kala Prakashan.

Mandelbaum, D.G. 1966. 'Transcendental and Pragmatic Aspects of Religion' *American Anthropologist* 68 (5): 1174–91.

Mauss, M. 1954. *The Gift* I. Cunnison (tr.). London: Cohen and West.

Mayer, A. 1966. *Caste and Kinship in Central India*. Berkeley and Los Angeles:

University of California Press.
Meisezahl, R.O. 1967. *Die Göttin Vajravārāhī: Eine ikonographische Studie nach einem Sādhana-Text von Advayavajra*. Leiden: E.J. Brill.
1985. *Hastapūjāvidhi-Texte: Der Handritus im annuttarayogischen Kult des Götterpaares Cakrasambara und Vajravārāhī*. Sankt Augustin: VGH Wissenschaftsverlag.
Michaels, A. 1989. 'Paśupati's Holy Field and the Temple Priests' Authority in Deopatan (Nepal)' in Bouillier and Toffin (eds.).
Mitra, D. 1971. *Buddhist Monuments*. Calcutta: Sahitya Samsad.
Mitra, R.L. 1971. *The Sanskrit Buddhist Literature of Nepal*. Calcutta: Sanskrit Pustak Bhandar. (First published 1882.)
Moffat, M. 1979. *An Untouchable Community in India*. Princeton, NJ: Princeton University Press.
Nagaraju, S. 1969. 'A Rare Saivo-Buddhist Work with Vaishnavite Interpolations' *Kannada Studies* 5: 67–75.
Narain, A.K. (ed.) 1980. *Studies in the History of Buddhism*. Delhi: B.R. Publishing House.
Nepali, G.S. 1965. *The Newars: An Ethno-Sociological Study of a Himalayan Community*. Bombay: United Asia Publications.
Obeyesekere, G. 1963. 'The Great Tradition and the Little in the Perspective of Sinhalese Buddhism' *JAS* 22 (2): 139–53.
1966. 'The Buddhist Pantheon in Ceylon and its Extensions' in M. Nash (ed.) *Anthropological Studies in Theravada Buddhism*. Yale University Southeast Asian Studies No. 13. Chicago and London: Chicago University Press.
1984. *The Cult of the Goddess Pattini*. Chicago and London: Chicago University Press.
Oldfield, H.A. 1981. *Sketches from Nepal*. 2 vols. Delhi: Cosmo Publications. (First published 1880.)
Orenstein, H. 1968. 'Towards a Grammar of Defilement in Hindu Law' in M. Singer and B.S. Cohn (eds.) *Structure and Change in Indian Society*. Chicago: Aldine.
Ortner, S.B. 1978. *Sherpas Through Their Rituals*. Cambridge: Cambridge University Press.
1989. *High Religion: A Cultural and Political History of Sherpa Buddhism*. Princeton, NJ: Princeton University Press.
Östör, A. 1980. *The Play of the Gods: Locality, Ideology, Structure and Time in the Festivals of a Bengali Town*. Chicago and London: Chicago University Press.
Owens, B.M. 1989. 'The Politics of Divinity in the Kathmandu Valley: The Festival of Bungadya/Rato Matsyendranath' Ph.D., Columbia University.
Pal, P. 1974. *The Arts of Nepal, Vol. I: Sculpture*. Leiden: E.J. Brill.
Pandey, R.B. 1969. *Hindu Saṁskāras: Socio-Religious Study of the Hindu Sacraments*. New Delhi: Motilal Banarsidass. (First published 1949.)
Parry, J. 1979. *Caste and Kinship in Kangra*. London: Routledge and Kegan Paul.
1980. 'Ghosts, Greed and Sin: The Occupational Identity of the Benares Funeral Priests' *Man* (N.S.) 15: 88–111.
1982. 'Sacrificial Death and the Necrophagous Ascetic' in M. Bloch and J. Parry (eds.) *Death and the Regeneration of Life*. Cambridge: Cambridge University Press.
1986. '*The Gift*, the Indian Gift and the "Indian Gift"' *Man* (N.S.) 21: 453–73.

Pott, P.H. 1966. *Yoga and Yantra: Their Interrelation and Their Significance for Indian Archaeology* R. Needham (tr.). The Hague: Martinus Nijhoff. (First published 1946.)

Pradhan, B. 1981. *The Newar Women of Bulu (Status of Women in Nepal, Vol. II: Field Studies, part 6)*. Kathmandu: CEDA, Tribhuvan University.

Pradhan, R.P. 1986. 'Domestic and Cosmic Rituals among the Hindu Newars of Kathmandu, Nepal' Ph.D., Dept. of Sociology, Delhi School of Economics.

Quigley, D. 1984. 'The Social Structure of a Newar Trading Community, East-Central Nepal' Ph.D., London School of Economics.

1985a. 'Household Organisation among Newar Traders' *CNS* 12 (2): 13–44.

1985b. 'The *Guthi* Organisations of Dhulikhel Shresthas' *Kailash* 12 (1–2): 5–61.

1986. 'Introversion and Isogamy: Marriage Patterns of the Newars of Nepal' *CIS* (N.S.) 20 (1): 75–95.

1987. 'Ethnicity without Nationalism: The Newars of Nepal' *EJS* 28: 152–70.

Raheja, G.G. 1988a. *The Poison in the Gift: Ritual, Prestation, and the Dominant Caste in a North Indian Village*. Chicago and London: Chicago University Press.

1988b. 'India: Caste, Kingship, and Dominance Reconsidered' *Annual Review of Anthropology* 17: 497–522.

Regmi, D.R. 1965. *Medieval Nepal*. 4 vols. (vols. 2–4: 1966.) Calcutta: Firma K.L. Mukhopadhyay.

Regmi, M.C. 1976. *Landownership in Nepal*. Berkeley and Los Angeles: University of California Press.

1978. *Land Tenure and Taxation in Nepal*. 4 vols. Kathmandu: Ratna Pustak Bhandar. (First published 1963–8.)

Reynell, J. 1985. 'Renunciation and Ostentation: A Jain Paradox' *Cambridge Anthropology* 9 (3): 20–33.

Riccardi, T. 1980. 'Buddhism in Ancient and Early Medieval Nepal' in A.K. Narain (ed.).

1985. Review of Slusser 1982 *JAS* 44 (2): 445–7.

Riley-Smith, T. 1982. 'Buddhist God-Makers of the Kathmandu Valley' Ph.D., Cambridge University.

Robinson, K.S. 1989. *Escape from Kathmandu*. New York: Tom Doherty Associates.

Roerich, G.N. 1959. *Biography of Dharmasvāmin*. Patna: K.P. Jayaswal Research Institute.

Rosser, C. 1966. 'Social Mobility in the Newar Caste System' in C. von Fürer-Haimendorf (ed.) *Caste and Kin in Nepal, India and Ceylon*. Bombay: Asia Publishing House.

Sahlins, M. 1974. *Stone Age Economics*. London: Tavistock.

Sakya, H. and T.R. Vaidya (eds.) 1970. *Medieval Nepal (Colophons and Inscriptions)*. Kathmandu: T.R. Vaidya.

Samuel, G. 1978. 'Religion in Tibetan Society: A New Approach' *Kailash* 6 (1): 45–66, (2): 99–114.

1982. 'Tibet as a Stateless Society and Some Islamic Parallels' *JAS* 41 (2): 215–29.

Sanderson, A. 1985. 'Purity and Power among the Brahmans of Kashmir' in M. Carrithers, S. Collins, and S. Lukes (eds.) *The Category of the Person*.

Cambridge: Cambridge University Press.
1986. 'Mandala and Agamic Identity in the Trika of Kashmir' in A. Padoux (ed.) *Mantras et diagrammes rituels dans l'hindouisme*. Paris: CNRS.
1988. 'Śaivism and the Tantric Traditions' in S. Sutherland, L. Houlden, P. Clarke, and F. Hardy (eds.) *The World's Religions*. Boston: G.K. Hall; London: Routledge.
in press. 'Vajrayāna: Origin and Function' in *Buddhism Towards the Year 2000* (Conference Proceedings). Bangkok: Dhammakaya Foundation.
Shaha, R. 1982. *Essays in the Practice of Government in Nepal*. Delhi: Manohar.
Shakya, R.J. 1980. *A Brief Introduction to Shiva Deva Sanskarita Om Kuli Shri Rudra Varna Mahavihar*. Lalitpur: Sangha Ratna Shakya *et al.*
Sharma, P.R. 1977. 'Caste, Social Mobility and Sanskritization: A Study of Nepal's Old Legal Code' *Kailash* 5 (4): 277–99.
1983. 'The Land System of the Licchavis of Nepal' *Kailash* 10 (1–2): 11–62.
Shastri, H. 1927. *Advayavajrasaṃgraha*. Baroda: GOS 90.
Shepard, J.W. 1985. 'Symbolic Space in Newar Culture' Ph.D., University of Michigan. UMI 8520981.
Singer, M. 1972. *When a Great Tradition Modernizes: An Anthropological Approach to Indian Civilization*. New York: Praeger.
Skorupski, T. 1989 (ed.) *The Buddhist Heritage*. (Buddhica Britannica 1.) Tring: The Institute of Buddhist Studies.
Slusser, M.S. 1982. *Nepal Mandala: A Cultural Study of the Kathmandu Valley*. Vol. I. Princeton, NJ: Princeton University Press.
Snellgrove, D.L. 1957. *Buddhist Himalaya: Travels and Studies in Quest of the Origins and Nature of Tibetan Religion*. Oxford: Cassirer.
1959a. *The Hevajra Tantra: A Critical Study*. 2 vols. (London Oriental Series 6.). London: Oxford University Presss.
1959b. 'The Notion of Divine Kingship in Tantric Buddhism' in *Studies in the History of Religions* (supplements to *Numen*) 4: 204–18.
1987. *Indo-Tibetan Buddhism: Indian Buddhists and Their Tibetan Successors*. London: Serindia.
1989. 'Multiple Features of the Buddhist Heritage' in T. Skorupski (ed.).
Southwold, M. 1983. *Buddhism in Life: The Anthropological Study of Religion and the Sinhalese Practice of Buddhism*. Manchester: Manchester University Press.
Spiro, M.E. 1982. *Buddhism and Society: A Great Tradition and its Burmese Vicissitudes*. (First published 1970.) Berkeley and Los Angeles: University of California Press.
Sresthacharya, I. with N.M. Tuladhar 1976. *Jyapu Vocabulary (Preliminary Report)*. Tribhuvan University, Kathmandu: INAS.
Srinivas, M.N. 1980. *The Remembered Village*. Delhi: Oxford University Press. (First published 1976.)
Stein, B. 1980. *Peasant, State and Society in Medieval South India*. Delhi: Oxford University Press.
Stein, M.A. 1900. *Kalhaṇa's Rājataraṅgiṇī: A Chronicle of the Kings of Kaśmīr*. London: Archibald Constable.
Stevenson, H.N.C. 1954. 'Status Evaluation in the Hindu Caste System' *JRAI* 84 (1–2): 45–65.

Stevenson, S. 1971. *The Rites of the Twice Born*. Delhi: Oriental Reprint Corporation. (First published 1920.)

Stoddard, R.H. 1979. 'Perceptions about the Geography of Religious Sites in the Kathmandu Valley' *CNS* 7 (1–2): 97–118

Strenski, I. 1983. 'On Generalized Exchange and the Domestication of the *Sangha*' *Man* (N.S.) 18: 463–77.

Strong, J.S. 1979. 'The Transforming Gift: An Analysis of Devotional Acts of Offering in Buddhist *Avadāna* Literature' *History of Religions* 18 (3): 221–37.

1983. *The Legend of King Aśoka: A Study and Translation of the* Aśokāvadāna. New Delhi: Motilal Banarsidass.

Takaoka, H. (ed.) 1981. *A Microfilm Catalogue of the Buddhist Manuscripts in Nepal*, vol. I. Nagoya: Buddhist Library.

Tambiah, S.J. 1970. *Buddhism and the Spirit Cults in North-East Thailand*. Cambridge: Cambridge University Press.

1976. *World Conqueror and World Renouncer*. Cambridge: Cambridge University Press.

1984. *The Buddhist Saints of the Forest and the Cult of the Amulets*. Cambridge: Cambridge University Press.

Tatz, M. 1977. 'The Vow of Benevolent Conduct (Introduction, Translation and Commentary)' in L. Chandra and P. Ratnam (eds.) *Studies in Indo-Asian Art and Culture*, Vol. V. (Śatapiṭaka Series 238.) Delhi: International Academy of Indian Culture.

Tewari, R.C. 1983. 'Socio-Cultural Aspects of Theravada Buddhism in Nepal' *JIABS* 6 (2): 67–93.

Thomas, E.J. 1933. *The History of Buddhist Thought*. London: Kegan Paul, Trench, Trübner.

Thomas, K. 1978. *Religion and the Decline of Magic*. London: Penguin.

Toffin, G. 1975. 'La Terminologie de parenté néwar: analyse descriptive et comparative' *L'Homme* 15 (3–4): 81–98.

1976a. 'La Presse à huile néwar de la vallée de Kathmandou (Népal): analyse technologique et socio-économique' *Journal d'Agriculture Tropicale et de Botanique Appliquée* 23 (7–12): 183–204.

1976b. 'La *Si Kā Bheāy*, "Festin de la Tête", chez les Néwar' *Kailash* 4 (4): 329–38.

1977. *Pyangaon: une communauté néwar de la vallée de Kathmandou: la vie matérielle*. Paris: CNRS.

1979a. 'Les Aspects religieux de la royauté néwar au Népal' *Archives des Sciences Sociales des Religions* 48 (1): 53–82.

1979b. 'Les Rites funéraires des hautes castes hindouistes néwar (Népal)' in J. Guiart (ed.) *Les Hommes et la mort*. Paris: Le Sycamore – Objets et Mondes.

1981a. 'Cultes des déesses et fête du Dasaĩ chez les Néwar (Népal)' *Puruṣārtha* 5: 55–81.

1981b. 'Espace urbain et religion: à propos des villes néwar' in G. Toffin (ed.) *L'Homme et la maison en Himalaya*. Paris: CNRS.

1984. *Société et religion chez les Néwar du Népal*. Paris: CNRS.

1987. 'Funeral Priests and the Caste System in the Kathmandu Valley' in Gutschow and Michaels (eds.).

1989. 'La Voie des "Héros": Tantrisme et héritage védique chez les Brahmans Rājopādhyāya au Népal' in Bouillier and Toffin (eds.).

n.d. 'Rājopādhyāya Brahmans': see under Gellner and Pradhan.
Trautmann, T.R. 1981. *Dravidian Kinship*. Cambridge: Cambridge University Press.
Tsuda, S. 1974. *The Saṁvarodaya-Tantra: Selected Chapters*. Tokyo: Yokuseido Press.
Tucci, G. 1958. *Minor Buddhist Texts*, Part II. Rome: ISMEO.
1980. *The Religions of Tibet* G. Samuel (tr.). London: Routledge and Kegan Paul. (First published 1970.)
Tuladhar, S.K. 1979. 'Gwaye Da Tayegu: An Initial Ritual of the Samyaka Guthi' *CNS* 7 (1–2): 48–70.
Turner, R.L. 1980. *A Comparative and Etymological Dictionary of the Nepali Language*. Delhi: Allied Publishers. (First published 1931.)
Turner, V.W. 1977. 'Symbols in African Ritual' in J.L. Dolgin, D.S. Kemnitzer, and D.M. Schneider (eds.) *Symbolic Anthropology: A Reader in the Study of Symbols and Meaning*. New York: Columbia University Press.
UNICEF 1987. *Children and Women of Nepal: A Situation Analysis*. Kathmandu: UNICEF.
Vaidya, Karunakar 1986. *Buddhist Traditions and Culture of the Kathmandu Valley (Nepal)*. Kathmandu: Sajha.
Vajracharya, Dibya Vajra 1986. 'The Path to Enlightenment' in Locke (ed.).
van der Veer, P. 1987. 'Taming the Ascetic: Devotionalism in a Hindu Monastic Order' *Man* (N.S.) 22: 680–95.
van Kooij, K.R. 1977. 'The Iconography of the Buddhist Wood-Carvings in a Newar Buddhist Monastery in Kathmandu (Chuṣya-Bāhā)' *JNRC* 1: 39–82.
1978. *Religion in Nepal*. (Iconography of Religions XIII.15.) Leiden: E.J. Brill.
Varṣa Kriyā: manuscript CA 6–2 of Takaoka 1981.
Vergati, A. 1975. 'M. Greenwold et les Néwars; doit-on vraiment recourir à deux modèles du système des castes au Népal?' *EJS* 16: 310–16.
1979. 'Une Divinité lignagère des Néwar: Digu-dyo' *BEFEO* 66: 115–27.
1982a. 'Social Consequences of Marrying Viṣṇu Nārāyaṇa: Primary Marriage among the Newars of Kathmandu Valley' *CIS* (N.S.) 16 (2): 271–87.
1982b. 'Le Culte et l'iconographie du Buddha Dîpankara dans la vallée de Kathmandou' *Arts Asiatiques* 37: 22–7.
1985. 'Le Roi faiseur de pluie: une nouvelle version de la légende d'Avalokiteś-vara rouge au Népal' *BEFEO* 74: 287–303.
Waddell, L.A. 1978. *Buddhism and Lamaism of Tibet*. Kathmandu: Educational Enterprises. (First published 1894.)
Wadley, S.S. 1975. *Shakti: Power in the Conceptual Structure of Karimpur Religion*. Chicago and London: Chicago University Press.
Warder, A.K. 1980. *Indian Buddhism*. New Delhi: Motilal Banarsidass.
Wayman, A. 1973. *The Buddhist Tantras: Light on Indo-Tibetan Esoterism*. New York: Samuel Weiser.
Weber, M. 1968. *Economy and Society* G. Roth and C. Wittich (eds.). 3 vols. New York: Bedminster Press.
Webster, P. 1981. 'To Plough or Not to Plough? A Newar Dilemma: Taboo and Technology in the Kathmandu Valley, Nepal' *Pacific Viewpoint* 22 (2): 99–135.
1983. 'Peasants and Landlords: Land tenure in the Kathmandu Valley, Nepal' *Pacific Viewpoint* 24 (2): 140–66.

1987. 'Bolajyā: the social organisation of labour amongst the Newars of the Kathmandu Valley' in Gutschow and Michaels (eds.) 1987.

Wegner, G.-M. 1988. *The Nāykhībājā of the Newar Butchers*. (Nepal Research Centre Publications 13.) Stuttgart: Franz Steiner.

Wiesner, U. 1976. *Nepal, Königriech im Himalaya: Geschichte, Kunst und Kultur im Kathmandu-Tal.* (Dumont Kunst-Reiseführer.) Cologne: Dumont.

Williams, P. 1989. *Mahāyāna Buddhism: The Doctrinal Foundations*. London and New York: Routledge.

Wilson, H.H. 1862. *Works of the Late H.H. Wilson*, vol. II. London: Trübner and Co.

Winternitz, M. 1972. *A History of Indian Literature*, vol. II: *Buddhist and Jaina Literature*. Delhi: Oriental Books Reprint Corporation. (First published 1933.)

Witzel, M. 1986. 'Agnihotra-Rituale in Nepal' in Kölver and Lienhard (eds.).

n.d. 'On Buddhist Homa in Nepal and Japan'.

Wright, D. (ed.) 1972. *History of Nepal* (tr. from Nepali by Munshi Shew Shanker Singh and Pandit Shri Gunanand). Kathmandu: Nepal Antiquated Book Publishers. (First published 1877.)

Yamasaki, Taikô 1988. *Shingon: Japanese Esoteric Buddhism* R. and C. Peterson (tr.), Y. Morimoto and D. Kidd (eds.). Boston and London: Shambhala.

Yokoyama, Kimizane 1983. *Mikkyo: The Virtue of Avalokiteśvara* A. Gleason and E. Takeda (tr.). Tokyo: Tama.

Zanen, S.M. 1986. 'The Goddess Vajrayogini and the Kingdom of Sankhu (Nepal)' *Puruṣārtha* 10: 125–66.

Index of opening phrases of Sanskrit verses cited

Index of persons (including authors)

General Index

Italicized entries indicate where a term is defined or discussed in detail.

Enjoyment Body (*saṃbhogakāya*), 293, 301; *see also trikāya*
enlightenment, 97, 100, 143, 158–9, 186, 188, 228, 230, 251, 261, 288, 292, 295, 298, 323, 356 n.43, 377 n.27; *see also* soteriology, *nirvāṇa*
equality, 248–50, 343
  within caste, 62–3
  within *guthi*, 248, 312
esoteric sphere, 77–9, 82, 113, 142–3, 253, 257, 273, 282, 287, 293, 315–16, 319–20, 330–1, 345; *see also āgā̃*, Diamond Way, Tantrism
essentially contested concepts, 67
evil eye (*mikhā wāgu*), 332
exchange
  between kin, 201–4
  between people, *see cipa*, *dān*, feast, marriage
  between people and gods, 107, *122–3*, 181, 211, 292, 344: *see also prasād, pūjā*
exclusiveness, *see* closure
exogamy, *see* marriage

family priest, *see purohit*
Farmer, *see* Maharjan
fast/fasting, 216, 221, 223–5, 245, 279, 302, 334–5
  month-long fast (*māy apasā̃ cwane*), 52, 369 n.55
  see also Observance
father's sister (*nini*), 123, *201–3*
father's sister's husband (*jicā pāju*), 25, *202–3*
feast (*bhway*), 26, *30–1*, 62, 143, 156, 175, 177, 182, 216–18, 231, 236, 243, 245–6, 280, 303, 306, 308, 371 n.1, 378 n.31; *see also samay*, food
festivals, 61, 68, 83, 91, 114, 126, 136–7, 203, 208, 213–20, 231, 313, 339–40
  local versus calendrical, 213–14, 218
  types of, 145, 190
Fire Sacrifice (*yajña*, *homa*), 92, 148, 150, *157–8*, 167, 169, 259, 266–8, 279, 286, 290, 303, 320
  types of, 157, 159
  see also Agni
First Head-Shaving (*busā̃ khāyegu*, *busākhā*), 199–200, 202
First Rice-Feeding (*annaprāśana*, (*macā*) *jā̃kwa*), 144, 153, 156, 199–200, 204
Five Buddhas (*pañcabuddha*, viz. Vairocana, Akṣobhya, Ratnasambhava, Amitābha, Amoghasiddhi, q.v.), 53, 82, 88, 96, *129*, 149, 151, 154, 158, 160, 183, 222, *251–2*, 259, 293, 375 n.33, 377 n.29; *see also* Buddha
Five-Coloured Thread, *see pasūkā*
Five Consecrations (*pañcābhiṣeka*), *267*, 289, 295
Five Lamps (*pañcapradīpa*), 301–3
Five Leaves (*pañcapallava*), 360 n.14
Five Nectars (*pañcāmṛta*), 301, 303, 360 n.14
  Tantric versions, 276, 278, 301–3
Five Offerings (*pañcopacāra*), *106*, 156
Five Precepts, *see* Precepts
Five Products of a Cow (*pañcagavya*), 153
Flask (*kalaśa*), 151–2, 154, 156, 203, 223, 268, 274, 279–80, 287, 291, 328
Flask Consecration (*kalaśābhiṣeka*), 268, 276, 374 n.17
Flask Worship (*kalaśa pūjā*), 148, *150–7*, 287
  Secret Flask Worship, 276; *see also* Alcohol Pot
folk religion, 72, 82, 103, 126, 344
food, 43, 122, 197, 209, 299
  in ritual, 78, 87, 106–7, 156–8, 310–13, 314
  types of, *30–1*
  see also alcohol, feast, *gaṇacakra*, meat, *pācāku*, *prajñābhū*, *prasād*, *samay*, *sikāḥ bhū*
foot-water, *see argha*
45th-Day Rite (*latyā*), 209, *210–13*
Fourth Consecration (*caturthābhiṣeka*), 267
Four Yoghurt Pots (*sagā̃ dhaupatti*), 152, 154, 160

Gaganagañja, 195
Gaḥchẽ, Lalitpur, 82, 310
Gāī Jātrā, *see* Sā Pāru
gālāybā̃, *see* Cow's Mouthful
gaṇacakra, 297, *303*
Gaṇapatihṛdaya, 359 n.39
Gandheśvara, 191, 195
Gaṇeś, 36, 53, 73–5, 79–80, 83–4, 106, 153–4, 169, 191, 216, 226, 228, 353 n.43
  set of four, 350 n.9
  see also Jala Vinayaka
Ganges, 189
Gā̃ Pyākhã (dance), 83
Garteśvara, 191, 195
Garuḍa Purāṇa, 210
Gathā̃ Mugaḥ, 214–15
gati, *see* rebirth
Gātilā, *see* Observance (of Vasundharā)
Gaurī, 154
Gayā, 169
Gāyatrī, *see* mantra
Gelukpa, 60, 99; *see also* monks (Tibetan), Tibetan Buddhism

gender, 76–7, 130–1, 200, 228–30, 273, 275, *280–1*, 313, 331, 367 n.26
and rates of taking Tantric Initiation, 270–1
see also women, position of
ghaḥkū, 269
ghaḥsū, *see* House Purification
Ghaḥsū Ācā/Karmācārya, *see* Karmācārya
ghaṇṭā, *see* bell
ghaṇṭābhiṣeka, *see* Bell Consecration
Ghaṇṭākarṇa, *see* Gathā̃ Mugaḥ
ghost (*pret* or *bhūt*), 36, 73–5, 121, 131–2, 134, 149, 157, 211, 256, 275, 277
Ghyaḥ Cāku Sãnhū (Makar Saṃkrānti), 181, 216
gift-giving, *see dān*
'gift-verses', *see* alms-receiving verses
god(s), *129–30*, 234
and merit, in Theravāda Buddhism, 338
and spirit-possession, 330
and urban space, 48
and worship, 106, 235–6, 243–6
as one of the rebirths, 132
avoided after a death, 205
'*dyaḥ*', use of, 74, 80–1, 129
exoteric Tantric, *see* Diamond Way (exoteric form of)
functional specialization of, 74, 76, 225–6, 363 n.17
Great Way as worship of, 75, 114
Hindu versus Buddhist, 61, 74–5, 154
images of, 111, 179, 264–5, 290, 299
in worship implements, 151, 154, 290
Maharjan attitude to, 69
pācāku as symbol of, 302
range of attitudes to, 292–4, 296
see also āgã̇ dyaḥ, *bodhisattva*, 'Durkheimian' deities, Lineage Deity, multivalency, pantheon, self-divinization, summoning
goddess, 27, 73, 75, 301, 314, 316, 379 n.17; *see also* Mother Goddess, Śāktism, and specific names
god-guardian (*dyaḥpāḥlāḥ*, *pūjārī*), *75–6*, 79, 140–1, 164, 169, 175–7, 180, 245, 249, 319–20, 379 n.13; *see also bāphā*
god-room (*dyaḥkwathā*), 29; *see also āgã̇*
gogrāsa, *see* Cow's Mouthful
Gokarṇa, 195
Gokarṇeśvara, 191, 195
goldsmith, 31, 49, 87, 91, 265, 372 n.17; *see also* artisan work
good-luck food, *see sagã*
Gopāla (dynasty), 9–10, 17, 348 n.11
Gorakhnāth (Gorakṣanāth), 292
Gorkha, 11–12, 19, 88, 350 n.13
Gorkhālī, *see* Parbatiyā, Nepali, Shah (dynasty)
gotra, 192
Govardhana Pūjā, 61
Grahamātṛkā, 359 n.39
Great Tradition, 53, 63, 81, 83, 98–9, 105, 300, 317, 347 n.3
Great Way (Mahāyāna), *111–14*
and monasticism, 59
and supernormal powers, 288, 346
and syncretism, 100–1
and worshipping all gods, 75, 114
as practice of *ahiṃsā*, 124, 133
history of, 1–3, *109–10*, 120, 180, 220, 227, 293, 318, 323, 338
influencing Disciples' Way, 179–80, 183
in monasteries, 113, 176, 184, 292
modern study of, 266, 321, 335
Newar practice of, 111, 114, 140, *189–250*, 163, 257, 262, 284, 296–7, 320, 343
relation to Diamond Way, 204, 251, 253–7, 287, 292, 314, 318, 345
Śākyas associated with, 113, 166, 257–8
scriptural teachings of, 119, 123, 150, 184, *261–3*, 292
subsuming Disciples' Way, 318, 345
see also Three Ways
gṛhapati-bodhisattva, 300
gṛhasthī, *see* householder
guardian, *see* god-guardian
Guardian Kings (*catur mahārāj*), 274
Gubhāju, 64, *66–7*, 267, 313, 328, 334; *see also* Vajrācārya
guhyābhiṣeka, *see* Secret Consecration
guhyakalaśa, *see* Alcohol Pot
Guhyakālī, 80–1
Guhyasamāja Tantra, 254, 256–7, 301
Guhyeśvarī, 19, 54, 75, 77, 80, 151, 154–5, 169, 191–3
Guita, Lalitpur, 42, 185–6, 358 n.23
Guji Bāhāḥ, Lalitpur, 176, 256, 265
Gũlā (Buddhist holy month), 69, 79, 93, 118, 181, 215–16, 218, 225, 245–6, 335, 363 n.25
gumbā, 34, 168, 174–6
Guṇakāraṇḍavyūha, 129
*guṇa*s, theory of three, 82, 359 n.36
Gũ Punhī, 215
guru, 88, 377 n.25
as teacher, 60, 116
Buddhist versus Hindu understanding of, 60, 141, 319
guru-disciple relationship, 140, 274, 324–5
rājguru, 338
recipient of *dān*, 121, 215
Vajrācāryas as, 60, 141–2, 222–3, 272–9, 328
Vajrasattva as, 150, 254, 262, 275

Cambridge Studies in Social and Cultural Anthropology

Editors: JACK GOODY, STEPHEN GUDEMAN, MICHAEL HERZFELD, JONATHAN PARRY

1 The Political Organisation of Unyamwezi
R.G. ABRAHAMS
2 Buddhism and the Spirit Cults in North-East Thailand*
S.J. TAMBIAH
3 Kalahari Village Politics: An African Democracy
ADAM KUPER
4 The Rope of Moka: Big-Men and Ceremonial Exchange in Mount Hagen, New Guinea
ANDREW STRATHERN
5 The Majangir: Ecology and Society of a Southwest Ethiopian People
JACK STAUDER
6 Buddhist Monk, Buddhist Layman: A Study of Urban Monastic Organisation in Central Thailand
JANE BUNNAG
7 Contexts of Kinship. An Essay in the Family Sociology of the Gonja of Northern Ghana
ESTHER N. GOODY
8 Marriage among a Matrilineal Elite: A Family Study of Ghanaian Civil Servants
CHRISTINE OPPONG
9 Elite Politics in Rural India: Political Stratification and Political Alliances in Western Maharashtra
ANTHONY T. CARTER
10 Women and Property in Morocco: Their Changing Relation to the Process of Social Stratification in the Middle Atlas
VANESSA MAHER
11 Rethinking Symbolism*
DAN SPERBER Translated by Alice L. Morton
12 Resources and Population: A Study of the Gurungs of Nepal
ALAN MACFARLANE
13 Mediterranean Family Structures
EDITED BY J.G. PERISTIANY
14 Spirits of Protest: Spirit Mediums and the Articulation of Consensus among the Zezuru of Southern Rhodesia (Zimbabwe)
PETER FRY
15 World Conqueror and World Renouncer: A Study of Buddhism and Polity in Thailand against a Historical Background*
S.J. TAMBIAH
16 Outline of a Theory of Practice*
PIERRE BOURDIEU. Translated by Richard Nice
17 Production and Reproduction: A Comparative Study of the Domestic Domain*
JACK GOODY
18 Perspectives in Marxist Anthropology*
MAURICE GODELIER. Translated by Robert Brain
19 The Fate of Shechem, or the Politics of Sex: Essays in the Anthropology of the Mediterranean
JULIAN PITT-RIVERS
20 People of the Zongo: The Transformation of Ethnic Identities in Ghana
ENID SCHILDKROUT

21 Casting out Anger: Religion among the Taita of Kenya
GRACE HARRIS
22 Rituals of the Kandyan State
H.L. SENEVIRATNE
23 Australian Kin Classification
HAROLD W. SCHEFFLER
24 The Palm and the Pleiades: Initiation and Cosmology in Northwest Amazonia*
STEPHEN HUGH-JONES
25 Nomads of Southern Siberia: The Pastoral Economies of Tuva
S.I. VAINSHTEIN. Translated by Michael Colenso
26 From the Milk River: Spatial and Temporal Processes in Northwest Amazonia*
CHRISTINE HUGH-JONES
27 Day of Shining Red: An Essay on Understanding Ritual*
GILBERT LEWIS
28 Hunters, Pastoralists and Ranchers: Reindeer Economies and their Transformations*
TIM INGOLD
29 The Wood-Carvers of Hong Kong: Craft Production in the World Capitalist Periphery
EUGENE COOPER
30 Minangkabau Social Formations: Indonesian Peasants and the World Economy
JOEL S. KAHN
31 Patrons and Partisans: A Study of Two Southern Italian Communes
CAROLINE WHITE
32 Muslim Society*
ERNEST GELLNER
33 Why Marry Her? Society and Symbolic Structures
LUC DE HEUSCH. Translated by Janet Lloyd
34 Chinese Ritual and Politics
EMILY MARTIN AHERN
35 Parenthood and Social Reproduction: Fostering and Occupational Roles in West Africa
ESTHER N. GOODY
36 Dravidian Kinship
THOMAS R. TRAUTMANN
37 The Anthropological Circle: Symbol, Function, History*
MARC AUGE. Translated by Martin Thorn
38 Rural Society in Southeast Asia
KATHLEEN GOUGH
39 The Fish-People: Linguistic Exogamy and Tukanoan Identity in Northwest Amazonia
JEAN E. JACKSON
40 Karl Marx Collective: Economy, Society and Religion in a Siberian Collective Farm*
CAROLINE HUMPHREY
41 Ecology and Exchange in the Andes
Edited by DAVID LEHMANN
42 Traders without Trade: Responses to Trade in two Dyula Communities
ROBERT LAUNAY
43 The Political Economy of West African Agriculture*
KEITH HART
44 Nomads and the Outside World
A.M. KHAZANOV. Translated by Julia Crookenden
45 Actions, Norms and Representations: Foundations of Anthropological Inquiry*
LADISLAV HOLY AND MILAN STUCHLIK
46 Structural Models in Anthropology*
PER HAGE AND FRANK HARARY
47 Servants of the Goddess: The Priests of a South Indian Temple
C.J. FULLER
48 Oedipus and Job in West African Religion*
MEYER FORTES

49 The Buddhist Saints of the Forest and the Cult of Amulets: A Study in Charisma, Hagiography, Sectarianism, and Millenial Buddhism*
S.J. TAMBIAH

50 Kinship and Marriage: An Anthropological Perspective (available in paperback in the USA only)
ROBIN FOX

51 Individual and Society in Guiana. A Comparative Study of Amerindian Social Organization*
PETER RIVIERE

52 People and the State: An Anthropology of Planned Development*
A.F. ROBERTSON

53 Inequality among Brothers: Class and Kinship in South China
RUBIE S. WATSON

54 On Anthropological Knowledge*
DAN SPERBER

55 Tales of the Yanomami: Daily Life in the Venezuelan Forest*
JACQUES LIZOT. Translated by Ernest Simon

56 The Making of Great Men: Male Domination and Power among the New Guinea Baruya*
MAURICE GODELIER. Translated by Rupert Swyer

57 Age Class Systems: Social Institutions and Politics Based on Age*
BERNARDO BERNARDI. Translated by David I. Kertzer

58 Strategies and Norms in a Changing Matrilineal Society: Descent, Succession and Inheritance among the Toka of Zambia
LADISLAV HOLY

59 Native Lords of Quito in the Age of the Incas: The Political Economy of North-Andean Chiefdoms
FRANK SALOMON

60 Culture and Class in Anthropology and History: A Newfoundland Illustration
GERALD SIDER

61 From Blessing to Violence: History and Ideology in the Circumcision Ritual of the Merina of Madagascar*
MAURICE BLOCH

62 The Huli Response to Illness
STEPHEN FRANKEL

63 Social Inequality in a Northern Portuguese Hamlet: Land, Late Marriage, and Bastardy, 1870–1978*
BRIAN JUAN O'NEILL

64 Cosmologies in the Making: A Generative Approach to Cultural Variation in Inner New Guinea*
FREDRIK BARTH

65 Kinship and Class in the West Indies: A Genealogical Study of Jamaica and Guyana*
RAYMOND T. SMITH

66 The Making of the Basque Nation
MARIANNE HEIBERG

67 Out of Time: History and Evolution in Anthropological Discourse
NICHOLAS THOMAS

68 Tradition as Truth and Communication
PASCAL BOYER

69 The Abandoned Narcotic: Kava and Cultural Instability in Melanesia
RON BRUNTON

70 The Anthropology of Numbers*
THOMAS CRUMP

71 Stealing People's Names: History and Politics in a Sepik River Cosmology
SIMON J. HARRISON

72 The Bedouin of Cyrenaica: Studies in Personal and Corporate Power
EMRYS L. PETERS. Edited by Jack Goody and Emanuel Marx

73 Property, Production and Family in Neckerhausen*
DAVID WARREN SABEAN

74 Bartered Brides: Politics, Gender and Marriage in an Afghan Tribal Society
NANCY TAPPER

75 Fifteen Generations of Bretons: Kinship and Society in Lower Brittany, 1720–1980
MARTINE SEGALEN. Translated by J.S. Underwood

76 Honor and Grace in Anthropology
Edited by J.G. PERISTIANY and JULIAN PITT-RIVERS

77 The Making of the Modern Greek Family: Marriage and Exchange in Nineteenth-Century Athens
PAUL SANT CASSIA WITH CONSTANTINA BADA

78 Religion and Custom in a Muslim Society: The Berti of Sudan
LADISLAV HOLY

79 Quiet Days in Burgundy: A Study of Local Politics
MARC ABELES. Translated by Annella McDermott

80 Sacred Void: Spatial Images of Work and Ritual Among the Giriama of Kenya
DAVID PARKIN

81 A Place of their Own: Family Farming in Eastern Finland
RAY ABRAHAMS

82 Power, Prayer and Production: The Jola of Casamance, Senegal
OLGA F. LINARES

83 Identity Through History: Living Stories in a Solomon Islands Society
GEOFFREY M. WHITE

* *available in paperback*